Complete Unity 2018 Game Development

Explore techniques to build 2D/3D applications using real-world examples

Alan Thorn
John P. Doran
Alan Zucconi
Jorge Palacios

Packt>

BIRMINGHAM - MUMBAI

Complete Unity 2018 Game Development

First published: January 2019

Production reference: 1310119

Published by Packt Publishing Ltd.
Livery Place
35 Livery Street
Birmingham
B3 2PB, UK.

ISBN 978-1-78995-286-5

www.packtpub.com

Contributors

About the authors

Alan Thorn is an educator, author, and multidisciplinary games-developer with 18 years of tech-industry experience. He is currently Head of Department for the Games Design and Development MA degree at the BAFTA-winning National Film and Television School, London. He has written 27 technical books on game development and presented 29 online training courses. He founded the game-studio Wax Lyrical Games and created the award-winning game Baron Wittard: Nemesis of Ragnarok.

John P. Doran is a passionate and seasoned technical game designer, software engineer, and author who is based in Redmond, Washington. For over a decade, John has built games in roles ranging from game designer to lead UI programmer. Additionally, John has taught game development in Singapore, South Korea, and the United States. To date, he has authored over 10 books pertaining to game development.

> *Thanks so much to my wife Hien and my family for all of their support while working on this book.*

Alan Zucconi is a passionate developer, author, and lecturer, recognized as one of Develop's 30 under 30. His expertise has been built over the past 10 years, working in the intersection between creativity and education. Starting in 2015, he published a series of educational tutorials for other developers and machine learning enthusiasts.

Jorge Palacios is a software and game developer with a BS in computer science and eight years of professional experience. He's been developing games for the last five years in different roles, from tool developer to lead programmer. Mainly focused on artificial intelligence and gameplay programming, he is currently working with Unity and HTML5.

He's also a game-programming instructor, speaker, and game-jam organizer.

Packt is searching for authors like you

If you're interested in becoming an author for Packt, please visit `authors.packtpub.com` and apply today. We have worked with thousands of developers and tech professionals, just like you, to help them share their insight with the global tech community. You can make a general application, apply for a specific hot topic that we are recruiting an author for, or submit your own idea.

Table of Contents

Preface

Through this Learning Path, you'll learn how to leverage the features of Unity and create amazing games, ranging from action shooters and mind-bending puzzle games to adventure and Virtual Reality (VR) games. If you have no prior experience of using Unity, you can still benefit from this Learning Path, which easily explains the complete working of the Unity toolset.

You'll start by learning how to create compelling shaders using Unity and understanding everything you need to know about vectors. This includes useful inputs on how lighting is constructed with vectors and how textures are used to create complex effects without the need for advanced math. In the succeeding chapters, you'll also be able to use popular AI techniques, such as A* and A*mbush to develop intelligent pathfinding agents for your games. The book will also guide you through different algorithms for creating decision-making agents that go beyond simple behaviors and movement.

By the end of this Learning Path, you will have developed all the basic skills to create highly engaging and replayable games.

This Learning Path includes content from the following Packt products:

- Unity 2018 By Example - Second Edition by Alan Thorn
- Unity 2018 Shaders and Effects Cookbook - Third Edition by John P. Doran, Alan Zucconi
- Unity 2018 Artificial Intelligence Cookbook - Second Edition by Jorge Palacios

Who this book is for

If you are a game developer who wants to learn tools that can transform your gameplay, this beginner-level Learning Path is ideal for you. Having basic knowledge of C# will help you grasp the concepts explained in the book easily.

What this book covers

`Chapter 1`, *Unity Fundamentals*, begins our journey into Unity by creating a first-person collection game. This is a great starting point if you're totally new to Unity and are ready to create your first game.

`Chapter 2`, *Creating a Collection Game*, continues from the previous chapter and completes the first project. It assumes that you have completed the first chapter and brings a closure to our project, leading neatly to the next chapter.

`Chapter 3`, *Post Processing Stack*, introduces readers to the Post Processing Stack, which will allow users to tweak their game's appearance without having to write any additional scripts.

`Chapter 4`, *Creating Your First Shader*, introduces you to the world of shader coding in Unity. You will build some basic shaders and learn how to introduce tweakable properties in your shaders to make them more interactive.

`Chapter 5`, *Surface Shaders and Texture Mapping*, covers the most common and useful techniques that you can implement with Surface Shaders, including how to use textures and normal maps for your models.

`Chapter 6`, *Understanding Lighting Models*, gives you an in-depth explanation of how shaders model the behavior of light. This chapter teaches you how to create custom lighting models used to simulate special effects, such as toon shading.

`Chapter 7`, *Physically-Based Rendering*, shows you that physically-based rendering is the standard technology used by Unity 5 to bring realism to your games. This chapter explains how to make the most out of it by mastering transparencies, reflective surfaces, and global illumination.

`Chapter 8`, *Vertex Functions*, teaches you how shaders can be used to alter the geometry of an object. This chapter introduces vertex modifiers and uses them to bring volumetric explosions, snow shaders, and other effects to life.

`Chapter 9`, *Fragment Shaders and Grab Passes*, explains how to use grab passes to make materials that emulate the deformations generated by semi-transparent materials.

`Chapter 10`, *Mobile Shader Adjustment*, helps you optimize your shaders to get the most out of any device.

`Chapter 11`, *Screen Effects with Unity Render Textures*, shows you how to create special effects and visuals that would otherwise be impossible to achieve.

`Chapter 12`, *Behaviors – Intelligent Movement*, explores some of the most interesting movement algorithms based on the steering behavior principles developed by Craig Reynolds and work from Ian Millington. They act as a foundation for most of the AI used in advanced games and other algorithms that rely on movement, such as the family of pathfinding algorithms.

`Chapter 13`, *Navigation*, covers path-finding algorithms for navigating complex scenarios. It will include some ways of representing the world using different kinds of graph structure, and several algorithms for finding a path, each aimed to different situations.

`Chapter 14`, *Decision Making*, explains different decision-making techniques that are flexible enough to adapt to different types of games, and robust enough to let us build modular decision-making systems.

`Chapter 15`, *The New NavMesh API*, shows the inner workings of the NavMesh API introduced in Unity 5.6, and explains how it enables us to grasp the power of the NavMesh engine and tune it in real time.

`Chapter 16`, *Coordination and Tactics*, deals with a number of different recipes for coordinating different agents as a whole organism, such as formations and techniques that allow us make tactical decisions based on graphs, such as waypoints and influence maps.

`Chapter 17`, *Agent Awareness*, explores different ways to simulate sense stimuli on an agent. We will learn how to use tools we already know to create these simulations: colliders and graphs.

`Chapter 18`, *Board Games and Applied Search AI*, covers a family of algorithms for developing board games, as well as turn-based-game techniques for creating AI.

`Chapter 19`, *Learning Techniques*, explores the field of machine learning. It will give us a great head-start in our endeavor to learn and apply machine learning techniques into our games.

`Chapter 20`, *Procedural Content Generation*, explores different techniques for enabling replayability in our games by creating content procedurally. It will give us some pointers in the right direction for different types of content.

To get the most out of this book

Readers are expected to have experience of working with Unity and some scripting experience (C# or JavaScript is fine).

The book learning path is written with Unity 2018.1.0f2.

You need an internet connection for downloading the Python libraries. Also, basic knowledge of Python and networking is required.

Download the example code files

You can download the example code files for this book from your account at `www.packt.com`. If you purchased this book elsewhere, you can visit `www.packt.com/support` and register to have the files emailed directly to you.

You can download the code files by following these steps:

1. Log in or register at `www.packt.com`.
2. Select the **SUPPORT** tab.
3. Click on **Code Downloads & Errata**.
4. Enter the name of the book in the **Search** box and follow the onscreen instructions.

Once the file is downloaded, please make sure that you unzip or extract the folder using the latest version of:

- WinRAR/7-Zip for Windows
- Zipeg/iZip/UnRarX for Mac
- 7-Zip/PeaZip for Linux

The code bundle for the book is also hosted on GitHub at `https://github.com/PacktPublishing/Complete-Unity-2018-Game-Development`. In case there's an update to the code, it will be updated on the existing GitHub repository.

We also have other code bundles from our rich catalog of books and videos available at `https://github.com/PacktPublishing/`. Check them out!

Conventions used

There are a number of text conventions used throughout this book.

`CodeInText`: Indicates code words in text, database table names, folder names, filenames, file extensions, pathnames, dummy URLs, user input, and Twitter handles. Here is an example: "Once selected, it will allow us to rename the item. Go ahead and set the name to `BloomProfile`."

A block of code is set as follows:

```
//-------------------------
using UnityEngine;
using System.Collections;
//-------------------------
public class Coin : MonoBehaviour
```

Bold: Indicates a new term, an important word, or words that you see onscreen. For example, words in menus or dialog boxes appear in the text like this. Here is an example: "To create a build for desktop platform, select **File** | **Build Settings** from the **File** menu"

Warnings or important notes appear like this.

Tips and tricks appear like this.

Get in touch

Feedback from our readers is always welcome.

General feedback: If you have questions about any aspect of this book, mention the book title in the subject of your message and email us at `customercare@packtpub.com`.

Errata: Although we have taken every care to ensure the accuracy of our content, mistakes do happen. If you have found a mistake in this book, we would be grateful if you would report this to us. Please visit `www.packt.com/submit-errata`, selecting your book, clicking on the Errata Submission Form link, and entering the details.

Piracy: If you come across any illegal copies of our works in any form on the Internet, we would be grateful if you would provide us with the location address or website name. Please contact us at `copyright@packt.com` with a link to the material.

If you are interested in becoming an author: If there is a topic that you have expertise in and you are interested in either writing or contributing to a book, please visit `authors.packtpub.com`.

Reviews

Please leave a review. Once you have read and used this book, why not leave a review on the site that you purchased it from? Potential readers can then see and use your unbiased opinion to make purchase decisions, we at Packt can understand what you think about our products, and our authors can see your feedback on their book. Thank you!

For more information about Packt, please visit `packt.com`.

1
Unity Fundamentals

This chapter starts the first project on our list, which will be a fun collection game. Remember, it doesn't matter if you've never used Unity before. We'll go through everything necessary step by step. By the end of the next chapter, you'll have pieced together a simple, but complete and functional, game. This is an important thing to achieve because you'll get familiar with a start-to-end game development workflow.

In this chapter, you will learn the following recipes:

- Game design
- Projects and folders
- Asset importing and configuration
- Level design
- Game objects
- Hierarchies

Game design

Let's make a coin collection game. Here, the player should control a character in the first-person mode, and he must wander the level, collecting all coins before a time limit runs out. If the timer runs out, the game is lost. On the other hand, if all coins are collected before the timer expires, the game is won. The first-person controls will use the default WASD keyboard setup, where *W* moves forward, *A* and *S* move left and right, and *D* walks backward. Head movement is controlled using the mouse, and coins are collected by simply walking into them. See *Figure 1.1*, featuring the coin collection game in action in the Unity Editor.

The great benefit in making this game is that it demonstrates all the core Unity features together and we don't need to rely on any external software to make assets, such as textures, meshes, and materials:

Figure 1.1: Preparing for a coin collection game (the completed game)

Getting started – Unity and projects

Every time you want to make a new Unity game, including coin collection games, you'll need to create New Project. Generally speaking, Unity uses the term Project to mean a Game. There are two main ways to make a new project, and it really doesn't matter which one you choose because both end up in the same place. If you're already in the Unity interface, looking at an existing scene or level, you can select **File** | **New Project** from the application menu. See *Figure 1.2*. It may ask if you want to save changes to the currently opened project and you should choose either **Yes** or **No**, depending on what you need.

After selecting the **New Project** option, Unity leads you to the project creation wizard:

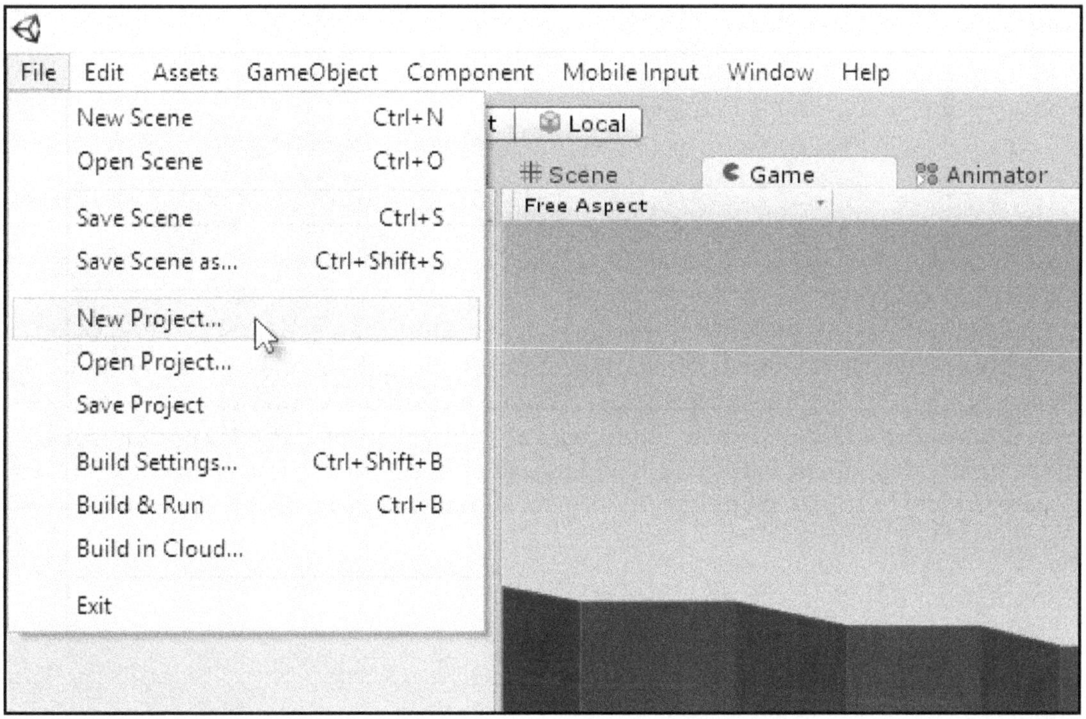

Figure 1.2: Creating a new project via the main menu

Alternatively, if you've just started Unity for the first time, you'll probably begin at the welcome dialog. See Figure 1.3. From here, you can access the new project creation wizard by choosing the **NEW PROJECT** button:

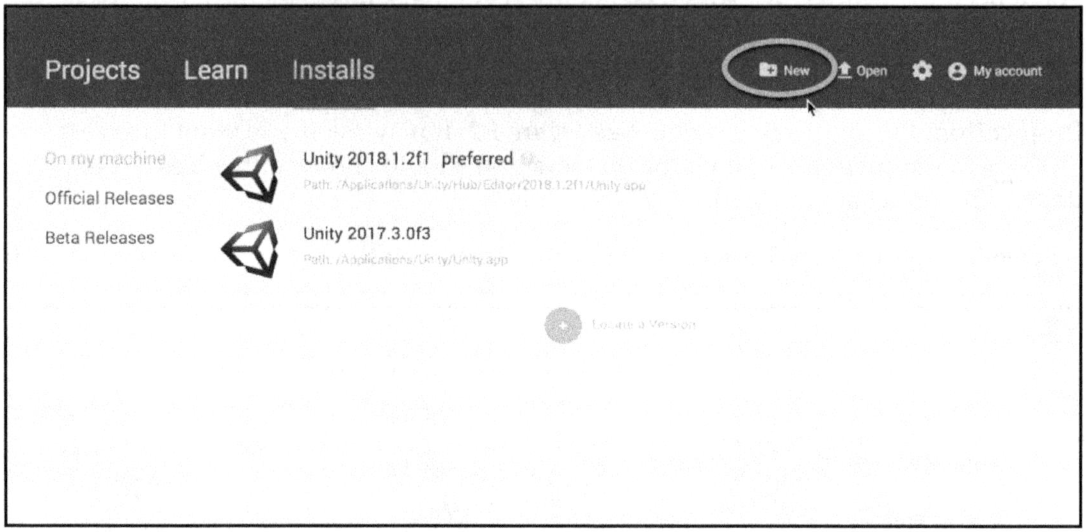

Figure 1.3: The Unity welcome screen

On reaching the **NEW PROJECT** creation wizard, Unity can generate a new project for you on the basis of some basic settings. Simply fill in the name of your project (such as `CollectionGame`), and select a folder on your computer to contain the project files that will be generated automatically. Finally, select the **3D** option from the template dropdown to create a 3D game, as opposed to **2D**, and then click on the **Create project** button to complete the project generation process. See *Figure 1.4*:

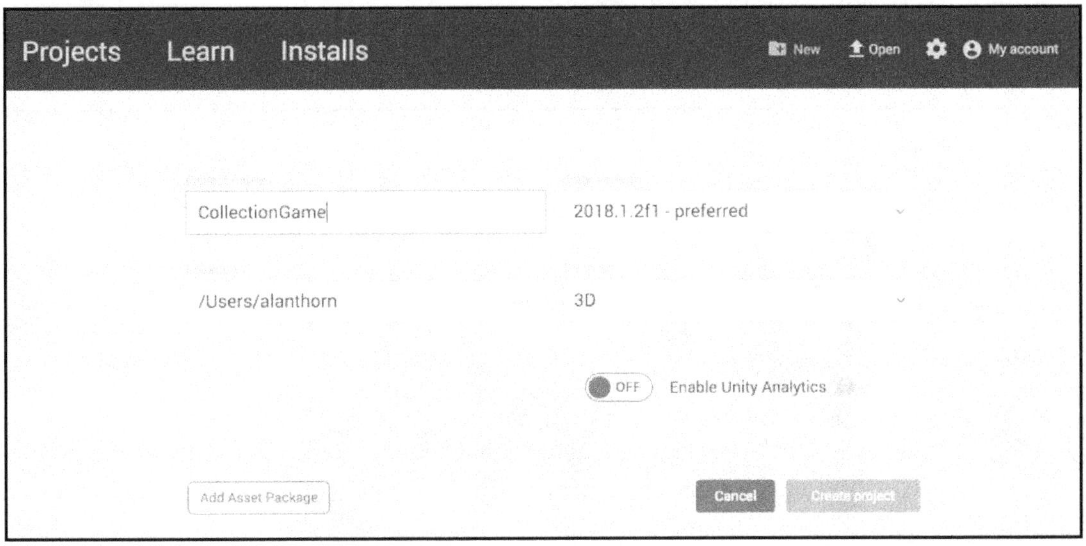

Figure 1.4: Creating a new project

Projects and project folders

Unity has now created a blank, new, and empty project. This represents the starting point for any game development project and is the place where development begins. The newly created project contains nothing initially: no meshes, textures, or any other **Assets**. You can confirm this by simply checking the **Project** panel area at the bottom of the editor interface. This panel displays the complete contents of the project folder, which corresponds to an actual folder on your local drive created earlier by the project wizard. This folder should be empty. See *Figure 1.5*.

- This panel will later be populated with more items, all of which we can use to build a game:

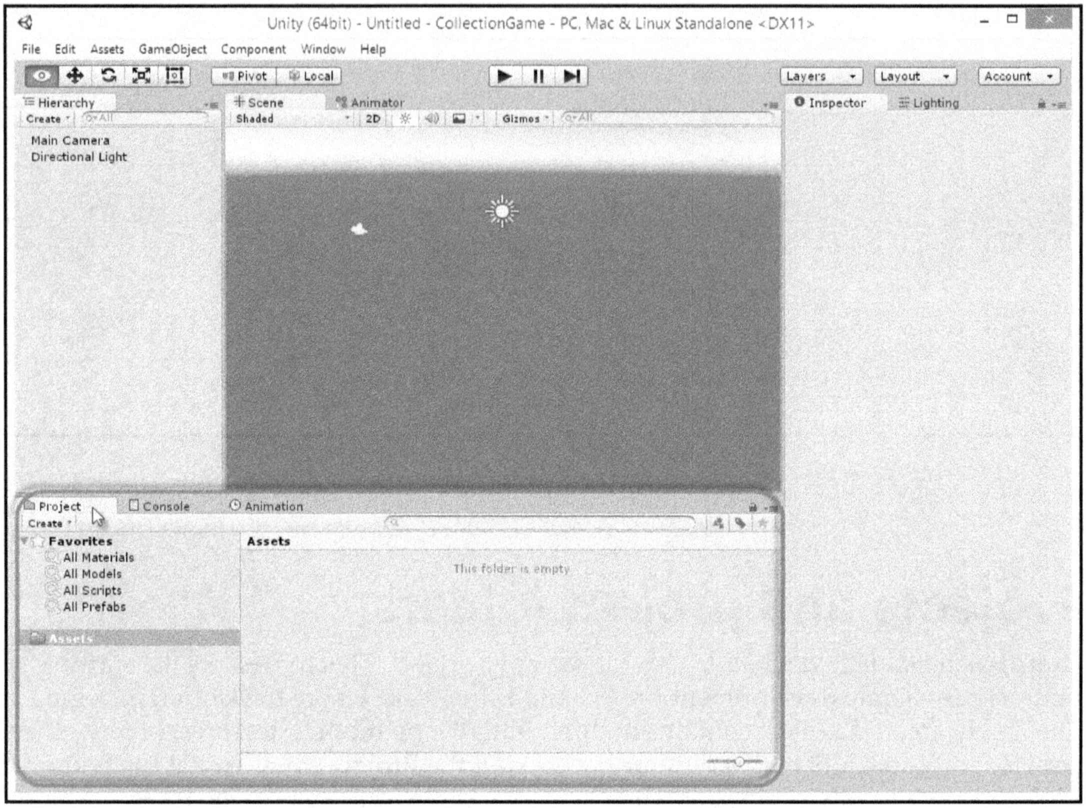

Figure 1.5: The Unity project panel docked at the bottom of the interface

If your interface looks radically different from *Figure 1.5,* in terms of its layout and arrangement, then you can reset the UI layout to its defaults. To do this, click on the **Layout** drop-down menu from the top-right corner of the editor interface, and choose **Default**. See *Figure 1.6:*

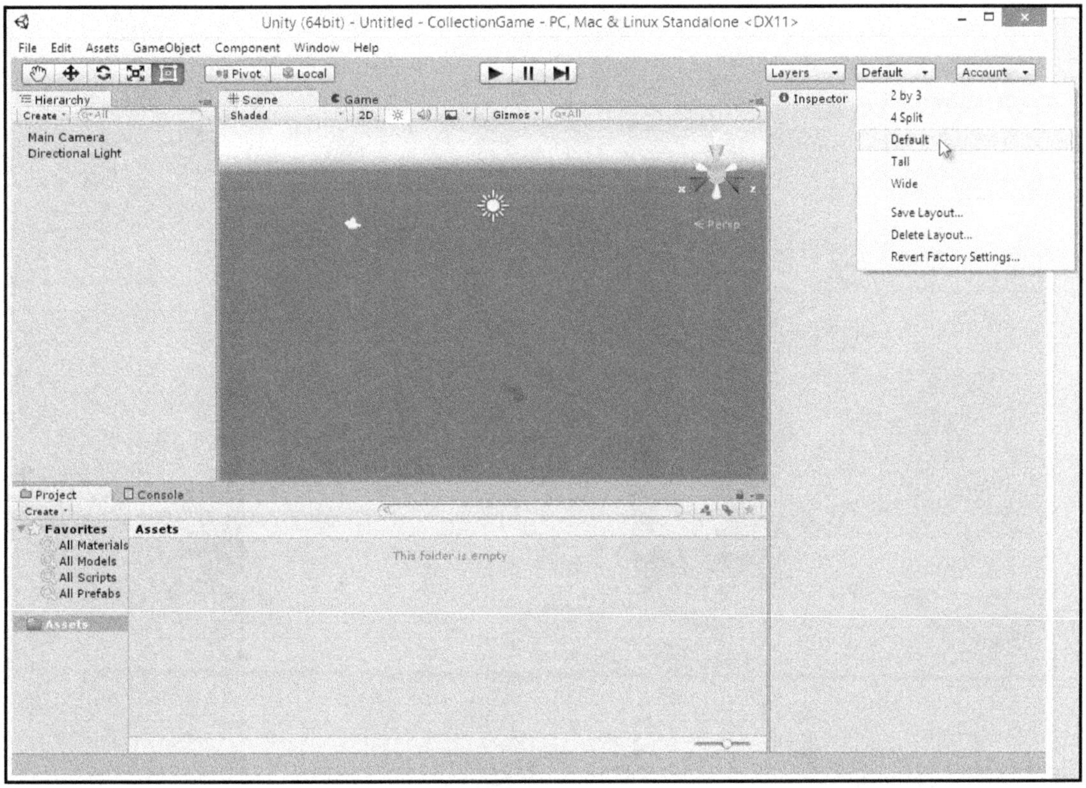

Figure 1.6: Switching to the default interface layout

You can view the contents of your project folder directly via either Windows Explorer or Mac Finder, by right-clicking the mouse in the **Project** panel from the **Unity Editor** to reveal a context menu, and from there, choose the **Show in Explorer** (Windows) or **Reveal in Finder** (Mac) option. See *Figure 1.7*:

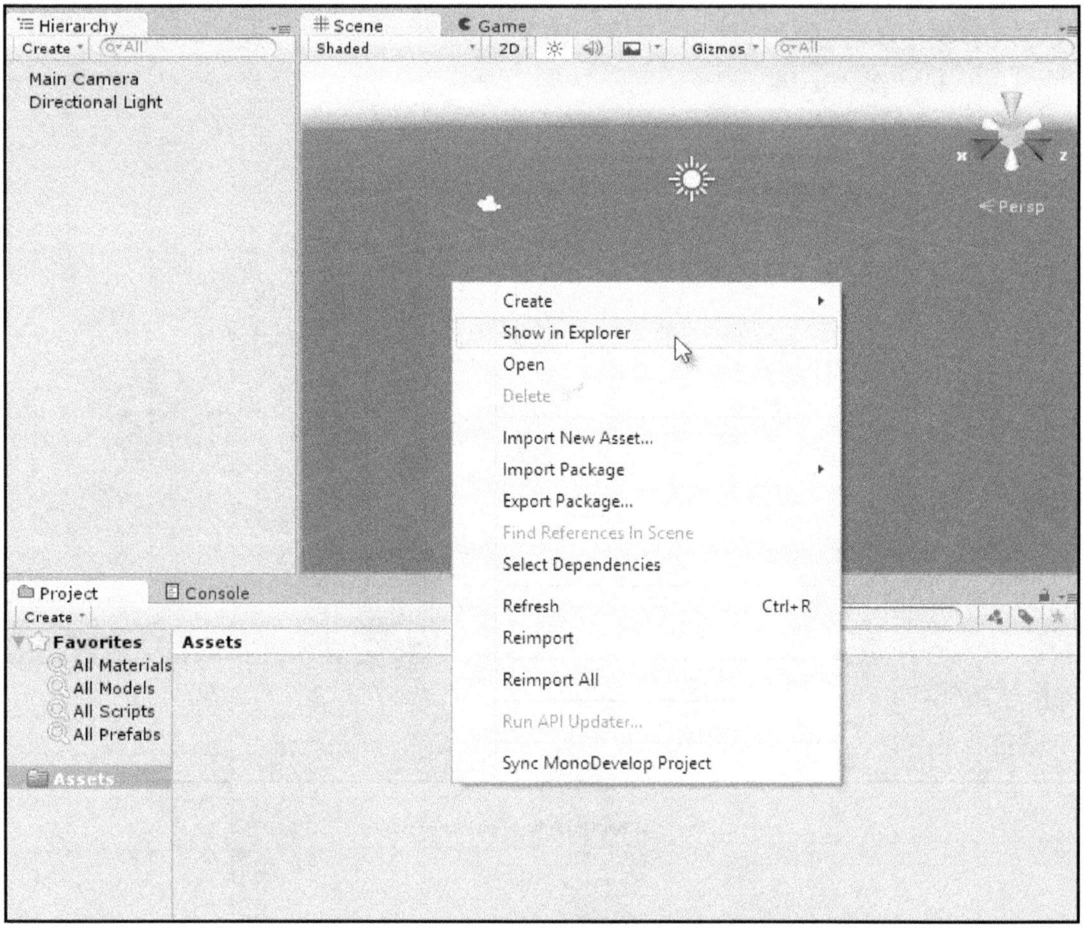

Figure 1.7: Displaying the project folder via the Project panel

Clicking on **Show in Explorer** displays the folder contents in the default system file browser. See *Figure 1.8*. This view is useful to inspect files, count them, or back them up. However, don't change the folder contents manually this way via Explorer or Finder. Specifically, don't move, rename, or delete files from here, because doing so can corrupt your Unity project irretrievably. Instead, delete and move files where needed within the **Project** panel in the **Unity Editor**. This way, Unity updates its metadata as appropriate, ensuring that your project continues to work properly:

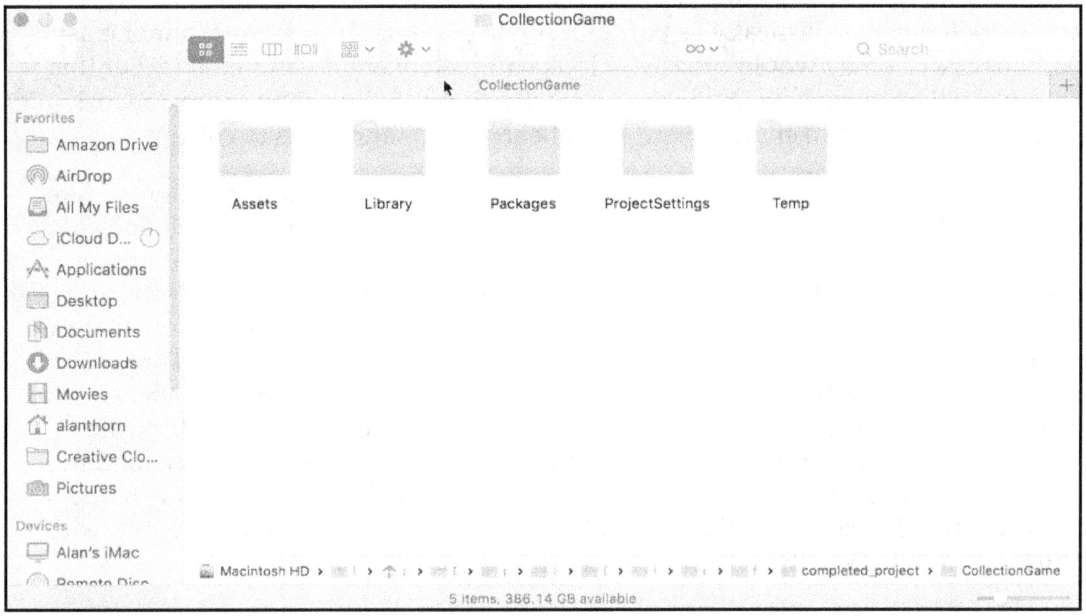

Figure 1.8: Viewing the Project panel from the OS file browser

Viewing the project folder in the OS file browser will display additional files and folders not visible in the **Project** panel, such as **Library** and **ProjectSettings**, and maybe a Temp folder. Together, these are known as the project metadata. This is not directly a part of your project per se, but contains additional settings and preferences that Unity needs to work properly. These folders and their files should not be edited or changed.

Importing assets

Assets are the ingredients or building blocks for games—the building blocks from which they're made. `Assets` include meshes (or 3D models), such as characters, props, trees, houses, and more: textures, which are image files such as JPEGs and PNGs (these determine how the surface of a mesh should look); music and sound effects to enhance the realism and atmosphere of your game, and finally, scenes, which are 3D spaces or worlds where meshes, textures, sounds, and music live, exist, and work together holistically as part of a single system. Thus, games cannot exist without assets—they would otherwise look completely empty and lifeless. For this reason, we'll need assets to make the coin collection game we're working toward. After all, we'll need an environment to walk around in and coins to collect!

Unity, however, is a game engine and not primarily an asset creation program, like Blender or Photoshop (though it can create assets). This means that assets, such as characters and props, are typically made first by artists in external, third-party software. From here, they are exported and transferred ready-made to Unity, and Unity is responsible only for bringing these assets to life in a coherent game that can be played. Third-party asset creation programs include Blender (which is free of charge), Maya or 3DS Max to make 3D models, Photoshop or GIMP (which is free of charge) to create textures, and Audacity (which is free of cost) to generate audio. There are plenty of other options too. The details of these programs are beyond the scope of this book. In any case, Unity assumes that you already have assets ready to import to build a game. For the coin collection game, we'll use assets that ship with Unity. So, let's import these to our project.

To do this, select **Assets** | **Import Package** from the application menu. Then select **Characters**, **ParticleSystems**, **Environment**, and **Prototyping**. See *Figure 1.9*:

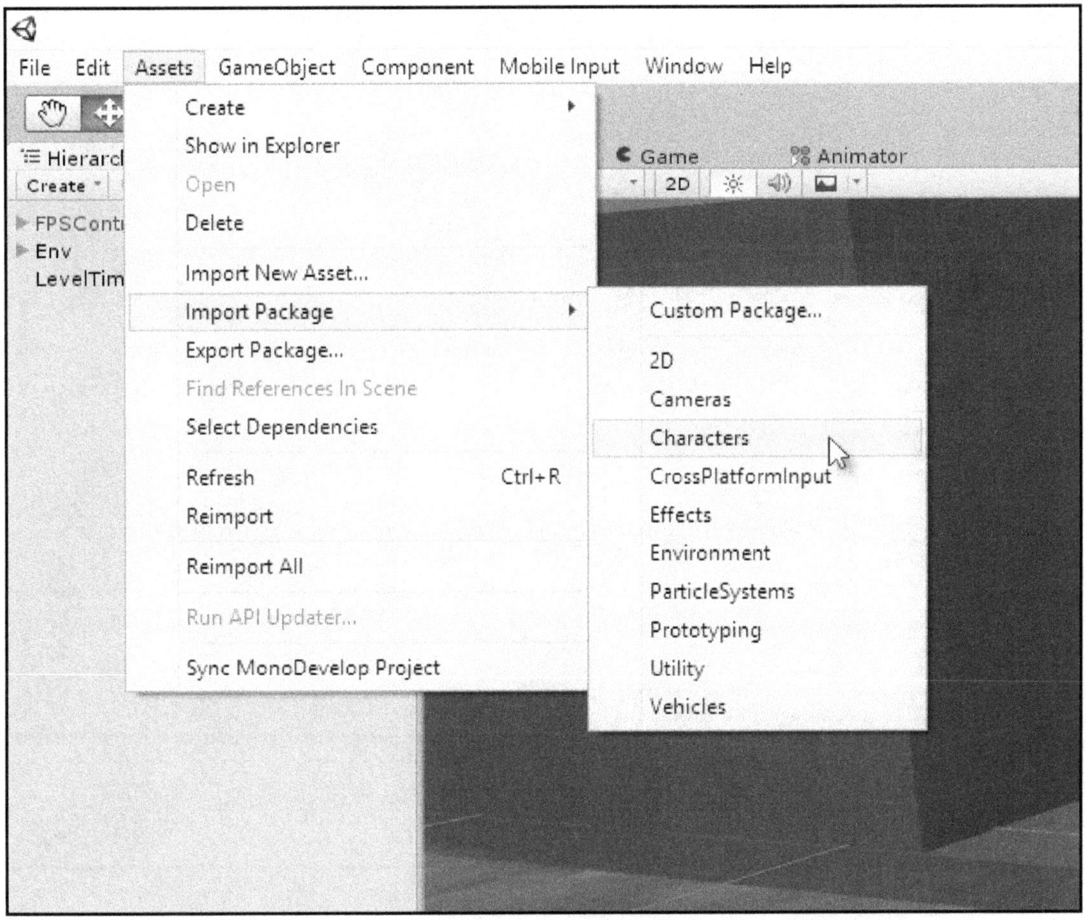

Figure 1.9: Importing assets via the Import Package menu

Each time you import a package from the menu, you'll be presented with an **Import** dialog. Simply leave all settings at their defaults, and click on **Import**. See *Figure 1.10*:

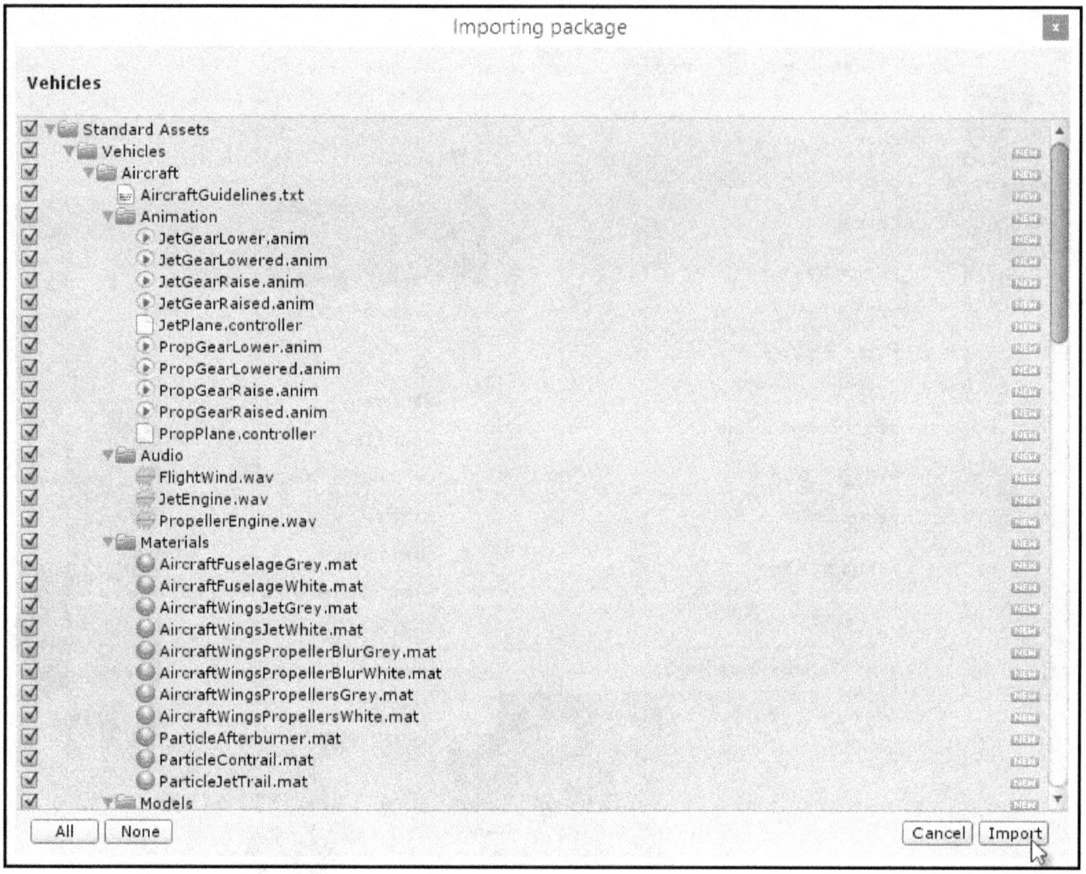

Figure 1.10: Choosing Assets to import

By default, Unity decompresses all files from the package (a library of assets) into the current project. After importing, lots of different assets and data will have been added to the **Project**, ready for use. These files are copies of the originals. So, any changes made to the imported files will not affect or invalidate the originals, which Unity maintains internally.

The files include models, sounds, textures, and more. These are listed in the **Unity Editor** from the **Project** panel. See the following screenshot:

Figure 1.11: Browsing imported assets from the Project panel

When selecting **Assets** | **Import** from the application menu, if you don't see all, or any, asset packages listed, you can download and install them separately from the Unity website at `https://unity3d.com/`. From the downloads page, choose the **Additional Downloads** option, and then select the Standard Assets package. See *Figure 1.12*.

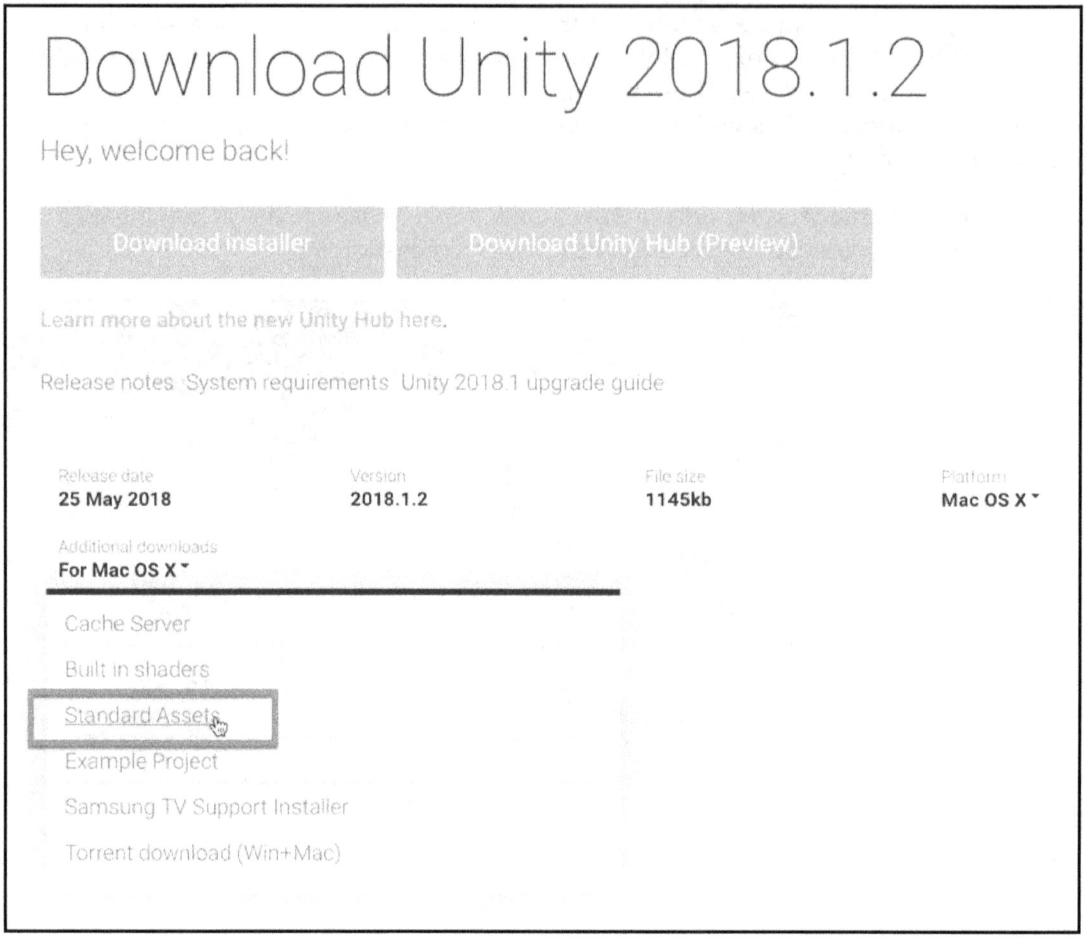

Figure 1.12: Downloading the Standard Assets package

The imported assets don't exist yet in our game scene or level. They don't appear in the game, and they won't do anything when the level begins! Rather, they're simply added to the **Project** panel, which behaves as a library or repository of assets, from which we can pick and choose to build up a game when needed. The assets imported thus far are built-in into Unity and we'll continually using them in subsequent sections to make a functional coin collection game. To get more information about each asset, you can select the asset by clicking on it with the mouse, and asset-specific details will be shown on the right-hand side of the **Unity Editor** in the **Inspector**. The **Inspector** is a property sheet editor that appears on the right-hand side of the interface.

It is context-sensitive and always changes to display properties for the selected object. See *Figure 1.13*:

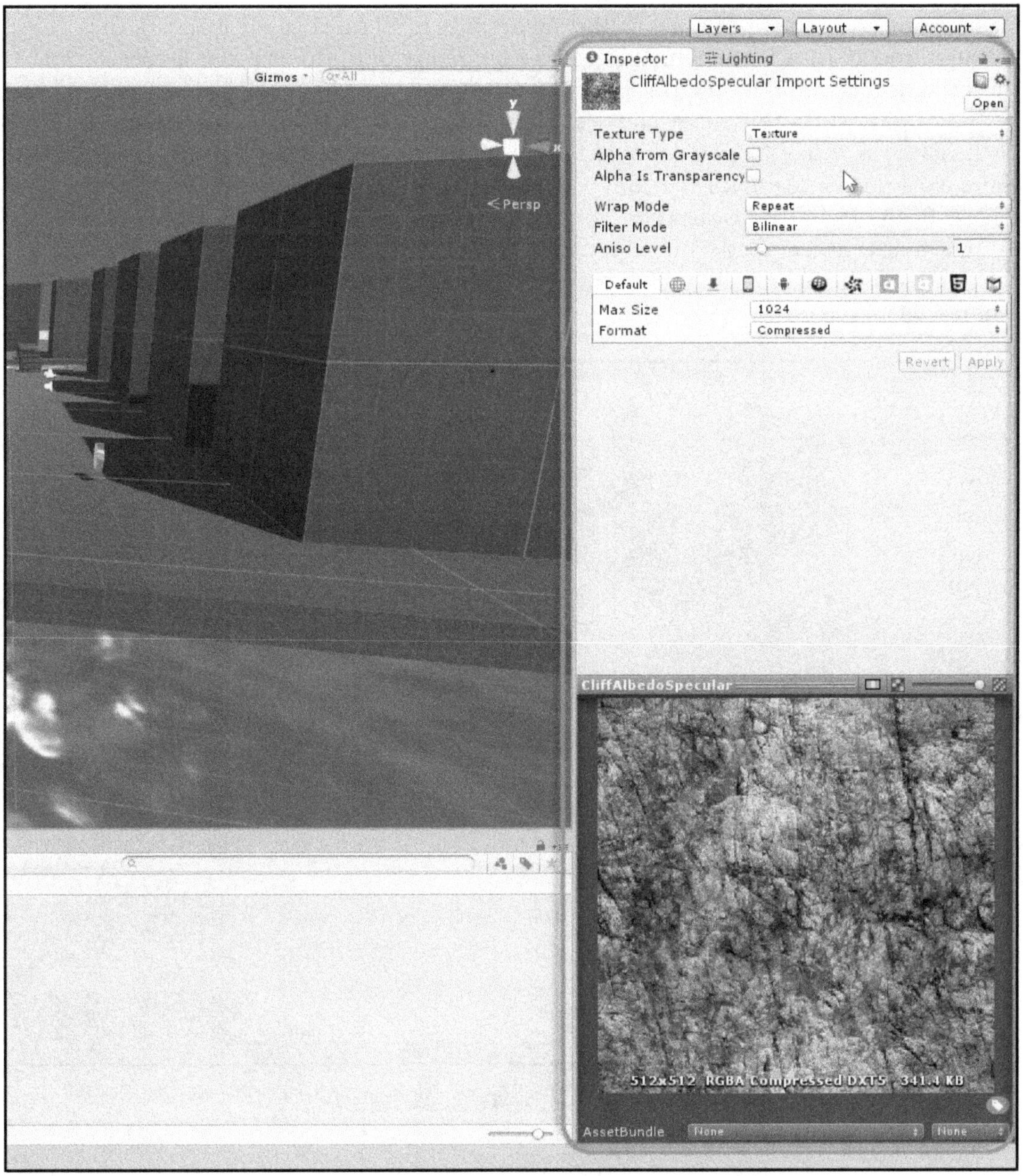

Figure 1.13: The Inspector displays all the properties for the currently selected object

Starting a level

We've now created a Unity project and imported a large library of assets via the **Unity Standard Asset** package, including architectural meshes for walls, floors, ceilings, and stairs. This means that we're now ready to build our first level using these assets! Remember, in Unity, a scene means a level. The word scene and level can be used interchangeably here. They refer simply to a 3D space, that is, the space-time of the game world—the place where things exist. Since all games happen in space and time, we'll need a scene for the coin collection game. To create a new scene, select **File | New Scene** from the application menu or press *Ctrl* + *N* on the keyboard. When you do this, a new and empty scene is created. You can see a visualization or preview of the scene via the **Scene** tab, which occupies the largest part of the Unity interface. See *Figure 1.14*:

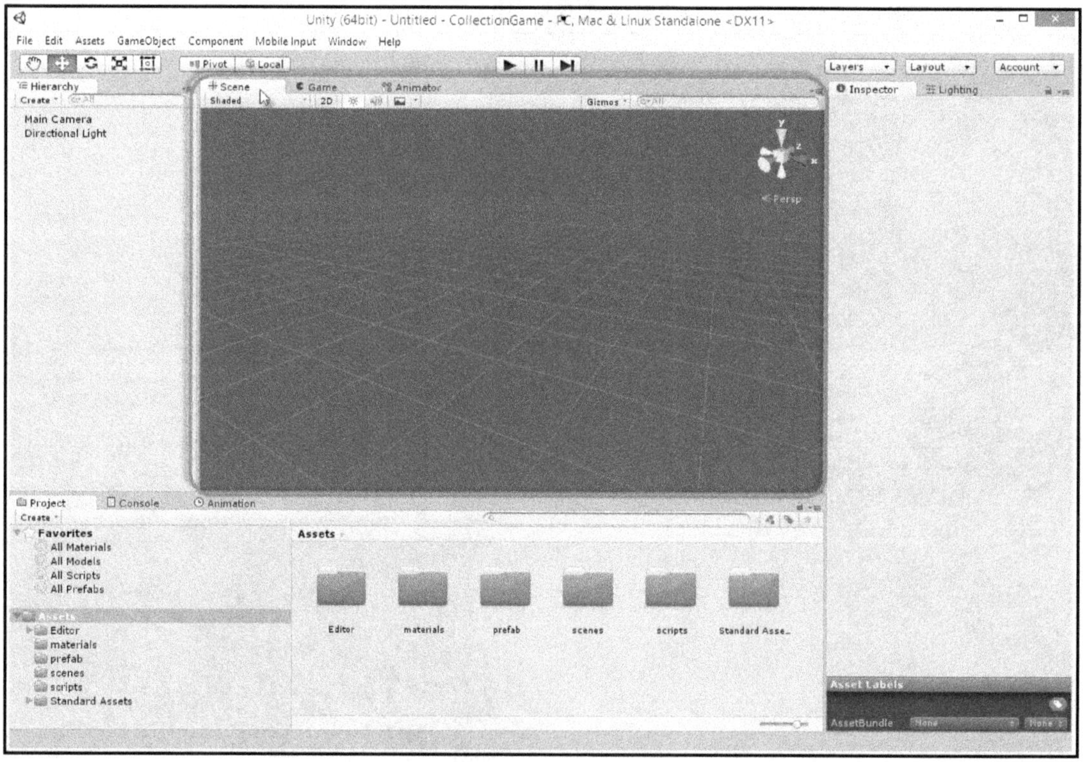

Figure 1.14: The Scene tab displays a preview of a 3D world

As shown in *Figure 1.14*, other tabs besides the scene are visible and available in Unity. These include a **Game** tab and an **Animator** tab; in some cases, there could be more as well. For now, we can ignore all the tabs except **Scene**. The **Scene** tab is designed for quick and easy previewing of a level during its construction.

Each new scene begins empty; well, almost empty. By default, each new scene begins with two objects; specifically, a **Light** to illuminate any other objects that are added and a **Camera** to display and render the contents of the scene from a specific vantage point. You can view a complete list of all the objects existing in the scene using the **Hierarchy** panel, which is docked to the left-hand side of the Unity interface. See Figure 1.15. This panel displays the name of every GameObject in the scene. In Unity, the word GameObject simply refers to a single, independent, and unique thing that lives within the scene, whether visible or not: meshes, lights, cameras, props, and more. Hence, the **Hierarchy** panel tells us about everything in the **Scene**:

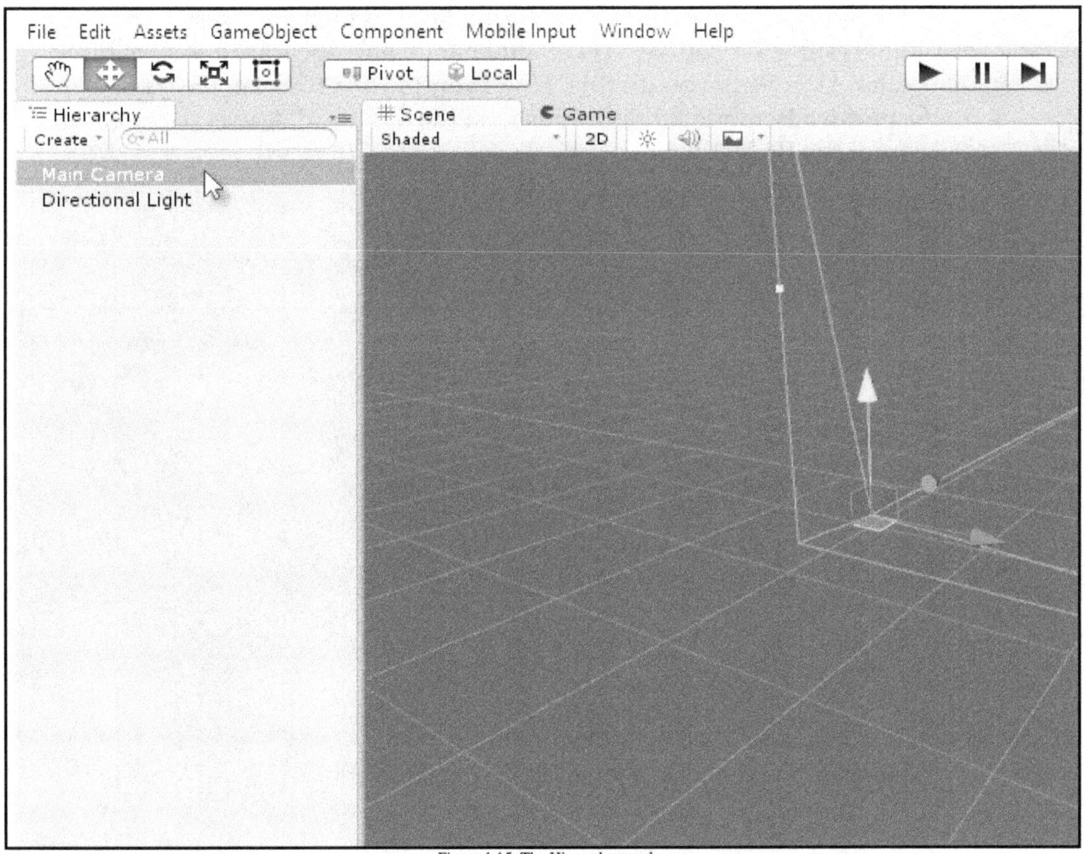

Figure 1.15: The Hierarchy panel

> You can even select objects in the scene by clicking on their name in the **Hierarchy** panel.

Next, let's add a floor to the scene. After all, the player needs something to stand on! We could build a floor mesh from scratch using third-party modeling software, such as Maya, 3DS Max, or Blender. However, the Unity Standard Asset package, which was imported earlier, contains floor meshes that we can use. This is very convenient. These meshes are part of the **Prototyping** package. To access them via the **Project** panel, open the `Standard Assets` folder by double-clicking it and then access the `Prototyping` | `Prefabs` folder. From here, you can select objects and preview them from the **Inspector**. See Figure 1.16:

> You could also quickly add a floor to the scene by choosing **GameObject** | **3D Object** | **Plane** from the application menu. However, this just adds a dull, grey floor, which isn't very interesting. Of course, you could change its appearance. As we'll see later, Unity lets you do this. However, for this tutorial, we'll use a specifically modeled floor mesh via the Standard Assets package from the Project panel.

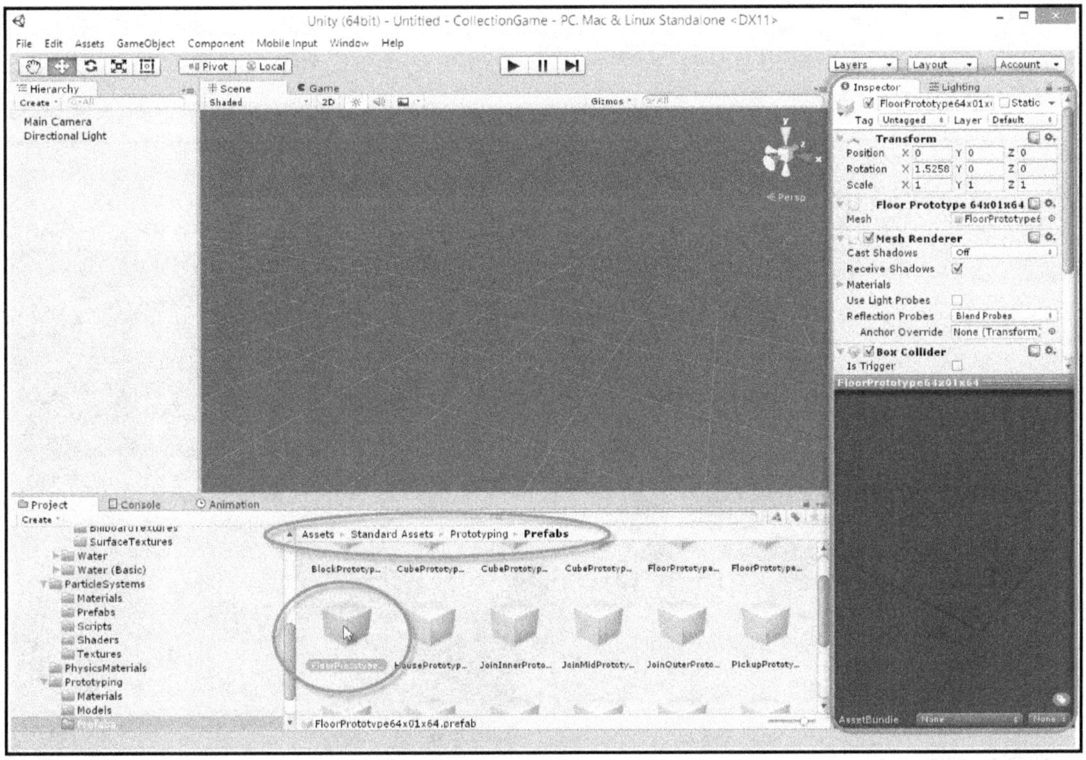

Figure 1.16: The Standard Assets/Prototyping package contains many meshes for quick scene building

The mesh named `FloorPrototype64x01x64` (as shown in *Figure 1.16*) is suitable as a floor. To add this mesh to the scene, simply drag and drop the object from the **Project** panel to the **Scene** view and then release the mouse.

See *Figure 1.17*. When you do this, notice how the **Scene** view changes to display the newly added mesh within the 3D space, and the mesh name also appears as a listing in the **Hierarchy** panel:

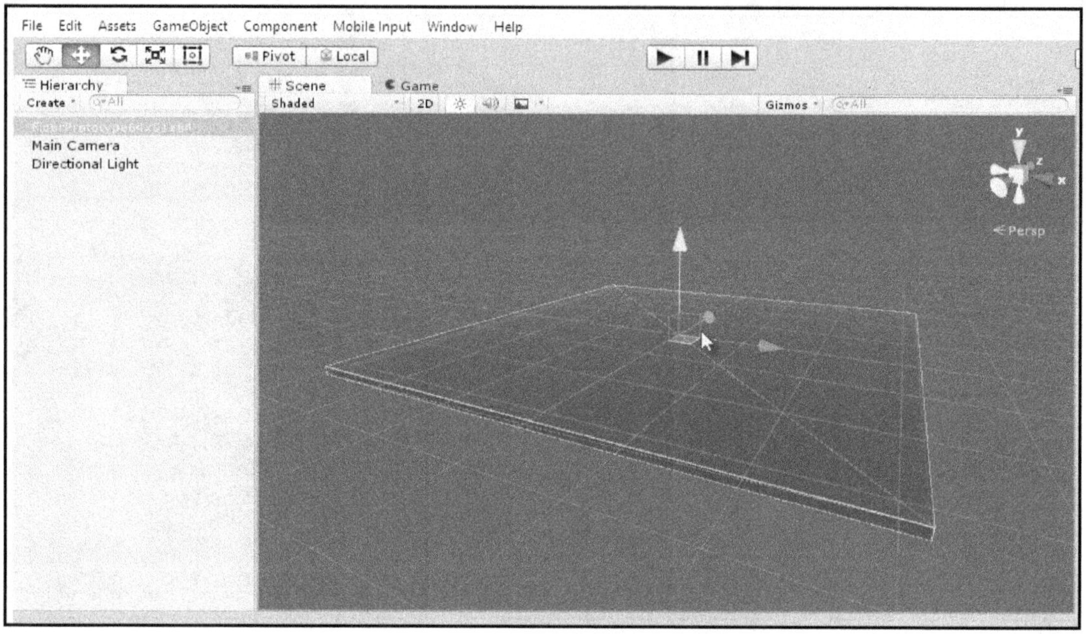

Figure 1.17: Dragging and dropping mesh assets from the Project panel to the Scene view will add them to the scene

The floor mesh asset from the **Project** panel has now been instantiated as a GameObject in the scene. This means that a copy or clone of the mesh asset, based on the original in the **Project** panel, has been added to the scene as a separate GameObject. The **Instance** (or GameObject) of the floor in the scene still depends on the floor asset in the **Project** panel. However, the asset does not depend on the instance. This means that, by deleting the floor in the scene, you will not delete the asset. However, if you delete the asset, you will invalidate the GameObject. You can also create more floors in **Scene** if you want by dragging and dropping the floor asset many times from the **Project** panel to the **Scene** view.

Each time, a new instance of the floor is created in the Scene as a separate and unique GameObject, although all the added instances will still depend on the single floor asset in the Project panel. See Figure 1.18:

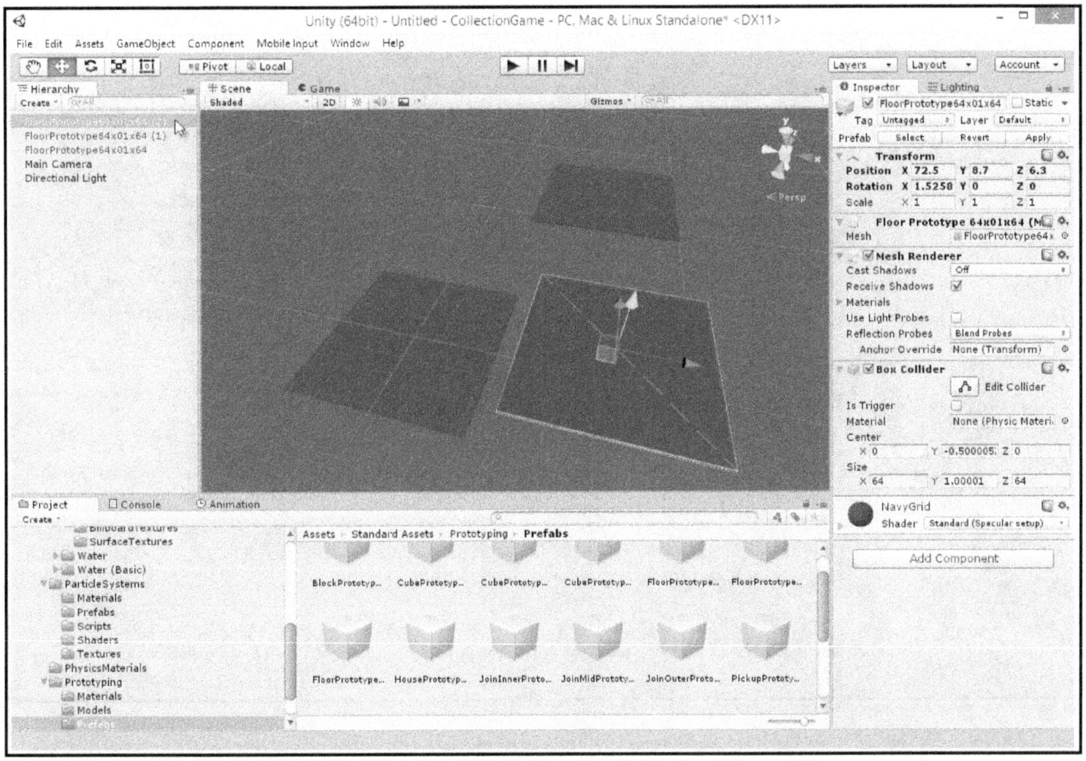

Figure 1.18: Adding multiple instances of the floor mesh to the scene

We don't actually need the duplicate floor pieces. So, let's delete them. Just click on the duplicates in the **Scene** view and then press *Delete* on the keyboard to remove them. Remember, you can also select and delete objects by clicking on their name in the **Hierarchy** panel and pressing *Delete*. Either way, this leaves us with a single floor piece and a solid start to building our scene. One remaining problem, though, concerns the floor and its name. By looking carefully in the **Hierarchy** panel, we can see that the floor name is `FloorPrototype64x01x64`. This name is long, obtuse, and unwieldy. We should change it to something more manageable and meaningful. This is not technically essential but is good practice to keep our work clean and organized. There are many ways to rename an object.

One way is to first select it and then enter a new name in the name field in the **Object Inspector**. I'll rename it `WorldFloor`. See *Figure 1.19*:

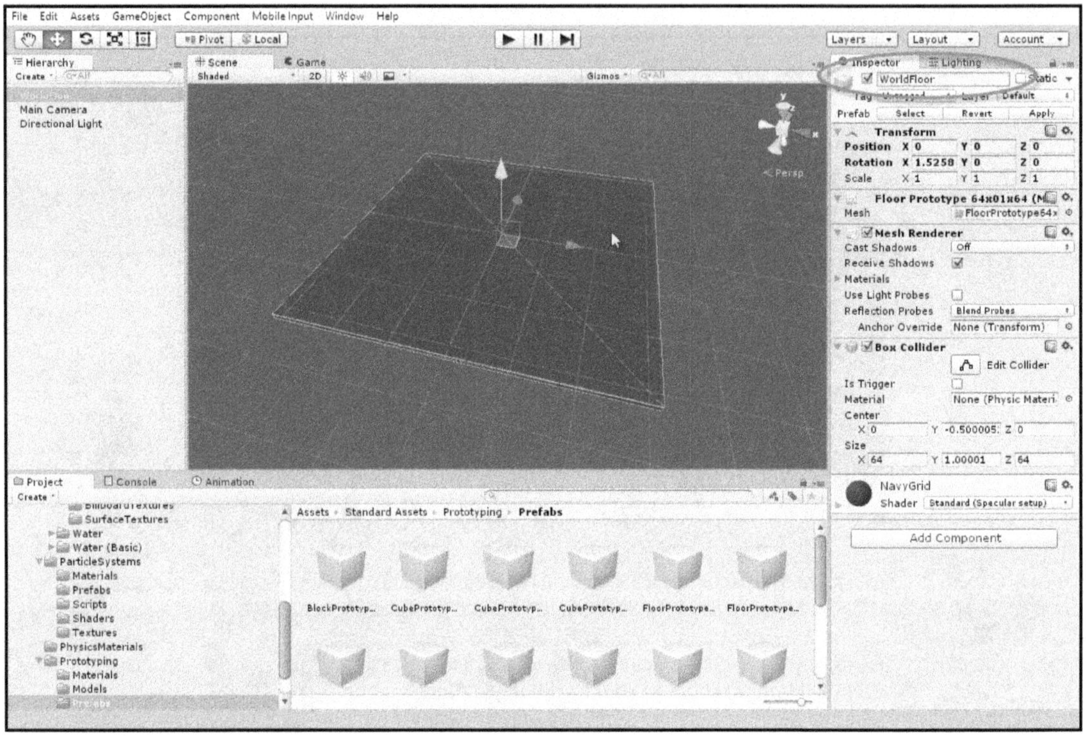

Figure 1.19: Renaming the floor mesh

Transformations and navigation

A scene with a floor mesh has been established, but this alone is uninteresting. We need to add more, such as buildings, stairs, columns, and perhaps more floor pieces. Otherwise, there would be no world for the player to explore. Before building on what we've got, however, let's make sure that the existing floor piece is centered at the world origin. Every point and location within a scene is uniquely identified by a coordinate, measured as an (X, Y, Z) offset from the world center (origin).

The current position for the selected object is always visible from the **Object Inspector**. In fact, the **Position**, **Rotation**, and **Scale** of an object are grouped together under a category (component) called **Transform**. **Position** indicates how far an object should be moved in three axes from the world center. **Rotation** indicates how much an object should be turned or rotated around its central axes. **Scale** indicates how much an object should be shrunk or expanded to smaller or larger sizes. A default **Scale** of one means that an object should appear at normal size, two means twice the size, and 0.5 means half the size, and so on. Together, the **Position**, **Rotation**, and **Scale** of an object constitute its transformation. To change the position of the selected object, you can simply type new values in the **X**, **Y**, and **Z** fields for Position. To move an object to the world center, simply enter (`0`, `0`, and `0`), as shown in *Figure 1.20*:

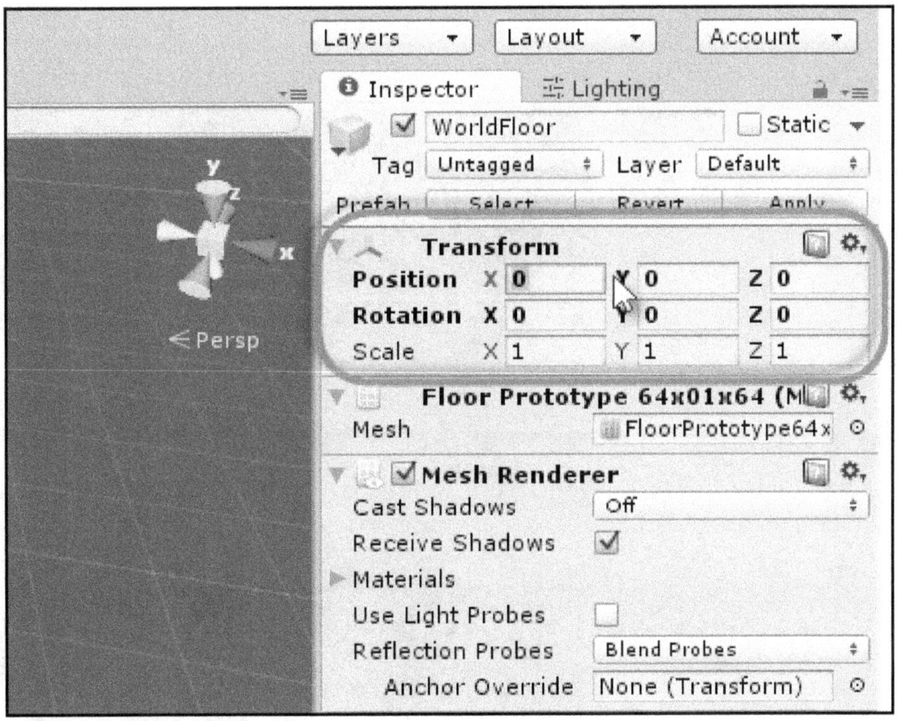

Figure 1.20: Centering an object to the world origin

Setting the position of an object, as we've done here, by typing numerical values is acceptable and appropriate for the specifying of exact positions. However, it's often more intuitive to move objects using mouse-based controls. To do this, let's add a second floor piece and position it away from the first instance. Drag and drop a floor piece from the **Project** panel in Scene to create a second floor GameObject. Then click on the new floor piece to select it and switch to the **Translate** tool. To do this, press *W* on the keyboard or click on the translate tool icon from the toolbar at the top of the editor interface. The translate tool allows you to reposition objects in **Scene**. See *Figure 1.21*:

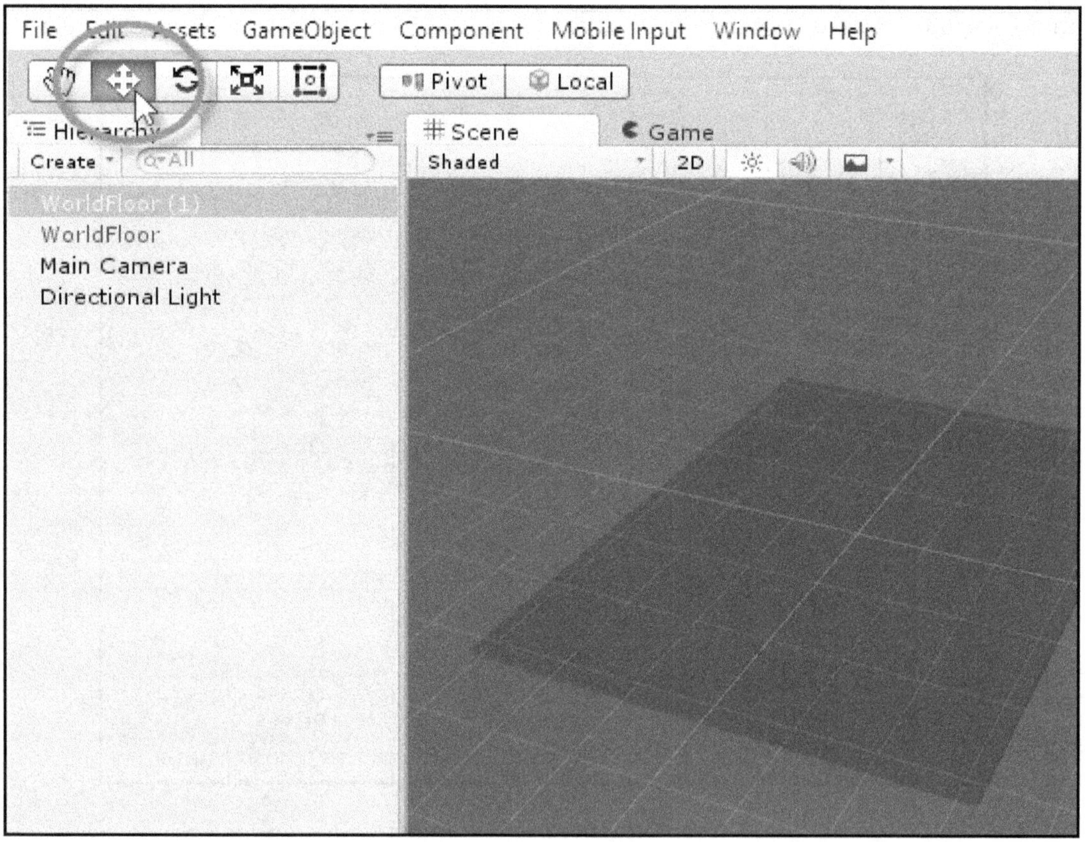

Figure 1.21: Accessing the translate tool

When the translate tool is active and an object is selected, a Gizmo appears centered on the object (three colored axes visible in the **Scene** tab). The translate Gizmo appears as three colored perpendicular axes: red, green, and blue corresponding to X, Y, and Z respectively.

To move an object, hover your cursor over one of the three axes (or planes between axes), and then click and hold the mouse while moving it to slide the object in that direction. You can repeat this process as often as needed to ensure that your objects are positioned where you need them to be. Use the translate tool to move the second floor piece away from the first. See *Figure 1.22*:

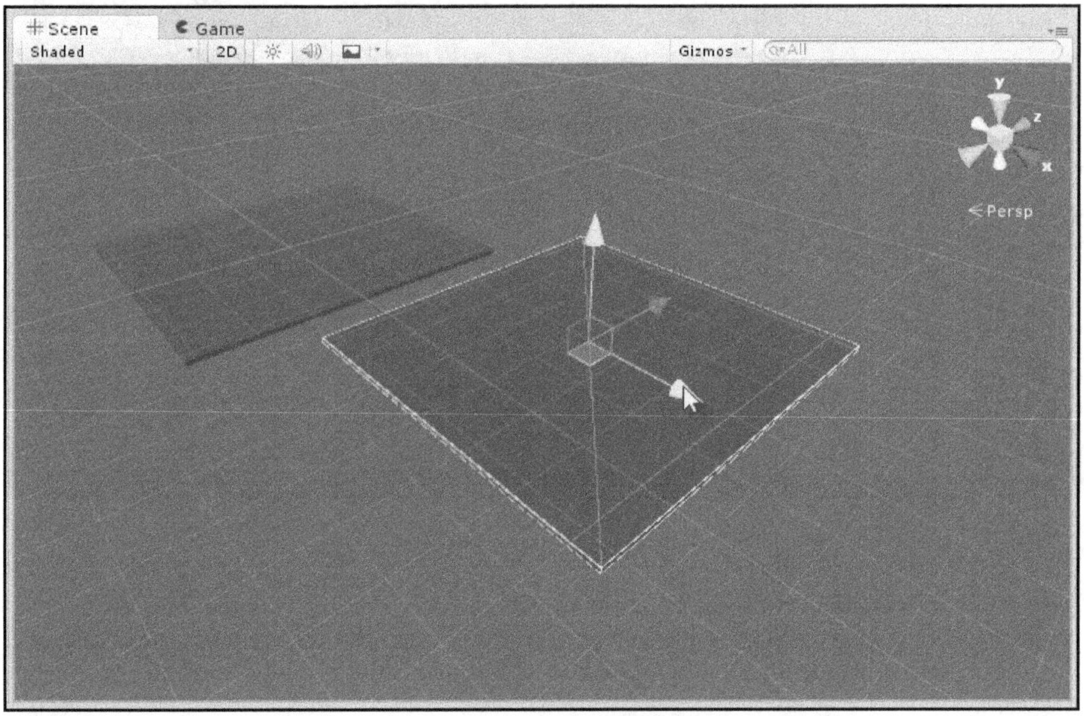

Figure 1.22: Translate an object using the translate Gizmo

You can also rotate and scale objects using the mouse, as with translate. Press *E* to access the rotate tool or *R* to access the scale tool, or you can activate these tools using their respective toolbar icons from the top of the editor. When these tools are activated, a Gizmo appears centered on the object, and you can click and drag the mouse over each specific axis to rotate or scale objects as needed. See *Figure 1.23*:

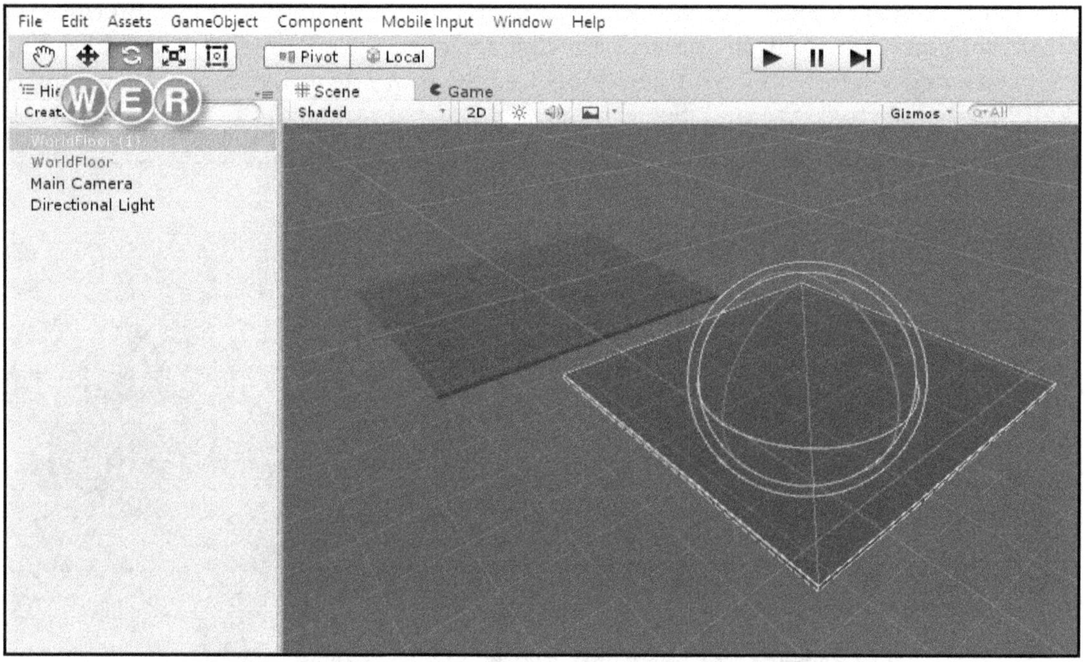

Figure 1.23: Accessing the rotate and scale tools

Being able to translate, rotate, and scale objects quickly through mouse and keyboard combinations is very important when working in Unity. For this reason, make using the keyboard shortcuts a habit, as opposed to accessing the tools continually from the toolbar.

However, in addition to moving, rotating, and scaling objects, you'll frequently need to move around yourself in the **Scene** view in order to see the world from different positions, angles, and perspectives. This means that you'll frequently need to reposition the scene preview camera in the world. You'll want to zoom in and zoom out of the world to get a better view of objects and change your viewing angle to see how objects align and fit together properly. To do this, you'll need to make extensive use of both the keyboard and mouse together.

To zoom closer or further from the object you're looking at, simply scroll the mouse wheel up or down—up zooms in and down zooms out. See *Figure 1.24*:

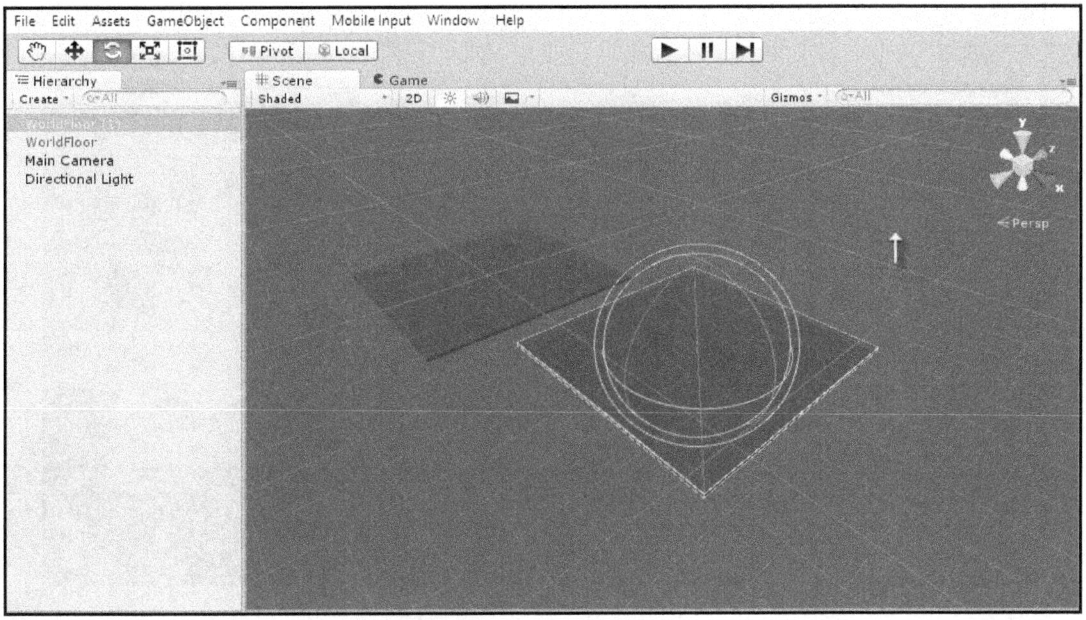

Figure 1.24: Zooming in and out

To pan the **Scene** view left or right, or up or down, hold down the middle mouse button while moving the mouse in the appropriate direction. Alternatively, you can access the pan tool from the application toolbar (or press Q on the keyboard) and then simply click and drag in the **Scene** view while the tool is active. Pan does not zoom in or out; it simply slides the camera left and right, or up and down:

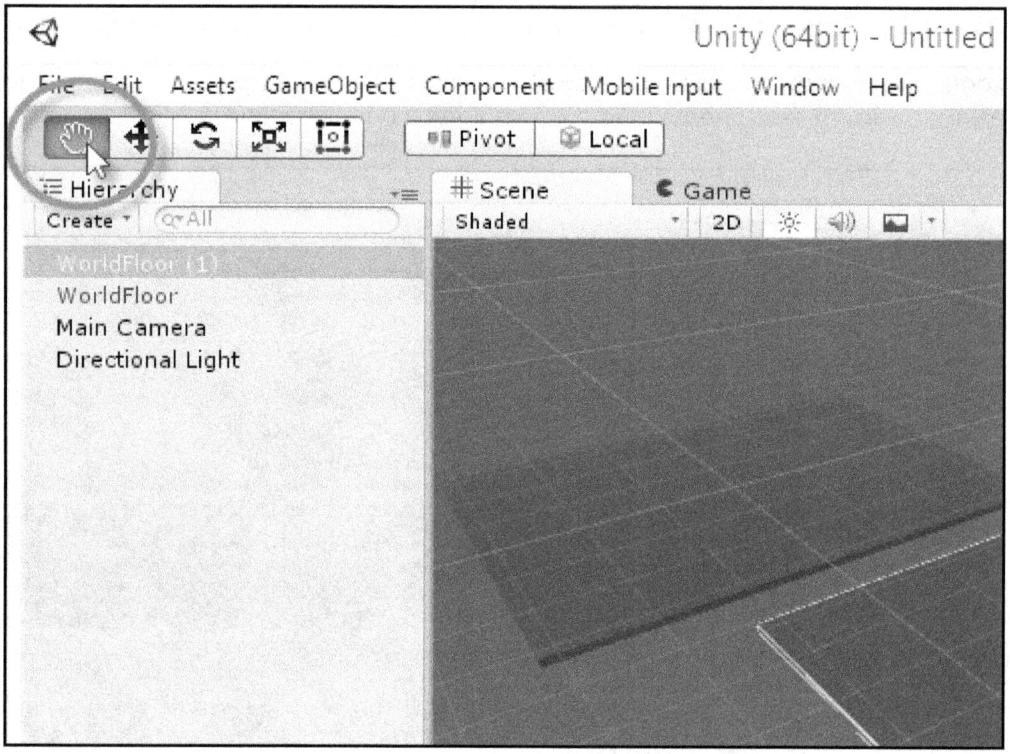

Figure 1.25: Accessing the Pan tool

Sometimes, while building levels, you'll lose sight entirely of the object that you need. For example, your viewport camera could be focusing on a completely different place from the object you really want to click or see. In this case, you'll often want to shift the viewport camera automatically in order to focus on that specific object.

Specifically, you'll want to reposition and rotate the viewport as necessary to bring a desired object to the center of the view. To do this automatically, select the object to focus on (or frame) by clicking on its name from the **Hierarchy** panel. Then, press the *F* key on the keyboard. Alternatively, you can double-click its name in the **Hierarchy** panel. See *Figure 1.26*:

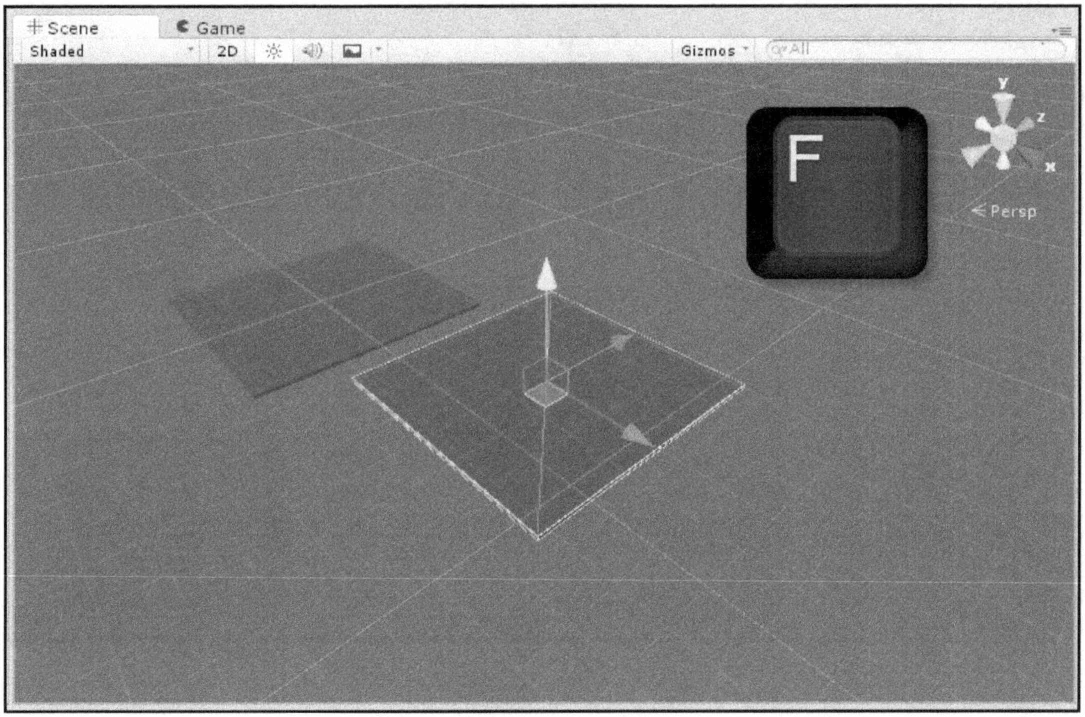

Figure 1.26: Framing a selected object

After framing an object, you'll often want to rotate around it in order to quickly and easily view it from all important angles. To achieve this, hold down the *Alt* key on the keyboard while clicking and dragging the mouse to rotate the view. See *Figure 1.27*:

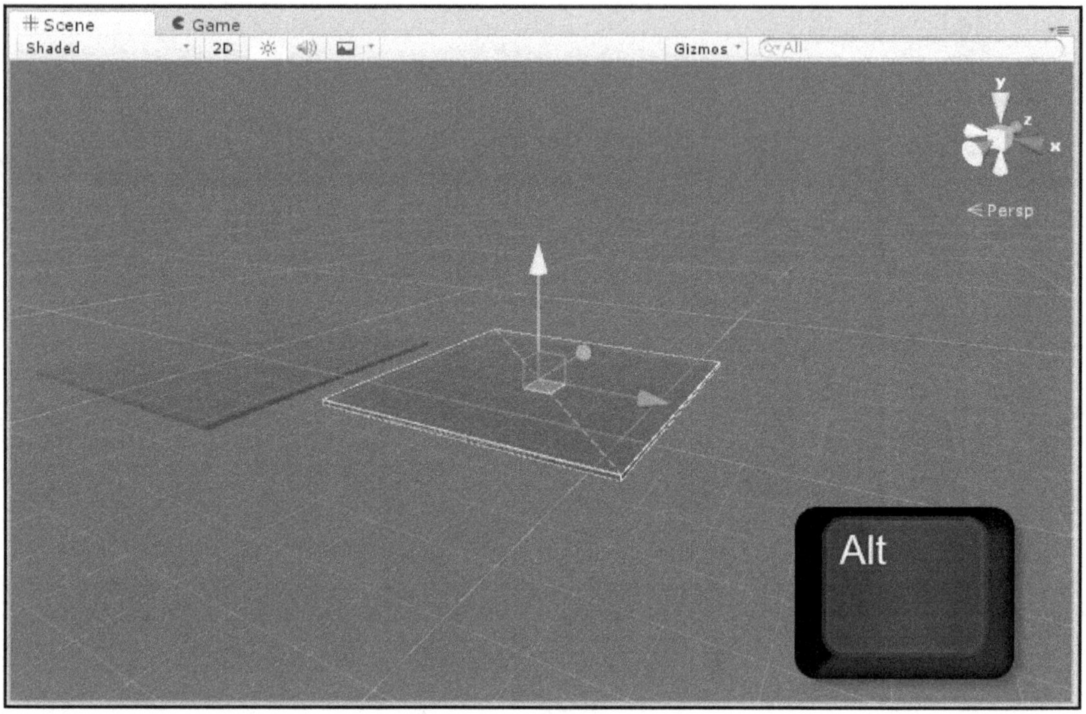

Figure 1.27: Rotating around the framed object

Lastly, it's helpful to navigate a level in the **Scene** view using first-person controls, that is, controls that mimic how first-person games are played. This helps you experience the scene at a more personal and immersive level.

To do this, hold down the right mouse button and (with the button depressed) use the WASD keys on the keyboard to control forward, backward, and strafing movement. Movement of the mouse controls head orientation. You can also hold down the *Shift* key while moving to increase movement speed. See *Figure 1.28*:

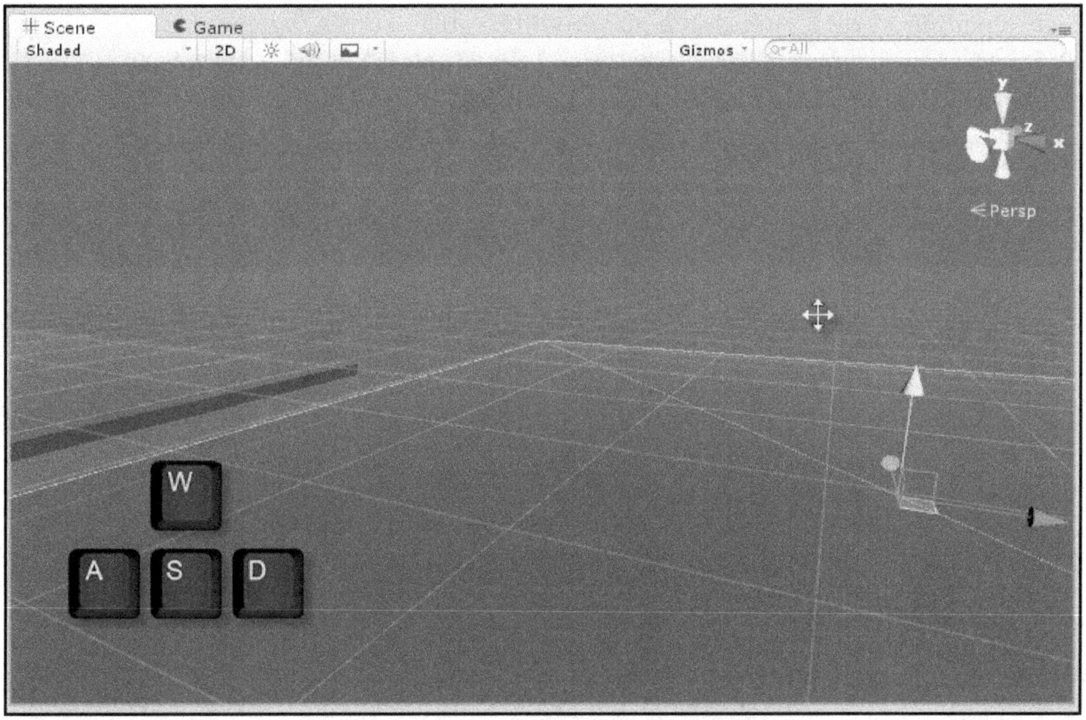

Figure 1.28: Using first-person controls

The great thing about learning the versatile transformation and navigation controls is that, on understanding them, you can move and orient practically any object in any way, and you can move and view the world from almost any position and angle. Being able to do this is critically important to build quality levels quickly. All of these controls, along with some others that we'll soon see, will be used frequently throughout this book to create scenes and work in Unity generally.

Scene building

Now that we've seen how to transform objects and navigate the scene viewport successfully, let's proceed to complete our first level for the coin collection game. Let's separate the two floor meshes apart in space, leaving a gap between them that we'll fix by creating a bridge, which the player will be able to cross, moving between the floor spaces like islands. We can use the translate tool (*W*) to move objects around. See *Figure 1.29*:

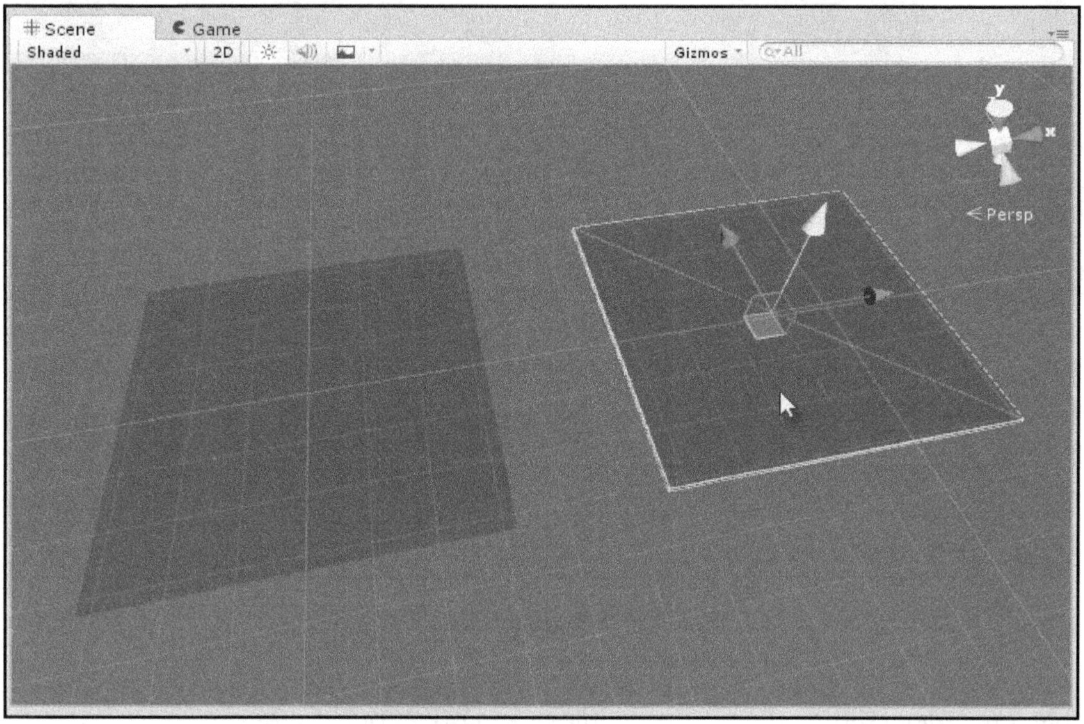

Figure 1.29: Separating the floor meshes into islands

If you want to create more floor objects, you can use the method that we've seen already by dragging and dropping the mesh asset in the **Project** panel in the Scene viewport. Alternatively, you can duplicate the selected object in the viewport by pressing *Ctrl* + *D* on the keyboard. Both methods produce the same result.

Next, we'll add some props and obstacles to the scene. Drag and drop some house objects onto the floor. The house object (`HousePrototype16x16x24`) is found in the `Assets` | `Standard Assets` | `Prototyping` | `Prefabs` folder. See *Figure 1.30*:

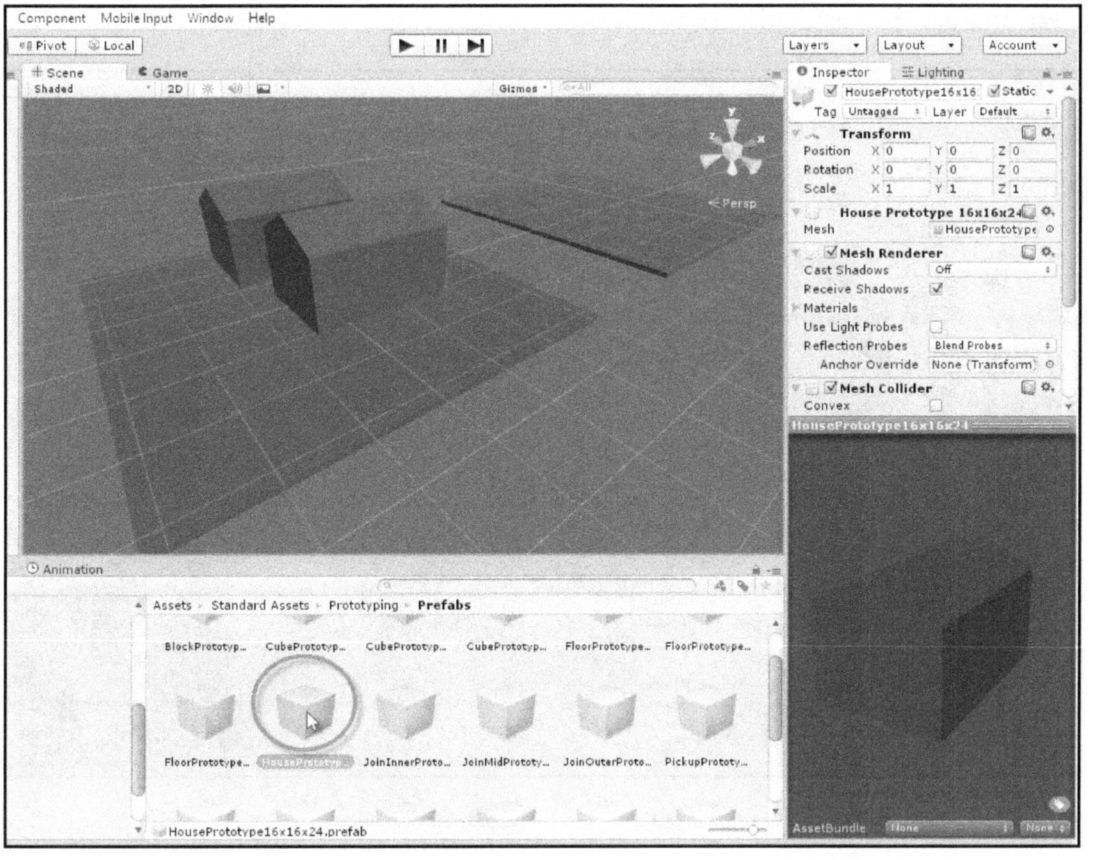

Figure 1.30: Adding house props to the scene

On dragging and dropping the house in the scene, it may align to the floor nicely with the bottom against the floor, or it may not align like that. If it does, that's splendid and great luck! However, we shouldn't rely on luck every time because we're professional game developers! Thankfully, we can make any two mesh objects align easily in Unity using vertex snapping. This feature works by forcing two objects into positional alignment within the scene by overlapping their vertices at a specific and common point.

For example, consider *Figure 1.31*. Here, a house object hovers awkwardly above the floor and we naturally want it to align level with the floor and perhaps over to the floor corner. To achieve this, start by selecting the house object (click on it or select it from the **Hierarchy** panel). The object to be selected is the one that *should move* to align and not the destination (which is the floor), which should remain in place:

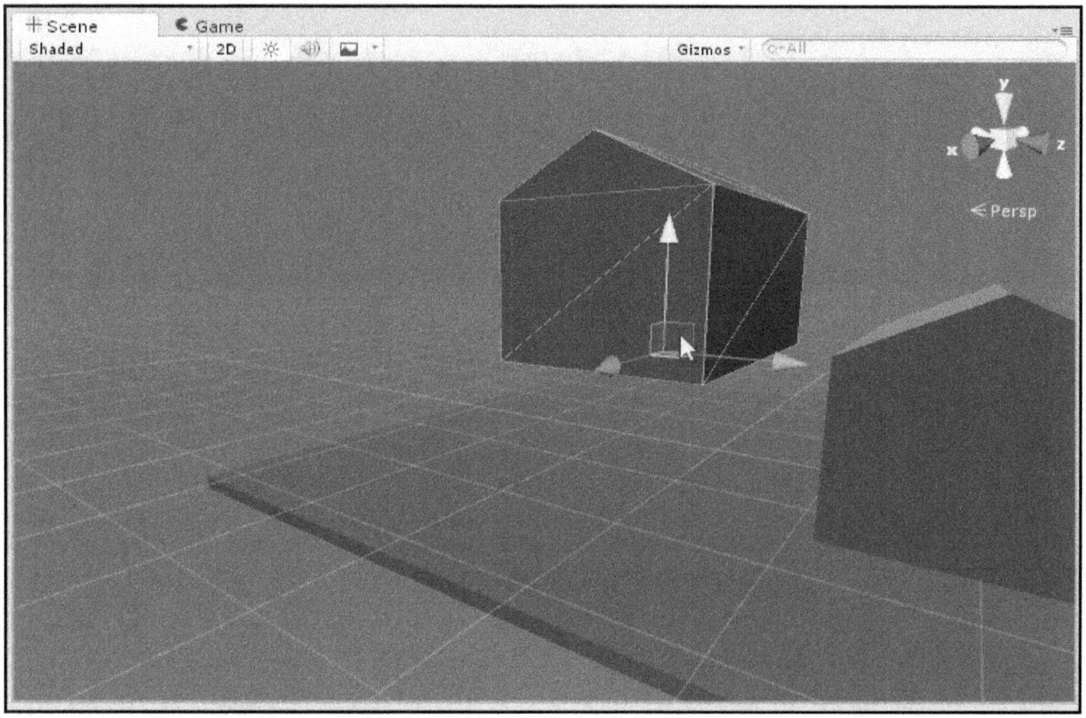

Figure 1.31: Misaligned objects can be snapped into place with Vertex Snapping

Next, activate the translate tool (*W*) and hold down the *V* key for vertex snapping. With *V* held down, move the cursor around and see how the Gizmo cursor sticks to the nearest vertex of the selected mesh. See *Figure 1.32*. Unity is asking you to pick a source vertex for the snapping:

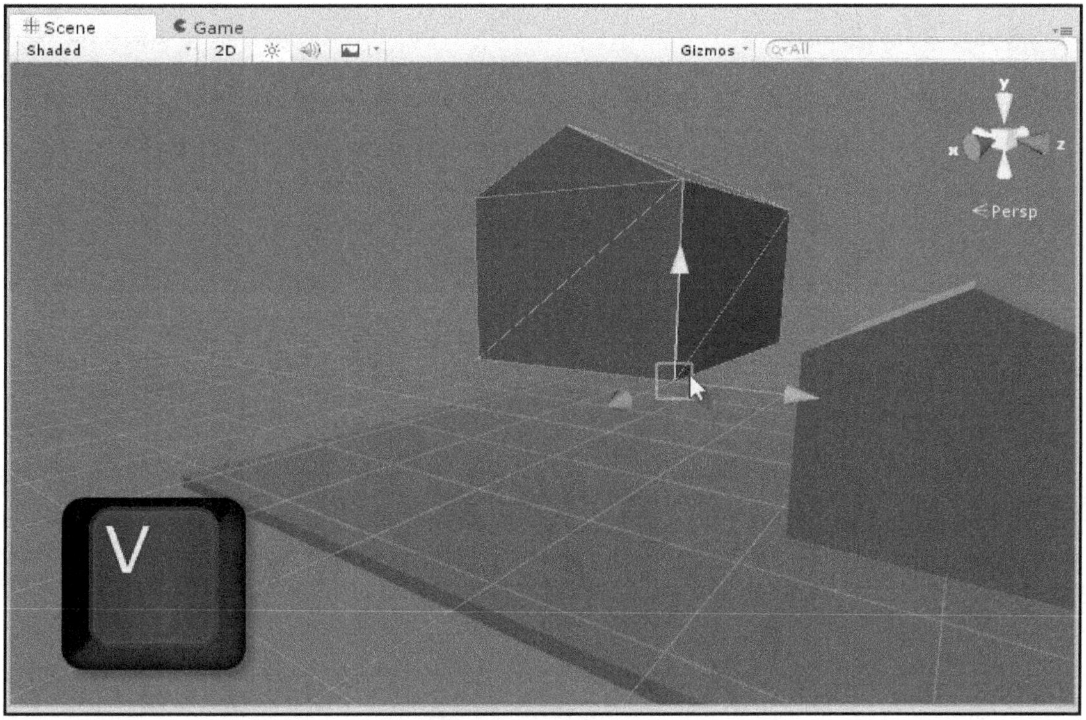

Figure 1.32: Hold down V to activate Vertex Snapping

With *V* held down, move the cursor to the bottom corner of the house, and then click and drag from the corner to the floor mesh corner. The house will then snap align to the floor, corner to corner. When aligned this way, it releases the *V* key, and the two meshes get aligned exactly at the vertices. See *Figure 1.33*:

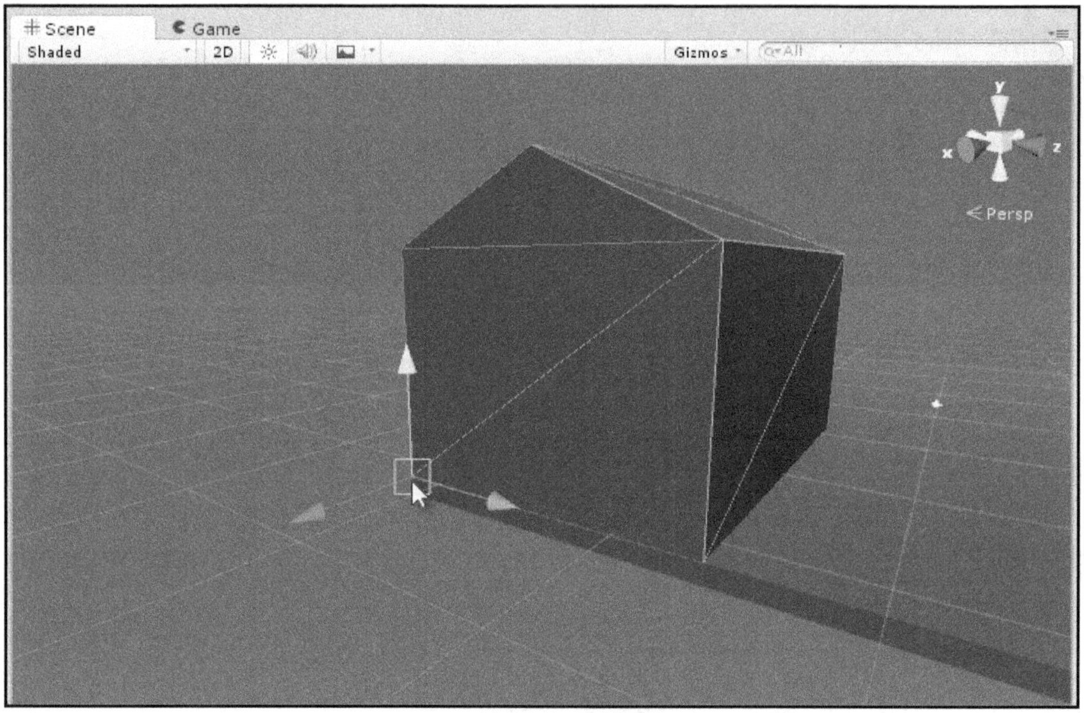

Figure 1.33: Align two meshes by vertices

Now you can assemble a complete scene using the mesh assets included in the `Prototyping` package. Drag and drop props in the scene, and using translate, rotate, and scale, you can reposition, realign, and rotate these objects; using vertex snapping, you can align them wherever you need. Give this some practice.

See *Figure 1.34* for the scene arrangement that I made using only these tools and assets:

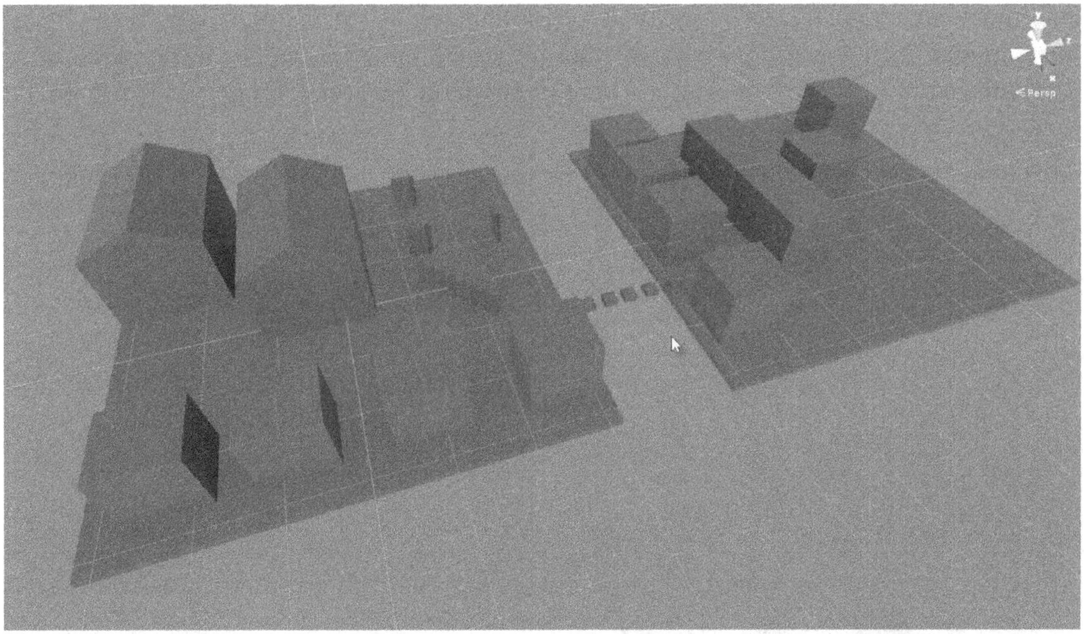

Figure 1.34: Building a complete level

Lighting and sky

The basic level has been created in terms of architectural models and layout; this was achieved using only a few mesh assets and some basic tools. Nevertheless, these tools are powerful and offer us a multitude of combinations and options to create great variety in game worlds. One important ingredient is missing for us, however. This ingredient is lighting. You'll notice from *Figure 1.34* that everything looks relatively flat, with no highlights, shadows, or light or dark areas. This is because scene lighting is not properly configured for best results, even though we already have a light in the scene, which was created initially by default.

Let's start setting the scene for the coin collection game by enabling the sky, if it's not already enabled. To do this, click on the **Extras** drop-down menu from the top toolbar in the **Scene** viewport. From the context menu, select **Skybox** to enable **Skybox** viewing. A **Skybox** simply refers to a large cube that surrounds the whole scene. Each interior side has a continuous texture (image) applied to simulate the appearance of a surrounding sky. For this reason, clicking the **Skybox** option displays a default sky in the **Scene** viewport. See Figure 1.35:

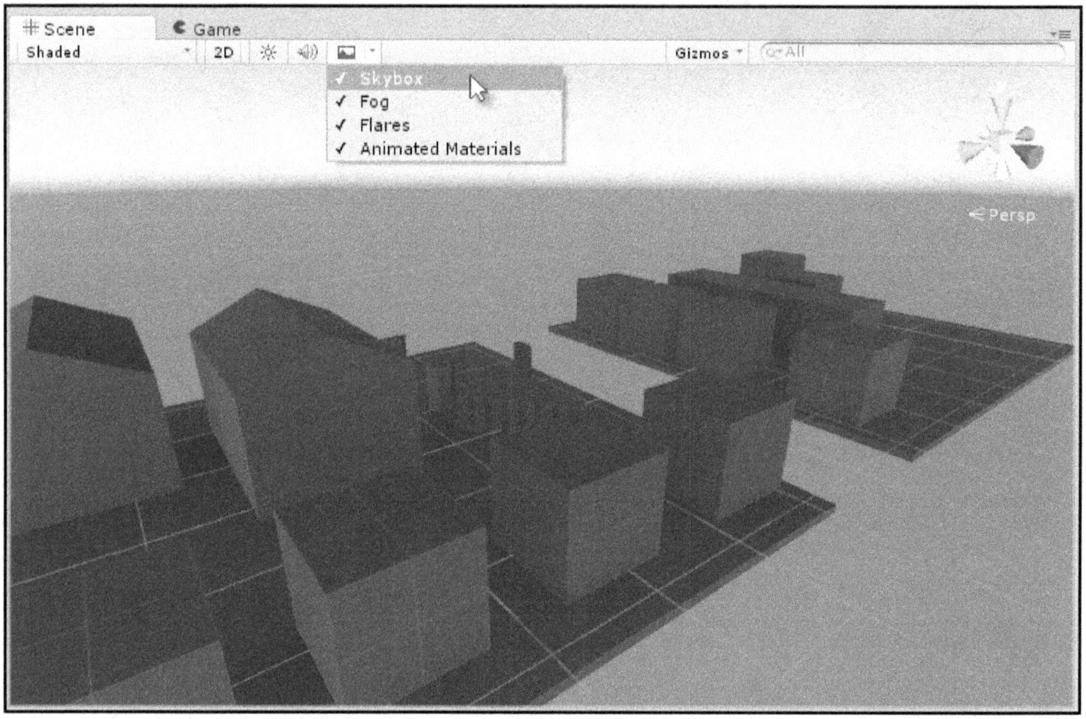

Figure 1.35: Enabling the sky

Now, although the **Skybox** is now enabled and the scene looks better than before, it's still not being illuminated properly—the objects lack shadows and highlights. To fix this, be sure that lighting is enabled for the scene by toggling on the lighting icon at the top of the **Scene** viewport. See *Figure 1.36*. This setting is for display purposes only. It only affects whether lighting effects are shown in the **Scene** viewport and not whether lighting is truly enabled for the final game:

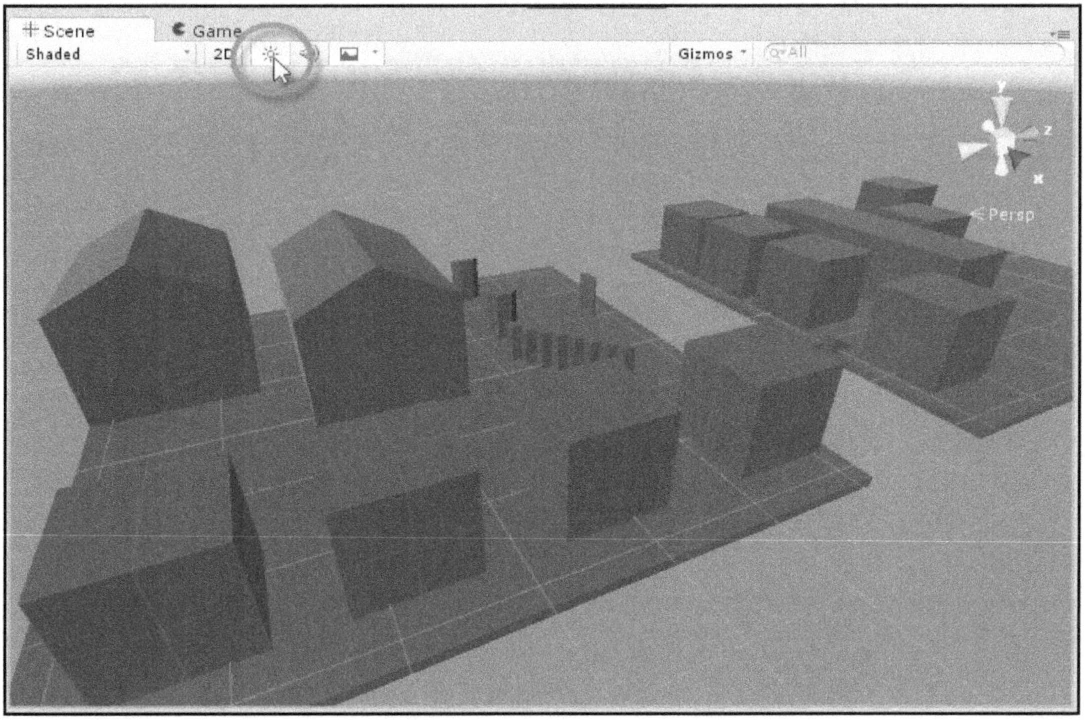

Figure 1.36: Enabling scene lighting in the Scene viewport

Enabling lighting display for the viewport will result in some differences to the scene appearance and, again, the scene should look better than before. You can confirm that scene lighting is taking effect by selecting **Directional Light** from the **Hierarchy** panel and rotating it. Doing this controls the time of day, rotating the light cycles between day and night and changing the light intensity and mood. This changes how the scene is rendered. See *Figure 1.37*:

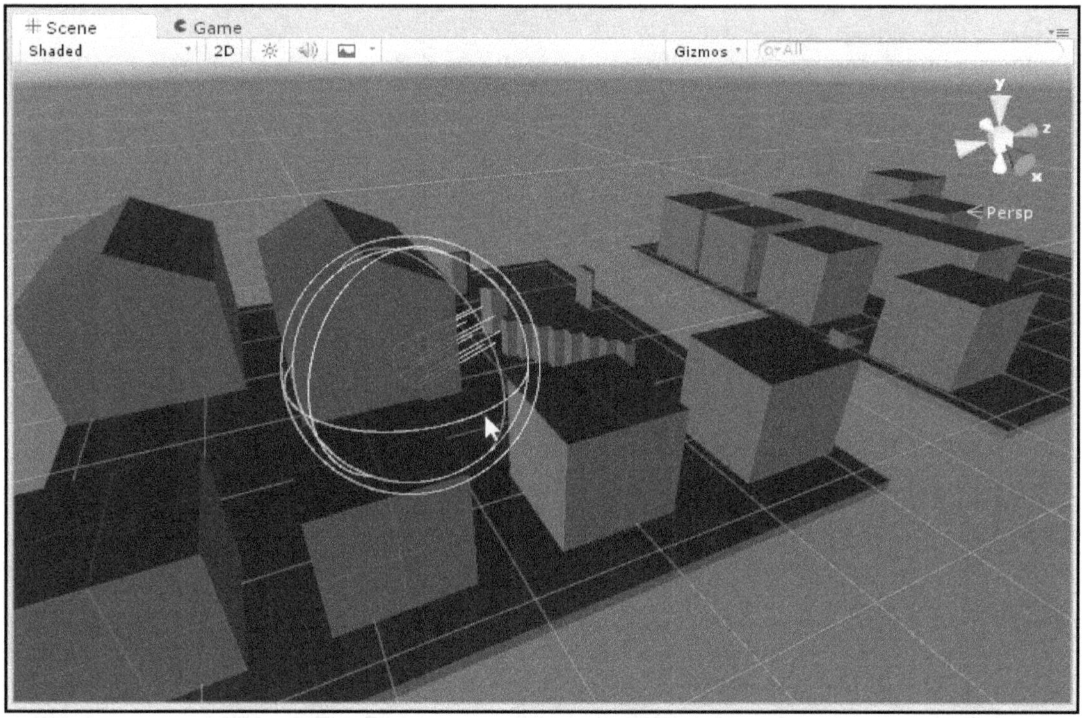

Figure 1.37: Rotating the scene directional light changes the time of day

Let's undo any rotations to the **Directional Light** by pressing *Ctrl* + *Z* on the keyboard. To prepare for final and optimal lighting, all non-movable objects in the scene (such as walls, floors, chairs, tables, ceilings, grass, hills, towers, and more) should be marked as **Static**. This signifies to Unity that the objects will never move, no matter what happens during gameplay. By marking non-movable objects ahead of time, you can help Unity optimize the way it renders and lights a scene. To mark objects as **Static**, simply select all non-movable objects (which includes practically the entire level so far), and then enable the Static checkbox via the **Object Inspector**.

Note that you don't need to enable the **Static** setting for each object separately. By holding down the *Shift* key while selecting objects, you can select multiple objects together, allowing you to adjust their properties as a batch through the **Object Inspector**. See *Figure 1.38*:

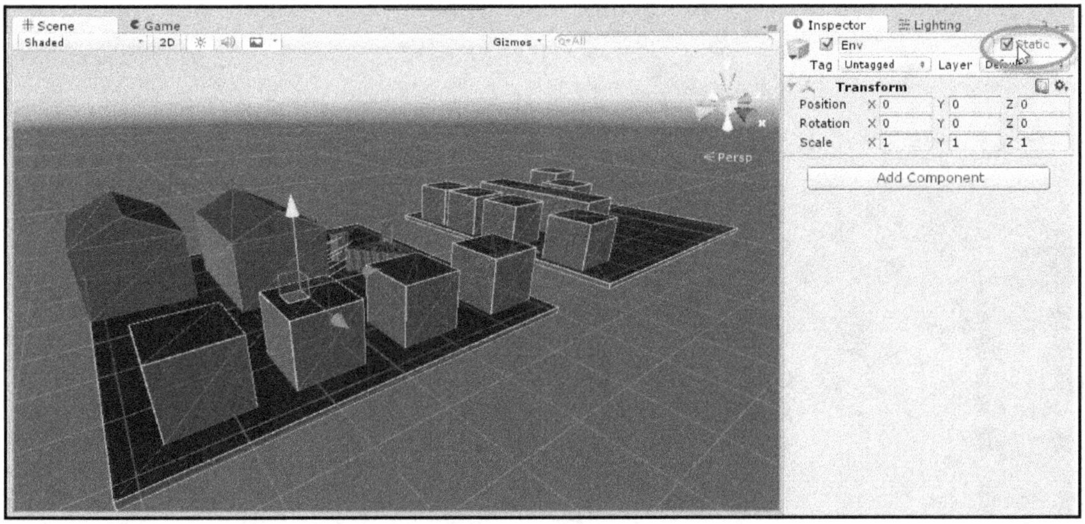

Figure 1.38: Enabling the Static option for multiple non-movable objects improves lighting and performance

When you enable the **Static** checkbox for geometry, Unity auto-calculates scene lighting in the background—effects such as shadows, indirect illumination, and more. It generates a batch of data called the **GI Cache**, featuring **Light Propagation Paths**, which instructs Unity how light rays should bounce and move around the scene to achieve greater realism. Even so, enabling the **Static** checkbox as we've done still won't produce cast shadows for objects, and this seriously detracts from realism. This happens because most mesh objects have the **Cast Shadows** option disabled.

To fix this, select all meshes in the scene. Then, from the **Object Inspector**, click on the **Cast Shadows** checkbox from the **Mesh Renderer** component, and choose the **On** option from the context menu. When you do this, all mesh objects should cast shadows. See *Figure 1.39*:

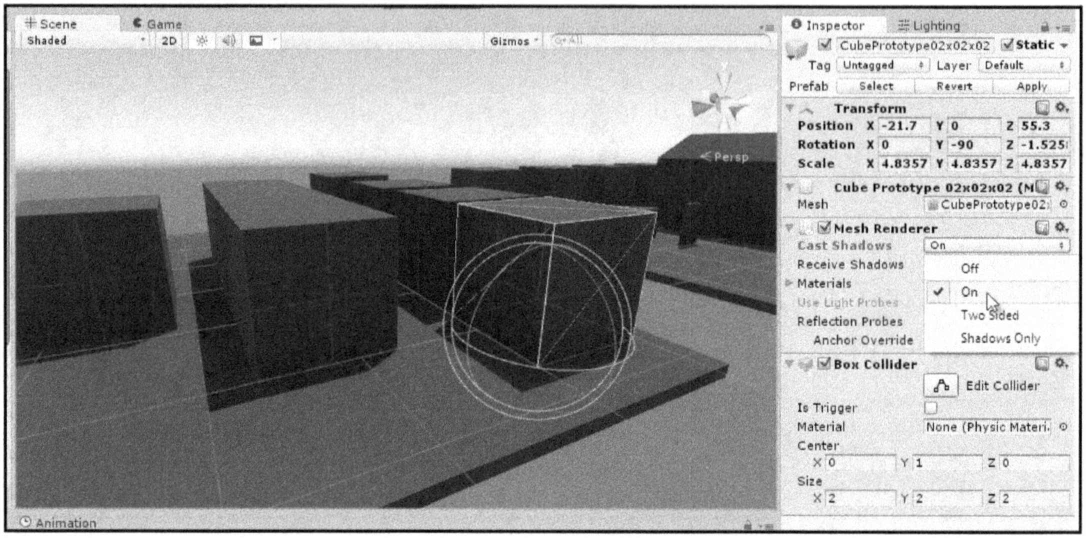

Figure 1.39: Enabling cast shadows from the Mesh Renderer component

Voila! Your meshes now cast shadows. Splendid work: in reaching this far, you've created a new project, populated a scene with meshes, and successfully illuminated them with directional lighting. That's excellent. However, it'd be even better if we could explore our environment in the first-person mode. We'll see how next.

Play testing and the Game tab

The environment created thus far for the coin collection game has been assembled using only the mesh assets included with the native **Prototyping** package. My environment, as shown in *Figure 1.40,* features two main floor islands with houses, and the islands themselves are connected together by a stepping-stone bridge. Your version may be slightly different, and that's fine: Figure 1.40:

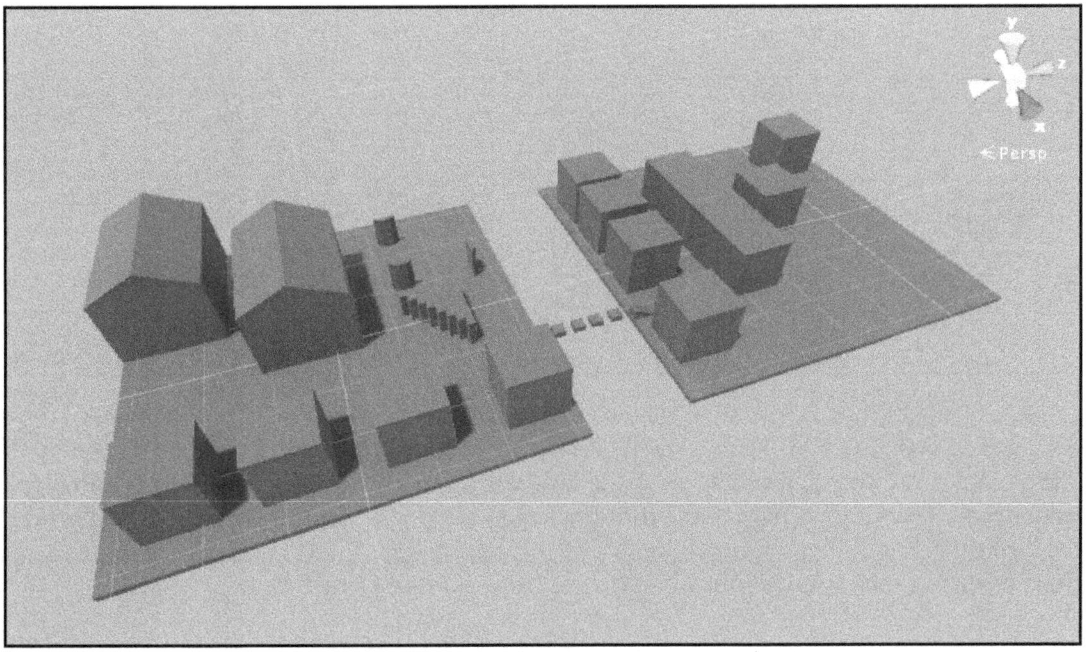

Figure 1.40: The scene created so far contains two island areas

Overall, the scene is good work. It's well worth saving (remember to save regularly!). To save the scene, press *Ctrl + S* on the keyboard or else choose **File** | **Save Scene** from the application menu. See *Figure 1.41.*

If you're saving the scene for the first time, Unity displays a pop-up **Save** dialog, prompting you to name the scene descriptively (we called it `Level_01`):

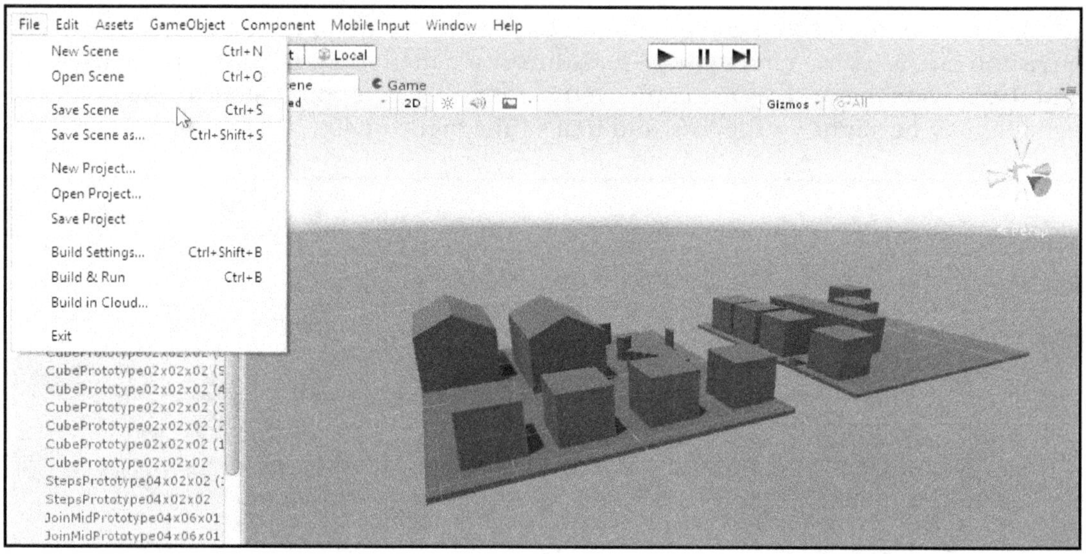

Figure 1.41: Saving a scene

After saving the scene, it becomes scene asset of the project and appears in the **Project** panel. See *Figure 1.42*. This means that the scene is now a genuine and integral part of the project and not just a temporary work-in-progress as it was before. Notice also that saving a scene is conceptually *different* from saving a project.

For example, the application menu has entries for **Save Scene** and **Save Project**. Remember, a Project is a collection of files and folders, including assets and scenes. A scene, by contrast, is one asset within the project and represents a complete 3D map that may be populated by other assets, such as meshes, textures, and sounds. Thus, saving a project saves the configuration between files and assets, including scenes. Saving a scene, in contrast, just retains the level changes within that specified scene.

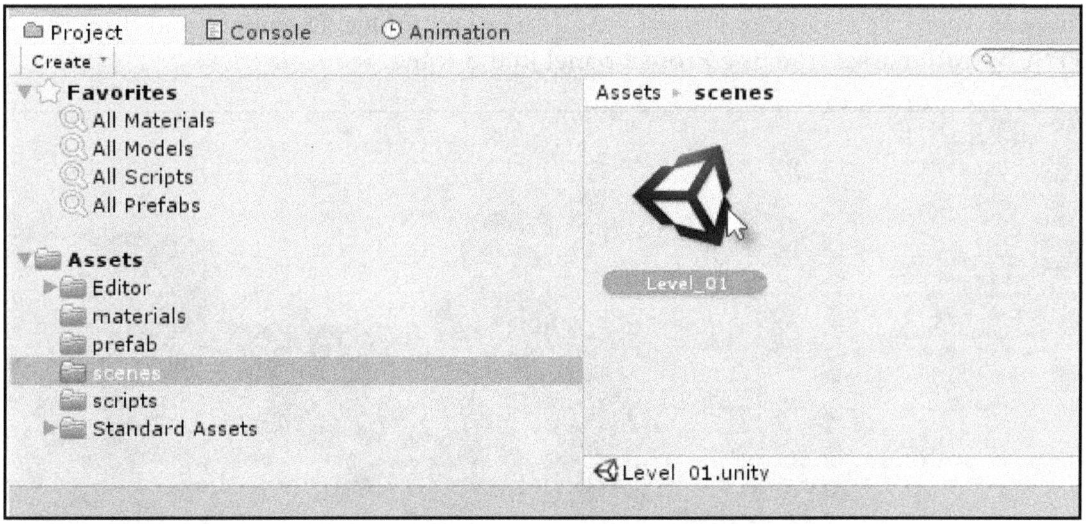

Figure 1.42: Saved scenes are added as assets within your project

> You can see from *Figure 1.42* that I've saved my scene in a folder named `scenes`. Folders can be created in your project by right-clicking on any empty area in the Project panel and choosing New Folder from the context menu, or else choose **Assets** | **Create** | **Folder** from the application menu. You can easily move and rearrange assets among folders by simply dragging and dropping them.

Now, the level, as it stands, contains nothing really playable. It's simply a static, lifeless, and non-interactive 3D environment made using the **Editor** tools. Let's correct this by making our scene playable, allowing the player to wander around and explore the world in first-person mode, controlled using the standard WASD keys on the keyboard. To achieve this, we'll add a first-person character controller to the scene. This is a ready-made asset included with Unity, which contains everything necessary to create quick and effective first-person controls. Open the `Standard Assets` | `Characters` | `FirstPersonCharacter` | `Prefabs` folder. Then drag and drop the **FPSController** asset from the **Project** panel in the scene. See *Figure 1.43*:

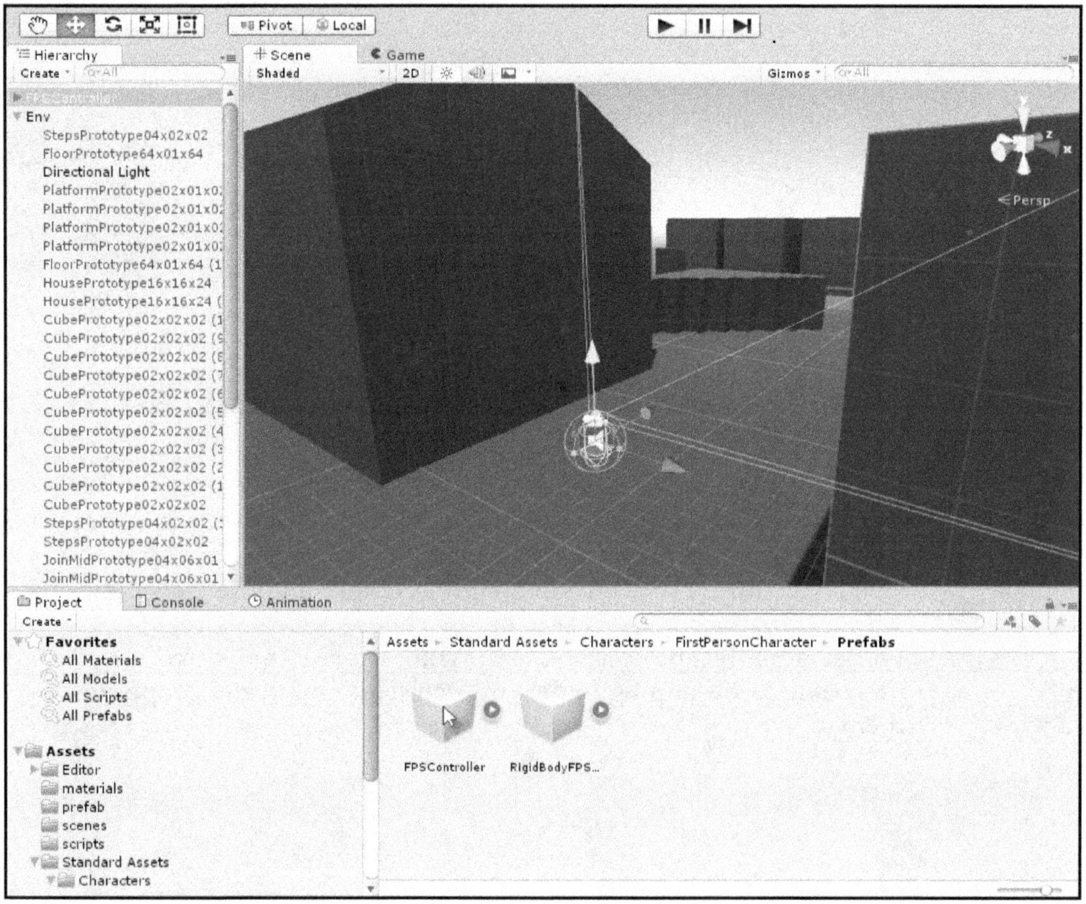

Figure 1.43: Adding an FPSController to the scene

After adding the first-person controller, click on the play button from the Unity toolbar to play test the game in first-person mode. See *Figure 1.44*:

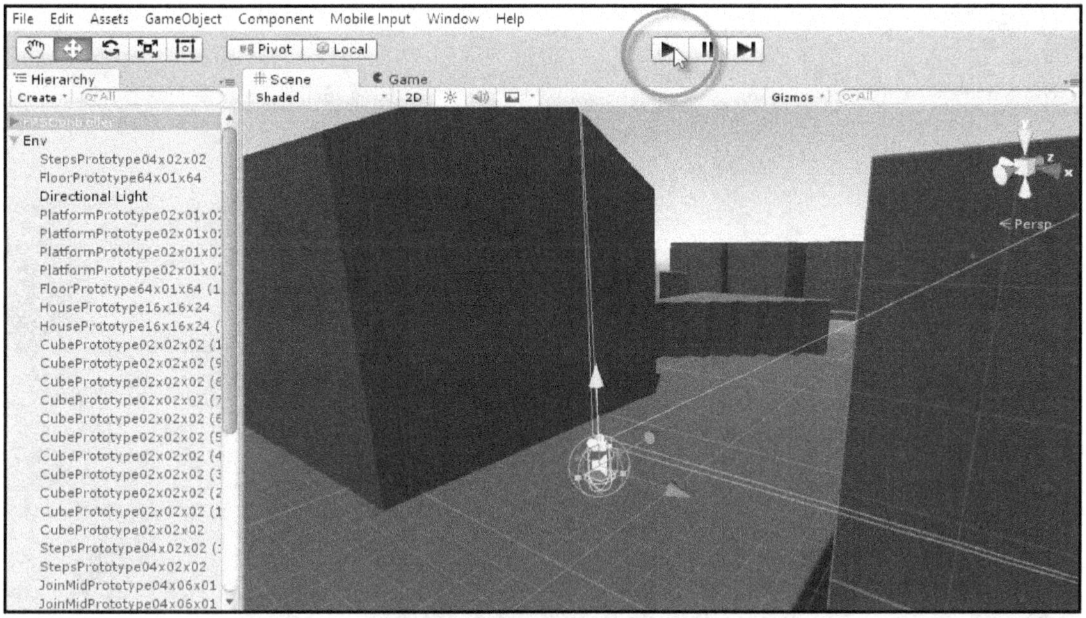

Figure 1.44: Unity scenes can be play tested by clicking on the play button from the toolbar

On clicking play, Unity typically switches from the **Scene** tab to the **Game** tab. As we've seen, the **Scene** tab is a director's-eye view of the active scene; it's where a scene is edited, crafted, and designed. In contrast, the **Game** tab is where the active scene is played and tested from the perspective of the gamer. From this view, the scene is displayed through the main game camera. While play mode is active, you can play test your game using the default game controls, provided that the **Game** tab is in focus.

The first-person controller uses the WASD keys on the keyboard and mouse movement controls head orientation. See Figure 1.45:

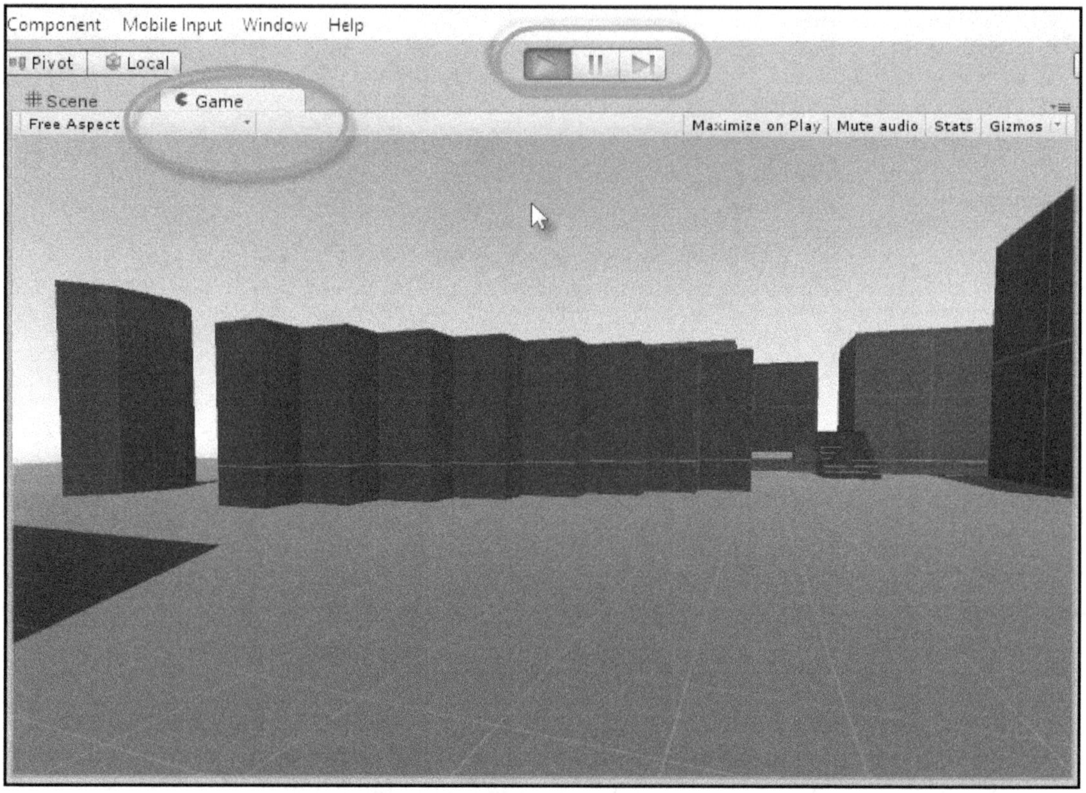

Figure 1.45: Play testing levels in the Game tab

You can switch back to the **Scene** tab while in play mode. You can even edit the scene and change, move, and delete objects there too! However, any and all scene changes made during play mode will automatically revert back to their original settings when play mode ends. This behavior is intentional. It lets you edit properties during gameplay to observe their effects and debug any issues without permanently changing the scene.

Congratulations! Your level should now be walkable in first-person mode. When completed, you can easily stop playback by clicking on the play button again or by pressing *Ctrl* + *P* on the keyboard. Doing this will return you to the **Scene** tab.

> Unity also features a Toggle-Pause button to suspend and resume gameplay.

You should notice that, on playing the level with a first-person controller, you receive an information message printed to the **Console** window. By default, this window appears at the bottom of the **Unity Editor**, docked beside the **Project** panel. This window is also accessible manually from the application menu, **Window** | **Console**. The **Console** window is where all encountered errors or warnings are displayed for your review as well as information messages. Errors are printed in red and warnings in yellow, and information messages appear as a default grey. Sometimes, a message appears just once, or sometimes it appears many times repeatedly. See *Figure 1.46*:

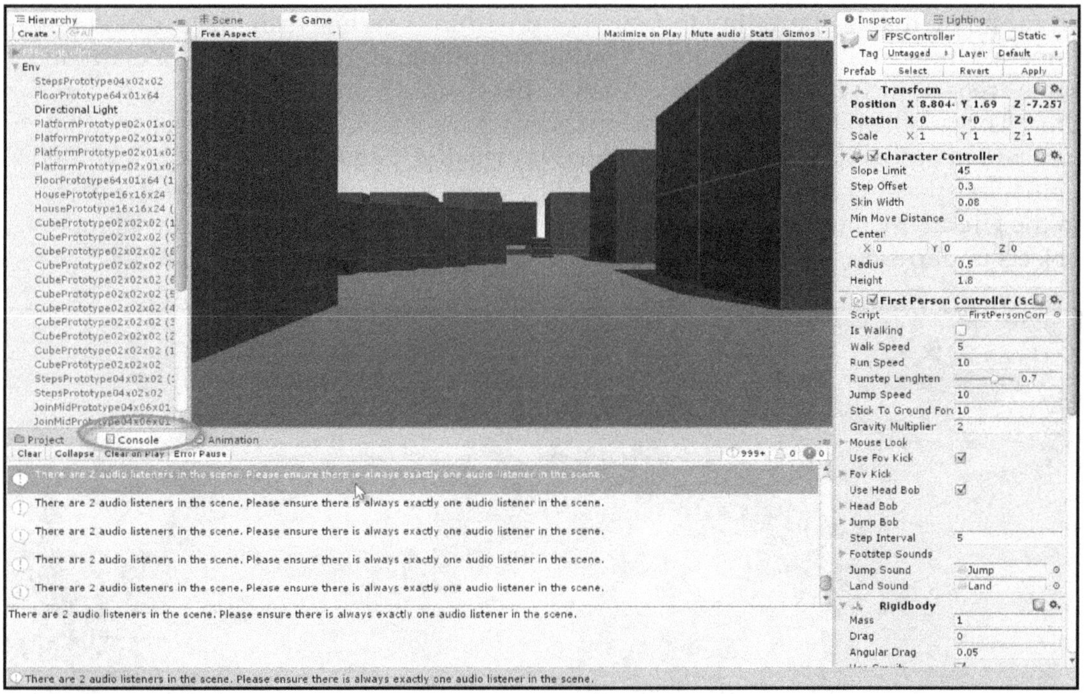

Figure 1.46: The Console outputs information, warnings, and errors

As mentioned, the **Console** window outputs three distinct types of message: information, warnings, and errors. Information messages are typically Unity's way of making best practice recommendations or suggestions based on how your project is currently working. Warnings are slightly more serious and represent problems either in your code or scene, which (if not corrected) could result in unexpected behaviors and suboptimal performance. Finally, errors describe areas in your scene or code that require careful and immediate attention. Sometimes, errors will prevent your game from working altogether and sometimes errors happen at runtime and can result in game crashes or freezes. The **Console** window, therefore, is helpful because it helps us debug and address issues with our games. *Figure 1.46* has identified an issue concerning duplicated audio listeners.

An audio listener is a component attached to a camera object. Specifically, each and every camera, by default, has an audio listener component attached. This represents an ear point, that is, the ability to hear sound within the scene from the position of the camera. Unfortunately, Unity doesn't support multiple active audio listeners in the same scene, which means that you can only hear audio from one place at any one time. This problem happens because our scene now contains two cameras, one that was added automatically when the scene was created, and the other that is included in the first-person controller. To confirm this, select the first-person controller object in the **Hierarchy** panel and click on the triangle icon beside its name to reveal more objects underneath, which are part of the first-person controller. See *Figure 1.47*:

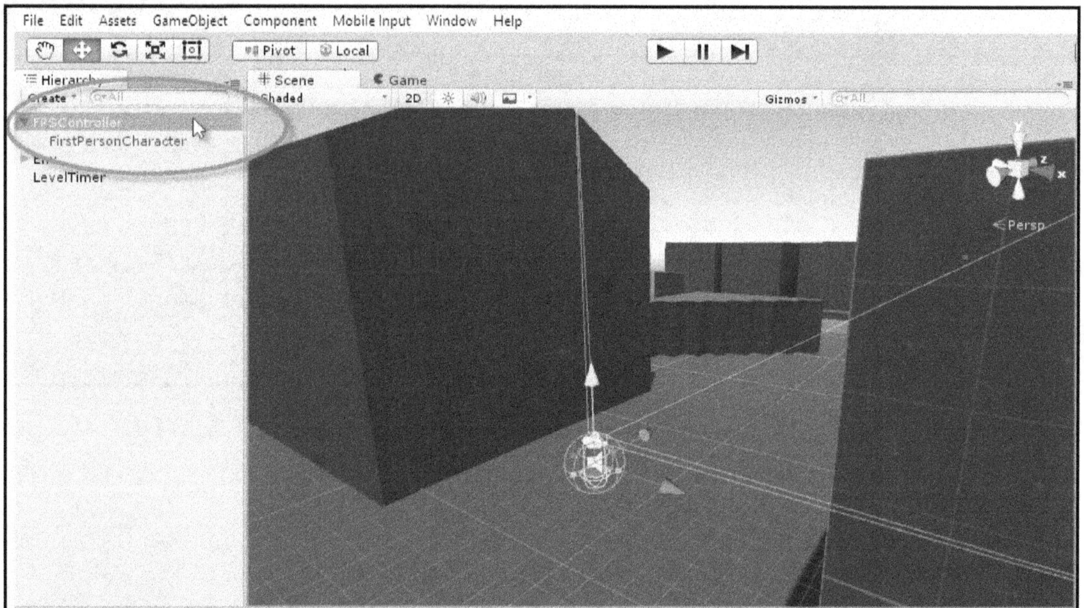

Figure 1.47: Finding the camera on a first-person controller

Select the `FirstPersonCharacter` object, which is underneath the `FPSController` object (as shown in *Figure 1.47*). The `FirstPersonCharacter` object is a child of the `FPSController`, which is the parent. This is because `FPSController` contains or encloses the `FirstPersonCharacter` object in the **Hierarchy** panel. Child objects inherit the transformations of their parents. This means that as parent objects move and rotate, all transformations will cascade downwards to all children. From the Object Inspector, you can see that the object has an **Audio Listener** component. See *Figure 1.48*:

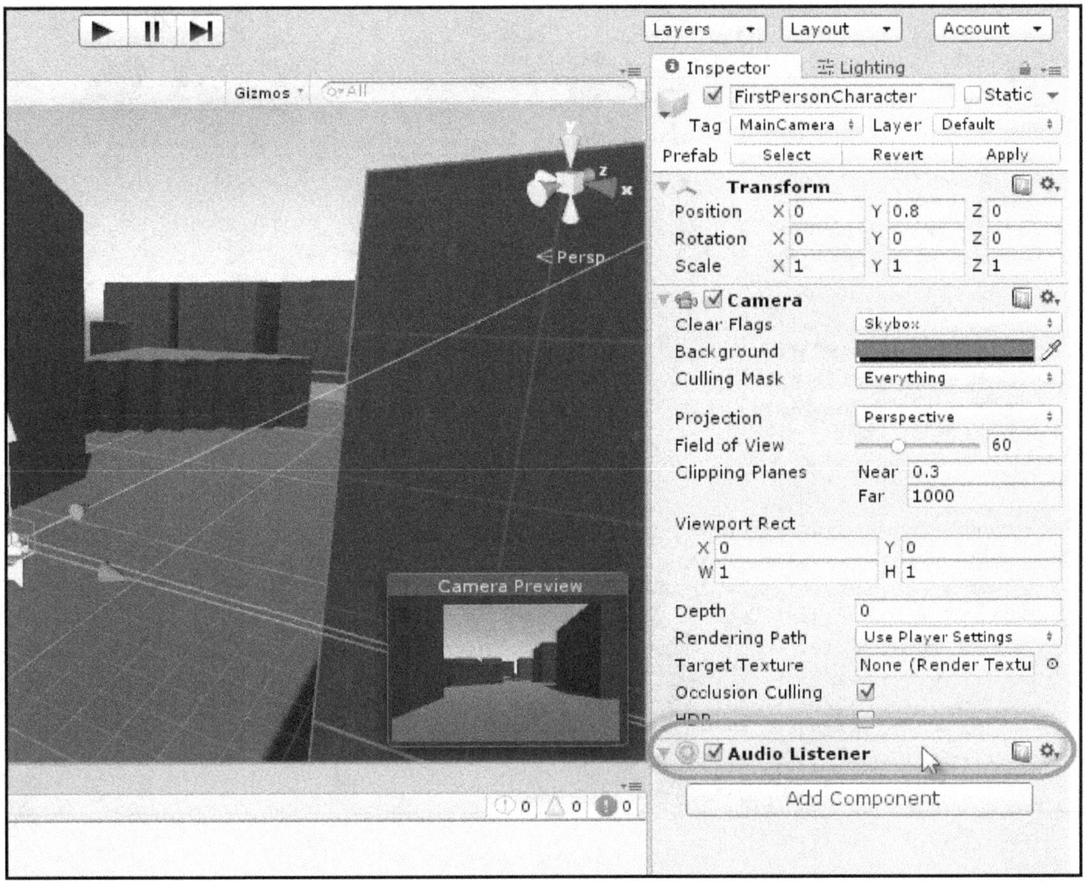

Figure 1.48: The FirstPersonController object contains an AudioListener component

We could remove the **Audio Listener** component from the `FPSController`, but this would prevent the player hearing sound in first-person perspective. So, instead, we'll delete the original camera created by default in the scene. To do this, select the original camera object in the hierarchy and press *Delete* on the keyboard. See *Figure 1.49*. This removes the **Audio Listener** warning in the **Console** during gameplay. Now, give the game a play test!

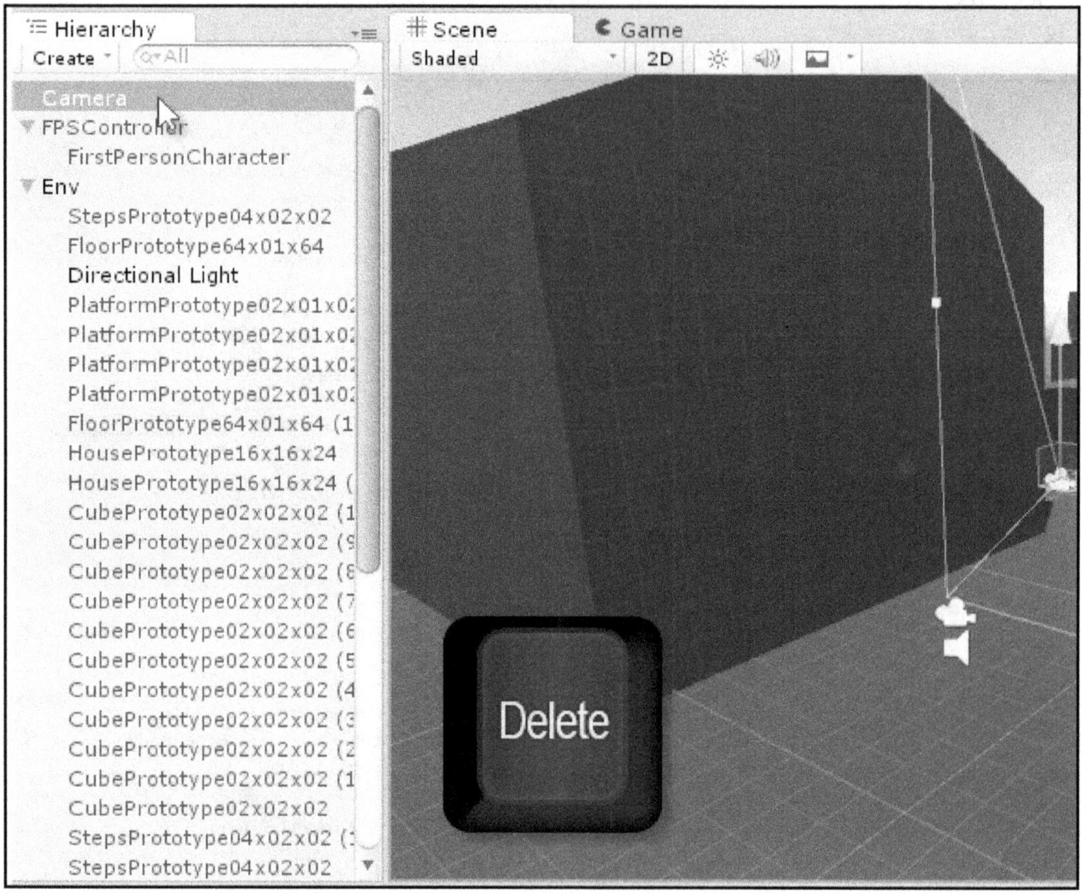

Figure 1.49: Deleting a camera object

Adding a water plane

The collection game is making excellent progress. We now have something playable insofar as we can run around and explore the environment in first-person mode. However, the environment could benefit from additional polish. Right now, for example, the floor meshes appear suspended in mid-air with nothing beneath them to offer support. See *Figure 1.50*. Further, it's possible to walk over the edge and fall into an infinite drop. So, let's add some water beneath the floors to complement the scene as a complete environment:

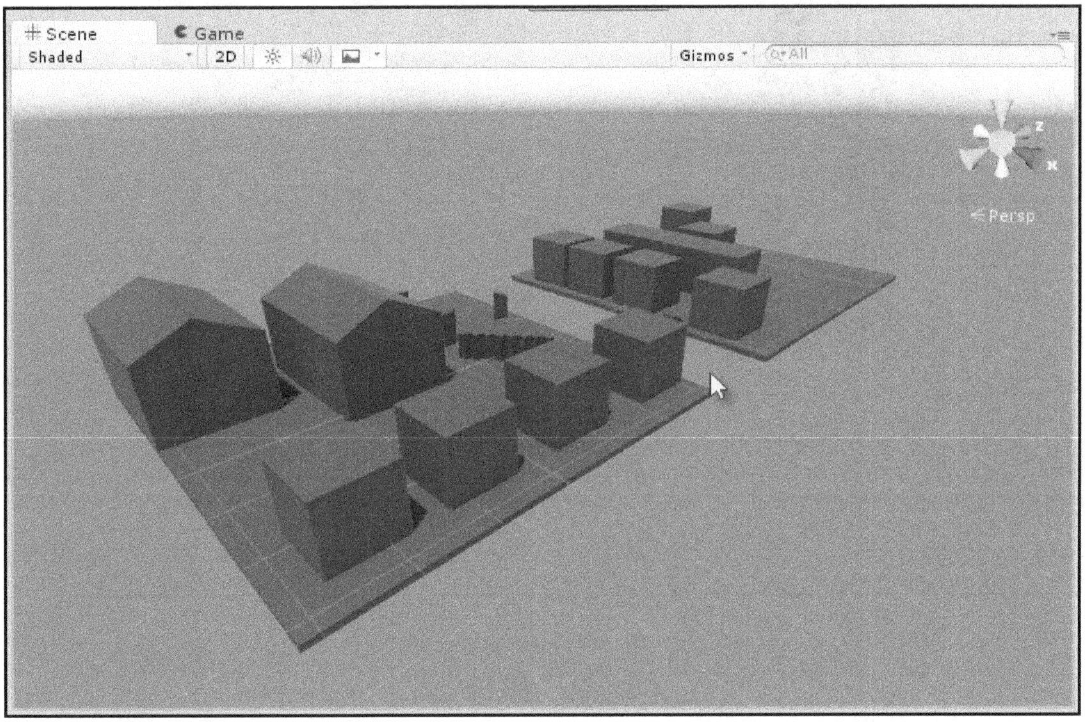

Figure 1.50: The world floor appears to float and have no support

To add water, we can use another ready-made Unity asset included in the **Project** panel. Open the `Standard Assets | Environment | Water | Water | Prefabs` folder. Then drag and drop the `WaterProDaytime` asset from the Project panel in the scene. See *Figure 1.51*. This appears as a circular object, which is initially smaller than needed:

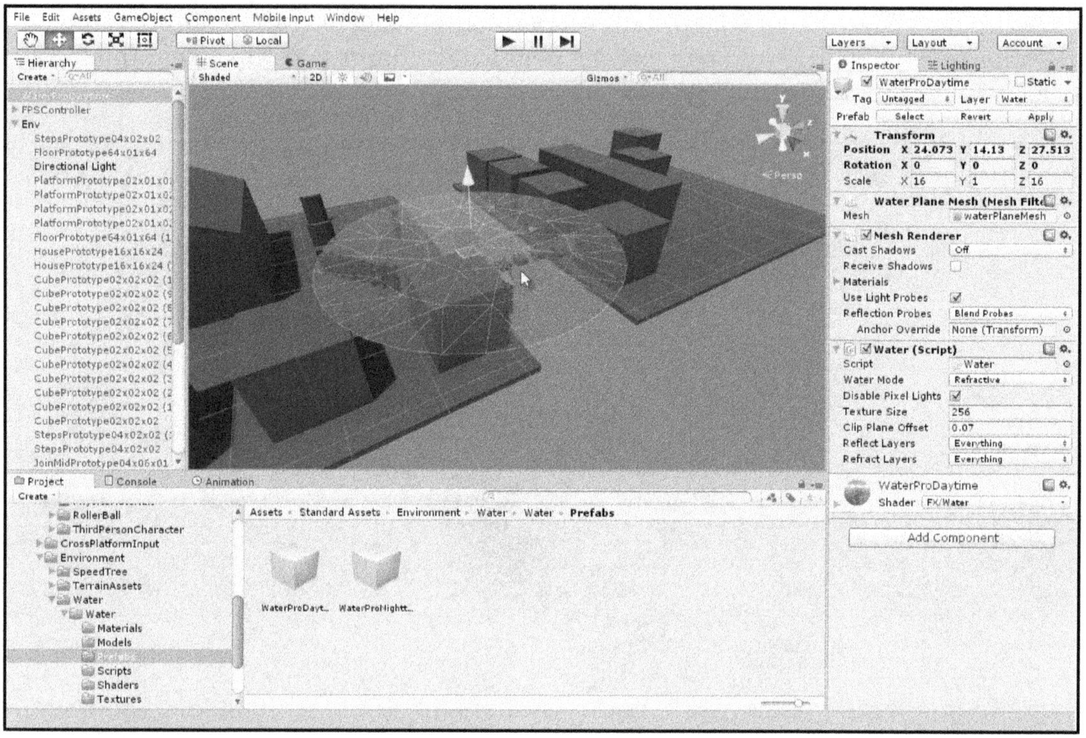

Figure 1.51: Adding water to the environment

After adding the `Water` prefab, position it below the floor level and use the scale tool (R) to increase its planar size (X, Z) to fill the environment outward into the distant horizon. This creates the feel that the floor meshes are smaller islands within an expansive world of water. See *Figure 1.52*:

Figure 1.52: Scaling and sizing water for the environment

Now, let's take another test run in the **Game** tab. Press play on the toolbar and navigate the character around in first-person mode. See *Figure 1.53*. You should see the water in the level. Of course, you can't walk on the water! Neither can you swim or dive beneath it. If you try walking on it, you'll simply fall through it, descending into infinity as though the water had never been there. Right now, the water is an entirely cosmetic feature, but it makes the scene look much better:

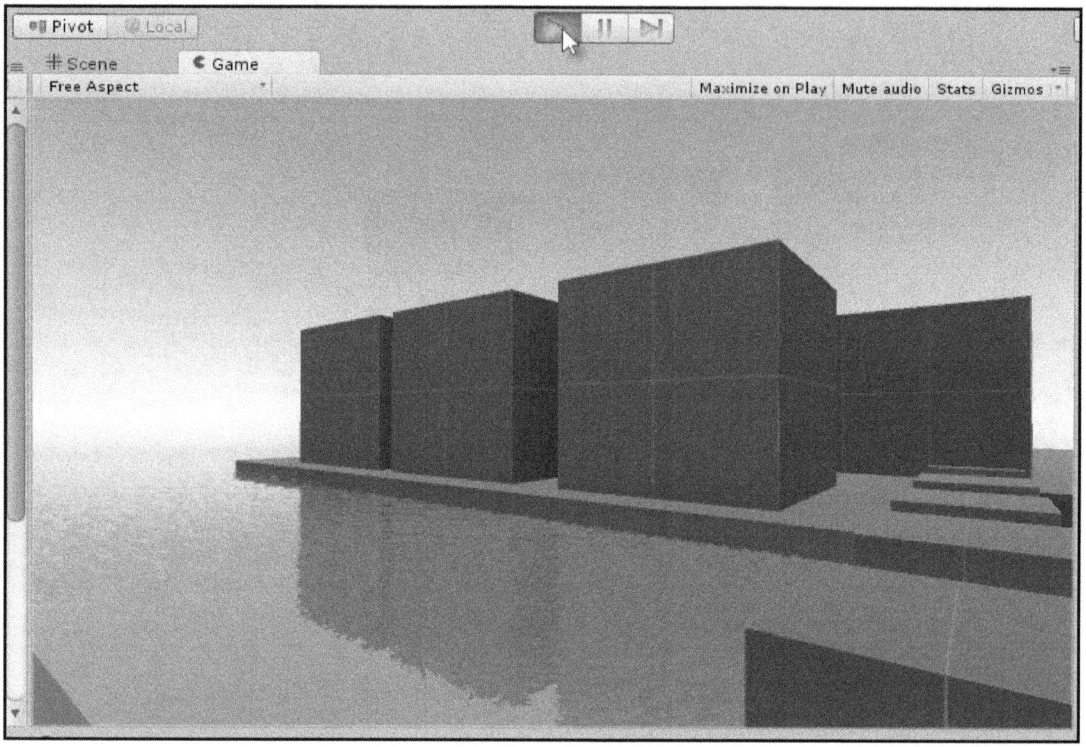

Figure 1.53: Testing the environment with water in FPS mode

The water is really a substanceless, ethereal object through which the player can pass easily. Unity doesn't recognize it as a solid or even a semi-solid object.

For now, however, we can add solidity to the water by first selecting the `Water` object from the **Hierarchy** panel (or in the **Scene** viewport) and then by choosing **Component** | **Physics** | **Box Collider** from the application menu. See *Figure 1.54*. Attaching a component to the selected object changes the object itself; it changes how it behaves. Essentially, components add behavior and functionality to objects, making them behave in different ways. Even so, resist the temptation to add lots of components to an object without reason and with the view that it makes them more versatile or powerful. It's better to have as few components on an object as necessary. This strategy of preferring relevant simplicity keeps your workflow neater, simpler, and optimized:

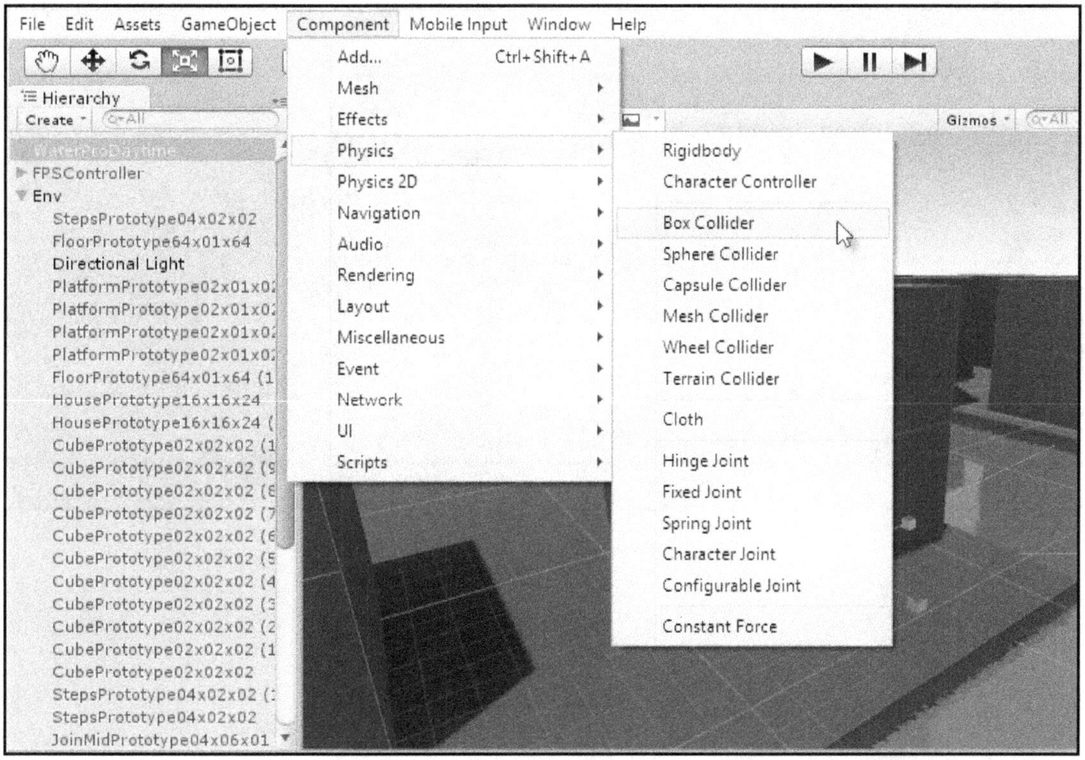

Figure 1.54: Attaching a Box Collider to a Water object

When a **Box Collider** is added to the water, a surrounding green cage or mesh appears. This approximates the volume and shape of the `Water` object and represents its physical volume, namely, the volume of the object that Unity recognizes as solid. See *Figure 1.55*:

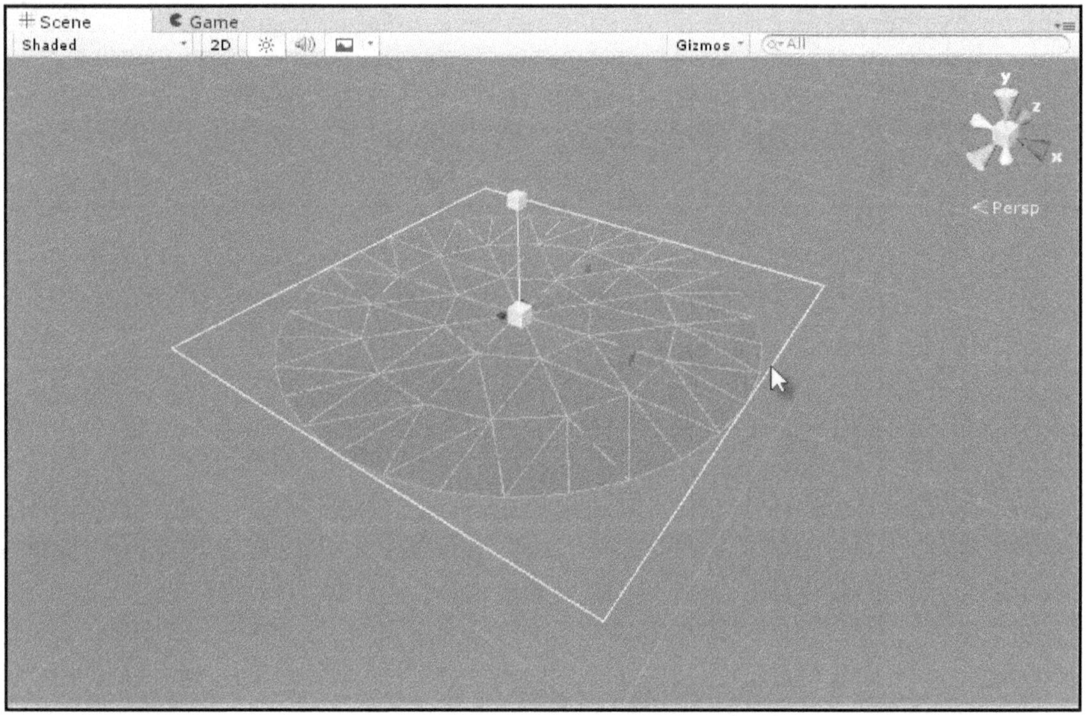

Figure 1.55: Box Colliders approximate physical volume

If you play the game now, your character will walk on water as opposed to falling through. True, the character should be able to swim properly, but walking might be better than falling. To achieve full swimming behavior would require significantly more work and is not covered here. If you want to remove the **Box Collider** functionality and return the water back to its original, ethereal state, then select the `Water` object, click on the cog icon on the **Box Collider** component, and then choose **Remove Component** from the context menu. See *Figure 1.56*:

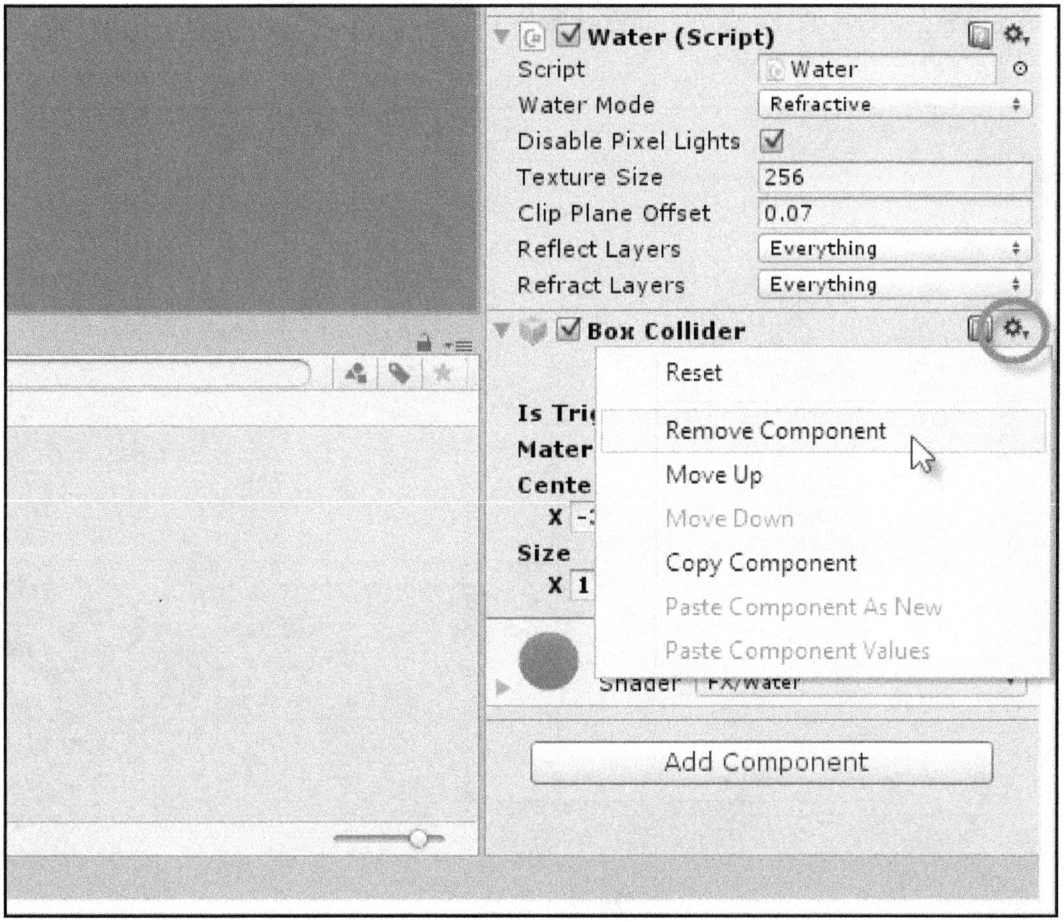

Figure 1.56: Removing a component

Adding a coin to collect

On reaching this far, our game has many features, namely, a complete environment, first-person controller, and water. However, we're supposed to be making a coin collection game and there aren't any coins for the player to collect yet. Now, to achieve fully collectible coins, we'll need to write some C# script, which will happen in the next chapter of this book. However, we can at least get started here at creating the coin object itself. To do this, we'll use a **Cylinder** primitive that's scaled to form a coin-looking shape. To create a cylinder, select **GameObject** | **3D Object** | **Cylinder** from the application menu:

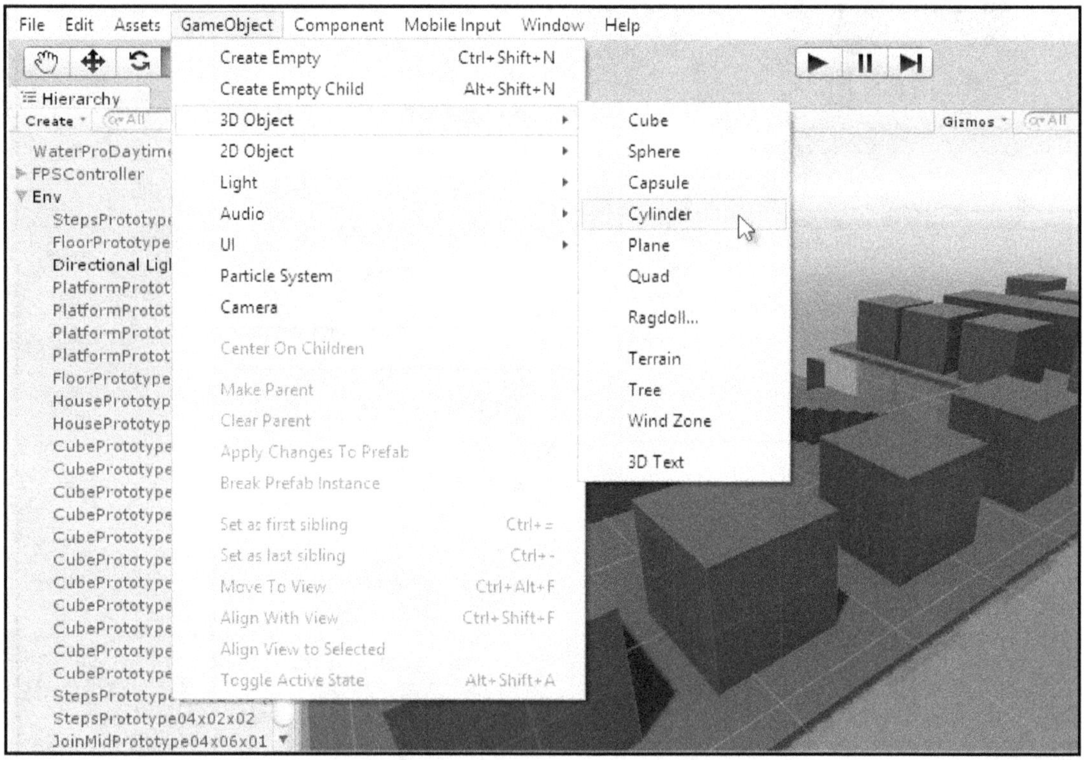

Figure 1.57: Create a Cylinder

Initially, the cylinder looks nothing like a coin. However, this is easily changed by scaling non-uniformly in the Z axis to make the cylinder thinner. Switch to the scale tool (R) and then scale the **Cylinder** inward. See Figure 1.58:

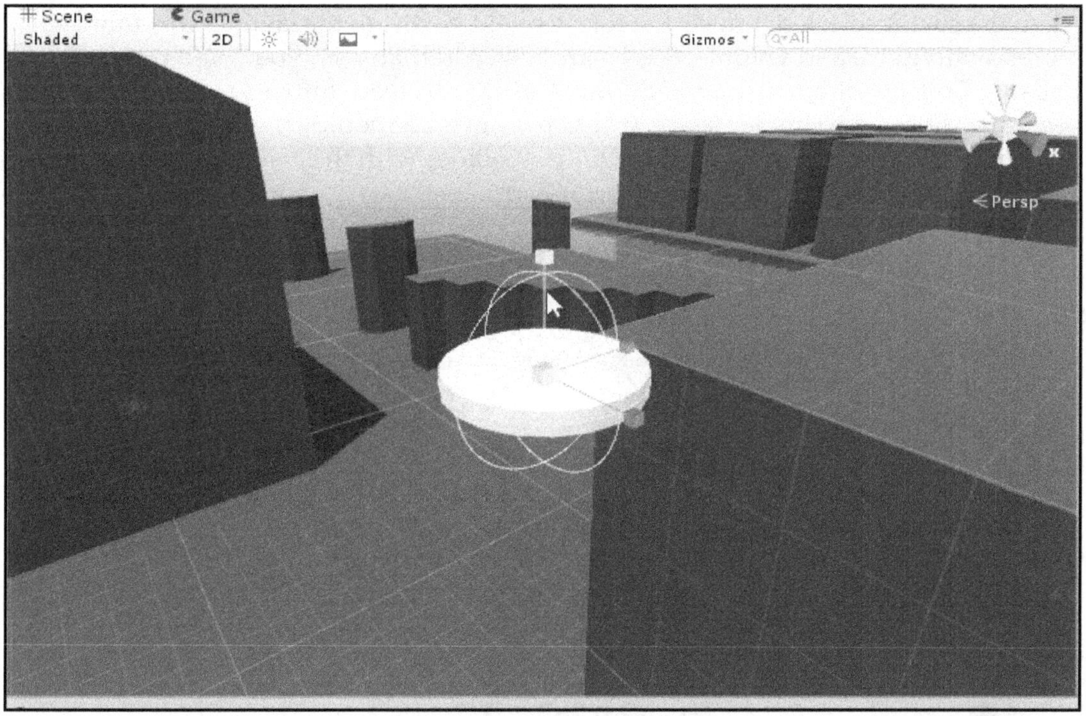

Figure 1.58: Scaling the cylinder to make a collectible coin

After rescaling the coin, its collider no longer represents its volume. It appears much larger than it should (see *Figure 1.58*). By default, the **Cylinder** is created with a **Capsule Collider** as opposed to a **Box Collider**. You can change the size of the **Capsule Collider** component by adjusting the **Radius** field from the **Object Inspector** when the coin is selected. Lower the **Radius** field to shrink the collider to a more representative size and volume. See *Figure 1.59*. Alternatively, you could remove **Capsule Collider** altogether and add **Box Collider** instead. Either way is fine; generally choose the simpler shape where possible. The colliders will be used in script in the next chapter to detect when the player collides with the coin to collect them:

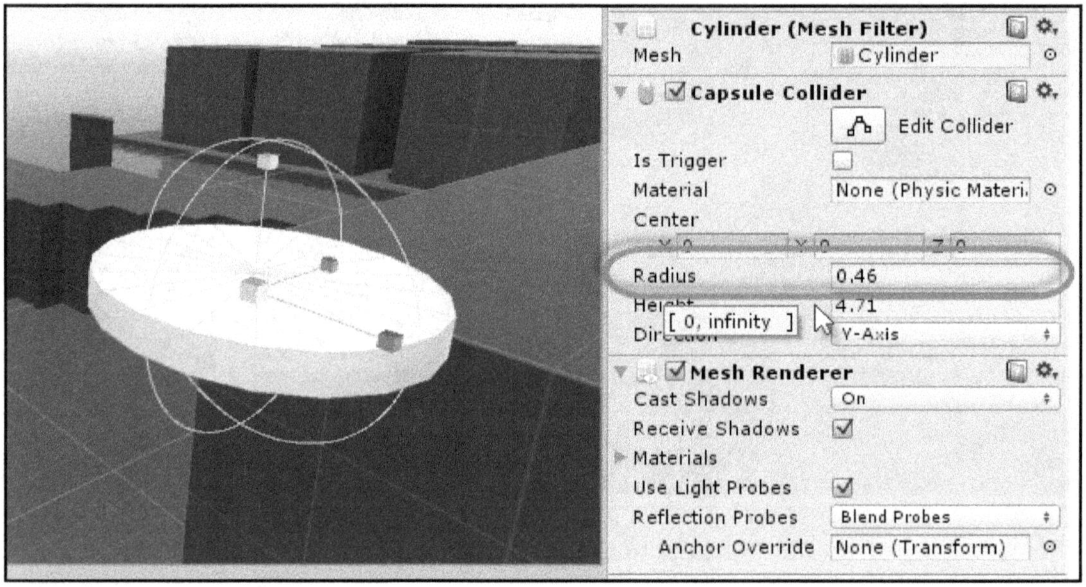

Figure 1.59: Adjusting the Capsule Collider for the coin

Here we are! We now have the basic shape and structure for a coin. We will, of course, improve it carefully and critically in many ways in the next chapter. For example, we'll make it collectible and assign it a material to make it look shiny. However, here, using only a basic Unity primitive and scale tool, we're able to generate a shape that truly resembles a coin.

Summary

Congratulations! On reaching this point, you have laid the foundations for a coin collection game that will be complete and functional in the next chapter. Here, we've seen how to create a Unity project from scratch and populate it with assets, such as meshes, textures, and scenes. In addition, we've seen how to create a scene for our game and use a range of assets to populate it with useful functionality that ships out of the box with the Unity engine, such as water, first-person controllers, and environment prototyping assets. In the next chapter, we'll resume work from where we ended here by making a coin that is collectible, and establishing a set of rules and logic for the game, making it possible to win and lose.

2
Creating a Collection Game

This chapter continues from the previous one by building a collection game with Unity. In this game, the player wanders an environment in first-person mode, searching for and collecting all the coins in a scene before a global timer expires. If all coins are collected before timer expiry, the game is won. However, if the timer expires before all coins are collected, the game is lost. The project created so far features a complete environment, with a floor, props, and water, and it also features a first-person controller along with a basic coin object, which looks correct in shape and form but still cannot be collected.

This chapter completes the project by creating a coin object to collect and adding a timer system to determine whether the total game time has elapsed. In essence, this chapter is about defining a system of logic and rules governing the game. To achieve this, we'll need to code in C# and so this chapter requires a basic understanding of programming.

In this chapter, you will learn the following recipes:

- Material creation
- Prefabs
- Coding with C#
- Writing script files
- Using particle systems
- Building and compiling games

Creating a coin material

The previous chapter closed by creating a basic coin object from a non-uniformly scaled cylinder primitive. This object was created by selecting **GameObject** | **3D Object** | **Cylinder** from the application menu. See *Figure 2.1*.

The coin object, as a concept, represents a basic or fundamental unit in our game logic because the player character should be actively searching the level looking for coins to collect before a timer runs out. This means that the coin is more than mere appearance; its purpose in the game is not simply eye candy, but is functional. It makes an immense difference to the game outcome whether the coin is collected by the player or not. Therefore, the coin object, as it stands, is lacking in two important respects. Firstly, it looks dull and grey—it doesn't really stand out and grab the player's attention. Secondly, the coin cannot actually be collected yet. Certainly, the player can walk into the coin, but nothing appropriate happens in response:

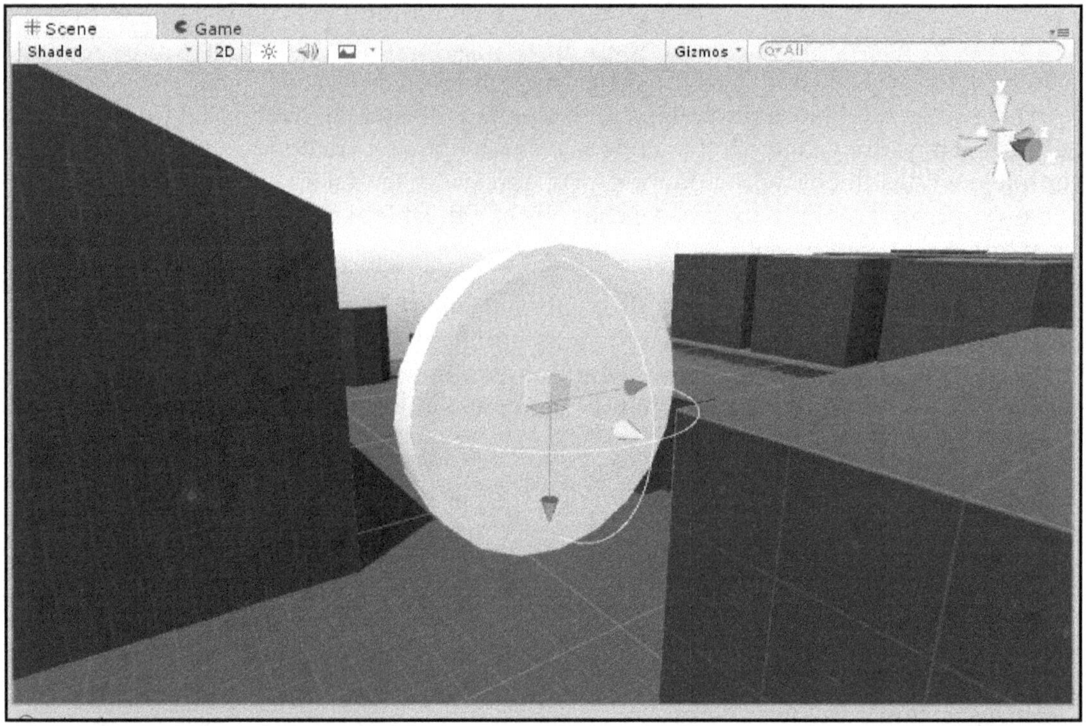

Figure 2.1: The coin object so far

> The CollectionGame project, as discussed in this chapter, can be found in the book companion files in the `Chapter02/CollectionGame` folder.

In this section, we'll focus on improving the coin appearance using a material. A material defines an algorithm (or instruction set) specifying how the coin should be rendered. A material doesn't just say what the coin should look like in terms of color; it defines how shiny or smooth a surface is, as opposed to rough and diffuse. This is important to recognize and is why a texture and material refer to different things. A texture is simply an image file loaded in memory, which can be wrapped around a 3D object via its UV mapping. In contrast, a material defines how one or more textures can be combined together and applied to an object to shape its appearance. To create a new material asset in Unity, right-click on an empty area in the Project panel, and from the context menu, choose **Create** | **Material**. See *Figure 2.2*. You can also choose **Assets** | **Create** | **Material** from the application menu:

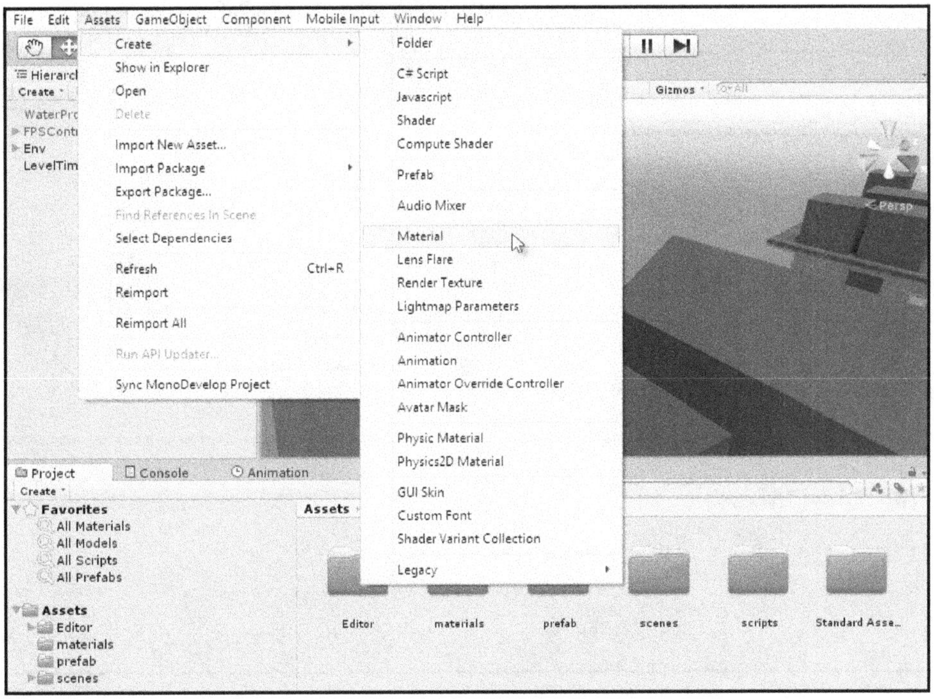

Figure 2.2: Creating a material

A material is sometimes called a Shader. If needed, you can create custom materials using a Shader language or you can use a Unity add-on, such as Shader Forge.

After creating a new material, assign it an appropriate name from the **Project** panel. As I'm aiming for a gold look, I'll name the material `mat_GoldCoin`. Prefixing the asset name with mat helps me know, just from the asset name, that it's a material asset. Simply type a new name in the text edit field to name the material. You can also click on the material name twice to edit the name at any time later. See *Figure 2.3*:

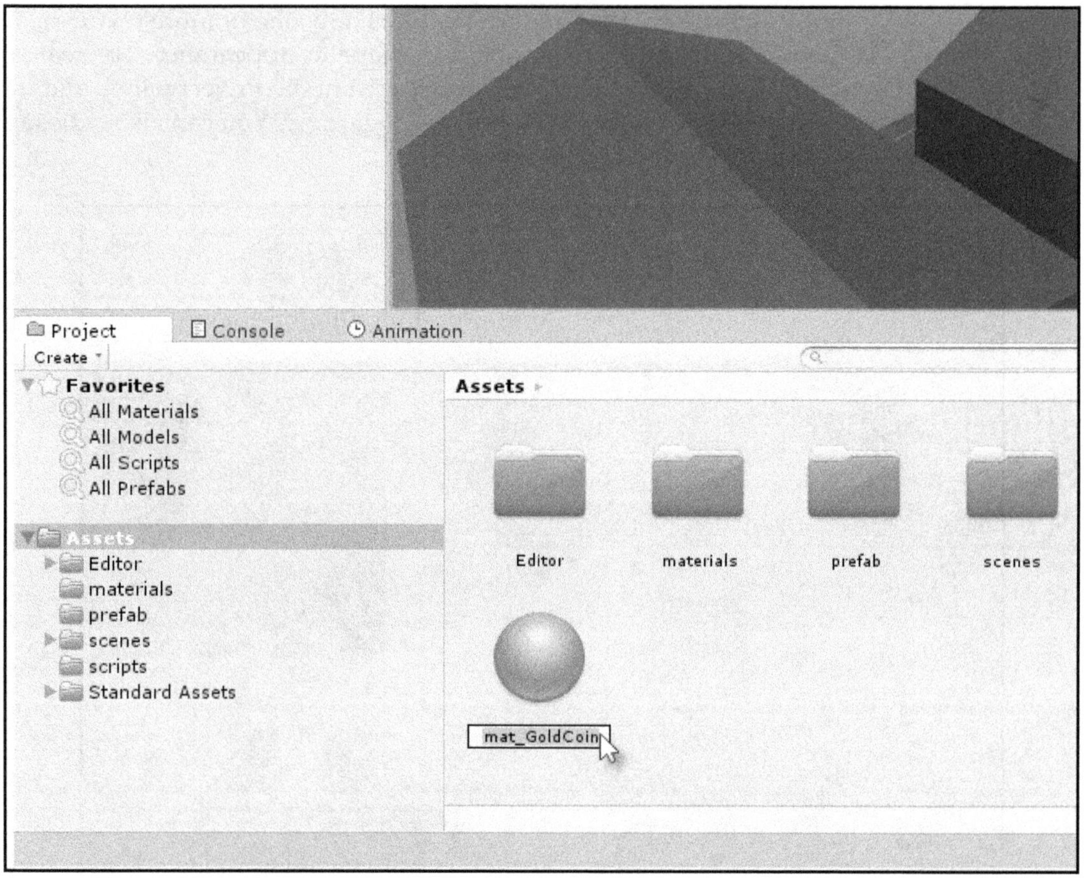

Figure 2.3: Naming a material asset

Next, select the material asset in the **Project** panel, if it's not already selected, and its properties display immediately in the Object Inspector. There are lots of properties listed! In addition, a material preview displays at the bottom of the **Object Inspector**, showing you how the material would look, based on its current settings, if it were applied to a 3D object, such as a sphere. As you change material settings from the Inspector, the preview panel updates automatically to reflect your changes, offering instant feedback on how the material would look.

See the following screenshot:

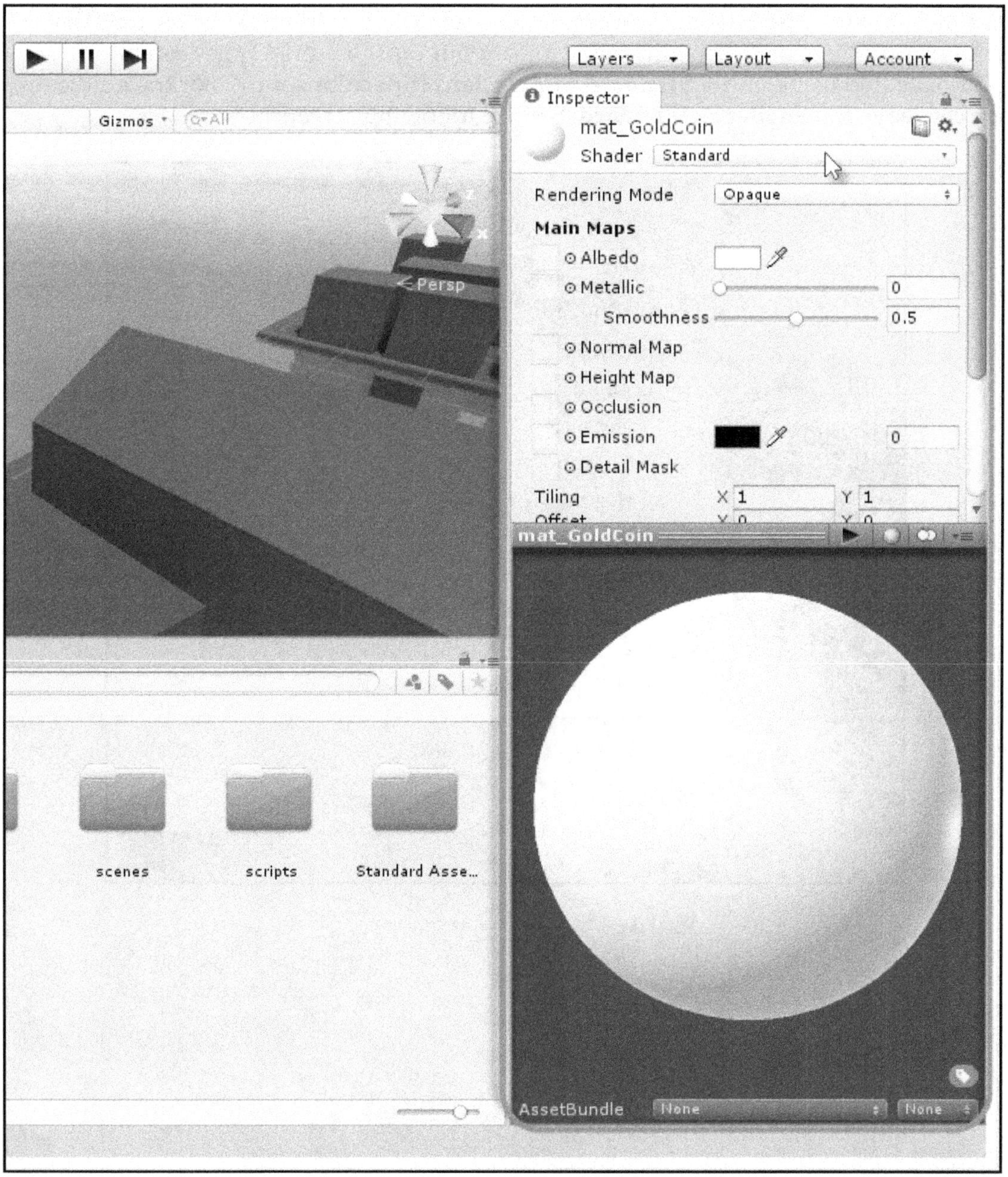

Figure 2.4: Material properties are changed from the Object Inspector

Let's now create a gold material for the coin. When creating any material, the first setting to choose is the **Shader** type because this setting affects all other parameters available to you. The **Shader** type determines which algorithm will be used to shade your object. There are many different choices, but most material types can be approximated using either **Standard** or **Standard** (**Specular setup**). For the gold coin, we can leave the **Shader** as **Standard**. See the following screenshot:

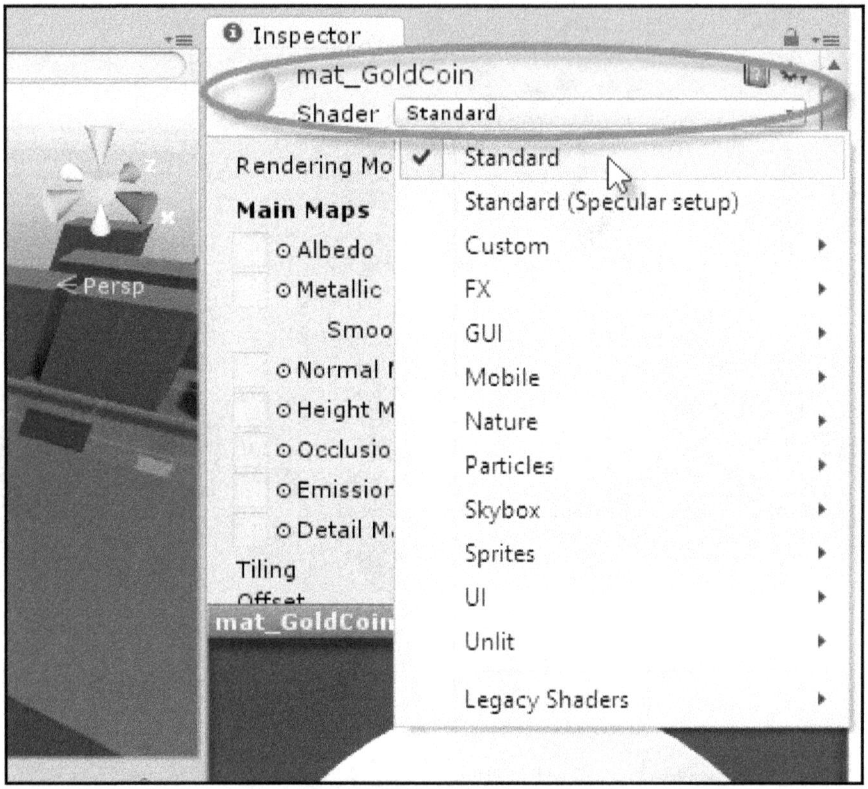

Figure 2.5: Setting the material Shader type

Right now, the preview panel displays the material as a dull grey, which is far from what we need. To define a gold color, we must specify the Albedo. To do this, click on the Albedo color slot to display a Color picker, and from the Color picker dialog, select a gold color. The material preview updates in response to reflect the changes. Refer to the following screenshot:

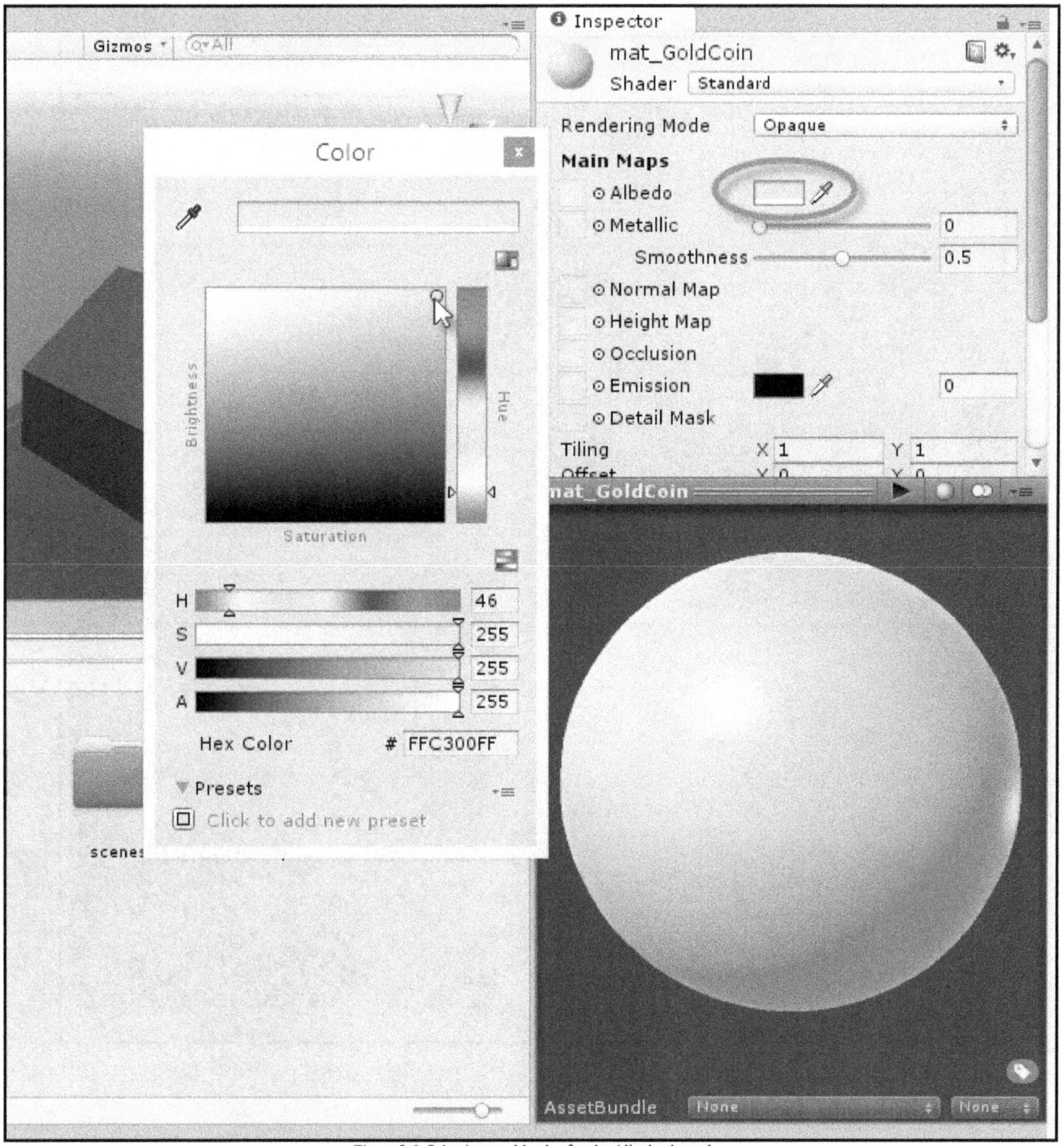

Figure 2.6: Selecting a gold color for the Albedo channel

The coin material is looking better than it did, but it's still supposed to represent a metallic surface, which tends to be shiny and reflective. To add this quality to our material, click and drag the Metallic slider in the Object Inspector to the right-hand side, setting its value to 1. This indicates that the material represents a fully metal surface as opposed to a diffuse surface such as cloth or hair. Again, the preview panel will update to reflect the change. See *Figure 2.7*:

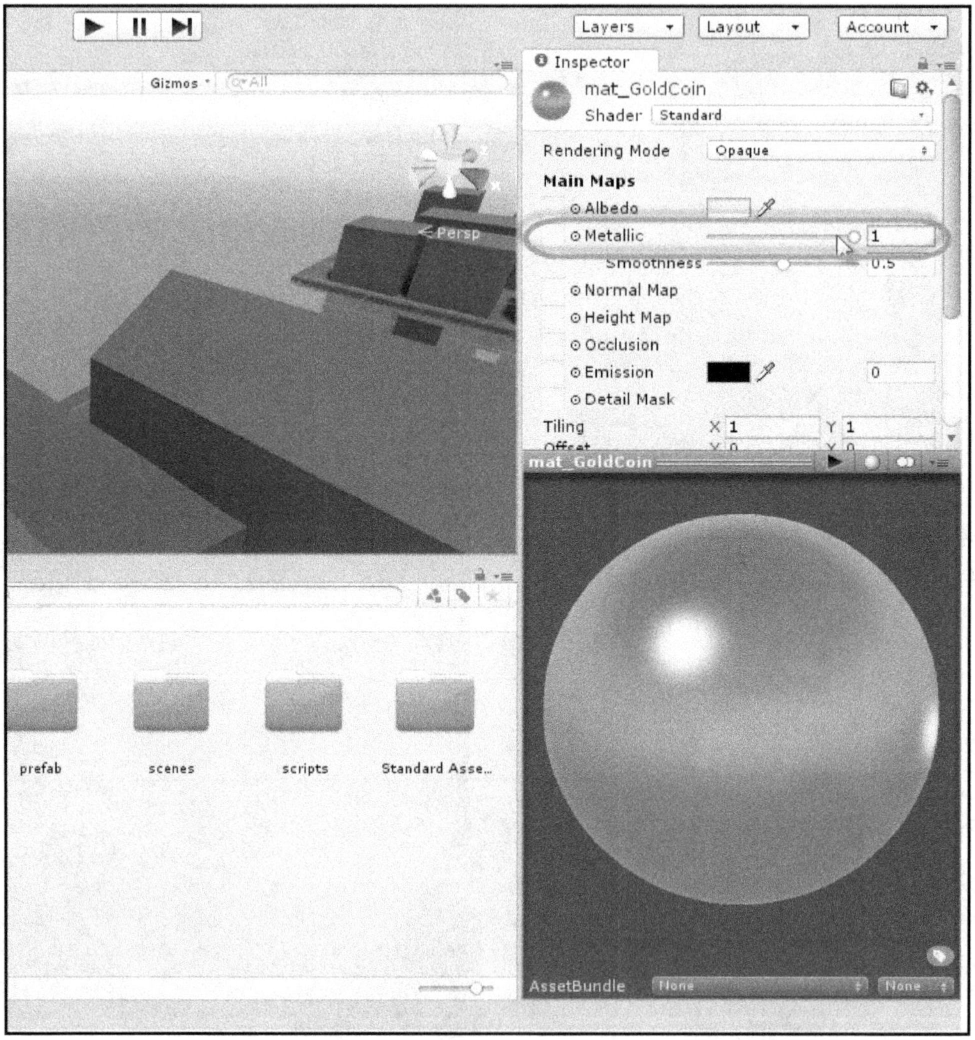

Figure 2.7: Creating a metallic material

We now have a gold material created, and it's looking good in the preview panel. If needed, you can change the kind of object used for a preview. By default, Unity assigns the created material to a sphere, but other primitive objects are allowed, including cubes, cylinders, and torus. This helps you preview materials under different conditions. You can change objects by clicking on the geometry button directly above the preview panel to cycle through them. See *Figure 2.8*:

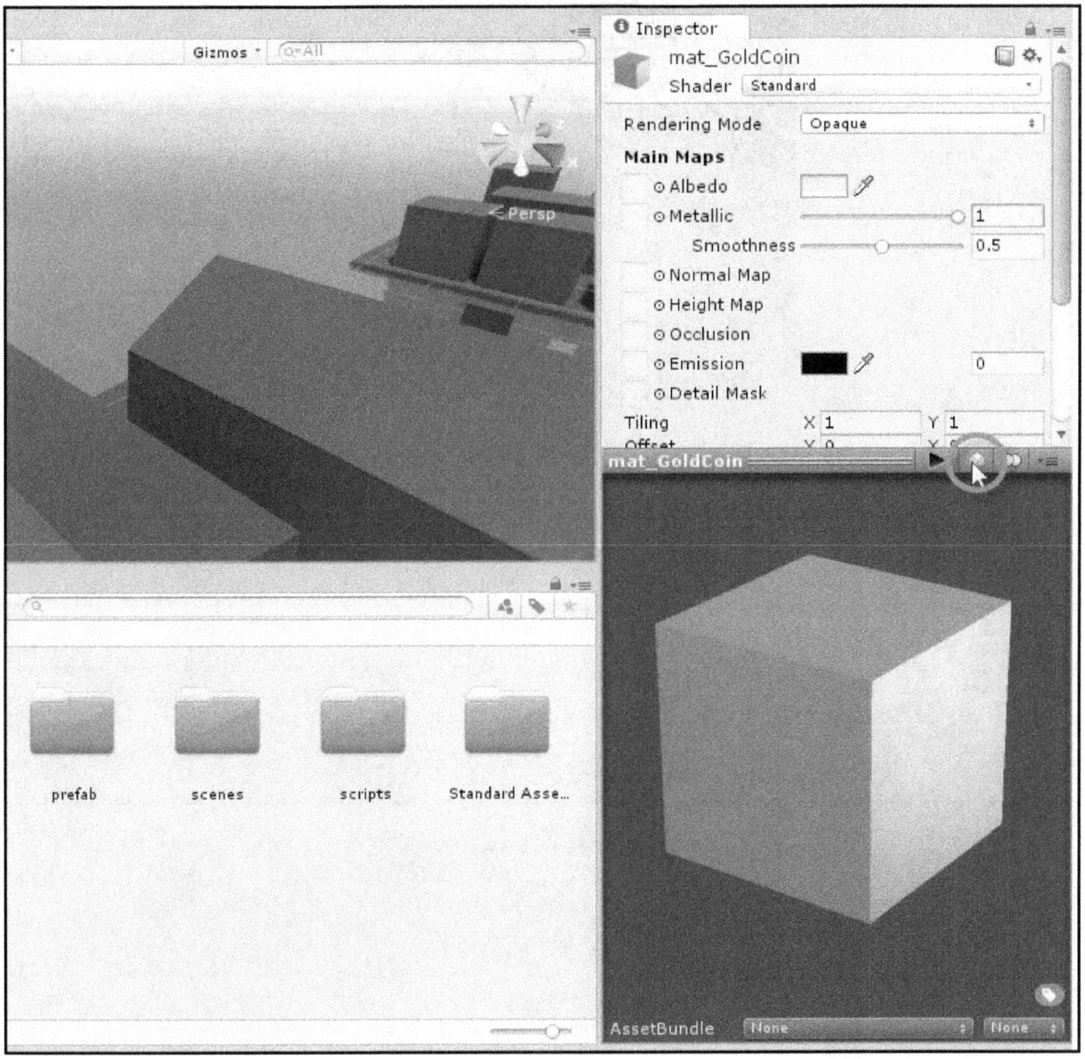

Figure 2.8: Previewing a material on an object

When your material is ready, you can assign it directly to meshes in your scene just by dragging and dropping. Let's assign the coin material to the coin. Click and drag the material from the Project panel to the coin object in the scene. On dropping the material, the coin will change appearance. See *Figure 2.9*:

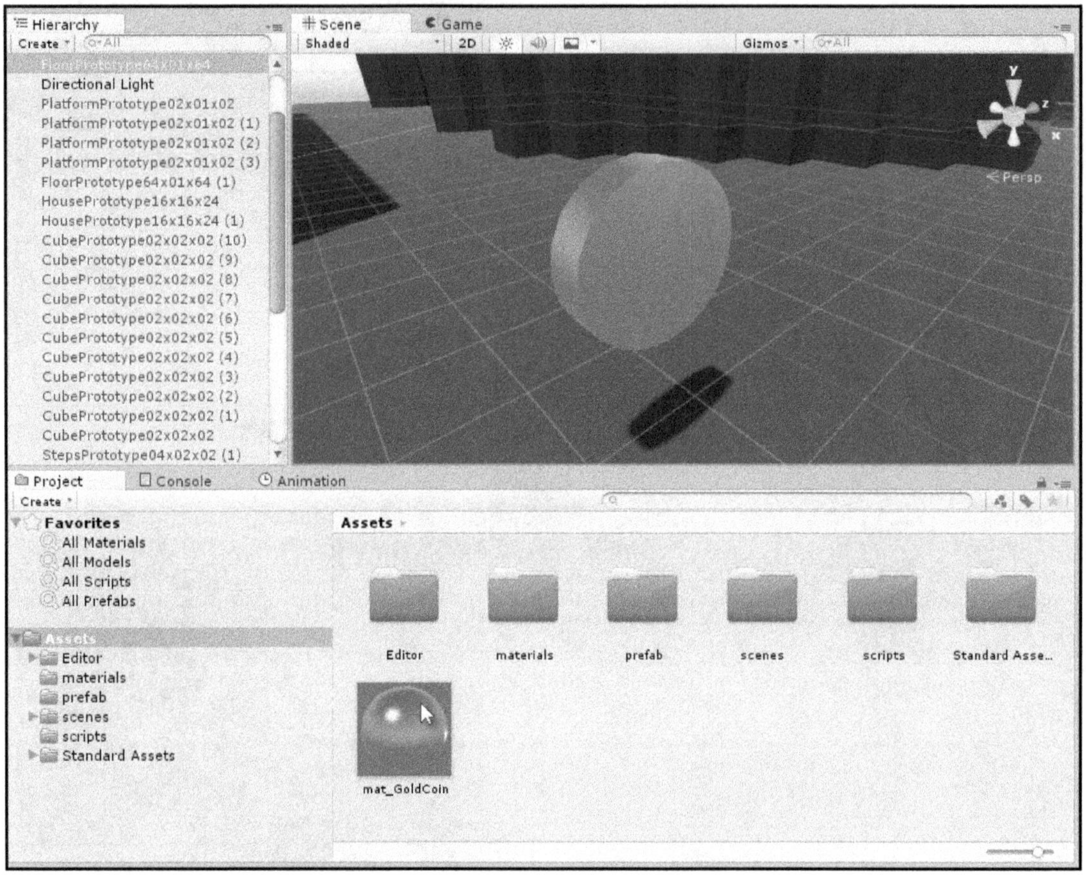

Figure 2.9: Assigning the material to the coin

You can confirm that material assignment occurred successfully and can even identify which material was assigned by selecting the Coin object in the Scene and viewing its Mesh Renderer component from the Object Inspector. The Mesh Renderer component is responsible for making sure that a mesh object is actually visible in the scene when the camera is looking. The Mesh Renderer component contains a Materials field. This lists all materials currently assigned to the object. By clicking on the material name from the Materials field, Unity automatically selects the material in the **Project** panel, making it quick and simple to locate materials. See *Figure 2.10*.

The Mesh Renderer component lists all materials assigned to an object:

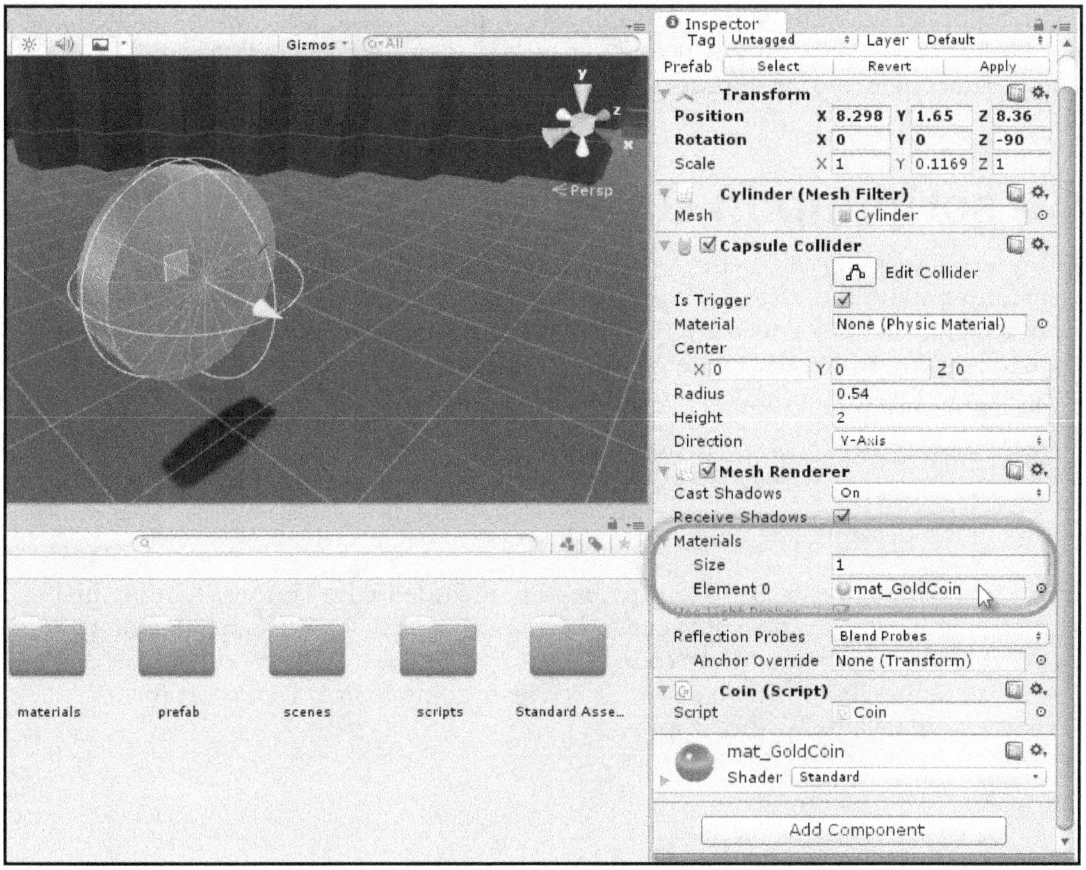

Figure 2.10: The Mesh Renderer component lists all materials assigned to an object

> Mesh objects may have multiple materials, with different materials assigned to different faces. For the best in-game performance, use as few unique materials on an object as necessary. Make the extra effort to share materials across multiple objects, if possible. Doing so can significantly enhance the performance of your game. For more information on optimizing rendering performance, see the online documentation at `http://docs.unity3d.com/Manual/OptimizingGraphicsPerformance.html`.

That's it! You now have a complete and functional gold material for the collectible coin. It's looking good. However, we're still not finished with the coin. The coin looks right, but it doesn't behave right. Specifically, it doesn't disappear when touched, and we don't yet keep track of how many coins the player has collected overall. To address this, then, we'll need to script.

C# scripting in Unity

Defining game logic, rules, and behavior often requires scripting. Specifically, to transform a static and lifeless scene with objects into an environment that does something, a developer needs to code behaviors. It requires someone to define how things should act and react under specific conditions. The coin collection game is no exception to this. In particular, it requires three main features:

- To know when the player collects a coin
- To keep track of how many coins are collected during gameplay
- To determine whether a timer has expired

There's no default out-of-the-box functionality included with Unity to handle this scenario. So we must write some code to achieve it. Unity supports two languages, namely, UnityScript (sometimes called JavaScript) and C#. Both are capable and useful languages, but this book uses C# because, going forward, support for JavaScript will eventually be dropped.

Let's start coding these three features in sequence. To create a new script file, right-click on an empty area in the Project panel, and from the context menu, choose **Create** | **C# Script**. Alternatively, you can navigate to **Assets** | **Create** | **C# Script** from the application menu. See *Figure 2.11*:

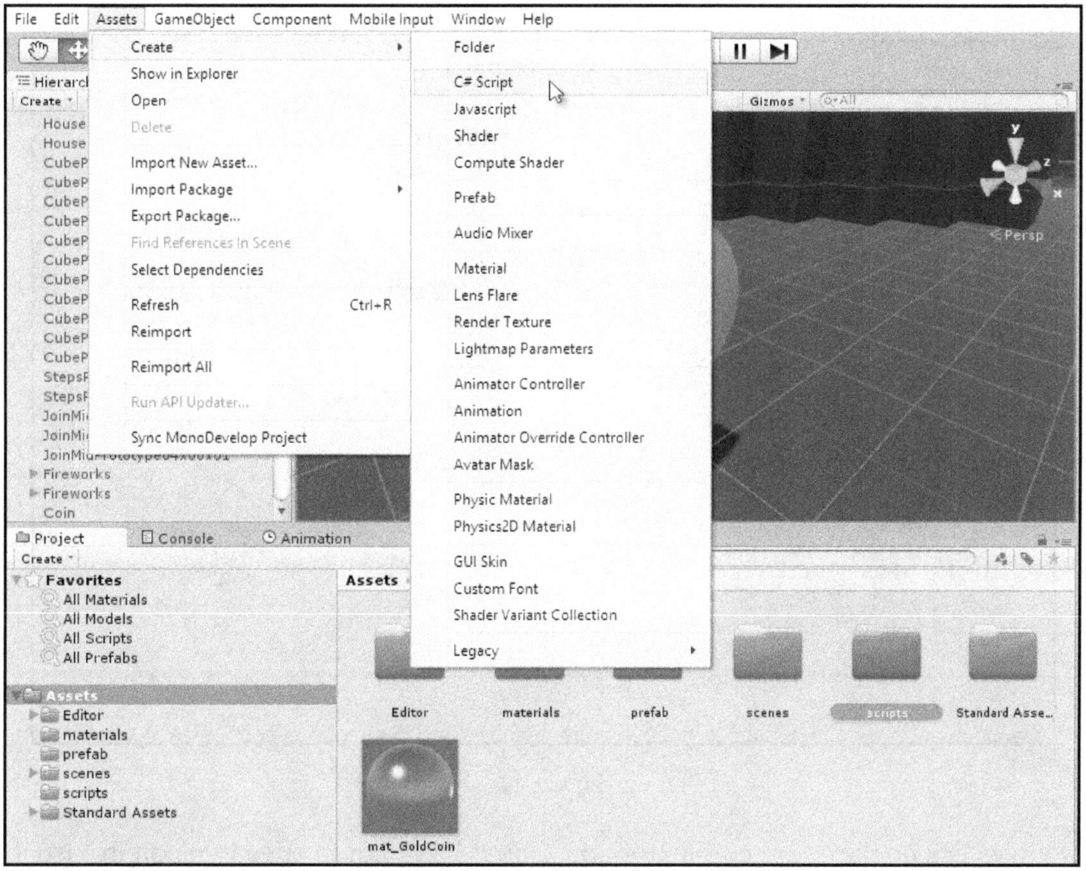

Figure 2.11: Creating a new C# script

After the file is created, you'll need to assign a descriptive name to it. I'll call it Coin.cs. In Unity, each script file represents a single, discrete class of matching names. Hence, the `Coin.cs` file encodes the `Coin` class. The `Coin` class will encapsulate the behavior of a Coin object and will, eventually, be attached to the Coin object in the scene. See *Figure 2.12*:

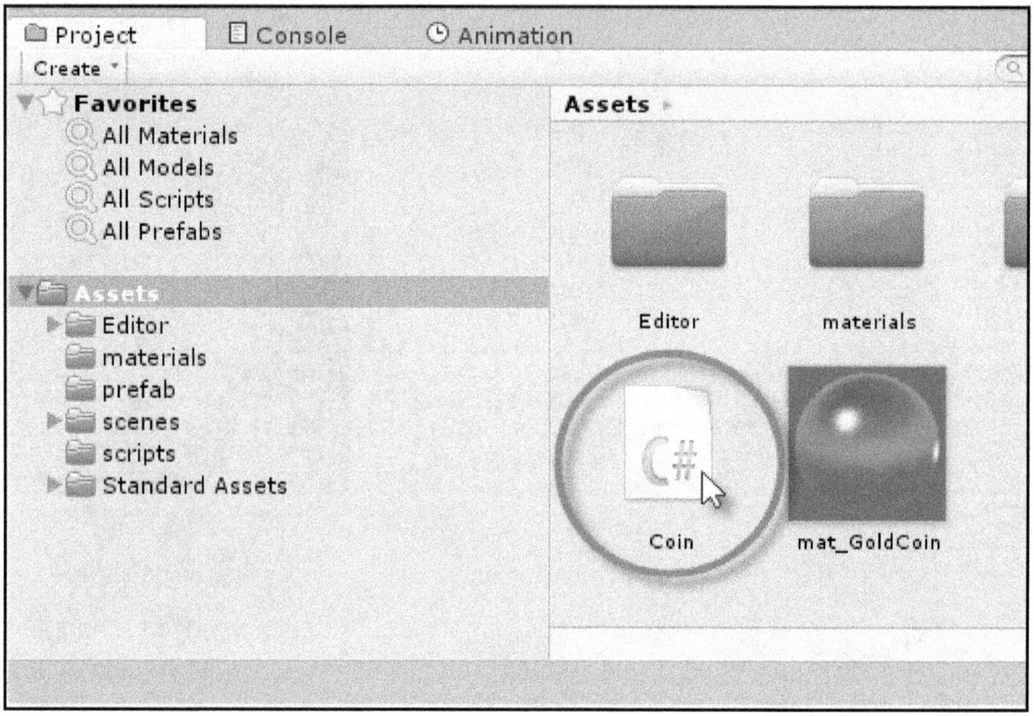

Figure 2.12: Naming a script file

Double-click on the `Coin.cs` file from the Object Inspector to open it to edit in Visual Studio, a third-party IDE application that ships with Unity. This program lets you edit and write code for your games. Once opened in Visual Studio, the source file will appear, as shown in *Code Sample 2.1*:

```
using UnityEngine;
using System.Collections;
public class Coin : MonoBehaviour
{
  // Use this for initialization
  void Start () {}
```

```
    // Update is called once per frame
    void Update () {}
}
```

By default, all newly created classes derive from MonoBehavior, which defines a common set of functionality shared by all components. The `Coin` class features two autogenerated functions, namely Start and Update. These functions are events invoked automatically by Unity. Start is called once as soon as the GameObject (to which the script is attached) is created in the Scene. Update is called once per frame on the object to which the script is attached. Start is useful for initialization code and Update is useful to create behaviors over time, such as motion and change. Now, before moving any further, let's attach the newly created script file to the Coin object in the Scene. To do this, drag and drop the `Coin.cs` script file from the Project panel on the Coin object. When you do this, a new Coin component is added to the object. This means that the script is instantiated and lives on the object. See *Figure 2.13*, attaching a script file to an object:

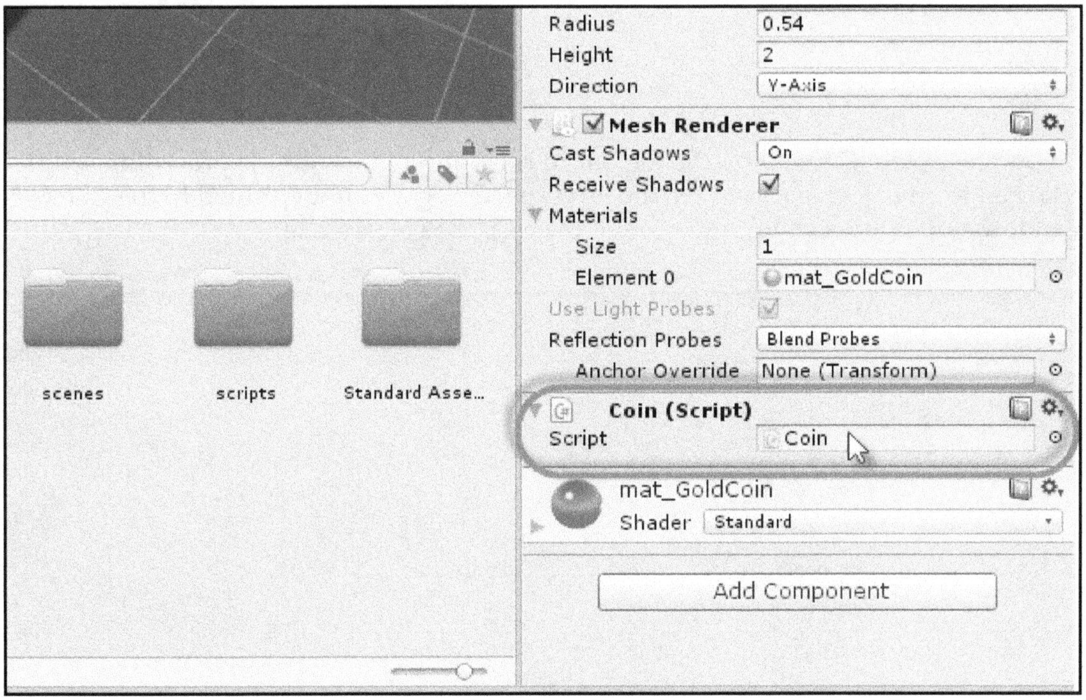

Figure 2.13: Attaching a script file to an object

When a script is attached to an object, it exists on the object as a component. A script file can normally be added to multiple objects and even to the same object multiple times. Each component represents a separate and unique instantiation of the class. When a script is attached in this way, Unity automatically invokes its events, such as Start and Update. You can confirm that your script is working normally by including a `Debug.Log` statement in the `Start` function.

This prints a debug message to the Console window when the GameObject is created in the Scene. Consider `Code Sample 2.2`, which achieves this:

```
using UnityEngine;
using System.Collections;
public class Coin : MonoBehaviour
{
// Use this for initialization
void Start () {
Debug.Log ("Object Created");
}
// Update is called once per frame
void Update () {
}
}
```

If you press play (*Ctrl + P*) on the toolbar to run your game with the preceding script attached to an object, you will see the message, Object Created, printed to the Console window—once for each instantiation of the class. See *Figure 2.14*:

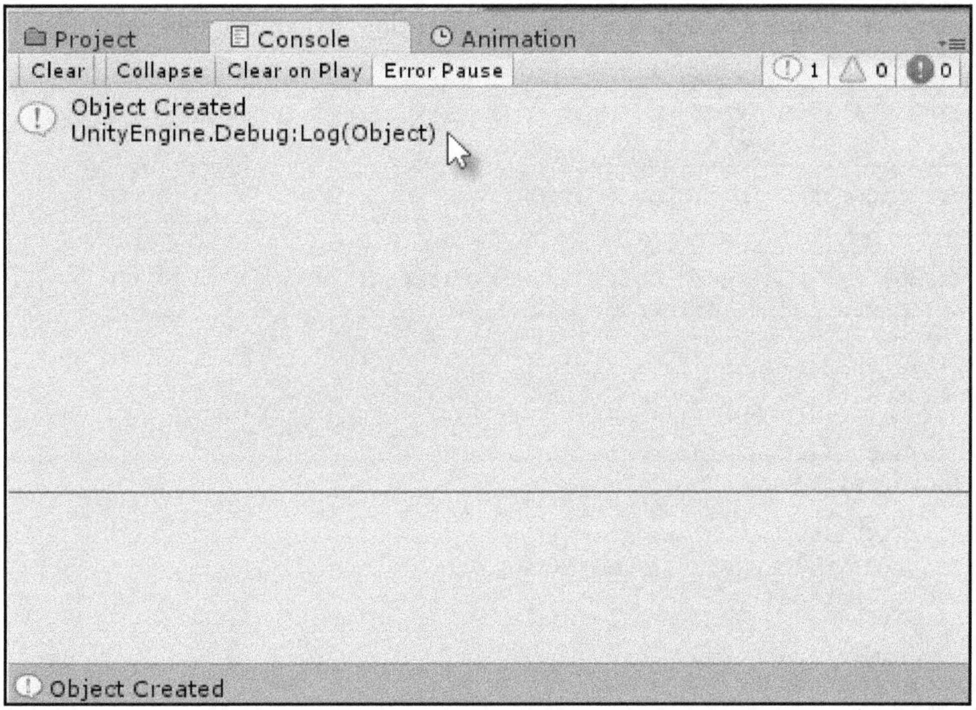

Figure 2.14: Printing messages to the Console window

Good work! We've now created a basic script for the `Coin` class and attached it to the coin. Next, let's define its functionality to keep track of coins as they are collected.

Counting coins

The coin collection game wouldn't really be much of a game if there were only one coin. The central idea is that a level should feature many coins, all of which the player should collect before a timer expires. Now, to know whether all coins have been collected, we'll need to know how many coins there are in total in the scene. After all, if we don't know how many coins there are, then we can't know if we've collected them all. So, our first task in scripting is to configure the Coin class so that we can know the total number of coins in the scene at any moment easily.

Consider *Code Sample 2.3*, which adapts the `Coin` class to achieve this:

```
//-------------------------
using UnityEngine;
using System.Collections;
//-------------------------
public class Coin : MonoBehaviour
{
//-------------------------
//Keeps track of total coin count in scene
public static int CoinCount = 0;
//-------------------------
// Use this for initialization
void Start ()
{
//Object created, increment coin count
++Coin.CoinCount;
}
//-------------------------
//Called when object is destroyed
void OnDestroy()
{
//Decrement coin count
--Coin.CoinCount;
//Check remaining coins
if(Coin.CoinCount <= 0)
{
//We have won
}
}
//-------------------------
}
//-------------------------
```

Code Sample 2.3

The following points summarize the code sample:

- The `Coin` class maintains a static member variable, `CoinCount,` which, being static, is shared across all instances of the class. This variable keeps count of the total number of coins in the scene and each instance has access to it.
- The Start function is called once per Coin instance when the object is created in the Scene. For coins that are present when the scene begins, the Start event is called at scene startup. This function increments the `CoinCount` variable by one per instance, thus keeping count of all coins.
- The `OnDestroy` function is called once per instance when the object is destroyed. This decrements the `CoinCount` variable, reducing the count for each coin destroyed.

Altogether, *Code Sample 2.3* maintains a `CoinCount` variable. In short, this variable allows us to always keep track of the total coin count. We can query it easily to determine how many coins remain. This is good, but is only the first step towards completing the coin collection functionality.

Collecting coins

Previously, we developed a coin counting variable telling us how many coins are in the scene. However, regardless of the count, the player still can't collect the coins during gameplay. Let's fix this now. To start, we need to think about collisions. Thinking carefully, we know that a coin is considered collected whenever the player walks into it, that is, a coin is collected when the player and the coin intersect or collide.

To determine when a collision happens like that, we must approximate the volume of both the player and coin in order to determine when the two volumes overlap in space. This is achieved in Unity through colliders. Colliders are special physics objects attached to meshes. They tell us when two meshes intersect. The FPSController object (First-person controller) already has a collider on it, through its Character Controller component. This approximates the physical body of a generic person. This can be confirmed by selecting FPSController in the Scene and examining the green wireframe cage surrounding the main camera. It is capsule-shaped. See *Figure 2.15*.

The Character Controller features a Collider to approximate the player body:

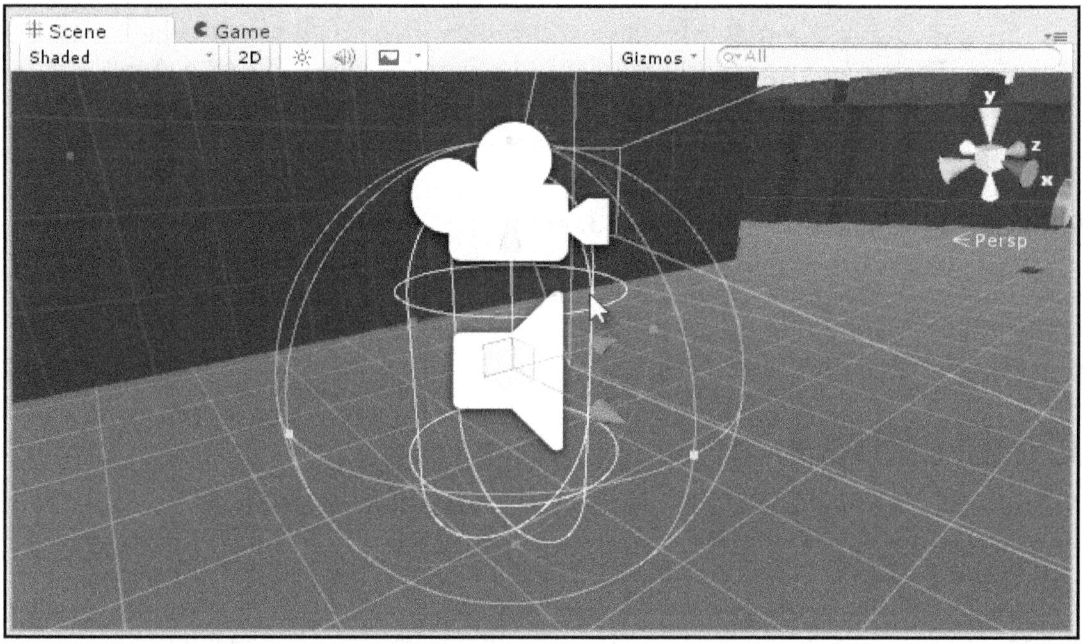

Figure 2.15: The Character Controller features a collider to approximate the player body

FPSController features a Character Controller component attached, which is configured by default with Radius, Height, and Center settings, defining the physical extents of the character in the scene. See *Figure 2.16*, FPSController features Character Controller. These settings can be left unchanged for our game:

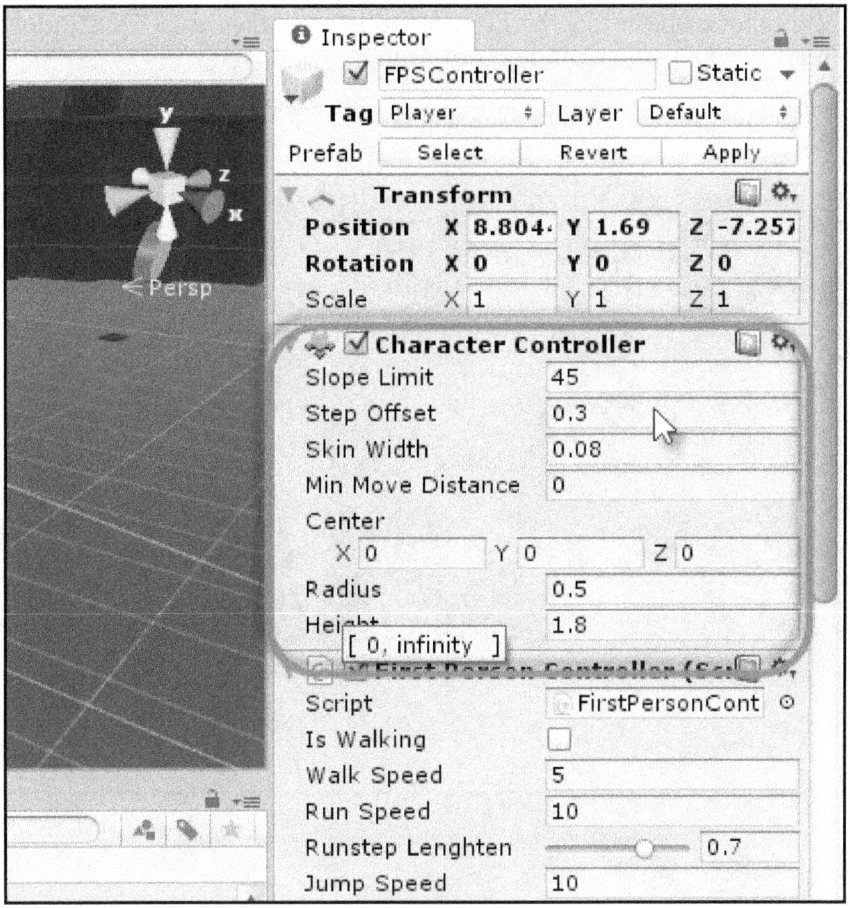

Figure 2.16: FPSController features a Character Controller

The Coin object, in contrast, features only a Capsule Collider component, which was added automatically when we created the Cylinder primitive earlier to resemble a coin. This approximates the coin's physical volume in the scene without adding any additional features specific to characters and motion as found in the Character Controller component. This is fine, because the coin is a Static object as opposed to a moving and dynamic object like the FPSController. See *Figure 2.17*, Cylinder primitives feature a Capsule Collider component:

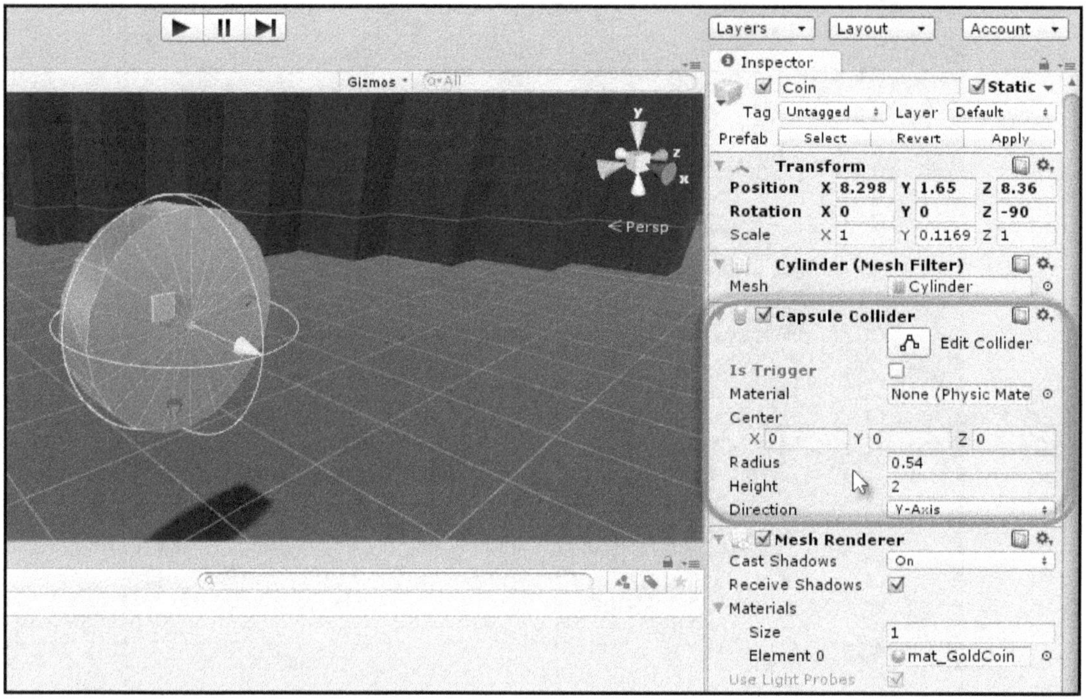

Figure 2.17: Cylinder primitives feature a Capsule Collider component

For this project, I'll stick to using a Capsule Collider component for the Coin object. However, if you want to change the attached collider to a different shape instead, such as a box or sphere, you can do this by first removing any existing collider components on the coin—click on the cog icon of the component in the Object Inspector and then select Remove Component from the context menu. See *Figure 2.18*:

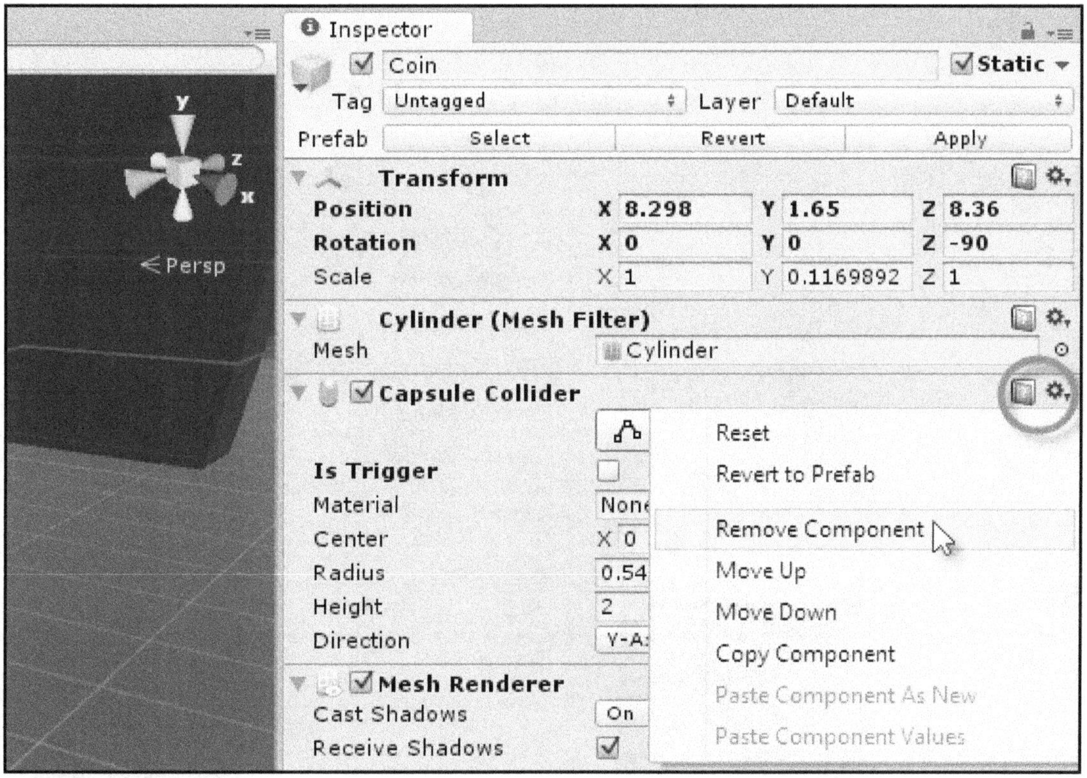

Figure 2.18: Removing a component from an object

You can then add a new collider component to the selected object by choosing **Component** | **Physics** from the application menu and then choosing a suitably shaped collider. See *Figure 2.19*:

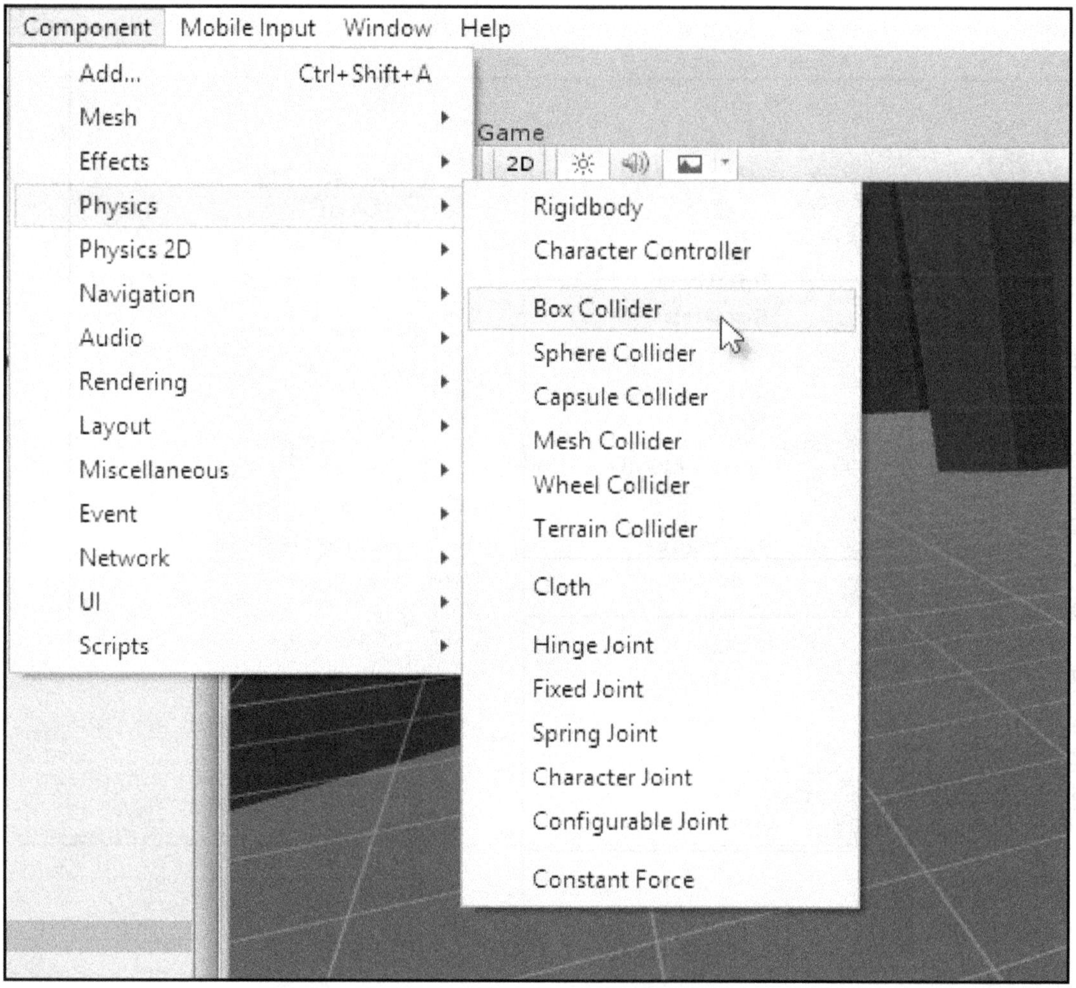

Figure 2.19: Adding a component to the selected object

Regardless of the collider type used, there's a minor problem. If you play the game now and try to run through the coin, it'll block your path. The coin acts as a solid, physical object through which FPSController cannot pass. However, for our purposes, this isn't how the coin should behave. It's supposed to be a collectible object.

The idea is that when we walk through it, the coin is collected and disappears. We can fix this easily by selecting the Coin object and enabling the Is Trigger checkbox in the Capsule Collider component, in the Object Inspector. The Is Trigger setting appears for almost all collider types. It lets us detect collisions and intersections with other colliders while allowing them to pass through. See *Figure 2.20*:

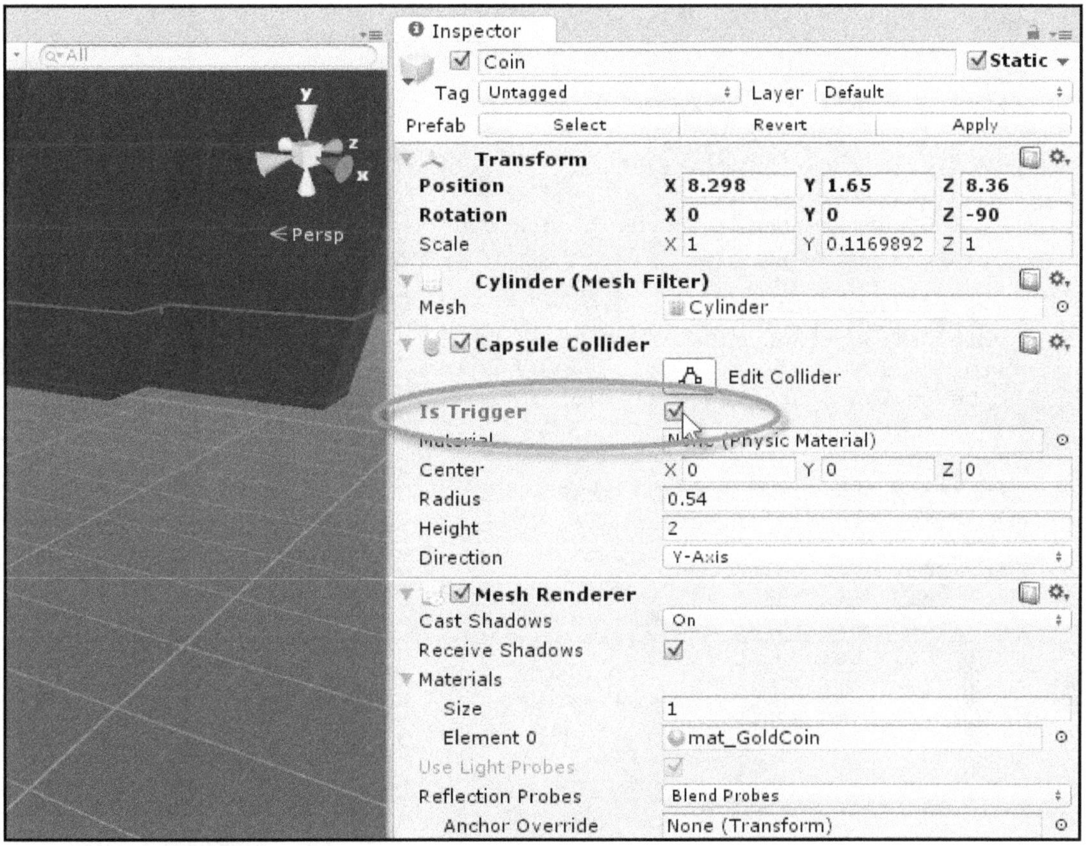

Figure 2.20: The Is Trigger setting allows objects to pass through colliders

If you play the game now, FPSController will easily walk through all coin objects in the scene. This is a good start. However, the coins don't actually disappear when touched; they still don't get collected. To achieve this, we'll need to add more script to the `Coin.cs` file. Specifically, we'll add an `OnTriggerEnter` function. This function is called automatically when an object, like the player, enters a collider.

For now, we'll add a Debug.Log statement to print a debug message when the player enters the collider, just for test purposes. See *Code Sample 2.4*:

```
//-------------------------
using UnityEngine;
using System.Collections;
//-------------------------
public class Coin : MonoBehaviour
{
  //-------------------------
  public static int CoinCount = 0;
  //-------------------------
  // Use this for initialization
  void Start () {
    //Object created, increment coin count
    ++Coin.CoinCount;
  }
  //-------------------------
  void OnTriggerEnter(Collider Col)
  {
    Debug.Log ("Entered Collider");
  }
  //-------------------------
  //Called when object is destroyed
  void OnDestroy()
  {
    //Decrement coin count
    --Coin.CoinCount;
    //Check remaining coins
    if(Coin.CoinCount <= 0)
    {
      //We have won
    }
  }
  //-------------------------
}
//-------------------------
```

More information on the OnTriggerEnter function can be found at the online Unity documentation here: `http://docs.unity3d.com/ScriptReference/ MonoBehaviour.OnTriggerEnter.html`

Test the *Code Sample 2.4* by pressing play on the toolbar. When you run into a coin, the `OnTriggerEnter` function will be executed and the message displayed. However, the question remains as to what object initiated this function in the first place. It's true that something collided with the coin, but what exactly? Was it the player, an enemy, a falling brick, or something else? To check this, we'll use Tag. The Tag feature lets you mark specific objects in the scene with specific tags or labels, allowing these objects to be easily identified in code so that we can check quickly that the player, rather than other objects, are colliding with the coins. After all, it should only be the player that can collect coins. So, firstly, we'll tag the player object with a tag called Player. To do this, select the FPSController object in the scene and then click on the Tag drop-down box in the Object Inspector. From here, select the Player tag. This marks FPSController as the Player object. See *Figure 2.21*:

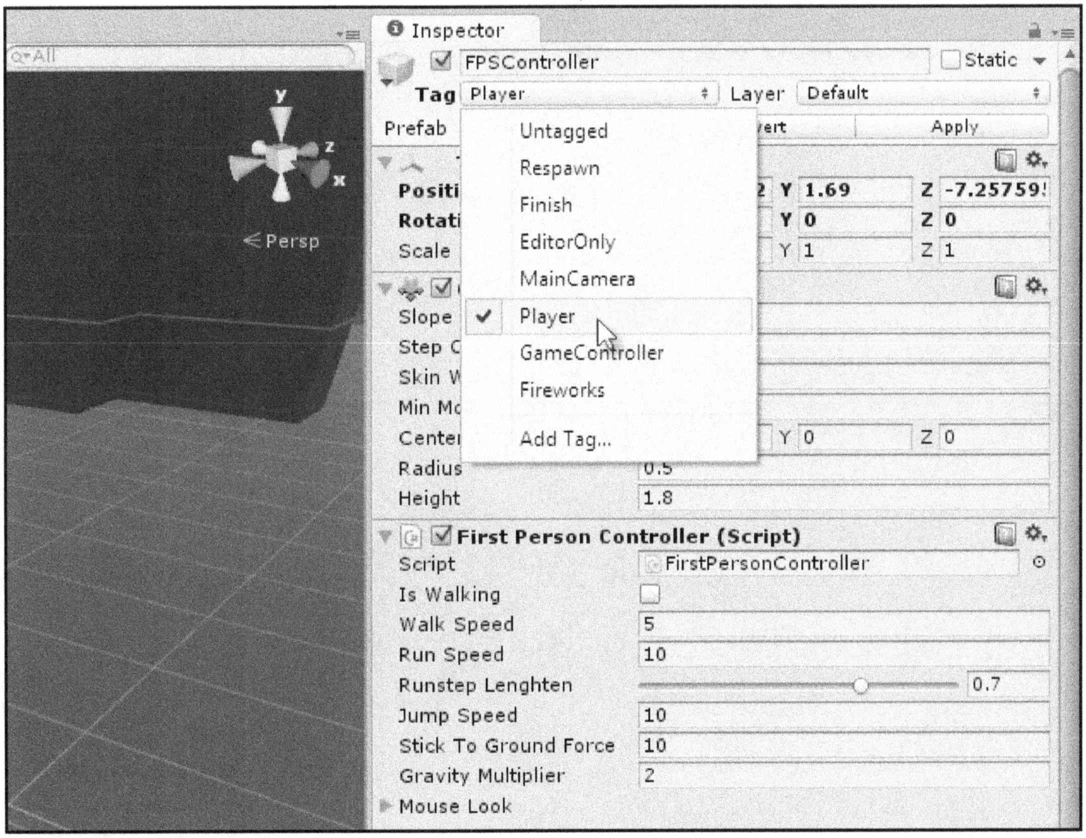

Figure 2.21: Tagging FPSController as Player

With FPSController now tagged as Player, we can refine the `Coin.cs` file, as shown in *Code Sample 2.5*. This handles coin collection, making the coin disappear on touch and decreasing the coin count:

```
//-------------------------
using UnityEngine;
using System.Collections;
//-------------------------
public class Coin : MonoBehaviour
{
  //-------------------------
  public static int CoinCount = 0;
  //-------------------------
  // Use this for initialization
  void Start () {
    //Object created, increment coin count
    ++Coin.CoinCount;
  }
  //-------------------------
  void OnTriggerEnter(Collider Col)
  {
    //If player collected coin, then destroy object
    if(Col.CompareTag("Player"))
    Destroy(gameObject);
  }
  //-------------------------
  //Called when object is destroyed
  void OnDestroy()
  {
    //Decrement coin count
    --Coin.CoinCount;
    //Check remaining coins
    if(Coin.CoinCount <= 0)
    {
      //We have won
    }
  }
  //-------------------------
}
//-------------------------
```

Code Sample 2.5

The following points summarize the code sample:

- `OnTriggerEnter` is called once automatically by Unity each time FPSController intersects the Coin collider
- When `OnTriggerEnter` is called, the Col argument contains information about the object that entered the collider on this occasion
- The `CompareTag` function is used to determine if the colliding object is the Player as opposed to a different object
- The `Destroy` function is called to destroy the Coin object itself, represented internally by the inherited member variable, gameObject
- When the `Destroy` function is called, the OnDestroy event is invoked automatically, which decrements the Coin count

Excellent work! You've just created your first working coin. The player can now run into the coin, collect it, and remove it from the scene. This is a great beginning, but the scene should contain more than one coin. We could solve this by duplicating the existing coin many times and repositioning each duplicate to a different place. However, there's a better way, as we'll see next.

Coins and prefabs

The basic coin functionality is now created, but the scene needs more than one coin. The problem with simply duplicating a coin and scattering the duplicates is that if we make a change later to one coin and need to propagate that change to all other coins, we'd need to delete the former duplicates and manually replace those with newer and amended duplicates. To avoid this tedious repetition, we can use prefabs. Prefabs let you convert an object in the scene to Assets in the Project panel. This can be instantiated in the scene as frequently as needed, as though it were a mesh asset. The advantage is that changes made to the asset are automatically applied to all instances automatically, even across multiple scenes.

This makes it easier to work with custom assets, so let's prefab the coin right now. To do this, select the Coin object in the scene and then drag and drop it in the Project panel. When this happens, a new prefab is created. The object in the scene is automatically updated to be an instance of prefab. This means that if the asset is deleted from the Project panel, the instance will become invalidated. See *Figure 2.22*:

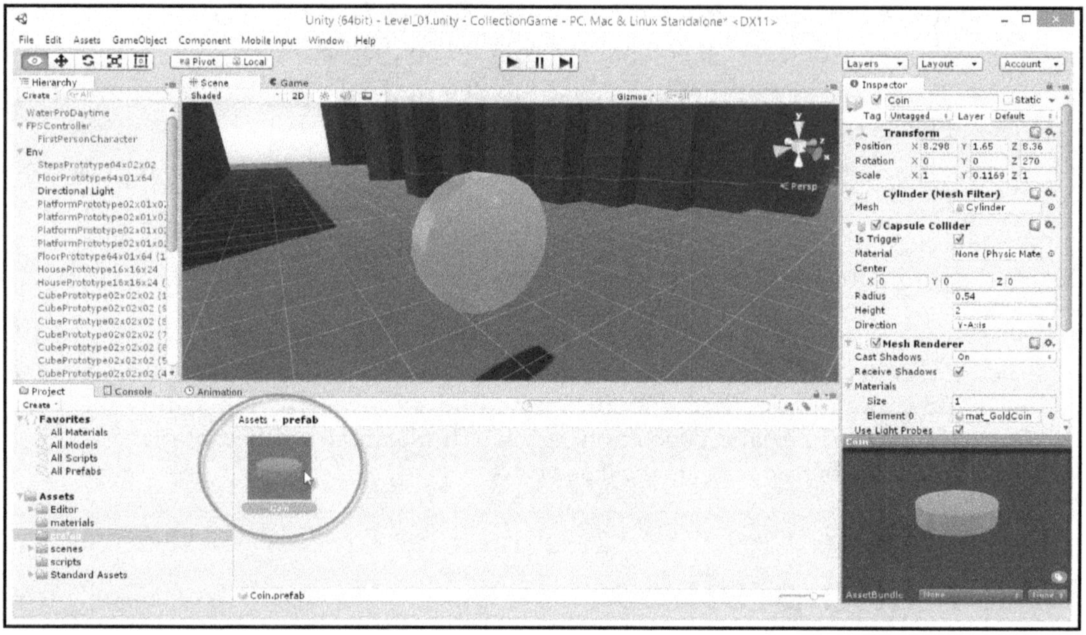

Figure 2.22: Creating a coin prefab

After prefab is created, you can add more instances of the coin easily to the level by dragging and dropping prefab from the **Project** panel to the Scene. Each instance is linked to the original prefab asset, which means that all changes made to the asset will immediately be made to all instances.

With this in mind, go ahead now and add as many Coin prefabs to the level as suitable for your coin collection game. Refer to the following figure for my arrangement:

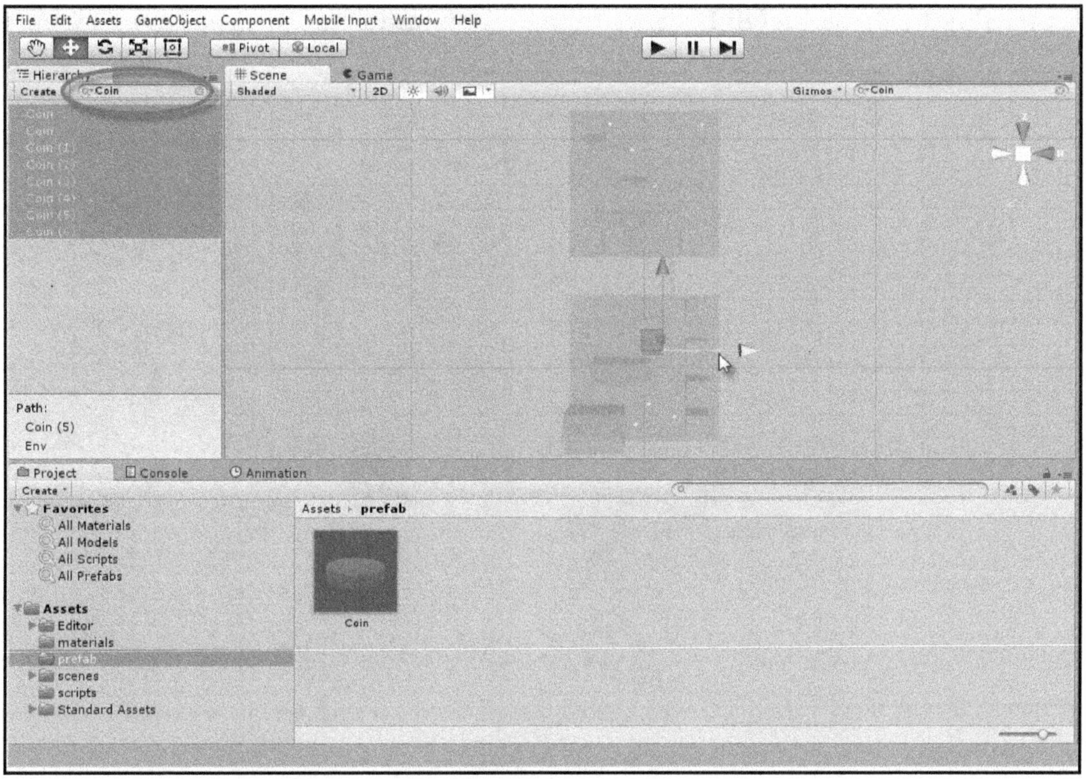

Figure 2.23: Adding coin prefabs to the level

One question that naturally arises is how you can transform prefab back into an independent GameObject that is no longer connected to the prefab asset. This is useful to do if you want some objects to be based on prefab but deviate from it slightly. To achieve this, select a prefab instance in the Scene, and then navigate to **GameObject** | **Break Prefab Instance** from the application menu. See *Figure 2.24*:

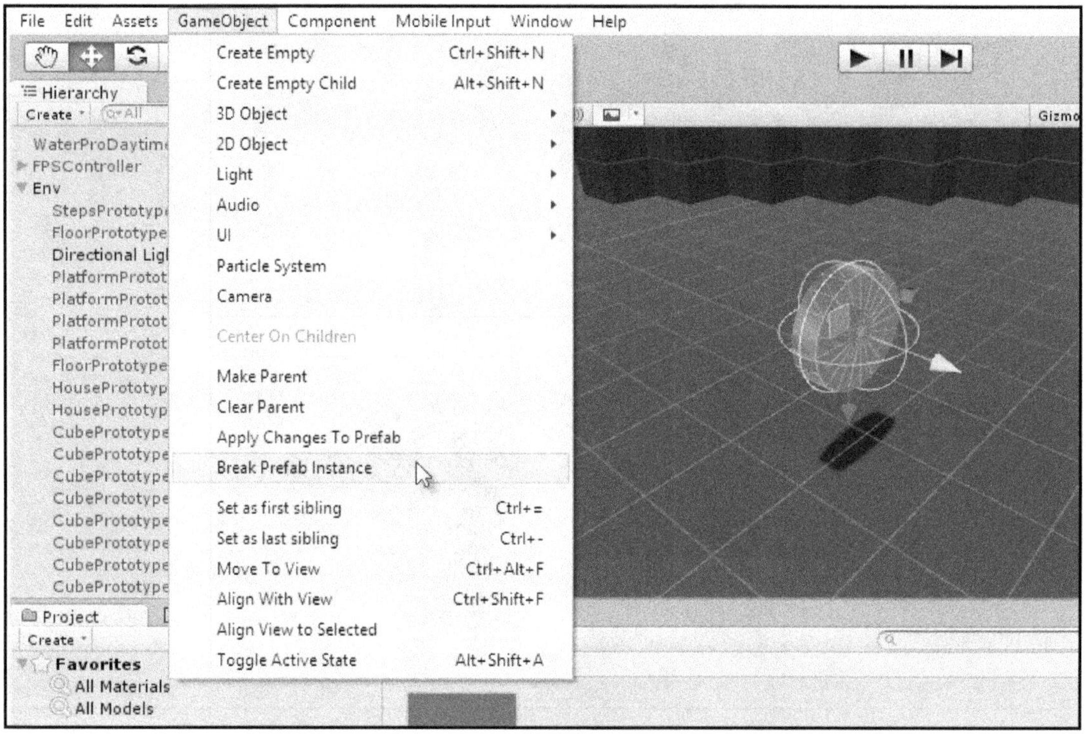

Figure 2.24: Breaking the prefab instance

If you add a prefab instance to Scene and make changes to it that you like and want to distribute upstream back to the prefab asset, then select the object and choose **GameObject** | **Apply Changes to Prefab**.

Timers and countdowns

You should now have a level complete with geometry and coin objects. Thanks to our newly added `Coin.cs` script, the coins are both countable and collectible. Even so, the level still poses little or no challenge to the player because there's no way the level can be won or lost. Specifically, there's nothing for the player to achieve. This is why a time limit is important for the game: it defines a win and loss condition. Namely, collecting all coins before the timer expires results in a win condition and failing to achieve this results in a loss condition. Let's get started at creating a timer countdown for the level. To do this, create a new and empty game object by selecting **GameObject** | **Create Empty** and rename this LevelTimer. See *Figure 2.25*:

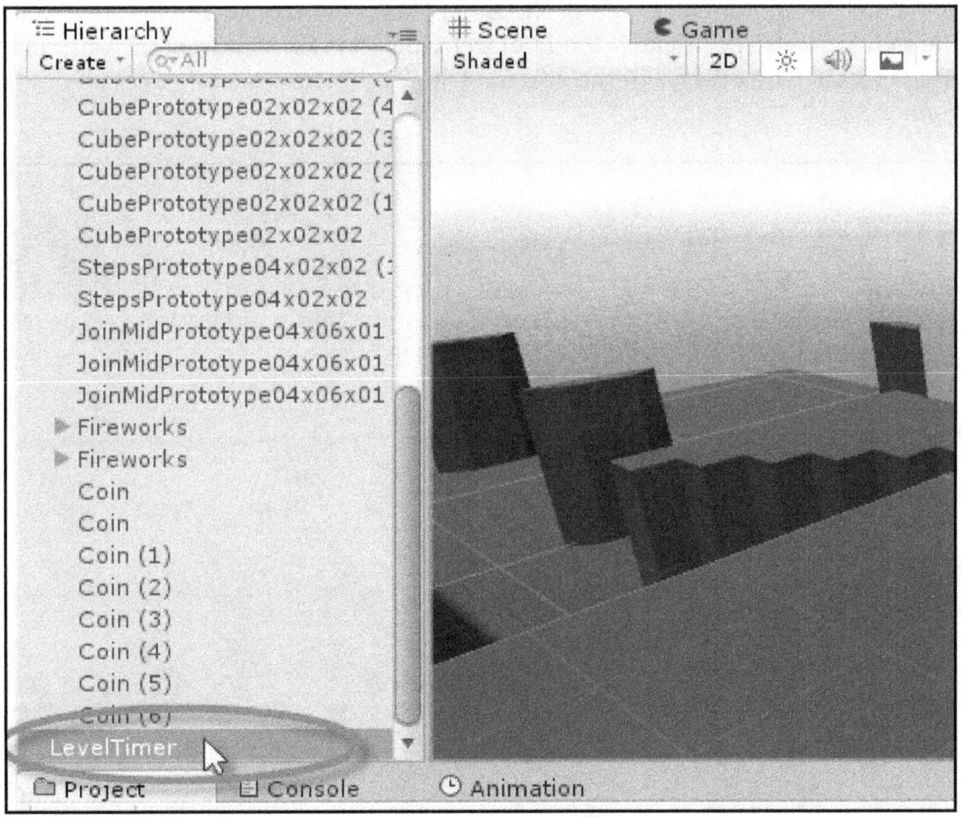

Figure 2.25: Renaming the timer object

Remember that empty game objects cannot be seen by the player because they have no mesh renderer component. They are especially useful to create functionality and behaviors that don't correspond directly to physical and visible entities, such as timers, managers, and game logic controllers.

Next, create a new script file named `Timer.cs` and add it to the LevelTimer object in Scene. By doing this, the timer functionality will exist in the scene. Make sure, however, that the timer script is added to one object, and no more than one. Otherwise, there will effectively be multiple, competing timers in the same scene. You can always search a scene to find all components of a specified type by using the Hierarchy panel. To do this, click in the Hierarchy search box and type `t:Timer`. Then press *Enter* on the keyboard to confirm the search. This search the scene for all objects with a component attached of the timer type, and the results are displayed in the Hierarchy panel. Specifically, the Hierarchy panel is filtered to show only the matching objects. The t prefix in the search string indicates a search by type operation. See *Figure 2.26*:

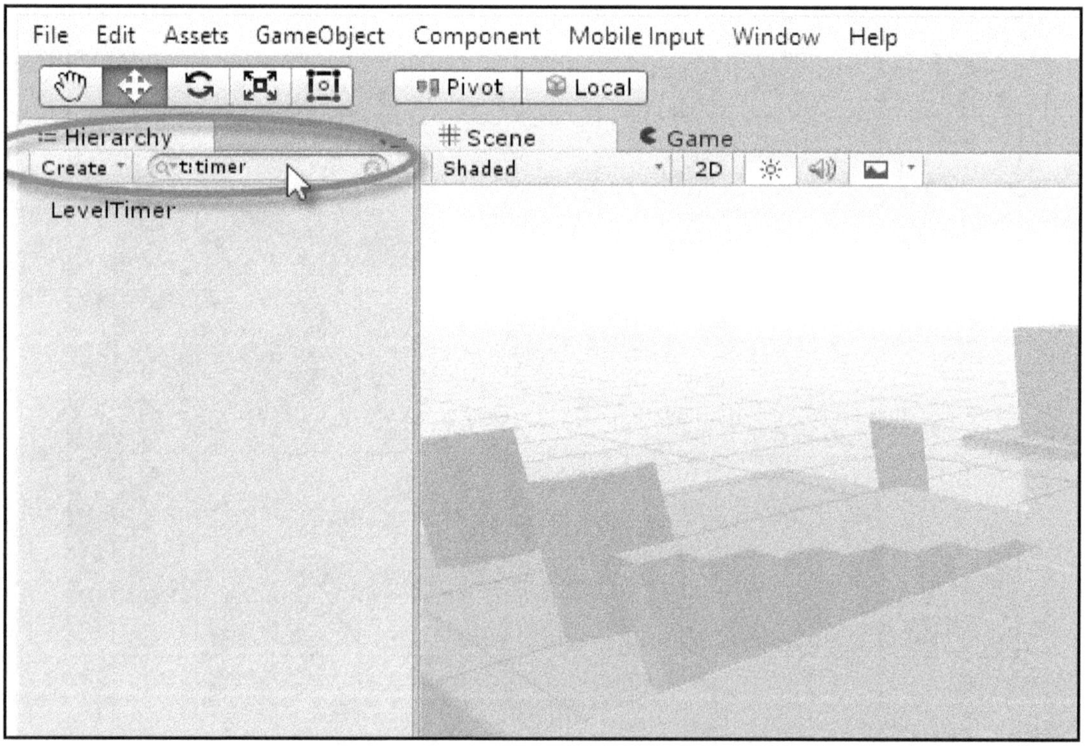

Figure 2.26: Searching for objects with a component of matching type

You can easily cancel a search and return the Hierarchy panel back to its original state by clicking on the small cross icon aligned to the right-hand side of the search field. This button can be tricky to spot. See *Figure 2.27*:

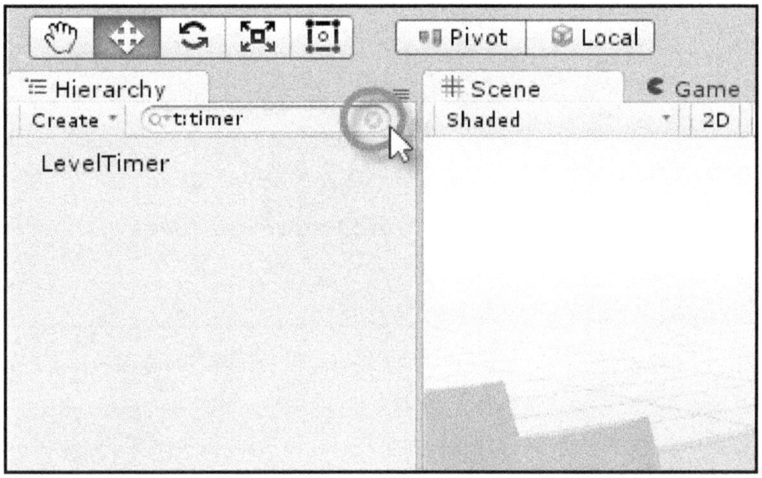

Figure 2.27: Canceling a type search

The timer script itself must be coded if it's to be useful. The full source code for the `Timer.cs` file is given in the following *Code Sample 2.6*. This source code is highly important if you've never scripted in Unity before. It demonstrates so many critical features. See the comments for a fuller explanation.

```
//------------------------
using UnityEngine;
using System.Collections;
//------------------------
public class Timer : MonoBehaviour
{
  //------------------------
  //Maximum time to complete level (in seconds)
  public float MaxTime = 60f;
  //------------------------
  //Countdown
  [SerializeField]
  private float CountDown = 0;
  //------------------------
  // Use this for initialization
  void Start ()
  {
    CountDown = MaxTime;
```

```
    }
    //------------------------
    // Update is called once per frame
    void Update ()
    {
      //Reduce time
      CountDown -= Time.deltaTime;
      //Restart level if time runs out
      if(CountDown <= 0)
      {
        //Reset coin count
        Coin.CoinCount=0;
        Application.LoadLevel(Application.loadedLevel);
      }
    }
    //------------------------
  }
  //------------------------
```

Code Sample 2.6

The following points summarize the code sample:

- In Unity, class variables declared as public (such as `public float MaxTime`) are displayed as editable fields in the Object Inspector of the editor. However, this applies to a range of supported data types only, but it's a highly useful feature. It means that developers can monitor and set public variables for classes directly from the Inspector as opposed to changing and recompiling code every time a change is needed. The private variables, in contrast, are hidden from the Inspector by default. However, you can force them to be visible, if needed, using the `SerializeField` attribute. The private variables prefixed with this attribute, such as the `CountDown` variable, will be displayed in the Object Inspector just like a public variable, even though the variable's scope still remains private.

- The `Update` function is a Unity native event supported for all classes derived from MonoBehaviour. `Update` is invoked automatically once per frame for all active GameObjects in the scene. This means that all active game objects are notified about frame change events. In short, `Update` is therefore called many times per second; the game FPS is a general indicator as to how many times each second. The actual number of calls will vary in practice from second to second. In any case, `Update` is especially useful to animate, update, and change objects over time. In the case of a `CountDown` class, it'll be useful to keep track of time as it passes, second by second. More information on the `Update` function can be found at the online Unity documentation at `http:// docs.unity3d.com/ScriptReference/ MonoBehaviour.Update.html`.

> In addition to the `Update` function called on each frame, Unity also supports two other related functions, namely, `FixedUpdate` and `LateUpdate`. `FixedUpdate` is used when coding with Physics, as we'll see later, and is called a fixed number of times per frame. `LateUpdate` is called once per frame for each active object, but the `LateUpdate` call will always happen after every object has received an Update event. Thus, it happens after the Update cycle, making it a late update. There are reasons for this late update and we'll see them later in the book.
>
> More information on `FixedUpdate` can be found in the online Unity documentation at `http://docs.unity3d.com/ ScriptReference/ MonoBehaviour.FixedUpdate.html` More information on the `LateUpdate` function can be found in the online Unity documentation at http://docs.unity3d.com/ ScriptReference/MonoBehaviour.LateUpdate.html.

- When scripting, the static `Time.deltaTime` variable is constantly available and updated automatically by Unity. It always describes the amount of time (in seconds) that has passed since the previous frame ended. For example, if your game has a frame rate of 2 FPS (a very low frame rate!) then `deltaTime` will be 0.5. This is because, in each second, there would be two frames, and thus each frame would be half a second. The `deltaTime` is useful because, if added over time, it tells you how much time in total has elapsed or passed since the game began. For this reason, `deltaTime` floating point variable is used heavily in the `Update` function for the timer to subtract the elapsed time from the countdown total. More information can be found on deltaTime at the online documentation at `http://docs.unity3d.com/ ScriptReference/Time-deltaTime.html`.
- The static `Application.LoadLevel` function can be called anywhere in code to change the active scene at runtime. Thus, this function is useful to move the gamer from one level to another. It causes Unity to terminate the active scene, destroying all its contents, and load a new scene. It can also be used to restart the active scene, simply by loading the active level again. Application. LoadLevel is most appropriate for games with clearly defined levels that are separate from each other and have clearly defined beginnings and endings. It is not, however, suitable for large open-world games in which large sprawling environments stretch on, seemingly without any breakage or disconnection. More information on `Application.LoadLevel` can be found in the online Unity documentation at `http://docs.unity3d.com/ScriptReference/Application.LoadLevel.html`.

After the timer script is created, select the LevelTimer object in the scene. From the Object Inspector, you can set the maximum time (in seconds) that the player is allowed in order to complete the level. See *Figure 2.28*. I've set the total time to 60 seconds. This means that all coins must be completed within 60 seconds from the level start.

If the timer expires, the level is restarted.

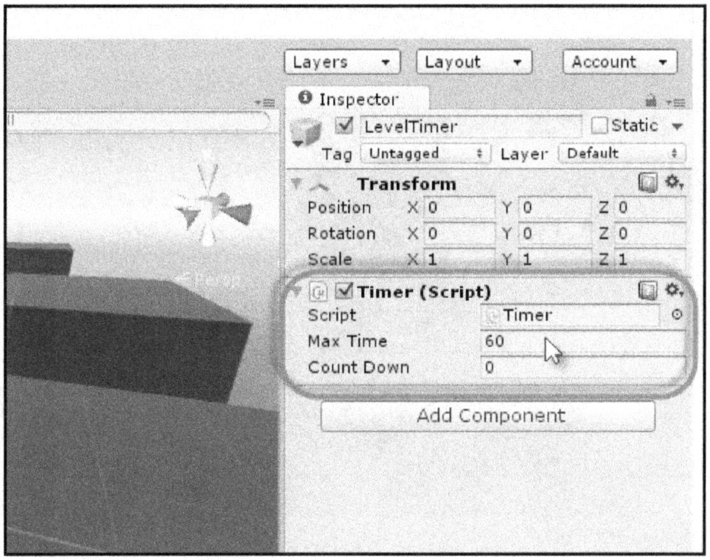

Figure 2.28: Setting the level total time

Great work! You should now have a completed level with a countdown that works. You can collect coins and the timer can expire. Overall, the game is taking shape. There is a further problem, however, which we'll address next.

Celebrations and fireworks!

The coin collection game is nearly finished. Coins can be collected and a timer expires, but the win condition itself is not truly handled. That is, when all coins are collected before time expiry, nothing actually happens to show the player that they've won. The countdown still proceeds and even restarts the level as though the win condition hadn't been satisfied at all. Let's fix this now. Specifically, when the win scenario happens, we should delete the timer object to prevent further countdown and show visual feedback to signify that the level has been completed. In this case, I'll add some fireworks! So, let's start by creating the fireworks. You can add these easily from the Unity Particle System packages. Navigate to the `Standard Assets` | `ParticleSystems` | `Prefabs` folder. Then, drag and drop the Fireworks particle system in Scene.

Add a second or even a third one if you want:

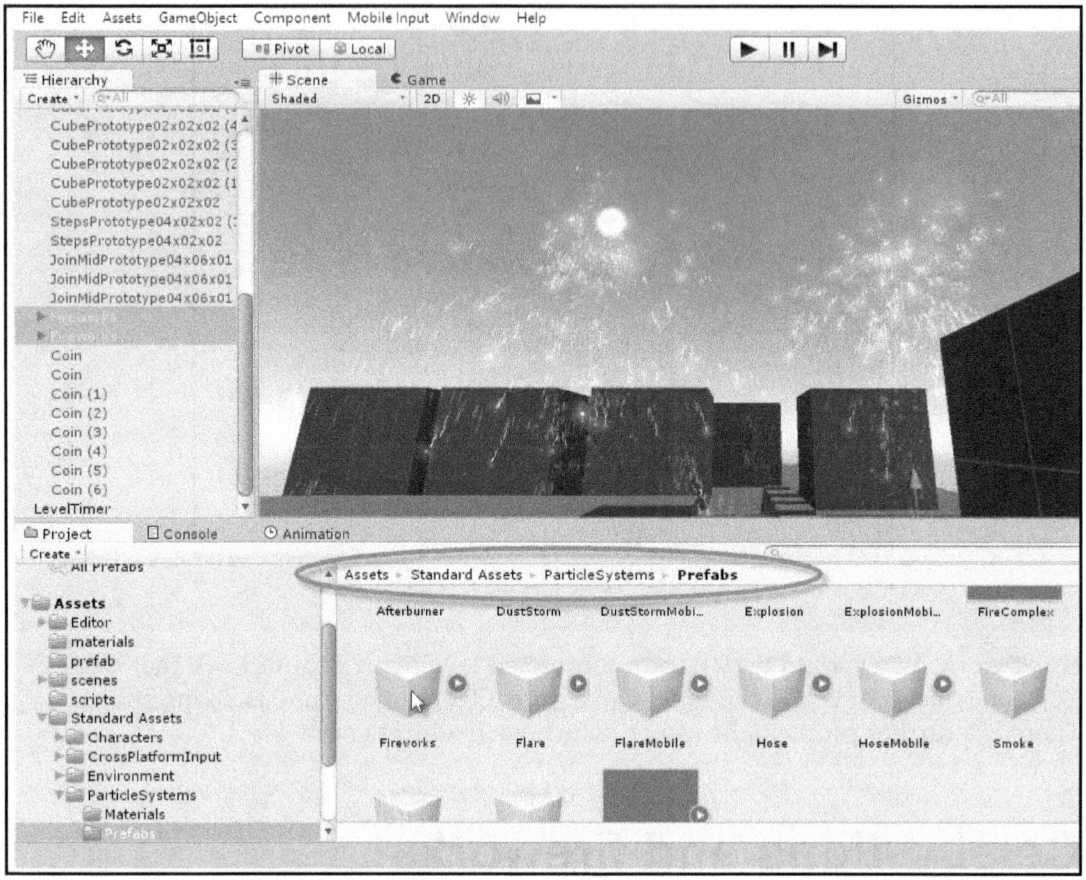

Figure 2.29: Adding two Fireworks prefabs

By default, all firework particle systems will play when the level begins. You can test this by pressing play on the toolbar. This is not the behavior that we want. We only want the fireworks to play when the win condition has been satisfied. To disable playback on level startup, select the Particle System object in the Scene and, from the Object Inspector, disable the **Play On Awake** checkbox, which can be found in the Particle System component. See *Figure 2.30*, Disabling Play On Awake:

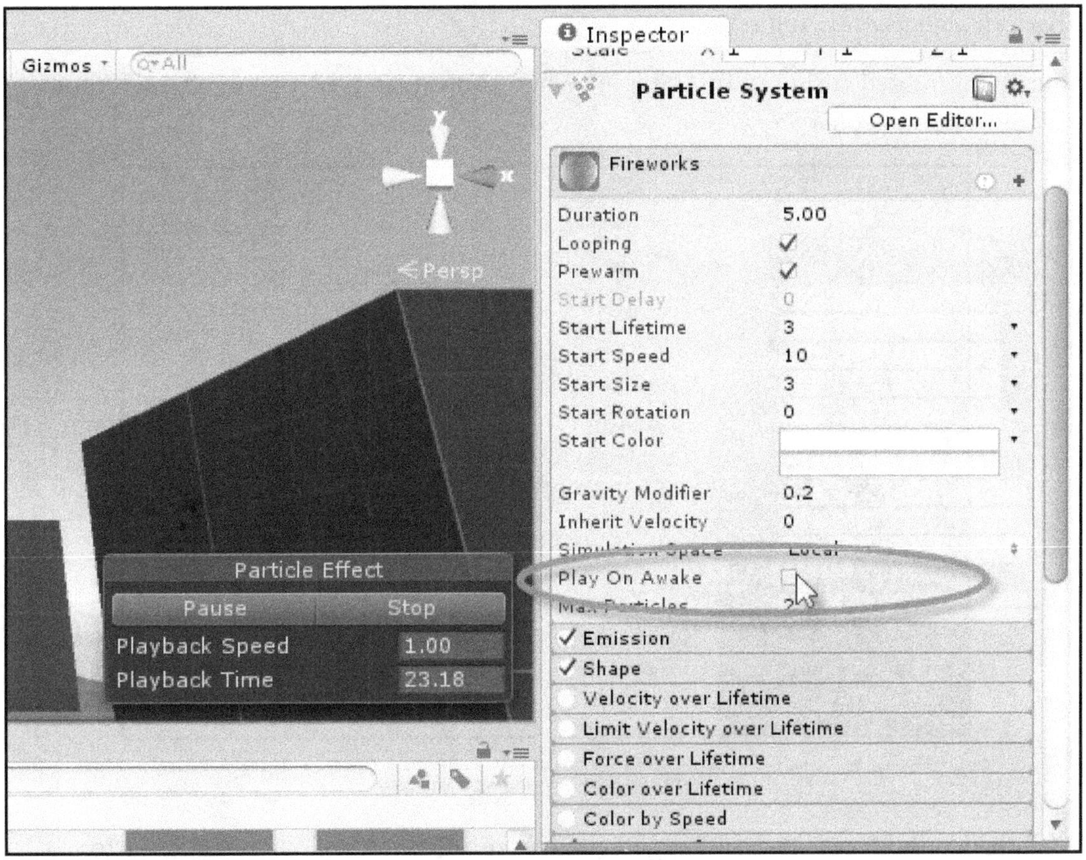

Figure 2.30: Disabling Play On Awake

Disabling **Play On Awake** prevents particle systems playing automatically at level startup. This is fine, but if they are ever to play at all, something must manually start them at the right time. We can achieve this through code. Before resorting to a coding solution, however, we'll first mark all firework objects with an appropriate tag. The reason for this is that, in code, we'll want to search for all firework objects in the scene and trigger them to play when needed. To isolate the firework objects from all other objects, we'll use tags. So, let's create a new Fireworks tag and assign them to the firework objects only in the Scene.

Tags were created earlier in this chapter when configuring the player character for coin collisions. See *Figure 2.31*:

Figure 2.31: Tagging firework objects

With the firework objects now tagged, we can refine the `Coin.cs` script class to handle a win condition for the scene, as shown in *Code Sample 2.7*. Comments follow:

```
//-------------------------
using UnityEngine;
using System.Collections;
//-------------------------
public class Coin : MonoBehaviour
{
  //-------------------------
  public static int CoinCount = 0;
```

```
    //------------------------
    // Use this for initialization
    void Awake ()
    {
      //Object created, increment coin count
      ++Coin.CoinCount;
    }
    //------------------------
    void OnTriggerEnter(Collider Col)
    {
      //If player collected coin, then destroy object
      if(Col.CompareTag("Player"))
      Destroy(gameObject);
    }
    //------------------------
    void OnDestroy()
    {
      --Coin.CoinCount;
      //Check remaining coins
      if(Coin.CoinCount <= 0)
      {
        //Game is won. Collected all coins
        //Destroy Timer and launch fireworks
        GameObject Timer = GameObject.Find("LevelTimer");
        Destroy(Timer);
        GameObject[] FireworkSystems =
        GameObject.FindGameObjectsWithTag("Fireworks");
        foreach(GameObject GO in FireworkSystems)
        GO.GetComponent<ParticleSystem>().Play();
      }
    }
    //------------------------
  }
  //------------------------
```

Code Sample 2.7

The following points summarize the code sample:

- The `OnDestroy` function is critical. It occurs when a coin is collected and features an if statement to determine when all coins are collected (the win scenario).

- When a win scenario happens, the `GameObject.Find` function is called to search the complete scene hierarchy for any active object named `LevelTimer`. If found, the object is deleted. This happens to delete the timer and prevent any further countdown when the level is won. If the scene contains multiple objects of a matching name, then only the first object is returned. This is one reason why the scene should contain one and only one timer.

> Avoid using the `GameObject.Find` function wherever possible. It's slow for performance. Instead, use `FindGameObjectsWithTag`. It's been used here only to demonstrate its existence and purpose. Sometimes, you'll need to use it to find a single, miscellaneous object that has no specific tag.

In addition to deleting the `LevelTimer` object, the `OnDestroy` function finds all firework objects in the scene and initiates them. It finds all objects of a matching tag using the `GameObject.FindGameObjectsWithTag` function. This function returns an array of all objects with the Fireworks tag and the ParticleSystem is initiated for each object by calling the `Play` function.

As mentioned, each GameObject in Unity is really made from a collection of attached and related components. An object is the sum of its components. For example, a standard cube (created using **GameObject** | **3D Object** | **Cube**) is made from a Transform component, Mesh Filter component, Mesh Renderer component, and Box Collider component. These components together make the cube what it is and behave how it does. The `GetComponent` function can be called in script to retrieve a reference to any specified component, giving you direct access to its public properties. The `OnDestroy` function in the preceding code uses `GetComponent` to retrieve a reference to the ParticleSystem component attached to the object. `GetComponent` is a highly useful and important function. More information on `GetComponent` can be found at the online Unity documentation at `http://docs.unity3d.com/ ScriptReference/GameObject.GetComponent.html`.

Play testing

You've now completed your first game in Unity! It's time to take it for a test run and then finally build it. Testing in Unity firstly consists of pressing play on the toolbar and simply playing your game to see that it works as intended from the perspective of a gamer. In addition to playing, you can also enable debugging mode from the Object Inspector to keep a watchful eye on all public and private variables during runtime, making sure that no variable is assigned an unexpected value.

To activate the Debug mode, click on the menu icon at the top right corner of the Object Inspector and, from the context menu that appears, select the **Debug** option. See *Figure 2.32*:

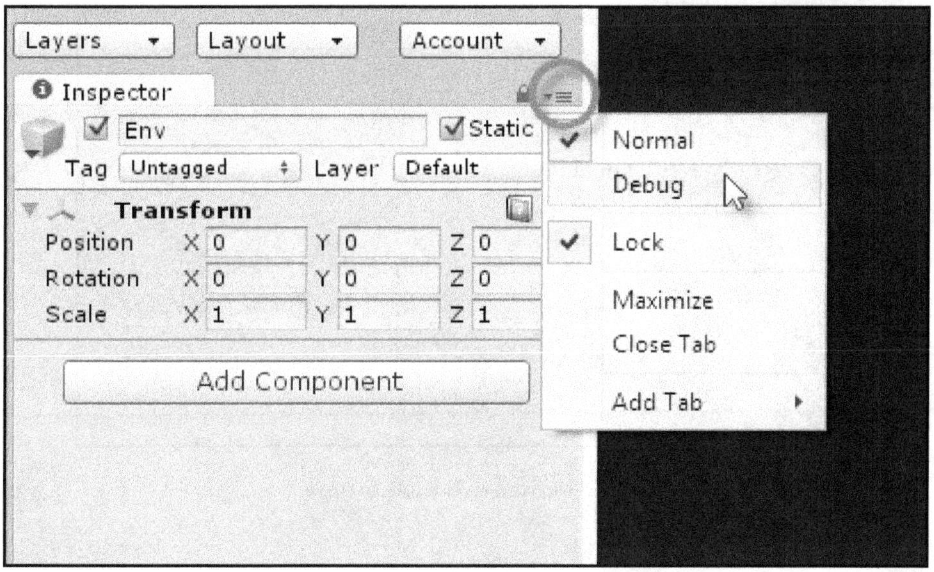

Figure 2.32: Activating Debug mode from the Object Inspector

After activating the Debug mode, the appearance of some variables and components in the Object Inspector may change. Typically, you'll get a more detailed and accurate view of your variables, and you'll also be able to see most private variables. See *Figure 2.33* for the Transform component in Debug mode:

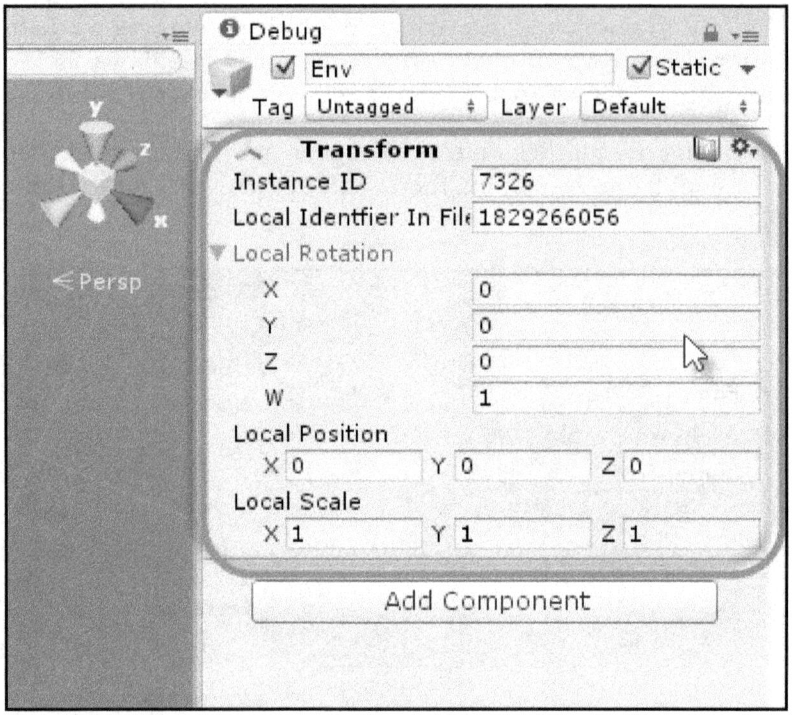

Figure 2.33: Viewing the Transform component in Debug mode

Another useful debugging tool at runtime is the Stats panel. This can be accessed from the Game tab by clicking on the Stats button from the toolbar. See *Figure 2.34*:

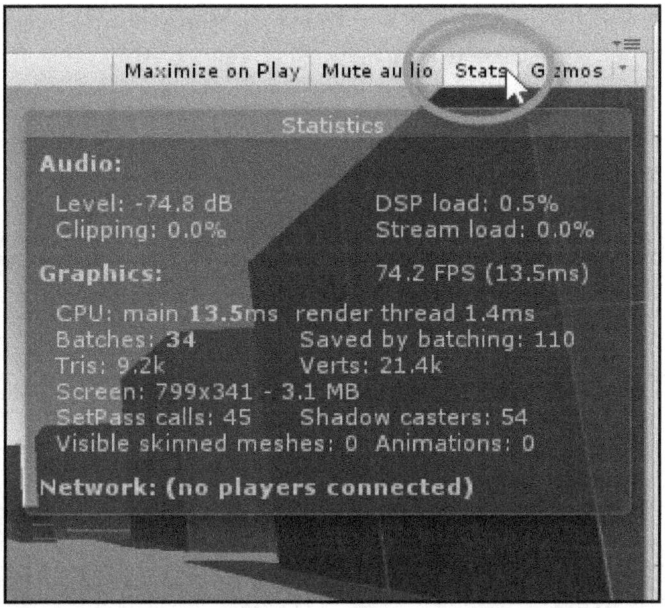

Figure 2.34: Accessing the Stats panel from the Game tab

The Stats panel is only useful during the play mode. In this mode, it details the critical performance statistics for your game, such as Frame Rate (FPS) and memory usage. This lets you diagnose or determine whether any problems may be affecting your game. The FPS represents the total number of frames (ticks or cycles) per second that your game can sustain on average. There is no right, wrong, or magical FPS, but higher values are better than lower ones. Higher values represent better performance because it means that your game can sustain more cycles in one second. If your FPS falls below 20 or 15, it's likely that your game will appear choppy or laggy as the performance weight of each cycle means it takes longer to process. Many variables can affect FPS, some internal and some external to your game. Internal factors include the number of lights in a scene, vertex density of meshes, number of instructions, and complexity of the code. Some external factors include the quality of your computer's hardware, number of other applications and processes running at the same time, and amount of hard drive space, among others.

In short, if your FPS is low, then it indicates a problem that needs attention. The solution to that problem varies depending on the context and you'll need to use judgement, for example, are your meshes too complex? Do they have too many vertices? Are your textures too large? Are there too many sounds playing? See *Figure 2.35* for the coin collection game up and running. The completed game can be found in the book companion files in the `Chapter02/End` folder:

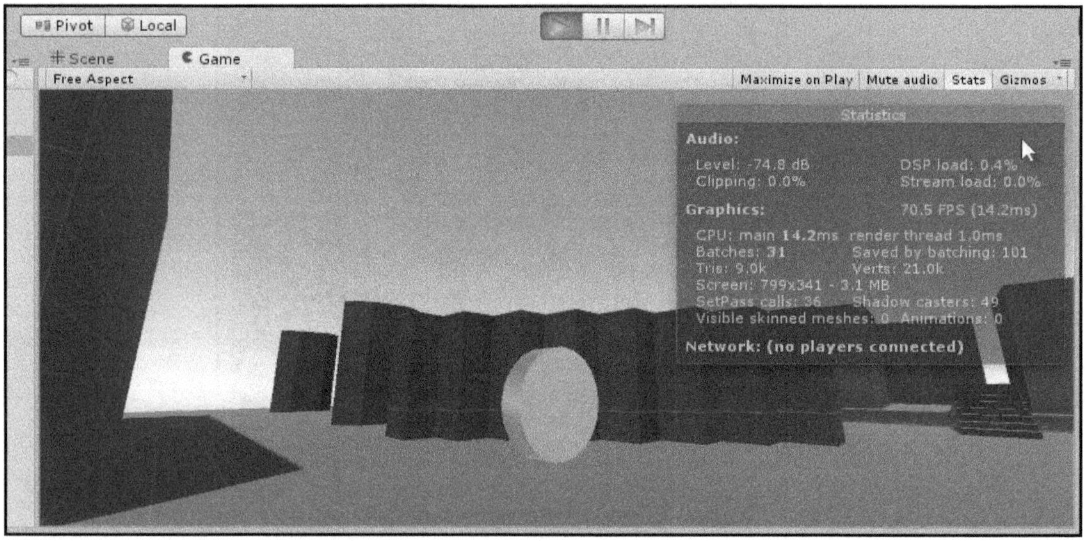

Figure 2.35: Testing the coin collection game

Building

So, now it's time to build the game! That is, to compile and package the game into a standalone and self-executing form, which the gamer can run and play without needing to use the Unity Editor. Typically, when developing games, you'll reach a decision about your target platform (such as Windows, iOS, Android, and others) during the design phase and not at the end of development. It's often said that Unity is a 'develop once, deploy everywhere tool. This slogan can conjure up the unfortunate image that, after a game is made, it'll work just as effortlessly on every platform supported by Unity as it does on the desktop.

Unfortunately, things are not so simple; games that work well on desktop systems don't necessarily perform equally well on mobiles and vice versa. This is largely due to the great differences in target hardware and industry standards that hold between them. Due to these differences, I'll focus our attention here to the Windows and Mac desktop platforms, ignoring mobiles and consoles and other platforms. To create a build for desktop platform, select **File** | **Build Settings** from the **File** menu:

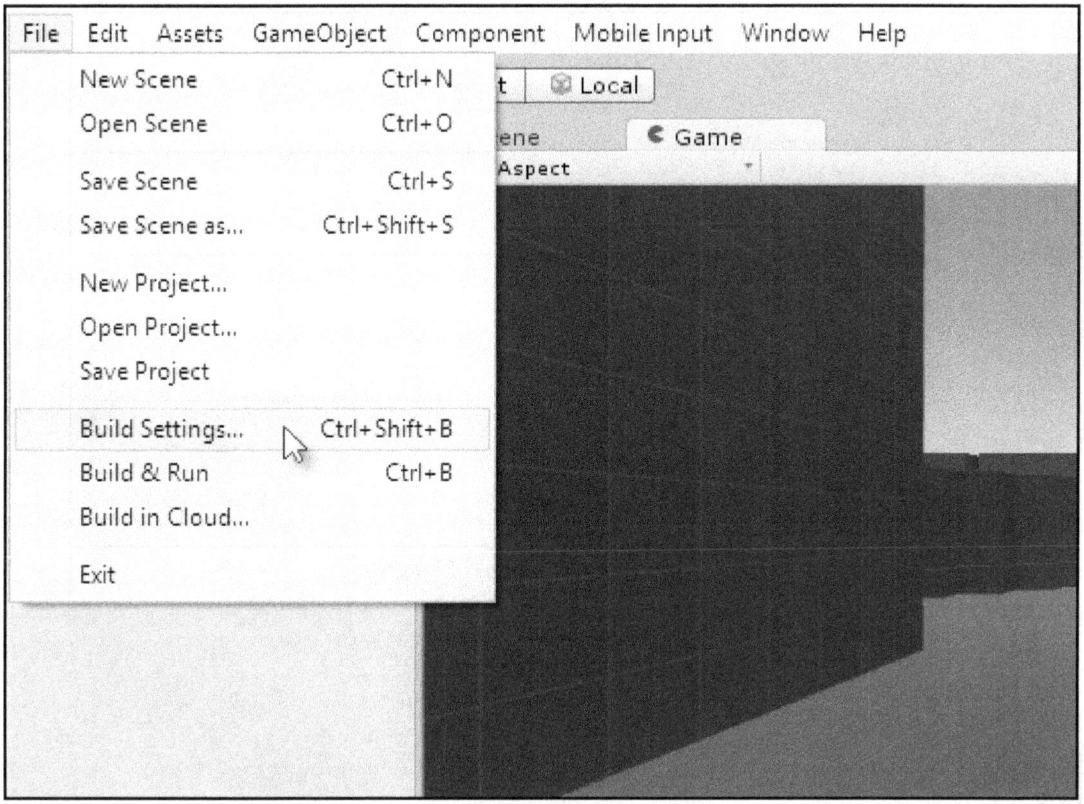

Figure 2.36: Accessing the Build Settings for the project

The **Build Settings** dialog is displayed and its interface consists of three main areas. The **Scenes In Build** list is a complete list of all scenes to be included in the build, regardless of whether the gamer will actually visit them in the game. It represents the totality of all scenes that could ever be visited in the game.

In short, if you want or need a scene in your game, then it needs to be in this list. Initially, the list is empty. See *Figure 2.37*:

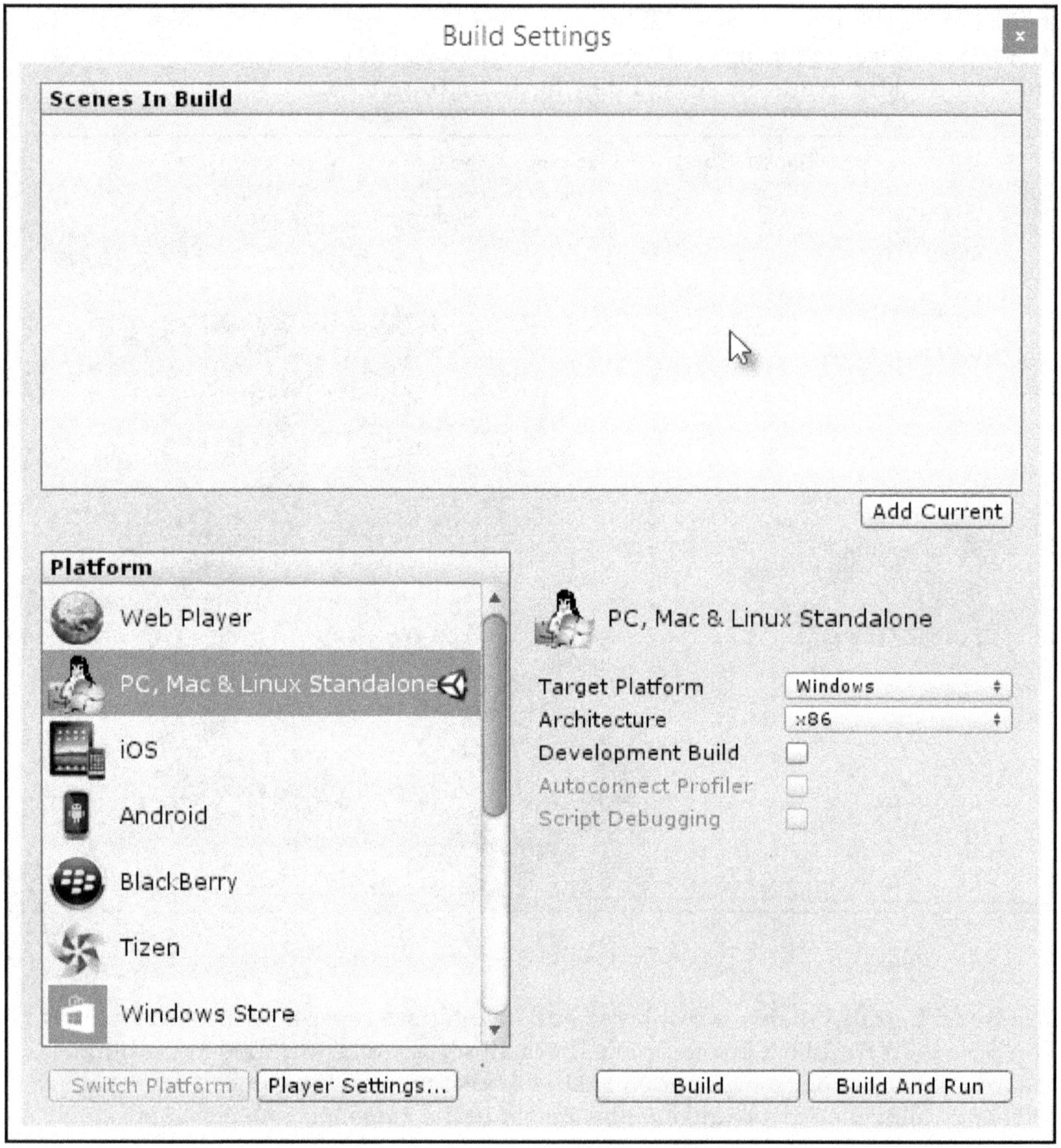

Figure 2.37: The Build Settings dialog

You can easily add scenes to the list by simply dragging and dropping the scene asset from the **Project** panel to the **Scenes In Build** list. For the coin collection game, I'll drag and drop the `Level_01` scene to the list. As scenes are added, Unity automatically assigns them a number, depending on their order in the list. 0 represents the topmost item, 1 the next item, and so on. This number is important insofar as the 0 item is concerned. The topmost scene (scene 0) will always be the starting scene. That is, when the build runs, Unity automatically begins execution from scene 0. Thus, scene 0 will typically be your splash or intro scene. See *Figure 2.38*:

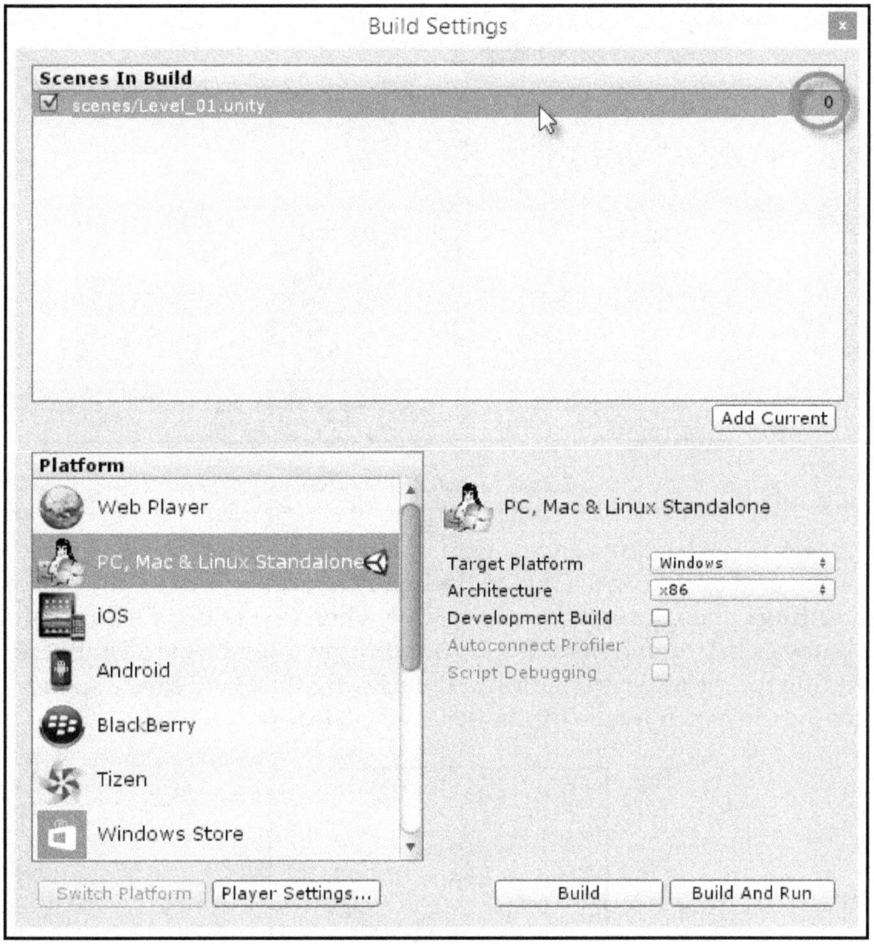

Figure 2.38: Adding a level to the Build Settings dialog

Next, be sure to select your target platform from the Platform list at the bottom left-hand side of the Build Settings dialog. For desktop platforms, choose **PC, Mac & Linux Standalone**, which should be selected by default. Then, from the options, set the **Target Platform** dropdown list to either Windows, Linux, or Mac OS X, depending on your system. See *Figure 2.39*:

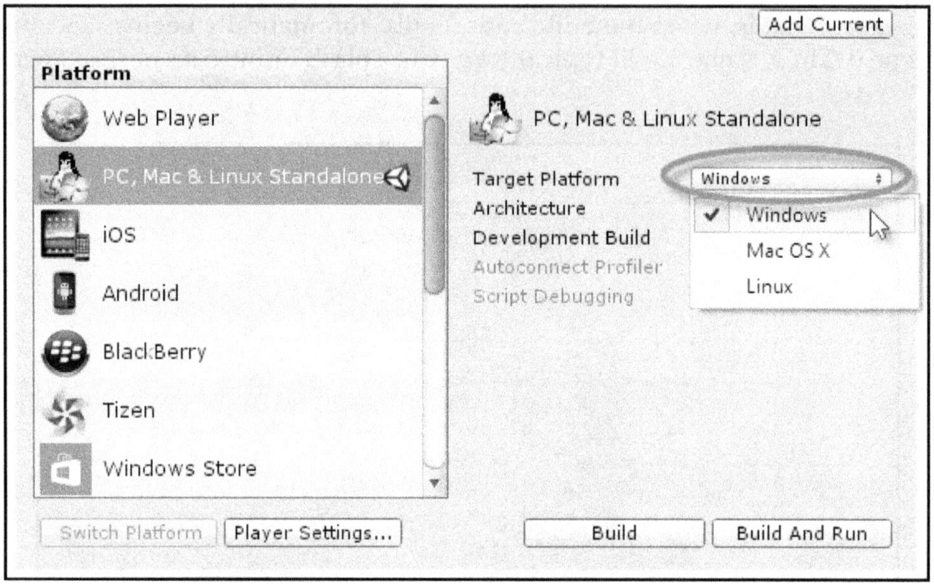

Figure 2.39: Choosing a target build platform

If you've previously been testing your game for multiple platforms or trying out other platforms such as Android and iOS, the **Switch Platform** button (at the bottom left of the **Build Settings** dialog) might become active when you select the **Standalone** option. If it does, click on the **Switch Platform** button to confirm to Unity that you intend building for the selected platform. On clicking this, Unity may spend a few minutes configuring your assets for the selected platform:

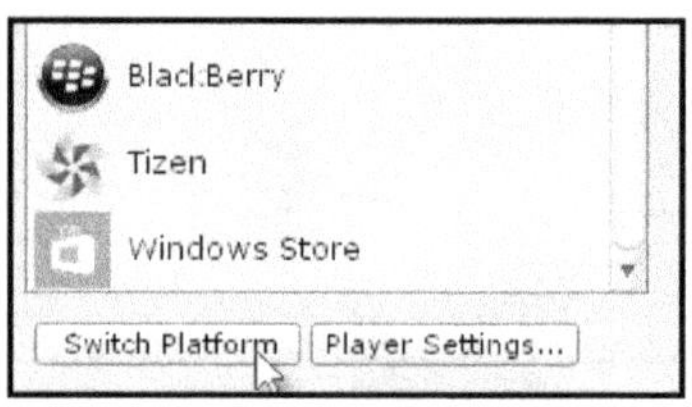

Figure 2.40: Switching platforms

Before building for the first time, you'll probably want to view the **Player Settings** options to fine-tune important build parameters, such as game resolution, quality settings, executable icon, and information, among other settings. To access the Player Settings, you can simply click on the **Player Settings** button from the **Build** dialog. This displays the Player Settings in the Object Inspector. The same settings can also be accessed via the application menu by navigating to **Edit** | **Project Settings** | **Player**. See *Figure 2.4*:

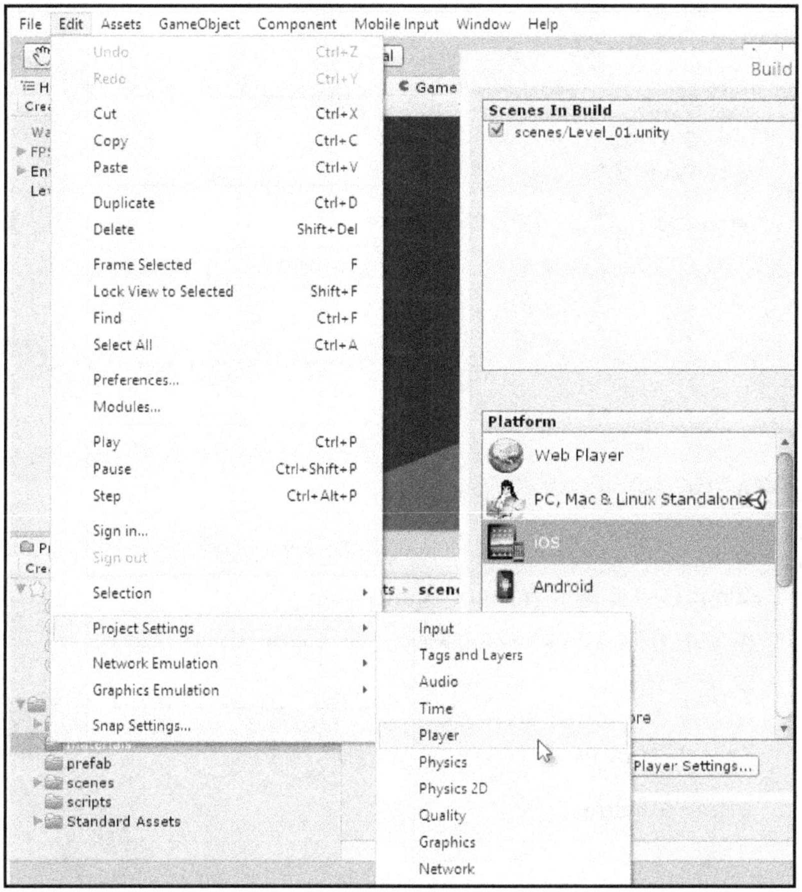

Figure 2.41: Accessing the Player Settings options

From the Player Settings options, set Company Name and Product Name as this information is baked and stored within the built executable. You can also specify an icon image for the executable as well as a default mouse cursor, if one is required. For the collection game, however, these latter two settings will be left empty. See *Figure 2.42*:

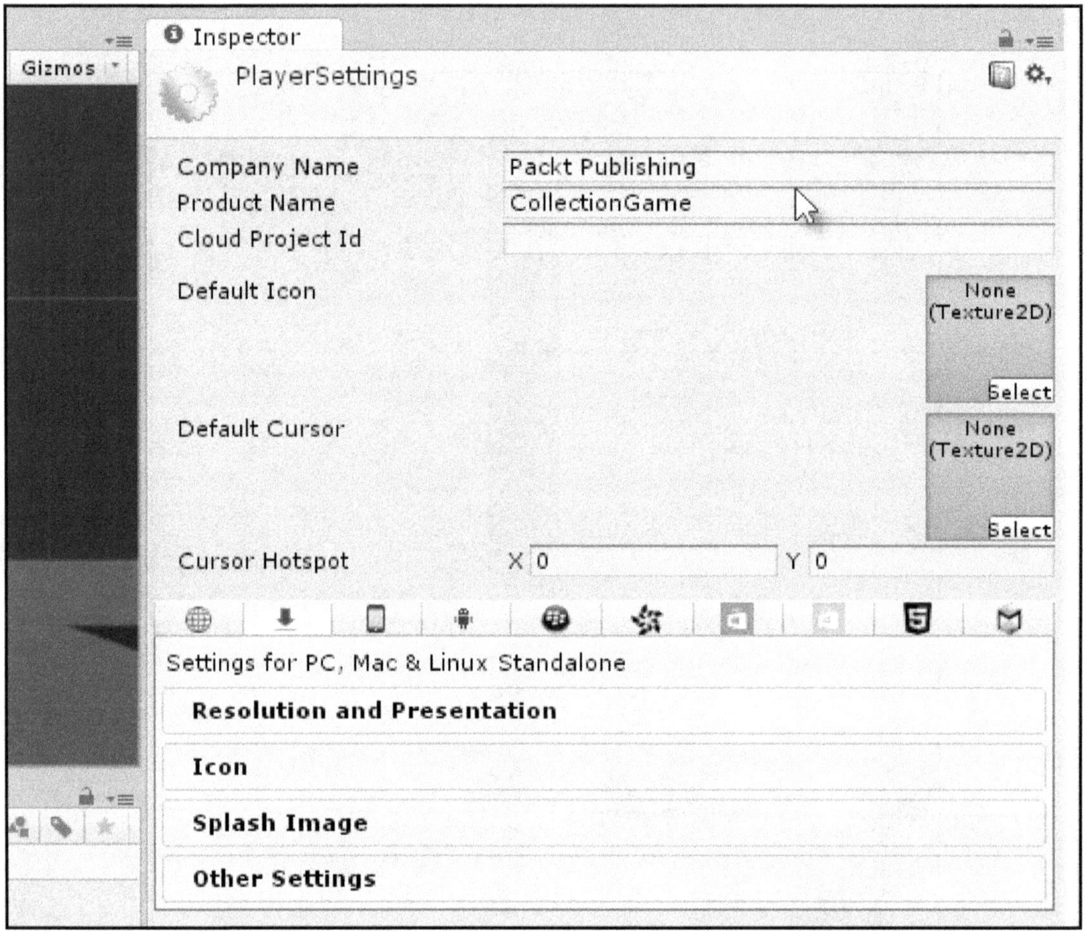

Figure 2.42: Setting a publisher name and product name

The **Resolution and Presentation** tab is especially important as it specifies the game screen size and whether a default splash screen (Resolution dialog) should appear at the application startup. From this tab, ensure that the **Default Is Full Screen** option is enabled, meaning that the game will run at the complete size of the system's screen as opposed to a smaller and movable window. In addition, enable the **Display Resolution Dialog** drop-down list. See *Figure 2.43*. When this is enabled, your application will display an options screen at startup, allowing the user to select a target resolution and screen size and customize controls.

For a final build, you'll probably want to disable this option, presenting the same settings through your own customized options screen in-game instead. However, for test builds, the **Resolution** dialog can be a great help. It lets you test your build easily at different sizes:

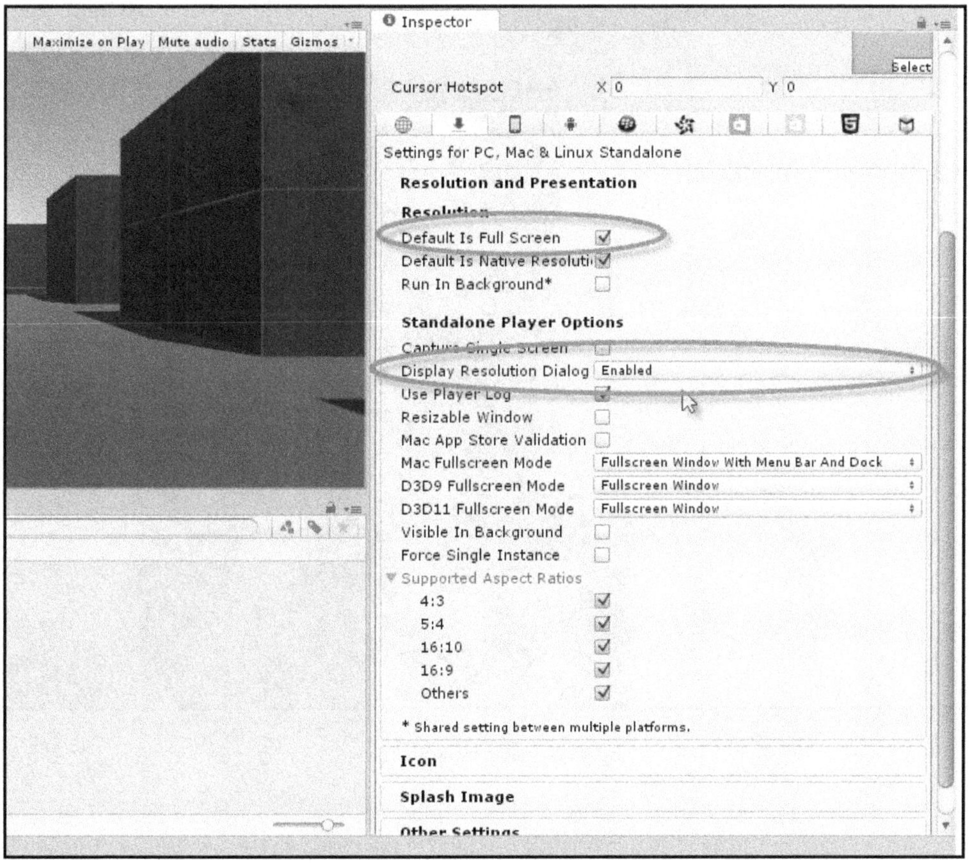

Figure 2.43: Enabling the Resolution dialog

Now you're ready to make your first compiled build. So, click on the **Build** button from the **Build Settings** dialog or else, choose **File** | **Build & Run** from the application menu. When you do this, Unity presents you with a **Save** dialog, asking you to specify a target location on your computer where the build should be made. Select a location and choose **Save**, and the build process will be completed. Occasionally, this process can generate errors, which are printed in red in the Console window. This can happen, for example, when you save to a read-only drive, have insufficient hard drive space, or don't have the necessary administration privileges on your computer. However, generally, the build process succeeds if your game runs properly in the editor. See *Figure 2.44*:

Figure 2.44: Building and running a game

After the Build is completed, Unity generates new files at your destination location. For Windows, it generates an executable file and data folder. See *Figure 2.45*. Both are essential and interdependent. That is, if you want to distribute your game and have other people play it without needing to install Unity, then you'll need to send users both the executable file and associated data folder and all its contents.

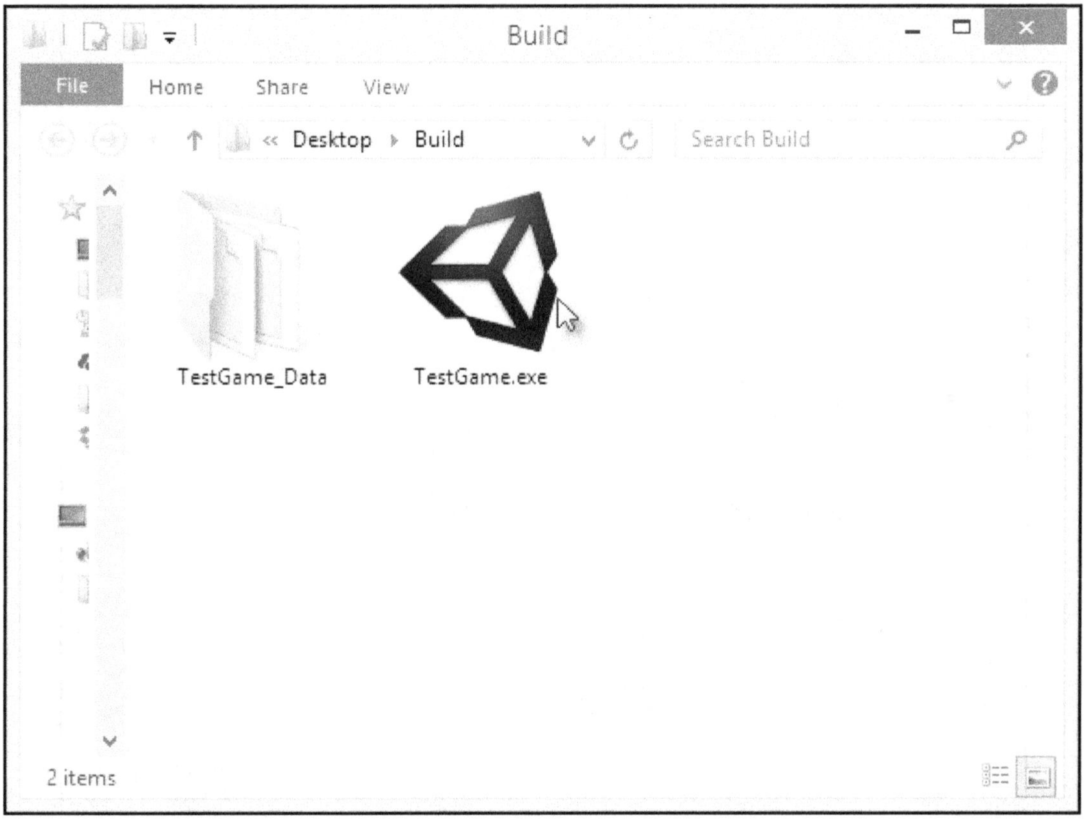

Figure 2.45: Unity builds several files

On running your game, the **Resolution** dialog will show, assuming that you enabled the **Display Resolution Dialog** option from the Player Settings. From here, users can select the game resolution, quality, and output monitor and configure player controls:

Figure 2.46: Preparing to run your game from the Resolution dialog

On clicking the play button, your game will run by default in fullscreen mode. Congratulations! Your game is now completed and built and you can send it to your friends and family for play testing! See *Figure 2.47*:

Figure 2.47: Running the coin collection game in fullscreen mode

But wait! How do you exit your game when you're finished playing? There's no quit button or main menu option in the game. For Windows, you just need to press *Alt* + *F4* on the keyboard. For Mac, you press *cmd* + *Q* and for Ubuntu, it's *Ctrl* + *Q*.

Excellent work! On reaching this point, you've completed the coin collection game, as well as your first game in Unity. On achieving this, you've seen a wide range of Unity features including level editing and design, prefabs, particle systems, meshes, components, script files, and build settings. Next, we'll embark on a journey to write our own shaders and effects.

3
Post Processing Stack

In this chapter, you will learn the following recipes:

- Installing the Post Processing Stack
- Getting a filmic look using grain, vignetting, and anti-aliasing
- Mimicking real life with bloom and anti-aliasing
- Setting the mood with color grading
- Creating a horror game look with fog

Introduction

It's great to write your own shaders and effects so that you can fine-tune your project to look just the way that you want, and this is what we will be spending the majority of the book looking into. However, it's also good to point out that Unity already comes with some prebuilt ways to get some of the more common effects that users like to have through the use of the Post Processing Stack.

For those who just want to get something up and running, the Post Processing Stack can be an excellent way for you to tweak the appearance of your game without having to write any additional code. Using the Post Processing Stack can also be useful in showing you just what shaders can do and how they can improve your game projects as, behind the scenes, the Post Processing Stack is itself a shader that is applied to the screen, aptly called a screen shader.

Installing the Post Processing Stack

Before we can use the Post Processing Stack, we must first get it from the newly introduced **Package Manager**. A Unity package is a single file that contains various assets that can be used in Unity in a similar manner to a `.zip` file. Previously, Unity used the **Asset Store** to share these files with users, but as time has gone on, the **Package Manager** has been added to give users an easy way to get free content from Unity.

Getting ready

To get started with this recipe, you will need to have Unity running and have created a new project. This chapter also requires you to have an environment to work from. The code files provided with this book will contain a basic scene and content to create the scene Unity's Standard Assets.

Open the `Chapter 1 | Starting Point` scene inside of the `Asset | Chapter 01 | Scenes` folder from the **Project** browser. If all goes well, you should see something like this from the **Game** tab:

This is a simple environment that will allow us to easily see how changes made in post-processing effects can modify how things are drawn on the screen.

> If you are interested in learning how to create the environment used, check out my previous book, *Unity 5.x Game Development Blueprints*, also available from Packt Publishing.

How to do it...

To begin:

1. Open up the **Package Manager** by going to **Window** | **Package Manager** (or by pressing *Ctrl* + *9*):

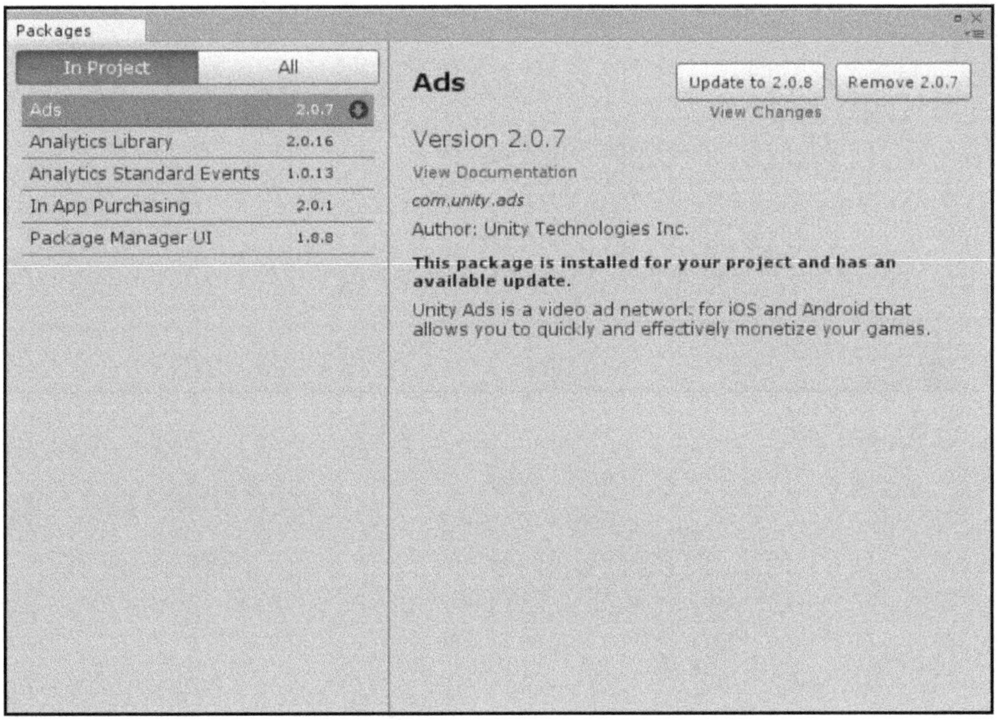

2. From the list view, click on the **All** button to display a list of all of the possible packages that are there. Once the list populates with all of the choices, select the **Post-processing** option:

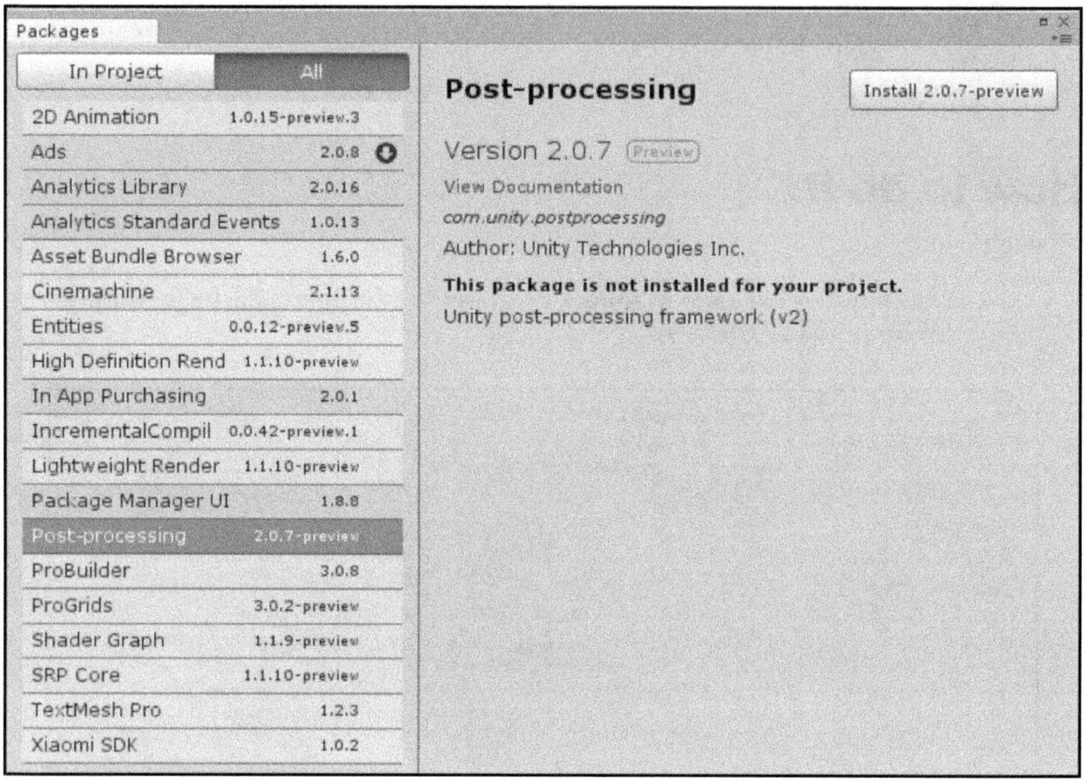

3. From there, at the top right of the menu, click on the **Install 2.0.7-preview** button. You may need to wait for a while for it to complete downloading the content. Once it's completed, you should be brought back to the **In Project** selection and now you'll see **Post-processing** added to the list:

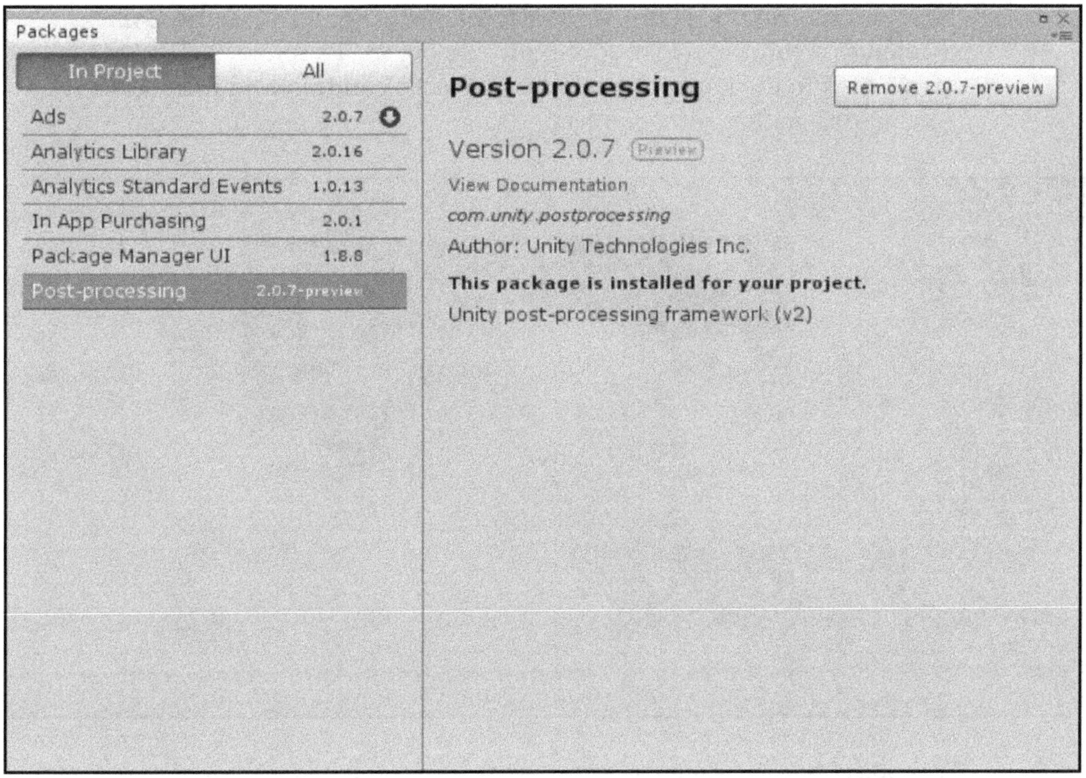

4. Close out of the **Packages** tab and go back to the **Scene** window to see the level. Then, from the **Hierarchy** window, we want to select the object that has our **Camera** component attached to it, as the Post Processing Stack needs to know which screen we want to modify. If you are using your own project, you may select the **MainCamera** object that comes with the default Unity scene, but the example project that is being used has the **Camera** located as a child of the `FPSController` object. To select it, click on the arrow next to the name to extend the object's children and then select the `FirstPersonCharacter` object:

This object has the **Camera** component on it, which is in charge of drawing what it sees to the **Game** tab when the game starts.

> **TIP:** You can double-click on a game object in the **Hierarchy** tab to zoom the camera from the **Scene** tab to its location. This makes it very easy to find things, even in a large game level.

5. With the object selected and our **Camera** component attached to it, next we need to add the **Post-processing Behavior** component to the object by going into **Component** | **Rendering** | **Post-process Layer**:

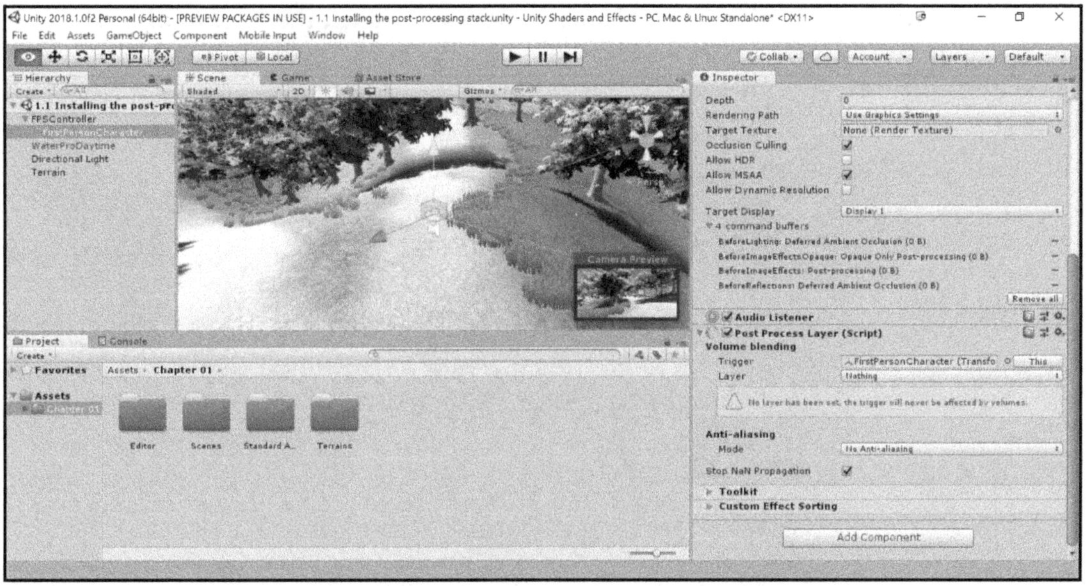

6. Once added, from the **Inspector** tab, scroll down to the **Post Process Layer (Script)** component and, under **Layer**, change the dropdown to `PostProcessing`.
7. This tells the component which objects we want to draw on the screen. When setting this, an object must have its **Layer** property set to `PostProcessing` in order to be seen.

8. To create a **Post Process Volume**, go to the menu and select **GameObject** | **3D Object** | **Post Process Volume**. From there, go to the **Inspector** tab and change the **Layer** property to `PostProcessing`. Finally, to make it easier to work with, change the **Position** to `0`, `0`, `0`, and under the **Post Process Volume** component, check the **Is Global** property:

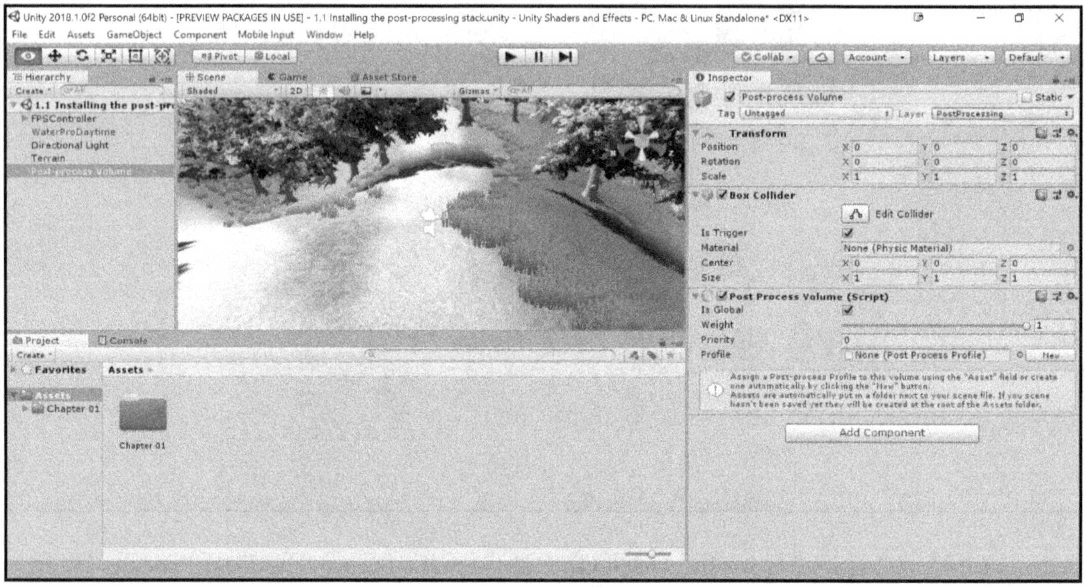

Notice that there is a **Profile** property to the volume. This property will contain information about how we wish to modify the screen. By checking **Is Global**, we are saying that this information should always be drawn on an object. By unchecking it, the effects will only be visible from a certain distance from where the volume is placed. Depending on the game, this could allow you to drastically modify how the game appears in certain areas, but we care only about getting the visual effect at this point.

Getting a filmic look using grain, vignetting, and depth of field

Now that we have the Post Processing Stack installed, we can create our first **Post-processing Volume**. The new Post Processing Stack relies on using volumes that describe how things should be drawn, either globally or within a certain area.

One of the most common appearances people like projects to have is that of a film. This is used quite frequently in titles such as the *Uncharted* series and *Grand Theft Auto V*. It's also used quite effectively in the *Left 4 Dead* series, as its creator are trying to emulate the B-movie zombie films that the games are based on.

Getting ready

Make sure you have completed the *Installing the Post Processing Stack* recipe before starting this one.

How to do it...

1. We first create a new **Post Processing Profile** by right-clicking within the `Assets | Chapter 1` folder in the **Project** window and then selecting **Create | Post Processing Profile**. Once selected, it will allow us to rename the item. Go ahead and set the name to `FilmicProfile`:

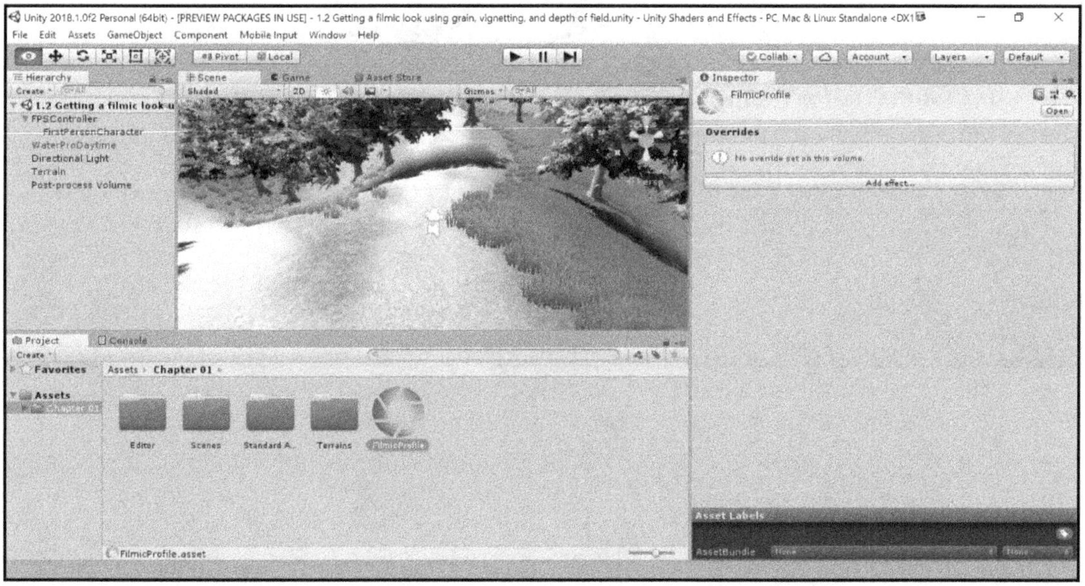

> **TIP**
> If you happen to not enter the name correctly, you can rename an item from the **Project** tab by clicking on the name and then clicking again.

2. Once created, you should notice that, when selected, the **Inspector** window will now contain a button that says **Add effect...** (as you can see in the preceding image), which will allow us to augment what is normally drawn on the screen.
3. From the **Hierarchy** tab, select the **Post-process Volume** object again and from the **Inspector** tab go to the **Post Process Volume** component and assign the **Profile** property to the `FilmicProflie` we just created:

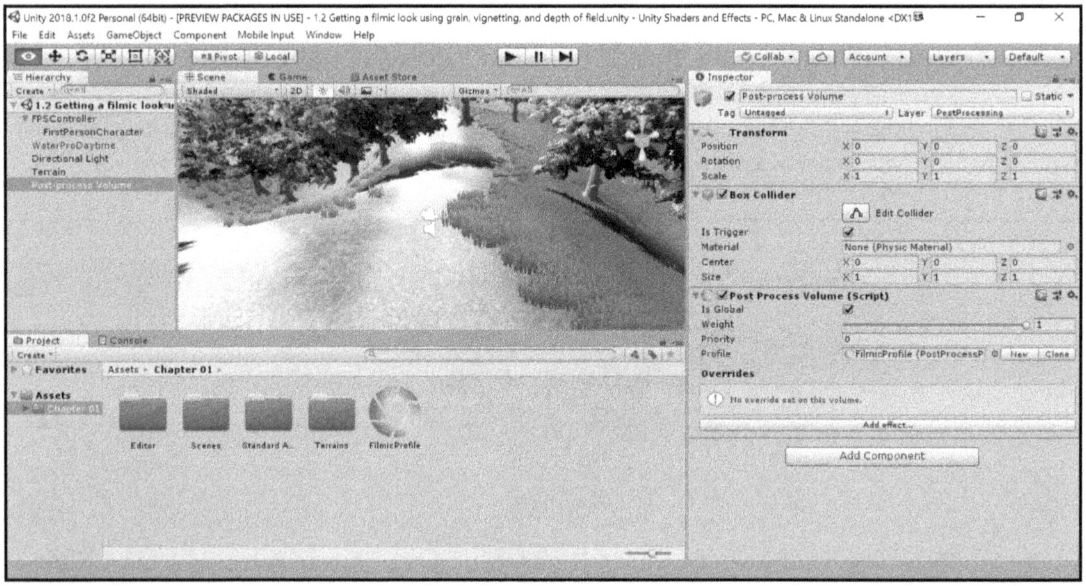

Notice that, once the **Profile** has been set, the **Add effect...** button shows up here as well. We can use this at either place and the changes will be saved in the file.

4. To get started, click on the **Add effect...** button and select the **Unity | Grain** option. By default, you'll only see the **Grain** option with a check, so click on the arrow to expand its contents:

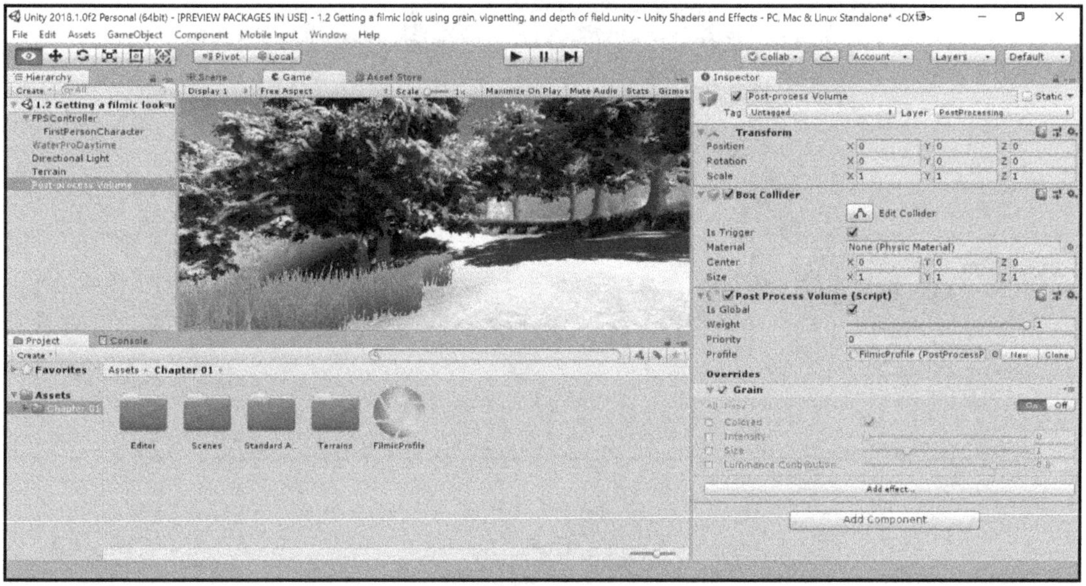

By default, you'll see that everything is greyed out. In order to have it affect anything, you have to click on the checkbox on the left-hand side. You can quickly turn them all on or off by pressing the **All** or **None** buttons on the screen.

5. In our case, check the **Intensity** option and set it to `0.2`. Then, check the **Size** property and set it to `0.3`. Afterward, switch to the **Game** tab to see a representation of what our tweaks have done:

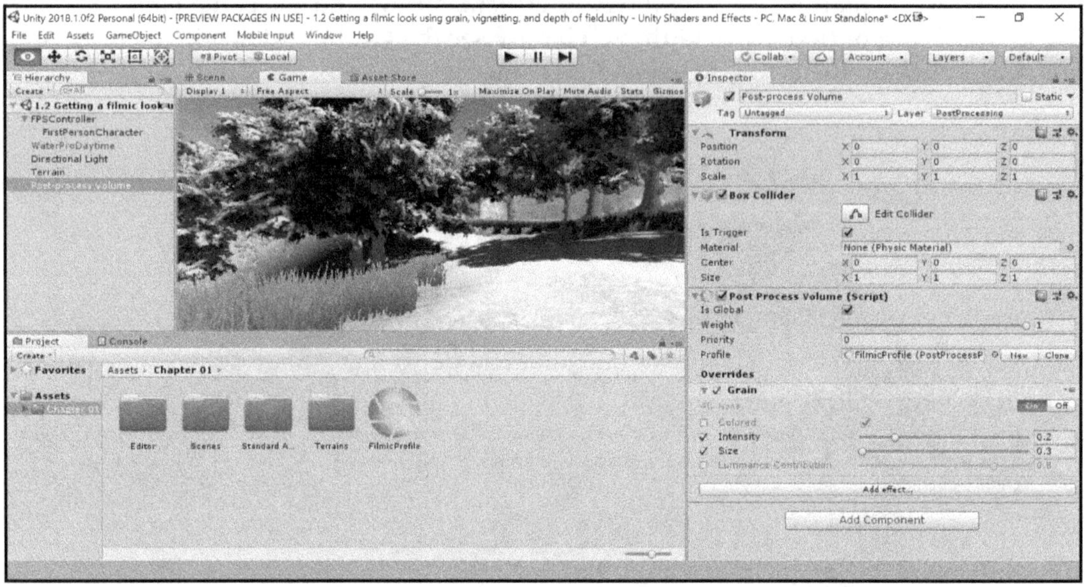

6. You will notice that the screen has become much fuzzier than before. Decrease the **Intensity** to `0.2`, the **Size** to `0.3`, and uncheck the **Colored** option.

> TIP: Unlike how users typically work in Unity, due to Post Processing Profiles being filed, you can modify them while playing your game and, upon stopping the game, the values are still saved. This can be useful for tweaking values to achieve the exact look that you're after.

7. The next property we want to tweak is the **Vignette** property. Note the blackened edges around the screen. Click on **Add effect...** and select **Unity** | **Vignette**. Open up the properties and change the **Intensity** to `0.5` and the **Smoothness** to `0.35`:

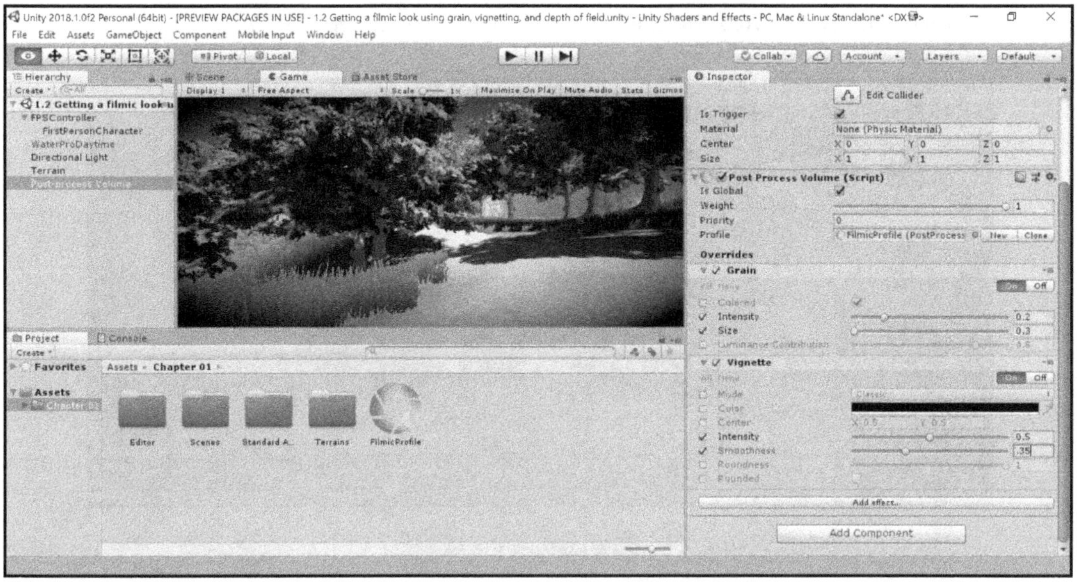

8. Next, select **Add effect...** again and, this time, select **Unity** | **Depth of Field**. Check the **Depth of Field** option. It may be difficult to see a change right off the bat, but change the **Focus Distance** to `6` and **Focal Length** to `80` and you should notice the grass in front of the background and the mountain in the distance are now blurred:

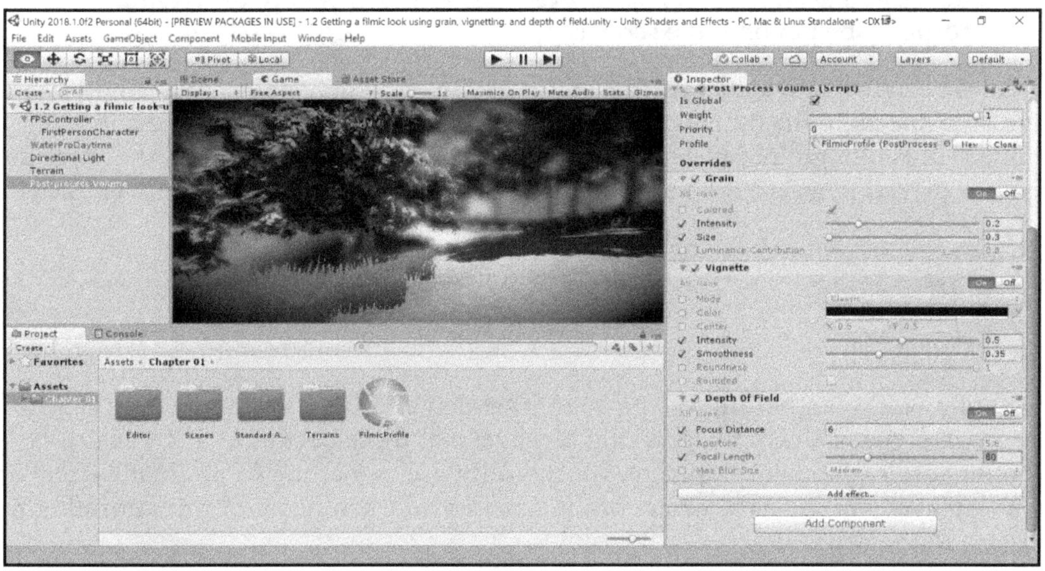

9. Now, if we go into the game itself, you should see our filmic look in action:

The final result of the filmic look

And with that, we now have a scene that looks much more like a film than what we had to begin with!

How it works...

Each time we add an effect to a **Post-processing Volume**, we are overriding what would normally be put onto the screen.

If you've been to a movie theater that still uses film, you may have noticed how there were little specks in the filmstock while the film was playing. The **grain** effect simulates this film grain, causing the effect to become more pronounced the more the movie is played. This is often used in horror games to obscure the player's vision.

> For more information on the grain effect, check out: `https://github.com/Unity-Technologies/PostProcessing/wiki/Grain`.

In the film world, **vignetting** can be an unintended effect of using the wrong type of lens for the type of shot you are trying to achieve or the aspect ratio that you are shooting for. In game development, we typically use vignetting for dramatic effect or to have players focus on the center of the screen by darkening and/or desaturating the edges of the screen compared to the center.

For more information on the vignette effect, check out: `https://github.com/Unity-Technologies/PostProcessing/wiki/Vignette`.

The **depth of field** setting basically determines what is blurry and what isn't. The idea is to have items of importance in focus while items in the background are not.

For more information on the depth of field effect, check out: `https://github.com/Unity-Technologies/PostProcessing/wiki/Depth-of-Field`.

Mimicking real life with bloom and anti-aliasing

The **bloom** optical effect aims to mimic the imaging effects of real-world cameras, where things in areas with lights will glow along the edges, thus overwhelming the camera. The bloom effect is very distinctive and you've likely seen it employed in areas in a game that are magical or heaven-like.

Getting ready

Make sure you have completed the *Installing the Post Processing Stack* recipe before starting this one.

How to do it...

1. We first create a new **Post Processing Profile** by right-clicking within the `Assets` folder in the **Project** window and then selecting **Create** | **Post Processing Profile**. Once selected, it will allow us to rename the item. Go ahead and set the name to `BloomProfile`.
2. Select the `Post-process volume` object and, from the **Inspector** window, go to the **Post Processing Volume** component and assign the **Profile** property to the `BloomProflie` we just created.

3. Afterward, select the **Game** tab, if it hasn't been selected already to see the results of the changes we are about to make in the following steps.
4. Select the **Add effect...** button and select **Unity** | **Bloom**. Once the effect has been added to the **Overrides** section of the **Post Processing Volume** component, select the arrow to open its properties. Check the **Intensity** property and set it to `3`. Afterward, check and set the **Threshold** to `0.75`, the **Soft Knee** to `0.1`, and the **Radius** to `3`:

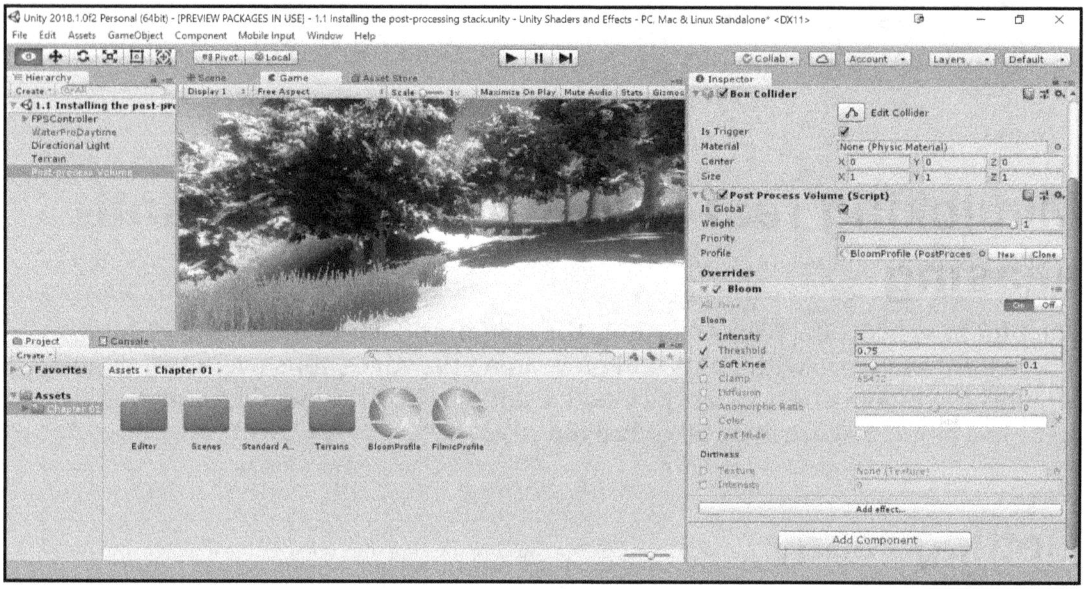

5. Next, select the object with the **Post Process Layer** component attached to it (in the example, it is the `FPSController` | `FirstPersonCharacter` object) and, from the **Inspector** tab, scroll down to the **Post Process Layer** script. From there, change the **Anti-aliasing** property dropdown to `Fast Approximate Anti-aliasing`:

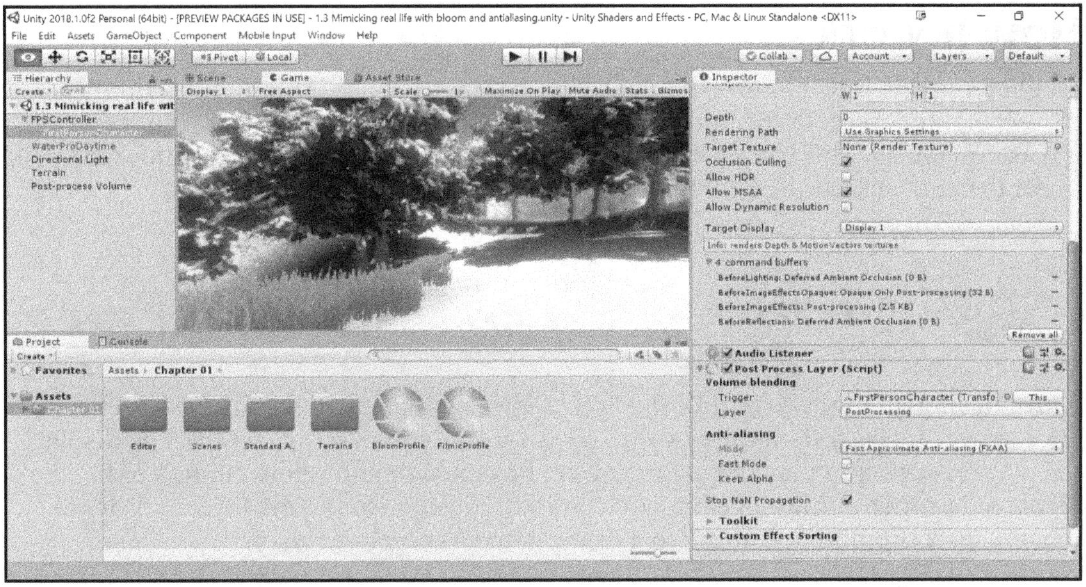

6. Afterward, save your scene and hit the Play button to check out your project:

The final result of using bloom and anti-aliasing

How it works...

As mentioned before, bloom will make bright things even brighter while adding a glow to lighter areas. In this recipe, you may notice that the path is much lighter than it was previously. This can be used in order to ensure that players will follow the path to get to the next section of gameplay.

For more information on bloom, check out: `https://github.com/Unity-Technologies/PostProcessing/wiki/Bloom`.

Anti-aliasing attempts to reduce the appearance of aliasing, which is the effect of lines appearing jagged on the screen. This is typically due to the fact that the display the player is using to play the game doesn't have a high enough resolution to be displayed properly. Anti-aliasing will combine colors with nearby lines in order to remove their prominence, at the cost of the game appearing blurry.

For more information on anti-aliasing and what each mode means, check out: `https://github.com/Unity-Technologies/PostProcessing/wiki/Anti-aliasing`.

Setting mood with color grading

One of the best ways to easily change the mood of a scene is by changing the colors a scene uses. One of the best examples of this is in the *Matrix* series of films, where the real world is always blue-tinted, while the computer-generated world of the Matrix is always tinted green. We can emulate this in our games through the use of color grading.

Getting ready

Make sure you have completed the *Installing the Post Processing Stack* recipe before starting this one.

How to do it...

1. We first create a new **Post Processing Profile** by right-clicking within the `Assets` folder in the **Project** window and then selecting **Create** | **Post Processing Profile**. Once selected, it will allow us to rename the item. Go ahead and set it to `ColorProfile`.
2. Select the `Post-process volume` object and, from the **Inspector** window, go to the **Post Processing Volume** component and assign the **Profile** property to the `ColorProflie` we just created.
3. Afterward, select the **Game** tab, if it hasn't been selected already, to see the results of the changes to be made.
4. Select the **Add effect...** button and select **Unity** | **Color Grading**.
5. Check the **Mode** property and set it to **Low Definition Range** (LDR). From there, you'll see a number of properties that can be used to adjust the colors on the screen in a similar manner to how Photoshop's hue/saturation menu works. Check the **Temperature** property and set it to `30`. Afterward, set the **Hue Shift** property to `-20` and the **Saturation** to `15`:

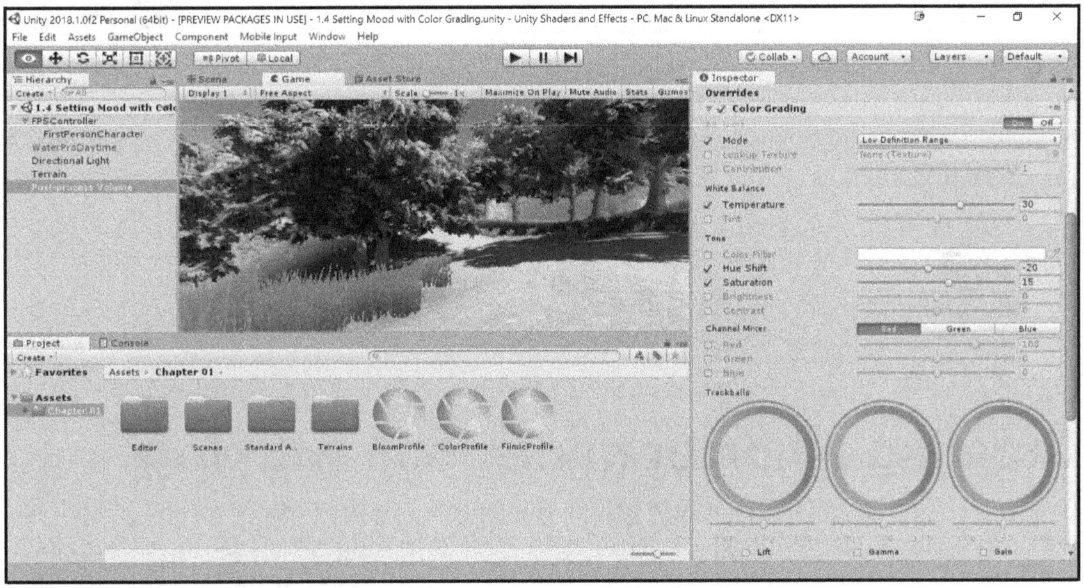

6. After making the changes, dive into the game to see what it looks like when playing:

The final result of using color grading

Notice how the previously very green environment is now much warmer and more yellow than before.

For more information on the color grading effect, check out: `https://github.com/Unity-Technologies/PostProcessing/wiki/Color-Grading`.

Creating a horror game look with fog

One of the types of games that best utilize the features of the Post Processing Stack is the horror genre. Using things such as depth of field to hide scary objects, as well as static to make the screen more menacing, can really help set your game firmly in the right place and provide the mood you are going for.

Getting ready

Make sure you have completed the *Installing the Post Processing Stack* recipe before starting this one.

How to do it...

1. We first create a new Post Processing Profile by right-clicking within the `Assets` folder in the **Project** window and then selecting **Create** | **Post Processing Profile**. Once selected, it will allow us to rename the item. Go ahead and set the name to `HorrorProfile`.
2. Select the `Post-process volume` object and, from the **Inspector** window, go to the **Post Processing Volume** component and assign the **Profile** property to the `HorrorProflie` we just created.
3. Unlike previous settings, though, the fog settings are located in the **Lighting** window, which can be accessed by going into **Window** | **Lighting**.
4. From there, scroll all the way to the bottom until you reach the **Other Settings** option. Once there, check **Fog** and set the color to a value that is close to the skybox. I used the following settings:

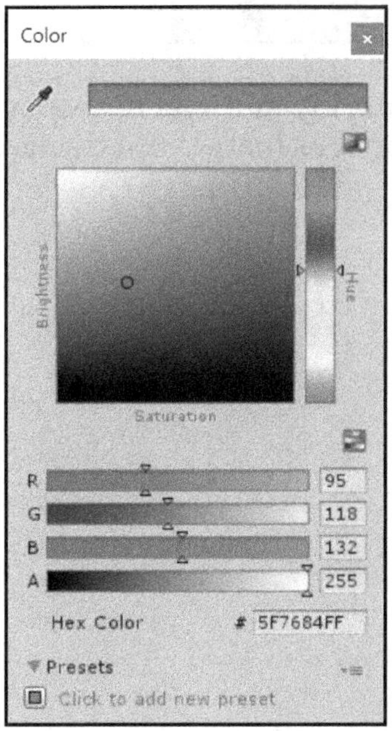

If you know the hex values of the color from your graphic editing software you can just type it in the **Hex Color** property of the **Color** window.

5. Next, change the **Mode** to `Exponential` and the **Density** to `0.03`:

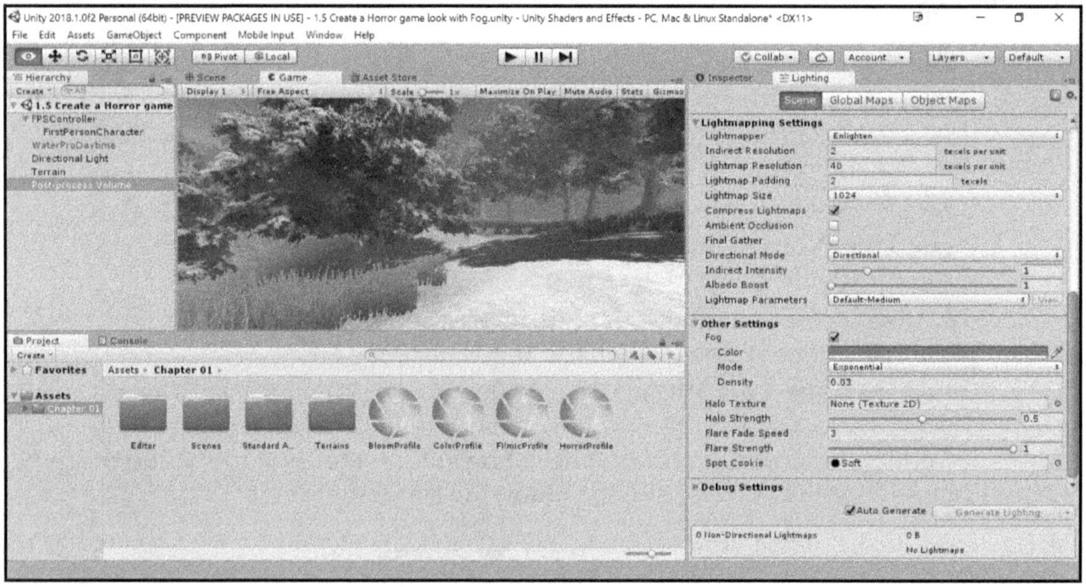

As you can see, it's already much more spooky that it was previously, but there are still more options that we can change.

6. Open up the **HorrorProfile** again and go to the **Inspector** tab. Press the **Add effect...** button and select **Unity | Ambient Occlusion**. Check the **Mode** option and select `Scalable Ambient Obscurance`. Afterward, change the **Intensity** to `2` and the **Radius** to `20`:

7. Lastly, lighting often has a big effect on the theme of a scene as well. If you're using the example map, select the `Directional Light` object in the **Hierarchy** tab and, from the **Inspector** tab under the **Light** component, change the **Intensity** to `0.5` and then adjust the **Color** to something darker. (I used the same color as in *step 4* with a **HEX** of `5F7684FF`.)

8. Save your game and then start it to see the effect of all of the changes:

The final result of our horror look

How it works...

The **Ambient Occlusion** option will calculate areas that should have additional shadows. Since our scene is filled with trees, this will make the undersides much darker than they were previously.

> For more information on the Ambient Occlusion effect, check out: `https://github.com/Unity-Technologies/PostProcessing/wiki/Ambient-Occlusion`. If you are interested in looking into the other options that the Post Processing stack has, check out: `https://github.com/Unity-Technologies/PostProcessing/wiki`.

4
Creating Your First Shader

In this chapter, you will learn the following recipes:

- Creating a basic Standard Shader
- Adding properties to a shader
- Using properties in a Surface Shader

Introduction

This chapter will cover some of the more common diffuse techniques found in today's game development shading pipelines. Let's imagine a cube that has been painted white uniformly in a 3D environment with a directional light. Even if the color used is the same on each face, they will all have different shades of white on them depending on the direction that the light is coming from and the angle that we are looking at it from. This extra level of realism is achieved in 3D graphics through the use of shaders, special programs that are mostly used to simulate how light works. A wooden cube and a metal one may share the same 3D model, but what makes them look different is the shader that they use.

This first chapter will introduce you to shader coding in Unity. If you have little to no previous experience with shaders, this chapter is what you need in order to understand what shaders are, how they work, and how to customize them. By the end of this chapter, you will have learned how to build basic shaders that perform basic operations. Armed with this knowledge, you will be able to create just about any Surface Shader.

Creating a basic Standard Shader

In Unity, when we create a game object, we then attach additional functionality through the use of **components**. In fact, every game object is required to have a Transform component; there are a number of components included in Unity already, and we create components of our own when we write scripts that extend from `MonoBehaviour`.

All the objects that are part of a game contain a number of components that affect their look and behavior. While scripts determine how objects should behave, renderers decide how they should appear on the screen. Unity comes with several renderers, depending on the type of object that we are trying to visualize; every 3D model typically has a `MeshRenderer` component attached to it. An object should have only one renderer, but the renderer itself can contain several materials. Each material is a wrapper for a single shader, the final ring in the food chain of 3D graphics. The relationships between these components can be seen in the following diagram:

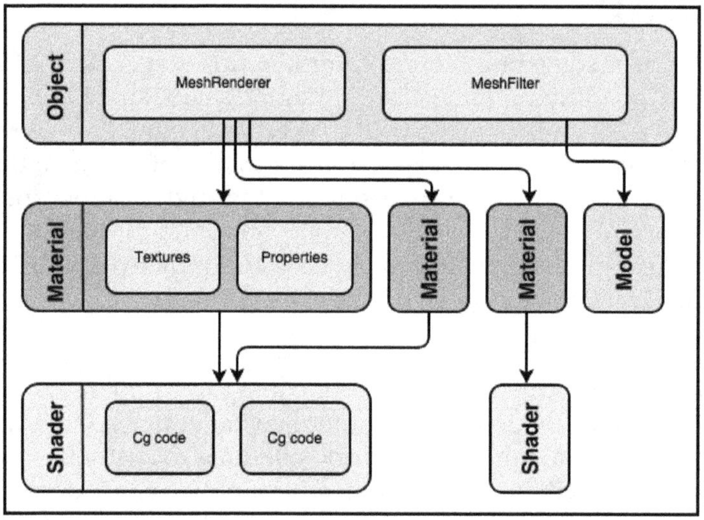

Understanding the difference between these components is essential for understanding how shaders work.

Getting ready

To get started with this recipe, you will need to have Unity running and must have a project opened. As mentioned before, there will also be a Unity project included with this cookbook, so you can use that one as well and simply add your own custom shaders to it as you step through each recipe. With this completed, you are now ready to step into the wonderful world of real-time shading!

Before getting into our first shader, let's create a small scene for us to work with:

1. Let's create a scene by navigating to **File** | **New Scene.**
2. Once you create the scene, create a plane to act as the ground by going to **GameObject** | **3D Objects** | **Plane** in the Unity editor. Next, select the object in the **Hierarchy** tab and then go into the **Inspector** tab. From there, right-click on the **Transform** component and select the **Reset Position** option:

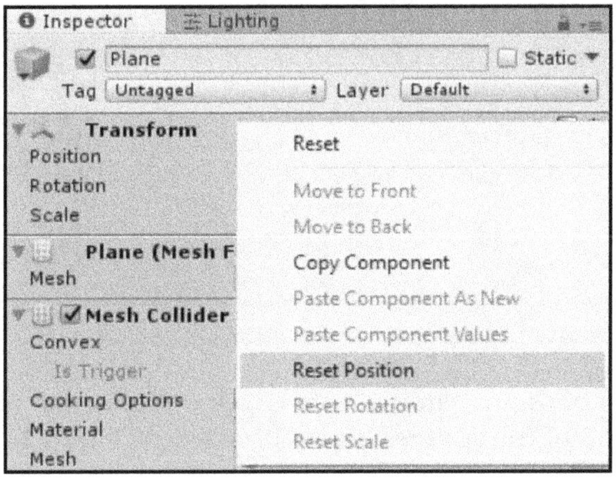

This will reset the position property of the object to be at `0, 0, 0`:

3. To make it easier to see what our shaders will look like when applied, let's add some shapes to visualize what each of our shaders will do. Create a sphere by going to **GameObject** | **3D Objects** | **Sphere**. Once created, select it and go to the **Inspector** tab. Next, change the **Position** to `0, 1, 0` so it is above the origin of the world (which is at `0, 0, 0`) and our previously created plane:

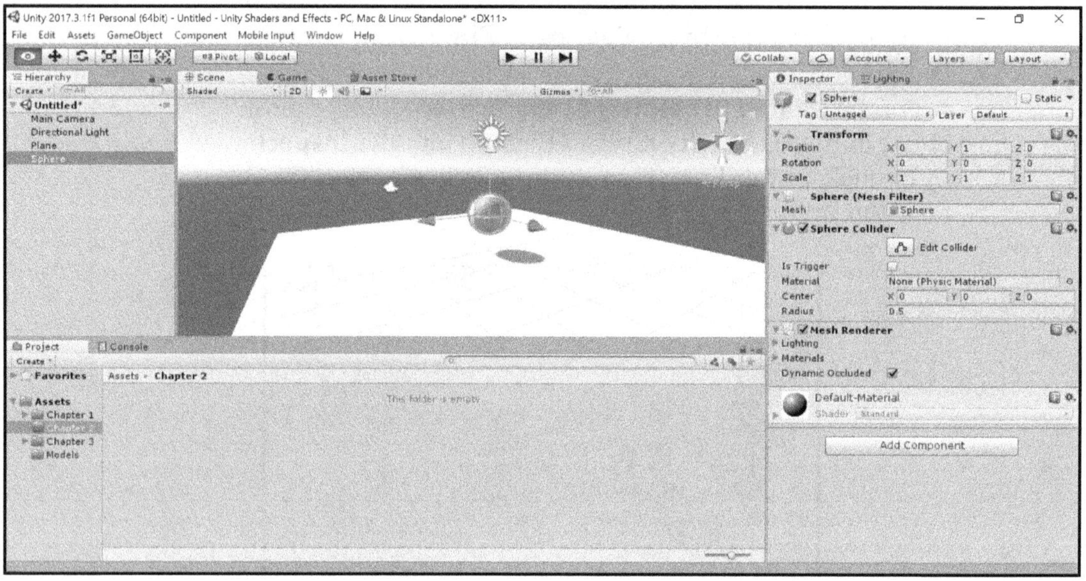

4. Once this sphere is created, create two more spheres, placing them to the left and right of the spheres at positions `-2, 1, 0` and `2, 1, 0` respectively:

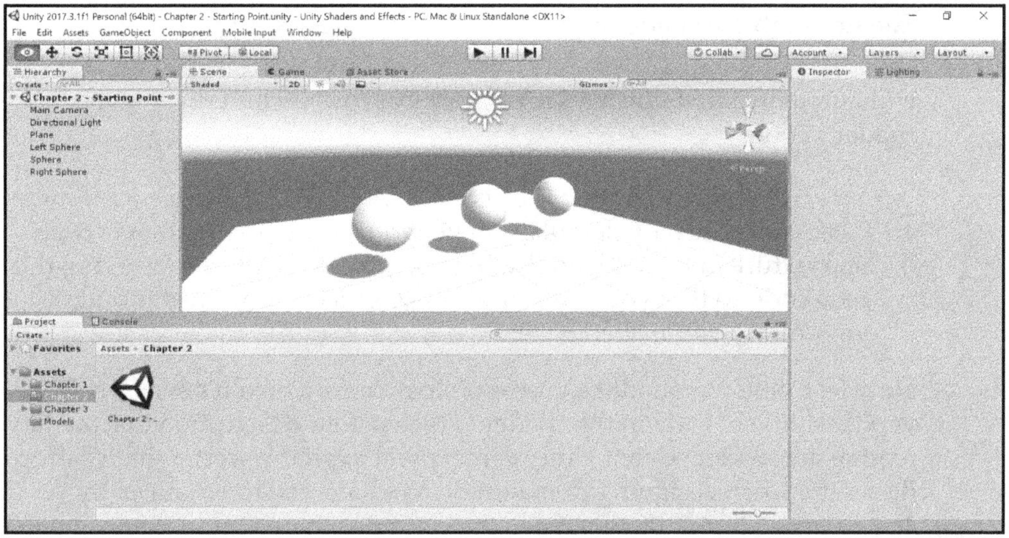

5. Lastly, confirm that you have a directional light (it should be seen in the Hierarchy tab). If not, you can add one by selecting **GameObject** | **Light** | **Directional Light** to make it easier to see the effect of your changes and how your shaders react to light.

> If you are using the Unity project that came with the cookbook, you can open up the `Chapter 2 | Starting Point` scene instead as it has been set up already.

How to do it...

With our scene generated, we can move on to the shader writing steps:

1. In the **Project** tab in your Unity editor, right-click on the `Chapter 2` folder and select **Create** | **Folder**.
2. Rename the folder that you created as `Shaders` by right-clicking on it and selecting **Rename** from the drop-down list, or by selecting the folder and hitting *F2* on the keyboard.
3. Create another folder and rename it as `Materials`.
4. Right-click on the `Shaders` folder and select **Create** | **Shader** | **Standard Surface Shader**. Then, right-click on the `Materials` folder and select **Create** | **Material**.

5. Rename both the shader and material as `StandardDiffuse`.
6. Launch the `StandardDiffuse` shader by double-clicking on the file. This will automatically launch a scripting editor for you and display the shader's code.

> You will see that Unity has already populated our shader with some basic code. This, by default, will get you a basic shader that accepts one texture in the Albedo (RGB) property. We will be modifying this base code so that you can learn how to quickly start developing your own custom shaders.

7. Now let's give our shader a custom folder from which it's selected. The very first line of code in the shader is the custom description that we have to give the shader so that Unity can make it available in the shader drop-down list when assigning to materials. We have renamed our path as `Shader "CookbookShaders/StandardDiffuse"`, but you can name it whatever you want and rename it at any time so don't worry about any dependencies at this point. Save the shader in your script editor and return to the Unity editor. Unity will automatically compile the shader when it recognizes that the file has been updated. This is what your shader should look like at this point:

```
Shader "CookbookShaders/StandardDiffuse" {
  Properties {
    _Color ("Color", Color) = (1,1,1,1)
    _MainTex ("Albedo (RGB)", 2D) = "white" {}
    _Glossiness ("Smoothness", Range(0,1)) = 0.5
    _Metallic ("Metallic", Range(0,1)) = 0.0
  }
  SubShader {
    Tags { "RenderType"="Opaque" }
    LOD 200

    CGPROGRAM
    // Physically based Standard lighting model, and enable
shadows on all light types
    #pragma surface surf Standard fullforwardshadows

    // Use shader model 3.0 target, to get nicer looking
lighting
    #pragma target 3.0

    sampler2D _MainTex;

    struct Input {
```

```
        float2 uv_MainTex;
      };

      half _Glossiness;
      half _Metallic;
      fixed4 _Color;

      // Add instancing support for this shader. You need to
check 'Enable Instancing' on materials that use the shader.
      // See https://docs.unity3d.com/Manual/GPUInstancing.html
for more information about instancing.
      // #pragma instancing_options assumeuniformscaling
      UNITY_INSTANCING_BUFFER_START(Props)
        // put more per-instance properties here
      UNITY_INSTANCING_BUFFER_END(Props)

      void surf (Input IN, inout SurfaceOutputStandard o) {
        // Albedo comes from a texture tinted by color
        fixed4 c = tex2D (_MainTex, IN.uv_MainTex) * _Color;
        o.Albedo = c.rgb;
        // Metallic and smoothness come from slider variables
        o.Metallic = _Metallic;
        o.Smoothness = _Glossiness;
        o.Alpha = c.a;
      }
      ENDCG
    }
    FallBack "Diffuse"
}
```

8. Technically speaking, this is a Surface Shader based on **physically-based rendering** (**PBR**). As the name suggests, this type of shader achieves realism by simulating how light physically behaves when hitting objects.
9. After your shader is created, we need to connect it to a material. Select the material called `StandardDiffuse` that we created in *step 4* and look at the **Inspector** tab. From the **Shader** drop-down list, select **CookbookShaders** | **StandardDiffuse**. (Your shader path might be different if you chose to use a different path name.) This will assign your shader to your material and make it ready for you to assign to an object.

> To assign material to an object, you can simply click and drag your material from the **Project** tab to the object in your scene. You can also drag material to the **Inspector** tab of an object in the Unity editor in order to assign it.

The screenshot of an example is as follows:

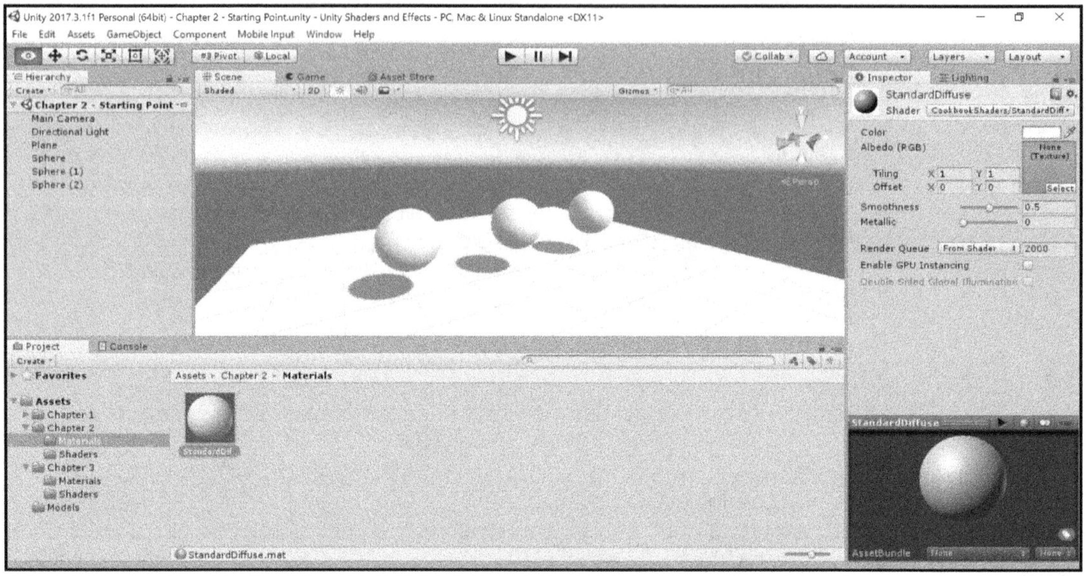

Not much to look at this point, but our shader development environment is set up and we can now start to modify the shader to suit our needs.

How it works...

Unity has made the task of getting your shader environment up and running very easy for you. It is simply a matter of a few clicks and you are good to go. There are a lot of elements working in the background with regard to the Surface Shader itself. Unity has taken the Cg shader language and made it more efficient to write by doing a lot of the heavy Cg code lifting for you. The Surface Shader language is a more component-based way of writing shaders. Tasks such as processing your own texture coordinates and transformation matrices have already been done for you, so you don't have to start from scratch any more. In the past, we would have to start a new shader and rewrite a lot of code over and over again. As you gain more experience with Surface Shaders, you will naturally want to explore more of the underlying functions of the Cg language and how Unity is processing all of the low-level **graphics processing unit** (GPU) tasks for you.

All the files in a Unity project are referenced independently from the folder that they are in. We can move shaders and materials from within the editor without the risk of breaking any connection. Files, however, should never be moved from outside the editor as Unity will not be able to update their references.

So, by simply changing the shader's path name to a name of our choice, we have got our basic diffuse shader working in the Unity environment, with lights and shadows and all that, just by changing one line of code!

There's more...

The source code of the built-in shaders is typically hidden in Unity. You cannot open this from the editor as you do with your own shaders. For more information on where to find a large portion of the built-in Cg functions for Unity, go to your Unity install directory and navigate to the `Editor | Data | CGIncludes` folder:

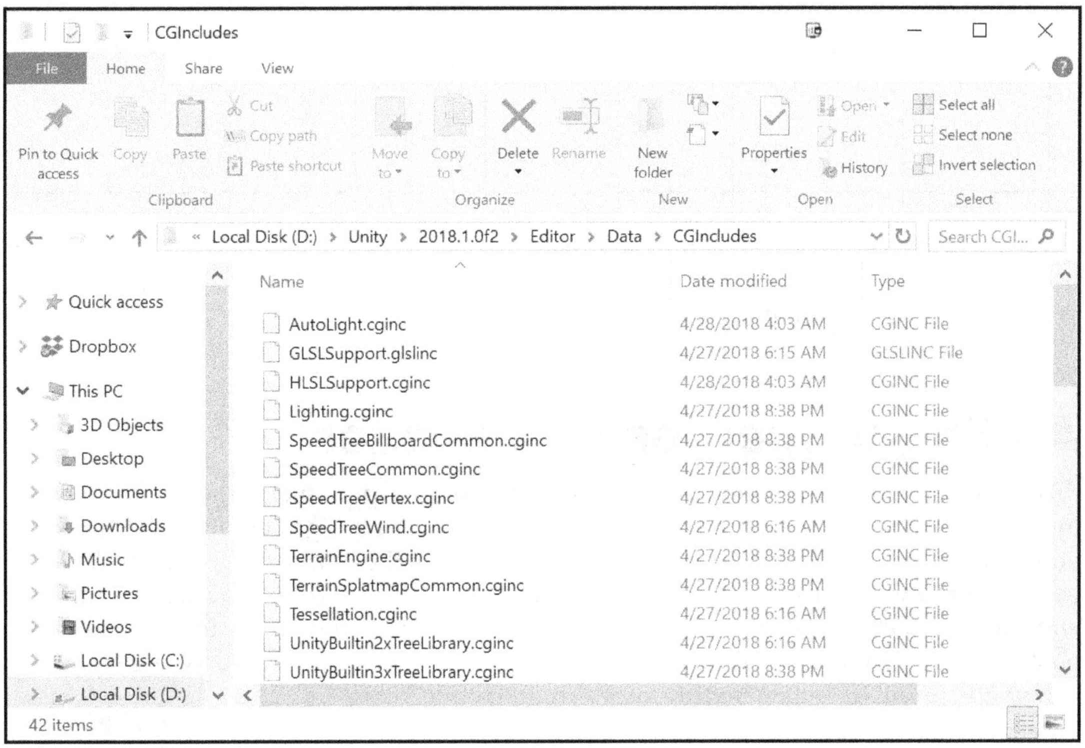

In this folder, you can find the source code of the shaders shipped with Unity. Over time, they have changed a lot; you can visit the **Unity download archive** (`https://unity3d.com/get-unity/download/archive`) if you need to access the source codes of a shader used in a different version of Unity. After choosing the right version, select **Built in shaders** from the drop-down list, as shown in the following screenshot:

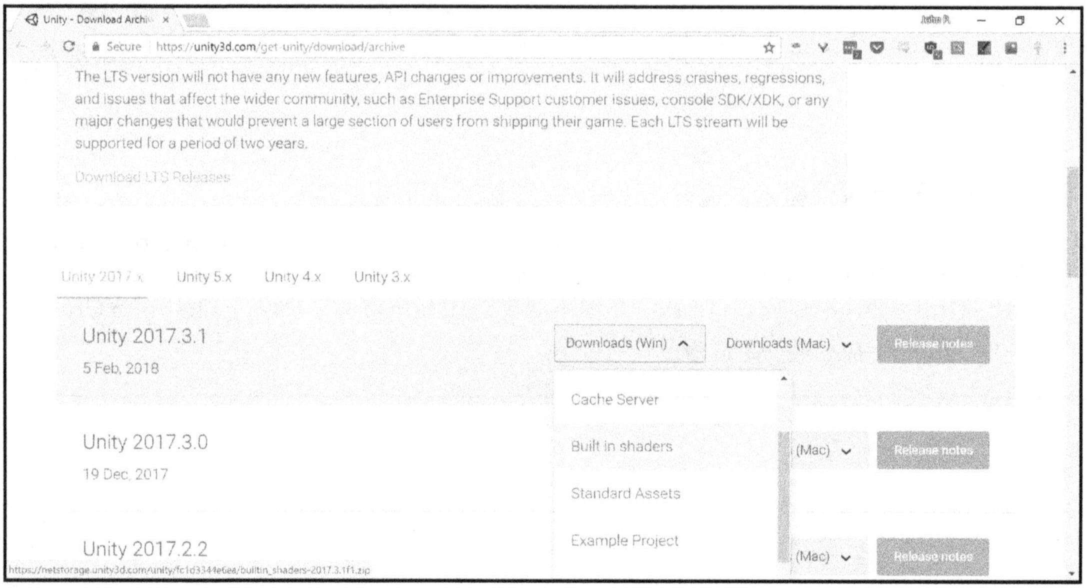

There are three files that are of note at this point: `UnityCG.cginc`, `Lighting.cginc`, and `UnityShaderVariables.cginc`. Our current shader is making use of all these files at the moment.

Adding properties to a shader

Properties of a shader are very important for the shader pipeline as they are the method that you use to let the artist or user of the shader assign textures and tweak your shader values. Properties allow you to expose GUI elements in a material's **Inspector** tab without you having to use a separate editor, which provides visual ways to tweak a shader. With your shader opened in your IDE of choice, look at the block of lines two through seven. This is called the `Properties` block of the script. Currently, it will have one texture property in it called `_MainTex`.

If you look at your material that has this shader applied to it, you will notice that there is one **texture** GUI element in the **Inspector** tab. These lines of code in our shader are creating this GUI element for us. Again, Unity has made this process very efficient in terms of coding and the amount of time it takes to iterate through changing your properties.

Getting ready

Let's see how this works in our current shader called `StandardDiffuse` by creating our own properties and learning more about the syntax involved. For this example, we will refit the shader previously created. Instead of using a texture, it will only use its color and some other properties that we will be able to change directly from the **Inspector** tab. Start by duplicating the `StandardDiffuse` shader. You can do this by selecting it in the **Inspector** tab and pressing *Ctrl* + *D*. This will create a copy called `StandardDiffuse 1`. Go ahead and rename it as `StandardColor`.

> You can give a friendlier name to your shader in its first line. For instance, `Shader "CookbookShaders/StandardDiffuse"` tells Unity to call this shader `StandardDiffuse` and move it to a group called `CookbookShaders`. If you duplicate a shader using *Ctrl* + *D*, your new file will share the same name. To avoid confusion, make sure to change the first line of each new shader so that it uses a unique alias in this and future recipes.

How to do it...

Once the `StandardColor` shader is ready, we can start changing its properties:

1. In the first line of the script, update the name to the following:

```
Shader "CookbookShaders/Chapter 02/StandardColor" {
```

2. In the `Properties` block of our shader, remove the current property by deleting the following code from our current shader:

```
_MainTex ("Albedo (RGB)", 2D) = "white" {}
```

3. As we have removed an essential property, this shader will not compile until the other references to `_MainTex` are removed. Let's remove this other line inside of the `SubShader` section:

```
sampler2D _MainTex;
```

4. The original shader used `_MainTex` to color the model. Let's change this by replacing the first line of code of the `surf()` function with this:

```
fixed4 c = _Color;
```

Just as you may be used to the `float` type being used for floating point values when writing code in C# and other programming languages, `fixed` is used for fixed-point values and is the type used when writing shaders. You may also see the `half` type used as well, which is like the `float` type but takes up half the space. This is useful for saving memory but is less precise in how it is presented. We will be discussing this in much greater detail in the *Techniques to make shaders more efficient* recipe in `Chapter 10`, *Mobile Shader Adjustment*.

For more information on fixed-point values, check out `https://en.wikipedia.org/wiki/Fixed-point_arithmetic`.

The `4` in `fixed4` stands for the fact that the color is a single variable that contains four `fixed` values: red, green, blue, and alpha. You will learn more about how this works and how to modify these values in more detail in the next chapter, `Chapter 5`, *Surface Shaders and Texture Mapping*.

5. When you save and return to Unity, the shader will compile, and you will see that now our material's **Inspector** tab doesn't have a texture swatch any more. To complete the refit of this shader, let's add one more property to the `Properties` block and see what happens. Enter the following code:

```
_AmbientColor ("Ambient Color", Color) = (1,1,1,1)
```

6. We have added another color swatch to the material's **Inspector** tab. Now let's add one more in order to get a feel for other kinds of properties that we can create. Add the following code to the `Properties` block:

```
_MySliderValue ("This is a Slider", Range(0,10)) = 2.5
```

7. We have now created another GUI element that allows us to visually interact with our shader. This time, we created a slider with the name **This is a Slider**, as shown in the following screenshot:

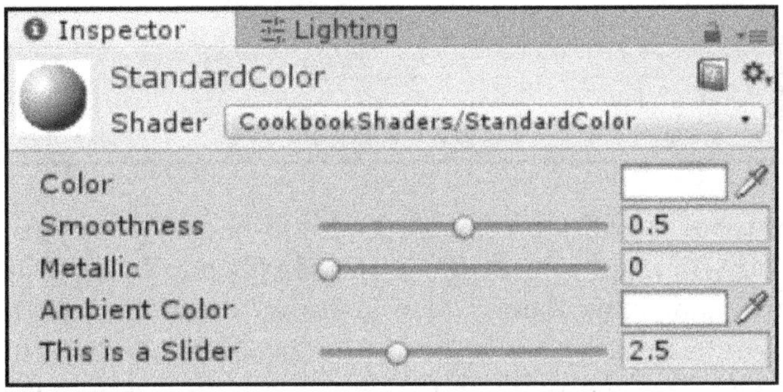

8. Properties allow you to create a visual way to tweak shaders without having to change values in the shader code itself. The next recipe will show you how these properties can actually be used to create a more interesting shader.

While properties belong to shaders, the values associated with them are stored in materials. The same shader can be safely shared between many different materials. On the other hand, changing the property of a material will affect the look of all the objects that are currently using it.

How it works...

Every Unity shader has a built-in structure that it is looking for in its code. The **Properties** block is one of those functions that are expected by Unity. The reason behind this is to give you, the shader programmer, a means of quickly creating GUI elements that tie directly into your shader code. These properties (variables) that you declare in the **Properties** block can then be used in your shader code to change values, colors, and textures. The syntax to define a property is as follows:

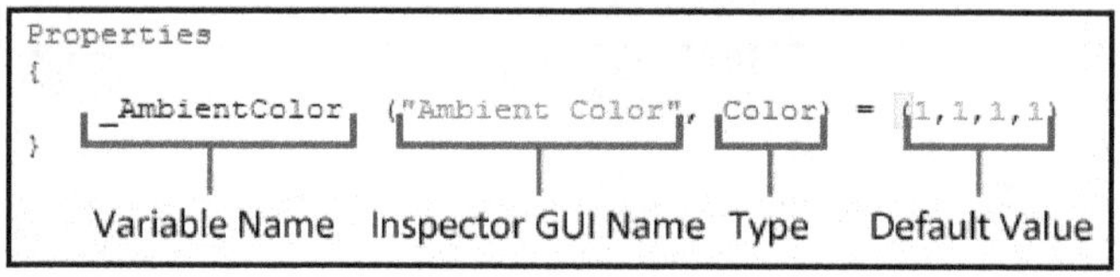

Let's take a look at what is going on under the hood here. When you first start writing a new property, you will need to give it a **Variable Name**. The **Variable Name** is going to be the name that your shader code is going to use in order to get the value from the GUI element. This saves us a lot of time because we don't have to set up this system ourselves. The next elements of a property are the **Inspector GUI Name** and **Type** of the property, which is contained within parentheses. The **Inspector GUI Name** is the name that is going to appear in the material's **Inspector** tab when the user is interacting with and tweaking the shader. The **Type** is the type of data that this property is going to control. There are many types that we can define for properties inside of Unity shaders. The following table describes the types of variables that we can have in our shaders:

Surface Shader property types	**Description**
`Range` (min, max)	This creates a `float` property as a slider from the minimum value to the maximum value
`Color`	This creates a color swatch in the **Inspector** tab that opens up a `color picker = (float,float,float,float)`
`2D`	This creates a texture swatch that allows a user to drag a texture into the shader
`Rect`	This creates a non-power of two texture swatch and functions the same as the `2D` GUI element
Cube	This creates a cube map swatch in the **Inspector** tab and allows a user to drag and drop a cube map into the shader
`float`	This creates a float value in the **Inspector** tab but without a slider
Vector	This creates a four-float property that allows you to create directions or colors

Finally, there is the **Default Value**. This simply sets the value of this property to the value that you place in the code. So, in the previous example diagram, the default value for the property named `_AmbientColor`, which is of the `Color` type, is set to a value of `1, 1, 1, 1`. As this is a `Color` property expecting a color that is `RGBA` or `float4` or `r, g, b, a = x, y, z, w`, this `Color` property, when first created, is set to white.

See also

The properties are documented in the Unity manual at `http://docs.unity3d.com/Documentation/Components/SL-Properties.html`.

Using properties in a Surface Shader

Now that we have created some properties, let's actually hook them up to the shader so that we can use them as tweaks to our shader and make the material process much more interactive. We can use the **Properties** values from the material's **Inspector** tab because we have attached a variable name to the property itself, but in the shader code, you have to set up a couple of things before you can start calling the value by its variable name.

How to do it...

The following steps show you how to use the properties in a Surface Shader:

1. Continuing from the previous example, let's create another shader with the name `ParameterExample`. Just like before, remove the `_MainTex` property in the same manner as was done in the *Adding properties to a shader* recipe of this chapter:

```
// Inside the Properties block
_MainTex ("Albedo (RGB)", 2D) = "white" {}

// Below the CGPROGRAM line
sampler2D _MainTex;

// Inside of the surf function
fixed4 c = tex2D (_MainTex, IN.uv_MainTex) * _Color;
```

2. Afterward, update the `Properties` section to the following code:

```
Properties {
  _Color ("Color", Color) = (1,1,1,1)
  _AmbientColor ("Ambient Color", Color) = (1,1,1,1)
  _MySliderValue ("This is a Slider", Range(0,10)) = 2.5

  _Glossiness ("Smoothness", Range(0,1)) = 0.5
  _Metallic ("Metallic", Range(0,1)) = 0.0
}
```

3. Next, add the following lines of code to the shader, below the `CGPROGRAM` line:

```
float4 _AmbientColor;
float _MySliderValue;
```

4. With *step 3* complete, we can now use the values from the properties in our shader. Let's do this by adding the value from the `_Color` property to the `_AmbientColor` property and giving the result of this to the `o.Albedo` line of code. So, let's add the following code to the shader in the `surf()` function:

```
void surf (Input IN, inout SurfaceOutputStandard o) {
      // We can then use the properties values in our shader
      fixed4 c = pow((_Color + _AmbientColor),
_MySliderValue);

      // Albedo comes from property values given from slider
and colors
      o.Albedo = c.rgb;

      // Metallic and smoothness come from slider variables
      o.Metallic = _Metallic;
      o.Smoothness = _Glossiness;
      o.Alpha = c.a;
    }
    ENDCG
```

5. Finally, your shader should look like the following shader code. If you save your shader and re-enter Unity, your shader will compile. If there were no errors, you will now have the ability to change the ambient and emissive colors of the material as well as increase the saturation of the final color using the slider value. Pretty neat:

```
Shader "CookbookShaders/Chapter02/ParameterExample" {
  // We define Properties in the properties block
  Properties {
    _Color ("Color", Color) = (1,1,1,1)
    _Glossiness ("Smoothness", Range(0,1)) = 0.5
    _Metallic ("Metallic", Range(0,1)) = 0.0
  }
  SubShader {
    Tags { "RenderType"="Opaque" }
    LOD 200

    // We need to declare the properties variable type inside
of the
    // CGPROGRAM so we can access its value from the
properties block.

    CGPROGRAM
    // Physically based Standard lighting model, and enable
shadows on all light types
    #pragma surface surf Standard fullforwardshadows

    // Use shader model 3.0 target, to get nicer looking
lighting
    #pragma target 3.0

    float4 _AmbientColor;
    float _MySliderValue;

    struct Input {
      float2 uv_MainTex;
    };

    half _Glossiness;
    half _Metallic;
    fixed4 _Color;

    // Add instancing support for this shader. You need to
check 'Enable Instancing' on materials that use the shader.
    // See https://docs.unity3d.com/Manual/GPUInstancing.html
for more information about instancing.
    // #pragma instancing_options assumeuniformscaling
```

```
    UNITY_INSTANCING_BUFFER_START(Props)
      // put more per-instance properties here
    UNITY_INSTANCING_BUFFER_END(Props)

    void surf (Input IN, inout SurfaceOutputStandard o) {
      // We can then use the properties values in our shader
      fixed4 c = pow((_Color + _AmbientColor),
_MySliderValue);

      // Albedo comes from property values given from slider
and colors
      o.Albedo = c.rgb;

      // Metallic and smoothness come from slider variables
      o.Metallic = _Metallic;
      o.Smoothness = _Glossiness;
      o.Alpha = c.a;
    }
    ENDCG
  }
  FallBack "Diffuse"
}
```

The `pow(arg1, arg2)` function is a built-in function that will perform the equivalent `math` function of power. So, argument `1` is the value that we want to raise to a power and argument `2` is the power that we want to raise it to.
To find out more about the `pow()` function, look at the Cg tutorial. It is a great free resource that you can use to learn more about shading and there is a glossary of all the functions available to you in the Cg shading language at `http://http.developer.nvidia.com/CgTutorial/cg_tutorial_appendix_e.html`.

The following screenshot demonstrates the result obtained using our properties to control our material's colors and saturation from within the material's **Inspector** tab:

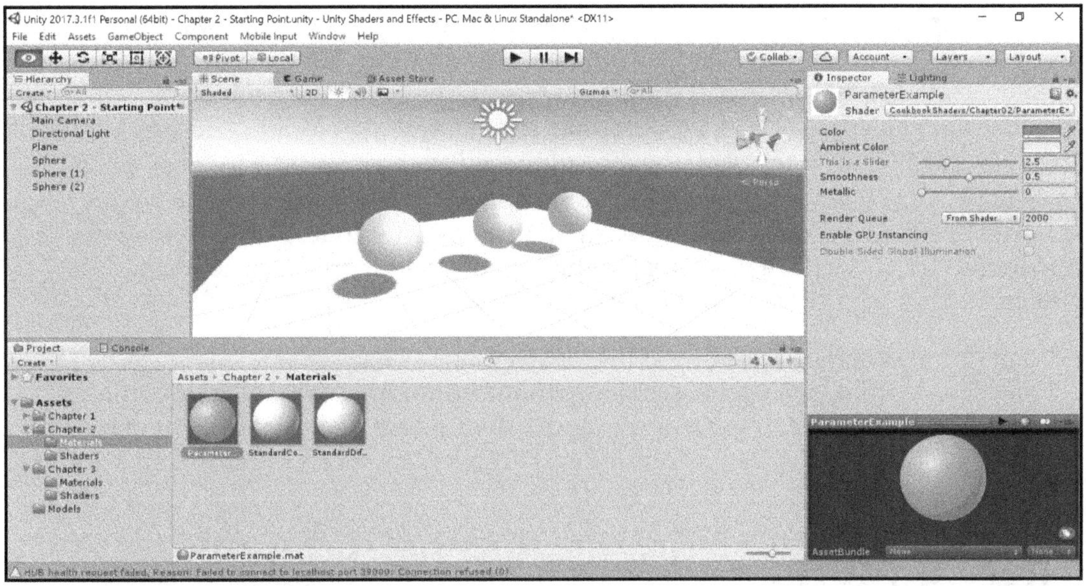

How it works...

When you declare a new property in the `Properties` block, you are providing a way for the shader to retrieve the tweaked value from the material's **Inspector** tab. This value is stored in the variable name portion of the property. In this case, `_AmbientColor`, `_Color`, and `_MySliderValue` are the variables in which we are storing the tweaked values.

In order for you to be able to use the value in the `SubShader` block, you need to create three new variables with the same names as the property's variable name. This automatically sets up a link between these two so that they know they have to work with the same data. Additionally, it declares the type of data that we want to store in our `SubShader` variables, which will come in handy when we look at optimizing shaders in a later chapter. Once you have created the `SubShader` variables, you can then use the values in the `surf()` function. In this case, we want to add the `_Color` and `_AmbientColor` variables together and take it to a power of whatever the `_MySliderValue` variable is equal to in the material's **Inspector** tab. The vast majority of shaders start out as Standard Shaders and get modified until they match the desired look. We have now created the foundation for any Surface Shader you will create that requires a diffuse component.

> Materials are assets. This means that any change made to them while your game is running in the editor are permanent. If you have changed the value of a property by mistake, you can undo it using *Ctrl* + *Z*.

There's more...

Like any other programming language, Cg does not allow mistakes. As such, your shader will not work if you have a typo in your code. When this happens, your materials are rendered in unshaded magenta:

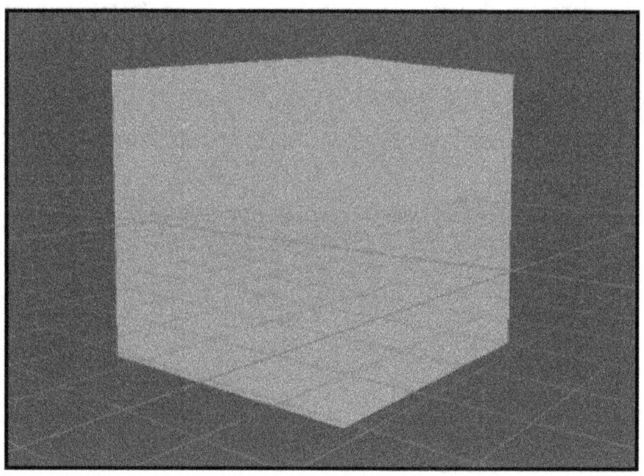

When a script does not compile, Unity prevents your game from being exported or even executed. Conversely, errors in shaders do not stop your game from being executed. If one of your shaders appears as magenta, it is time to investigate where the problem is. If you select the incriminated shader, you will see a list of errors displayed in its **Inspector** tab:

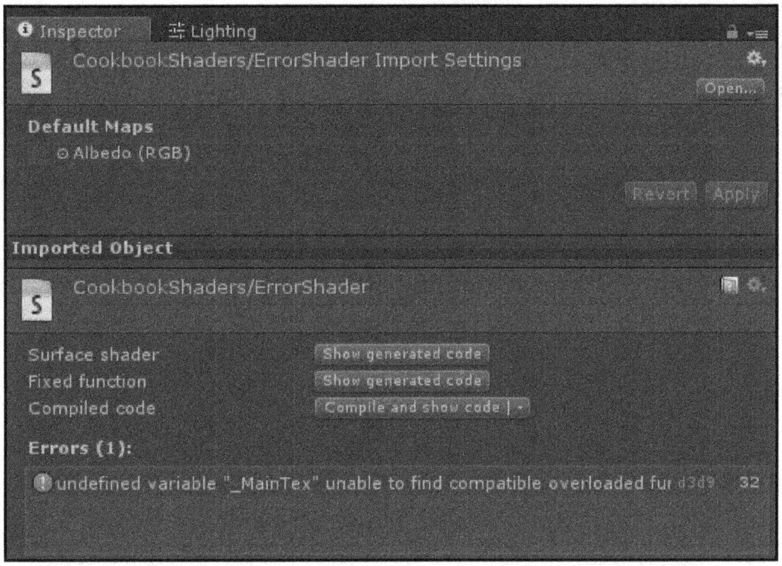

Despite showing the line that raised the error, it rarely means that this is the line that has to be fixed. The error message shown in the previous screenshot is generated by deleting the `sampler2D _MainTex` variable from the `SubShader{}` block. However, the error is raised by the first line that tries to access such a variable. Finding and fixing what's wrong with code is a process called **debugging**. The most common mistakes that you should check for are as follows:

- A missing bracket. If you forgot to add a curly bracket to close a section, the compiler is likely to raise errors at the end of the document, at the beginning, or in a new section.
- A missing semicolon. One of the most common mistakes, but luckily one of the easiest to spot and fix. When looking at the Error definition, first check if the line above it has a semicolon or not.
- A property that has been defined in the `Properties` section but has not been coupled with a variable in the `SubShader{}` block.
- Compared to what you might be used to in C# scripts, the floating point values in Cg do not need to be followed by an `f`. It's `1.0`, not `1.0f`.

The error messages raised by shaders can be very misleading, especially due to their strict syntactic constraints. If you are in doubt about their meaning, it's best to search the internet. The Unity forums are filled with other developers who are likely to have encountered (and fixed) your problem before.

See also

- More information on how to master Surface Shaders and their properties can be found in `Chapter 5`, *Surface Shaders and Texture Mapping*

5
Surface Shaders and Texture Mapping

In this chapter, we will explore the topic of Surface Shaders in greater detail than in the previous chapter. We will start from building a very simple matte material and end with holographic projections and the advanced blending of terrains. We will also see how you can use textures to animate, blend, and drive any other property that they like.

In this chapter, you will learn the following recipes:

- Diffuse shading
- Accessing and modifying packed arrays
- Adding a texture to a shader
- Scrolling textures by modifying UV values
- Creating a shader with normal mapping
- Creating a transparent material
- Creating a Holographic Shader
- Packing and blending textures
- Creating a circle around your terrain

Introduction

Surface Shaders were introduced in `Chapter 4`, *Creating Your First Shader*, as the main type of shader that's used in Unity. This chapter will show you in detail what these actually are and how they work. Generally speaking, there are two essential steps in every Surface Shader. First, you have to specify certain physical properties of the material that you want to describe, such as its diffuse color, smoothness, and transparency. These properties are initialized in a function called the **surface function** and are stored in a structure called the `SurfaceOutput`. Secondly, the `SurfaceOutput` is passed to a lighting model. This is a special function that will also take information about the nearby lights in the scene. Both of these parameters are then used to calculate the final color for each pixel of your model. The lighting function is where the real calculations of a shader take place as it's the piece of code that determines how light should behave when it touches a material.

The following diagram loosely summarizes how a Surface Shader works. Custom lighting models will be explored in `Chapter 6`, *Understanding Lighting Models*, while `Chapter 8`, *Vertex Functions*, will focus on vertex modifiers:

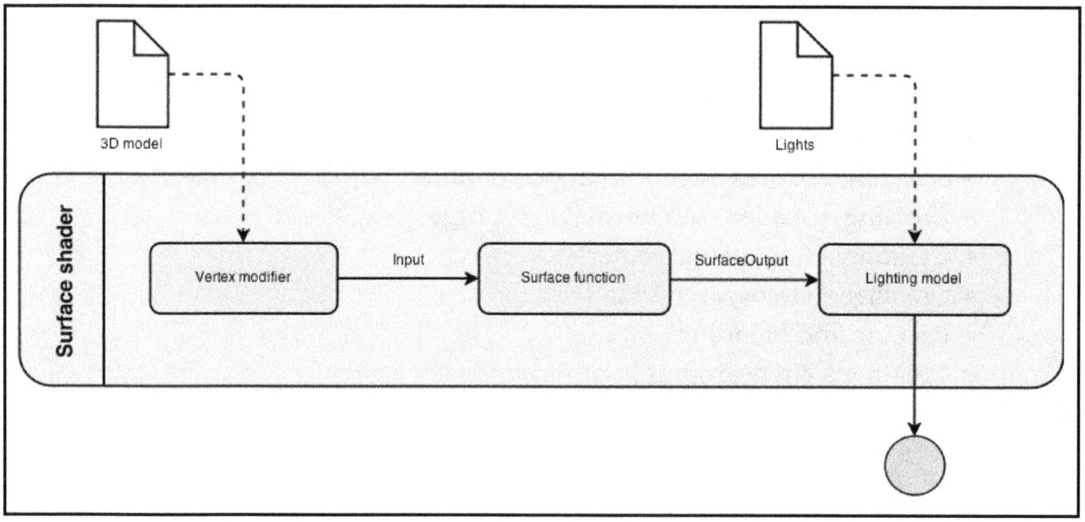

Diffuse shading

Before starting our journey into texture mapping, it is important to understand how diffuse materials work. Certain objects might have a uniform color and smooth surface, but are not smooth enough to shine in reflected light. These matte materials are best represented with a Diffuse Shader. While, in the real world pure diffuse materials do not exist, Diffuse Shaders are relatively cheap to implement and are largely applied in games with low-poly aesthetics, so they're worth learning about.

There are several ways in which you can create your own Diffuse Shader. A quick way is to start with Unity's Standard Surface Shader and edit it to remove any additional texture information.

Getting ready

Before starting this recipe, you should have created a Standard Surface Shader with the name `SimpleDiffuse`. For instructions on creating a Standard Surface Shader, look at the *Creating a basic Standard Surface Shader* recipe located in `Chapter 4`, *Creating Your First Shader,* if you haven't done so already.

How to do it...

Open up the `SimpleDiffuse` shader you've created and make the following changes:

1. In the `Properties` section, remove all of the variables except for `_Color`:

```
Properties
{
  _Color ("Color", Color) = (1,1,1,1)
}
```

2. From the `SubShader{}` section, remove the `_MainTex`, `_Glossiness`, and `_Metallic` variables. You should not remove the reference to `uv_MainTex` as Cg does not allow the `Input` struct to be empty. The value will simply be ignored.
3. Also, remove the `UNITY_INSTANCING_BUFFER_START/END` macros and the comments used with them.

4. Remove the content of the `surf()` function and replace it with the following:

```
void surf (Input IN, inout SurfaceOutputStandard o)
{
  o.Albedo = _Color.rgb;
}
```

5. Your shader should look as follows:

```
Shader "CookbookShaders/Chapter03/SimpleDiffuse" {
  Properties
  {
    _Color ("Color", Color) = (1,1,1,1)
  }
  SubShader
  {
    Tags { "RenderType"="Opaque" }
    LOD 200

    CGPROGRAM
    // Physically based Standard lighting model, and enable
shadows on all light types
    #pragma surface surf Standard fullforwardshadows

    // Use shader model 3.0 target, to get nicer looking
lighting
    #pragma target 3.0


    struct Input
    {
      float2 uv_MainTex;
    };

    fixed4 _Color;

    void surf (Input IN, inout SurfaceOutputStandard o)
    {
      o.Albedo = _Color.rgb;
    }

    ENDCG
  }
  FallBack "Diffuse"
}
```

TIP

The two lines below `CGPROGRAM` is actually one line and is cut off due to the size of the book.

6. As this shader has been refitted with a Standard Shader, it will use physically-based rendering to simulate how light behaves on your models.

TIP

If you are trying to achieve a non-photorealistic look, you can change the first `#pragma` directive so that it uses `Lambert` rather than `Standard`. If you do so, you should also replace the `SurfaceOutputStandard` parameter of the `surf` function with `SurfaceOutput`. For more information on this and the other lighting models that Unity supports, Jordan Stevens put together a very nice article about it, which you can see here: `http://www.jordanstevenstechart.com/lighting-models`

7. Save the shader and dive back into Unity. Using the same instructions as in the *Creating a basic Standard Surface Shader* recipe located in `Chapter 4`, *Creating Your First Shader*, create a new material called `SimpleDiffuseMat` and apply our newly created shader to it. Change the color to something different, such as red, by clicking on the window next to the **Color** property in the **Inspector** window while selected.
8. Then, go into the `Models` folder of this book's example code and bring the bunny object into our scene by dragging and dropping it from the **Project** window into the **Hierarchy** window. From there, assign the `SimpleDiffuseMat` material to the object:

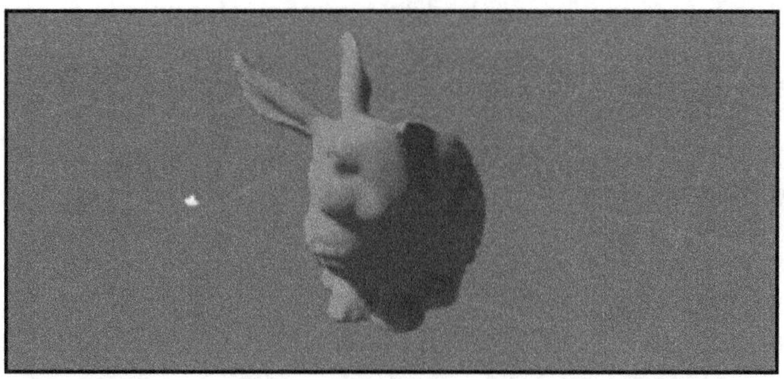

9. You can double-click on an object in the **Hierarchy** tab in order to center the camera on the object that's been selected.

How it works...

The way shaders allow you to communicate the rendering properties of your material to their lighting model is via their `SurfaceOutput`. It is basically a wrapper around all the parameters that the current lighting model needs. It should not surprise you that different lighting models have different `SurfaceOutput` structs. The following table shows the three main output structs used in Unity and how they can be used:

Type of shaders	Standard	Physically-Based Lighting Models
Diffuse	Any Surface Shader `SurfaceOutput`	**Standard** `SurfaceOutputStandard`
Specular	Any Surface Shader `SurfaceOutput`	**Standard (Specular setup)** `SurfaceOutputStandardSpecular`

The `SurfaceOutput` struct has the following properties:

- `fixed3 Albedo;`: This is the diffuse color of the material
- `fixed3 Normal;`: This is the tangent space, normal, if written
- `fixed3 Emission;`: This is the color of the light emitted by the material (this property is declared as `half3` in the Standard Shaders)
- `fixed Alpha;`: This is the transparency of the material
- `half Specular;`: This is the specular power from `0` to `1`
- `fixed Gloss;`: This is the specular intensity

The `SurfaceOutputStandard` struct has the following properties:

- `fixed3 Albedo;`: This is the base color of the material (whether it's diffuse or specular)
- `fixed3 Normal;`
- `half3 Emission;`: This property is declared as `half3`, while it was defined as `fixed3` in `SurfaceOutput`
- `fixed Alpha;`
- `half Occlusion;`: This is the occlusion (default `1`)
- `half Smoothness;`: This is the smoothness (`0` = rough, `1` = smooth)
- `half Metallic;`: `0` = non-metal, `1`= metal

The `SurfaceOutputStandardSpecular` struct has the following properties:

- `fixed3 Albedo;`
- `fixed3 Normal;`
- `half3 Emission;`
- `fixed Alpha;`
- `half Occlusion;`
- `half Smoothness;`
- `fixed3 Specular;`: This is the specular color. This is very different from the `Specular` property in `SurfaceOutput` as it allows you to specify a color rather than a single value.

Using a Surface Shader correctly is a matter of initializing the `SurfaceOutput` with the correct values.

For more information on creating Surface Shaders, check out the following link: `https://docs.unity3d.com/Manual/SL-SurfaceShaders.html`

Accessing and modifying packed arrays

Loosely speaking, the code inside a shader has to be executed for at least every pixel in your screen. This is the reason why GPUs are highly optimized for parallel computing; they can execute multiple processes at the same time. This philosophy is also evident in the standard type of variables and operators available in Cg. Understanding them is essential, not just so that you can use the shaders correctly, but also to write highly optimized ones.

How to do it...

There are two types of variables in Cg: single values and packed arrays. The latter can be identified because their type ends with a number such as `float3` or `int4`. As their names suggest, these types of variables are similar to structs, which means that they each contain several single values. Cg calls them packed arrays, though they are not exactly *arrays* in the traditional sense.

The elements of a packed array can be accessed as a normal struct. They are typically called `x`, `y`, `z`, and `w`. However, Cg also provides you with another alias for them, that is, `r`, `g`, `b`, and `a`. Despite there being no difference between using `x` or `r`, it can make a huge difference for the readers. Shader coding, in fact, often involves calculation with positions and colors. You might have seen this in the Standard Shaders:

```
o.Alpha = _Color.a;
```

Here, `o` was a struct and `_Color` was a packed array. This is also why Cg prohibits the mixed usage of these two syntaxes: you cannot use `_Color.xgz`.

There is also another important feature of packed arrays that has no equivalent in C#: **swizzling**. Cg allows addressing and reordering elements within packed arrays in just a single line. Once again, this appears in the Standard Shader:

```
o.Albedo = _Color.rgb;
```

`Albedo` is `fixed3`, which means that it contains three values of the `fixed` type. However, `_Color` is defined as a `fixed4` type. A direct assignment would result in a compiler error as `_Color` is bigger than `Albedo`. The C# way of doing this would be as follows:

```
o.Albedo.r = _Color.r;
o.Albedo.g = _Color.g;
o.Albedo.b = _Color.b;
```

However, it can be compressed in Cg:

```
o.Albedo = _Color.rgb;
```

Cg also allows reordering elements, for instance, using `_Color.bgr` to swap the red and blue channels.

Lastly, when a single value is assigned to a packed array, it is copied to all of its fields:

```
o.Albedo = 0; // Black =(0,0,0)
o.Albedo = 1; // White =(1,1,1)
```

This is referred to as **smearing**.

Swizzling can also be used on the left-hand side of an expression, allowing only certain components of a packed array to be overwritten:

```
o.Albedo.rg = _Color.rg;
```

In this case, it is called **masking**.

There's more...

Where swizzling really shows its full potential is when it's applied to packed matrices. Cg allows types such as `float4x4`, which represents a matrix of floats with four rows and four columns. You can access a single element of the matrix using the `_mRC` notation, where *R* is the row and *C* is the column:

```
float4x4 matrix;
// ...
float first = matrix._m00;
float last = matrix._m33;
```

The `_mRC` notation can also be chained:

```
float4 diagonal = matrix._m00_m11_m22_m33;
```

An entire row can be selected using squared brackets:

```
float4 firstRow = matrix[0];
// Equivalent to
float4 firstRow = matrix._m00_m01_m02_m03;
```

See also

- In addition to being easier to write, swizzling, smearing, and masking properties have performance benefits as well
- However, inappropriate use of swizzling can also make your code harder to understand at first glance, and may make it harder for the compiler to automatically optimize your code
- Packed arrays are one of the nicest features of Cg. You can discover more about them here: `http://http.developer.nvidia.com/CgTutorial/cg_tutorial_chapter02.html`

Adding a texture to a shader

Textures can bring our shaders to life very quickly in terms of achieving very realistic effects. In order to effectively use textures, we need to understand how a 2D image is mapped to a 3D model. This process is called texture mapping, and it requires some work to be done on the shader and 3D model that we want to use. Models, in fact, are made out of triangles, which are often referred to as polygons; each vertex on the model can store data that shaders can access and use to determine what to draw.

One of the most important pieces of information that are stored in vertices is the **UV data**. It consists of two coordinates, *U* and *V*, ranging from 0 to 1. They represent the *XY* position of the pixel in the 2D image that will be mapped to the vertices. UV data is present only for vertices; when the inner points of a triangle have to be texture-mapped, the GPU interpolates the closest UV values to find the right pixel in the texture to be used. The following diagram shows you how a **2D Texture** is mapped to a triangle from a 3D model:

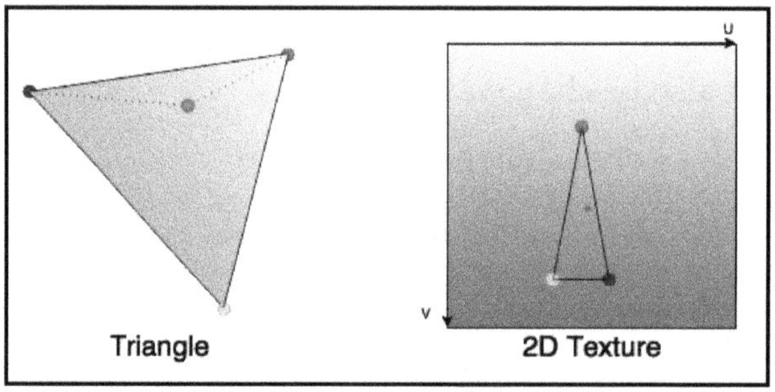

The UV data is stored in the 3D model and requires modeling software to be edited. Some models lack the UV component, hence they cannot support texture mapping. The Stanford bunny, for example, was not originally provided with one.

Getting ready

For this recipe, you'll need a 3D model with UV data and its texture. They both need to be imported to Unity before starting. You can do this simply by dragging them to the editor. As the Standard Shader supports texture mapping by default, we'll use this and then explain how it works in detail.

How to do it...

Adding a texture to your model using the Standard Shader is incredibly simple, as follows:

1. In the Sample Code for this chapter that's provided with this book, you can find the `basicCharacter` model which, by default, has UV information embedded into it, making it so that when we attach a material, it will draw the texture using that information.
2. Create a new Standard Surface Shader called `TexturedShader` by going to the **Project** tab and then selecting **Create** | **Shaders** | **Standard Surface Shader**. Once created, you can type in a new name for the shader and then press *Enter*.
3. For organization's sake, open the shader and change the first line to the following:

```
Shader "CookbookShaders/Chapter03/TexturedShader" {
```

4. This will allow us to find the shader inside of the organization we have been using so far for this book.
5. Create a new material called `TexturedMaterial` by going to the **Project** tab and then selecting **Create** | **Material**. Once created, you can type in a new name for the material and then press *Enter* to confirm the change.

6. Assign the shader to the material by going to the **Inspector** tab and then clicking on the **Shader** dropdown before selecting `CookbookShaders/Chapter 03/TexturedShader`:

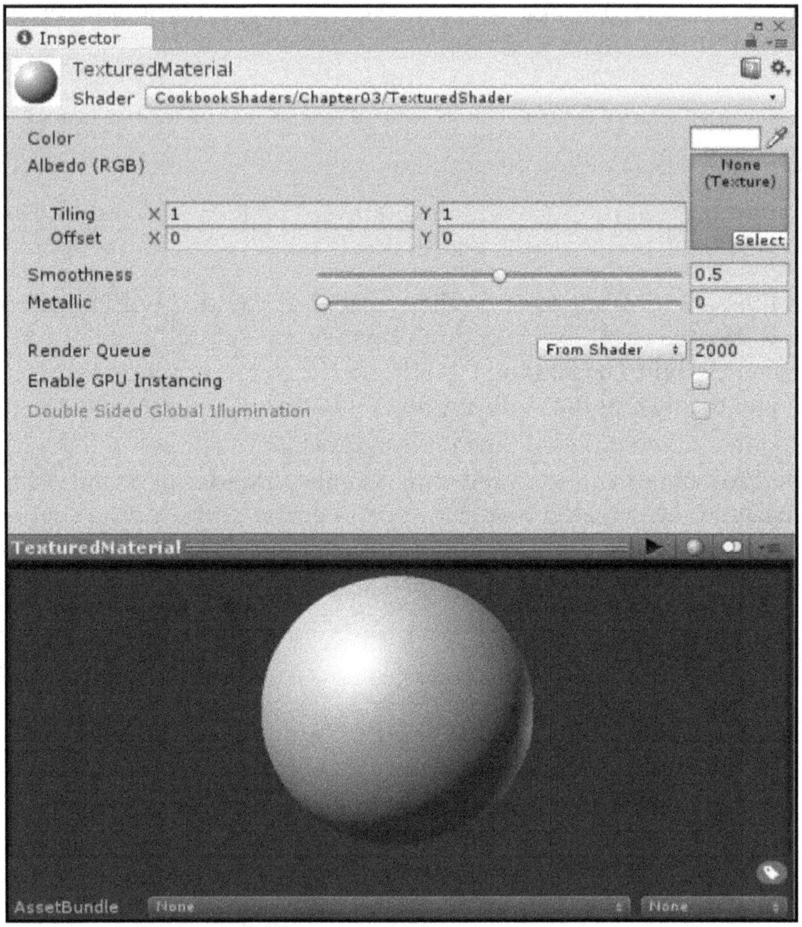

You may also do this by first selecting the material and then dragging the shader file over it in the **Project** tab.

7. After selecting the material, drag your texture to the empty rectangle called **Albedo (RGB)**. If you are missing some, there are textures located in this chapter's example code that can be used. If you have followed all of these steps correctly, your material **Inspector** tab should look like this:

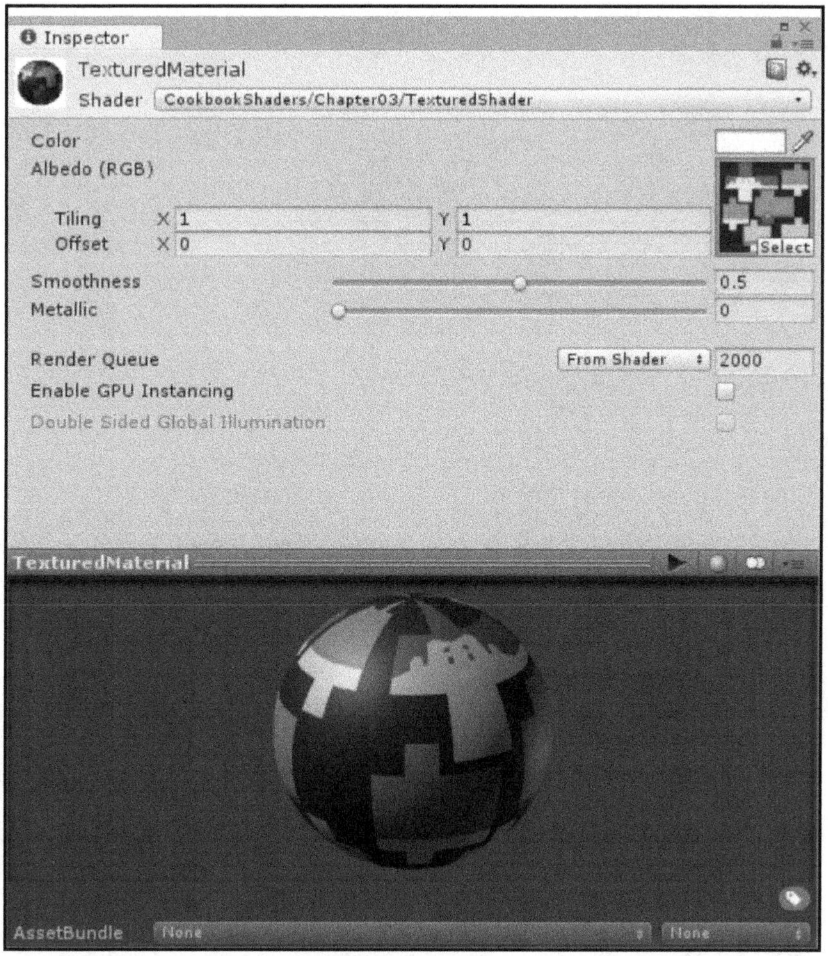

The Standard Shader knows how to map a 2D image to a 3D model using its UV models and textures used in this example were created by Kenney Vleugels and Casper Jorissen. You can find these and many other public domain game assets at `Kenney.nl`.

8. To see the UV data in action, in the example code's `Models` folder, drag and drop the model into the **Hierarchy** tab. Once there, double-click on the newly created object to zoom in so that you can see the object:

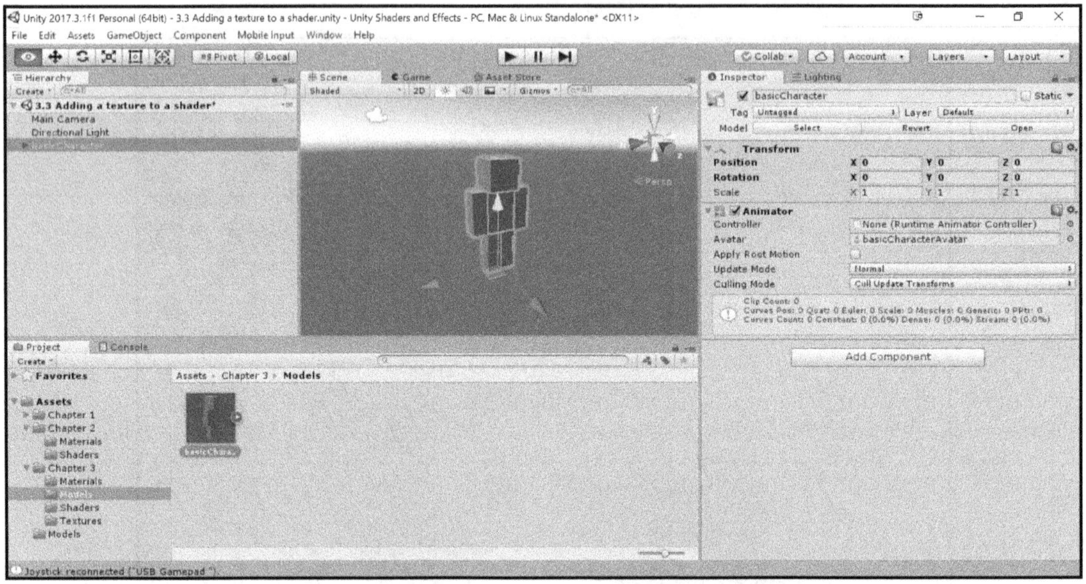

9. Once there, you may go to the **Project** tab and open up the `Chapter 3 | Materials` folder and drag and drop our `Textured Material` onto the character. Note that the model consists of different objects, each of which provides direction to draw in a particular place. This means that you will need to drop the material on each part of the model (`ArmLeft1`, `ArmRight1`, `Body1`, and so on); trying to apply this to the top level of the hierarchy only (`basicCharacter`) will not work:

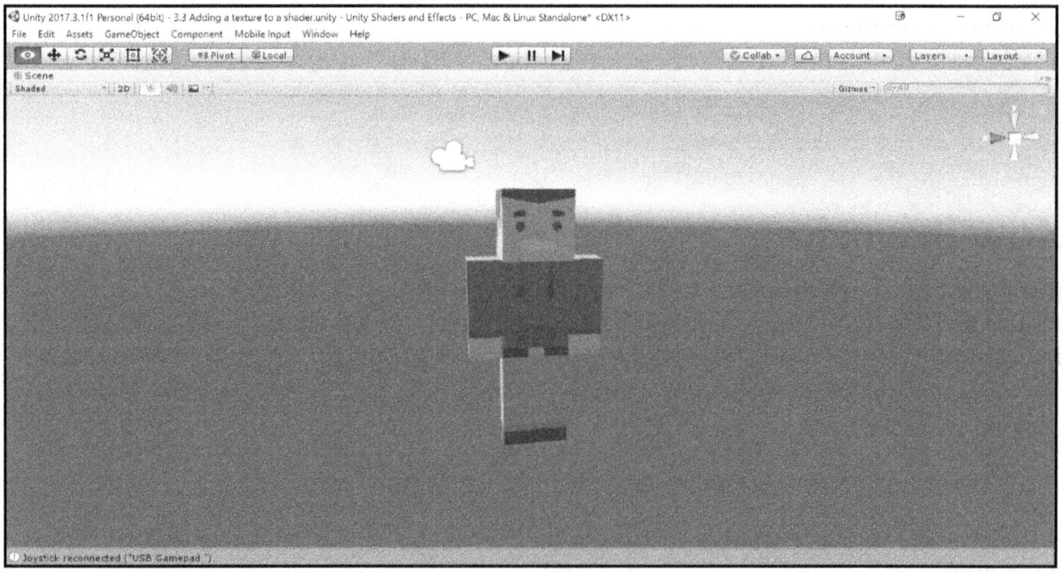

10. It is also possible to change what the object looks like by changing the texture that's being used. For instance, if we use the other texture provided (`skin_womanAlternative`), we have a very different looking character:

This is often used in games to provide different kinds of characters with minimal cost.

How it works...

When the Standard Shader is used from the **Inspector** of a material, the process behind texture mapping is completely transparent to developers. If we want to understand how it works, it's necessary to take a closer look at `TexturedShader`. From the `Properties` section, we can see that the `Albedo (RGB)` texture is actually referred to in the code as `_MainTex`:

```
_MainTex ("Albedo (RGB)", 2D) = "white" {}
```

In the `CGPROGRAM` section, this texture is defined as `sampler2D`, the standard type for 2D textures:

```
sampler2D _MainTex;
```

The following line shows a `struct` called `Input`. This is the input parameter for the surface function and contains a packed array called `uv_MainTex`:

```
struct Input {
  float2 uv_MainTex;
};
```

Every time the `surf()` function is called, the `Input` structure will contain the UV of `_MainTex` for the specific point of the 3D model that needs to be rendered. The Standard Shader recognizes that the name `uv_MainTex` refers to `_MainTex` and initializes it automatically. If you are interested in understanding how the UV is actually mapped from a 3D space to a 2D texture, you can check out `Chapter 7`, *Understanding Lighting Models*.

Finally, the UV data is used to sample the texture in the first line of the surface function:

```
fixed4 c = tex2D (_MainTex, IN.uv_MainTex) * _Color;
```

This is done using the `tex2D()` function of Cg; it takes a texture and UV and returns the color of the pixel at that position.

> The *U* and *V* coordinates go from *0* to *1*, where (0,0) and (1,1) correspond to two opposite corners. Different implementations associate UV with different corners; if your texture happens to appear reversed, try inverting the V component.

There's more...

When you import a texture to Unity, you are setting up some of the properties that `sampler2D` will use. The most important is the **Filter** mode, which determines how colors are interpolated when the texture is sampled. It is very unlikely that the UV data will point exactly to the center of a pixel; in all other cases, you might want to interpolate between the closest pixels to get a more uniform color. The following is a screenshot of the **Inspector** tab of an example texture:

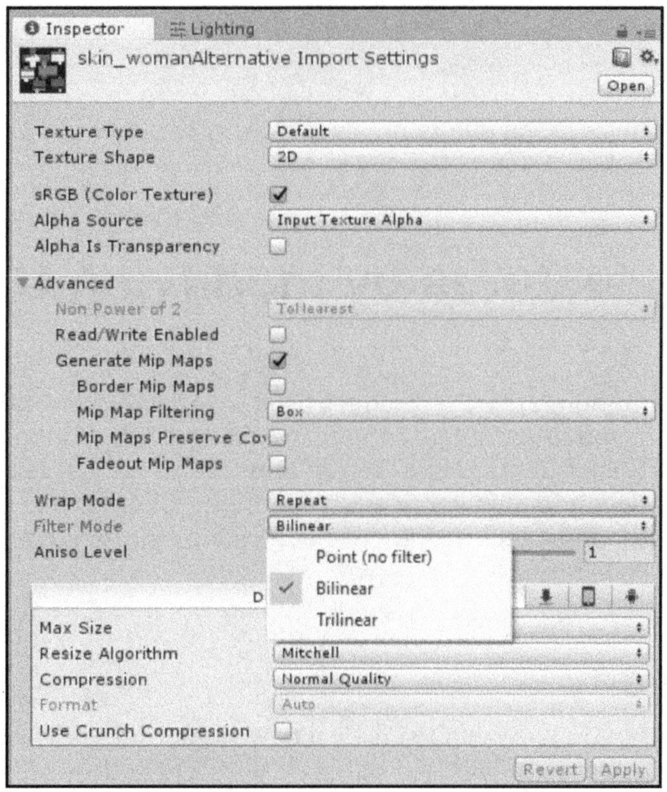

For most applications, **Bilinear** provides an inexpensive, yet effective, way to smooth the texture. If you are creating a 2D game, however, **Bilinear** might produce blurred tiles. In this case, you can use **Point** to remove any interpolation from the texture sampling.

When a texture is seen from a steep angle, texture sampling is likely to produce visually unpleasant artifacts. You can reduce them by setting the **Aniso Level** to a higher value. This is particularly useful for floor and ceiling textures, where glitches can break the illusion of continuity.

See also

- If you would like to know more about the inner workings of how textures are mapped to a 3D surface, you can read the information available at `http://developer.nvidia.com/CgTutorial/cg_tutorial_chapter03.html`.
- For a complete list of the options available when importing a 2D texture, you can refer to the following website: `http://docs.unity3d.com/Manual/class-TextureImporter.html`

Scrolling textures by modifying UV values

One of the most common texture techniques used in today's game industry is the process of allowing you to scroll the textures over the surface of an object. This allows you to create effects such as waterfalls, rivers, and lava flows. It's also a technique that is the basis of creating animated sprite effects, but we will cover this in a subsequent recipe of this chapter. First, let's see how we will create a simple scrolling effect in a Surface Shader.

Getting ready

To begin this recipe, you will need to create a new shader file (`ScrollingUVs`) and material (`ScrollingUVMat`). This will set us up with a nice clean shader that we can use to study the scrolling effect by itself.

How to do it...

To begin with, we will launch our new shader file that we just created and enter the code mentioned in the following steps:

1. The shader will need two new properties that will allow us to control the speed of the texture scrolling. So, let's add a speed property for the *X* direction and a speed property for the *Y* direction, as shown in the following code:

```
Properties {
  _Color ("Color", Color) = (1,1,1,1)
  _MainTex ("Albedo (RGB)", 2D) = "white" {}
  _ScrollXSpeed ("X Scroll Speed", Range(0,10)) = 2
  _ScrollYSpeed ("Y Scroll Speed", Range(0,10)) = 2
}
```

2. When working in ShaderLab, `Properties` has a syntax that looks like the following:

```
Properties
{
    _propertyName("Name in Inspector", Type) = value
}
```

Each property contained in the `Properties` block first has a name that is used in code to refer to the object, here specified as `_propertyName`. The underscore isn't required but is a common standard in place. Inside the parenthesis, you'll see two parameters. The first is a string that defines what text will be displayed in the **Inspector** for what this property is. The second parameter is the type of data we wish to store.

In our case, for the *X* and *Y* Scroll Speed, we are creating a number with a possible Range from 0 to 10. Lastly, we can initialize the property with a default value which is done on the end. As we've seen before, these properties will show up in the **Inspector** if you select a material that is using this shader.

For more information on Properties and how to create them, check out `https://docs.unity3d.com/Manual/SL-Properties.html`.

For this example, we don't need the `Smoothness` or `Metallic` properties, so we can remove them as well.

3. Modify the Cg properties in the `CGPROGRAM` section above the definition of `_MainTex` and create new variables so that we can access the values from our properties:

```
fixed _ScrollXSpeed;
fixed _ScrollYSpeed;
sampler2D _MainTex;
```

4. We also need to remove the `_Glossiness` and `_Metallic` definitions as we are not using them anymore.
5. Modify the surface function to change the UVs given to the `tex2D()` function. Then, use the built-in `_Time` variable to animate the UVs over time when the **Play** button is pressed in the editor:

```
void surf (Input IN, inout SurfaceOutputStandard o) {
    // Create a separate variable to store our UVs
    // before we pass them to the tex2D() function
    fixed2 scrolledUV = IN.uv_MainTex;
    // Create variables that store the individual x and y
    // components for the UV's scaled by time
    fixed xScrollValue = _ScrollXSpeed * _Time;
    fixed yScrollValue = _ScrollYSpeed * _Time;
    // Apply the final UV offset
    scrolledUV += fixed2(xScrollValue, yScrollValue);
    // Apply textures and tint
    half4 c = tex2D(_MainTex, scrolledUV);
    o.Albedo = c.rgb * _Color;
    o.Alpha = c.a;
}
```

6. Once the script is finished, save it and then go back to the Unity editor. Go to the `Materials` folder and assign `ScrollingUVsMat` to use our `ScrollingUVs` shader. Once that is done, under the **Albedo (RGB)** property, drag and drop the water texture from the example code provided with this book to assign the property:

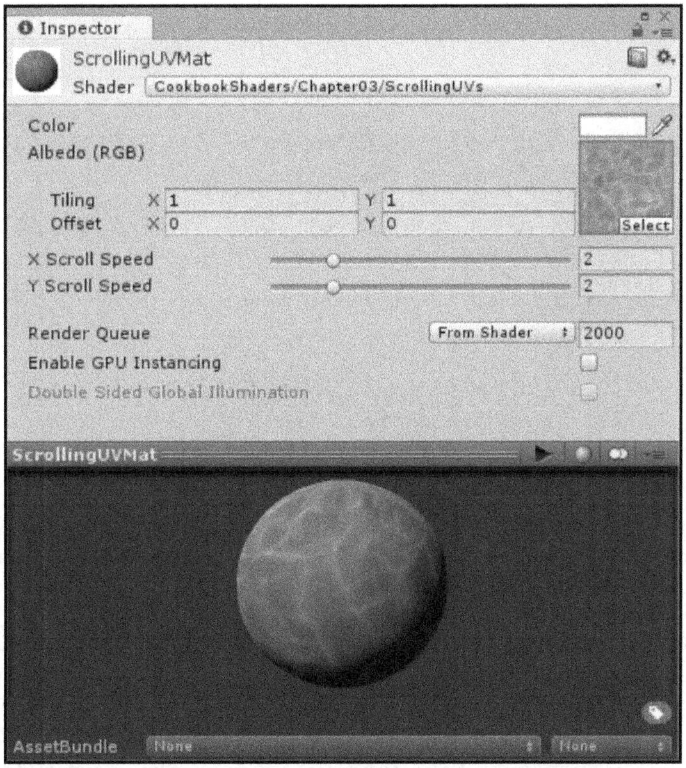

7. After this is created, we need to create an object that can use the shader. From a new scene, go ahead and select **GameObject** | **3D Object** | **Plane** and drag and drop the `ScrollingUVMat` material onto it.

8. Once applied, go ahead and play the game to see the shader in action:

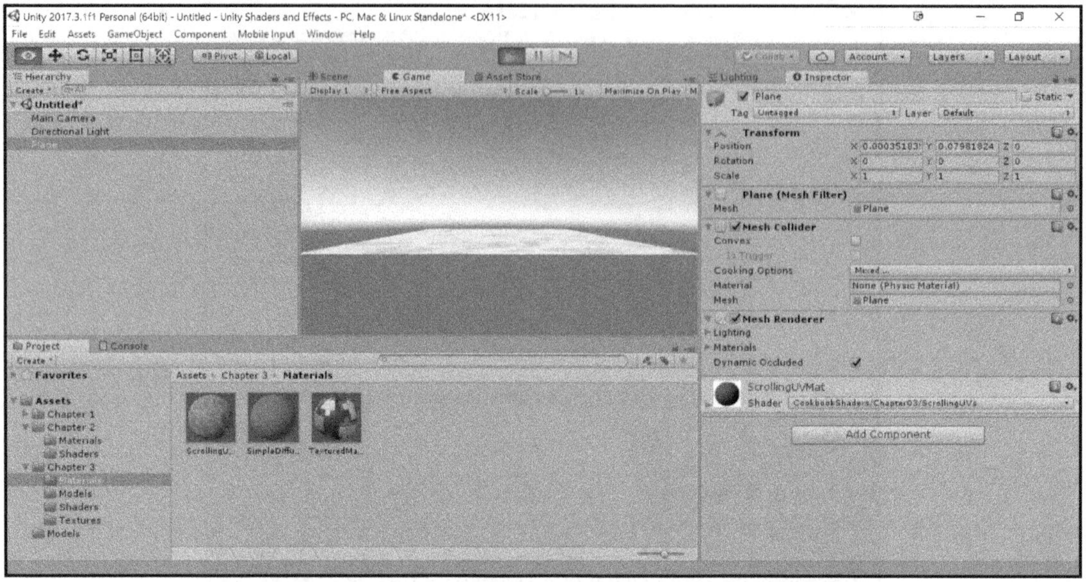

While it's not visible in this still image, you will notice that in the Unity editor, the object will now move in both the *X* and *Y* axes! Feel free to drag the **X Scroll Speed** and **Y Scroll Speed** properties in the **Inspector** tab to see how the changes affect how the object moves. Also, feel free to move the camera to make it easier to see if you would like.

TIP

If you modify a variable on a **Material** during gameplay, the value will stay changed, unlike how Unity typically works.

Pretty cool! With this knowledge, we can take this concept much further to create interesting visual effects. The following screenshot demonstrates the result of utilizing the scrolling UV system with multiple materials in order to create a simple river motion for your environments:

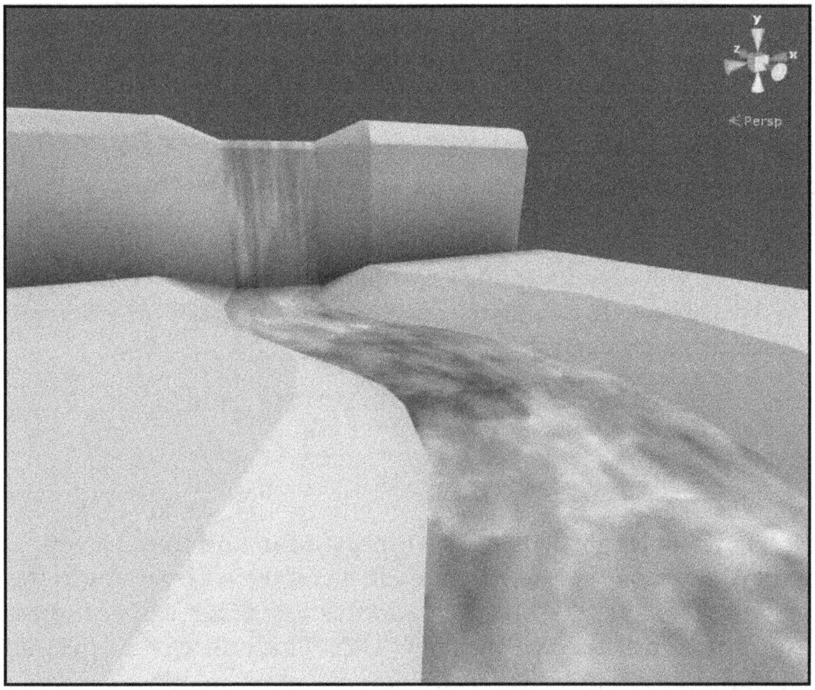

How it works...

The scrolling system starts with the declaration of a couple of properties, which will allow the user of this shader to increase or decrease the speed of the scrolling effect itself. At their core, they are float values being passed from the material's **Inspector** tab to the surface function of the shader. For more information on shader properties, see `Chapter 4`, *Creating Your First Shader*.

Once we have these float values from the material's **Inspector** tab, we can use them to offset our UV values in the shader.

To begin this process, we first store the UVs in a separate variable called `scrolledUV`. This variable has to be `float2`/`fixed2` because the UV values are being passed to us from the `Input` structure:

```
struct Input
{
  float2 uv_MainTex;
}
```

Once we have access to the mesh's UVs, we can offset them using our scroll speed variables and built-in `_Time` variable. This built-in variable returns a variable of the `float4` type, meaning that each component of this variable contains different values of time as it pertains to game time.

A complete description of these individual time values is described at the following link: `http://docs.unity3d.com/Manual/SL-UnityShaderVariables.html`

This `_Time` variable will give us an incremented float value based on Unity's game time clock. So, we can use this value to move our UVs in a UV direction and scale that time with our scroll speed variables:

```
// Create variables that store the individual x and y
// components for the uv's scaled by time
fixed xScrollValue = _ScrollXSpeed * _Time;
fixed yScrollValue = _ScrollYSpeed * _Time;
```

With the correct offset being calculated by time, we can add the new offset value back to the original UV position. This is why we are using the += operator in the next line. We want to take the original UV position, add the new offset value, and then pass this to the `tex2D()` function as the texture's new UVs. This creates the effect of the texture moving on the surface. What we are really doing is manipulating the UVs, so we are faking the effect of the texture moving:

```
scrolledUV += fixed2(xScrollValue, yScrollValue);
half4 c = tex2D (_MainTex, scrolledUV);
```

Creating a shader with normal mapping

Every triangle of a 3D model has a *facing direction*, which is the direction that it is pointing toward. It is often represented with an arrow placed in the center of the triangle and is orthogonal to the surface. The facing direction plays an important role in the way light reflects on a surface. If two adjacent triangles face different directions, they will reflect lights at different angles, hence they'll be shaded differently. For curved objects, this is a problem: it is obvious that the geometry is made out of flat triangles.

To avoid this problem, the way the light reflects on a triangle doesn't take into account its facing direction, but its *normal direction* instead. As stated in the *Adding a texture to a shader* recipe, vertices can store data; the normal direction is the most used information after the UV data. This is a vector of unit length (which means it has a length of 1) that indicates the direction faced by the vertex.

Regardless of the facing direction, every point within a triangle has its own normal direction that is a linear interpolation of the ones stored in its vertices. This gives us the ability to fake the effect of high-resolution geometry on a low-resolution model.

The following screenshot shows the same geometric shape rendered with different per-vertex normals. In the image, on the left, normals are orthogonal to the face represented by its vertices; this indicates that there is a clear separation between each face. On the right, normals are interpolated along the surface, indicating that even if the surface is rough, a light should reflect as if it's smooth. It's easy to see that even if the three objects in the following screenshot share the same geometry, they reflect light differently. Despite being made out of flat triangles, the object on the right reflects light as if its surface was actually curved:

Smooth objects with rough edges are a clear indication that per-vertex normals have been interpolated. This can be seen if we draw the direction of the normal stored in every vertex, as shown in the following screenshot. You should note that every triangle has only three normals, but as multiple triangles can share the same vertex, more than one line can come out of it:

Calculating the normals from the 3D model is a technique that has rapidly declined in favor of a more advanced one-normal mapping. Similar to what happens with texture mapping, the normal directions can be provided using an additional texture, usually called a normal map or bump map.

Normal maps are usually images where the red, green, and blue channels of the image are used to indicate the *X*, *Y*, and *Z* components of the normal direction.

There are many ways to create normal maps these days. Some applications, such as CrazyBump (`http://www.crazybump.com/`) and NDO Painter (`http://quixel.se/ndo/`), will take in 2D data and convert it to normal data for you. Other applications such as Zbrush 4R7 (`http://www.pixologic.com/`) and AUTODESK (`http://usa.autodesk.com`) will take 3D-sculpted data and create normal maps for you. The actual process of creating normal maps is out of the scope of this book, but the links in the previous text should help you get started.

Unity makes the process of adding normals to your shaders quite an easy process in the Surface Shader realm using the `UnpackNormals()` function. Let's see how this is done.

Getting ready

To begin this recipe, first create a new scene by selecting **File | New Scene**. Then, create a sphere game object by going to **GameObject | 3D Objects | Sphere**. Double-click on the object in the **Hierarchy** tab to bring the object into focus in the **Scene** tab. You will also need to create a new standard Surface Shader file (`NormalShader`) and material (`NormalShaderMat`). Once created, set the material to a sphere in the **Scene** view. This will give us a clean workspace in which we can look at just the normal mapping technique:

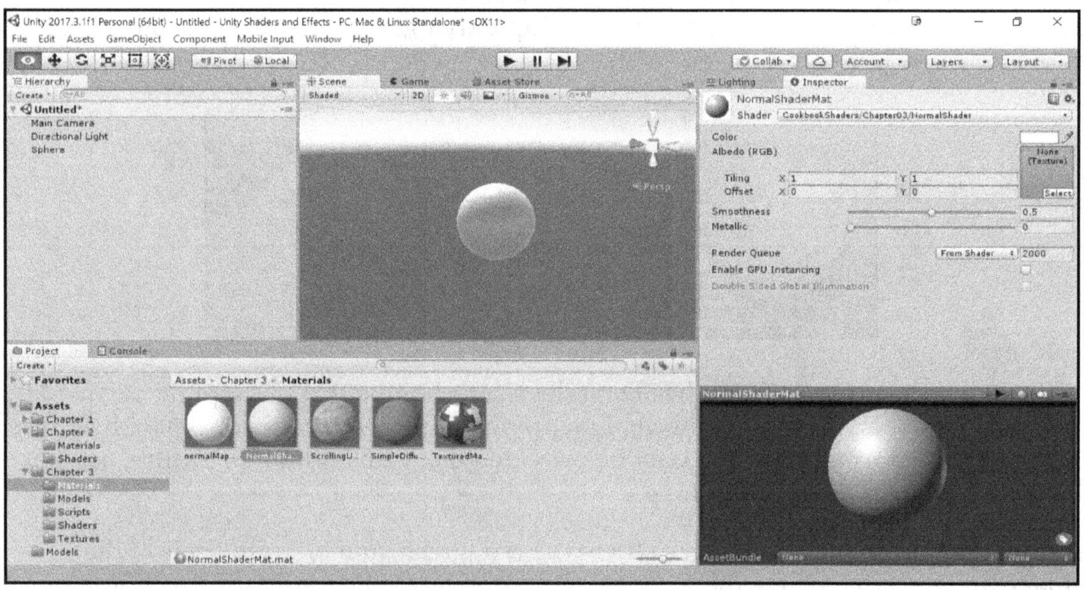

You will need a normal map for this recipe, but there is also one in the Unity project included with this book.

An example normal map included with this book's content is shown here:

You can see it for yourself in the `Assets | Chapter 03 | Textures` folder under `normalMapExample`.

How to do it...

The following are the steps to create a normal map shader:

1. Let's get the `Properties` block set up in order to have a color `Tint` and texture:

```
Properties
{
  _MainTint ("Diffuse Tint", Color) = (0,1,0,1)
  _NormalTex ("Normal Map", 2D) = "bump" {}
}
```

In this case, I have 1 in the green and alpha channels and `0` for red and blue, so the default color will be green. For the `_NormalTex` property, we are using a 2D type, which means we can use a 2D image to dictate what each pixel will use. By initializing the texture as `bump`, we are telling Unity that `_NormalTex` will contain a normal map (sometimes referred to as bump maps as well, hence the bump name). If the texture is not set, it will be replaced by a grey texture. The color used (`0.5`, `0.5`, `0.5`, `1`) indicates no bump at all.

2. In the `SubShader{}` block, scroll below the `CGPROGRAM` statement and remove the original `_MainText`, `_Glossiness`, `_Metallic`, and `_Color` definitions. Afterward, add in our `_NormalTex` and `_MainTint`:

```
    CGPROGRAM
    // Physically based Standard lighting model, and enable
shadows
    // on all light types
    #pragma surface surf Standard fullforwardshadows

    // Use shader model 3.0 target, to get nicer looking
lighting
    #pragma target 3.0

    // Link the property to the CG program
    sampler2D _NormalTex;
    float4 _MainTint;
```

3. We need to make sure that we update the `Input` struct with the proper variable name so that we can use the model's UVs for the normal map texture:

```
// Make sure you get the UVs for the texture in the struct
struct Input
{
  float2 uv_NormalTex;
}
```

4. Finally, we extract the normal information from the normal map texture using the built-in `UnpackNormal()` function. Then, you only have to apply these new normals to the output of the Surface Shader:

```
void surf (Input IN, inout SurfaceOutputStandard o) {
  // Use the tint provided as the base color for the
material
  o.Albedo = _MainTint;

  // Get the normal data out of the normal map texture
  // using the UnpackNormal function
  float3 normalMap = UnpackNormal(tex2D(_NormalTex,
    IN.uv_NormalTex));

  // Apply the new normal to the lighting model
  o.Normal = normalMap.rgb;
}
```

5. Save your script and return to the Unity editor. You should notice that the sphere has now become green by default if added. More importantly though, notice the **Normal Map** property that has been added. Drag and drop the normal map texture into the slot.

6. You may notice some changes, but it may be hard to visually see what is going on. In the **Normal Map** property, change the **Tiling** to (`10`, `10`). This way, you can see the normal map duplicated 10 times over the course of the sphere in the *X* and *Y* axes instead of only once:

7. The following screenshot demonstrates the result of our normal map shader:

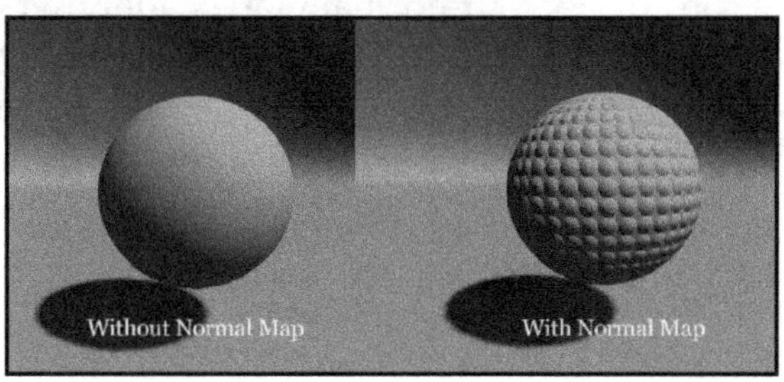

Shaders can have both a texture map and a normal map. It is not uncommon to use the same UV data to address both. However, it is possible to provide a secondary set of UVs in the vertex data (UV2), which are specifically used for the normal map.

How it works...

The actual math to perform the normal mapping effect is definitely beyond the scope of this chapter, but Unity has done it all for us already. It has created the functions for us so that we don't have to keep doing it over and over again. This is another reason why Surface Shaders are a really efficient way to write shaders.

If you look in the `UnityCG.cginc` file found in the `Editor | Data| CGIncludes` folder in your Unity installation directory, you will find the definitions for the `UnpackNormal()` function. When you declare this function in your Surface Shader, Unity takes the normal map provided and processes it for you, giving you the correct type of data so that you can use it in your per-pixel lighting function. It's a huge time-saver! When sampling a texture, you get RGB values from `0` to `1`; however, the directions of a normal vector range from `-1` to `1`. `UnpackNormal()` brings these components into the right range.

Once you have processed the normal map with the `UnpackNormal()` function, you send it back to your `SurfaceOutput` struct so that it can be used in the lighting function. This is done by using `o.Normal = normalMap.rgb;`. We will see how the normal is actually used to calculate the final color of each pixel in `Chapter 6`, *Understanding Lighting Models.*

There's more...

You can also add some controls to your normal map shader that lets a user adjust the intensity of the normal map. This is easily done by modifying the `x` and `y` components of the normal map variable and then adding it all back together. Add another property to the `Properties` block and name it `_NormalMapIntensity`:

```
_NormalMapIntensity("Normal intensity", Range(0,3)) = 1
```

In this case, we are giving the property the ability to be between `0` and `3` with a default value of `1`. Once created, you'll need to add the variable inside the SubShader:

```
// Link the property to the CG program
sampler2D _NormalTex;
float4 _MainTint;
float _NormalMapIntensity;
```

After the property is added, we can make use of it. Multiply the `x` and `y` components of the unpacked normal map and reapply this value to the normal map variable with the bolded changes:

```
void surf (Input IN, inout SurfaceOutputStandard o) {
  // Use the tint provided as the base color for the material
  o.Albedo = _MainTint;

  // Get the normal data out of the normal map texture
  // using the UnpackNormal function
  float3 normalMap = UnpackNormal(tex2D(_NormalTex,
    IN.uv_NormalTex));

  normalMap.x *= _NormalMapIntensity;
  normalMap.y *= _NormalMapIntensity;

  // Apply the new normal to the lighting model
  o.Normal = normalize(normalMap.rgb);
}
```

Normal vectors are supposed to have lengths equal to one. Multiplying them for `_NormalMapIntensity` changes their length, making normalization necessary. The normalize function will take the vector and adjust it so that it is pointing in the correct direction but with a length of one, which is what we are looking for.

Now, you can let a user adjust the intensity of the normal map in the material's **Inspector** tab, as follows:

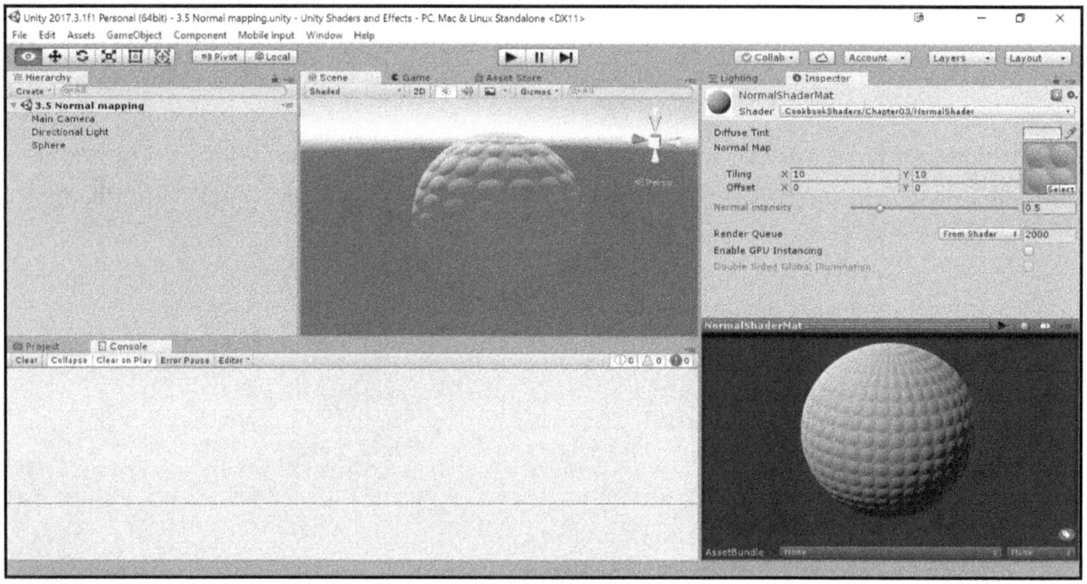

The following screenshot shows the result of modifying the normal map with our scalar values:

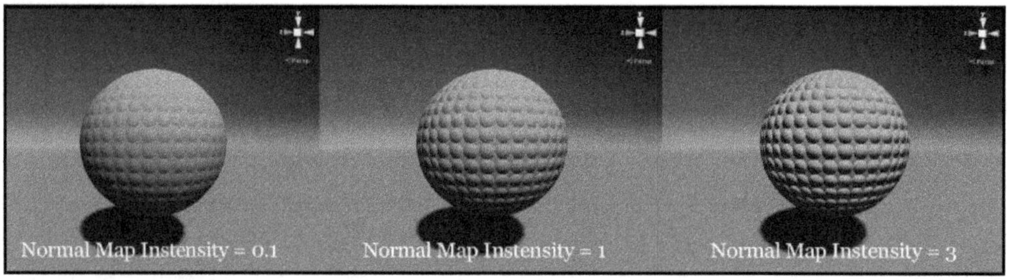

Creating a transparent material

All the shaders we have seen so far have something in common; they are used for solid materials. If you want to improve the look of your game, transparent materials are often a good way to start. They can be used for anything from a fire effect to a glass window. Working with them, unfortunately, is slightly more complicated. Before rendering solid models, Unity orders them according to the distance from the camera (*Z ordering*) and skips all the triangles that are facing away from the camera (**culling**). When rendering transparent geometries, there are instances in which these two aspects can cause problems. This recipe will show you how to solve some of these issues when it comes to creating a transparent Surface Shader. This topic will be heavily revisited in `Chapter 9`, *Fragment Shaders and Grab Passes*, where realistic glass and water shaders will be provided.

Getting ready

This recipe requires a new shader, which we'll be calling `Transparent`, and a new material (`TransparentMat`) so that it can be attached to an object. As this is going to be a transparent glass window, a quad or plane is perfect (**GameObject** | **3D Objects** | **Quad**). We will also need several other non-transparent objects to test the effect:

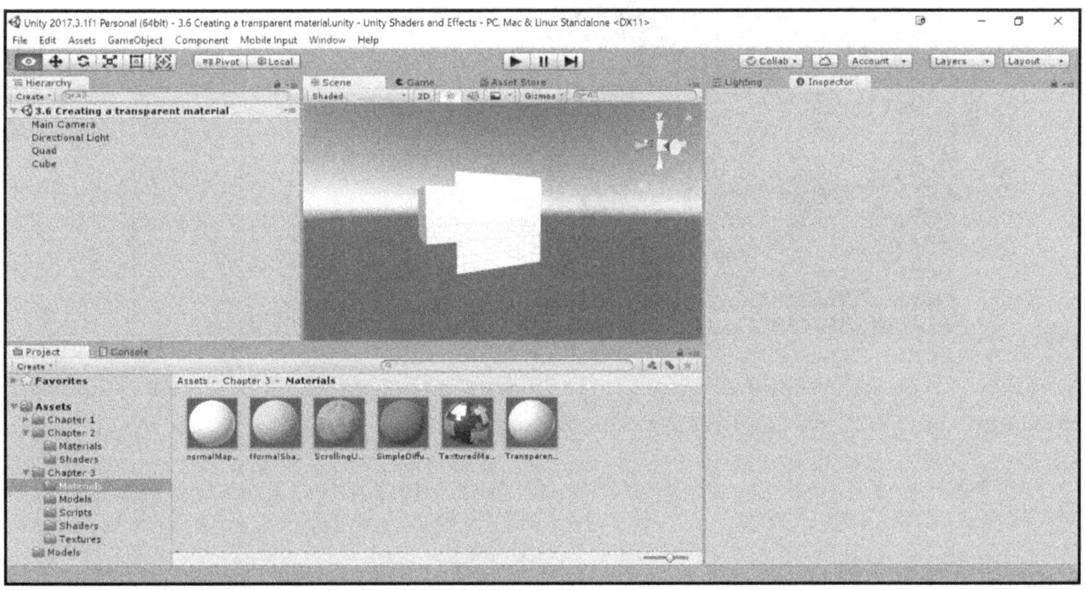

In this example, we will use a PNG image file for the glass texture since it has support for an alpha channel that will be used to determine the transparency of the glass. The process of creating such an image depends on the software that you are using. However, these are the main steps that you will need to follow:

1. Find the image of the glass you want for your windows.
2. Open it with a photo editing software, such as *GIMP* or *Photoshop*.
3. Select the parts of the image that you want to be semi-transparent.
4. Create a white (full opacity) layer mask on your image.
5. Use the selection previously made to fill the layer mask with a darker color. White is treated as fully visible, black will be treated as invisible, and grey will be somewhere in the middle.
6. Save the image and import it into Unity.

The toy image used in this recipe is a picture of stained glass from the *Meaux Cathedral* in *France* (`https://en.wikipedia.org/wiki/Stained_glass`). If you have followed all of these steps, your image should look like this (**RGB** channels on the left, and **A** channel on the right):

You can also make use of the image file in provided the example code for this book in `Chapter 3 | Textures` folder (`Meaux_Vitrail.psd`).

Attaching this image to the material will cause the image to show up, but we cannot see it behind the glass:

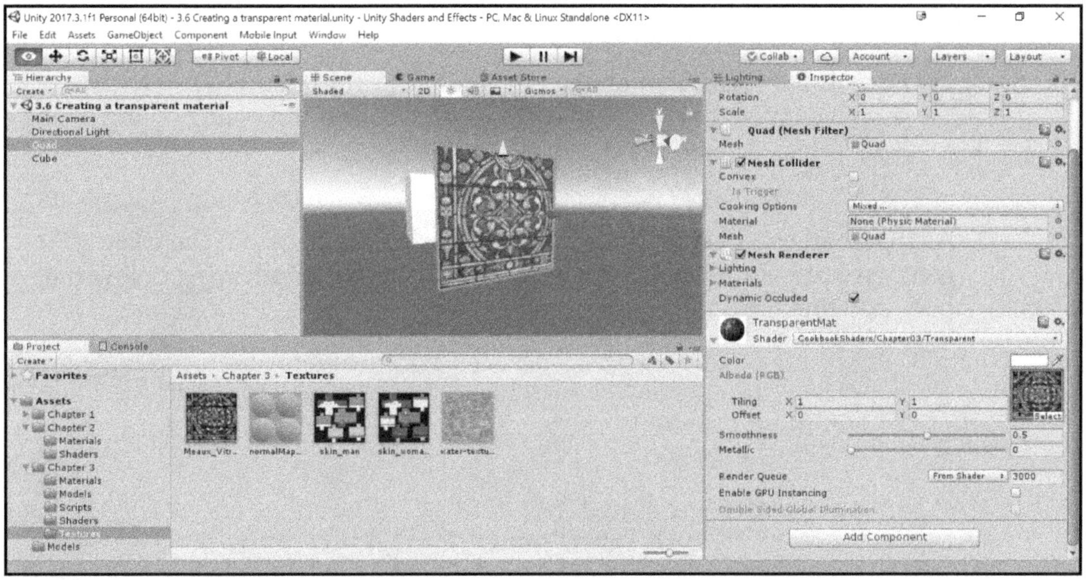

As we would like to see behind this, we can make adjustments to the shader to do exactly that.

How to do it...

As mentioned previously, there are a few aspects that we need to take care of while using a Transparent Shader:

1. Remove the `_Glossiness` and `_Metallic` variables from the `Properties` and `SubShader` sections of the code as they aren't needed for this example.
2. In the `SubShader{}` section of the shader, modify the `Tags` section to the following so that we can signal that the shader is transparent:

```
Tags
{
  "Queue" = "Transparent"
  "IgnoreProjector" = "True"
  "RenderType" = "Transparent"
}
```

Tags are used by the `SubShader` to know how and when items should be rendered. Similar to the dictionary type, tags are key-value pairs where the left-hand side is the tag name and the right-hand side is the value you wish for it to be set to.

For more information on tags in ShaderLab, check out: `https://docs.unity3d.com/Manual/SL-SubShaderTags.html`

3. As this shader is designed for 2D materials, make sure that the back geometry of your model is not drawn by adding the following below the `LOD 200` line:

```
    LOD 200

    // Do not show back
    Cull Back

    CGPROGRAM
    // Physically based Standard lighting model, and enable
shadows on all light types
    #pragma surface surf Standard alpha:fade
```

4. Tell the shader that this material is transparent and needs to be blended with what was drawn on the screen before:

```
#pragma surface surf Standard alpha:fade
```

5. Use this Surface Shader to determine the final color and transparency of the glass:

```
void surf(Input IN, inout SurfaceOutputStandard o)
{
  float4 c = tex2D(_MainTex, IN.uv_MainTex) * _Color;
  o.Albedo = c.rgb;
  o.Alpha = c.a;
}
```

6. Afterward, save your script and dive back to the Unity editor:

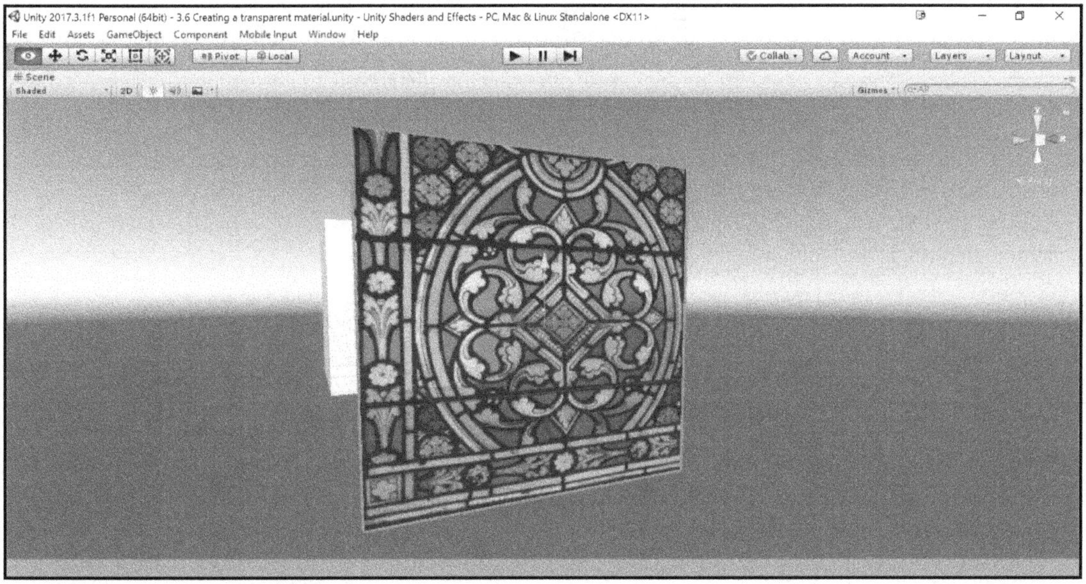

Notice that you can now see the cube behind the glass. Perfect!

How it works...

This shader introduces several new concepts. First of all, `Tags` are used to add information about how the object is going to be rendered. The really interesting one here is `Queue`. Unity, by default, will sort your objects for you based on the distance from the camera. So, as an object gets nearer to the camera, it is going to be drawn over all the objects that are further away from the camera. For most cases, this works out just fine for games, but you will find yourself in certain situations where you will want to have more control over the sorting of your objects in your scene. Unity has provided us with some default render queues, each with a unique value that directs Unity when to draw the object to the screen. These built-in render queues are called `Background`, `Geometry`, `AlphaTest`, `Transparent`, and `Overlay`. These queues weren't just created arbitrarily; they actually serve a purpose to make our lives easier when writing shaders and interacting with the real-time renderer.

Refer to the following table for descriptions on the usage of each of these individual render queues:

Render queue	Render queue description	Render queue value
`Background`	This render queue is rendered first. It is used for skyboxes and so on.	`1000`
`Geometry`	This is the default render queue. This is used for most objects. Opaque geometry uses this queue.	`2000`
`AlphaTest`	Alpha-tested geometry uses this queue. It's different from the `Geometry` queue as it's more efficient to render alpha-tested objects after all the solid objects are drawn.	`2450`
`Transparent`	This render queue is rendered after `Geometry` and `AlphaTest` queues in back-to-front order. Anything alpha-blended (that is, shaders that don't write to the depth buffer) should go here, for example, glass and particle effects.	`3000`
`Overlay`	This render queue is meant for overlay effects. Anything rendered last should go here, for example, lens flares.	`4000`

So, once you know which render queue your object belongs to, you can assign its built-in render queue tag. Our shader used the `Transparent` queue, so we wrote `Tags{"Queue"="Transparent"}`.

The fact that the `Transparent` queue is rendered after `Geometry` does *not* mean that our glass will appear on top of all the other solid objects. Unity will draw the glass last, but it will not render pixels that belong to pieces of geometry hidden behind something else. This control is done using a technique called **ZBuffering**. More information on how models are rendered can be found at the following link: `http://docs.unity3d.com/Manual/SL-CullAndDepth.html`.

The `IgnoreProjector` tag makes this object unaffected by Unity's projectors.

The last concept introduced is `alpha:fade`. This indicates that all the pixels from this material have to be blended with what was on the screen before according to their alpha values. Without this directive, the pixels will be drawn in the correct order, but they won't have any transparency.

Creating a Holographic Shader

More and more space-themed games are being released every year. An important part of a good sci-fi game is the way futuristic technology is presented and integrated into gameplay. There's nothing that screams futuristic more than holograms. Despite being present in many flavors, holograms are often represented as semi-transparent, thin projections of an object. This recipe shows you how to create a shader that simulates such effects. Take this as a starting point: you can add noise, animated scan lines, and vibrations to create a truly outstanding holographic effect. The following screenshot shows an example of a Holographic effect:

Getting ready

Create a shader called `Holographic`. Attach it to a material (`HolographicMat`) and assign it to a 3D model in your scene:

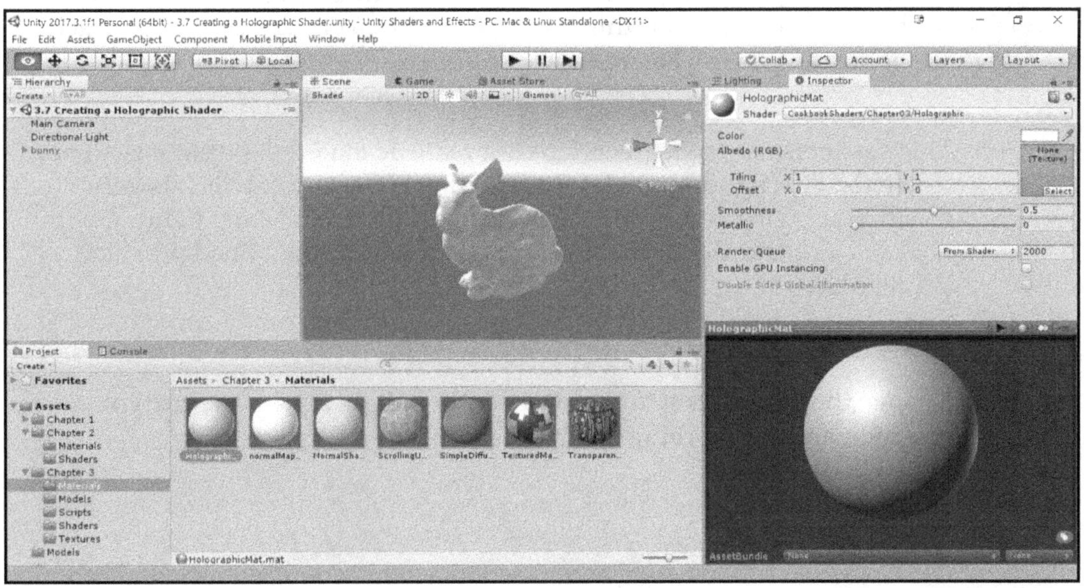

How to do it...

The following changes will change our existing shader into a holographic one:

1. Remove the following properties as they will not be used:
    - `_Glossiness`
    - `_Metallic`
2. Add the following property to the shader:

```
_DotProduct("Rim effect", Range(-1,1)) = 0.25
```

3. Add its respective variable to the `CGPROGRAM` section:

```
float _DotProduct;
```

4. As this material is transparent, add the following tags:

```
Tags
{
  "Queue" = "Transparent"
  "IgnoreProjector" = "True"
  "RenderType" = "Transparent"
}
```

According to the type of object that you will use, you might want its backside to appear. If this is the case, add `Cull Off` so that the back of the model won't be removed (*culled*).

5. This shader is not trying to simulate a realistic material, so there is no need to use the PBR lighting model. **Lambertian reflectance**, which is very cheap, is used instead. Additionally, we should disable any lighting with `nolighting` and signal to Cg that this is a Transparent Shader using `alpha:fade`:

```
#pragma surface surf Lambert alpha:fade nolighting
```

6. Change the `Input` structure so that Unity will fill it with the current view direction and the world normal direction:

```
struct Input
{
  float2 uv_MainTex;
  float3 worldNormal;
```

```
    float3 viewDir;
  };
```

7. Use the following surface function. Remember that since this shader is using Lambertian reflectance as its lighting function, the name of the `SurfaceOutput` structure should be changed accordingly to `SurfaceOutput` instead of `SurfaceOutputStandard`:

```
void surf(Input IN, inout SurfaceOutput o)
{
  float4 c = tex2D(_MainTex, IN.uv_MainTex) * _Color;
  o.Albedo = c.rgb;

  float border = 1 - (abs(dot(IN.viewDir,
     IN.worldNormal)));
  float alpha = (border * (1 - _DotProduct) + _DotProduct);
  o.Alpha = c.a * alpha;
}
```

8. Save your script and dive into Unity. From there, change the **Color** property in the **HolographicMat** and see your hologram come to life:

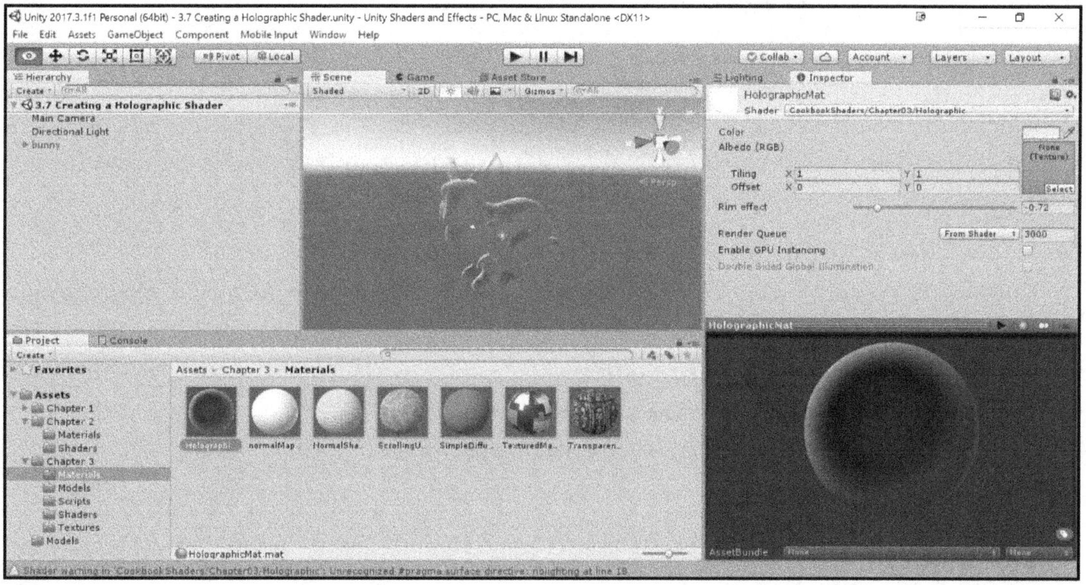

You can now use the **Rim effect** slider to choose the strength of the holographic effect.

How it works...

As mentioned previously, this shader works by showing only the silhouette of an object. If we look at the object from another angle, its outline will change. Geometrically speaking, the edges of a model are all those triangles whose *normal direction* is orthogonal (90 degrees) to the current *view direction*. The `Input` structure declares these parameters, `worldNormal` and `viewDir`, respectively.

The problem of understanding when two vectors are orthogonal can be solved using `_DotProduct`. This is an operator that takes two vectors and returns zero if they are orthogonal. We use `_DotProduct` to determine how close to zero the `_DotProduct` has to be for the triangle to fade completely.

The second aspect that is used in this shader is the gentle fading between the edge of the model (fully visible) and the angle determined by `_DotProduct` (invisible). This linear interpolation is effected as follows:

```
float alpha = (border * (1 - _DotProduct) + _DotProduct);
```

Finally, the original `alpha` from the texture is multiplied with the newly calculated coefficient to achieve the final look.

There's more...

This technique is very simple and relatively inexpensive, and yet it can be used for a large variety of effects, such as the following:

- The slightly colored atmosphere of a planet in sci-fi games
- The edge of an object that has been selected or is currently under the mouse
- A ghost or specter
- Smoke coming out of an engine
- The shockwave of an explosion
- The bubble shield of a spaceship under attack

See also

The `_DotProduct` plays an important role in the way reflections are calculated. `Chapter 6`, *Understanding Lighting Models*, will explain in detail how it works and why it is widely used in so many shaders.

Packing and blending textures

Textures are useful for storing not only loads of data, not just pixel colors as we generally tend to think of them, but also for multiple sets of pixels in both the *x* and *y* directions and RGBA channels. We can actually pack multiple images into a single RGBA texture and use each of the R, G, B, and A components as individual textures themselves by extracting each of these components from the shader code.

The result of packing individual grayscale images into a single RGBA texture can be seen in the following screenshot:

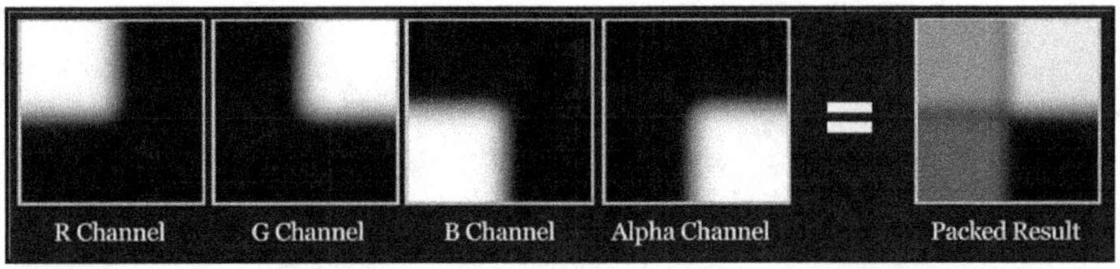

Why is this helpful? Well, in terms of the amount of actual memory that your application takes up, textures are a large portion of your application's size. We can, of course, reduce the size of the image, but then we would lose details in how it can be represented. So, to begin reducing the size of your application, we can look at all of the images that we are using in our shader and see if we can merge these textures into a single texture. Using a single texture with multiple images in them requires fewer draw calls and less overhead than separate files. We can also use this concept to combine irregularly shaped textures (that being, those that are not squares) into a single one to take up less space than giving them their own full texture.

Any texture that is grayscale can be packed into one of the RGBA channels of another texture. This might sound a bit odd at first, but this recipe is going to demonstrate one of the uses of packing a texture and using these packed textures in a shader.

One example of using these packed textures is when you want to blend a set of textures together onto a single surface. You see this most often in terrain type shaders, where you need to blend into another texture nicely using some sort of control texture or the packed texture, in this case. This recipe covers this technique and shows you how to construct the beginnings of a nice four-texture blended terrain shader.

Getting ready

Let's create a new shader file in your `Shaders` folder (`TextureBlending`) and then create a new material for this shader (`TextureBlendingMat`). The naming convention is entirely up to you for your shader and material files, so try your best to keep them organized, and easy to reference later on.

Once you have your shader and material ready, create a new scene in which we can test our shader. Inside to the scene, place the `Terrain_001` object from the `Chapter 3 | Models` folder and assign the `TextureBlendingMat` material to it:

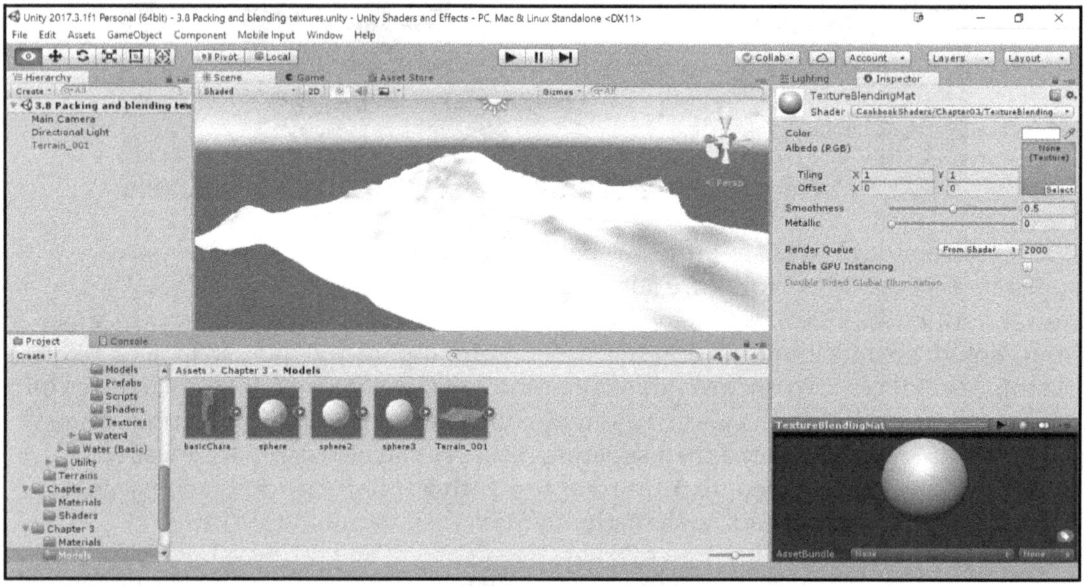

You will also need to gather up four textures that you would want to blend together. These can be anything, but for a nice terrain shader, you will want grass, dirt, rocky dirt, and rock textures. You can find these assets in `Chapter 1 | Standard Assets | Environment | TerrainAssets | SurfaceTextures` folder in the example code for this book.

Finally, we will also need a blending texture that is packed with grayscale images. This will give us the four blending textures that we can use to direct how the color textures will be placed on the object surface.

We can use very intricate blending textures to create a very realistic distribution of terrain textures over a terrain mesh, as shown in the following screenshot:

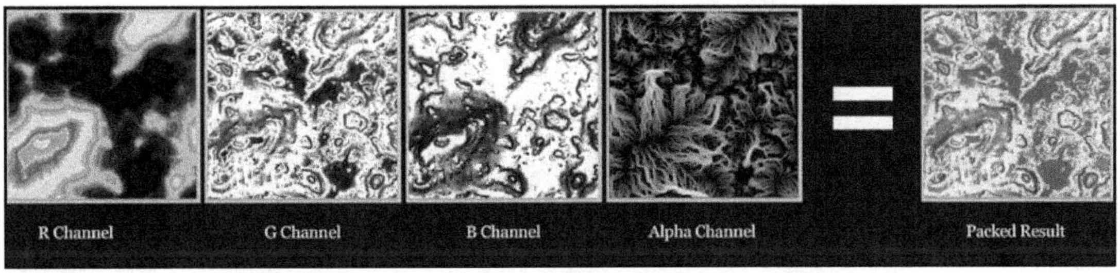

How to do it...

Let's learn how to use packed textures by entering the code shown in the following steps:

1. We need to add a few properties to our `Properties` block. We will need five `sampler2D` objects, or textures, and two `Color` properties:

```
Properties
{
 _MainTint ("Diffuse Tint", Color) = (1,1,1,1)
//Add the properties below so we can input all of our
   textures
  _ColorA ("Terrain Color A", Color) = (1,1,1,1)
  _ColorB ("Terrain Color B", Color) = (1,1,1,1)
  _RTexture ("Red Channel Texture", 2D) = ""{}
  _GTexture ("Green Channel Texture", 2D) = ""{}
  _BTexture ("Blue Channel Texture", 2D) = ""{}
  _ATexture ("Alpha Channel Texture", 2D) = ""{}
  _BlendTex ("Blend Texture", 2D) = ""{}
}
```

TIP: As always, remove the properties we are not using from the base shader from our code.

2. We then need to create the `SubShader{}` section variables that will be our link to the data in the `Properties` block:

```
CGPROGRAM
#pragma surface surf Lambert

// Use shader model 3.5 target, to support enough textures
#pragma target 3.5
float4 _MainTint;
float4 _ColorA;
float4 _ColorB;
sampler2D _RTexture;
sampler2D _GTexture;
sampler2D _BTexture;
sampler2D _BlendTex;
sampler2D _ATexture;
```

3. Due to the number of items inside of our shader, we will need to update the target level version of our shader model to `3.5`:

For more information on Shader Compilation Target Levels, check out: `https://docs.unity3d.com/Manual/SL-ShaderCompileTargets.html`.

4. So, now we have our texture properties and we are passing them to our `SubShader{}` function. In order to allow the user to change the tiling rates on a per-texture basis, we will need to modify our `Input` struct. This will allow us to use the tiling and offset parameters on each texture:

```
struct Input
{
  float2 uv_RTexture;
  float2 uv_GTexture;
  float2 uv_BTexture;
  float2 uv_ATexture;
  float2 uv_BlendTex;
};
```

5. In the `surf()` function, get the texture information and store it in its own variables so that we can work with the data in a clean, easy-to-understand way:

```
void surf (Input IN, inout SurfaceOutput o) {
  //Get the pixel data from the blend texture
  //we need a float 4 here because the texture
  //will return R,G,B,and A or X,Y,Z, and W
  float4 blendData = tex2D(_BlendTex, IN.uv_BlendTex);
  //Get the data from the textures we want to blend
  float4 rTexData = tex2D(_RTexture, IN.uv_RTexture);
  float4 gTexData = tex2D(_GTexture, IN.uv_GTexture);
  float4 bTexData = tex2D(_BTexture, IN.uv_BTexture);
  float4 aTexData = tex2D(_ATexture, IN.uv_ATexture);
```

TIP: Remember that due to us using Lambert, we will be using `SurfaceOutput` instead of `SurfaceOutputStandard` for the `surf` function.

6. Let's blend each of our textures together using the `lerp()` function. It takes three arguments, `lerp(value : a, value : b,` and `blend: c)`. The `lerp()` function takes in two textures and blends them with the float value given in the last argument:

```
//No we need to construct a new RGBA value and add all
//the different blended texture back together
float4 finalColor;
finalColor = lerp(rTexData, gTexData, blendData.g);
finalColor = lerp(finalColor, bTexData, blendData.b);
finalColor = lerp(finalColor, aTexData, blendData.a);
finalColor.a = 1.0;
```

7. Finally, we multiply our blended texture by the color tint values and use the red channel to determine where the two different terrain tint colors go:

```
  //Add on our terrain tinting colors
  float4 terrainLayers = lerp(_ColorA, _ColorB, blendData.r);
  finalColor *= terrainLayers;
  finalColor = saturate(finalColor);
  o.Albedo = finalColor.rgb * _MainTint.rgb;
  o.Alpha = finalColor.a;
}
```

8. Save your script and go back into Unity. Once there, you can assign the `TerrainBlend` texture to the **Blend Texture** property. Once you've done that, place different textures in the different channels in order to see our script in action:

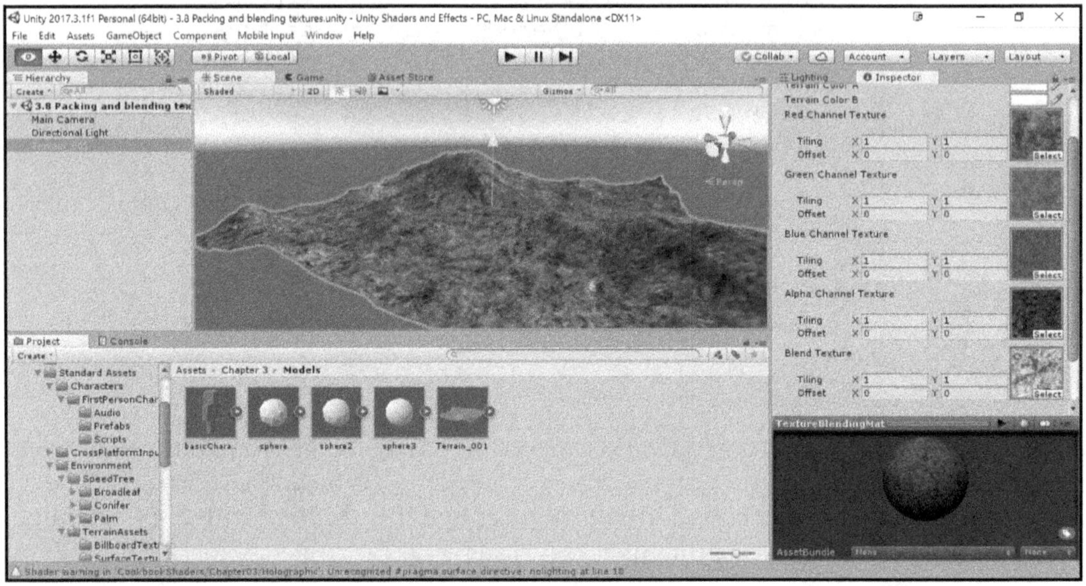

9. This effect can be taken even further by using different textures and terrain tinting to create some great looking terrains with minimal effort. The result of blending together four terrain textures and creating a terrain tinting technique can be seen in the following screenshot:

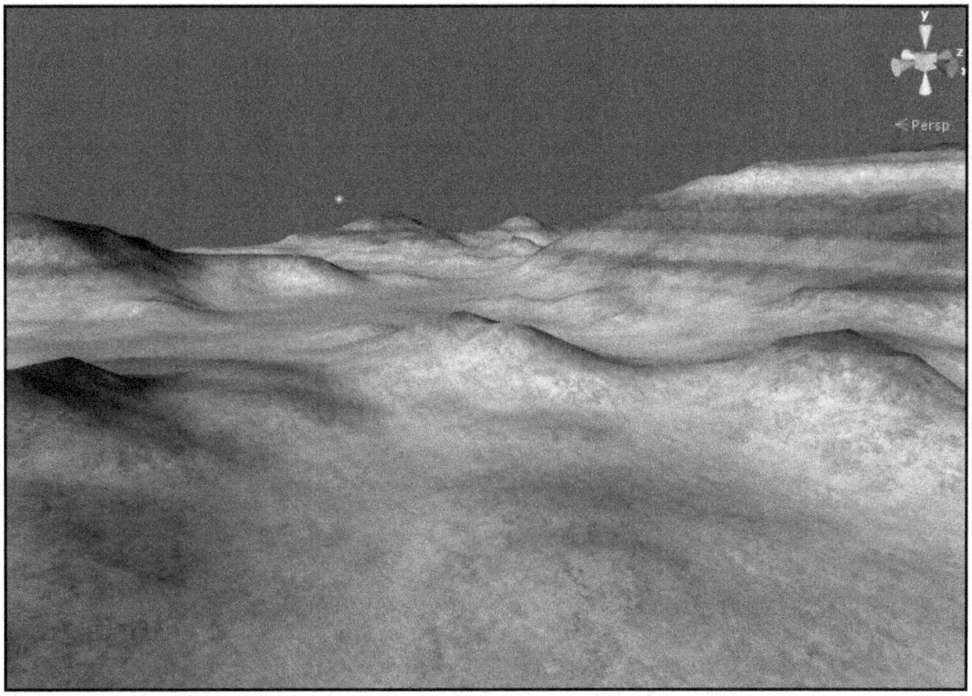

How it works...

This might seem like quite a few lines of code, but the concept behind blending is actually quite simple. For the technique to work, we have to employ the built-in `lerp()` function from the `CgFX` standard library. This function allows us to pick a value between argument one and argument two using argument three as the blend amount:

Function	Description
`lerp(a, b, f )`	This involves linear interpolation: $(1 - f)^{*} a + b * f$ Here, `a` and `b` are matching vector or scalar types. The `f` parameter can be either a scalar or vector of the same type as `a` and `b`.

So, for example, if we wanted to find the mid-value between `1` and `2`, we could feed the value `0.5` as the third argument to the `lerp()` function and it would return the value `1.5`. This works perfectly for our blending needs as the values of an individual channel in an RGBA texture are single float values, usually in the range of `0` to `1`.

In the shader, we simply take one of the channels from our **Blend Texture** and use it to drive the color that is picked in a `lerp()` function for each pixel. For instance, we take our grass texture and dirt texture, use the red channel from our blending texture, and feed this to a `lerp()` function. This will give us the correct blended color result for each pixel on the surface.

A more visual representation of what is happening when using the `lerp()` function is shown in the following diagram:

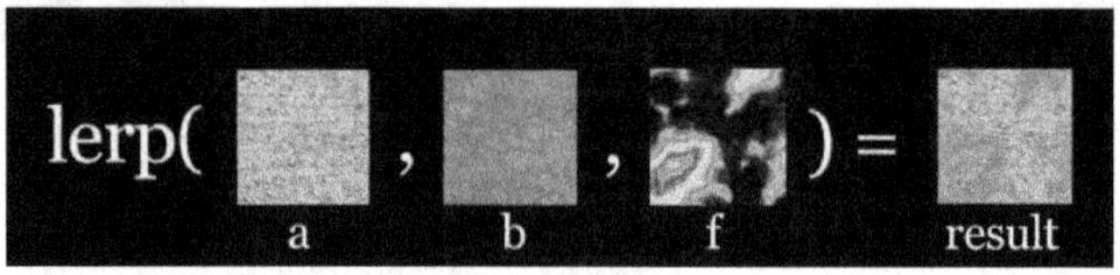

The shader code simply uses the four channels of the **Blend Texture** and all the color textures to create a final **Blended Texture**. This final texture then becomes the color that we can multiply with our diffuse lighting.

Creating a circle around your terrain

Many RTS games display distances (range attack, moving distance, sight, and so on) by drawing a circle around the selected unit. If the terrain is flat, this can be done simply by stretching a quad with the texture of a circle. If that's not the case, the quad will most likely be clipped behind a hill or another piece of geometry. This recipe will show you how to create a shader that allows you to draw circles around an object of arbitrary complexity. If you want to be able to move or animate your circle, we will need both a shader and C# script.

The following screenshot shows an example of drawing a circle in a hilly region using a shader:

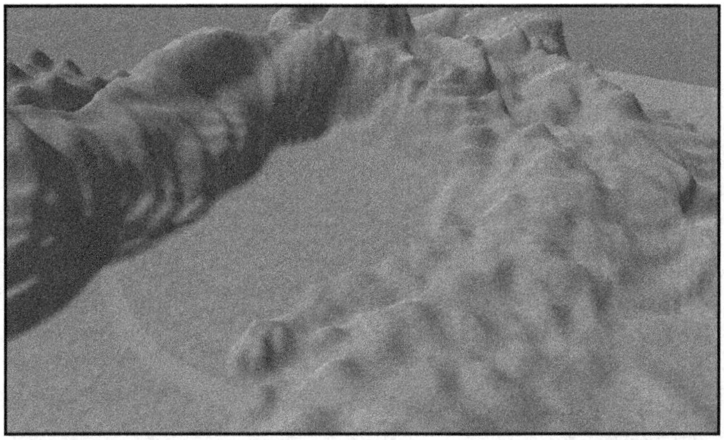

Getting ready

Despite working with every piece of geometry, this technique is oriented to terrains. Hence, the first step is setting up a terrain in Unity, but instead of using a model, we will create one within the Unity editor:

1. Let's start by creating a new shader called `RadiusShader` and the respective material, `RadiusMat`.
2. Have the character for your object ready; we will draw a circle around it.
3. From the menu, navigate to **GameObject** | **3D Object** | **Terrain** to create a new terrain.
4. Create the geometry for your terrain. You can either import an existing one or draw your own using the tools available (**Raise/Lower Terrain**, **Paint Height**, **Smooth Height**).

5. The terrains are special objects in Unity, and the way texture mapping works on them is different from traditional 3D models. You cannot provide `_MainTex` from a shader as it needs to be provided directly from the terrain itself. To do this, select **Paint Texture** and then click on **Add Texture...**:

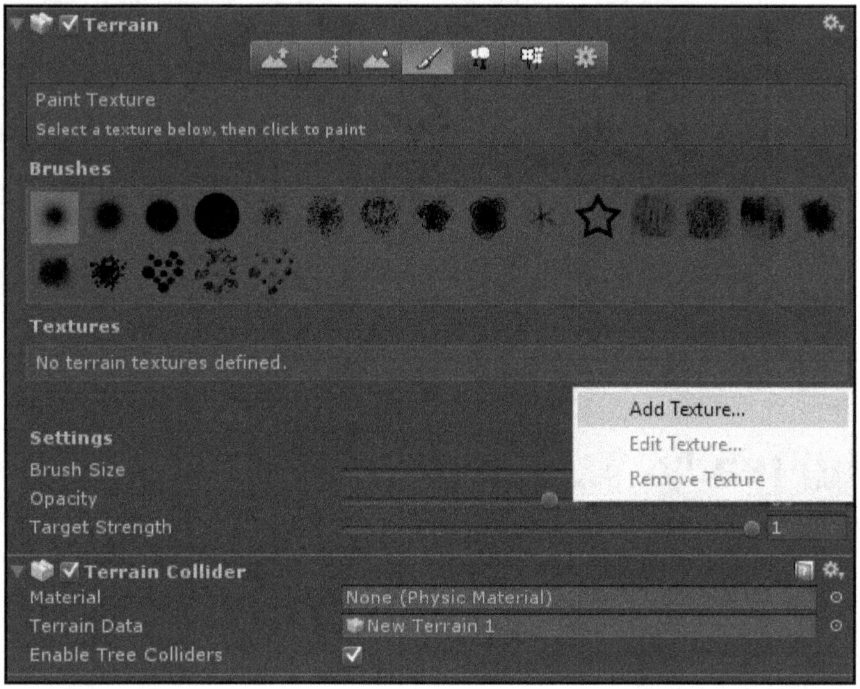

The creation of a terrain isn't covered in this book, but if you would like to learn more about it, check out the following link: `https://docs.unity3d.com/Manual/terrain-UsingTerrains.html`

6. Now that the texture is set, you have to change the material of the terrain so that a custom shader can be provided. From **Terrain Settings**, change the **Material** property to `Custom`, and then drag the **Radius** material to the `Custom Material` box:

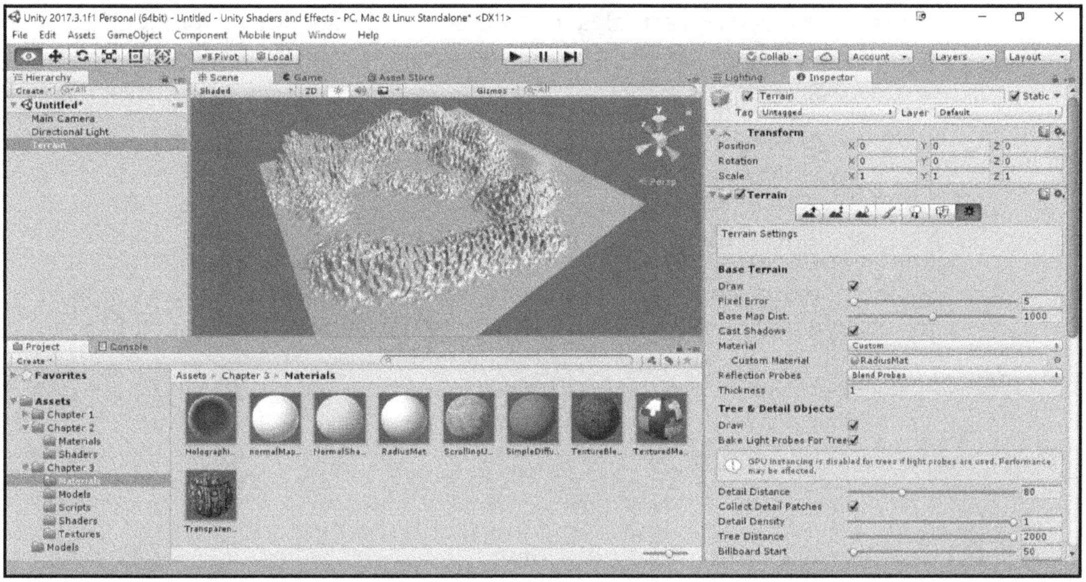

You are now ready to create your shader.

How to do it...

Let's start by editing the `RadiusShader` file:

1. In the new shader, remove the `_Glossiness` and `_Metallic` properties and add these four properties:

```
_Center("Center", Vector) = (200,0,200,0)
_Radius("Radius", Float) = 100
_RadiusColor("Radius Color", Color) = (1,0,0,1)
_RadiusWidth("Radius Width", Float) = 10
```

2. Add their respective variables to the `CGPROGRAM` section, remembering to remove the declaration of `_Glossiness` and `_Metallic`:

```
float3 _Center;
float _Radius;
fixed4 _RadiusColor;
float _RadiusWidth;
```

3. `Input` to our surface function requires not only the UV of the texture but also the position (in world coordinates) of every point of the terrain. We can retrieve this parameter by changing the `struct Input` as follows:

```
struct Input
{
  float2 uv_MainTex; // The UV of the terrain texture
  float3 worldPos;   // The in-world position
};
```

4. Lastly, we use this surface function:

```
void surf(Input IN, inout SurfaceOutputStandard o)
{
  // Get the distance between the center of the
  // place we wish to draw from and the input's
  // world position
  float d = distance(_Center, IN.worldPos);

  // If the distance is larger than the radius and
  // it is less than our radius + width change the color
  if ((d > _Radius) && (d < (_Radius + _RadiusWidth)))
  {
    o.Albedo = _RadiusColor;
  }
  // Otherwise, use the normal color
  else
  {
    o.Albedo = tex2D(_MainTex, IN.uv_MainTex).rgb;
  }
}
```

These steps are all it takes to draw a circle on your terrain. You can use the material's Inspector tab to change the position, radius, and color of the circle:

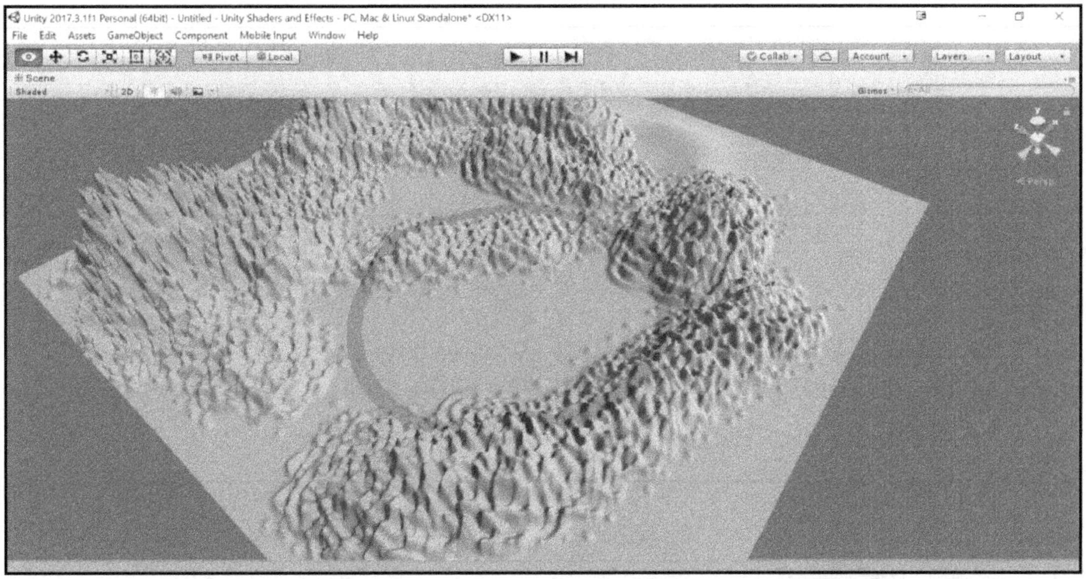

Moving the circle

This is great, but you'll likely also want to change where the circle is at run-time, which we can do via code. If you want the circle to follow your character, other steps are necessary:

1. Create a new C# script called `SetRadiusProperties`.
2. Since you may wish to see this change both in the game and outside, we can add a tag to the top of the class saying to execute this code while in the editor, in addition to when the game is being played, by adding the following tag:

```
[ExecuteInEditMode]
public class SetRadiusProperties : MonoBehaviour
```

3. Add these properties to the script:

```
public Material radiusMaterial;
public float radius = 1;
public Color color = Color.white;
```

4. In the `Update()` method, add these lines of code:

```
if(radiusMaterial != null)
{
    radiusMaterial.SetVector("_Center", transform.position);
    radiusMaterial.SetFloat("_Radius", radius);
    radiusMaterial.SetColor("_RadiusColor", color);
}
```

5. Attach the script to the object you wish to have the circle drawn around.
6. Finally, drag the `RadiusMat` material to the **Radius Material** slot of the script:

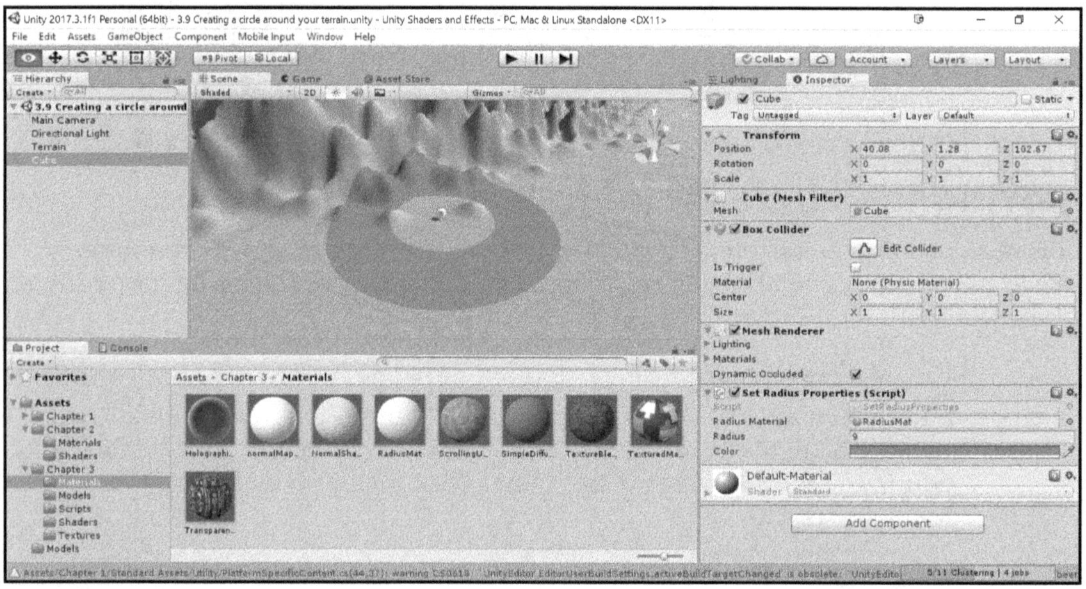

You can now move your character around and this will create a nice circle around it. Changing the properties of the `Radius` script will change the radius as well.

How it works...

The relevant parameters to draw a circle are its center, radius, and color. They are all available in the shader with the names `_Center`, `_Radius`, and `_RadiusColor`. By adding the `worldPos` variable to the `Input` structure, we are asking Unity to provide us with the position of the pixel that we are drawing expressed in world coordinates. This is the actual position of an object in the editor.

The `surf()` function is where the circle is actually drawn. It calculates the distance from the point being drawn and the center of the radius, and then it checks whether it is between `_Radius` and `_Radius + _RadiusWidth`; if this is the case, it uses the chosen color. In the other case, it just samples the texture map like all the other shaders we have seen so far.

6 Understanding Lighting Models

In the previous chapters, we introduced Surface Shaders and explained how we can change physical properties (such as Albedo and Specular) to simulate different materials. How does this really work? At the heart of every Surface Shader, there is its **lighting model**. It's the function that takes these properties and calculates the final shade of each pixel. Unity usually hides this from the developers because in order to write a lighting model, you have to understand how light reflects and refracts onto surfaces. This chapter will finally show you how lighting models work and give you the basics to create your own.

In this chapter, you will learn the following recipes:

- Creating a custom diffuse lighting model
- Creating a toon shader
- Creating a Phong Specular type
- Creating a BlinnPhong Specular type
- Creating an Anisotropic Specular type

Introduction

Simulating the way light works is a very challenging and resource-consuming task. For many years, video games have used very simple lighting models which, despite lacking realism, were very believable. Even if most 3D engines are now using physically-based renderers, it is worth exploring some simpler techniques. The ones presented in this chapter are reasonably realistic and widely adopted on devices with low resources such as mobile phones. Understanding these simple lighting models is also essential if you want to create your own.

Creating a custom diffuse lighting model

If you are familiar with Unity 4, you may know that the default shader it provided was based on a lighting model called **Lambertian reflectance**. This recipe will show you how it is possible to create a shader with a custom lighting model and explains the mathematics involved and implementation. The following diagram shows the same geometry rendered with a Standard Shader (right) and a diffuse Lambert one (left):

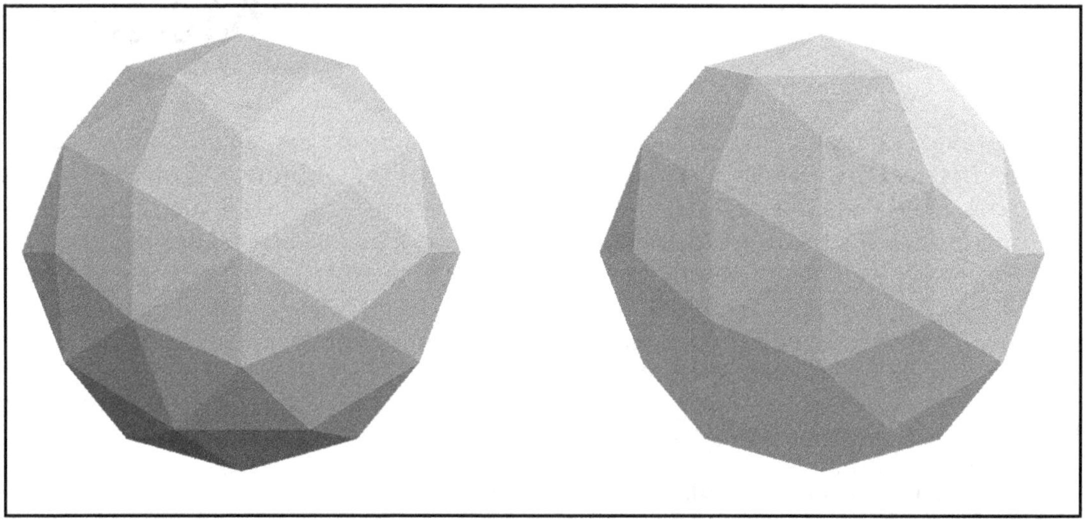

Shaders based on Lambertian reflectance are classified as non-photorealistic; no object in the real world really looks like this. However, Lambert Shaders are still often used in low-poly games as they produce a neat contrast between the faces of complex geometries. The lighting model used to calculate the Lambertian reflectance is also very efficient, making it perfect for mobile games.

Unity has already provided us with a lighting function that we can use for our shaders. It is called the Lambertian lighting model. It is one of the more basic and efficient forms of reflectance, which you can find in a lot of games even today. As it is already built in the Unity Surface Shader language, we thought it best to start with this first and build on it. You can also find an example in the Unity reference manual, but we will go into more depth and explain where the data is coming from and why it is working the way it is. This will help you get a nice grounding in setting up custom lighting models so that we can build on this knowledge in the future recipes in this chapter.

Getting ready

Let's start by carrying out the following steps:

1. Create a new shader and give it a name (`SimpleLambert`).
2. Create a new material, give it a name (`SimpleLambertMat`), and assign the new shader to its `shader` property.
3. Then, create a sphere object and place it roughly in the center of the scene and attach the new material to it.
4. Finally, let's create a directional light to cast some light on our object if one isn't created already.
5. When your assets have been set up in Unity, you should have a scene that resembles the following screenshot:

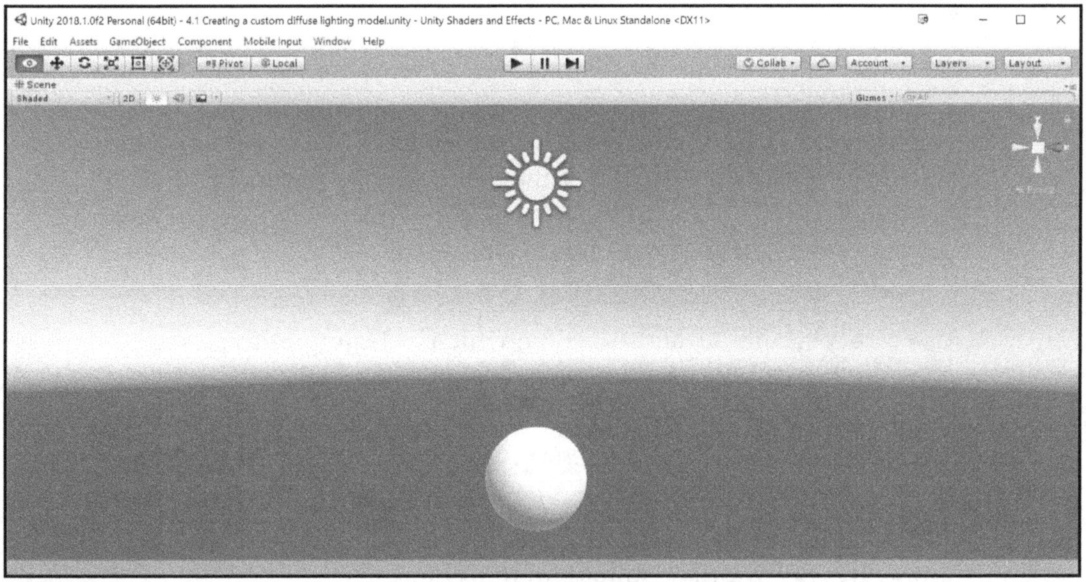

How to do it...

The Lambertian reflectance can be achieved with the following changes to the shader:

1. Begin by replacing the shader's `Properties` block with the following :

```
Properties
{
  _MainTex("Texture", 2D) = "white"
}
```

2. Since we are removing all of the other properties, remove the `_Glossiness`, `_Metallic`, and `_Color` declarations inside of the `SubShader` section.
3. Change the `#pragma` directive of the shader so that, instead of `Standard`, it uses our custom lighting model:

```
#pragma surface surf SimpleLambert
```

If you try to run the script now, it will complain that it doesn't know what the `SimpleLambert` lighting model is. We will need to create a function called `Lighting` + the name that we gave here with instructions on how to light the object, which we will be writing later on in this recipe. In this case, it would be `LightingSimpleLambert`.

4. Use a very simple surface function, which just samples the texture according to its UV data:

```
void surf(Input IN, inout SurfaceOutput o) {
  o.Albedo = tex2D(_MainTex, IN.uv_MainTex).rgb;
}
```

5. Add a function called `LightingSimpleLambert()` that will contain the following code for the Lambertian reflectance:

```
// Allows us to use the SimpleLambert lighting mode
half4 LightingSimpleLambert (SurfaceOutput s, half3 lightDir,
                             half atten)
{
  // First calculate the dot product of the light direction
and the
  // surface's normal
  half NdotL = dot(s.Normal, lightDir);

  // Next, set what color should be returned
```

```
    half4 color;

    color.rgb = s.Albedo * _LightColor0.rgb * (NdotL * atten);
    color.a = s.Alpha;

    // Return the calculated color
    return color;
}
```

6. Save your script and return to the Unity editor. You should notice that it looks somewhat different than what was there before:

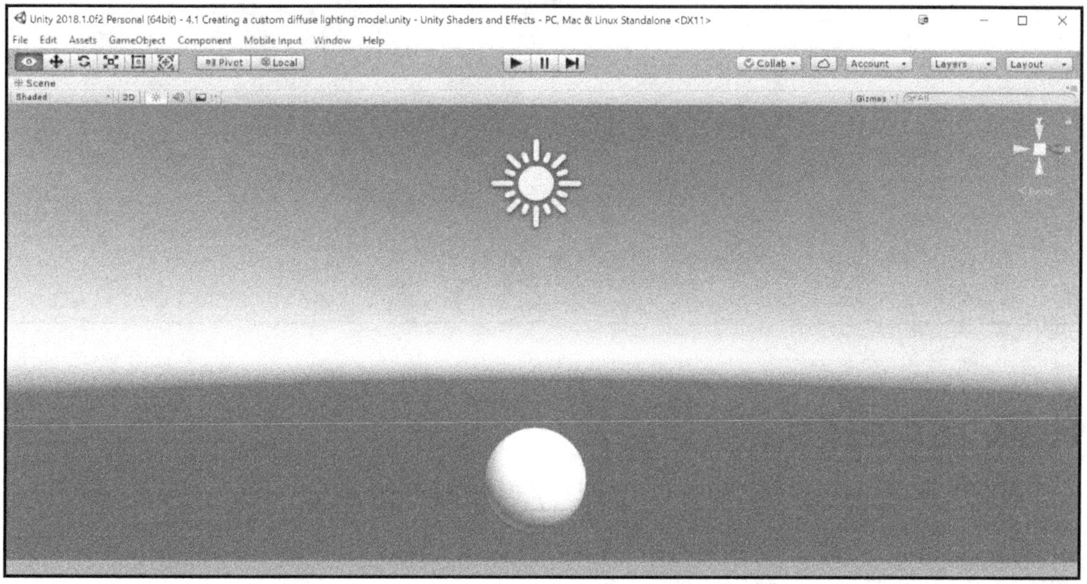

7. The effect is even easier to see if we use the cylinders we used in the previous chapter, `Chapter 5`, *Surface Shaders and Texture Mapping*:

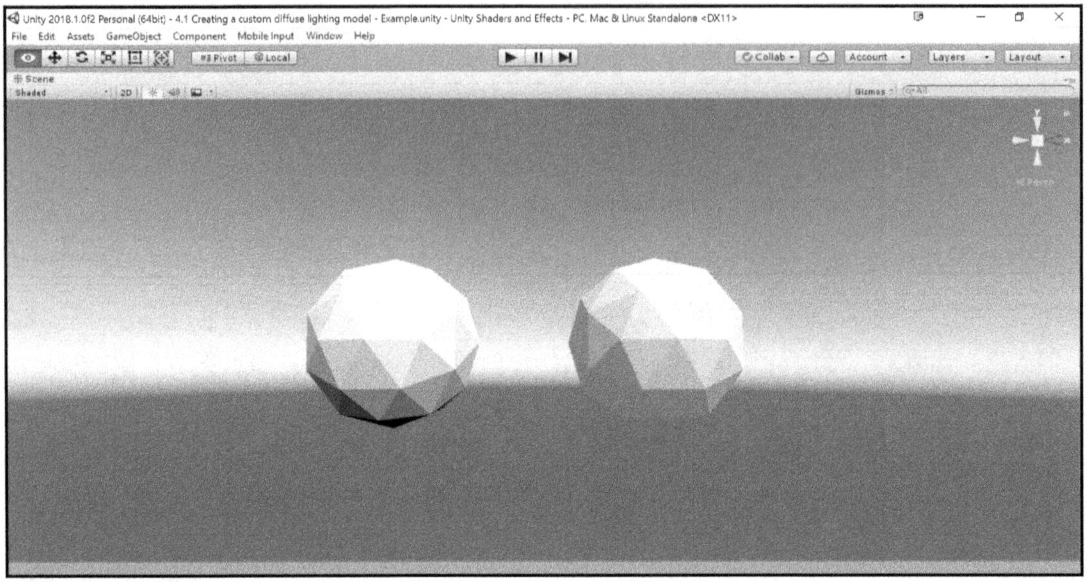

How it works...

As previously seen in `Chapter 4`, *Creating Your First Shader*, the `#pragma` directive is used to specify which surface function to use. Choosing a different lighting model works in a similar fashion: `SimpleLambert` forces Cg to look for a function called `LightingSimpleLambert()`. Note the `Lighting` at the beginning, which is omitted in the directive.

The `Lighting` function takes three parameters: the *surface output* (which contains the physical properties such as the albedo and transparency), the *direction* the light is coming from, and its *attenuation*.

According to Lambertian reflectance, the amount of light a surface reflects depends on the angle between the incident light and surface normal. If you have played pool billiards, you are surely familiar with this concept; the direction of a ball depends on its incident angle against the wall. If you hit a wall at a 90 degree angle, the ball will come back at you; if you hit it with a very low angle, its direction will be mostly unchanged. The Lambertian model makes the same assumption; if the light hits a triangle at a 90 degree angle, all the light gets reflected back. The lower the angle, the less light is reflected back to you. This concept is shown in the following diagram:

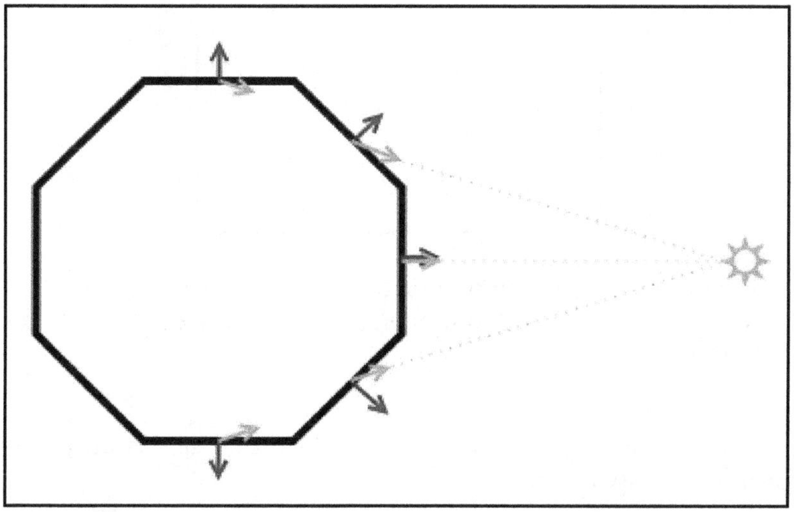

This simple concept has to be translated into a mathematical form. In vector algebra, the angle between two unit vectors can be calculated via an operator called **dot product**. When the dot product is equal to zero, two vectors are orthogonal, which means that they make a 90-degree angle. When it is equal to one (or minus one), they are parallel to each other. Cg has a function called `dot()`, which implements the dot product extremely efficiently.

The following diagram shows a light source (sun) shining on a complex surface. **L** indicates the light direction (called `lightDir` in the shader) and **N** is the normal to the surface. The light is reflected with the same angle that it hits the surface with:

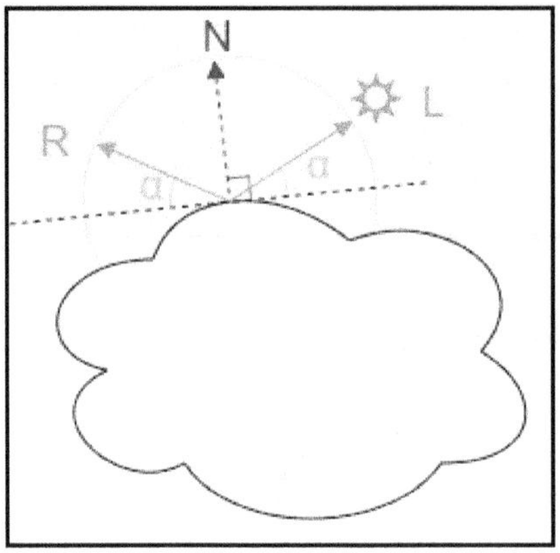

For more information on normals and what they mean mathematically check out: https://en.wikipedia.org/wiki/Normal_(geometry)

Lambertian reflectance simply uses the `NdotL` dot product as a multiplicative coefficient for the intensity of light:

$$I = N \cdot L$$

When *N* and *L* are parallel, all the light is reflected back to the source, causing the geometry to appear brighter. The `_LightColor0` variable contains the color of the light that is calculated.

Prior to Unity 5, the intensity of the lights was different. If you are using an old diffuse shader based on the Lambertian model, you may notice that `NdotL` is multiplied by two: `(NdotL * atten * 2)`, rather than `(NdotL * atten)`. If you are importing a custom shader from Unity 4, you will need to correct this manually. Legacy Shaders, however, have already been designed taking this aspect into account.

When the dot product is negative, the light is coming from the opposite side of the triangle. This is not a problem for opaque geometries as triangles that are not facing the camera frontally are culled (discarded) and not rendered.

This basic Lambert is a great starting point when you are prototyping your shaders as you can get a lot accomplished in terms of writing the core functionality of the shader while not having to worry about the basic `Lighting` functions.

Unity has provided us with a lighting model that has already taken the task of creating a Lambert lighting for you. If you look at the `UnityCG.cginc` file found in your Unity's installation directory under the `Data` folder, you will notice that you have Lambert and BlinnPhong lighting models available for you to use. The moment you compile your shader with `#pragma surface surf Lambert`, you are telling the shader to utilize Unity's implementation of the Lambert `Lighting` function in the `UnityCG.cginc` file so that you don't have to write that code over and over again. We will explore how the BlinnPhong model works later in this chapter.

Creating a toon shader

One of the most used effects in games is **toon shading**, which is also known as **celluloid** (**CEL**) shading. It is a non-photorealistic rendering technique that makes 3D models appear flat. Many games use it to give the illusion that the graphics are being hand-drawn rather than being 3D modeled. You can see, in the following diagram, a sphere rendered with a toon Shader (left) and a Standard Shader (right):

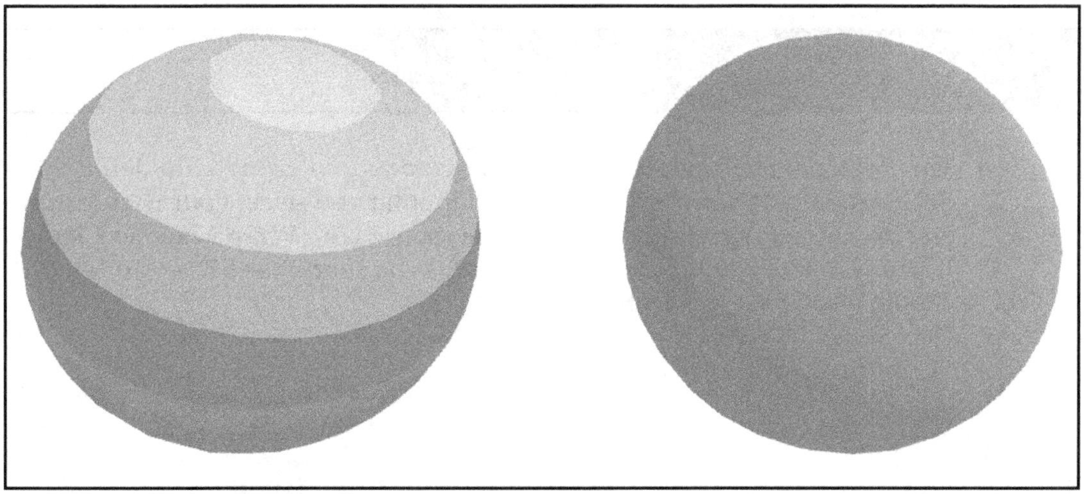

Achieving this effect using just surface functions is not impossible, but it would be extremely expensive and time consuming. The surface function, in fact, only works on the properties of the material, not its actual lighting condition. As toon shading requires us to change the way light reflects, we need to create our custom lighting model instead.

Getting ready

Let's start this recipe by creating a shader and its material and importing a special texture, as follows:

1. Start by creating a new shader; in this example, we will duplicate the one made in the previous recipe by selecting it in the **Project** tab and then hit *Ctrl* + *D*. We will change the name of this new `shader` to `ToonShader`.

> TIP: You can rename an object in the **Project** window by single-clicking on the name.

2. Create a new material for the shader (`ToonShaderMat`) and attach it to a 3D model. Toon shading works best on curved surfaces.
3. This recipe requires an additional texture called a **ramp map**, which will be used to dictate when we want to use certain colors depending on the shade received:

4. This book has an example texture in `Chapter 4 | Textures` folder. If you decide to import your own, it is important that you select your next texture and, from the **Inspector** tab, change the ramp map's **Wrap Mode** to **Clamp**. If you want the edges between the colors to be sharp, the **Filter Mode** should also be set to **Point**:

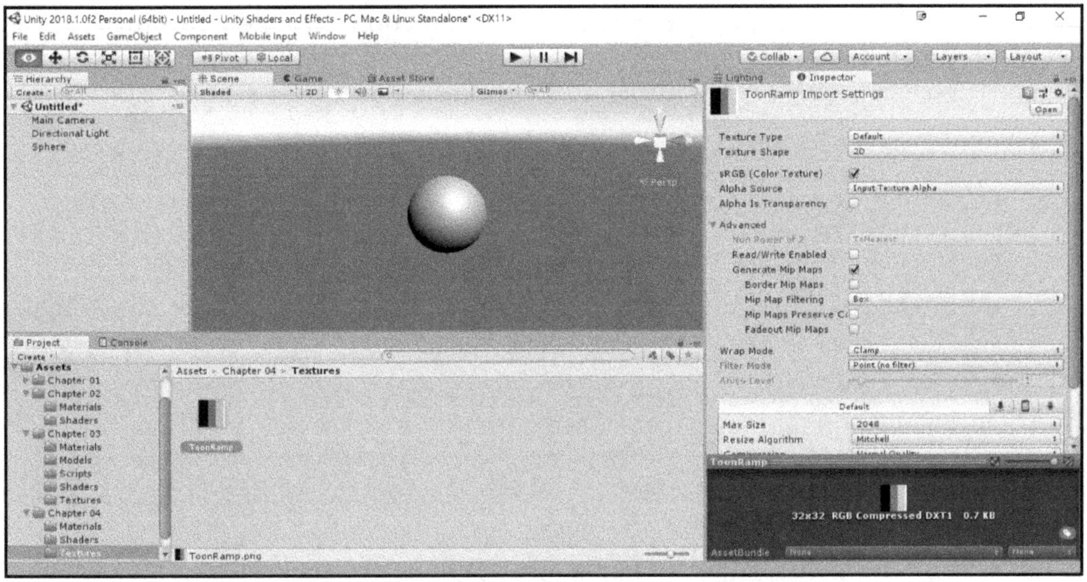

The example project included with this book already has this step completed in the `Assets | Chapter 4 | Texture | ToonRamp` file, but it is a good idea to verify that this is the case before moving forward.

How to do it...

The toon aesthetic can be achieved with the following changes to the shader:

1. Add a new property for a texture called `_RampTex`:

```
_RampTex ("Ramp", 2D) = "white" {}
```

2. Add its relative variable in the `CGPROGRAM` section:

```
sampler2D _RampTex;
```

3. Change the `#pragma` directive so that it points to a function called `LightingToon()`:

```
#pragma surface surf Toon
```

4. Replace the `LightingSimpleLambert` function with the following function instead:

```
fixed4 LightingToon (SurfaceOutput s, fixed3 lightDir,
            fixed atten)
{
  // First calculate the dot product of the light direction
and the
  // surface's normal
  half NdotL = dot(s.Normal, lightDir);
  // Remap NdotL to the value on the ramp map
  NdotL = tex2D(_RampTex, fixed2(NdotL, 0.5));

  // Next, set what color should be returned
  half4 color;

  color.rgb = s.Albedo * _LightColor0.rgb * (NdotL * atten );
  color.a = s.Alpha;

  // Return the calculated color
  return color;
}
```

5. Save the script, open up the `ToonShaderMat`, and assign the `Ramp` property to your ramp map. If all goes well, you should see something like the following in your scene:

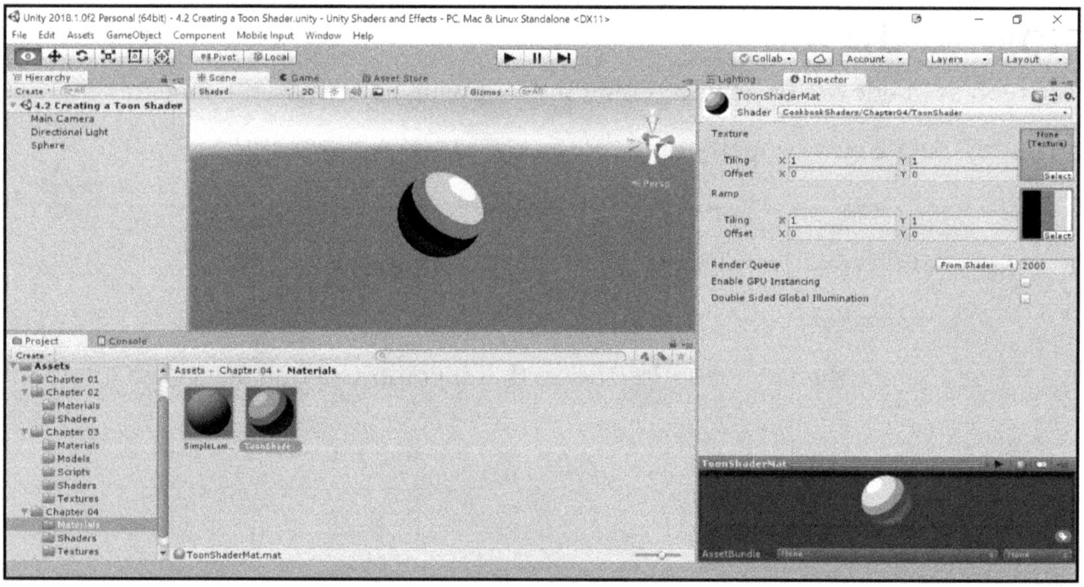

This effect may be modified by the lighting in the scene. You can change the illumination of the scene by going to **Window** | **Lighting** | **Settings** and changing the **Environment** | **Environment Lighting** | **Intensity Multiplier** property to `0`.

How it works...

The main characteristic of toon shading is the way the light is rendered; surfaces are not shaded uniformly. To achieve this effect, we need a ramp map. Its purpose is to remap the Lambertian light intensity `NdotL` to another value. Using a ramp map without a gradient, we can force the lighting to be rendered in steps. The following diagram shows how the ramp map is used to correct the light intensity:

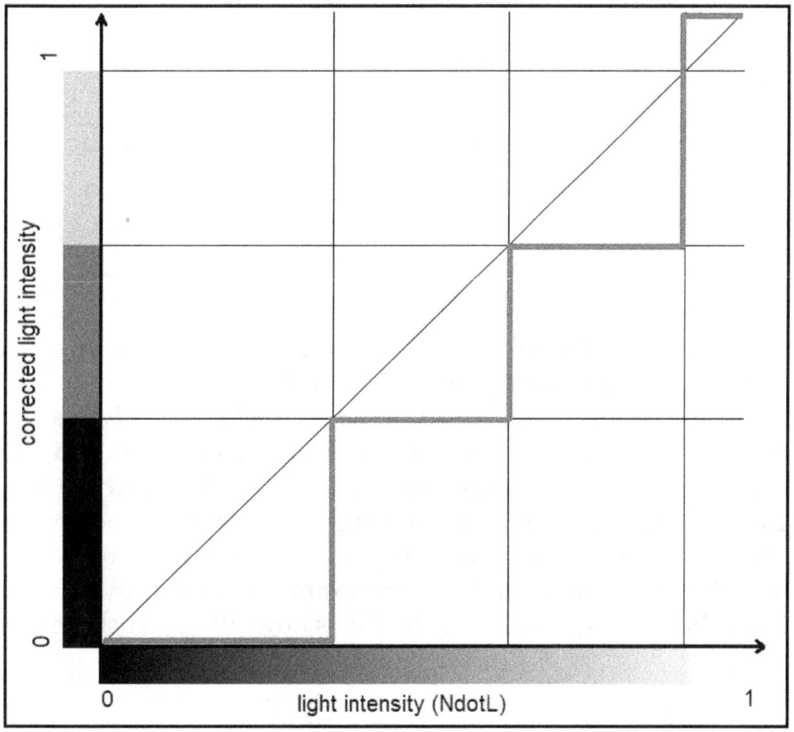

There's more...

There are many different ways whereby you can achieve a toon shading effect. Using different ramps can produce dramatic changes in the way your models look, so you should experiment in order to find the best one.

An alternative to ramp textures is to **snap** the light intensity `NdotL` so that it can only assume a certain number of values equidistantly sampled from `0` to `1`:

```
half4 LightingCustomLambert (SurfaceOutput s, half3 lightDir,
               half3 viewDir, half atten)
{
  half NdotL = dot (s.Normal, lightDir);

  // Snap instead
  half cel = floor(NdotL * _CelShadingLevels) /
           (_CelShadingLevels - 0.5);

  // Next, set what color should be returned
  half4 color;

  color.rgb = s.Albedo * _LightColor0.rgb * (cel * atten );
  color.a = s.Alpha;

  // Return the calculated color
  return color;
}
```

To snap a number we first multiply `NdotL` by the `_CelShadingLevels` variable, round the result to an integer through the `floor` function, and then divides it back. This rounding is done by the `floor` function which will effectively remove the decimal point from a number. By doing this, the `cel` quantity is forced to assume one of the `_CelShadingLevels` equidistant values from `0` to `1`. This removes the need for a ramp texture and makes all the color steps of the same size. If you are going for this implementation, remember to add a property called `_CelShadingLevels` to your shader. You can find an example of this in the example code for this chapter. Try dragging the **Levels** property to see how it affects how the screenshot is shown:

Creating a Phong Specular type

The specularity of an object surface simply describes how shiny it is. These types of effects are often referred to as view-dependent effects in the shader world. This is because, in order to achieve a realistic Specular effect in your shaders, you need to include the direction of the camera or the user facing the object's surface. The most basic and performance-friendly Specular type is the Phong Specular effect. It is the calculation of the light direction reflecting off of the surface compared to the user's view direction. It is a very common Specular model used in many applications, from games to movies. While it isn't the most realistic in terms of accurately modeling the reflected Specular, it gives a great approximation of what is expected of shininess that performs well in most situations. Additionally, if your object is further away from the camera and there is no need for a very accurate Specular, this is a great way to provide a Specular effect to your shaders.

In this recipe, we will be covering how to implement the per-vertex version of the shader and also the per-pixel version using some new parameters in the Surface Shader's `Input` struct. We will see the difference and discuss when and why to use these two different implementations for different situations.

Getting ready

To start with this recipe, perform the following steps:

1. Create a new shader (`Phong`), material(`PhongMat`), and a new scene with a sphere in it with a **Plane** underneath it (**GameObject | 3D Objects | Plane**).
2. Attach the shader to the material and the material to the object. To finish off your new scene, create a new directional light if one is not there already, so that you can see your Specular effect as you code it:

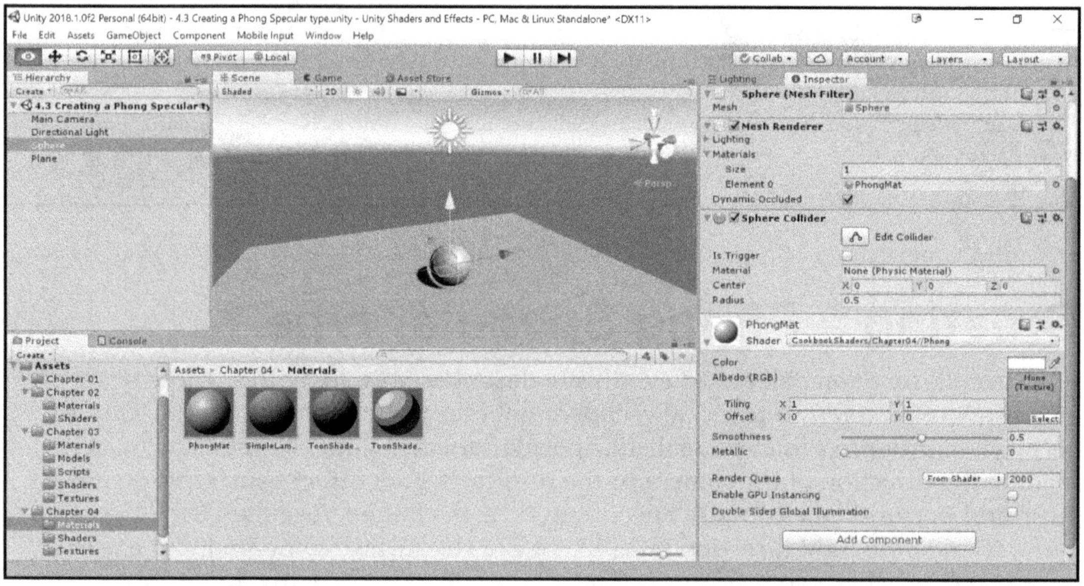

How to do it...

Follow these steps to create a Phong lighting model:

1. You might be seeing a pattern at this point, but we always like to start out with our most basic part of the shader writing process: the creation of properties. So, let's remove all of the current properties with their definitions in the `SubShader` block and then add the following properties to the shader:

```
Properties
```

```
{
  _MainTint ("Diffuse Tint", Color) = (1,1,1,1)
  _MainTex ("Base (RGB)", 2D) = "white" {}
  _SpecularColor ("Specular Color", Color) = (1,1,1,1)
  _SpecPower ("Specular Power", Range(0,30)) = 1
}
```

2. We then have to make sure to add the corresponding variables to our `CGPROGRAM` block in our `SubShader{}` block:

```
float4 _SpecularColor;
sampler2D _MainTex;
float4 _MainTint;
float _SpecPower;
```

3. Now, we have to add our custom lighting model so that we can compute our own Phong Specular. Don't worry if it doesn't make sense at this point; we will cover each line of code in the *How it works...* section of this recipe. Add the following code to the shader's `SubShader{}` function:

```
fixed4 LightingPhong (SurfaceOutput s, fixed3 lightDir,
                      half3 viewDir, fixed atten)
{
  // Reflection
  float NdotL = dot(s.Normal, lightDir);
  float3 reflectionVector = normalize(2.0 * s.Normal *
     NdotL - lightDir);

  // Specular
  float spec = pow(max(0, dot(reflectionVector, viewDir)),
     _SpecPower);
  float3 finalSpec = _SpecularColor.rgb * spec;

  // Final effect
  fixed4 c;
  c.rgb = (s.Albedo * _LightColor0.rgb * max(0,NdotL) *
     atten) + (_LightColor0.rgb * finalSpec);
  c.a = s.Alpha;
  return c;
}
```

4. Next, we have to tell the `CGPROGRAM` block that it needs to use our custom Lighting function instead of one of the built-in ones. We do this by changing the `#pragma` statement to the following:

```
CGPROGRAM
#pragma surface surf Phong
```

5. Finally, let's update the `surf` function to the following:

```
void surf (Input IN, inout SurfaceOutput o)
{
 half4 c = tex2D (_MainTex, IN.uv_MainTex) * _MainTint;
 o.Albedo = c.rgb;
 o.Alpha = c.a;
}
```

6. The following screenshot demonstrates the result of our custom Phong lighting model using our own custom reflection vector:

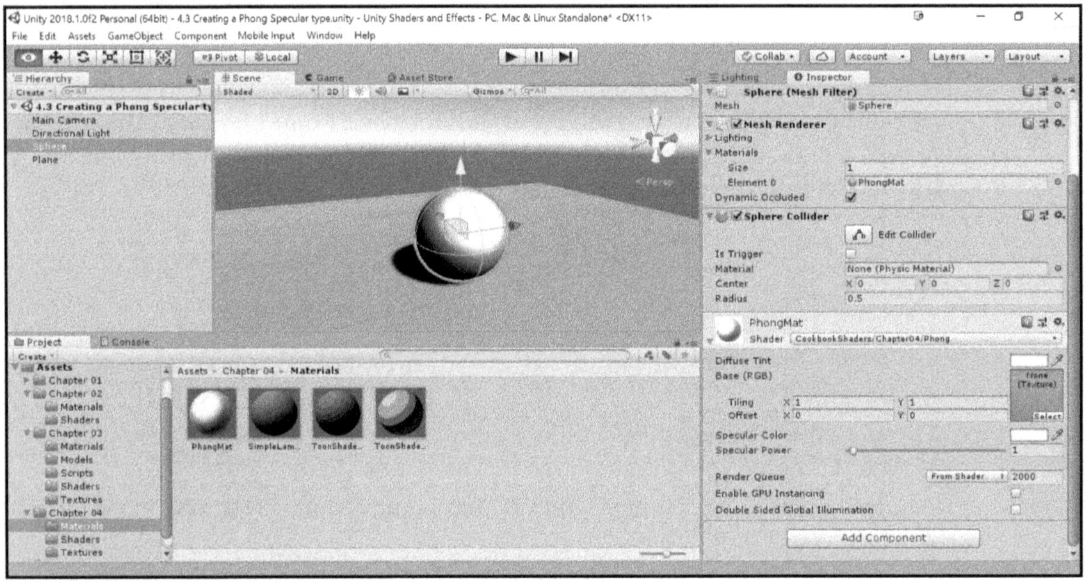

Try changing the **Specular Power** property and notice the effect that you see.

How it works...

Let's break down the Lighting function by itself, as the rest of the shader should be pretty familiar to you at this point.

In the previous recipes, we have used a Lighting function that provided only the light direction, `lightDir`.

Unity comes with a set of Lighting functions that you can use, including one that provides the view direction, `viewDir`.

To figure out how to write your own custom lighting mode refer to the following table replacing NameYouChoose with the lighting function name you gave in the `#pragma` statement or go to `http://docs.unity3d.com/Documentation/Components/SL-SurfaceShaderLighting.html` for more details:

Not view-dependent	`half4 LightingNameYouChoose (SurfaceOutput s, half3 lightDir, half atten);`
View-dependent	`half4 LightingNameYouChoose (SurfaceOutput s, half3 lightDir, half3 viewDir, half atten);`

In our case, we are using a Specular shader, so we need to have the view-dependent `Lighting` function structure. We have to write the following:

```
CPROGRAM
#pragma surface surf Phong
fixed4 LightingPhong (SurfaceOutput s, fixed3 lightDir, half3 viewDir,
fixed atten)
{
  // ...
}
```

This will tell the shader that we want to create our own view-dependent shader. Always make sure that your Lighting function name is the same in your `Lighting` function declaration and the `#pragma` statement, or Unity will not be able to find your lighting model.

The components that play a role in the `Phong` model are described in the following image. We have the light direction **L** (coupled with its perfect reflection **R**) and normal direction **N**. They have all been encountered before in the Lambertian model, with the exception of **V**, which is the **view direction**:

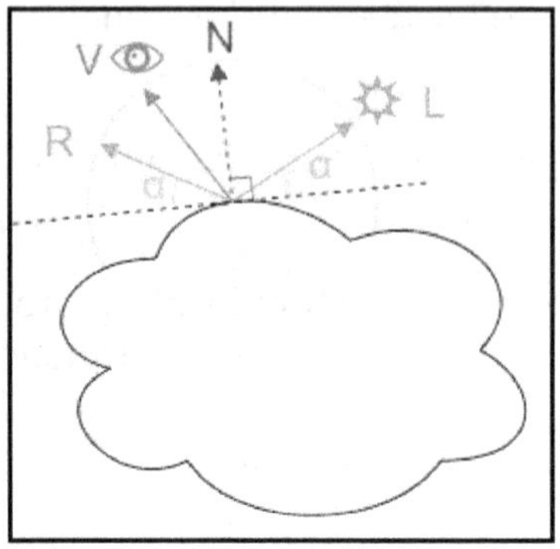

The `Phong` model assumes that the final light intensity of a reflective surface is given by two components, its diffuse color, and Specular value, as follows:

$$I = D + S$$

The diffuse component *D* remains unchanged from the Lambertian model:

$$D = N \cdot L$$

The Specular component *S* is defined as follows:

$$S = (R \cdot V)^p$$

Here, *p* is the Specular power defined as `_SpecPower` in the shader. The only unknown parameter is *R*, which is the reflection of *L* according to *N*. In vector algebra, this can be calculated as follows:

$$R = 2N \cdot (N \cdot L) - L$$

This is exactly what is calculated in the following:

```
float3 reflectionVector = normalize(2.0 * s.Normal * NdotL -
                                    lightDir);
```

This has the effect of bending the normal towards the light; as a vertex, normal is pointing away from the light, it is forced to look at the light. Refer to the following diagram for a more visual representation. The script that produces this debug effect is included in this book's support page at `https://www.packtpub.com/books/content/support`:

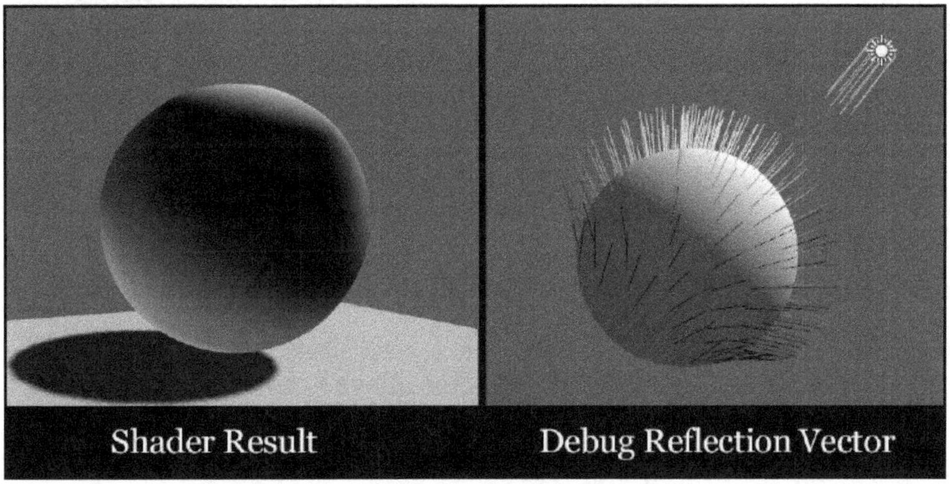

The following diagram displays the final result of our Phong Specular calculation isolated in the shader:

Creating a BlinnPhong Specular type

Blinn is another more efficient way of calculating and estimating specularity. It is done by getting the half vector from the view direction and light direction. It was brought into the world of Cg by Jim Blinn. He found that it was much more efficient to just get the half vector instead of calculating our own reflection vectors. It cut down on the code and processing time. If you actually look at the built-in BlinnPhong lighting model included in the `UnityCG.cginc` file, you will notice that it is using the half vector as well, hence it is named BlinnPhong. It is just a simpler version of the full Phong calculation.

Getting ready

To start with this recipe, perform the following steps:

1. This time, instead of creating a whole new scene, let's just use the objects and scene that we have by using **File** | **Save Scene As...**, and create a new shader (BlinnPhong) and material (`BlinnPhongMat`):

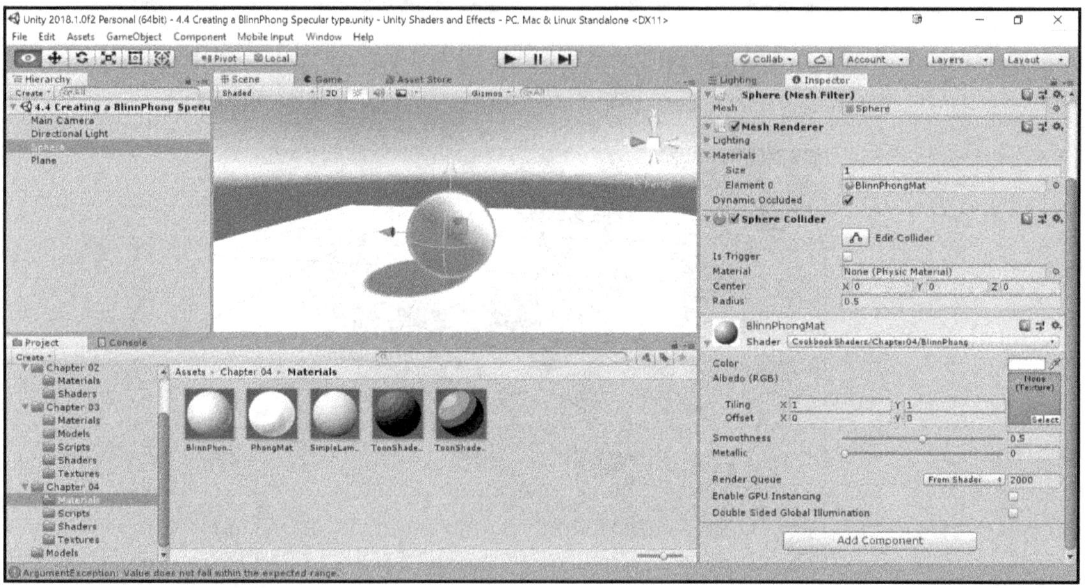

2. Once you have a new shader, double-click on it to launch your IDE of choice so that you can start editing your shader.

How to do it...

Perform the following steps to create a BlinnPhong lighting model:

1. First, let's remove all of the current properties with their definitions in the `SubShader` block. Then we need to add our own properties to the `Properties` block so that we can control the look of the Specular highlight:

```
Properties
{
  _MainTint ("Diffuse Tint", Color) = (1,1,1,1)
  _MainTex ("Base (RGB)", 2D) = "white" {}
  _SpecularColor ("Specular Color", Color) = (1,1,1,1)
  _SpecPower ("Specular Power", Range(0.1,60)) = 3
}
```

2. Then we need to make sure that we have created the corresponding variables in our `CGPROGRAM` block so that we can access the data from our `Properties` block, in our subshader:

```
sampler2D _MainTex;
float4 _MainTint;
float4 _SpecularColor;
float _SpecPower;
```

3. Now it's time to create our custom lighting model that will process our Diffuse and Specular calculations. The code is as follows:

```
fixed4 LightingCustomBlinnPhong (SurfaceOutput s,
                        fixed3 lightDir,
                        half3 viewDir,
                        fixed atten)
{
  float NdotL = max(0,dot(s.Normal, lightDir));

  float3 halfVector = normalize(lightDir + viewDir);
  float NdotH = max(0, dot(s.Normal, halfVector));
  float spec = pow(NdotH, _SpecPower) * _SpecularColor;

  float4 color;
  color.rgb = (s.Albedo * _LightColor0.rgb * NdotL) +
        (_LightColor0.rgb * _SpecularColor.rgb * spec) *
atten;
  color.a = s.Alpha;
  return color;
}
```

4. Then update the `surf` function to the following:

```
void surf (Input IN, inout SurfaceOutput o)
{
 half4 c = tex2D (_MainTex, IN.uv_MainTex) * _MainTint;
 o.Albedo = c.rgb;
 o.Alpha = c.a;
}
```

5. To complete our shader, we will need to tell our CGPROGRAM block to use our custom lighting model rather than a built-in one by modifying the `#pragma` statement with the following code:

```
CPROGRAM
#pragma surface surf CustomBlinnPhong
```

6. The following screenshot demonstrates the results of our BlinnPhong lighting model:

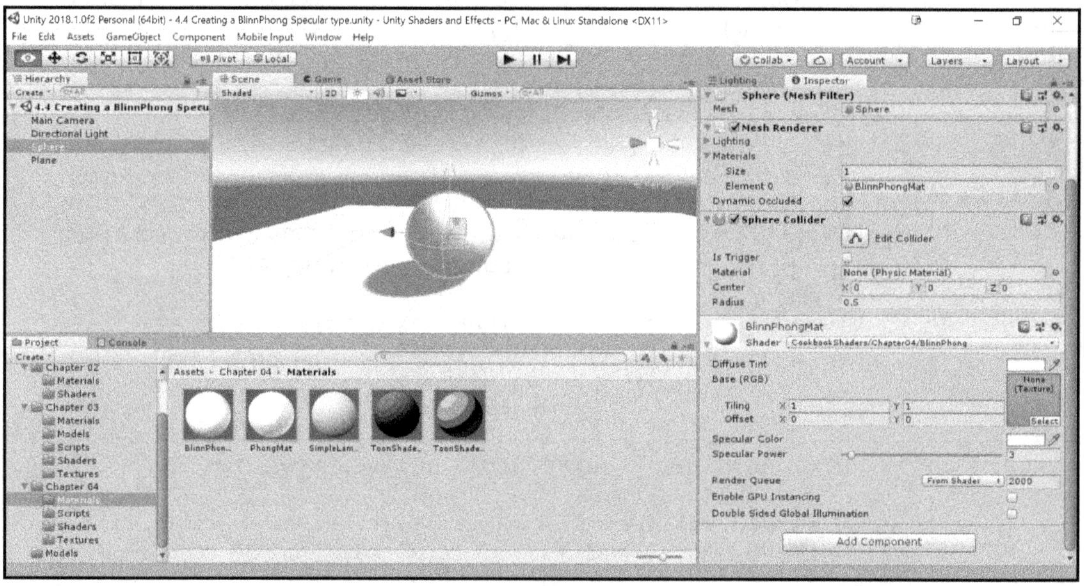

How it works...

The BlinnPhong Specular is almost exactly like the Phong Specular, except that it is more efficient because it uses less code to achieve almost the same effect. Before the introduction of physically-based rendering, this approach was the default choice for Specular reflection in Unity 4.

Calculating the reflection vector **R** is generally expensive. The BlinnPhong Specular replaces it with the half vector **H** between the view direction **V** and light direction **L**:

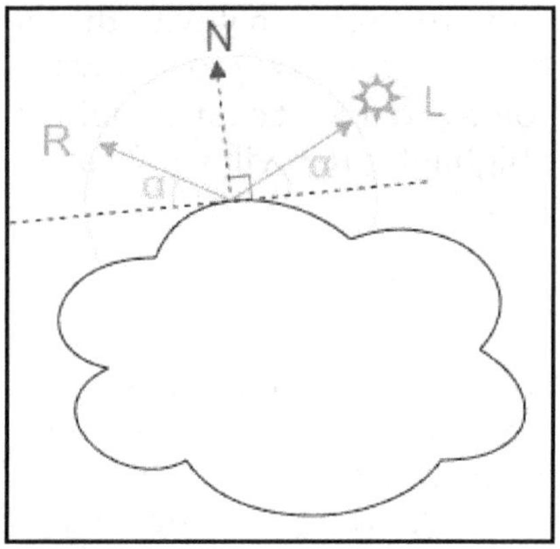

Instead of calculating our own reflection vector, we are simply going to get the vector halfway between the view direction and light direction, basically simulating the reflection vector. It has actually been found that this approach is more physically accurate than the last approach, but we thought it necessary to show you all the possibilities:

$$S_{Phong} = (R \cdot V)^p, \qquad S_{BlinnPhong} = (N \cdot H)^p$$

According to vector algebra, the half vector can be calculated as follows:

$$H = \frac{V + L}{|V + L|}$$

Here |V+L| is the length of the vector V+L. In Cg, we simply need to add the view direction and light direction together and then normalize the result to a unity vector:

```
float3 halfVector = normalize(lightDir + viewDir);
```

Then, we simply need to dot the vertex normal with this new half vector to get our main Specular value. After this, we just take it to a power of `_SpecPower` and multiply it by the Specular color variable. It's much lighter on the code and math, but still gives us a nice Specular highlight that will work for many real-time situations.

See also

The light models seen in this chapter are extremely simple; no real material is perfectly matte or perfectly specular. Moreover, it is not uncommon for complex materials such as clothing, wood, and skin to require knowledge of how light scatters in the layers beneath the surface. Use the following table to recap the different lighting models encountered so far:

Technique	**Type**	**Light Intensity (I)**
Lambertian	Diffuse	$I = N \cdot L$
`Phong`	Specular	$I = N \cdot L + (R \cdot V)^p$ $R = 2N \cdot (N \cdot L) - L$
BlinnPhong	Specular	$I = N \cdot L + (N \cdot H)^p$ $H = \frac{V + L}{\lvert V + L \rvert}$

There are other interesting models such as the Oren-Nayar lighting model for rough surfaces: `https://en.wikipedia.org/wiki/Oren%E2%80%93Nayar_reflectance_model`.

Creating an Anisotropic Specular type

Anisotropic is a type of Specular or reflection that simulates the directionality of grooves in a surface and modifies/stretches the Specular in the perpendicular direction. It is very useful when you want to simulate brushed metals, not a metal with a clear, smooth, and polished surface. Imagine the Specular that you see when you look at the data side of a CD or DVD or the way Specular is shaped at the bottom of a pot or pan. You will notice that if you carefully examine the surface, there is a direction to the grooves, usually in the way the metal was brushed. When you apply a Specular to this surface, you get a Specular stretched in the perpendicular direction.

This recipe will introduce you to the concept of augmenting your Specular highlights to achieve different types of brushed surfaces. In future recipes, we will look at the ways in which we can use the concepts of this recipe to achieve other effects, such as stretched reflections and hair, but here, you are going to learn the fundamentals of the technique first. We will be using this shader as a reference for our own custom Anisotropic Shader:
`http://wiki.unity3d.com/index.php?title=Anisotropic_Highlight_Shader`.
The following diagram shows examples of different types of Specular effects that you can achieve using Anisotropic Shaders in Unity:

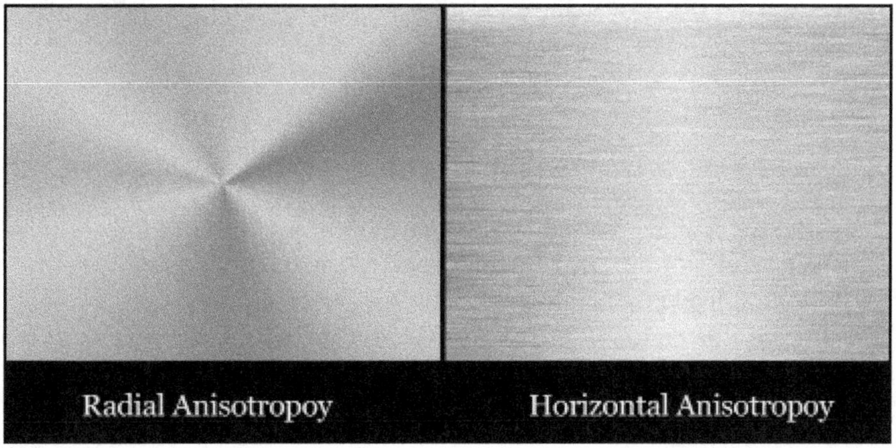

Getting ready

Let's start this recipe by creating a shader, its material, and some lights for our scene:

1. Create a new scene with some objects and lights so that we can visually debug our shader. In this case, we will be using some capsules, a sphere, and a cylinder.
2. Then create a new shader and material, and hook them up to your objects:

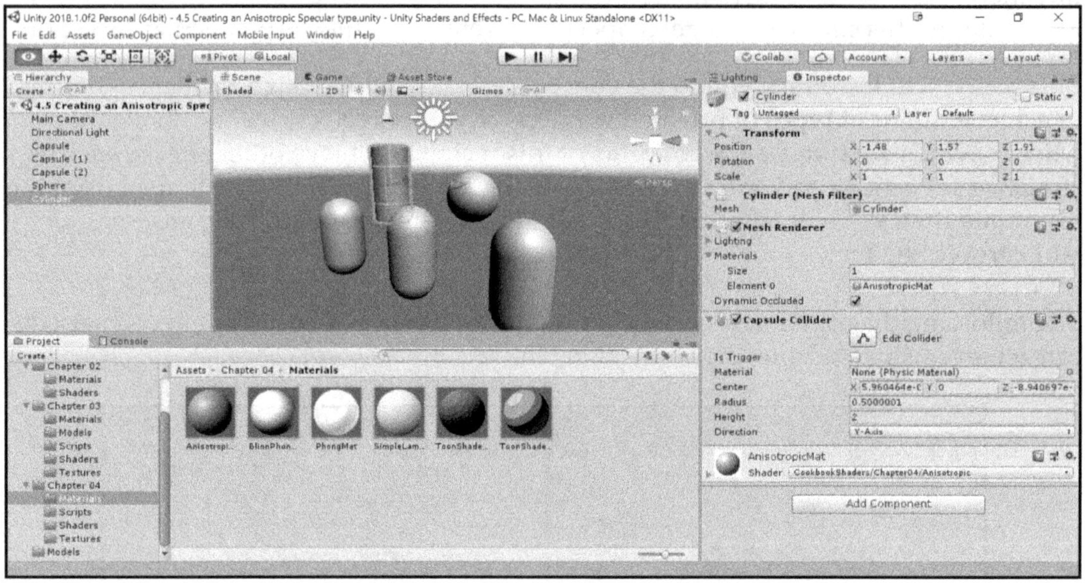

3. Lastly, we will need some sort of normal map that will indicate the directionality of our Anisotropic Specular highlight.
4. The following screenshot shows the Anisotropy normal map we will be using for this recipe. It is available from this book's support page at `https://www.packtpub.com/books/content/support`:

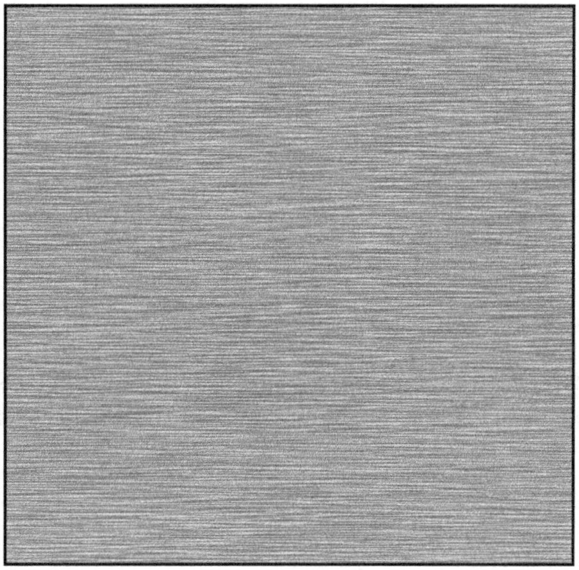

How to do it...

To create an Anisotropic effect, we need to make the following changes to the shader previously created:

1. We first need to remove the old properties and then add the properties that we are going to need for our shader. These will allow a lot of artistic control over the final appearance of the surface:

```
Properties
{
  _MainTint ("Diffuse Tint", Color) = (1,1,1,1)
  _MainTex ("Base (RGB)", 2D) = "white" {}
  _SpecularColor ("Specular Color", Color) = (1,1,1,1)
  _Specular ("Specular Amount", Range(0,1)) = 0.5
  _SpecPower ("Specular Power", Range(0,1)) = 0.5
  _AnisoDir ("Anisotropic Direction", 2D) = "" {}
  _AnisoOffset ("Anisotropic Offset", Range(-1,1)) = -0.2
}
```

2. We then need to make the connection between our `Properties` block and our `SubShader{}` block so that we can use the data being provided by the `Properties` block:

```
sampler2D _MainTex;
sampler2D _AnisoDir;
float4 _MainTint;
float4 _SpecularColor;
float _AnisoOffset;
float _Specular;
float _SpecPower;
```

3. Now we can create our `Lighting` function that will produce the correct Anisotropic effect on our surface. We will use the following code for this:

```
fixed4 LightingAnisotropic(SurfaceAnisoOutput s, fixed3
   lightDir, half3 viewDir, fixed atten)
{
  fixed3 halfVector = normalize(normalize(lightDir) +
     normalize(viewDir));
  float NdotL = saturate(dot(s.Normal, lightDir));

  fixed HdotA = dot(normalize(s.Normal +
s.AnisoDirection),
     halfVector);  float aniso = max(0, sin(radians((HdotA
+ _AnisoOffset) *
     180)));  float spec = saturate(pow(aniso, s.Gloss *
128) *
     s.Specular);

  fixed4 c;
  c.rgb = ((s.Albedo * _LightColor0.rgb * NdotL) +
     (_LightColor0.rgb * _SpecularColor.rgb * spec)) *
     atten;
  c.a = s.Alpha;
  return c;
}
```

4. In order to use this new `Lighting` function, we need to tell the subshader's `#pragma` statement to look for it instead of using one of the built-in `Lighting` functions:

```
CGPROGRAM
#pragma surface surf Anisotropic
```

5. We have also given the Anisotropic normal map its own UVs by declaring the following code in the `struct Input`. This isn't entirely necessary as we could just use the UVs from the main texture, but this gives us independent control over the tiling of our brushed metal effect so that we can scale it to any size we want:

```
struct Input
{
  float2 uv_MainTex;
  float2 uv_AnisoDir;
};
```

6. We also need to add the `struct SurfaceAnisoOutput`:

```
struct SurfaceAnisoOutput
{
  fixed3 Albedo;
  fixed3 Normal;
  fixed3 Emission;
  fixed3 AnisoDirection;
  half Specular;
  fixed Gloss;
  fixed Alpha;
};
```

7. Finally, we need to use the `surf()` function to pass the correct data to our `Lighting` function. Hence, we will get the per-pixel information from our Anisotropic normal map and set our Specular parameters as follows:

```
void surf(Input IN, inout SurfaceAnisoOutput o)
{
  half4 c = tex2D(_MainTex, IN.uv_MainTex) * _MainTint;
  float3 anisoTex = UnpackNormal(tex2D(_AnisoDir,
     IN.uv_AnisoDir));

  o.AnisoDirection = anisoTex;
  o.Specular = _Specular;
  o.Gloss = _SpecPower;
  o.Albedo = c.rgb;
  o.Alpha = c.a;
}
```

8. Save your script and return to the Unity editor. Select the `AnisotropicMat` material and assign the **Anisotropic Direction** property to the texture we talked about in the *Getting ready* section of this recipe. Afterward, adjust the Anisotopic `Offset` property using the slider and notice the changes.

The Anisotropic normal map allows us to give the surface direction and helps us disperse the Specular highlight around the surface. The following screenshot demonstrates the result of our Anisotropic Shader:

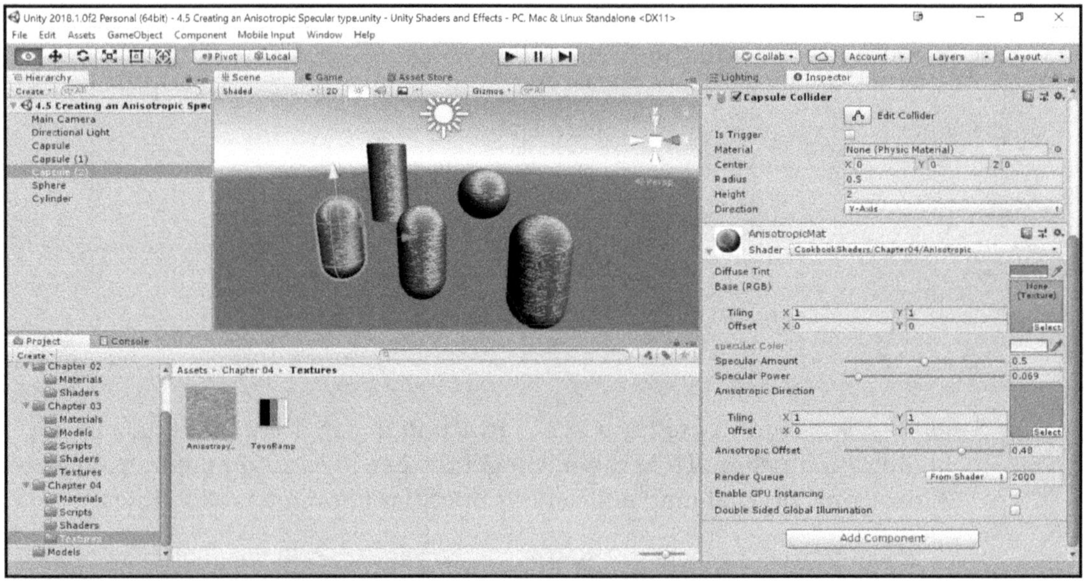

How it works...

Let's break down this shader into its core components and explain why we are getting the effect. We will mostly be covering the custom Lighting function here, as the rest of the shader should be pretty self-explanatory at this point.

We first start by declaring our own `SurfaceAnisoOutput struct`. We need to do this in order to get the per-pixel information from the Anisotropic normal map, and the only way we can do this in a Surface Shader is to use a `tex2D()` function in the `surf()` function. The following code shows the custom surface output structure used in our shader:

```
struct SurfaceAnisoOutput
{
  fixed3 Albedo;
  fixed3 Normal;
  fixed3 Emission;
  fixed3 AnisoDirection;
  half Specular;
  fixed Gloss;
  fixed Alpha;
};
```

We can use the `SurfaceAnisoOutput` struct as a way of interacting between the Lighting function and the surface function. In our case, we are storing the per-pixel texture information in the variable called `anisoTex` in our `surf()` function and then passing this data to the `SurfaceAnisoOutput` struct by storing it in the `AnisoDirection` variable. Once we have this, we can use the per-pixel information in the `Lighting` function using `s.AnisoDirection`.

With this data connection set up, we can move on to our actual lighting calculations. This begins by getting the usual out of the way, the half vector, so that we don't have to do the full reflection calculation and diffuse lighting, which is the vertex normal dotted with the light vector or direction. This is done in Cg with the following lines:

```
fixed3 halfVector = normalize(normalize(lightDir) +
                    normalize(viewDir));
float NdotL = saturate(dot(s.Normal, lightDir));
```

Then, we start the actual modification to the Specular to get the right look. We first dot the normalized sum of the vertex normal and per-pixel vectors from our Anisotropic normal map with the `halfVector` calculated in the previous step. This gives us a float value that gives a value of `1` as the surface normal, which is modified by the Anisotropic normal map as it becomes parallel with `halfVector` and `0` as it is perpendicular. Finally, we modify this value with a `sin()` function so that we can basically get a darker middle highlight and ultimately a ring effect based on `halfVector`. All the previously mentioned operations are summarized in the following two lines of Cg code:

```
fixed HdotA = dot(normalize(s.Normal + s.AnisoDirection),
                  halfVector);
float aniso = max(0, sin(radians((HdotA + _AnisoOffset) * 180)));
```

Finally, we scale the effect of the `aniso` value by taking it to a power of `s.Gloss`, and then globally decrease its strength by multiplying it by `s.Specular`:

```
float spec = saturate(pow(aniso, s.Gloss * 128) * s.Specular);
```

This effect is great for creating more advanced metal type surfaces, especially the ones that are brushed and appear to have directionality to them. It also works well for hair or any sort of soft surface with directionality to it. The following screenshot shows the result of displaying the final Anisotropic lighting calculation:

7 Physically-Based Rendering

Introduced in Unity 5, PBR is a shading model that seeks to render graphics in a way that acts in a similar manner to how light works in the real world. Previous chapters have repeatedly mentioned it without revealing too much about it. If you want to understand not only how PBR works, but how to make the most out of it, this is the chapter you should read.

In this chapter, you will learn the following recipes:

- Understanding the metallic setup
- Adding transparency to PBR
- Creating mirrors and reflective surfaces
- Baking lights in your scene

Introduction

All the lighting models encountered in `Chapter 6`, *Understanding Lighting Models*, were very primitive descriptions of how light behaves. The most important aspect during their making was *efficiency*. Real-time shading is expensive, and techniques such as Lambertian or BlinnPhong are a compromise between computational cost and realism.

Having a more powerful GPU has allowed us to write progressively more sophisticated lighting models and rendering engines, with the aim of simulating how light actually behaves. This is, in a nutshell, the philosophy behind PBR. As the name suggests, it tries to get as close as possible to the physics behind the processes that give a unique look at each material. Despite this, the term PBR has been widely used in marketing campaigns and is more of a synonym for **state-of-the-art rendering** rather than a well-defined technique.

Unity implements PBR in two main ways:

- The first is a completely new lighting model (called Standard). Surface Shaders allow developers to specify the physical properties of a material, but they do not impose actual physical constraints on them. PBR fills this by gap using a lighting model that enforces principles of physics such as **energy conservation** (an object cannot reflect more light than the amount it receives), **microsurface scattering** (rough surfaces reflect light more erratically compared to smooth ones), **Fresnel reflectance** (specular reflections appear at grazing angles), and **surface occlusion** (the darkening of corners and other geometries that are hard to light). All these aspects, and many others, are used to calculate the standard lighting model.
- The second aspect that makes PBR so realistic is called **Global Illumination** (**GI**) and is the simulation of physically-based light transport. It means that objects are not drawn in the scene as if they were separate entities. They all contribute to the final rendering as light can reflect on them before hitting something else. This aspect is not captured in the shaders themselves, but is an essential part of how the rendering engine works. Unfortunately, accurately simulating how light rays actually bounce over surfaces in real time is beyond the capabilities of modern GPUs. Unity makes some clever optimizations that allow us to retain visual fidelity without sacrificing performance. Some of the most advanced techniques (such as reflections), however, require user input.

All of these aspects will be covered in this chapter. It is important to remember that PBR and GI do not automatically guarantee that your game will be photorealistic. Achieving photorealism is a very challenging task and, like every art, it requires great expertise and exceptional skills.

Understanding the metallic setup

Unity provides three different types of PBR shaders; they are referred to in the drop-down menu of the material's **Inspector** tab as **Standard**, **Standard (Roughness Setup)**, and **Standard (Specular setup)**. The main difference is that **Standard** and **Standard (Roughness Setup)** expose the **Metallic** property, but **Standard** contains a **Smoothness** property while the second replaces **Smoothness** with **Roughness. Standard (Specular setup)** contains **Smoothness**, but replaces the **Metallic** property with **Specular**. **Smoothness** and **Roughness** are opposites of each other, so a `1` **Smoothness** means `0` **Roughness** and vice versa. You can generally get the same result no matter which shader you use, so it mostly comes down to personal preference.

These setups represent different ways in which you can initialize PBR materials. One of the concepts that has driven PBR is the ability to provide meaningful, physically-related properties that artists and developers can tweak and play with. The properties of some materials are easier to represent, indicating how *metallic* they are. For others, it is more important to specify how they reflect lights directly through its **specularity**. This recipe will show you how to use the **metallic setup** effectively. It's important to remember that the metallic workflow is not just for metallic materials; it is a way of defining how materials will look according to how metallic or non-metallic their surface is. Despite being presented as two different types of shaders, both **Metallic** and **Specular** setups are generally equally expressive.

As shown in the Unity documentation at `http://docs.unity3d.com/Manual/StandardShaderMetallicVsSpecular.html` and mentioned earlier, the same materials can usually be recreated with both setups (see the following screenshot):

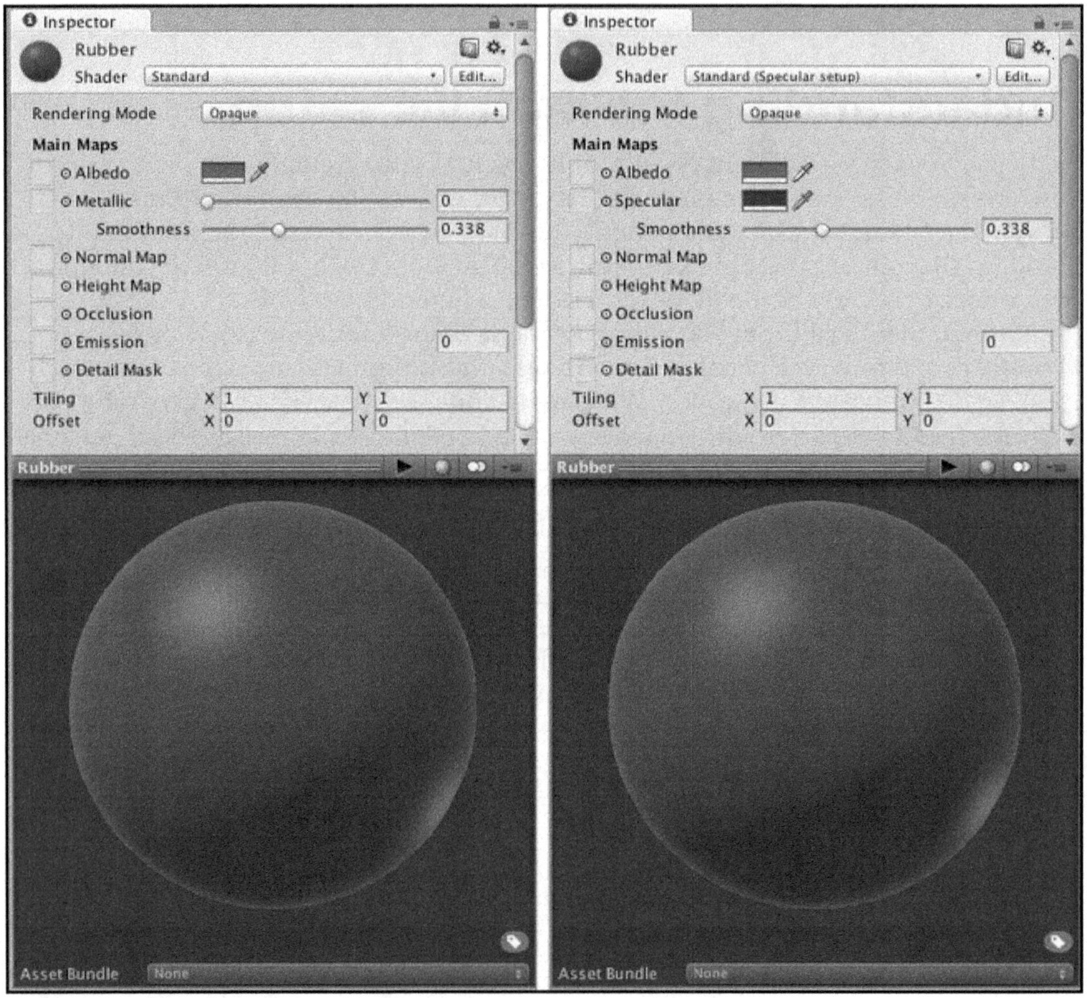

Getting ready

This recipe will use the Standard Shader, so there is no need to create a new one. The steps to start the recipe are as follows:

1. Create a new material (`MetallicMat`).
2. From its **Inspector**, make sure that **Standard** is selected from its **Shader** drop-down menu.
3. You will also need a textured 3D model. Our basic character we've been using previously will work perfectly. Drag and drop it into the scene. Afterward, drag and drop the `MetallicMat` material onto each of the parts of the character. Also, assign the texture for the m**aterial** to the **Albedo** property:

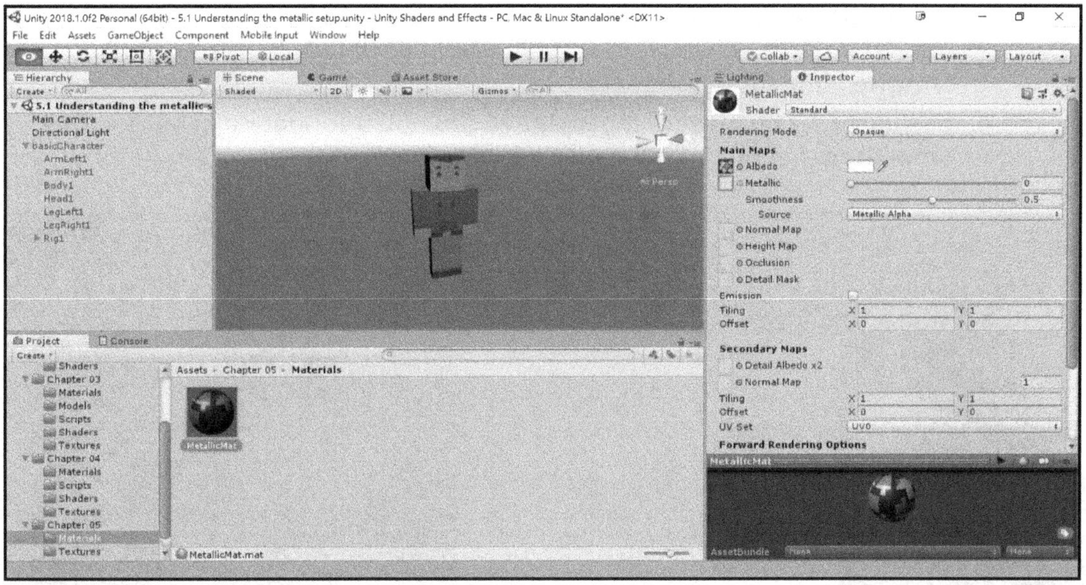

How to do it...

There are two main textures that need to be configured in the Standard Shader: **Albedo** and **Metallic**. To use the metallic workflow effectively, we need to initialize these maps correctly:

1. The **Albedo** map should be initialized with the unlit texture of the 3D model.
2. To create the **Metallic** map, start by duplicating the file for your **Albedo** map. You can do this by selecting the map from the **Project** tab and pressing *Ctrl* + *D*.
3. Use white (`#ffffff`) to color the regions of the map that correspond to materials that are made of pure metal. Use black (`#000000`) for all the other colors. Shades of grey should be used for dusty, weathered, or worn-out metal surfaces, rust, scratched paint, and so on. As a matter of fact, Unity uses only the red channel to store the metallic value; the green and blue ones are ignored.
4. Use the alpha channel of the image to provide information about the **Smoothness** of the material:

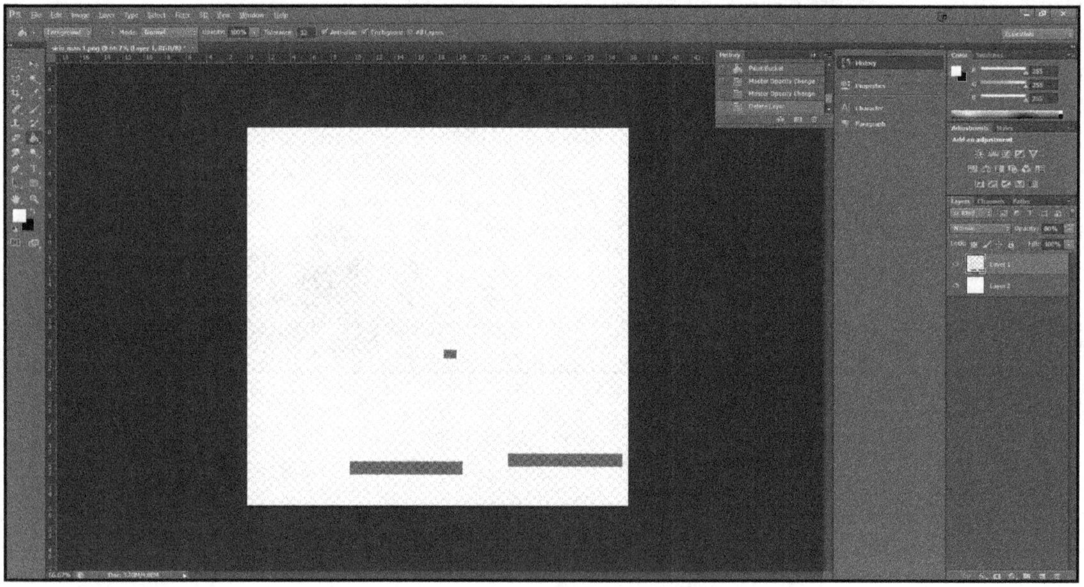

An example of a Metallic map opened in Photoshop

For our simple character, the belt and the little ends of the hoodie are the only parts we need to be metallic. I've also made the opacity around 55% for the main character, with the belt having a higher opacity of 80%:

5. Assign the **Metallic** map to the material. The **Metallic** slider will disappear as these two properties are now controlled by the map. You may use the **Smoothness** slider to provide a modifier on the map you've provided:

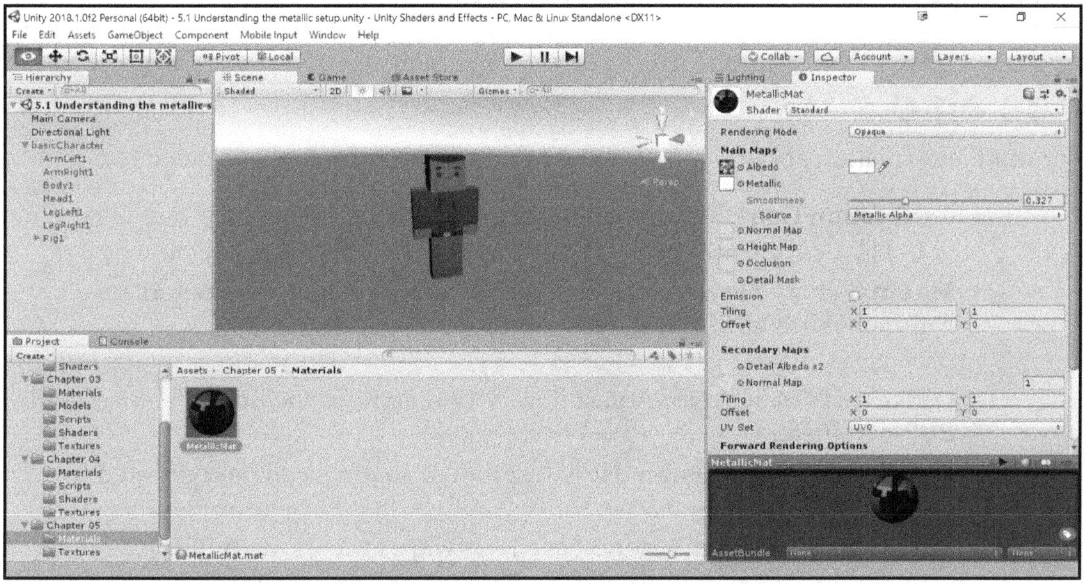

How it works...

Metals are known for the conducting of electricity; light is in the form of electromagnetic waves, meaning that almost all metals behave in a similar way compared to non-conductors (often referred as **insulators**). Conductors tend to reflect most photons (70-100%), resulting in high reflectance. The remaining light is absorbed, rather than diffused, suggesting that conductors have a very dark diffuse component. Insulators, conversely, have a low reflectance (4%); the rest of the light is scattered on the surface, contributing to their diffused looks.

In the Standard Shader, purely metallic materials have dark diffuse components, and the color of their specular reflections is determined by the **Albedo** map. Conversely, the diffuse component of purely non-metallic materials is determined by the **Albedo** map; the color of their specular highlights is determined by the color of the incoming light. Following these principles allows the metallic workflow to combine the **Albedo** and specular into the **Albedo** map, enforcing physically-accurate behaviors. This also allows for saving more space, resulting in a significant speed increase at the expenses of reduced control over the look of your materials.

See also

For more information about the metallic setup, you can refer to these links:

- **Calibration chart**: How to calibrate a metallic material (`http://blogs.unity3d.com/wp-content/uploads/2014/11/UnityMetallicChart.png`)
- **Material chart**: How to initialize the Standard Shader parameters for common materials (`http://docs.unity3d.com/Manual/StandardShaderMaterialCharts.html`)
- **Quixel MEGASCANS**: A vast library of materials, including textures and PBR parameters (`https://megascans.se/`)
- **PBR Texture Conversion**: How traditional shaders can be converted to PBR shaders (`http://www.marmoset.co/toolbag/learn/pbr-conversion`)
- **Substance Designer**: A node-based software to work with PBR (`https://www.allegorithmic.com/products/substance-designer`)
- **The Theory of Physically-Based Rendering**: A complete guide about PBR (`https://www.allegorithmic.com/pbr-guide`)

Adding transparency to PBR

Transparency is such an important aspect in games that the Standard Shader supports three different ways of doing it. This recipe is useful if you need to have realistic materials with transparent or semi-transparent properties. Glasses, bottles, windows, and crystals are good candidates for PBR transparent shaders. This is because you can still have all the realism introduced by PBR with the addition of a transparent or translucent effect. If you need transparency for something different, such as UI elements or pixel art, there are more efficient alternatives that are explored in the *Creating a transparent material* recipe in `Chapter 5`, *Surface Shaders and Texture Mapping*.

> In order to have a transparent standard material, changing the alpha channel of its **Albedo** color property is not enough. Unless you properly set its **Rendering Mode**, your material will not appear transparent.

Getting ready

This recipe will use the Standard Shader, so there is no need to create a new one:

1. Create a new material (`TransparencyMat`).
2. Make sure that the **Shader** property is set to either **Standard** or **Standard (Specular setup)** from the material's **Inspector** tab.
3. Assign the newly created material to the 3D object that you want to be transparent:

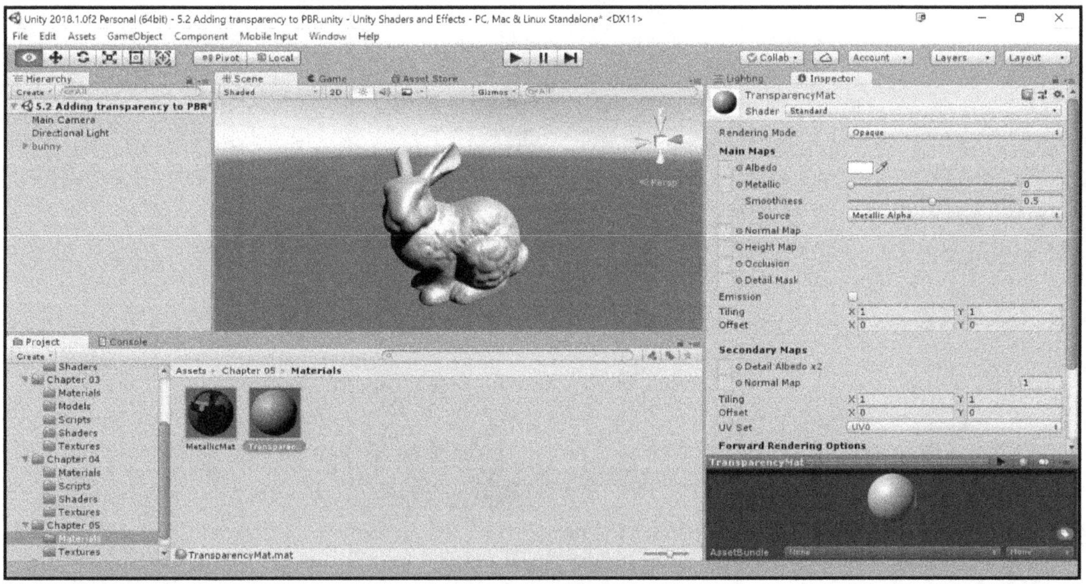

How to do it...

The Standard Shader provides three different types of transparencies. Despite being very similar, they have subtle differences and fit in different contexts.

Semi-transparent materials

Some materials such as clear plastics, crystal, and glass are semi-transparent. This means that they both require all the realistic effects of PBR (such as specular highlights and Fresnel refraction and reflection), but allow the geometry behind an object with the material attached to be seen. If this is what you need, perform the following steps:

1. From the material's **Inspector** tab, set **Rendering Mode** to **Transparent**.
2. The amount of transparency is determined by the alpha channel of the **Albedo** color or the **Albedo** map (if any). If you click on the box to the right of the **Albedo** section, you'll bring up a **Color** menu. Adjusting the **A** channel will make the item more visible or less visible:

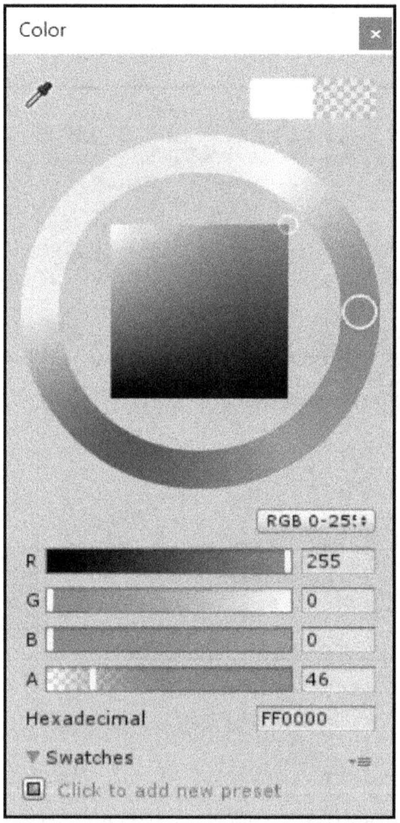

3. Setting the **A** channel to `44` provides the following effect:

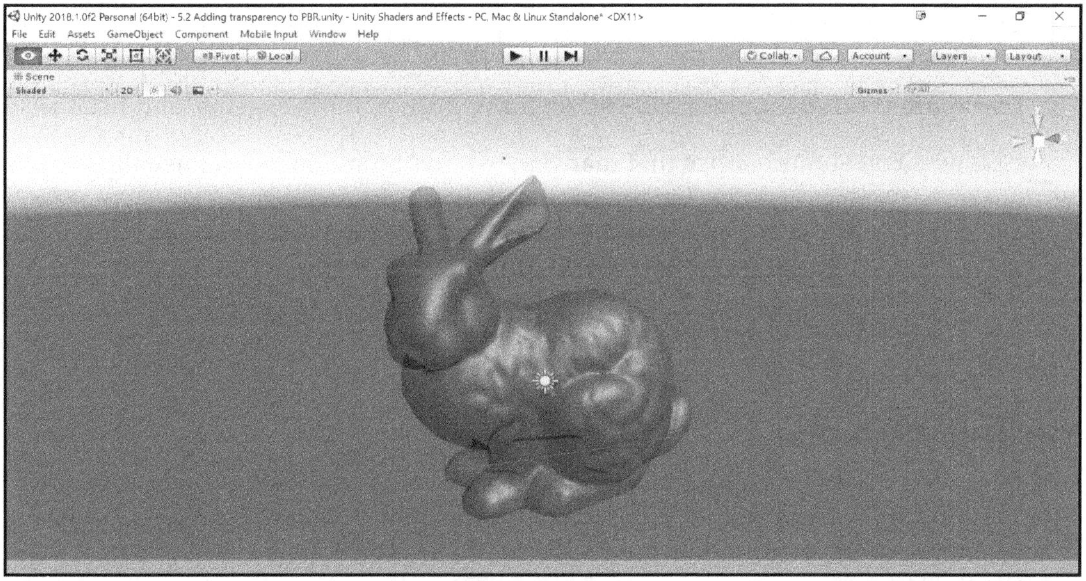

4. The following screenshot shows the Unity calibration scene with four different highly polished plastic spheres. From left to right, their transparency is increasing. The last sphere is fully transparent, but retains all the added effects of PBR:

The Unity Calibration Scene can be downloaded for free from the Asset Store at `https://www.assetstore.unity3d.com/en/#!/content/25422`.

The **Transparent** rendering mode is perfect for windows, bottles, gems, and headsets.

You should notice that many transparent materials don't usually project shadows. On top of this, the **Metallic** and **Smoothness** properties of a material can interfere with the transparency effect. A mirror-like surface can have the alpha set to zero, but if it reflects all the incoming light, it won't appear transparent.

Fading objects

Sometimes, you want an object to fully disappear with a fading effect. In this case, specular reflections and Fresnel refraction and reflection should disappear as well. When a fading object is fully transparent, it should also be invisible. To do this, perform the following steps:

1. From the material's **Inspector** tab, set **Rendering Mode** to **Fade**.
2. As before, use the alpha channel of the **Albedo** color or map to determine the final transparency:

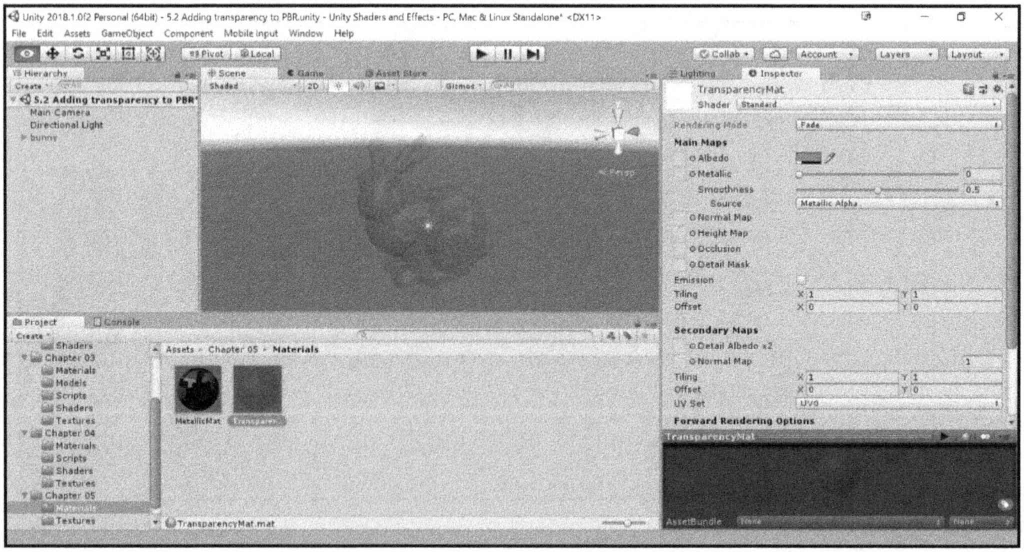

3. The following screenshot shows four fading spheres. It is clear from the screenshot that the PBR effects fade with the sphere as well. As you can see in the following image, the last one on the right is almost invisible:

4. This rendering mode works best for non-realistic objects, such as holograms, laser rays, faux lights, ghosts, and particle effects.

Solid geometries with holes

Most of the materials encountered in a game are solid, meaning that they don't allow light to pass through them. At the same time, many objects have a very complex (yet flat) geometry. Modeling leaves and grass with 3D objects is often overkilled. A more efficient approach is to use a quad (rectangle) with a leaf texture. While the leaf itself is solid, the rest of the texture should be fully transparent. If this is what you want, then perform the following steps:

1. From the material's **Inspector** tab, set **Rendering Mode** to **Cutout**.
2. Use the **Alpha Cutoff** slider to determine the cutoff threshold. All the pixels in the **Albedo** map with an alpha value equal to or less than **Alpha Cutoff** will be hidden.

The following image, taken from the *Unity Official Tutorials* on PBR (`https://www.youtube.com/watch?v=fD_ho_ofY6A`), shows you how the effect of the **Cutout** rendering mode can be used to create a hole in the geometry:

It's worth noticing that **Cutout** does not allow the back of the geometry to be seen. In the previous example, you could not see the inner volume of the sphere. If you require such an effect, you need to create your own shader and make sure that the back geometry is not culled.

See also

- As mentioned previously, some of the examples in this recipe have been created using the Unity **Shader Calibration Scene**, which is freely available in the Asset Store at `https://www.assetstore.unity3d.com/en/#!/content/25422`.
- More information about **Albedo** and **Transparency** can be found at `http://docs.unity3d.com/Manual/StandardShaderMaterialParameterAlbedoColor.html`.

Creating mirrors and reflective surfaces

Specular materials reflect lights when objects are viewed from certain angles. Unfortunately, even the Fresnel reflection, which is one of the most accurate models, does not correctly reflect lights from nearby objects. The lighting models examined in the previous chapters took into account only light sources, but ignored light that is reflected from other surfaces. With what you've learned about shaders so far, making a mirror is simply not possible.

Global illumination makes this possible by providing PBR shaders with information about their surroundings. This allows objects to have not just specular highlights, but also real reflections, which depend on the other objects around them. Real-time reflections are very costly and require manual setting up and tweaking in order to work. When done properly, they can be used to create mirror-like surfaces, as seen in the following diagram:

Getting ready

This recipe will not feature any new shader. Quite the opposite; most of the work is done directly in the editor. Perform the following steps:

1. Create a new scene.

2. Create a quad (**GameObject** | **3D Object** | **Quad**), which will serve as a mirror. I've rotated it to -65 in the Y axis to make it easy to see.
3. Create a new material (`MirrorMat`) and attach it to the mirror.
4. Place the quad in a scene with other objects.
5. Create a new reflection probe from **GameObject** | **Light** | **Reflection Probe** and place it in front of the quad:

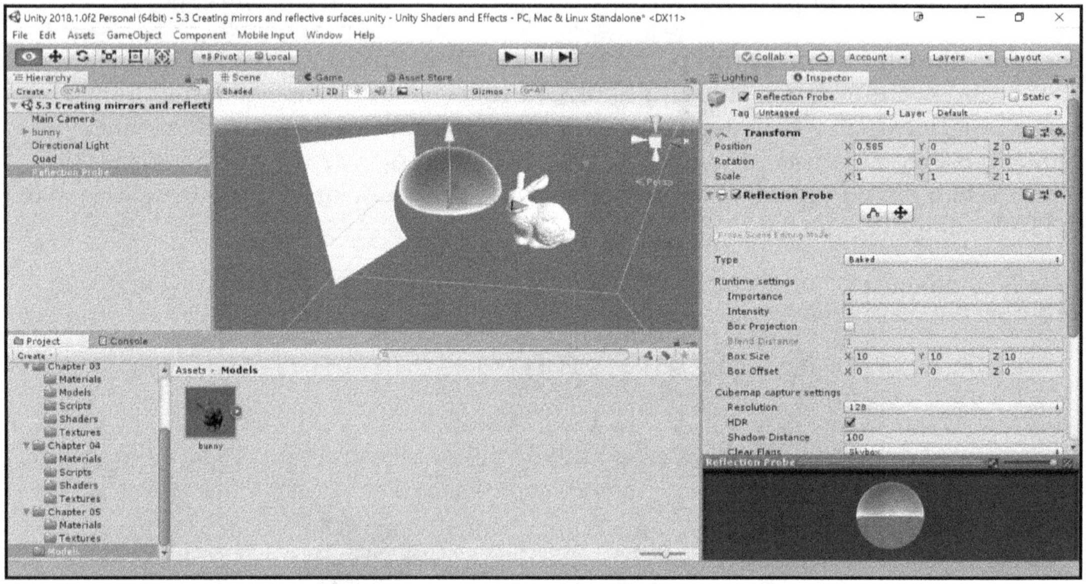

How to do it...

If the preceding steps have been followed correctly, you should have a quad in the middle of your scene, close to a reflection probe. In order to make it in a mirror, some changes need to be made:

1. Change the shader of the material to **Standard** and its **Rendering Mode** to **Opaque**.
2. Change its **Metallic** and **Smoothness** properties to one. You should see the material reflecting the sky more clearly.
3. Select the reflection probe and change its **Size** and **Probe Origin** until it is in front of the quad and it encloses all the objects that you want to reflect.

4. To make the item more clear under the **Cubemap capture settings**, change the **Resolution** to `2048`.
5. Finally, change its **Type** to **Realtime** and the **Refresh Mode** to **Every frame**. Also, make sure that **Culling Mask** is set to **Everything**.
6. Your reflection probe should be configured, as shown in the following screenshot:

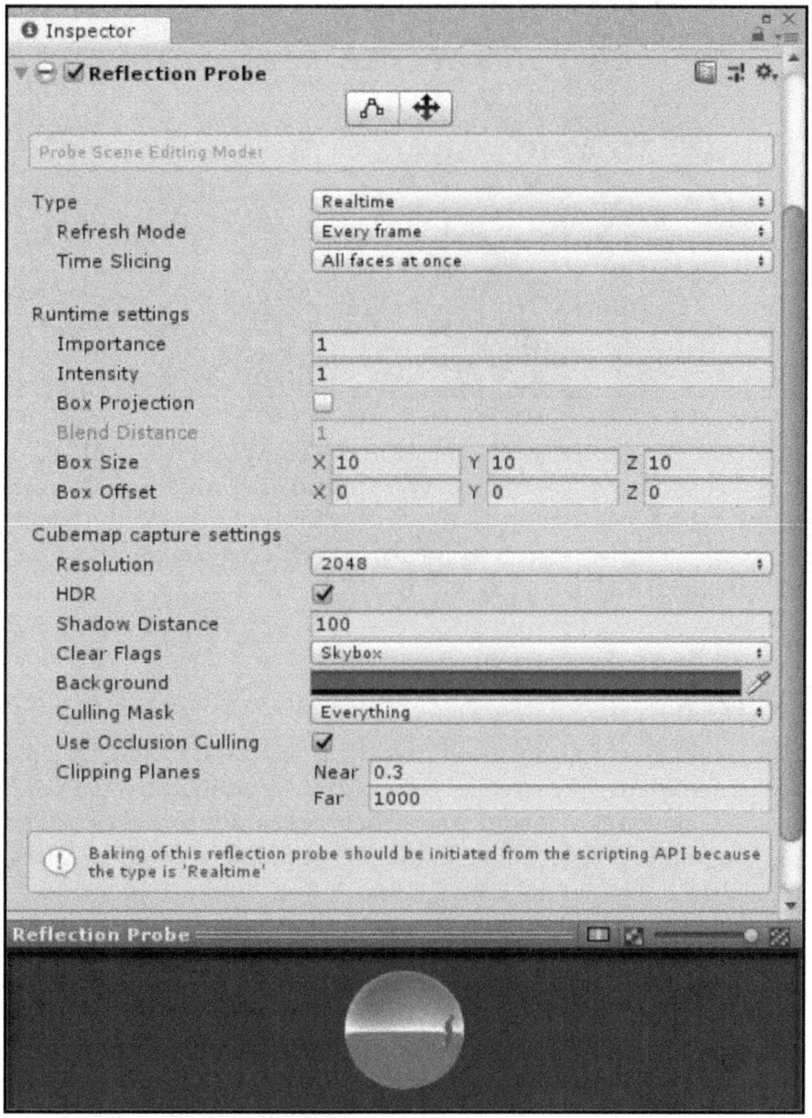

7. Using these settings, you should see something similar to this:

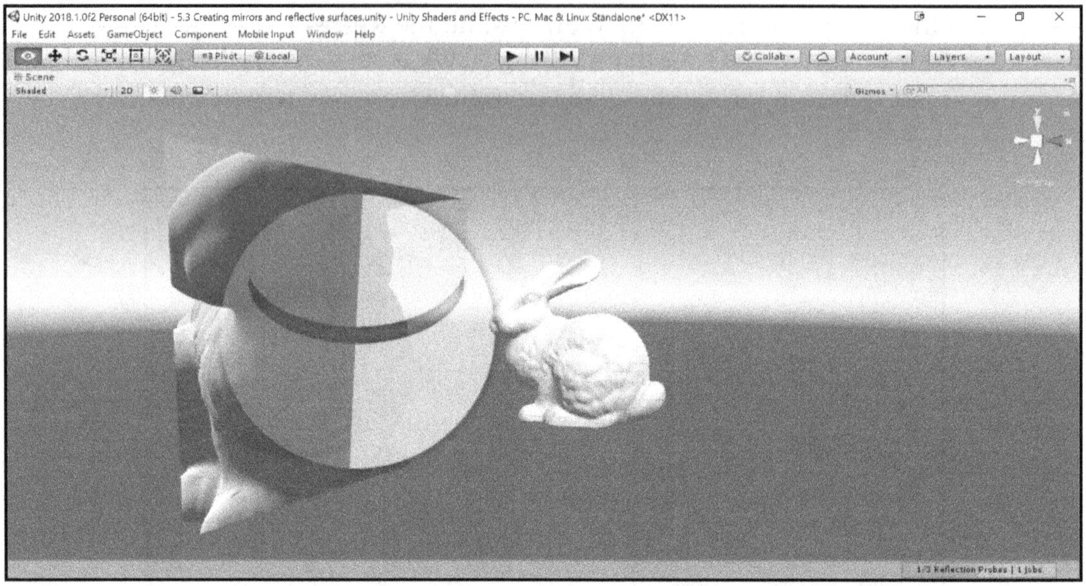

You may notice that the bunny seems larger in the reflection rather than what's beside it. If your probe is used for a real mirror, you should check the **Box Projection** flag (in this example, setting the box size to `1, 1, 1` does a pretty good job of looking like a mirror). If it is used for other reflective surfaces, such as shiny pieces of metal or glass tables, you can uncheck it.

How it works...

When a shader wants information about its surroundings, it is usually provided in a structure called **cube maps**. They have been briefly mentioned in `Chapter 4`, *Creating Your First Shader*, as one of the shader property types, among `Color`, `2D`, `Float`, and `Vector`. Loosely speaking, cube maps are the 3D equivalent of 2D textures; they represent a 360-degree view of the world, as seen from a center point.

Unity previews cube maps with a spherical projection, as seen in the following diagram:

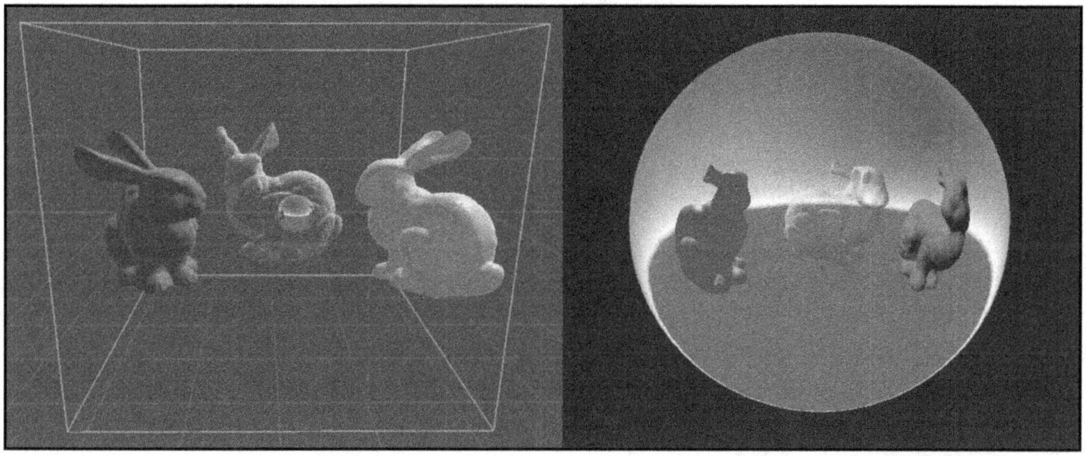

When cube maps are attached with a camera, they are referred to as **skyboxes**, as they are used to provide a way to reflect the sky. They can be used to reflect geometries that are not in the actual scene, such as nebulae, clouds, and stars.

The reason why they are called cube maps is because of the way they are created: a cube map is made up of six different textures, each one attached to the face of a cube. You can create a cube map manually or delegate it to a **reflection probe**. You can imagine a reflection probe as a collection of six cameras, creating a 360-degree mapping of the surrounding area. This also gives you an idea as to why probes are so expensive. By creating one in our scene, we allow Unity to know which objects are around the mirror. If you need more reflective surfaces, you can add multiple probes. You need no further action for the reflection probes to work. The Standard Shaders will use them automatically.

You should notice that when they are set to **Realtime**, they render their cube map at the beginning of every frame. There is a trick to make this faster; if you know that part of the geometry that you want to reflect does not move, you can bake the reflection. This means that Unity can calculate the reflection before starting the game, allowing more precise (and computationally expensive) calculations. In order to do this, your reflection probe must be set to **Baked** and will work only for objects that are flagged as **Static**. Static objects cannot move or change, which makes them perfect for terrain, buildings, and props. Every time a static object is moved, Unity will regenerate the cube maps for its baked reflection probes. This might take a few minutes to several hours.

You can mix **Realtime** and **Baked** probes to increase the realism of your game. Baked probes will provide very high-quality reflections, environmental reflections, while the real-time ones can be used to move objects such as cars or mirrors. The *Baking lights in your scene* section will explain in detail how light baking works.

See also

If you are interested in learning more about reflection probes, you should check these links:

- Unity manual about the Reflection Probe: `http://docs.unity3d.com/Manual/class-ReflectionProbe.html`
- Box projection and other advanced Reflection Probe settings: `https://docs.unity3d.com/Manual/AdvancedRefProbe.html`

Baking lights in your scene

Rendering lighting is a very expensive process. Even with state-of-the-art GPUs, accurately calculating the **light transport** (which is how light bounces between surfaces) can take hours. In order to make this process feasible for games, real-time rendering is essential. Modern engines compromise between realism and efficiency; most of the computation is done beforehand in a process called **light baking**. This recipe will explain how light baking works and how you can get the most out of it.

Getting ready

Light baking requires you to have a scene ready. It should have geometries and, obviously, lights. For this recipe, we will rely on Unity's standard features so there is no need to create additional shaders or materials. We will be reusing the map that we used previously in `Chapter 3`, *Post Processing Stack*. For better control, you might want to access the **Lighting** window. If you don't see it, select **Window** | **Lighting** | **Settings** from the menu and dock it where it is more convenient for you.

How to do it...

Light baking requires some manual configuration. There are three essential, yet independent, steps that you need to take.

Configuring the static geometry

These steps must be followed for the configuration:

1. Identify all the objects in your scene that do not change position, size, and material. Possible candidates are buildings, walls, terrain, props, trees, and others. In our case, it will be all of the objects aside from the `FPSController` and its children.
2. Select these objects and check the **Static** box from the **Inspector** tab, as shown in the following screenshot. If any of the selected objects have children, Unity will ask if you want them to be considered static as well. If they meet the requirements (fixed position, size, and material), select **Yes, change children** in the pop-up box:

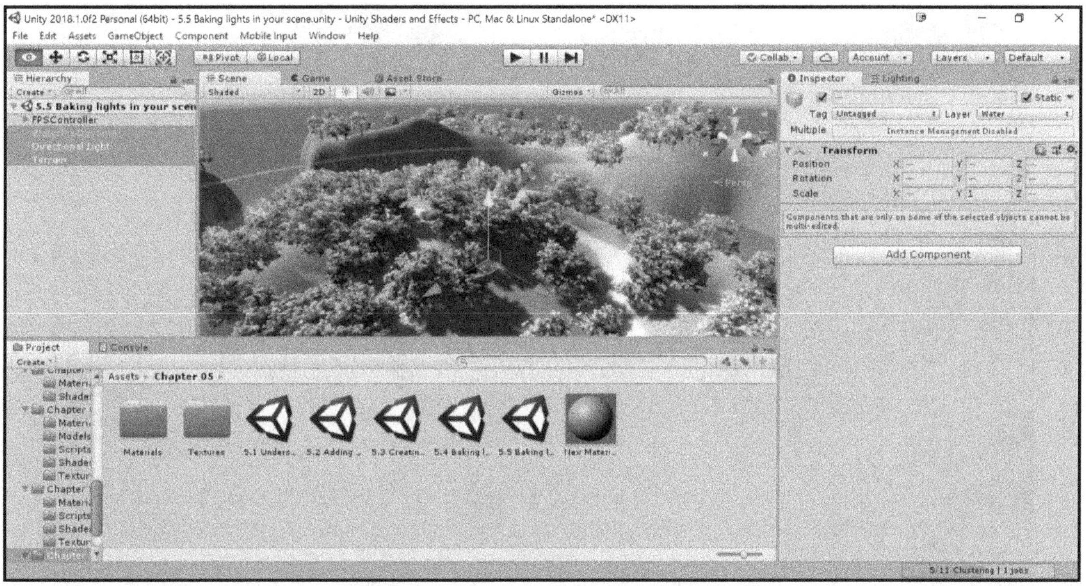

> If a light qualifies as a static object but illuminates non-static geometry, make sure that its **Baking** property is set to **Mixed**. If it will affect only static objects, set it to **Baked**.

Configuring the light probes

There are objects in your game that will move, such as the main character, enemies, and the other **non-playable characters** (**NPCs**). If they enter a static region that is illuminated, you might want to surround it with light probes. To do this, follow the given steps:

1. From the menu, navigate to **GameObject** | **Light** | **Light Probe Group**. A new object called **Light Probe Group** will appear in **Hierarchy**.
2. Once selected, eight interconnected spheres will appear. Click and move them around the scene so that they enclose the static region in which your characters can enter. The following screenshot shows an example of how light probes can be used to enclose the volume of a static office space:

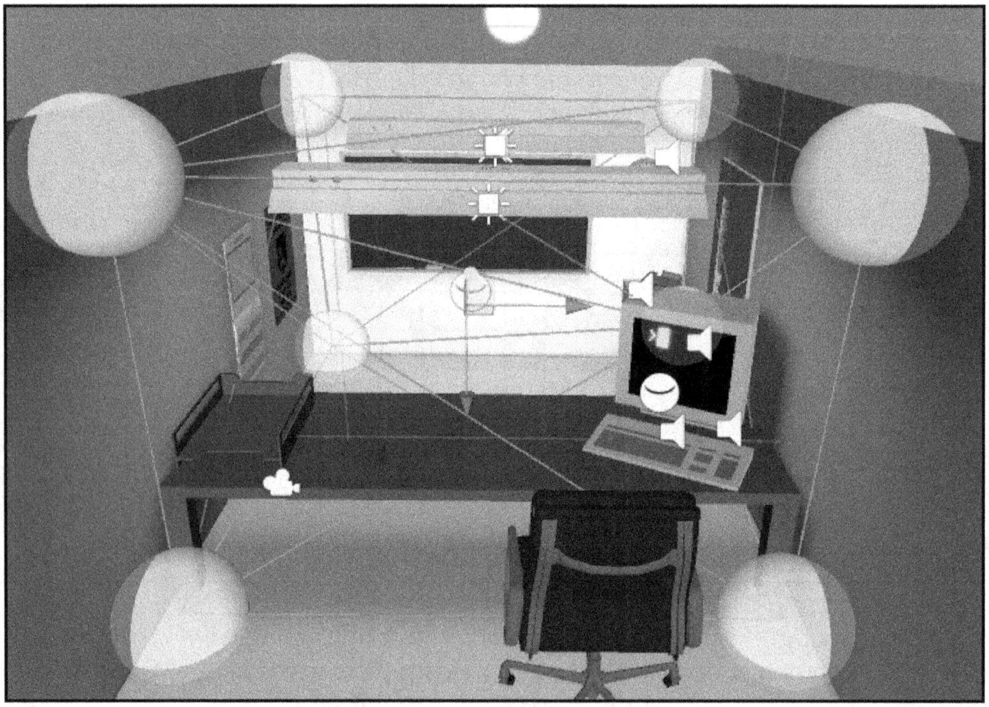

For our example, it would just be the center area the player is able to enter:

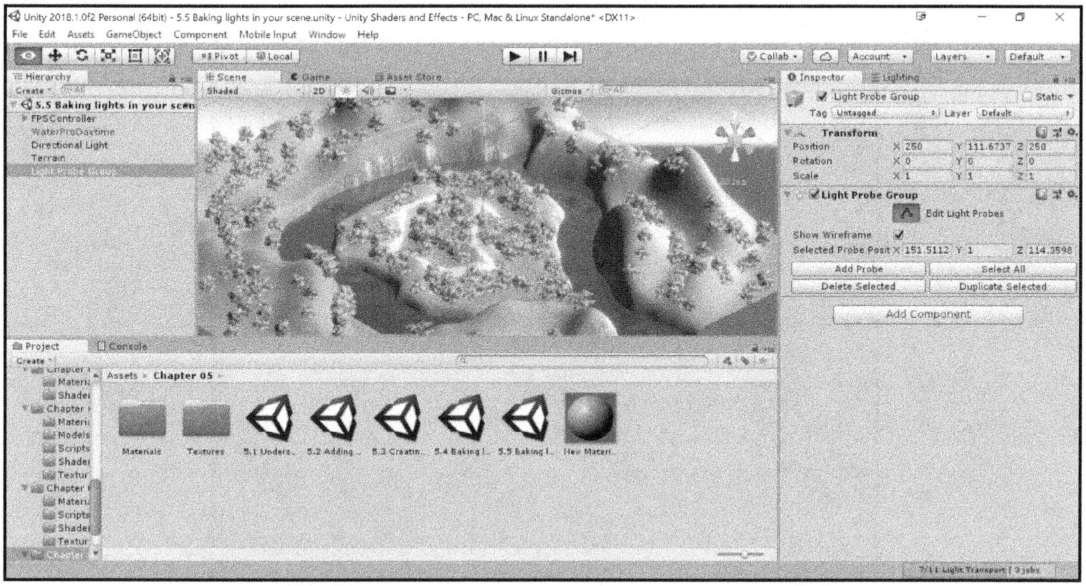

3. Select the moving objects that will enter the light probe region.

4. From their **Inspector**, expand their **renderer component** (usually **Mesh Renderer**) and make sure that **Light Probes** is not set to **Off checked** (see the following screenshot):

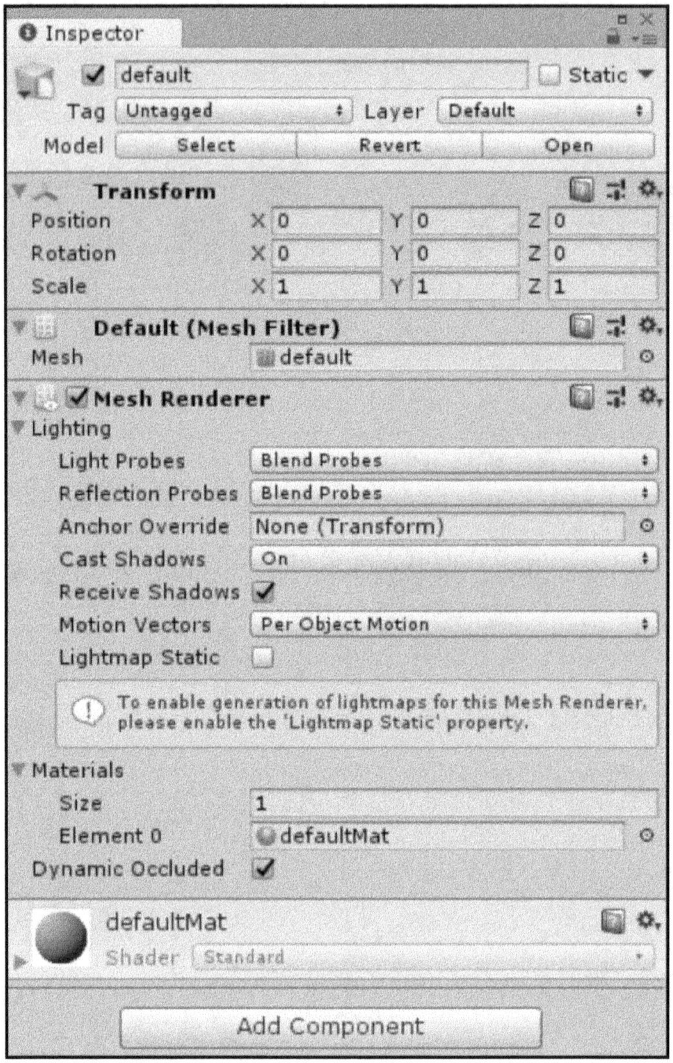

Deciding where and when to use light probes is a critical problem; more information about this can be found in the *How it works...* section for this recipe.

Baking the lights

To bake the lights, follow the given steps:

1. First, select the lights you'd like to bake. Confirm from the **Inspector** tab that the **Mode** is set to **Baked** in the **Light** component:

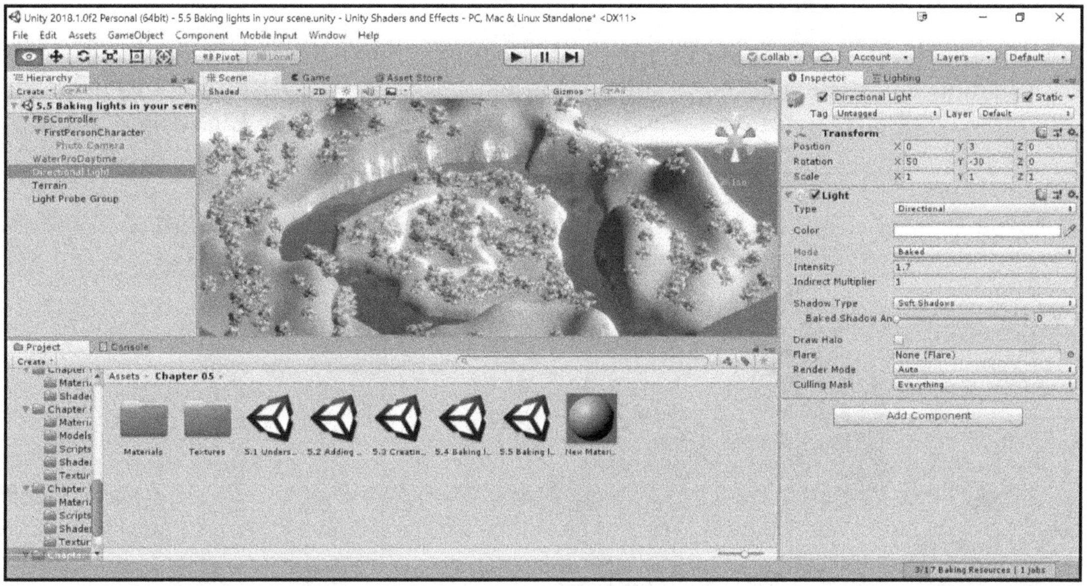

2. To finally bake the lights, open the **Lighting** window by going to **Window** | **Lighting** | **Settings**. Once there, select the **Global Maps** tab.
3. If the **Auto Generate** checkbox is enabled, Unity will automatically execute the baking process in the background. If not, click on **Generate Lighting**.

> Light baking can take several hours even for a relatively small scene. If you are constantly moving static objects or lights, Unity will restart the process from scratch, causing a severe slowdown in the editor. You can uncheck the **Auto** checkbox from the **Lighting** | **Lightmaps** | **Settings** tab to prevent this so that you can decide when to start the process manually.

How it works...

The most complicated part of rendering is the light transport. During this phase, the GPU calculates how the rays of light bounce between objects. If an object and its lights don't move, this calculation can be done only once as it will never change during the game. Flagging an object as **Static** is how to tell Unity that such an optimization can be made.

Loosely speaking, light baking refers to the process of calculating the global illumination of a static object and saving it in what is called a **lightmap**. Once baking is completed, lightmaps can be seen in the **Global Maps** tab of the **Lighting** window:

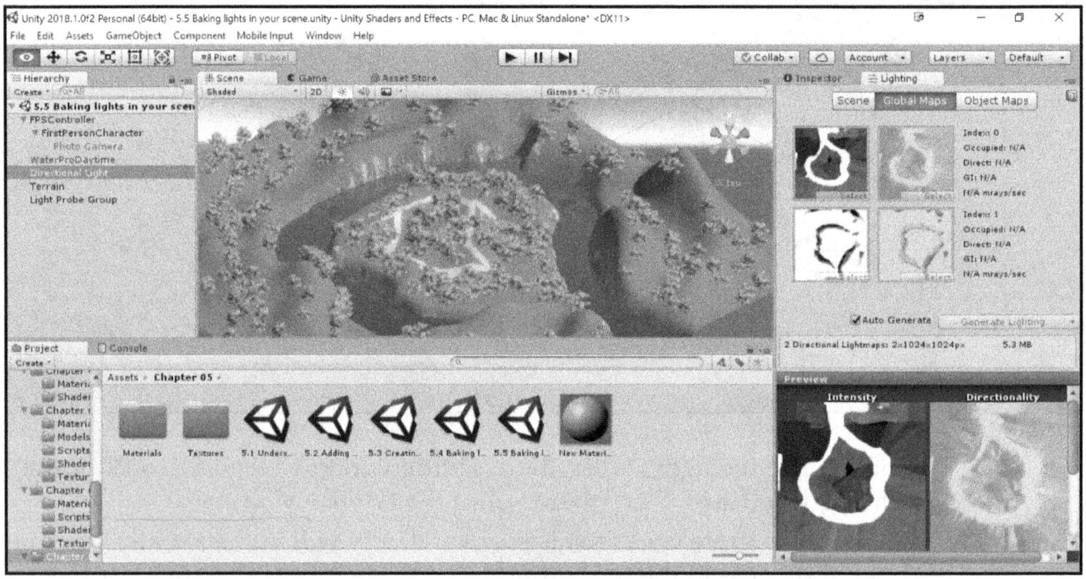

Light baking comes at a great expense: memory. Every static surface is, in fact, retextured so that it already includes its lighting condition. Let's imagine that you have a forest of trees, all sharing the same texture. Once they are made static, each tree will have its very own texture. Light baking not only increases the size of your game, but can take a lot of texture memory if used indiscriminately.

The second aspect introduced in this recipe is **light probing**. Light baking produces extremely high-quality results for static geometries, but does not work on moving objects. If your character is entering a static region, it can look somehow *detached* from the environment. Its shading will not match the surroundings, resulting in an aesthetically unpleasant result. Other objects, such as **skinned mesh renderers**, will not receive global illumination even if made static. Baking lights in real-time is not possible, although light probes offer an effective alternative. Every light probe samples the global illumination at a specific point in space. A light probe group can sample several points in space, allowing the interpolation of global illumination within a specific volume. This allows us to cast a better light on moving objects, even despite the fact that global illumination has been calculated only for a few points. It is important to remember that light probes need to enclose a volume in order to work. It is best to place light probes in regions where there is a sudden change in light conditions. Similar to lightmaps, probes consume memory and should be placed wisely; remember that they exist only for non-static geometry. Since there are no visible objects in the demoscene, this was done purely for demonstration purposes.

Even while using light probes, there are a few aspects that Unity's global illumination cannot capture. Non-static objects, for instance, cannot reflect light on other objects.

See also

You can read more about light probes at `http://docs.unity3d.com/Manual/LightProbes.html`.

8
Vertex Functions

The term shader originates from the fact that Cg has been used mainly to simulate realistic lighting conditions (shadows) on 3D models. Despite this, shaders are now much more than that. They not only define the way the objects are going to look, they can also redefine their shapes entirely. If you want to learn how to manipulate the geometry of a 3D object via shaders, this is the chapter for you.

In this chapter, you will learn the following recipes:

- Accessing a vertex color in a Surface Shader
- Animating vertices in a Surface Shader
- Extruding your models
- Implementing a snow shader
- Implementing a volumetric explosion

Introduction

In `Chapter 4`, *Creating Your First Shader*, we explained that 3D models are not just a collection of triangles. Each vertex can contain data that is essential to render the model itself correctly. This chapter will explore how to access this information in order to use it in a shader. We will also explore in detail how the geometry of an object can be deformed simply using Cg code.

Accessing a vertex color in a Surface Shader

Let's begin this chapter by taking a look at how we can access the information of a model's vertex using the vertex function in a Surface Shader. This will arm us with the knowledge to start utilizing the elements contained within a model's vertex in order to create really useful and visually appealing effects.

A vertex in a vertex function can return information about itself that we need to be aware of. You can actually retrieve the vertices' normal directions as a float3 value and the position of the vertex as float3, and you can even store color values in each vertex and return that color as float4. This is what we will take a look at in this recipe. We need to see how to store color information and retrieve this stored color information inside each vertex of a Surface Shader.

Getting ready

In order to write this shader, we need to prepare a few assets.

In order to view the colors of a vertex, we need to have a model that has had color applied to its vertices. While you could use Unity to apply colors, you would have to write a tool to allow an individual to apply the colors or write some scripts to achieve the color application.

In the case of this recipe, you can use a 3D modeling tool such as Maya or Blender to apply the colors to our model. There is a model available in the example code provided with the book in the `Chapter 06 | Models` folder (`VertexColorObject.fbx`) that you can obtain at the book's *Support* page at `https://www.packtpub.com/books/content/support`.

The following steps will set us up to create this Vertex Shader:

1. Create a new scene and place the imported model (`VertexColorObject`) in the scene.
2. Create a new **Shader** (`SimpleVertexColor`) and **Material** (`SimpleVertexColorMat`).
3. When completed, assign the shader to the material and then the material to the imported model.

Your scene should now look similar to the following screenshot:

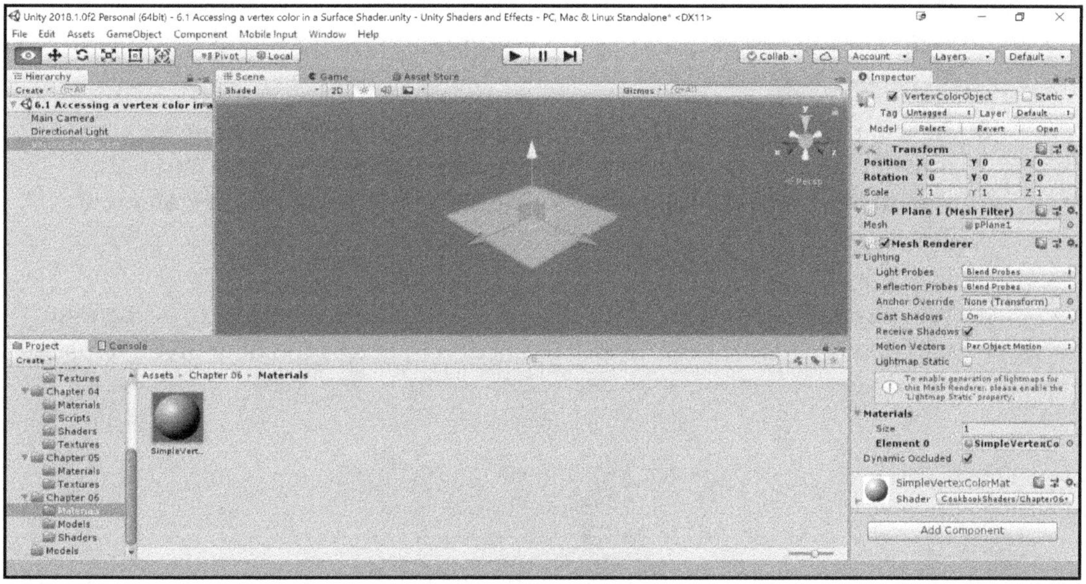

How to do it...

With our scene, shader, and material created and ready to go, we can begin to write the code for our shader. Launch the shader by double-clicking on it in the **Project** tab in the Unity editor. Perform the following steps:

1. As we are creating a very simple shader, we will not need to include any properties in our `Properties` block. We will still include a `Global Color Tint`, just to stay consistent with the other shaders in this book. Enter the following code in the `Properties` block of your shader:

```
Properties
{
  _MainTint("Global Color Tint", Color) = (1,1,1,1)
}
```

2. This next step tells Unity that we will be including a vertex function in our shader:

```
CGPROGRAM
#pragma surface surf Lambert vertex:vert
```

3. As usual, if we have included properties in our `Properties` block, we must make sure to create a corresponding variable in our `CGPROGRAM` statement. Enter the following code just below the `#pragma` statement:

```
float4 _MainTint;
```

4. We now turn our attention to the `Input struct`. We need to add a new variable in order for our `surf()` function to access the data given to us by our `vert()` function:

```
struct Input
{
  float2 uv_MainTex;
  float4 vertColor;
};
```

5. Now we can write our simple `vert()` function to gain access to the colors stored in each vertex of our mesh:

```
void vert(inout appdata_full v, out Input o)
{
  UNITY_INITIALIZE_OUTPUT(Input,o);
  o.vertColor = v.color;
}
```

6. Finally, we can use the vertex color data from our `Input struct` to be assigned to the `o.Albedo` parameters in the built-in `SurfaceOutput` struct:

```
void surf (Input IN, inout SurfaceOutput o)
{
  o.Albedo = IN.vertColor.rgb * _MainTint.rgb;
}
```

7. With our code completed, we can now re-enter the Unity editor and let the shader compile. If all goes well, you should see something similar to the following screenshot:

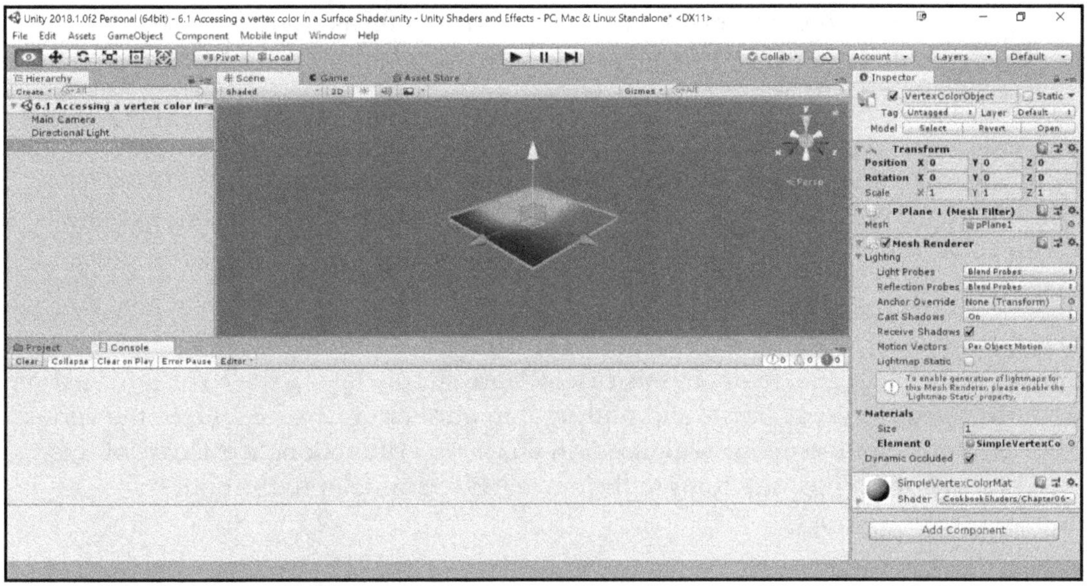

How it works...

Unity provides us with a way to access the vertex information of the model to which a shader is attached. This gives us the power to modify things such as the vertices' position and color. With this recipe, we have imported a mesh from Maya (though just about any 3D software application can be used), where vertex colors were added to `Verts`. You'll notice that by importing the model, the default material will not display the vertex colors. We actually have to write a shader to extract the vertex color and display it on the surface of the model. Unity provides us with a lot of built-in functionality when using Surface Shaders, which makes the process of extracting this vertex information quick and efficient.

Our first task is to tell Unity that we will be using a vertex function when creating our shader. We do this by adding the `vertex:vert` parameter to the `#pragma` statement of `CGPROGRAM`. This automatically makes Unity look for a vertex function named `vert()` when it goes to compile the shader. If it doesn't find one, Unity will throw a compiling error and ask you to add a `vert()` function to your shader.

This brings us to our next step. We have to actually code the `vert()` function, as seen in *step 5*. We first use a built-in macro to make sure that the `o` variable is initialized to 0 if it doesn't have anything that is a requirement if you are targeting DirectX 11 or above.

> For more information on the macro, as well as all of the other macros that ShaderLab has to offer, check out: `https://docs.unity3d.com/Manual/SL-BuiltinMacros.html`.

By having this function, we can access the built-in data struct called `appdata_full`. This built-in struct is where the vertex information is stored. So, we then extract the vertex color information by passing it to our `Input struct` by adding the code, `o.vertColor = v.color`.

The `o` variable represents our `Input struct` and the `v` variable is our `appdata_full vertex` data. In this case, we are simply taking the color information from the `appdata_full` struct and putting it in our `Input struct`. Once the vertex color is in our Input struct, we can use it in our `surf()` function. In the case of this recipe, we simply apply the color to the `o.Albedo` parameter to the built-in `SurfaceOutput` struct.

There's more...

You can also access the fourth component from the `vert` color data. If you notice, the `vertColor` variable we declared in the `Input struct` is of the `float4` type. This means that we are also passing the alpha value of the vertex colors. Knowing this, you can use it to your advantage for the purpose of storing a fourth vertex color to perform effects such as transparency or giving yourself one more mask to blend two textures. It's really up to you and your production to determine if you really need to use the fourth component, but it is worth mentioning here.

Animating vertices in a Surface Shader

Now that we know how to access data on a per-vertex basis, let's expand our knowledge set to include other types of data and the position of a vertex.

Using a vertex function, we can access the position of each vertex in a mesh. This allows us to actually modify each individual vertex while the shader does the processing.

In this recipe, we will create a shader that will allow us to modify the positions of each vertex on a mesh with a sine wave. This technique can be used to create animations for objects such as flags or waves on an ocean.

Getting ready

Let's gather our assets together so that we can create the code for our Vertex Shader:

1. Create a new scene and place a plane mesh in the center of the scene (**GameObject** | **3D Objects** | **Plane**).

> **TIP:** The `Plane` object created may seem to be a single quad but, in fact, has 121 verts, which we are going to be moving. Using a quad would provide unexpected results. To check for yourself, select the `Plane` object and, under the **Plane (Mesh Filter)** component, double-click on the **Mesh** property.

2. Create a new shader (`VertexAnimation`) and material (`VertexAnimationMat`).
3. Finally, assign the shader to the material and the material to the plane mesh.

Your scene should look similar to the following screenshot:

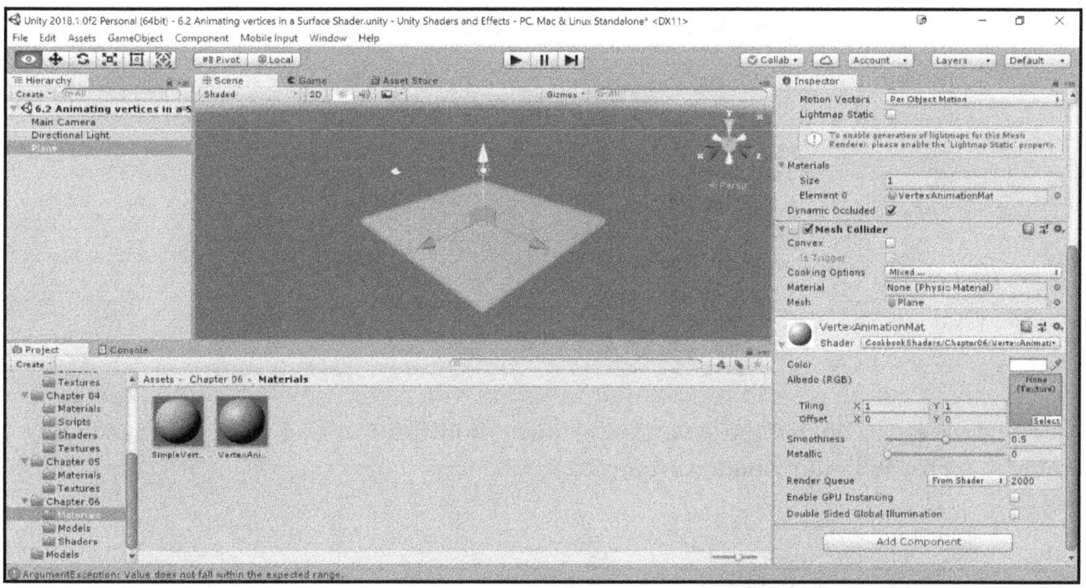

How to do it...

With our scene ready to go, let's double-click on our newly created shader to open it in the code editor:

1. Let's begin with our shader and populate the `Properties` block:

```
Properties
{
  _MainTex ("Base (RGB)", 2D) = "white" {}
  _tintAmount ("Tint Amount", Range(0,1)) = 0.5
  _ColorA ("Color A", Color) = (1,1,1,1)
  _ColorB ("Color B", Color) = (1,1,1,1)
  _Speed ("Wave Speed", Range(0.1, 80)) = 5
  _Frequency ("Wave Frequency", Range(0, 5)) = 2
  _Amplitude ("Wave Amplitude", Range(-1, 1)) = 1
}
```

2. We now need to tell Unity that we are going to be using a vertex function by adding the following to the `#pragma` statement:

```
CGPROGRAM
#pragma surface surf Lambert vertex:vert
```

3. In order to access the values that have been given to us by our properties, we need to declare a corresponding variable in our `CGPROGRAM` block:

```
sampler2D _MainTex;
float4 _ColorA;
float4 _ColorB;
float _tintAmount;
float _Speed;
float _Frequency;
float _Amplitude;
float _OffsetVal;
```

4. We will be using the vertex position modification as a `vert` color as well. This will allow us to tint our object:

```
struct Input
{
  float2 uv_MainTex;
  float3 vertColor;
}
```

5. At this point, we can perform our vertex modification using a sine wave and vertex function. Enter the following code after the `Input struct`:

```
void vert(inout appdata_full v, out Input o)
{
  UNITY_INITIALIZE_OUTPUT(Input,o);
  float time = _Time * _Speed;
  float waveValueA = sin(time + v.vertex.x * _Frequency) *
_Amplitude;

  v.vertex.xyz = float3(v.vertex.x, v.vertex.y +
waveValueA, v.vertex.z);
  v.normal = normalize(float3(v.normal.x + waveValueA,
v.normal.y, v.normal.z));
  o.vertColor = float3(waveValueA,waveValueA,waveValueA);
}
```

6. Finally, we complete our shader by performing a `lerp()` function between two colors so that we can tint the peaks and valleys of our new mesh, modified by our vertex function:

```
void surf (Input IN, inout SurfaceOutput o)
{
  half4 c = tex2D (_MainTex, IN.uv_MainTex);
  float3 tintColor = lerp(_ColorA, _ColorB,
IN.vertColor).rgb;
  o.Albedo = c.rgb * (tintColor * _tintAmount);
  o.Alpha = c.a;
}
```

7. After completing the code for your shader, switch back to Unity and let the shader compile. Once compiled, select the **Material** and assign the **Base (RGB) Texture** to the `UV Checker` material that is included in `Chapter 6 | Textures` folder of this book's example code.

8. From there, assign **Color A** and **Color B** to different colors. After the changes, you should see something similar to the following screenshot:

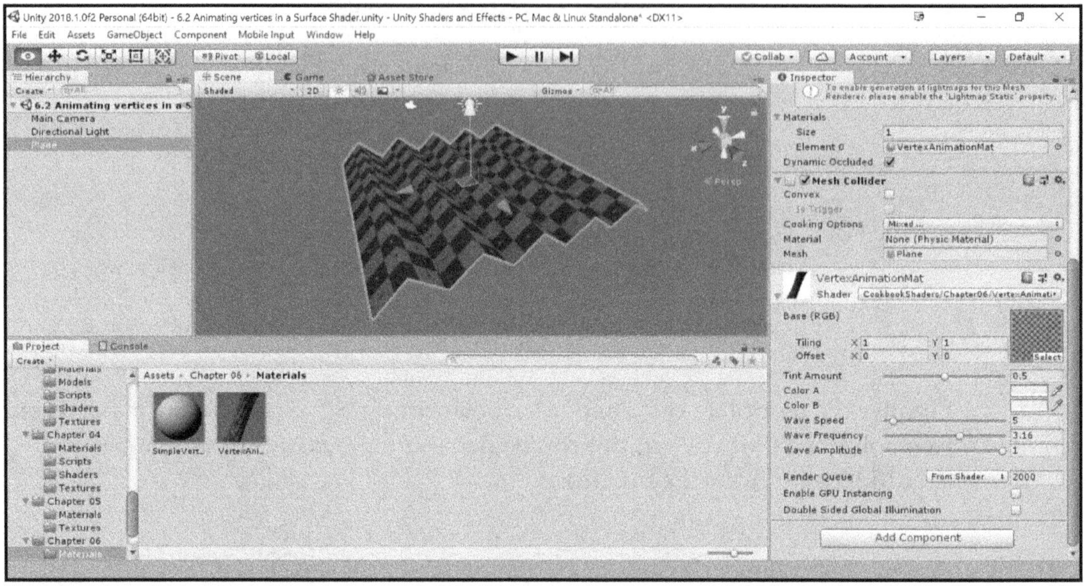

How it works...

This particular shader uses the same concept from the last recipe, except that this time, we are modifying the positions of the vertices in the mesh. This is really useful if you don't want to rig up simple objects, such as a flag, and then animate them using a skeleton structure or hierarchy of transforms.

We simply create a sine wave value using the `sin()` function that is built into the Cg language. After calculating this value, we add it to the *y* value of each vertex position, creating a wave-like effect.

We also modified the normal on the mesh just to give it more realistic shading based on the sine wave value.

You will see how easy it is to perform more complex vertex effects by utilizing the built-in vertex parameters that Surface Shaders give us.

Extruding your models

One of the biggest problems in games is repetition. Creating new content is a time-consuming task, and when you have to face thousands of enemies, chances are that they will all look the same. A relatively cheap technique to add variation to your models is using a shader that alters its basic geometry. This recipe will show you a technique called **normal extrusion**, which can be used to create a chubbier or skinnier version of a model, as shown in the following screenshot of a soldier from the Unity camp demo:

For ease of use, I have provided a prefab of the solider in the example code for this book under the `Chapter 6 | Prefabs` folder.

Getting ready

For this recipe, you need to have access to the shader used by the model that you want to alter. Once you have it, we duplicate it so that we can edit it safely. It can be done as follows:

1. Find the shader your model is using and, once selected, duplicate it by pressing *Ctrl* + *D*. If it is just using the Standard Shader, as in this example, it is also possible to just create a new Standard Material such as normal, and the Albedo map will automatically transfer over. Either way, rename this new shader `NormalExtrusion`.

2. Duplicate the original material of the model and assign the cloned shader to it.
3. Assign the new material to your model (`NormalExtrusionMat`) and start editing it.

In order for this effect to work, your model should have **normals**.

How to do it...

To create this effect, start by modifying the duplicated shader:

1. Let's start by adding a property to our shader, which will be used to modulate its extrusion. The range presented here goes from `-0.0001` to `0.0001`, but you might have to adjust this according to your own needs:

```
__Amount ("Extrusion Amount", Range(-0.0001, 0.0001)) = 0
```

2. Couple the property with its respective variable:

```
float _Amount;
```

3. Change the `#pragma` directive so that it now uses a vertex modifier. You can do this by adding `vertex:function_name` at the end of it. In our case, we have called the `vert:` function:

```
#pragma surface surf Standard vertex:vert
```

4. Add the following vertex modifier:

```
void vert (inout appdata_full v)
{
  v.vertex.xyz += v.normal * _Amount;
}
```

5. The shader is now ready; you can use the Extrusion Amount slider in the material's **Inspector** tab to make your model skinnier or chubbier. Also, feel free to create a clone of the material in order to have different extrusion amounts for each character:

How it works...

Surface Shaders work in two steps. In all the previous chapters, we only explored its last one: the surface function. There is another function that can be used: the vertex modifier. It takes the data structure of a vertex (which is usually called `appdata_full`) and applies a transformation to it. This gives us the freedom to do virtually anything with the geometry of our model. We signal to the GPU that such a function exists by adding `vertex:vert` to the `#pragma` directive of the Surface Shader. You can refer to `Chapter 9`, *Fragment Shaders and Grab Passes,* to learn how vertex modifiers can be defined in a Vertex and Fragment Shader instead.

One of the most simple yet effective techniques that can be used to alter the geometry of a model is called normal extrusion. It works by projecting a vertex along its normal direction. This is done by the following line of code:

```
v.vertex.xyz += v.normal * _Amount;
```

The position of a vertex is displaced by `_Amount` units toward the vertex normal. If `_Amount` gets too high, the results can be quite unpleasant. With smaller values, however, you can add a lot of variation to your models.

There's more...

If you have multiple enemies and want each one to have its own weight, you have to create a different material for each one of them. This is necessary as materials are normally shared between models and changing one will change all of them. There are several ways in which you can do this; the quickest one is to create a script that automatically does it for you. The following script, once attached to an object with a `Renderer`, will duplicate its first material and set the `_Amount` property automatically:

```
using UnityEngine;
public class NormalExtruder : MonoBehaviour {
  [Range(-0.0001f, 0.0001f)]
  public float amount = 0;
  // Use this for initialization
  void Start ()
  {
    Material material = GetComponent<Renderer>().sharedMaterial;
    Material newMaterial = new Material(material);
    newMaterial.SetFloat("_Amount", amount);
    GetComponent<Renderer>().material = newMaterial;
  }
}
```

Adding extrusion maps

This technique can actually be improved even further. We can add an extra texture (or use the alpha channel of the main one) to indicate the amount of extrusion. This allows for much better control over which parts are raised or lowered. The following code shows you how it is possible to achieve such an effect (the main difference from what we've done before is in bold):

```
Shader "CookbookShaders/Chapter06/Normal Extrusion Map"
{
  Properties
  {
    _MainTex("Texture", 2D) = "white" {}
    _ExtrusionTex("Extrusion map", 2D) = "white" {}
  _ Amount("Extrusion Amount", Range(-0.0001, 0.0001)) = 0
  }
  SubShader
  {
    Tags{ "RenderType" = "Opaque" }

    CGPROGRAM
```

```
    #pragma surface surf Standard vertex:vert
    struct Input
    {
      float2 uv_MainTex;
    };

    float _Amount;

    sampler2D _ExtrusionTex;
    void vert(inout appdata_full v)
    {
      float4 tex = tex2Dlod (_ExtrusionTex,
float4(v.texcoord.xy,0,0));
      float extrusion = tex.r * 2 - 1;
      v.vertex.xyz += v.normal * _Amount * extrusion;
    }

    sampler2D _MainTex;
    void surf(Input IN, inout SurfaceOutputStandard o)
    {
      float4 tex = tex2D(_ExtrusionTex, IN.uv_MainTex);
      float extrusion = abs(tex.r * 2 - 1);

      o.Albedo = tex2D(_MainTex, IN.uv_MainTex).rgb;
      o.Albedo = lerp(o.Albedo.rgb, float3(0, 0,0), extrusion *
_Amount
                        / 0.0001 * 1.1);
    }
  ENDCG
  }

  Fallback "Diffuse"
}
```

The red channel of `_ExtrusionTex` is used as a multiplying coefficient for normal extrusion. A value of `0.5` leaves the model unaffected; darker or lighter shades are used to extrude vertices inward or outward, respectively. You should note that in order to sample a texture within a vertex modifier, `tex2Dlod` should be used instead of `tex2D`.

In shaders, color channels go from zero to one, although sometimes you need to represent negative values as well (such as inward extrusion). When this is the case, treat `0.5` as zero; consider having smaller values as negative and higher values as positive. This is exactly what happens with normals, which are usually encoded in RGB textures. The `UnpackNormal()` function is used to map a value in the range (0,1) on the range (-1,+1). Mathematically speaking, this is equivalent to `tex.r * 2 -1`.

Extrusion maps are perfect for zombifying characters by shrinking the skin to highlight the shape of the bones underneath. The following screenshot shows you how a healthy soldier can be transformed into a corpse using just a shader and extrusion map. Compared to the previous example, you may notice how the clothing is unaffected. The shader used in the following screenshot also darkens the extruded regions to give an even more emaciated look to the soldier:

Implementing a snow shader

The simulation of snow has always been a challenge in games. The vast majority of games simply include snow directly in the model's texture so that their tops look white. However, what if one of these objects starts rotating? Snow is not just a lick of paint on a surface; it is a proper accumulation of material and should be treated as such. This recipe shows you how to give a snowy look to your models using just a shader.

This effect is achieved in two steps. First, white is used for all the triangles facing the sky. Second, their vertices are extruded to simulate the effect of snow accumulation. You can see the result in the following screenshot:

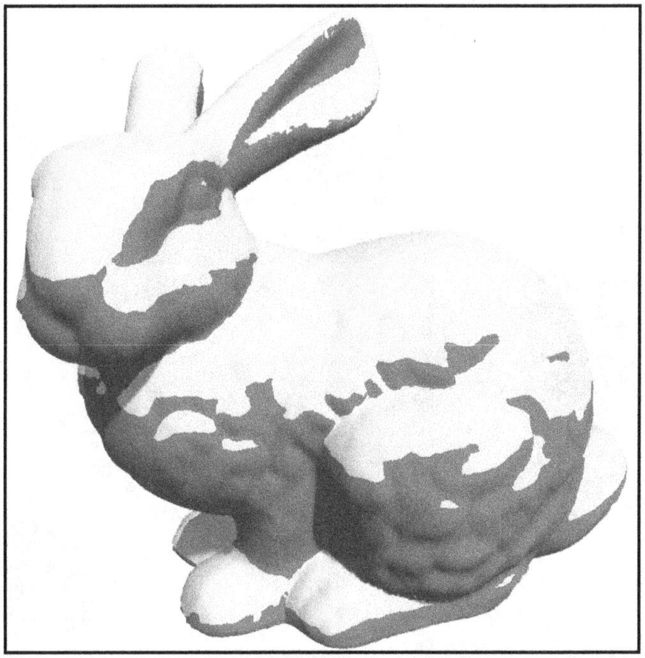

> Keep in mind that this recipe does not aim to create a photorealistic snow effect. It provides a good starting point, but it is up to the artist to create the right textures and find the right parameters to make it fit your game.

Getting ready

This effect is purely based on shaders. We will need the following:

1. Create a new shader for the snow effect (`SnowShader`).
2. Create a new material for the shader (`SnowMat`).
3. Assign the newly created material to the object that you want to be snowy and assign a color so it's easier to tell where the snow is:

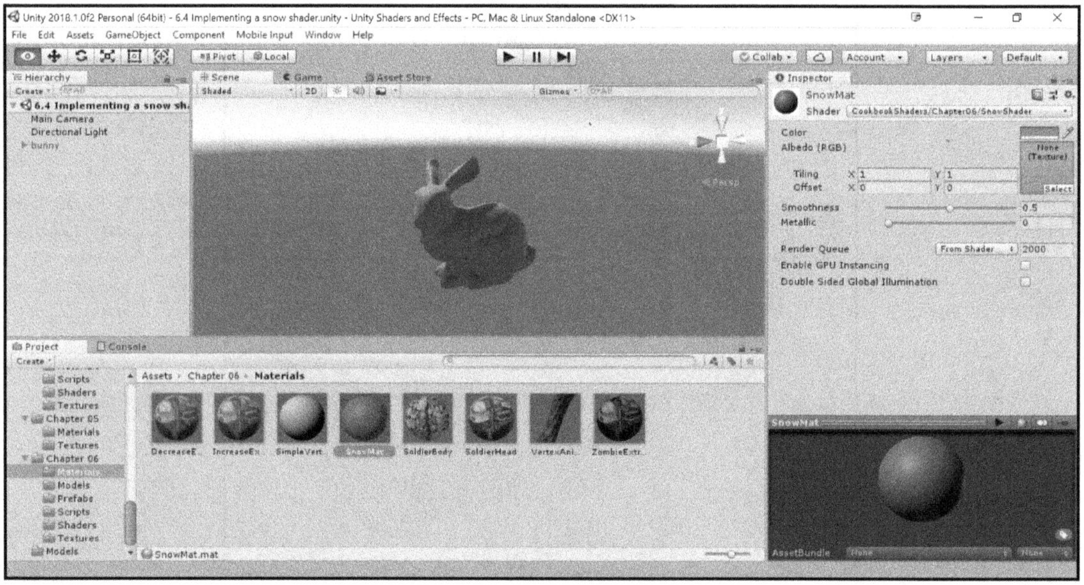

How to do it...

To create a snowy effect, open your shader and make the following changes:

1. Replace the properties of the shader with the following ones:

```
_Color("Main Color", Color) = (1.0,1.0,1.0,1.0)
_MainTex("Base (RGB)", 2D) = "white" {}
_Bump("Bump", 2D) = "bump" {}
_Snow("Level of snow", Range(1, -1)) = 1
_SnowColor("Color of snow", Color) = (1.0,1.0,1.0,1.0)
_SnowDirection("Direction of snow", Vector) = (0,1,0)
_SnowDepth("Depth of snow", Range(0,1)) = 0
```

2. Complete them with their relative variables:

```
sampler2D _MainTex;
sampler2D _Bump;
float _Snow;
float4 _SnowColor;
float4 _Color;
float4 _SnowDirection;
float _SnowDepth;
```

3. Replace the `Input` structure with the following one:

```
struct Input
{
  float2 uv_MainTex;
  float2 uv_Bump;
  float3 worldNormal;
  INTERNAL_DATA
};
```

4. Replace the surface function with the following one. It will color the snowy parts of the model white:

```
void surf(Input IN, inout SurfaceOutputStandard o)
{
  half4 c = tex2D(_MainTex, IN.uv_MainTex);

  o.Normal = UnpackNormal(tex2D(_Bump, IN.uv_Bump));
  if (dot(WorldNormalVector(IN, o.Normal), _SnowDirection.xyz)
      >= _Snow)
  {
  o.Albedo = _SnowColor.rgb;
  }
  else
  {
  o.Albedo = c.rgb * _Color;
  }
  o.Alpha = 1;
}
```

5. Configure the `#pragma` directive so that it uses vertex modifiers:

```
#pragma surface surf Standard vertex:vert
```

6. Add the following vertex modifiers, which extrude the vertices covered in snow:

```
void vert(inout appdata_full v)
{
  float4 sn = mul(UNITY_MATRIX_IT_MV, _SnowDirection);

  if (dot(v.normal, sn.xyz) >= _Snow)
  {
    v.vertex.xyz += (sn.xyz + v.normal) * _SnowDepth * _Snow;
  }
}
```

7. You can now use the material's **Inspector** tab to select how much of your model is going to be covered and how thick the snow should be:

How it works...

This shader works in two steps:

- Coloring the surface
- Altering the geometry.

Coloring the surface

The first step alters the color of the triangles that are facing the sky. It affects all the triangles with a normal direction similar to `_SnowDirection`. As seen before in `Chapter 5`, *Understanding Lighting Models*, comparing unit vectors can be done using the **dot product**. When two vectors are orthogonal, their dot product is zero; it is one (or minus one) when they are parallel to each other. The `_Snow` property is used to decide how aligned they should be in order to be considered as facing the sky.

If you look closely at the surface function, you can see that we are not dotting the normal and snow direction directly. This is because they are usually defined in a different space. The snow direction is expressed in world coordinates, while the object normals are usually relative to the model itself. If we rotate the model, its normals will not change, which is not what we want. To fix this, we need to convert the normals from their object coordinates to world coordinates. This is done with the `WorldNormalVector()` function, as seen in the following code:

```
if (dot(WorldNormalVector(IN, o.Normal), _SnowDirection.xyz) >=
  _Snow)
{
  o.Albedo = _SnowColor.rgb;
}
else
{
  o.Albedo = c.rgb * _Color;
}
```

This shader simply colors the model white; a more advanced one should initialize the `SurfaceOutputStandard` structure with textures and parameters from a realistic snow material.

Altering the geometry

The second effect of this shader alters the geometry to simulate the accumulation of snow. Firstly, we identify which triangles have been colored white by testing the same condition used in the surface function. This time, unfortunately, we cannot rely on `WorldNormalVector()` as the `SurfaceOutputStandard` structure is not yet initialized in the vertex modifier. We use this other method instead, which converts `_SnowDirection` to object coordinates:

```
float4 sn = mul(UNITY_MATRIX_IT_MV, _SnowDirection);
```

Then, we can extrude the geometry to simulate the accumulation of snow:

```
if (dot(v.normal, sn.xyz) >= _Snow)
{
    v.vertex.xyz += (sn.xyz + v.normal) * _SnowDepth * _Snow;
}
```

Once again, this is a very basic effect. You could use a texture map to control the accumulation of snow more precisely or give a peculiar, uneven look.

See also

If you need high-quality snow effects and props for your game, you can also check these resources on the Unity Asset Store:

- **Winter Suite ($30)**: A much more sophisticated version of the snow shader presented in this recipe can be found at `https://www.assetstore.unity3d.com/en/#!/content/13927`.
- **Winter Pack ($60)**: A very realistic set of props and materials for snowy environments can be found at `https://www.assetstore.unity3d.com/en/#!/content/13316`.

Implementing a volumetric explosion

The art of game development is a clever trade-off between realism and efficiency. This is particularly true for explosions; they are at the heart of many games, yet the physics behind them is often beyond the computational power of modern machines. Explosions are, essentially, nothing more than very hot balls of gas; hence, the only way to correctly simulate them is by integrating a fluid simulation into your game. As you can imagine, this is unfeasible for a runtime application, and many games simulate them simply with particles. When an object explodes, it is common to simply instantiate fire, smoke, and debris particles so that, together, they can achieve believable results. This approach, unfortunately, is not very realistic and is easy to spot. There is an intermediate technique that can be used to achieve a much more realistic effect: volumetric explosions. The idea behind this concept is that explosions are not treated like a bunch of particles; they are evolving 3D objects, not just flat 2D textures.

Getting ready

Complete this recipe with the following steps:

1. Create a new shader for this effect (`VolumetricExplosion`).
2. Create a new material to host the shader (`VolumetricExplosionMat`).
3. Attach the material to a sphere. You can create one directly from the editor, navigating to **GameObject** | **3D Object** | **Sphere**:

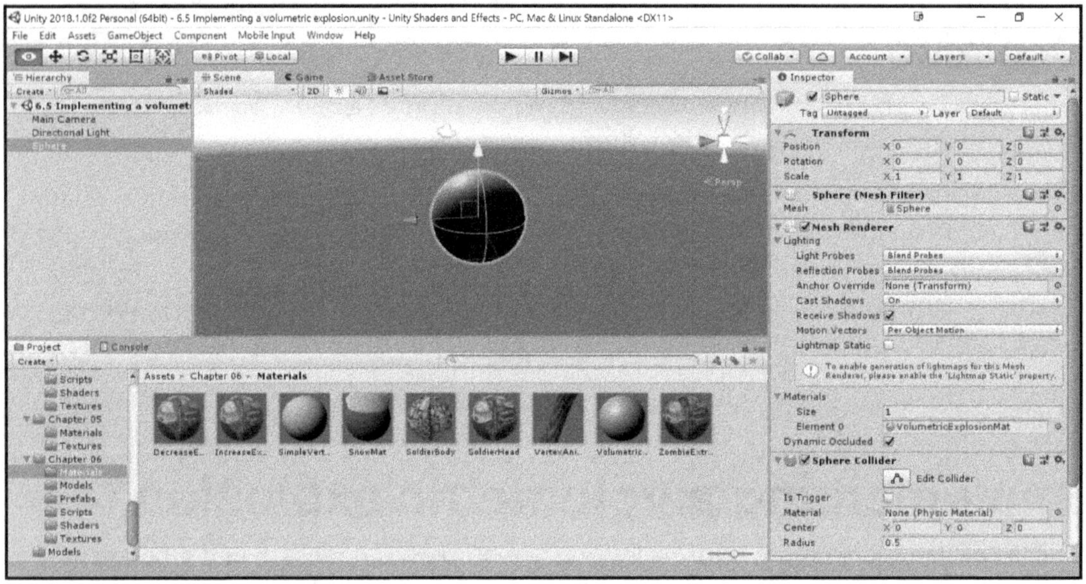

This recipe works well with the standard Unity Sphere, but if you need big explosions, you might need to use a high-poly sphere. In fact, a vertex function can only modify the vertices of a mesh. All the other points will be interpolated using the positions of the nearby vertices. Fewer vertices means a lower resolution for your explosions.

4. For this recipe, you will also need a ramp texture that has, in a gradient, all the colors your explosions will have. You can create a texture like the following screenshot using GIMP or Photoshop:

TIP: You can find this image (`explosionRamp`) in `Chapter 6 | Textures` folder in the example code provided with this book.

5. Once you have the picture, import it to Unity. Then, from its **Inspector**, make sure that **Filter Mode** is set to **Bilinear** and the **Wrap Mode** to **Clamp**. These two settings make sure that the ramp texture is sampled smoothly.
6. Lastly, you will need a noisy texture. You can search on the internet for freely available noise textures. The most commonly used ones are generated using Perlin noise. I have included an example in `Chapter 6 | Textures` folder for your use:

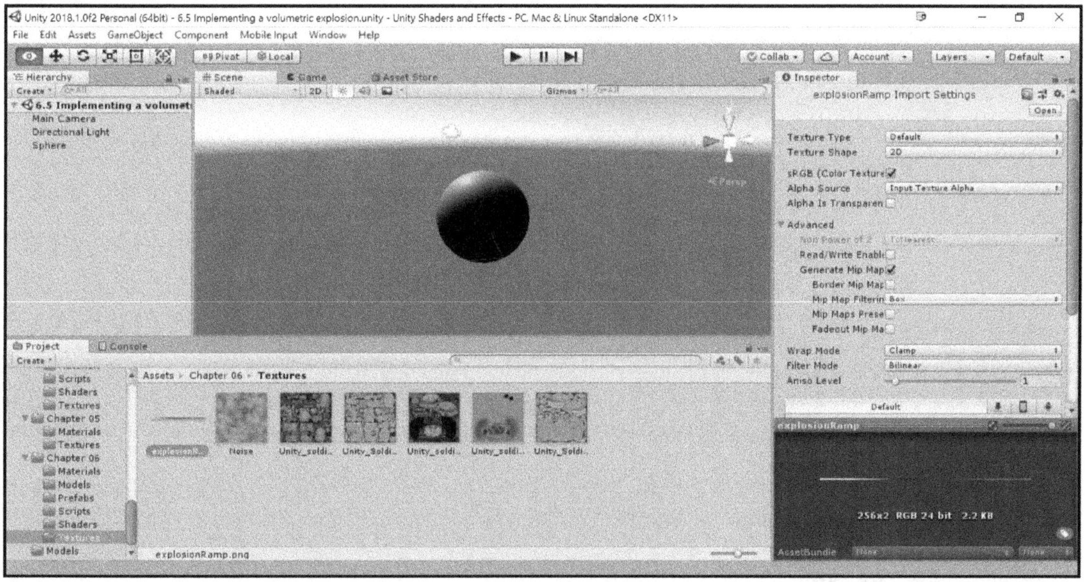

How to do it...

This effect works in two steps: a vertex function to change the geometry, and a surface function to give it the right color. The steps are as follows:

1. Remove the current properties and add the following properties to the shader:

```
Properties
{
  _RampTex("Color Ramp", 2D) = "white" {}
  _RampOffset("Ramp offset", Range(-0.5,0.5))= 0
  _NoiseTex("Noise Texture", 2D) = "gray" {}
  _Period("Period", Range(0,1)) = 0.5
  _Amount("_Amount", Range(0, 1.0)) = 0.1
  _ClipRange("ClipRange", Range(0,1)) = 1
}
```

2. Add their relative variables so that the Cg code of the shader can actually access them:

```
sampler2D _RampTex;
half _RampOffset;

sampler2D _NoiseTex;
float _Period;

half _Amount;
half _ClipRange;
```

3. Change the `Input` structure so that it receives the UV data of the ramp texture:

```
struct Input
{
  float2 uv_NoiseTex;
};
```

4. Add the following vertex function:

```
void vert(inout appdata_full v) {
  float3 disp = tex2Dlod(_NoiseTex,
float4(v.texcoord.xy,0,0));
  float time = sin(_Time[3] *_Period + disp.r*10);
  v.vertex.xyz += v.normal * disp.r * _Amount * time;
}
```

5. Add the following surface function:

```
void surf(Input IN, inout SurfaceOutput o)
{
  float3 noise = tex2D(_NoiseTex, IN.uv_NoiseTex);

  float n = saturate(noise.r + _RampOffset);

  clip(_ClipRange - n);

  half4 c = tex2D(_RampTex, float2(n,0.5));

  o.Albedo = c.rgb;
  o.Emission = c.rgb*c.a;
}
```

6. We specify the vertex function in the `#pragma` directive, adding the `nolightmap` parameter to prevent Unity from adding realistic lighting to our explosion:

```
#pragma surface surf Lambert vertex:vert nolightmap
```

7. The last step is selecting the material and, from its **Inspector**, attaching the two textures in the relative slots:

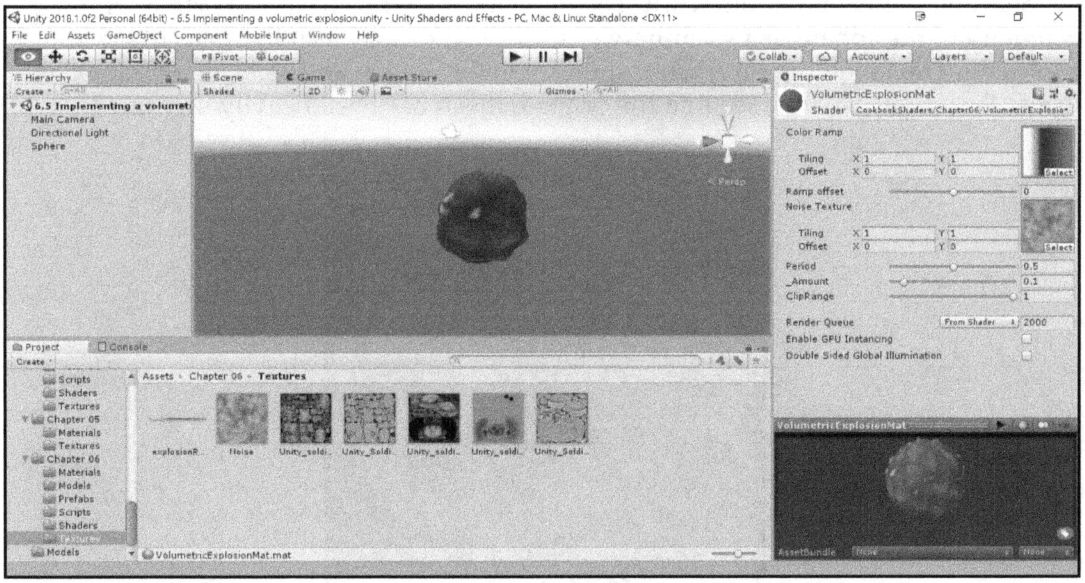

8. This is animated material, meaning that it evolves over time. You can watch the material changing in the editor by clicking on **Animated Materials** from the **Scene** window:

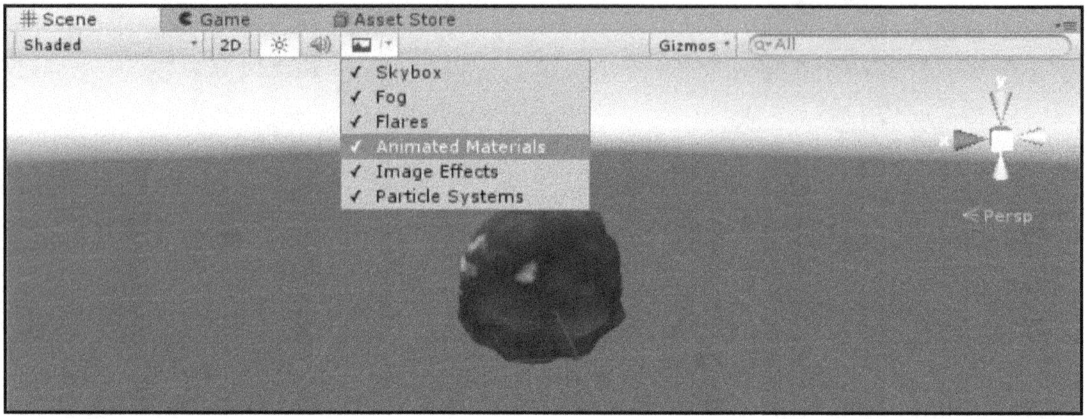

How it works...

If you are reading this recipe, you should already be familiar with how Surface Shaders and vertex modifiers work. The main idea behind this effect is to alter the geometry of the sphere in a seemingly chaotic way, exactly as it happens in a real explosion. The following screenshot shows you what such an explosion will look like inside the editor. You can see that the original mesh has been heavily deformed:

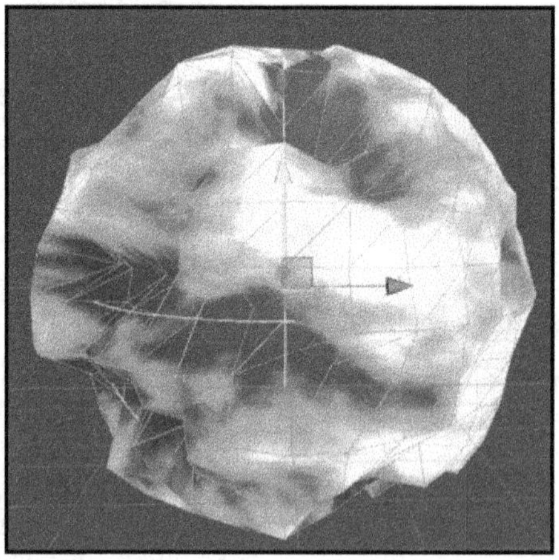

The vertex function is a variant of the technique called normal extrusion introduced in the *Extruding your models* recipe of this chapter. The difference here is that the amount of extrusion is determined both by the time and noise texture.

> When you need a random number in Unity, you can rely on the `Random.Range()` function. There is no standard way to get random numbers in a shader, so the easiest way is to sample a noise texture.

There is no standard way to do this, so take this as an example only:

```
float time = sin(_Time[3] *_Period + disp.r*10);
```

The built-in `_Time[3]` variable is used to get the current time from within the shader, and the red channel of the `disp.r` noise texture is used to make sure that each vertex moves independently. The `sin()` function makes the vertices go up and down, simulating the chaotic behavior of an explosion. Then, the normal extrusion takes place:

```
v.vertex.xyz += v.normal * disp.r * _Amount * time;
```

You should play with these numbers and variables until you find a pattern of movement that you are happy with.

The last part of the effect is achieved by the surface function. Here, the noise texture is used to sample a random color from the ramp texture. However, there are two more aspects that are worth noting. The first one is the introduction of `_RampOffset`. Its usage forces the explosion to sample colors from the left or right side of the texture. With positive values, the surface of the explosion tends to show more grey tones—exactly what happens when it is dissolving. You can use `_RampOffset` to determine how much fire or smoke there should be in your explosion. The second aspect introduced in the surface function is the usage of `clip()`. What `clip()` does is it clips (removes) pixels from the rendering pipeline. When invoked with a negative value, the current pixel is not drawn. This effect is controlled by `_ClipRange`, which determines which pixels of the volumetric explosions are going to be transparent.

By controlling both `_RampOffset` and `_ClipRange`, you have full control and can determine how the explosion behaves and dissolves.

There's more...

The shader presented in this recipe makes a sphere look like an explosion. If you really want to use it, you should couple it with some scripts in order to get the most out of it. The best thing to do is to create an explosion object and make it into a prefab so that you can reuse it every time you need to. You can do this by dragging the sphere back into the **Project** window. Once it is done, you can create as many explosions as you want using the `Instantiate()` function.

It is worth noticing, however, that all the objects with the same material share the same look. If you have multiple explosions at the same time, they should not use the same material. When you are instantiating a new explosion, you should also duplicate its material. You can do this easily with this piece of code:

```
GameObject explosion = Instantiate(explosionPrefab) as GameObject;
Renderer renderer = explosion.GetComponent<Renderer>();
Material material = new Material(renderer.sharedMaterial);
renderer.material = material;
```

Lastly, if you are going to use this shader in a realistic way, you should attach a script to it that changes its size, `_RampOffset`, and `_ClipRange` according to the type of explosion that you want to recreate.

See also

- Much more can be done to make explosions realistic. The approach presented in this recipe only creates an empty shell; inside it, the explosion is actually empty.
- An easy trick to improve this is to create particles inside it. However, you can only go so far with this.
- The short movie, *The Butterfly Effect* (`http://unity3d.com/pages/butterfly`), created by Unity Technologies in collaboration with Passion Pictures and Nvidia, is the perfect example.
- It is based on the same concept of altering the geometry of a sphere, but it renders it with a technique called **volume ray casting**.

- In a nutshell, it renders the geometry as if it's full. You can see an example in the following screenshot:

- If you are looking for high-quality explosions, check out Pyro Technix (`https://www.assetstore.unity3d.com/en/#!/content/16925`) in the Asset Store. It includes volumetric explosions and couples them with realistic shockwaves.

9
Fragment Shaders and Grab Passes

So far in this book, we have relied on Surface Shaders. They have been designed to simplify the way shader coding works, providing meaningful tools for artists. If we want to push our knowledge of shaders further, we need to venture into the territory of Vertex and Fragment Shaders.

In this chapter, you will learn the following recipes:

- Understanding Vertex and Fragment Shaders
- Using grab passes to draw behind objects
- Implementing a Glass Shader
- Implementing a Water Shader for 2D games

Introduction

Compared to Surface Shaders, Vertex and Fragment Shaders come with little to no information about the physical properties that determine how light reflects on surfaces. What they lack in expressivity, they compensate for with power: Vertex and Fragment Shaders are not limited by physical constraints and are perfect for non-photorealistic effects. This chapter will focus on a technique called the **grab pass**, which allows these shaders to simulate deformations.

Understanding Vertex and Fragment Shaders

The best way to understand how Vertex and Fragment Shaders work is by creating one yourself. This recipe will show you how to write one of these shaders, which will simply apply a texture to a model and multiply it by a given color, as shown in the following screenshot:

Notice how it works similarly to how the Multiply filter in Photoshop works. That's because we will be doing the same calculation done there!

The shader presented here is very simple, and it will be used as a starting base for all the other Vertex and Fragment Shaders.

Getting ready

For this recipe, we will need a new shader. Follow these steps:

1. Create a new shader (`Multiply`).
2. Create a new material (`MultiplyMat`) and assign the shader to it.
3. Bring the soldier prefab from the `Chapter 06 | Prefabs` folder into the scene, and attach the new material to the prefab's head. The head can be found in the `Soldier` child of the `Soldier` object.
4. From there, in the **Inspector** tab, scroll down to the **Skinned Mesh Renderer** component and, under **Materials**, set **Element 0** to the new materials. Lastly, in the `Albedo (RGB)` property, drag and drop the `Unity_soldier_Head_DIF_01` texture. The following screenshot should help demonstrate what we are looking for:

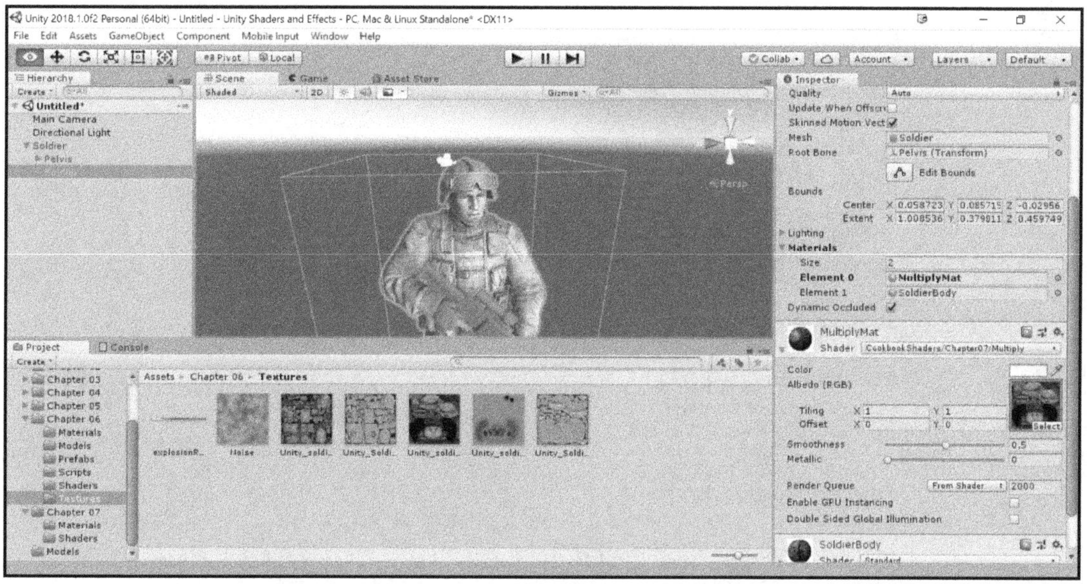

How to do it...

In all the previous chapters, we have always been able to refit Surface Shaders. This is not the case any more, as Surface and Fragment Shaders are structurally different. We will need to implement the following changes:

1. Delete all the properties of the shader, replacing them with the following:

```
Properties
{
 _Color ("Color", Color) = (1,0,0,1)
 _MainTex ("Albedo (RGB)", 2D) = "white" {}
}
```

2. Delete all the code in the `SubShader` block and replace it with this:

```
SubShader
{
 Pass
 {
 CGPROGRAM

 #pragma vertex vert
 #pragma fragment frag

 half4 _Color;
 sampler2D _MainTex;

 struct vertInput
 {
 float4 pos : POSITION;
 float2 texcoord : TEXCOORD0;
 };

 struct vertOutput
 {
 float4 pos : SV_POSITION;
 float2 texcoord : TEXCOORD0;
 };

 vertOutput vert(vertInput input)
 {
 vertOutput o;
 o.pos = mul(UNITY_MATRIX_MVP, input.pos);
 o.texcoord = input.texcoord;
 return o;
 }
```

```
        half4 frag(vertOutput output) : COLOR
        {
        half4 mainColour = tex2D(_MainTex, output.texcoord);
        return mainColour * _Color;
        }

        ENDCG
        }
      }
      FallBack "Diffuse"
```

3. Save your shader script and return to the Unity editor. Once finished, modify the **Color** property of the `MultiplyMat` material and see that we get the result we are looking for:

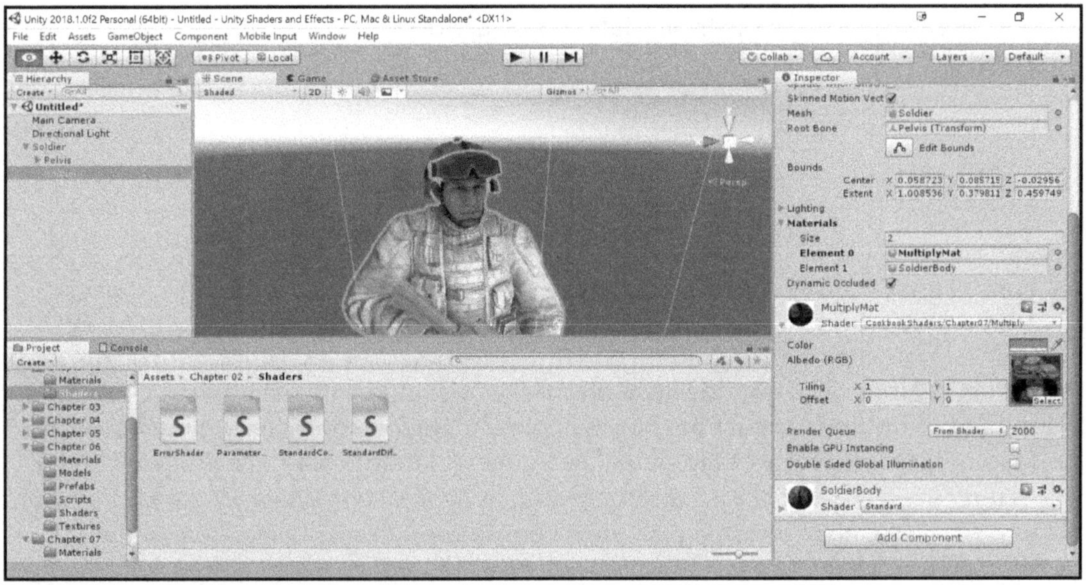

This will also be the base for all future Vertex and Fragment Shaders.

How it works...

As the name suggests, Vertex and Fragment Shaders work in two steps. The model is first passed through a vertex function; the result is then inputted to a Fragment function. Both these functions are assigned using `#pragma` directives:

```
#pragma vertex vert
#pragma fragment frag
```

In this case, they are simply called `vert` and `frag`.

Conceptually speaking, fragments are closely related to pixels; the term fragment is often used to refer to the collection of data necessary to draw a pixel. This is also why Vertex and Fragment Shaders are often called **Pixel Shaders**.

The vertex function takes the input data in a structure that is defined as `vertInput` in the shader:

```
struct vertInput
{
 float4 pos : POSITION;
 float2 texcoord : TEXCOORD0;
};
```

Its name is totally arbitrary, but its content is not. Each field of the `struct` must be decorated with a **binding semantic**. This is a feature of Cg that allows us to mark variables so that they will be initialized with certain data, such as normal vectors and the vertex position. The binding semantic, `POSITION`, indicates that when `vertInput` is inputted to the vertex function, `pos` will contain the position of the current vertex. This is similar to the vertex field of the `appdata_full` structure in a Surface Shader. The main difference is that `pos` is represented in model coordinates (relative to the 3D object), which we need to convert to view coordinates manually (relative to the position on the screen).

> The vertex function in a Surface Shader is used to alter the geometry of the model only. In a Vertex and Fragment Shader, instead, the vertex function is necessary to project the coordinates of the model to the screen.

The mathematics behind this conversion is beyond the scope of this chapter. However, this transformation can be achieved by using the `UnityObjectToClipPos` function, which will take a point from object space to the camera's clip space in homogeneous coordinates. This is done by multiplying by the **model-view-projection matrix**, and it is essential to find the position of a vertex on the screen:

```
vertOutput o;
o.pos = UnityObjectToClipPos(input.pos);
```

For more information on this and other helper functions that ShaderLab has built-in, check out `https://docs.unity3d.com/Manual/SL-BuiltinFunctions.html`.

The other piece of information initialized is `textcoord`, which uses the `TEXCOORD0` binding semantics to get the UV data of the first texture. No further processing is required, and this value can be passed directly to the fragment function (`frag`):

```
o.texcoord = input.texcoord;
```

While Unity will initialize `vertInput` for us, we are responsible for the initialization of `vertOutput`. Despite this, its fields still need to be decorated with binding semantics:

```
struct vertOutput
{
  float4 pos : SV_POSITION;
  float2 texcoord : TEXCOORD0;
};
```

Once the vertex function has initialized `vertOutput`, the structure is passed to the fragment function (`frag`). This samples the main texture of the model and multiplies it by the color provided.

As you can see, the Vertex and Fragment Shader have no knowledge of the physical properties of the material. This means that the material does not have the same effect by light sources, and it does not have data regarding how light reflects to create bumped surfaces compared to a Surface Shader; it works closer to the architecture of the graphics GPU.

There's more...

One of the most confusing aspects of Vertex and Fragment Shaders is binding semantics. There are many others that you can use, and their meanings depend on context.

Input semantics

The binding semantics in the following table can be used in `vertInput`, which is the structure that Unity provides to the vertex function. The fields decorated with this semantics will be initialized automatically:

Binding semantics	**Description**
`POSITION, SV_POSITION`	The position of a vertex in world coordinates (object space)
`NORMAL`	The normal of a vertex, relative to the world (not to the camera)
`COLOR, COLOR0, DIFFUSE, SV_TARGET`	The color information stored in the vertex
`COLOR1, SPECULAR`	The secondary color information stored in the vertex (usually the specular)
`TEXCOORD0, TEXCOORD1, ..., TEXCOORDi`	The i-th UV data stored in the vertex

Output semantics

When binding, semantics are used in `vertOutput`; they do not automatically guarantee that fields will be initialized. Quite the opposite; it's our responsibility to do so. The compiler will do its best to ensure that the fields are initialized with the right data:

Binding semantics	**Description**
`POSITION, SV_POSITION, HPOS`	The position of a vertex in camera coordinates (clip space, from zero to one for each dimension)
`COLOR, COLOR0, COL0, COL, SV_TARGET`	The front primary color
`COLOR1, COL1`	The front secondary color

`TEXCOORD0, TEXCOORD1, ..., TEXCOORDi, TEXi`	The i-th UV data stored in the vertex
`WPOS`	The position, in pixels, in the window (origin in the lower left corner)

If, for any reason, you need a field that will contain a different type of data, you can decorate it with one of the many `TEXCOORD` data available. The compiler will not allow fields to be left undecorated.

See also

You can refer to the NVIDIA Reference Manual to check the other binding semantics that are available in Cg:

`http://developer.download.nvidia.com/cg/Cg_3.1/Cg-3.1_April2012_ReferenceManual.pdf`

Using the grab pass to draw behind objects

In the *Adding transparency to PBR* recipe of `Chapter 7`, *Physically-Based Rendering*, we have seen how a material can be made transparent. Even if a transparent material can draw over a scene, it cannot change what has been drawn underneath it. This means that those Transparent Shaders cannot create distortions such as the ones typically seen in glass or water. In order to simulate them, we need to introduce another technique called a grab pass. This allows us to access what has been drawn on-screen so far, so that a shader can use it (or alter it) with no restrictions. To learn how to use grab passes, we will create a material that grabs what's rendered behind it and draws it again on the screen. It's a shader that, paradoxically, uses several operations to show no changes at all.

Getting ready

This recipe requires the following operations:

1. Create a shader (`GrabShader`) that we will initialize later.
2. Create a material (`GrabMat`) to host the shader.

3. Attach the material to a flat piece of geometry, such as a quad. Place it in front of some other object so that you cannot see through it. The quad will appear transparent as soon as the shader is complete:

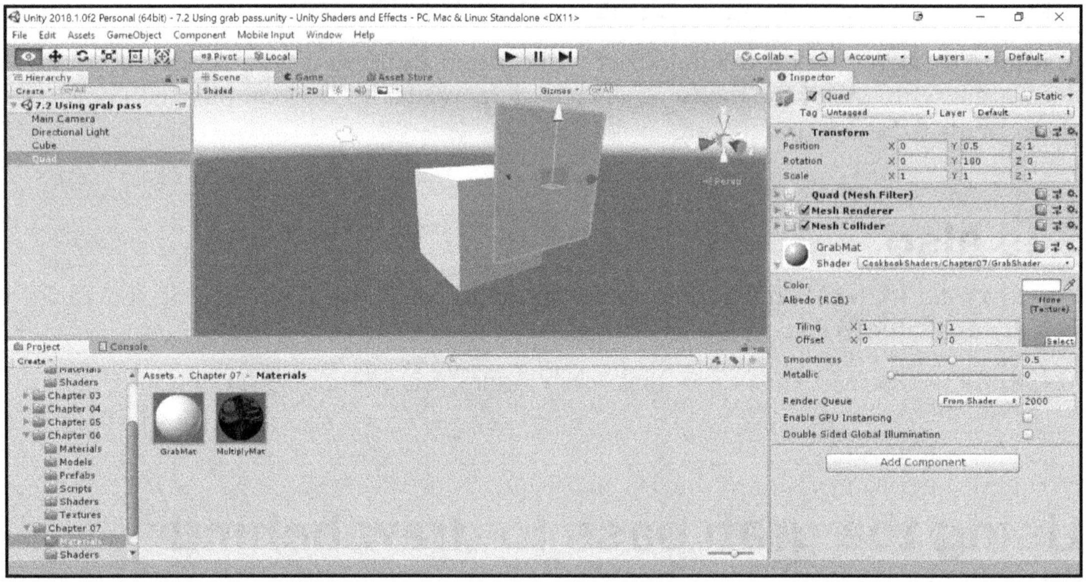

How to do it...

To use a grab pass, you need to follow these steps:

1. Remove the `Properties` section, and the `Input` section; this shader will not use any of them.
2. In the `SubShader` section, remove everything, and add the following to ensure the object is treated as being `Transparent`:

```
Tags{ "Queue" = "Transparent" }
```

3. Then, below that, add a grab pass:

```
GrabPass{ }
```

4. After the `GrabPass`, we will need to add this extra pass:

```
Pass
{
  CGPROGRAM
  #pragma vertex vert
  #pragma fragment frag

  #include "UnityCG.cginc"
  sampler2D _GrabTexture;

  struct vertInput
  {
    float4 vertex : POSITION;
  };

  struct vertOutput
  {
    float4 vertex : POSITION;
    float4 uvgrab : TEXCOORD1;
  };

  // Vertex function
  vertOutput vert(vertInput v)
  {
    vertOutput o;
    o.vertex = mul(UNITY_MATRIX_MVP, v.vertex);
    o.uvgrab = ComputeGrabScreenPos(o.vertex);
    return o;
  }
  // Fragment function
  half4 frag(vertOutput i) : COLOR
  {
    fixed4 col = tex2Dproj(_GrabTexture,
UNITY_PROJ_COORD(i.uvgrab));
    return col + half4(0.5,0,0,0);
  }
  ENDCG
}
```

5. Save your script and return to the Unity editor. Upon getting back, you should notice your material now works the way you intend it to:

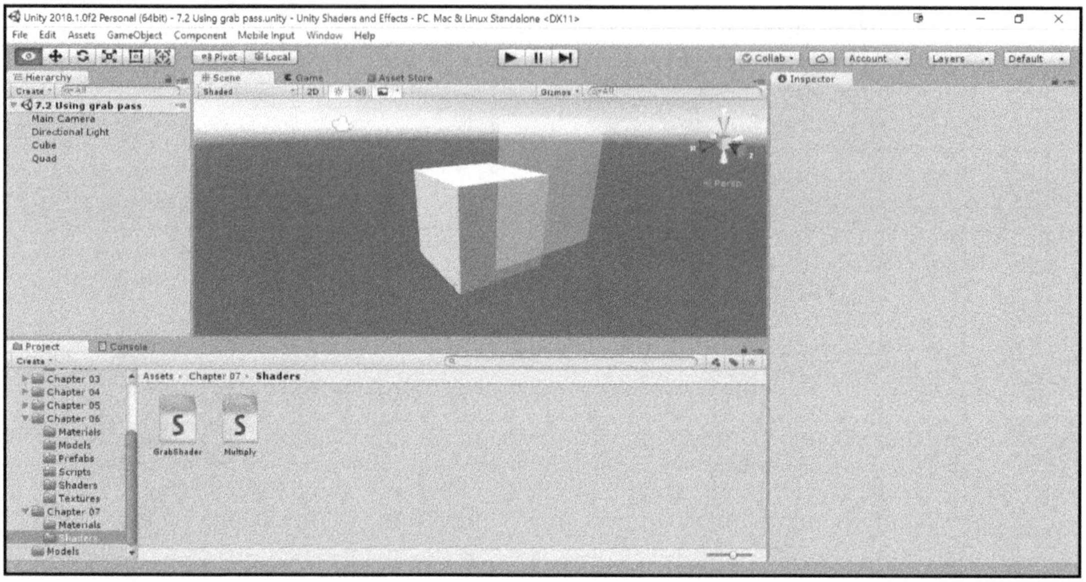

How it works...

This recipe not only introduces grab passes, but also Vertex and Fragment Shaders; for this reason, we have to analyze the shader in detail.

So far, all the code has always been placed directly in the `SubShader` section. This is because our previous shaders required only a single pass. This time, two passes are required. The first one is the `GrabPass{}`, which is defined simply by `GrabPass{}`. The rest of the code is placed in the second pass, which is contained in a `Pass` block.

The second pass is not structurally different from the shader shown in the first recipe of this chapter; we use the vertex function, `vert`, to get the position of the vertex, and then we give it a color in the Fragment function frag. The difference is that vert calculates another important detail: the UV data for the `GrabPass{}`. The `GrabPass{}` automatically creates a texture that can be referred to as follows:

```
sampler2D _GrabTexture;
```

In order to sample this texture, we need its UV data. The `ComputeGrabScreenPos` function returns data that we can use later to sample the grab texture correctly. This is done in the Fragment Shader using the following line:

```
fixed4 col = tex2Dproj(_GrabTexture, UNITY_PROJ_COORD(i.uvgrab));
```

This is the standard way in which a texture is grabbed and applied to the screen in its correct position. If everything has been done correctly, this shader will simply clone what has been rendered behind the geometry. We will see in the following recipes how this technique can be used to create materials such as water and glass.

There's more...

Every time you use a material with `GrabPass{}`, Unity will have to render the screen to a texture. This operation is very expensive and limits the number of `GrabPass` instances that you can use in a game. Cg offers a slightly different variation:

```
GrabPass {"TextureName"}
```

This line not only allows you to give a name to the texture, but also shares the texture with all the materials that have a `GrabPass` called `TextureName`. This means that if you have ten materials, Unity will only do a single `GrabPass` and share the texture with all of them. The main problem of this technique is that it doesn't allow for effects that can be stacked. If you are creating a glass with this technique, you won't be able to have two glasses one after the other.

Implementing a Glass Shader

Glass is a very complicated material; it should not be a surprise that other chapters have already created shaders to simulate it in the *Adding transparency to PBR* recipe of `Chapter 7`, *Physically-Based Rendering*. We already know how to make our glasses semi-transparent to show the objects behind it perfectly and that works for a number of applications. However, most glasses are not perfect. For instance, if you look through a stain glass window you may notice distortions or deformations when you look through them. This recipe will teach you how to achieve that effect. The idea behind this effect is to use a Vertex and Fragment Shader with a `GrabPass`, and then sample the grab texture with a little change to its UV data to create a distortion. You can see the effect in the following screenshot, using the glass-stained textures from the Unity Standard Assets:

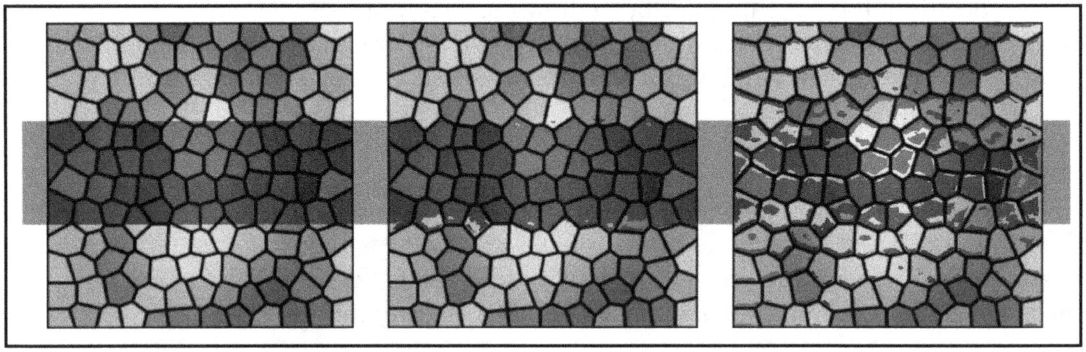

Getting ready

The setup for this recipe is similar to the one presented previously in `Chapter 8`, *Vertex Functions*:

1. Create a new Vertex and Fragment Shader. You can start by copying the one used in the previous recipe, *Using the grab pass to draw behind objects,* as a base by selecting it and hitting *Ctrl* + *D* to duplicate it. Once duplicated, change its name to `WindowShader`.
2. Create a material that will use the shader (`WindowMat`).
3. Assign the material to a quad or another flat geometry that will simulate your glass.

4. Place some objects behind it so that you can see the distortion effect:

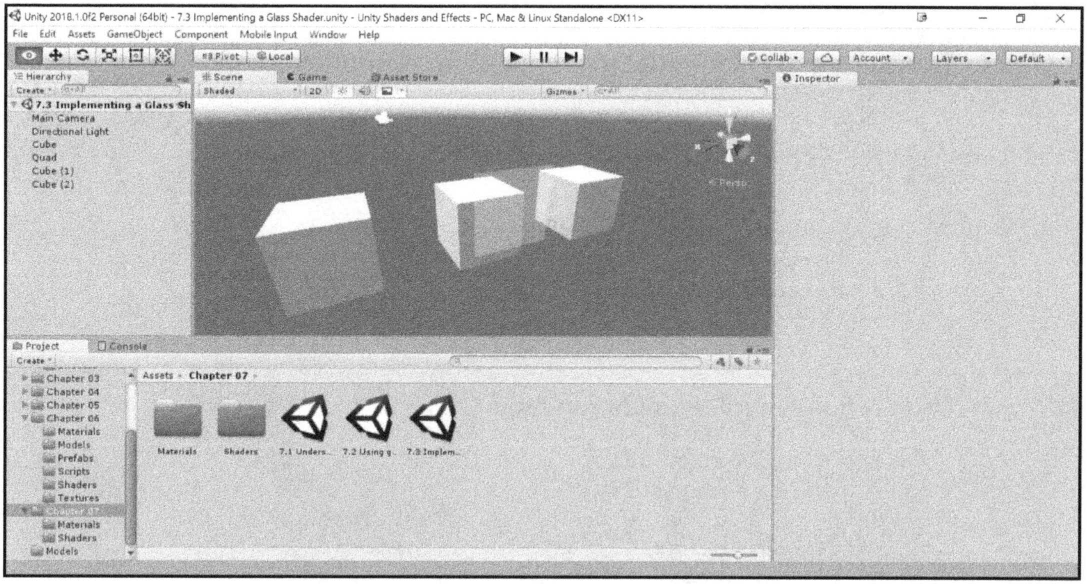

How to do it...

Let's start by editing the Vertex and Fragment Shaders:

1. Create a `Properties` block with these items in it:

```
Properties
{
  _MainTex("Base (RGB) Trans (A)", 2D) = "white" {}
  _Colour("Colour", Color) = (1,1,1,1)
  _BumpMap("Noise text", 2D) = "bump" {}
  _Magnitude("Magnitude", Range(0,1)) = 0.05
}
```

2. Add their variables in the second pass:

```
sampler2D _MainTex;
fixed4 _Colour;

sampler2D _BumpMap;
float _Magnitude;
```

3. Add the texture information to the input and output structures:

```
float2 texcoord : TEXCOORD0;
```

4. Transfer the UV data from the input to the output structure:

```
// Vertex function
vertOutput vert(vertInput v)
{
  vertOutput o;
  o.vertex = UnityObjectToClipPos(v.vertex);
  o.uvgrab = ComputeGrabScreenPos(o.vertex);
  o.texcoord = v.texcoord;
  return o;
}
```

5. Use the following Fragment function:

```
half4 frag(vertOutput i) : COLOR
{
  half4 mainColour = tex2D(_MainTex, i.texcoord);
  half4 bump = tex2D(_BumpMap, i.texcoord);
  half2 distortion = UnpackNormal(bump).rg;

  i.uvgrab.xy += distortion * _Magnitude;

  fixed4 col = tex2Dproj(_GrabTexture,
UNITY_PROJ_COORD(i.uvgrab));
  return col * mainColour * _Colour;
}
```

6. This material is transparent, so it changes its tags in the `SubShader` block:

```
Tags{ "Queue" = "Transparent" "IgnoreProjector" = "True"
"RenderType" =
  "Opaque" }
```

7. What's left now is to set the texture for the glass, and for a normal map to displace the grab texture:

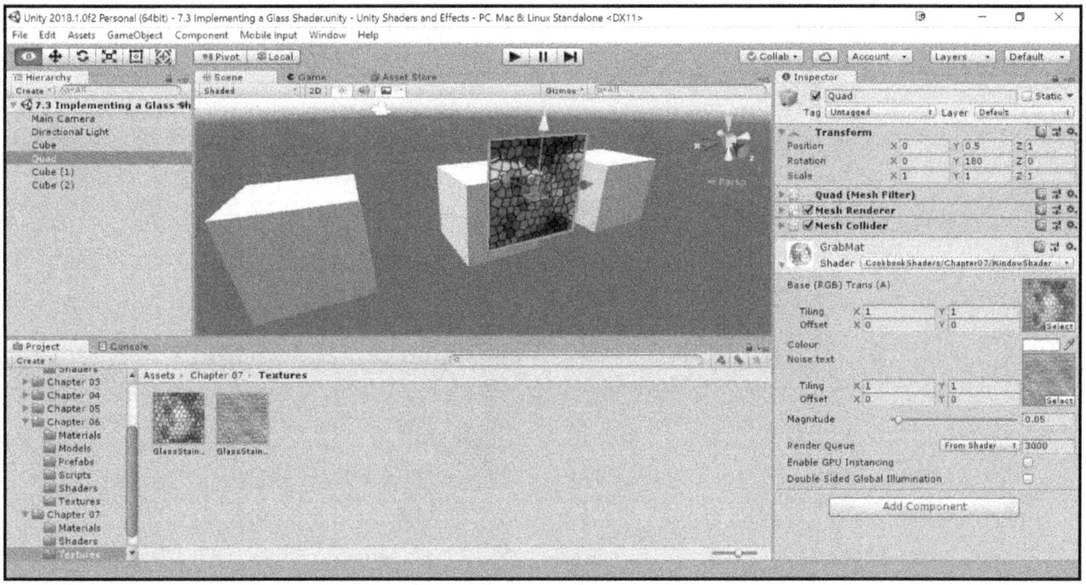

How it works...

The core that this shader uses is a grab pass to take what has already been rendered on the screen. The part where the distortion takes place is in the Fragment function. Here, a normal map is unpacked and used to offset the UV data of the grab texture:

```
half4 bump = tex2D(_BumpMap, i.texcoord);
half2 distortion = UnpackNormal(bump).rg;

i.uvgrab.xy += distortion * _Magnitude;
```

The `_Magnitude` slider is used to determine how strong the effect is:

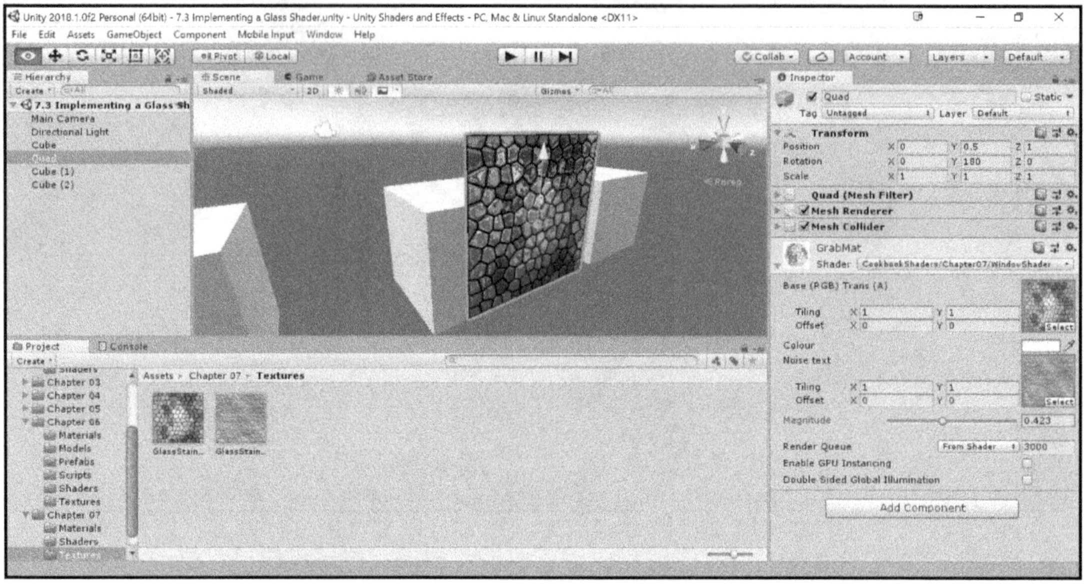

There's more...

This effect is very generic; it grabs the screen and creates a distortion based on a normal map. There is no reason why it shouldn't be used to simulate more interesting things. Many games use distortions around explosions or other sci-fi devices. This material can be applied to a sphere and, with a different normal map, it would simulate the heat wave of an explosion perfectly.

Implementing a Water Shader for 2D games

The Glass Shader introduced in the previous recipe is static; its distortion never changes. It takes just a few changes to convert it to an animated material, making it perfect for 2D games that feature water. This uses a similar technique to the one shown in `Chapter 8`, *Vertex Functions*, in the recipe entitled *Animating Vertices in a Surface Shader*:

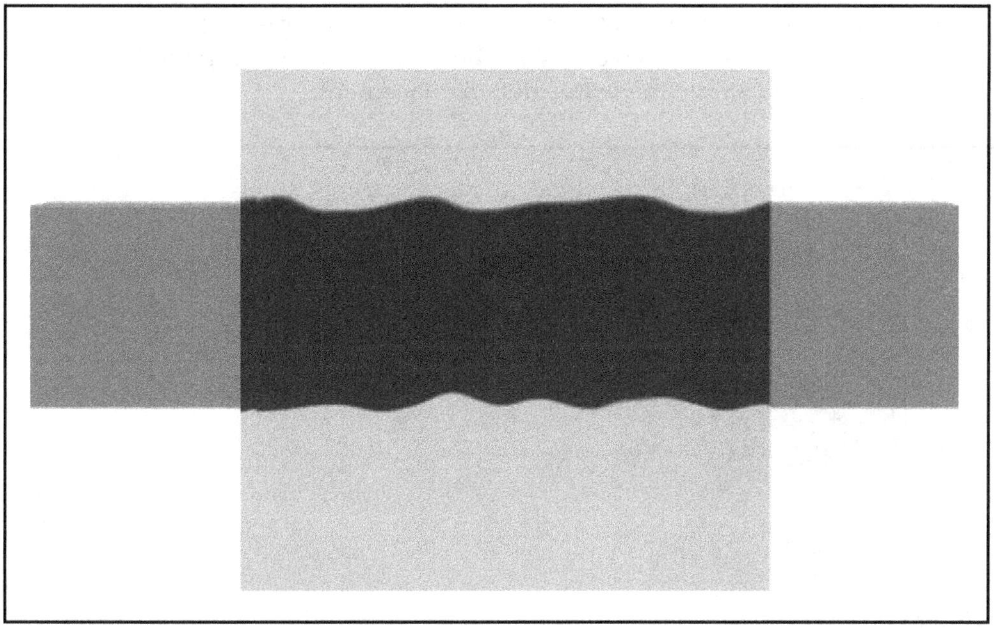

Getting ready

This recipe is based on the Vertex and Fragment Shaders described in the *Using the grab pass to draw behind objects* recipe, as it will rely heavily on `GrabPass`.

1. Create a new Vertex and Fragment Shader. You can start by copying the one used in the previous recipe, *Using the grab pass to draw behind objects,* as a base by selecting it and hitting *Ctrl+D* to duplicate it. Once duplicated, change its name to `WaterShader`.
2. Create a material that will use the shader (`WaterMat`).

3. Assign the material to a flat geometry that will represent your 2D water. In order for this effect to work, you should have something rendered behind it so that you can see the water-like displacement:

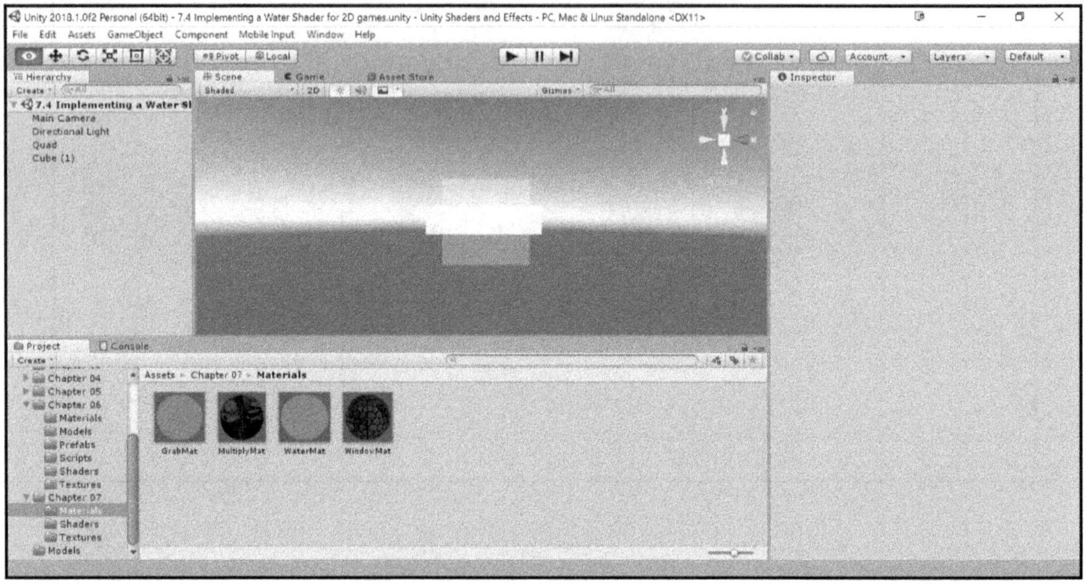

4. This recipe requires a noise texture, which is used to get pseudo-random values. It is important that you choose a seamless noise texture, such as the ones generated by tileable 2D Perlin noise, as shown in the following screenshot. This ensures that when the material is applied to a large object, you will not see any discontinuity. In order for this effect to work, the texture has to be imported in Repeat mode. If you want a smooth and continuous look for your water, you should also set it to Bilinear from Inspector. These settings ensure that the texture is sampled correctly from the shader:

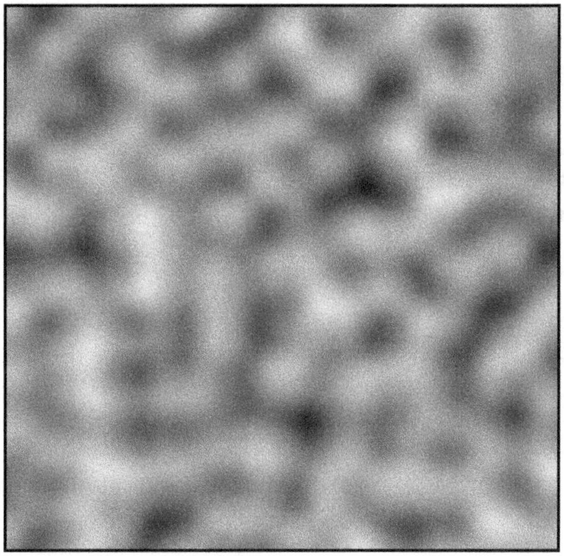

TIP: You can find an example noise texture in `Chapter 6 | Textures` folder of the book's example code.

How to do it...

To create this animated effect, you can start by refitting the shader. Follow these steps:

1. Add the following properties:

```
_NoiseTex("Noise text", 2D) = "white" {}
_Colour ("Colour", Color) = (1,1,1,1)
_Period ("Period", Range(0,50)) = 1
_Magnitude ("Magnitude", Range(0,0.5)) = 0.05
_Scale ("Scale", Range(0,10)) = 1
```

2. Add their respective variables to the second pass of the shader:

```
sampler2D _NoiseTex;
fixed4 _Colour;

float _Period;
```

```
float _Magnitude;
float _Scale;
```

3. Define the following input and output structures for the vertex function:

```
struct vertInput
{
  float4 vertex : POSITION;
  fixed4 color : COLOR;
  float2 texcoord : TEXCOORD0;
};

struct vertOutput
{
  float4 vertex : POSITION;
  fixed4 color : COLOR;
  float2 texcoord : TEXCOORD0;
  float4 worldPos : TEXCOORD1;
  float4 uvgrab : TEXCOORD2;
};
```

4. This shader needs to know the exact position of the space of every fragment. To do this, update the vertex function to the following:

```
// Vertex function
vertOutput vert(vertInput v)
{
  vertOutput o;
  o.vertex = UnityObjectToClipPos(v.vertex);
  o.color = v.color;
  o.texcoord = v.texcoord;

  o.worldPos = mul(unity_ObjectToWorld, v.vertex);
  o.uvgrab = ComputeGrabScreenPos(o.vertex);
  return o;
}
```

5. Use the following Fragment function:

```
fixed4 frag (vertOutput i) : COLOR
{
  float sinT = sin(_Time.w / _Period);

  float distX = tex2D(_NoiseTex, i.worldPos.xy / _Scale +
float2(sinT,
    0) ).r - 0.5;
  float distY = tex2D(_NoiseTex, i.worldPos.xy / _Scale +
float2(0,
```

```
        sinT) ).r - 0.5;

      float2 distortion = float2(distX, distY);
      i.uvgrab.xy += distortion * _Magnitude;
      fixed4 col = tex2Dproj( _GrabTexture,
    UNITY_PROJ_COORD(i.uvgrab));
      return col * _Colour;
    }
```

6. Save your script and return to the Unity editor. Afterward, select your Water Material (`WatMat`) and apply the noise texture. Afterward, tweak the properties in the Water Material and notice how it modifies the things behind it.

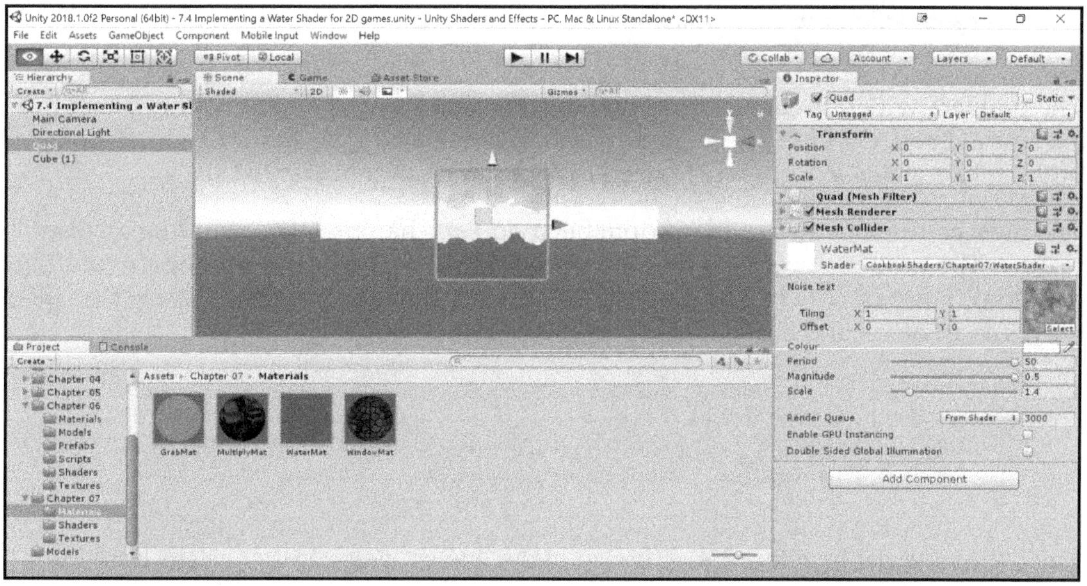

How it works...

This shader is very similar to the one introduced in the *Implementing a Glass Shader* recipe. The major difference is that this is an animated material; the displacement is not generated from a normal map, but takes into account the current time in order to create a constant animation. The code that displaces the UV data of the grab texture seems quite complicated; let's try to understand how it has been generated. The idea behind it is that a sinusoid function is used to make the water oscillate. This effect needs to evolve over time; to achieve this effect, the distortion generated by the shader depends on the current time that is retrieved with the built-in variable, `_Time`. The `_Period` variable determines the period of the sinusoid, which means how fast the waves appear:

```
float2 distortion = float2( sin(_Time.w/_Period),
  sin(_Time.w/_Period) ) - 0.5;
```

The problem with this code is that you have the same displacement on the *X* and *Y* axes; as a result, the entire grab texture will rotate in a circular motion, which looks nothing like water. We obviously need to add some randomness to this.

The most common way to add random behaviors to shaders is by including a noise texture. The problem now is to find a way to sample the texture at seemingly random positions. The best way to avoid seeing an obvious sinusoid pattern is to use the sine waves as an offset in the UV data of the `_NoiseTex` texture:

```
float sinT = sin(_Time.w / _Period);
float2 distortion = float2(
    tex2D(_NoiseTex, i.texcoord / _Scale + float2(sinT, 0) ).r - 0.5,
    tex2D(_NoiseTex, i.texcoord / _Scale + float2(0, sinT) ).r - 0.5
);
```

The `_Scale` variable determines the size of the waves. This solution is closer to the final version but has a severe issue—if the water quad moves, the UV data follows it and you can see the water waves following the material rather than being anchored to the background. To solve this, we need to use the world position of the current fragment as the initial position for the UV data:

```
float sinT = sin(_Time.w / _Period);
float2 distortion = float2(
    tex2D(_NoiseTex, i.worldPos.xy / _Scale + float2(sinT, 0) ).r -
0.5,
    tex2D(_NoiseTex, i.worldPos.xy / _Scale + float2(0, sinT) ).r -
0.5
);
i.uvgrab.xy += distortion * _Magnitude;
```

The result is a pleasant, seamless distortion, which doesn't move in any clear direction.

We can also improve the readability of the code by breaking apart the distortion into smaller steps:

```
float sinT = sin(_Time.w / _Period);

float distX = tex2D(_NoiseTex, i.worldPos.xy / _Scale +
  float2(sinT, 0) ).r - 0.5;
float distY = tex2D(_NoiseTex, i.worldPos.xy / _Scale +
  float2(0, sinT) ).r - 0.5;

float2 distortion = float2(distX, distY);
i.uvgrab.xy += distortion * _Magnitude;
```

That is what you should see in the final result.

> As happens with all these special effects, there is no perfect solution. This recipe shows you a technique to create water-like distortion, but you are encouraged to play with it until you find an effect that fits the aesthetics of your game.

10
Mobile Shader Adjustment

In the next two chapters, we are going to take a look at making the shaders that we write in a performance-friendly manner for different platforms. We won't be talking about any one platform specifically, but we are going to break down the elements of shaders we can adjust in order to make them more optimized for mobiles and efficient on any platform in general. These techniques range from understanding what Unity offers in terms of built-in variables that reduce the overhead of the shaders memory to learning about ways in which we can make our own shader code more efficient.

In this chapter, you will learn the following recipes:

- Techniques to make shaders more efficient
- Profiling your shaders
- Modifying our shaders for mobile

Introduction

Learning the art of optimizing your shaders will come up in just about any game project that you work on. There will always come a point in any production where a shader needs to be optimized, or maybe it needs to use fewer textures but produces the same effect. As a technical artist or shader programmer, you have to understand these core fundamentals to optimize your shaders so that you can increase the performance of your game while still achieving the same visual fidelity. Having this knowledge can also help in setting the way in which you write your shader from the start. For instance, by knowing that the game built using your shader will be played on a mobile device, we can automatically set all our `Lighting` functions to use a half-vector as the view direction or set all of our float variable types to fixed or half so as to reduce the amount of memory used. These, and many other techniques, all contribute to your shaders running efficiently on your target hardware. Let's begin our journey and start learning how to optimize our shaders.

Techniques to make shaders more efficient

What is a cheap shader? When first asked the question, it might be a little tough to answer, as there are many elements that go into making a more efficient shader. It could be the amount of memory used up by your variables. It could be the amount of textures the shader is using. It could also be that our shader is working fine, but we can actually produce the same visual effect with half the amount of data by reducing the amount of code we are using or data we are creating. We are going to explore a few of these techniques in this recipe and show how they can be combined to make your shader fast and efficient but still produce the high-quality visuals everyone expects from games today, whether on a mobile or PC.

Getting ready

In order to get this recipe started, we need to gather a few resources together. So, let's perform the following tasks:

1. Create a new scene and fill it with a simple sphere object and single directional light.
2. Create a new shader (`OptimizedShader01`) and material (`OptimizedShader01Mat`) and assign the shader to the material.
3. We then need to assign the material we just created to our sphere object in our
new scene:

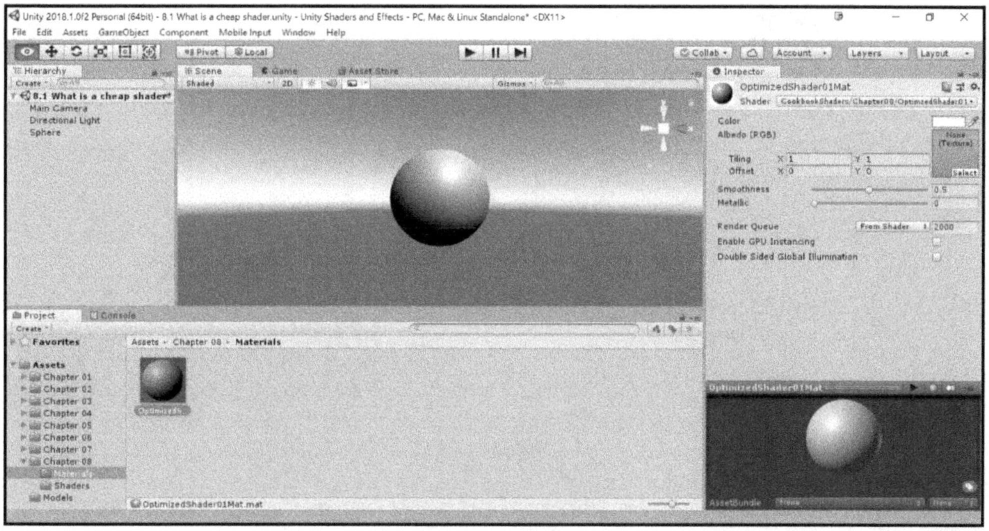

4. Finally, modify the shader so that it uses a diffuse texture and normal map and includes your own custom `Lighting` function.

```
Properties
{
  _MainTex ("Base (RGB)", 2D) = "white" {}
  _NormalMap ("Normal Map", 2D) = "bump" {}
}
SubShader
{
  Tags { "RenderType"="Opaque" }
  LOD 200
  CGPROGRAM
  #pragma surface surf SimpleLambert

  sampler2D _MainTex;
  sampler2D _NormalMap;

  struct Input
  {
    float2 uv_MainTex;
    float2 uv_NormalMap;
  };
  inline float4 LightingSimpleLambert (SurfaceOutput s,
                                        float3 lightDir,
                                        float atten)
  {
   float diff = max (0, dot (s.Normal, lightDir));
   float4 c;
```

```
        c.rgb = s.Albedo * _LightColor0.rgb * (diff * atten * 2);
        c.a = s.Alpha;
        return c;
      }

      void surf (Input IN, inout SurfaceOutput o)
      {
        fixed4 c = tex2D (_MainTex, IN.uv_MainTex);
        o.Albedo = c.rgb;
        o.Alpha = c.a;
        o.Normal = UnpackNormal(tex2D(_NormalMap,
    IN.uv_NormalMap));
      }
      ENDCG
    }
    FallBack "Diffuse"
```

5. Lastly, assign a base and normal map to your material (I used the `MudRockey` texture included in the assets for `Chapter 3`, *Post Processing Stack*). You should now have a setup similar to the following screenshot.
6. This setup will allow us to take a look at some of the basic concepts that go into optimizing shaders using Surface Shaders in Unity:

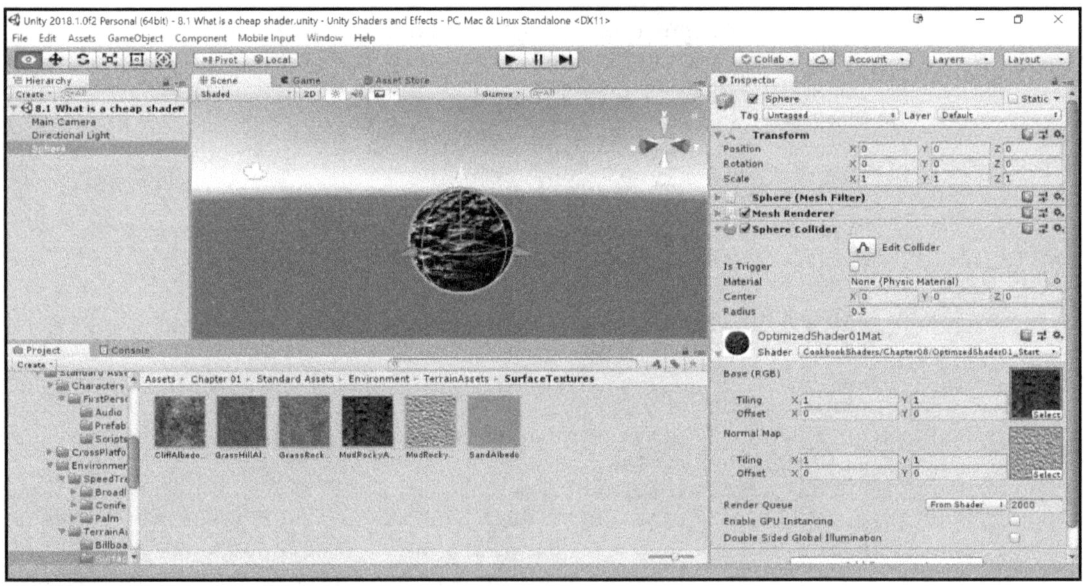

How to do it...

We are going to build a simple `DiffuseShader` to take a look at a few ways in which you can optimize your shaders in general.

First, we'll optimize our variable types so that they use less memory when they are processing data:

1. Let's begin with the `struct Input` in our shader. Currently, our UVs are being stored in a variable of the `float2` type.

2. Remember that floats provide the highest form of precision at a full 32 bits of memory. This is needed for complex trigonometry or exponents, but if you can handle less precision, it's much better to use either a half or a fixed instead. The half type provides up to 3 digits of precision using half the size, or 16 bits of memory. That means we can have a `half2` with the same amount of memory of a single float. We need to change this to use `half2` instead:

```
struct Input
{
    half2 uv_MainTex;
    half2 uv_NormalMap;
};
```

3. We can then move to our `Lighting` function and reduce the variables' memory footprint by changing their types to the following:

```
inline fixed4 LightingSimpleLambert (SurfaceOutput s, fixed3
lightDir, fixed atten)
{
  fixed diff = max (0, dot(s.Normal, lightDir));
  fixed4 c;
  c.rgb = s.Albedo * _LightColor0.rgb * (diff * atten * 2);
  c.a = s.Alpha;
  return c;
}
```

4. In this case, we are using the lowest precision type of `fixed`, which is only 11 bits as compared to the `float` type's 32. This is useful for simple calculations such as color or texture data, which is perfect for this particular case.

> In case you'd like a refresher on the fixed type as well as all of the other types we are using, please check out Chapter 4, *Creating Your First Shader*, or look at https://docs.unity3d.com/Manual/SL-DataTypesAndPrecision.html.

5. Finally, we can complete this optimization pass by updating the variables in our surf() function. Since we're using texture data, it's fine for us to use a fixed4 here instead:

```
void surf (Input IN, inout SurfaceOutput o)
{
  fixed4 c = tex2D (_MainTex, IN.uv_MainTex);
  o.Albedo = c.rgb;
  o.Alpha = c.a;
  o.Normal = UnpackNormal(tex2D(_NormalMap, IN.uv_NormalMap));
}
```

6. Now that we have our variables optimized, we are going to take advantage of a built-in Lighting function variable so that we can control how lights are processed by this shader. By doing this, we can greatly reduce the number of lights the shader processes. Modify the #pragma statement in your shader with the following code:

```
CGPROGRAM
#pragma surface surf SimpleLambert noforwardadd
```

7. We can optimize this further by sharing UVs between the normal map and diffuse texture. To do this, we simply change the UV lookup in our UnpackNormal() function to use _MainTex UVs instead of the UVs of _NormalMap:

```
void surf (Input IN, inout SurfaceOutput o)
{
  fixed4 c = tex2D (_MainTex, IN.uv_MainTex);
  o.Albedo = c.rgb;
  o.Alpha = c.a;
  o.Normal = UnpackNormal(tex2D(_NormalMap, IN.uv_MainTex));
}
```

8. As we have removed the need for the normal map UVs, we need to make sure that we remove the normal map UV code from the Input struct:

```
struct Input
{
```

```
    half2 uv_MainTex;
};
```

9. Finally, we can further optimize this shader by telling the shader that it only works with certain renderers:

```
CGPROGRAM
#pragma surface surf SimpleLambert exclude_path:prepass
noforwardadd
```

The result of our optimization passes show us that we really don't notice a difference in the visual quality, but we have reduced the amount of time it takes for this shader to be drawn to the screen. You will learn about finding out how much time it takes for a shader to render in the next recipe, but the idea to focus on here is that we achieve the same result with fewer data. So keep this in mind when creating your shaders. The following screenshot shows us the final result of our shader:

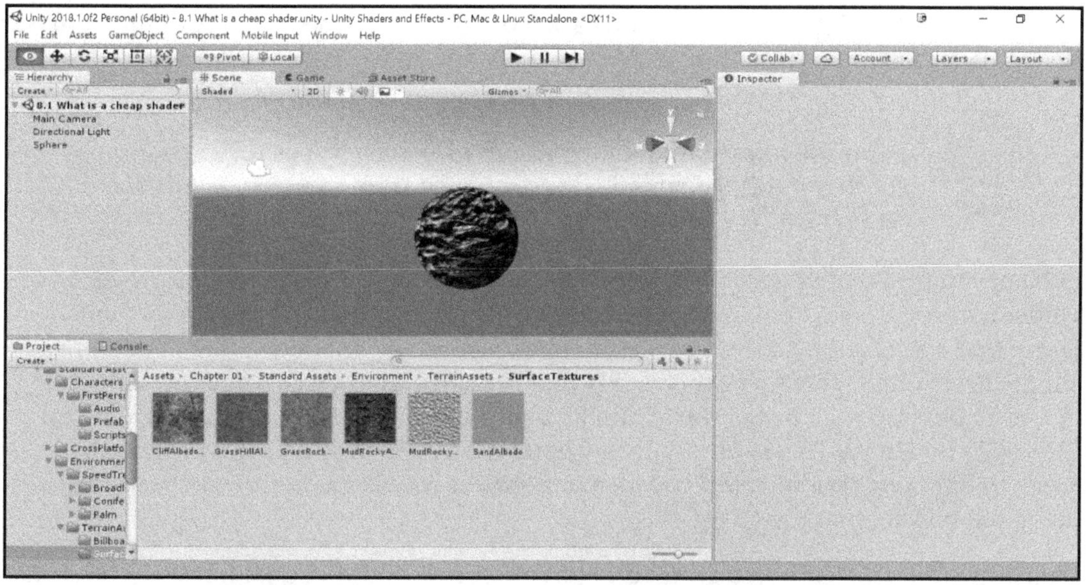

How it works...

Now that we have seen the ways in which we can optimize our shaders, let's dive in a bit deeper and really understand how all of these techniques work, why we should use them, and look at a couple of other techniques that you can try for yourself in your own shaders.

Let's first focus our attention on the size of the data each of our variables is storing when we declare them. If you are familiar with programming, then you will understand that you can declare values or variables with different sizes of types. This means that a float actually has a maximum size in memory. The following description will describe these variable types in much more detail:

- **Float**: A float is a full 32-bit precision value and is the slowest of the three different types we see here. It also has its corresponding values of `float2`, `float3`, and `float4`, which allow us to store multiple floats in one variable.
- **Half**: The half variable type is a reduced 16-bit floating point value and is suitable for store UV values and color values and much faster than using a float value. As with the float type, it has its corresponding values, which are `half2`, `half3`, and `half4`.
- **Fixed**: A fixed value is the smallest in size of the three types, but can be used for lighting calculations and colors and has the corresponding values of `fixed2`, `fixed3`, and `fixed4`.

TIP

For more information on working with array types for shaders, check out the *Using packed arrays* recipe from `Chapter 5`, *Surface Shaders and Texture Mapping*.

Our second phase of optimizing our simple shader was to declare the `noforwardadd` value to our `#pragma` statement. This is basically a switch that automatically tells Unity that any object with this particular shader receives only per-pixel light from a single directional light. Any other lights that are calculated by this shader will be forced to be processed as per-vertex lights using *spherical harmonic* values produced internally by Unity. This is especially obvious when we place another light in the scene to light our sphere object because our shader is doing a per-pixel operation using the normal map.

This is great, but what if you wanted to have a bunch of directional lights in the scene and control over which of these lights is used for the main per-pixel light? Well, if you notice, each light has a **Render Mode** drop-down. If you click on this drop-down, you will see a couple of flags that can be set. These are **Auto**, **Important**, and **Not Important**. By selecting a light, you can tell Unity that a light should be considered more as a per-pixel light than a per-vertex light, by setting its render mode to **Important** and vice versa. If you leave a light set to **Auto**, then you will let Unity decide the best course of action:

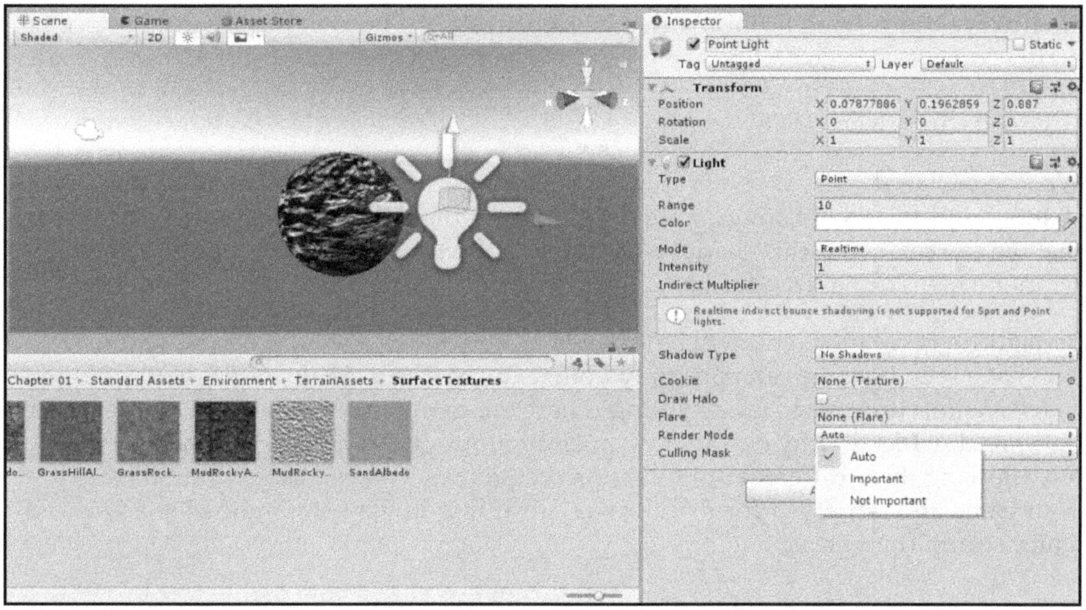

Place another light in your scene and remove the texture that is currently in the main texture for our shader. You will notice that the second point light does not react with the normal map, only the directional light that we created first. The concept here is that you save on per-pixel operations by just calculating all extra lights as vertex lights, and save performance by just calculating the main directional light as a per-pixel light. The following diagram visually demonstrates this concept as the point light is not reacting with the normal map:

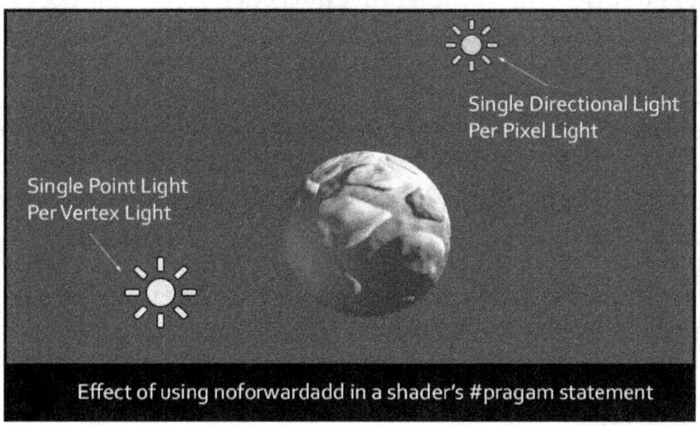

Finally, we did a bit of cleaning up and simply told the normal map texture to use the main texture's UV values, and we got rid of the line of code that pulled in a separate set of UV values specifically for the normal map. This is always a nice way to simplify your code and clean up any unwanted data.

We also declared `exclude_pass: prepass` in our `#pragma` statement so that this shader wouldn't accept any custom lighting from the deferred renderer. This means that we can really use this shader effectively in the forward renderer only, which is set in the main camera's settings.

By taking a bit of time, you will be amazed at how much a shader can be optimized. You have seen how we can pack grayscale textures into a single RGBA texture as well as use lookup textures to fake lighting. There are many ways in which a shader can be optimized, which is why it is always an ambiguous question to ask in the first place, but knowing these different optimization techniques, you can cater your shaders to your game and target platform, ultimately resulting in very streamlined shaders and a nice steady frame rate.

Profiling your shaders

Now that we know how we can reduce the overhead that our shaders might take, let's take a look at how to find problematic shaders in a scene where you might have a lot of shaders or a ton of objects, shaders, and scripts, all running at the same time. To find a single object or shader among a whole game can be quite daunting, but Unity provides us with its built-in **Profiler**. This allows us to actually see, on a frame-by-frame basis, what is happening in the game, and each item that is being used by the GPU and CPU.

Using the **Profiler**, we can isolate items such as shaders, geometry, and general rendering items using its interface to create blocks of profiling jobs. We can filter out items until we are looking at the performance of just a single object. This then lets us see the effects on the CPU and GPU that the object has while it is performing its functions at runtime.

Let's take a look through the different sections of the **Profiler** and learn how to debug our scenes and, most importantly, our shaders.

Getting ready

Let's use our **Profiler** by getting a few assets ready and launching the **Profiler** window:

1. Let's use the scene from the last recipe and launch the Unity **Profiler** from **Window** | **Profiler** or *Ctrl* + 7. Feel free to drag and drop or move it so you can see it well. I personally put it at the same spot as the **Inspector** tab.
2. Let's also duplicate our sphere a couple more times to see how that affects our rendering.
3. From the **Profiler** tab, click on the **Deep Profile** option to get additional information about the project and then play your game!

You should see something similar to the following image:

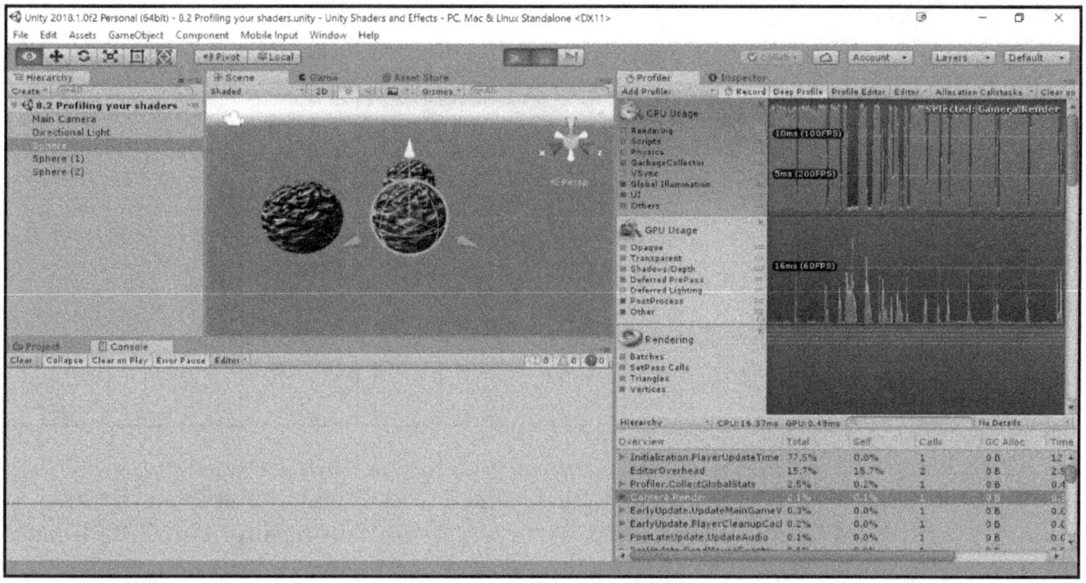

How to do it...

To use the **Profiler**, we will take a look at some of the UI elements of this window. Before we hit Play, let's take a look at how to get the information we need from the **Profiler**:

1. First, click on the larger blocks in the **Profiler** window called **GPU Usage**, **CPU Usage**, and **Rendering**. You will find these blocks on the left-hand side of the upper window:

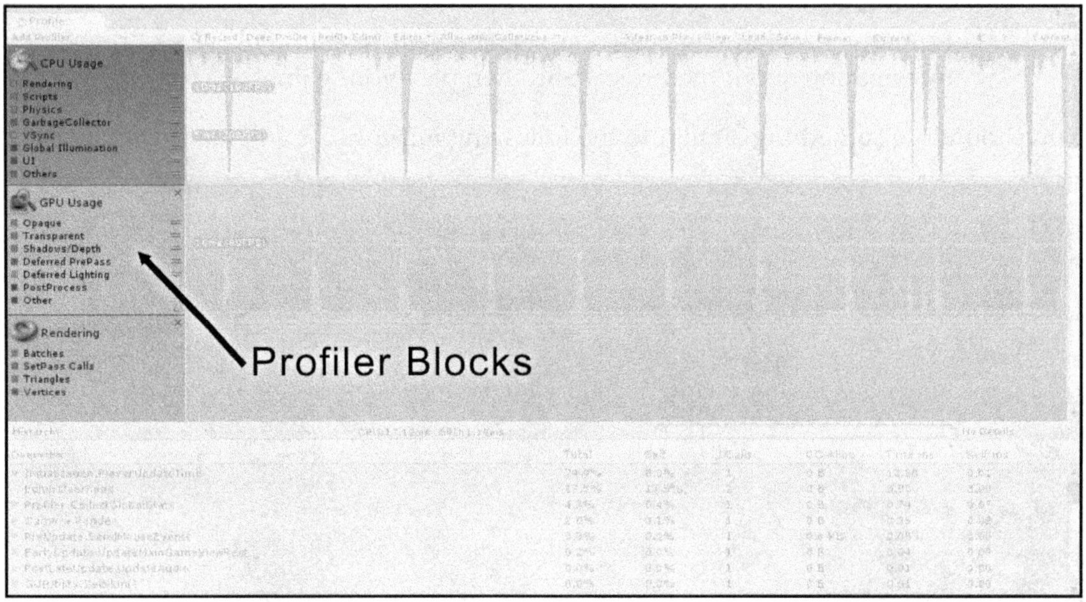

2. Using these blocks, we can see different data specific to those major functions of our game. The **CPU Usage** is showing us what most of our scripts are doing, as well as physics and overall rendering. The **GPU Usage** block is giving us detailed information about the elements that are specific to our lighting, shadows, and render queues. Finally, the **Rendering** block is giving us information about the drawcalls and amount of geometry we have in our scene at any one frame.

TIP

If you do not see the GPU Usage option, click on **Add Profiler** | **GPU**. It is possible that it may not show up if your graphics card drivers are not up to date.

By clicking on each of these blocks, we can isolate the type of data we see during our profiling session.

3. Now, click on the tiny colored blocks in one of these **Profile** blocks and hit Play, or *Ctrl* + *P*, to run the scene.
4. This lets us dive down even deeper into our profiling session so that we can filter out what is being reported back to us. While the scene is running, uncheck all of the boxes, except for **Opaque** in the **GPU Usage** block. Notice that we can now see just how much time is being used to render the objects that are set to the **Render Queue** of **Opaque**:

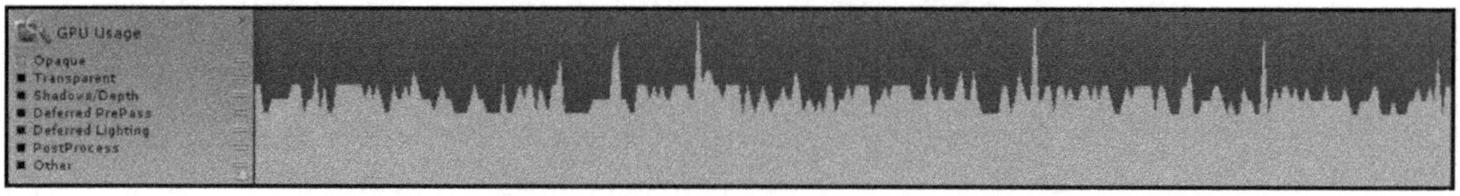

5. Another great function of the **Profiler** window is the action of clicking and dragging in the graph view.
6. This will automatically pause your game so that you can further analyze a certain spike in the graph to find out exactly which item is causing the performance problem. Click and drag around in the graph view to pause the game and see the effect of using this functionality:

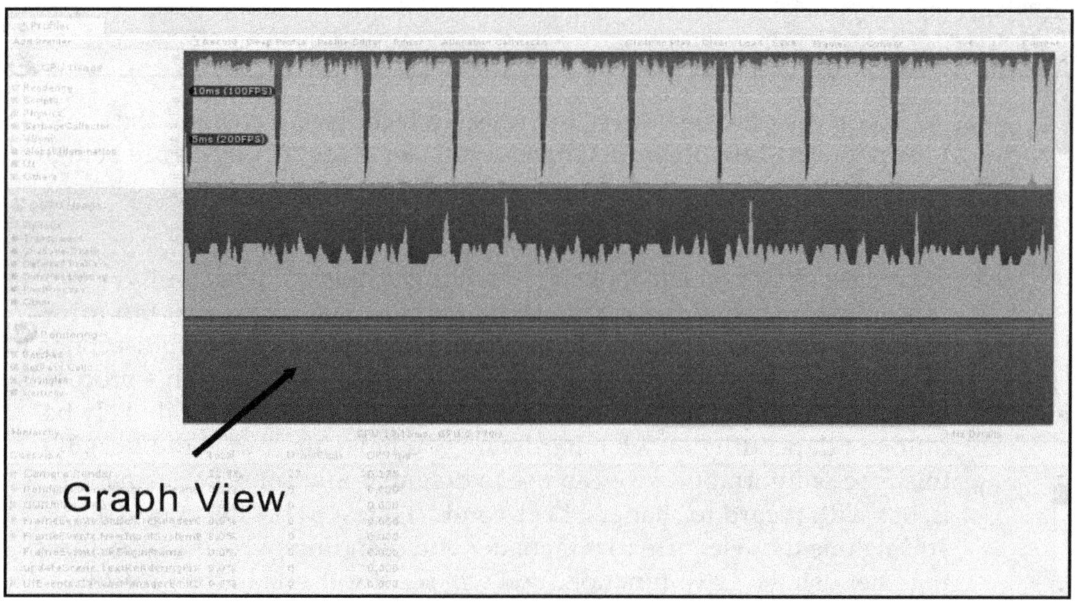

7. Turning our attention now towards the lower half of the **Profiler** window, you will notice that there is a dropdown item available when we have the **GPU Block** selected. We can expand this to get even more detailed information about the current active profiling session and, in this case, more information about what the camera is currently rendering and how much time it is taking up:

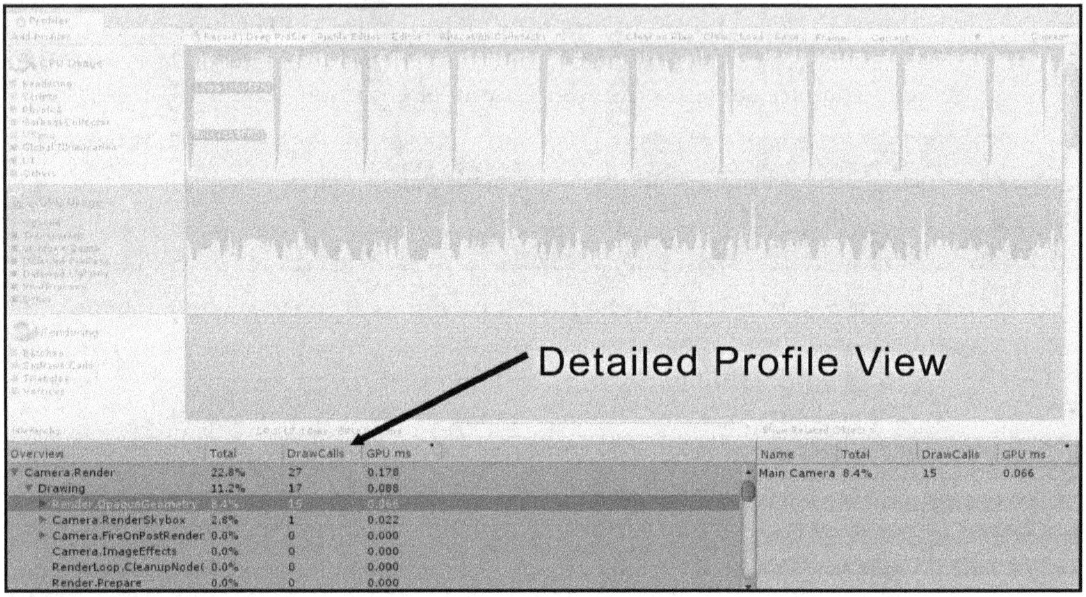

If you click on the button that says **No Details** and changes the option to **Show Related Objects**, you can see what objects are being used in the functions being called.

8. This gives us a complete look at the inner workings of what Unity is processing in this particular frame. In this case, we can see that our three spheres with our optimized shader are taking roughly **0.066** milliseconds to draw to the screen, they are taking up fifteen drawcalls, and this process is taking **8.4%** of the GPU's time in every frame (the numbers will likely be different depending on what hardware you have for your computer). It's this type of information we can use to diagnose and solve performance issues with regard to shaders. Let's conduct a test to see the effects of adding one more texture to our shader and blending two diffuse textures together using a `lerp` function. You will see the effects in the **Profiler** pretty clearly.

9. Modify the `Properties` block of your shader with the following code to give us another texture to use:

```
Properties
{
  _MainTex ("Base (RGB)", 2D) = "white" {}
  _BlendTex("Blend Texture", 2D) = "white" {}
  _NormalMap ("Normal Map", 2D) = "bump" {}
}
```

10. Then let's feed our texture to `CGPROGRAM`:

```
sampler2D _MainTex;
sampler2D _NormalMap;
sampler2D _BlendTex;
```

11. Now it's time to update our `surf()` function accordingly so that we blend our diffuse textures together:

```
void surf (Input IN, inout SurfaceOutput o)
{
  fixed4 c = tex2D (_MainTex, IN.uv_MainTex);
  fixed4 blendTex = tex2D(_BlendTex, IN.uv_MainTex);

  c = lerp(c, blendTex, blendTex.r);

  o.Albedo = c.rgb;
  o.Alpha = c.a;
  o.Normal = UnpackNormal(tex2D(_NormalMap, IN.uv_MainTex));
}
```

Once you save your modifications in your shader and return to Unity's editor, we can run our game and see the increase in milliseconds of our new shader.

12. Attach a new texture inside of your `Blend Texture`:

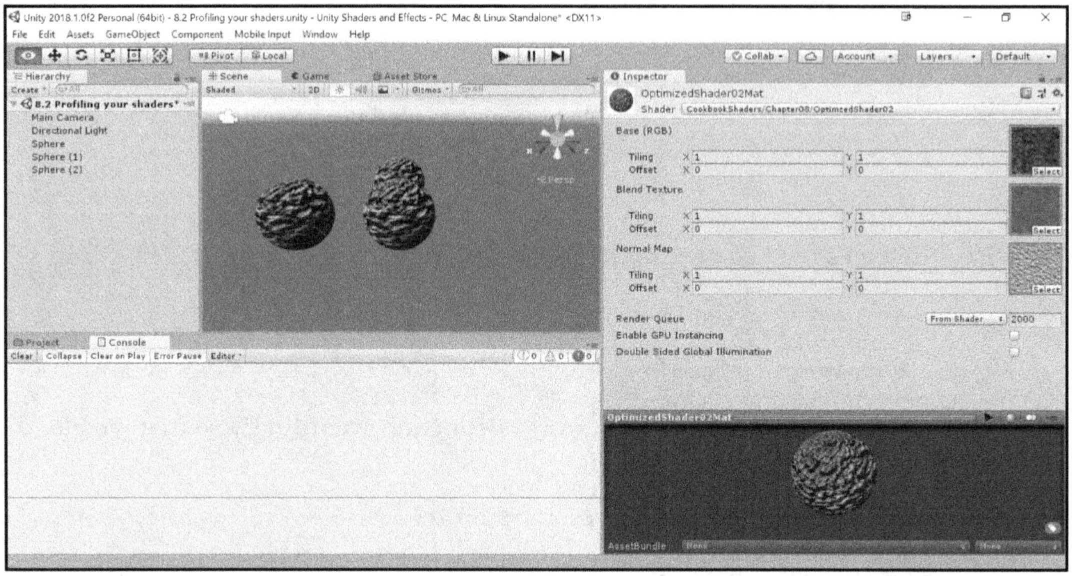

13. Press Play to start the game again with the **Profiler** turned on. Press Play once you have returned to Unity and let's take a look at the results in our **Profiler**:

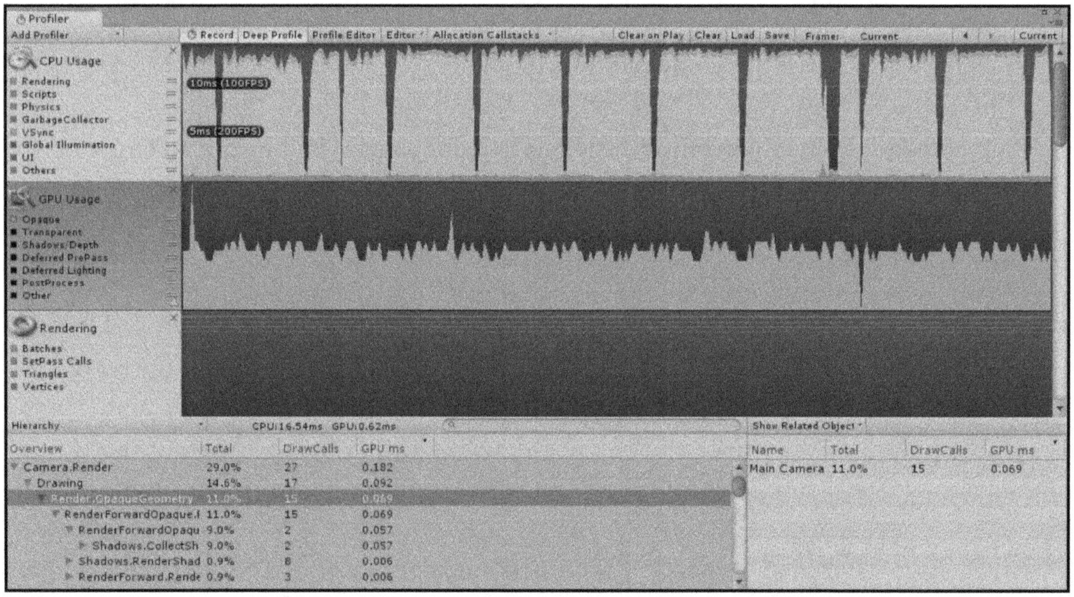

You can see now that the amount of time to render our **Opaque** Shaders in this scene is taking **0.069** milliseconds, up from **0.066** milliseconds. By adding another texture and using the `lerp()` function, we increased the render time for our spheres. While it's a small change, imagine having 20 shaders all working in different ways on different objects.

Using the information given here, you can pinpoint areas that are causing performance decreases more quickly and solve these issues using the techniques from the previous recipe.

How it works...

While it's completely out of the scope of this book to describe how this tool actually works internally, we can surmise that Unity has given us a way to view the computer's performance while our game is running. Basically, this window is tied very tightly to the CPU and GPU to give us real-time feedback of how much time is being taken for each of our scripts, objects, and render queues. Using this information, we have seen that we can track the efficiency of our shader writing to eliminate problem areas and code.

It's important to note that games running with the **Profiler** open, as well as from within the editor in general, will make the game slightly slower than it would be when compiled and running in a normal situation. You might even see the **Editor** in the **Profilers** list of CPU expenses.

There's more...

It is also possible to profile specifically for mobile platforms. Unity provides us with a couple of extra features when the Android or iOS build target is set in the **Build Settings**. We can actually get real-time information from our mobile devices while the game is running. This becomes very useful because you are able to profile directly on the device itself instead of profiling directly in your editor. To find out more about this process, refer to Unity's documentation at the following link: `http://docs.unity3d.com/Documentation/Manual/MobileProfiling.html`.

Modifying our shaders for mobile

Now that we have seen quite a broad set of techniques for making really optimized shaders, let's take a look at writing a nice, high-quality shader targeted for a mobile device. It is actually quite easy to make a few adjustments to the shaders we have written so that they run faster on a mobile device. This includes elements such as using the `approxview` or `halfasview Lighting` function variables. We can also reduce the amount of textures we need and even apply better compression for the textures we are using. By the end of this recipe, we will have a nicely optimized normal-mapped, Specular Shader for use in our mobile games.

Getting ready

Before we begin, let's get a fresh new scene and fill it with some objects to apply our `MobileShader`:

1. Create a new scene and fill it with a default sphere and single directional light.
2. Create a new material (`MobileMat`) and shader (`MobileShader`), and assign the shader to the material.
3. Finally, assign the material to our sphere object in our scene.

When completed, you should have a scene similar to the one in the following screenshot:

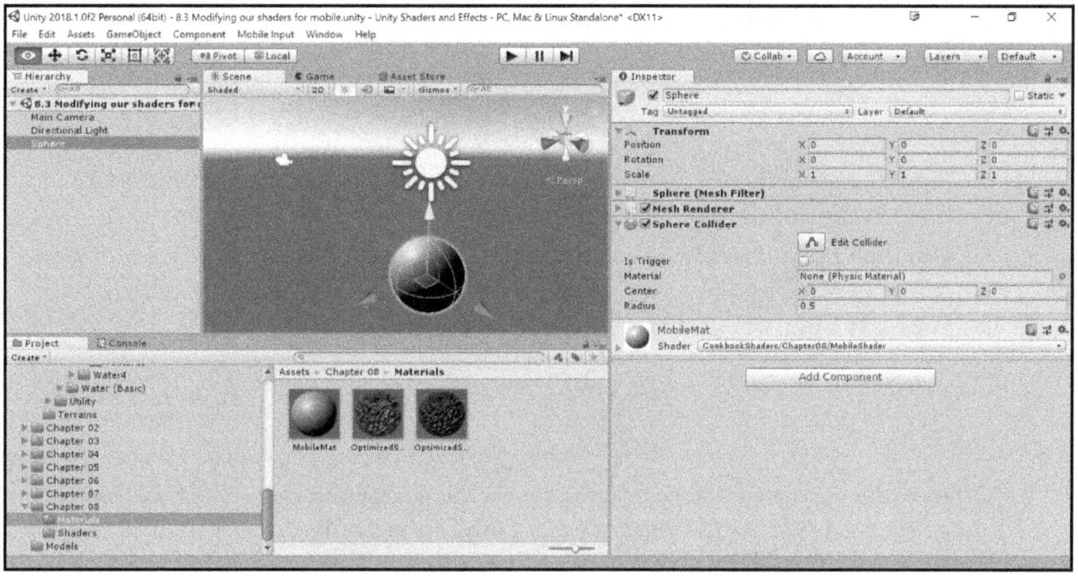

How to do it...

For this recipe, we will write a mobile-friendly shader from scratch and discuss the elements that make it more mobile friendly:

1. Let's first populate our `Properties` block with the textures required. In this case, we are going to use a single `_Diffuse` texture with the gloss map in its alpha channel, `Normal map`, and a slider for specular intensity:

```
Properties
{
  _Diffuse ("Base (RGB) Specular Amount (A)", 2D) = "white" {}
  _SpecIntensity ("Specular Width", Range(0.01, 1)) = 0.5
  _NormalMap ("Normal Map", 2D) = "bump"{}
}
```

2. Our next task is to set up our `#pragma` declarations. This will simply turn certain features of the Surface Shader on and off, ultimately making the shader cheaper or more expensive:

```
CGPROGRAM
#pragma surface surf MobileBlinnPhong exclude_path:prepass
nolightmap noforwardadd halfasview
```

> **TIP:** The highlighted line should be on one line.

3. Next, remove the `#pragma target 3.0` line, as we are not using any of the features of it.
4. We then need to make the connection between our `Properties` block and `CGPROGRAM`. This time, we are going to use the fixed variable type for our specular intensity slider in order to reduce its memory usage:

```
sampler2D _Diffuse;
sampler2D _NormalMap;
fixed _SpecIntensity;
```

5. In order for us to map our textures to the surface of our object, we need to get some UVs. In this case, we are going to get only one set of UVs to keep the amount of data in our shader down to a minimum:

```
struct Input
{
  half2 uv_Diffuse;
};
```

6. The next step is to fill in our `Lighting` function using a few of the new input variables that are available to us when using the new `#pragma` declarations:

```
inline fixed4 LightingMobileBlinnPhong (SurfaceOutput s,
fixed3 lightDir, fixed3 halfDir, fixed atten)
    {
      fixed diff = max (0, dot (s.Normal, lightDir));
      fixed nh = max (0, dot (s.Normal, halfDir));
      fixed spec = pow (nh, s.Specular*128) * s.Gloss;
      fixed4 c;
      c.rgb = (s.Albedo * _LightColor0.rgb * diff +
_LightColor0.rgb * spec) * (atten*2);
      c.a = 0.0;
      return c;
    }
```

7. Finally, we complete the shader by creating the `surf()` function and processing the final color of our surface:

```
void surf (Input IN, inout SurfaceOutput o)
{
  fixed4 diffuseTex = tex2D (_Diffuse, IN.uv_Diffuse);
  o.Albedo = diffuseTex.rgb;
  o.Gloss = diffuseTex.a;
  o.Alpha = 0.0;
  o.Specular = _SpecIntensity;
  o.Normal = UnpackNormal(tex2D(_NormalMap, IN.uv_Diffuse));
}
```

8. When finished with the code portion of this recipe, save your shader and return to the Unity editor to let the shader compile. If no errors occurred, assign some properties for the **Base** and **Normal Map** properties:

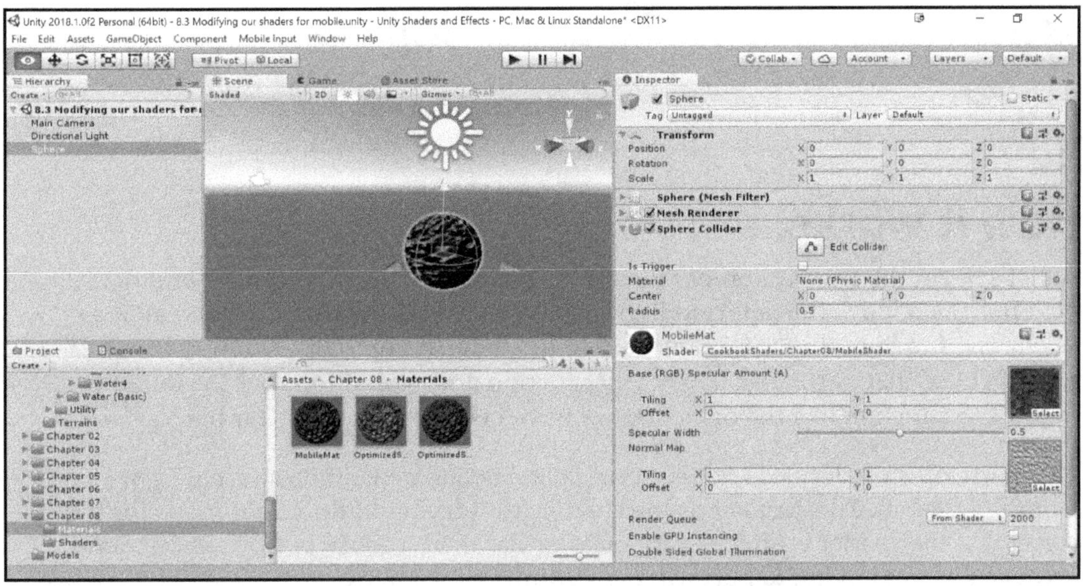

9. Add a few point lights and some copies of the new object and you should see a result similar to the following screenshot:

How it works...

So, let's begin the description of this shader by explaining what it does and doesn't do. First, it excludes the deferred lighting pass. This means that if you created a `Lighting` function that was connected to the deferred renderer's `prepass`, it wouldn't use that particular `Lighting` function and would look for the default `Lighting` function like the ones that we have been creating thus far in this book.

This particular shader does not support *lightmapping* by Unity's internal light-mapping system. This just keeps the shader from trying to find light maps for the object that the shader is attached to, making the shader more performance-friendly because it is not having to perform the lightmapping check.

We included the `noforwardadd` declaration so that we process only per-pixel textures with a single directional light. All other lights are forced to become per-vertex lights and will not be included in any per-pixel operations you might do in the `surf()` function.

Finally, we are using the `halfasview` declaration to tell Unity that we aren't going to use the main `viewDir` parameter found in a normal `Lighting` function. Instead, we are going to use the half vector as the view direction and process our specular with this. This becomes much faster for the shader to process as it will be done on a per-vertex basis. It isn't completely accurate when it comes to simulating specular in the real world, but visually, on a mobile device, it looks just fine and the shader is more optimized.

It's techniques like these that make a shader more efficient and cleaner, codewise. Always make sure that you are using only the data you need while weighing this against your target hardware and the visual quality that the game requires. In the end, a cocktail of these techniques is what ultimately makes up your shaders for your games.

11 Screen Effects with Unity Render Textures

In this chapter, you will learn the following recipes:

- Setting up the screen effects script system
- Using brightness, saturation, and contrast with screen effects
- Using basic Photoshop-like Blend modes with screen effects
- Using the Overlay Blend mode with screen effects

Introduction

One of the most impressive aspects of learning to write shaders is the process of creating your own screen effects, also known as post effects. With these screen effects, we can create stunning real-time images with Bloom, Motion Blur, HDR effects, and so on. Most modern games on the market today make heavy use of these screen effects for their depth of field effects, Bloom effects, and even color correction effects.

In `Chapter 3`, *Post Processing Stack*, we discussed how to use this with Unity's built-in Post Processing Stack, but in this chapter, you will learn how to build up the script system yourself. This system will give you the control to create many kinds of screen effects. We will cover `RenderTexture`, what the depth buffer is, and how to create effects that give you Photoshop-like control over the final rendered image of your game. By utilizing screen effects for your games, you not only round out your shader writing knowledge, but you will also have the power to create your own incredible real-time renders with Unity from scratch.

Setting up the screen effects script system

The process of creating screen effects is one in which we grab a full-screen image (or texture), use a shader to process its pixels on the GPU, and then send it back to Unity's renderer to apply it to the whole rendered image of the game. This allows us to perform per-pixel operations on the rendered image of the game in real time, giving us a more global artistic control.

Imagine if you had to go through and adjust each material on each object in your game to just adjust the contrast of the final look of your game. While not impossible, this would take a bit of labor to perform. By utilizing a screen effect, we can adjust the screen's final look as a whole, thereby giving us more Photoshop-like control over our game's final appearance.

In order to get a screen effect system up and running, we have to set up a single script to act as the courier of the game's current rendered image, or what Unity calls the `RenderTexture`. By utilizing this script to pass the `RenderTexture` to a shader, we can create a flexible system for establishing screen effects. For our first screen effect, we are going to create a very simple grayscale effect and make our game look black and white. Let's take a look at how this is done.

Getting ready

In order to get our screen effects system up and running, we need to create a few assets for our current Unity project. By doing this, we will set ourselves up for the steps in the following sections:

1. In the current project, create a new scene to work in.
2. Create a simple sphere in the scene and assign it a new material (I called mine `RedMat`). This new material can be anything, but for our example, we will make a simple red material using the Standard Shader.
3. Finally, create a new directional light and save the scene.
4. We need to create a new C# script and call it `TestRenderImage.cs`. For organization purposes, create a folder called `Scripts` from the **Project** tab to put it in.

With all of our assets ready, you should have a simple scene setup, which looks similar to the following screenshot:

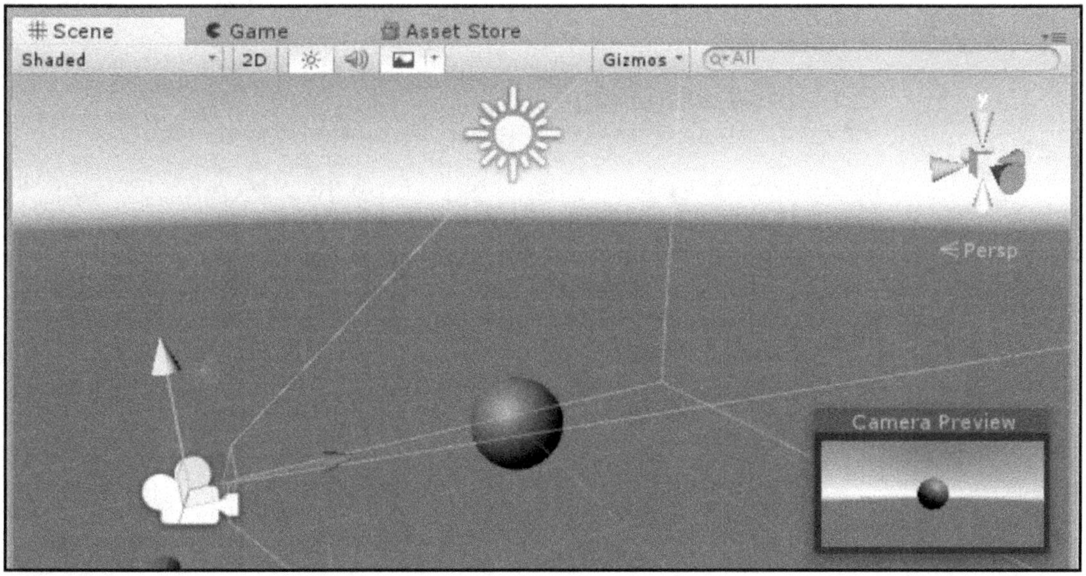

How to do it...

In order to make our grayscale screen effect work, we need a script and shader. So, we will complete these two new items here and fill them in with the appropriate code to produce our first screen effect. Our first task is to complete the C# script. This will get the whole system running. After this, we will complete the shader and see the results of our screen effect. Let's complete our script and shader with the following steps:

1. Open the `TestRenderImage.cs` C# script and begin by entering a few variables that we will need to store important objects and data. Enter the following code at the very top of the `TestRenderImage` class:

```
#region Variables
public Shader curShader;
public float greyscaleAmount = 1.0f;
private Material screenMat;
#endregion
```

2. In order for us to edit the screen effect in real time, when the Unity editor isn't playing, we need to enter the following line of code just above the declaration of the `TestRenderImage` class:

```
using UnityEngine;

[ExecuteInEditMode]
public class TestRenderImage : MonoBehaviour {
```

3. As our screen effect is using a shader to perform the pixel operations on our screen image, we have to create a material to run the shader. Without this, we can't access the properties of the shader. For this, we will create a C# property to check for a material, and create one if it doesn't find one. Enter the following code just after the declaration of the variables from *step 1*:

```
#region Properties
Material ScreenMat
{
    get
    {
        if (screenMat == null)
        {
            screenMat = new Material(curShader);
            screenMat.hideFlags =
HideFlags.HideAndDontSave;
        }
        return screenMat;
    }
}
#endregion
```

4. We now want to set up some checks in our script to see if the current target platform that we are building the Unity game on actually supports image effects. If it doesn't find anything at the start of this script, then the script will disable itself:

```
void Start()
{
    if (!SystemInfo.supportsImageEffects)
    {
        enabled = false;
        return;
    }

    if (!curShader && !curShader.isSupported)
```

```
        {
            enabled = false;
        }
    }
```

5. To actually grab the rendered image from the Unity renderer, we need to make use of the following built-in function that Unity provides us, called `OnRenderImage()`. Enter the following code so that we can have access to the current `RenderTexture`:

```
void OnRenderImage(RenderTexture sourceTexture,
RenderTexture destTexture)
{
    if (curShader != null)
    {
        ScreenMat.SetFloat("_Luminosity",
greyscaleAmount);

        Graphics.Blit(sourceTexture, destTexture,
ScreenMat);
    }
    else
    {
        Graphics.Blit(sourceTexture, destTexture);
    }
}
```

6. Our screen effect has a variable called `grayScaleAmount` with which we can control how much grayscale we want for our final screen effect. So, in this case, we need to make the value go from `0` to `1`, where `0` is no grayscale effect and `1` is a full grayscale effect. We will perform this operation in the `Update()` function, which will be called every frame while the game is running:

```
void Update ()
{
    greyscaleAmount = Mathf.Clamp(greyscaleAmount, 0.0f,
1.0f);
}
```

7. Finally, we complete our script by doing a little bit of clean-up on objects we created when the script started:

```
void OnDisable()
{
  if(screenMat)
  {
```

```
            DestroyImmediate(screenMat);
        }
    }
```

8. At this point, we can now apply this script to the camera, if it compiled without errors, in Unity. Let's apply the `TestRenderImage.cs` script to our main camera in our scene. You should see the `grayScaleAmount` value and a field for a shader, but the script throws an error to the console window. It says that it is missing an instance to an object and so won't process appropriately. If you recall from *step 4*, we are doing some checks to see whether we have a shader and if the current platform supports the shader. As we haven't given the screen effect script a shader to work with, then the `curShader` variable is just null, which throws an error. Let's continue with our screen effects system by completing the shader.
9. Create a new shader called `ScreenGrayscale`. To begin our shader, we will populate our `Properties` with some variables so that we can send data to this shader:

```
Properties
{
 _MainTex ("Base (RGB)", 2D) = "white" {}
 _Luminosity("Luminosity", Range(0.0, 1)) = 1.0
}
```

10. Our shader is now going to utilize pure CG shader code instead of utilizing Unity's built-in Surface Shader code. This will make our screen effect more optimized as we need to work only with the pixels of the `RenderTexture`. So, we will delete everything inside of the `Pass` that was there before and create a new `Pass` block in our shader and fill it with some new `#pragma` statements that we haven't seen before:

```
SubShader
{
  Pass
  {
    CGPROGRAM
    #pragma vertex vert_img
    #pragma fragment frag
    #pragma fragmentoption ARB_precision_hint_fastest
    #include "UnityCG.cginc"
```

11. In order to access the data being sent to the shader from the Unity editor, we need to create the corresponding variables in our `CGPROGRAM`:

```
uniform sampler2D _MainTex;
```

```
fixed _Luminosity;
```

12. Finally, all we need to do is set up our pixel function, in this case called `frag()`. This is where the meat of the screen effect is. This function will process each pixel of the `RenderTexture` and return a new image to our `TestRenderImage.cs` script:

```
fixed4 frag(v2f_img i) : COLOR
{
  //Get the colors from the RenderTexture and the uv's
  //from the v2f_img struct
  fixed4 renderTex = tex2D(_MainTex, i.uv);
  //Apply the Luminosity values to our render texture
  float luminosity = 0.299 * renderTex.r + 0.587 *
renderTex.g + 0.114 * renderTex.b;
  fixed4 finalColor = lerp(renderTex, luminosity,
_Luminosity);
  renderTex.rgb = finalColor;

  return renderTex;
}
```

13. Lastly, change the `FallBack` line to the following:

```
FallBack off
```

14. The final shader should look as follows:

```
Shader "CookbookShaders/Chapter09/Grayscale"
{
  Properties
  {
    _MainTex ("Base (RGB)", 2D) = "white" {}
    _Luminosity("Luminosity", Range(0.0, 1)) = 1.0
  }

  SubShader
  {
    Pass
    {
      CGPROGRAM
      #pragma vertex vert_img
      #pragma fragment frag
      #pragma fragmentoption ARB_precision_hint_fastest
      #include "UnityCG.cginc"

      uniform sampler2D _MainTex;
      fixed _Luminosity;
```

```
        fixed4 frag(v2f_img i) : COLOR
        {
          //Get the colors from the RenderTexture and the
uv's
          //from the v2f_img struct
          fixed4 renderTex = tex2D(_MainTex, i.uv);
          //Apply the Luminosity values to our render
texture
          float luminosity = 0.299 * renderTex.r + 0.587 *
renderTex.g + 0.114 * renderTex.b;
          fixed4 finalColor = lerp(renderTex, luminosity,
_Luminosity);

          renderTex.rgb = finalColor;
          return renderTex;
        }
      ENDCG
      }
    }
  FallBack off
}
```

Once the shader is complete, return to Unity and let it compile to see if any errors occurred. If not, assign the new shader to the `TestRenderImage.cs` script and change the value of the grayscale amount variable. You should see the game view go from a colored version of the game to a grayscale version of the game:

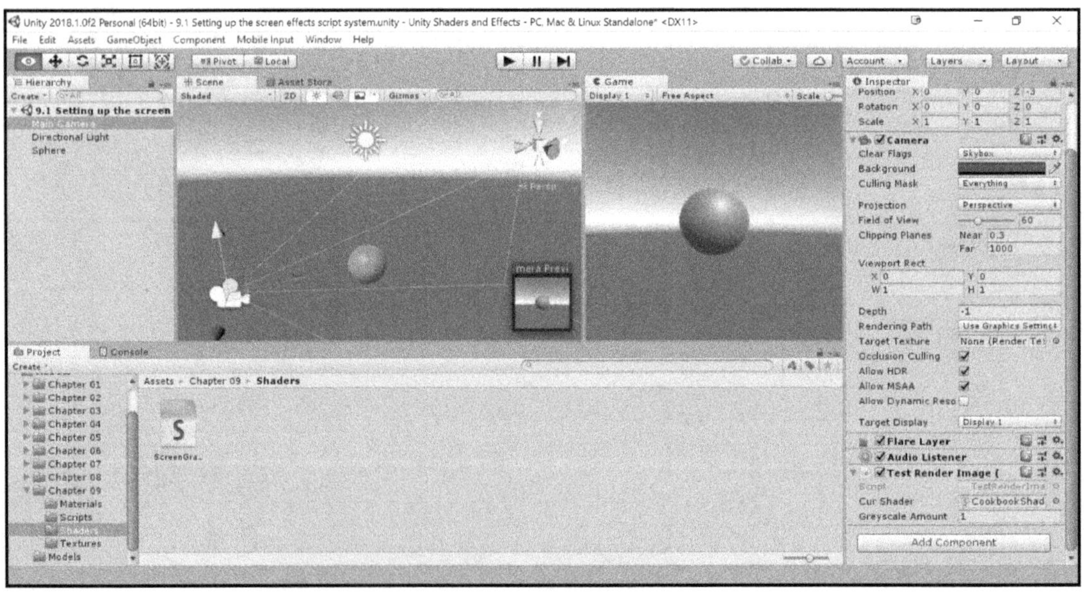

The following screenshot demonstrates this Screen Effect:

With this complete, we now have an easy way to test out new screen effect shaders without having to write our whole screen effect system over and over again. Let's dive in a little deeper and learn about what's going on with the `RenderTexture` and how it is processed throughout its existence.

How it works...

To get a screen effect up and running inside of Unity, we need to create a script and shader. The script drives the real-time update in the editor and is also responsible for capturing the `RenderTexture` from the main camera and passing it to the shader. Once the `RenderTexture` gets to the shader, we can use the shader to perform per-pixel operations.

At the start of the script, we perform a few checks to make sure that the current selected build platform actually supports screen effects and the shader itself. There are instances where a current platform will not support screen effects or the shader that we are using. So, the checks that we do in the `Start()` function ensure we don't get any errors if the platform doesn't support the screen system.

Once the script passes these checks, we initiate the screen effects system by calling the built-in `OnRenderImage()` function. This function is responsible for grabbing the `renderTexture`, giving it to the shader using the `Graphics.Blit()` function, and returning the processed image to the Unity renderer. You can find more information on these two functions at the following URLs:

- `OnRenderImage`: `http://docs.unity3d.com/Documentation/ScriptReference/MonoBehaviour.OnRenderImage.html`
- `Graphics.Blit`: `http://docs.unity3d.com/Documentation/ScriptReference/Graphics.Blit.html`

Once the current `RenderTexture` reaches the shader, the shader takes it, processes it through the `frag()` function, and returns the final color for each pixel.

You can see how powerful this becomes as it gives us Photoshop-like control over the final rendered image of our game. These screen effects work sequentially like Photoshop layers on top of what the camera sees. When you place these screen effects one after the other, they will be processed in that order. These are just the bare bones steps to get a screen effect working, but it is the core of how the screen effects system works.

There's more...

Now that we have our simple screen effect system up and running, let's take a look at some of the other useful information we can obtain from Unity's renderer:

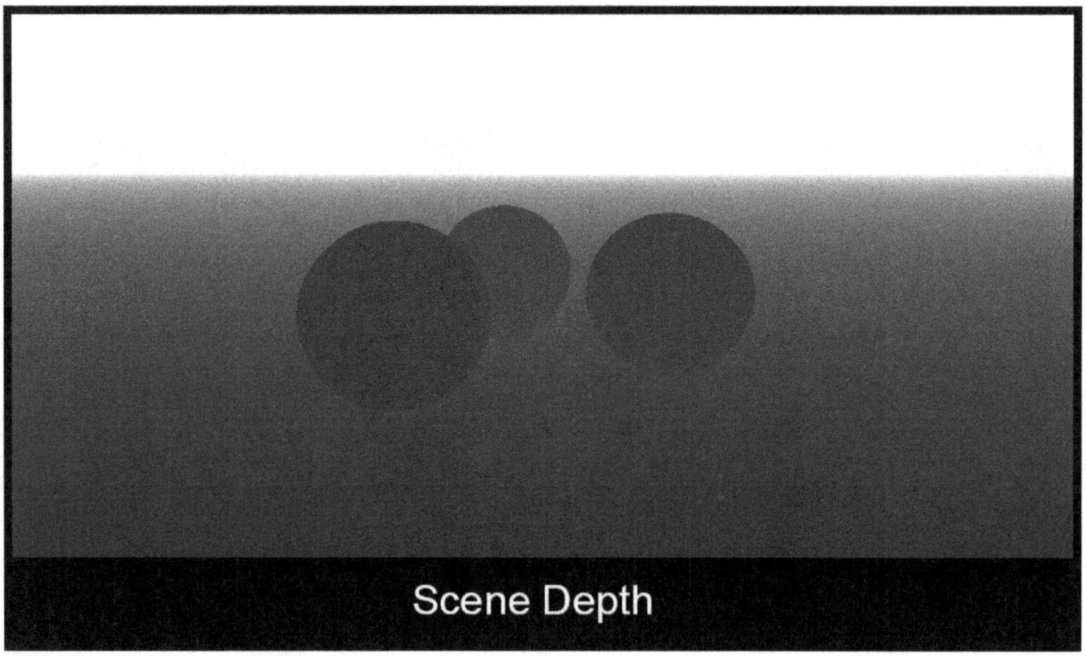

We can actually get the depth of everything in our current game by turning on Unity's built-in **Depth** mode. Once this is turned on, we can use the depth information for a ton of different effects. Let's take a look at how this is done:

1. Duplicate the sphere we created twice and create a plane underneath:

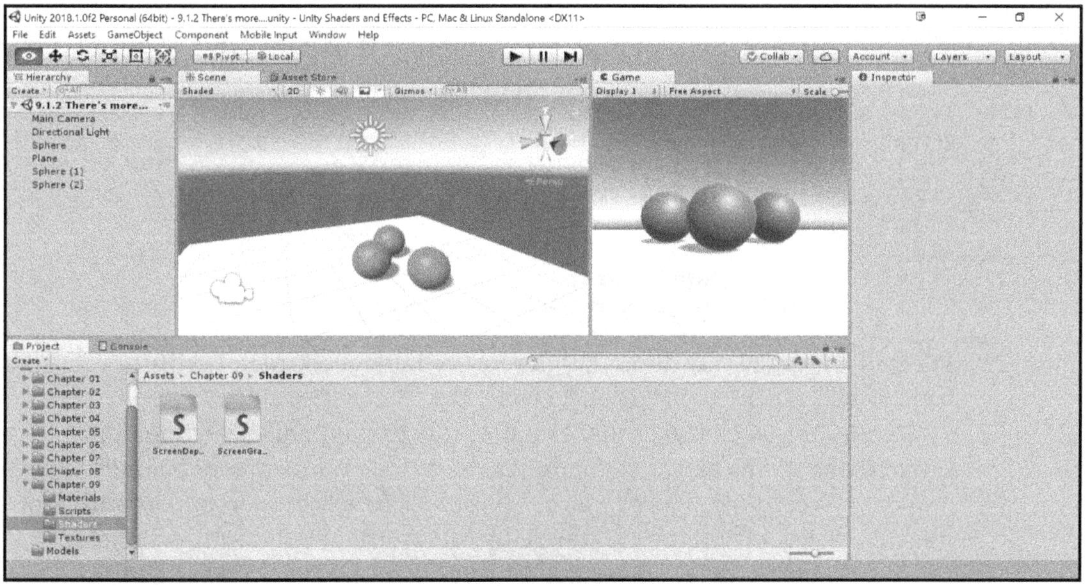

2. Create a new shader by duplicating the `ScreenGreyscale` code by selecting it and pressing *Ctrl* + *D*. Once duplicated, rename the script to `SceneDepth`. Then double-click on this shader to open it in your script editor.
3. We will create the main texture (`_MainTex`) property and a property to control the power of the scene depth effect. Enter the following code in your shader:

```
Properties
{
  _MainTex ("Base (RGB)", 2D) = "white" {}
  _DepthPower("Depth Power", Range(0, 1)) = 1
}
```

4. Now we need to create the corresponding variables in our `CGPROGRAM`. We are going to add one more variable called `_CameraDepthTexture`. This is a built-in variable that Unity has provided us with through the use of the `UnityCG.cginclude` file. It gives us the depth information from the camera:

```
Pass
{
  CGPROGRAM
  #pragma vertex vert_img
  #pragma fragment frag
  #pragma fragmentoption ARB_precision_hint_fastest
  #include "UnityCG.cginc"

  uniform sampler2D _MainTex;
  fixed _DepthPower;
  sampler2D _CameraDepthTexture;
```

5. We will complete our depth shader by utilizing a couple of built-in functions that Unity provides us with, the `UNITY_SAMPLE_DEPTH()` and `linear01Depth()` functions. The first function actually gets the depth information from our `_CameraDepthTexture` and produces a single float value for each pixel. The `Linear01Depth()` function then makes sure that the values are within the `0-1` range by taking this final depth value to a power we can control, where the mid-value in the `0-1` range sits in the scene based off of the camera position:

```
fixed4 frag(v2f_img i) : COLOR
{
  //Get the colors from the RenderTexture and the uv's
  //from the v2f_img struct
  float depth =
UNITY_SAMPLE_DEPTH(tex2D(_CameraDepthTexture, i.uv.xy));
  depth = pow(Linear01Depth(depth), _DepthPower);

  return depth;
}
```

6. With our shader complete, let's turn our attention to the Unity editor and create a new script to work with. Select our `TestRenderImage` script and duplicate it. Name this new script `RenderDepth` and open it up in your script editor.

7. Update the script to have the same class name as we renamed it to in the previous step (`RenderDepth`):

```
using UnityEngine;

[ExecuteInEditMode]
public class RenderDepth : MonoBehaviour {
```

8. We need to add the `depthPower` variable to the script so that we can let users change the value in the editor:

```
#region Variables
public Shader curShader;
public float depthPower = 0.2f;
private Material screenMat;
#endregion
```

9. Our `OnRenderImage()` function then needs to be updated so that it is passing the right value to our shader:

```
void OnRenderImage(RenderTexture sourceTexture,
RenderTexture destTexture)
{
    if (curShader != null)
    {
        ScreenMat.SetFloat("_DepthPower", depthPower);

        Graphics.Blit(sourceTexture, destTexture,
ScreenMat);
    }
    else
    {
        Graphics.Blit(sourceTexture, destTexture);
    }
}
```

10. To complete our depth screen effect, we need to tell Unity to turn on the depth rendering in the current camera. This is done by simply setting the main camera's `depthTextureMode`:

```
void Update ()
{
    Camera.main.depthTextureMode = DepthTextureMode.Depth;
    depthPower = Mathf.Clamp(depthPower, 0, 1);
}
```

With all the code set up, save your script and shader and return to Unity to let them both compile. Afterward, select the **Main Camera**, right-click on the **TextRenderImage** component, and select **Remove Component**. Afterward, attach this new component to the object and drag and drop our new shader inside. If no errors are encountered, you should see a result similar to the following screenshot:

Here's an example of what we can get if we tweak the values even more:

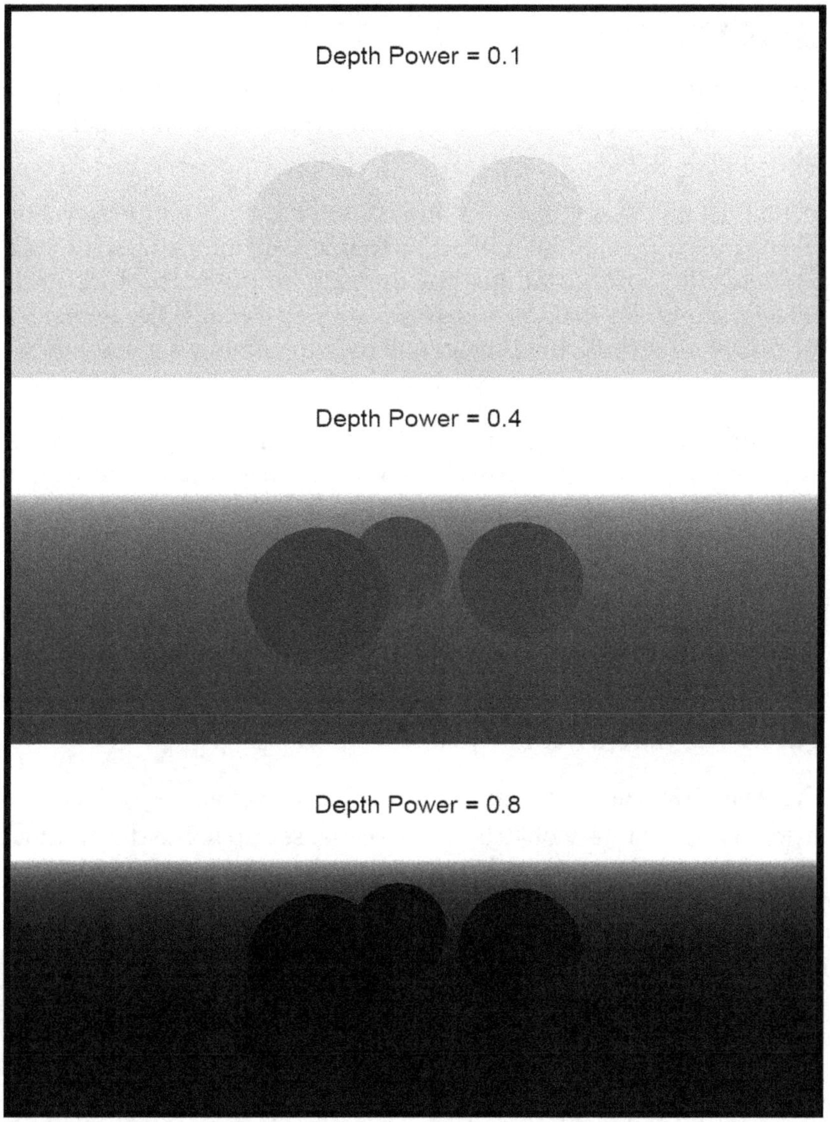

Using brightness, saturation, and contrast with screen effects

Now that we have our screen effects system up and running, we can explore how to create more involved pixel operations to perform some of the more common screen effects found in games today.

Using a screen effect to adjust the overall final colors of your game is crucial in giving artists global control over the final look of the game. Techniques such as color adjustment sliders allow users to adjust the intensity of the reds, blues, and greens of the final rendered game. This concept is also used with techniques such as putting a certain tone of color over the whole screen, as seen in something like a sepia film effect.

For this particular recipe, we are going to cover some of the more core color adjustment operations we can perform on an image. These are brightness, saturation, and contrast. Learning how to code these color adjustments gives us a nice base from which we can learn the art of screen effects.

Getting ready

We will need to create a couple of new assets. We can utilize the same scene as our test scene, but we will need a new script and shader:

1. Create a new scene by going to **File** | **New Scene**.
2. Add a couple of new objects to the scene, set up some different colored diffuse materials, and randomly assign them to the new objects in the scene. This will give us a good range of colors to test with our new screen effect:

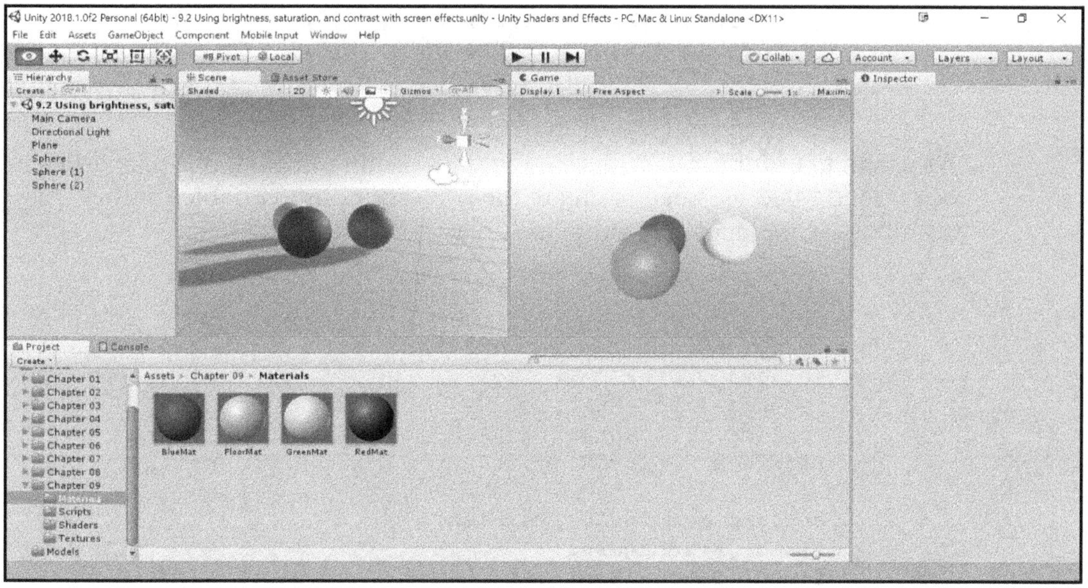

How to do it...

Now that we have completed our scene setup and created our new script and shader, we can begin to fill in the code necessary to achieve the brightness, saturation, and contrast screen effects. We will be focusing on just the pixel operation and variable setup for our script and shader, since getting a screen effect system up and running is described in the *Setting up the screen effects script system* recipe in this chapter:

1. Create a new shader by duplicating the `ScreenGreyscale` code by selecting it from the **Project** tab under the `Chapter 9 | Shaders` folder and pressing *Ctrl* + *D*. Once duplicated, rename the script to `ScreenBSC`. Then double-click on this shader to open it in your script editor.
2. Editing the shader first makes more sense so that we know what kind of variables we will need for our C# script. Let's begin by entering the appropriate properties for our brightness, saturation, and contrast effect. Remember that we need to keep the `_MainTex` property in our shader as this is the property that the `RenderTexture` targets when creating screen effects:

```
Properties
{
  _MainTex ("Base (RGB)", 2D) = "white" {}
```

```
    _Brightness("Brightness", Range(0.0, 1)) = 1.0
    _Saturation("Saturation", Range(0.0, 1)) = 1.0
    _Contrast("Contrast", Range(0.0, 1)) = 1.0
}
```

3. As usual, in order for us to access the data coming in from our properties in our CGPROGRAM, we need to create the corresponding variables in the CGPROGRAM, replacing the previous ones:

```
Pass
{
  CGPROGRAM
  #pragma vertex vert_img
  #pragma fragment frag
  #pragma fragmentoption ARB_precision_hint_fastest
  #include "UnityCG.cginc"

  uniform sampler2D _MainTex;
  fixed _Brightness;
  fixed _Saturation;
  fixed _Contrast;
```

4. Now, we need to create the operations that will perform the brightness, saturation, and contrast effects. Enter the following new function in our shader, just above the frag() function:

```
float3 ContrastSaturationBrightness(float3 color, float
brt, float sat, float con)
{
  // Increase or decrease these values to
  //adjust r, g and b color channels separately
  float AvgLumR = 0.5;
  float AvgLumG = 0.5;
  float AvgLumB = 0.5;
//Luminance coefficients for getting luminance from the
image
  float3 LuminanceCoeff = float3(0.2125, 0.7154, 0.0721);
  //Operation for brightness
  float3 AvgLumin = float3(AvgLumR, AvgLumG, AvgLumB);
  float3 brtColor = color * brt;
  float intensityf = dot(brtColor, LuminanceCoeff);
  float3 intensity = float3(intensityf, intensityf,
intensityf);
  //Operation for Saturation
  float3 satColor = lerp(intensity, brtColor, sat);
  //Operation for Contrast
  float3 conColor = lerp(AvgLumin, satColor, con);
```

```
    return conColor;
}
```

> **TIP:** Don't worry if it doesn't make sense just yet; all the code will be explained in the *How it works* section of this recipe.

5. Finally, we just need to update our `frag()` function to actually use the `ContrastSaturationBrightness()` function. This will process all the pixels of our `RenderTexture` and pass it back to our script:

```
fixed4 frag(v2f_img i) : COLOR
{
  //Get the colors from the RenderTexture and the uv's
  //from the v2f_img struct
  fixed4 renderTex = tex2D(_MainTex, i.uv);
  //Apply the Brughtness, saturation, contrast operations
  renderTex.rgb =
ContrastSaturationBrightness(renderTex.rgb,
                        _Brightness,
                        _Saturation,
                        _Contrast);
  return renderTex;
}
```

With the code entered in the shader, return to the Unity editor to let the new shader compile. If there are no errors, we can return to our code editor to work on our script. Let's begin by creating a couple of new lines of code that will send the proper data to our shader:

1. Now that the shader is finished, let's work on the script needed to make the effect show up. From the **Project** tab, go to the `Chapter 9 | Scripts` folder. Once there, select the `TestRenderImage` script and duplicate it by pressing *Ctrl* + *D*. Rename the newly created script to `RenderBSC`. Once renamed, double-click on it to enter your IDE of choice.

2. To modify our script, we need to rename the class to match our filename, `RenderBSC`:

```
[ExecuteInEditMode]
public class RenderBSC : MonoBehaviour {
```

3. Afterward, we need to add the proper variables that will drive the values of our screen effect. In this case, we will need a slider for brightness, a slider for saturation, and a slider for contrast:

```
#region Variables
public Shader curShader;
public float brightness = 1.0f;
public float saturation = 1.0f;
public float contrast = 1.0f;
private Material screenMat;
#endregion
```

4. With our variables set up, we now need to tell the script to send the values of the variables we created to the shader. We do this in the `OnRenderImage()` function:

```
void OnRenderImage(RenderTexture sourceTexture,
RenderTexture destTexture)
{
    if (curShader != null)
    {
        ScreenMat.SetFloat("_Brightness", brightness);
        ScreenMat.SetFloat("_Saturation", saturation);
        ScreenMat.SetFloat("_Contrast", contrast);

        Graphics.Blit(sourceTexture, destTexture,
ScreenMat);
    }
    else
    {
        Graphics.Blit(sourceTexture, destTexture);
    }
}
```

5. Finally, all we need to do is clamp the values of the variables within a range that is reasonable. These clamp values are entirely preferential, so you can use whichever values you see fit:

```
void Update()
{
    brightness = Mathf.Clamp(brightness, 0.0f, 2.0f);
    saturation = Mathf.Clamp(saturation, 0.0f, 2.0f);
    contrast = Mathf.Clamp(contrast, 0.0f, 3.0f);
}
```

With the script completed and shader finished, we simply assign our script to our **Main Camera** and our shader to the script, and you should see the effects of brightness, saturation, and contrast by manipulating the property values:

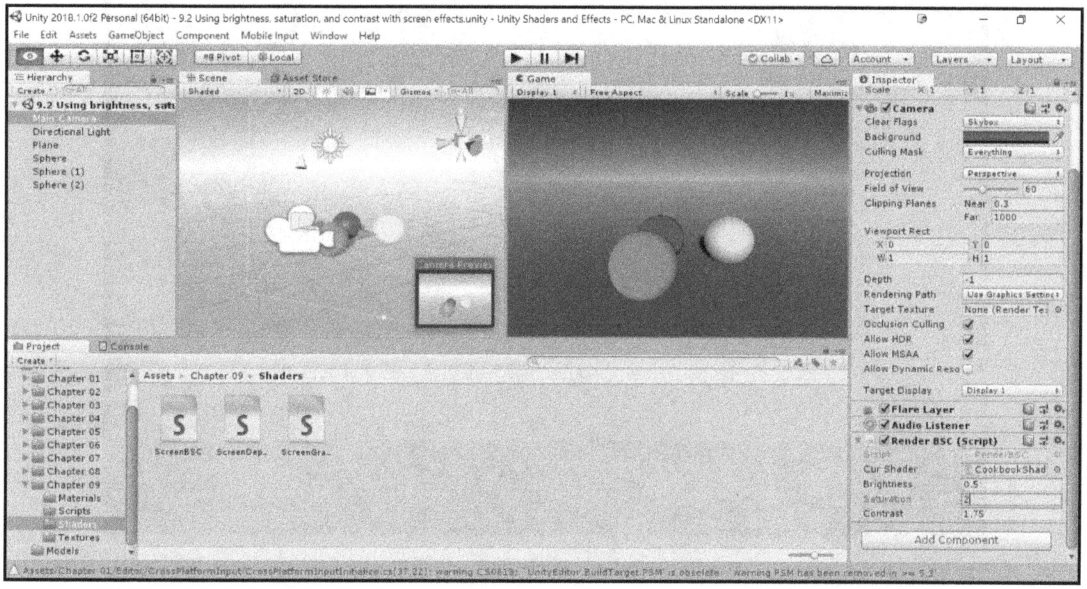

The following screenshot shows a result you can achieve with this screen effect:

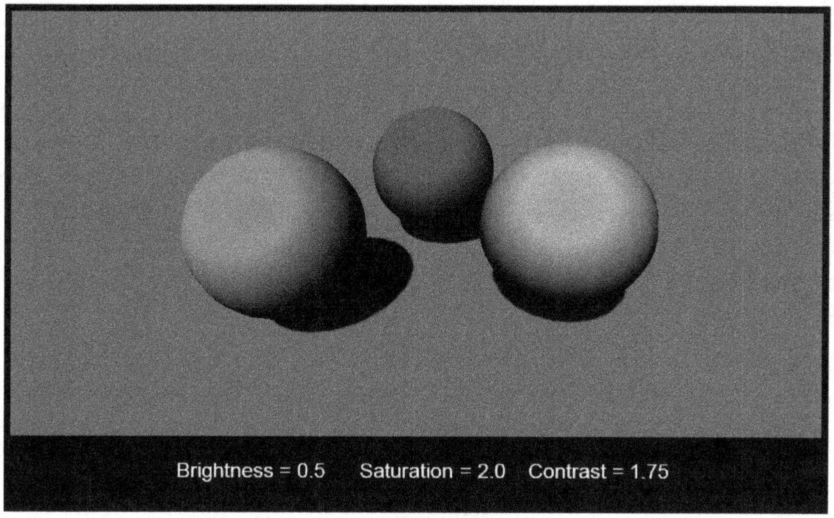

The following screenshot shows another example of what can be done by adjusting the colors of the render image:

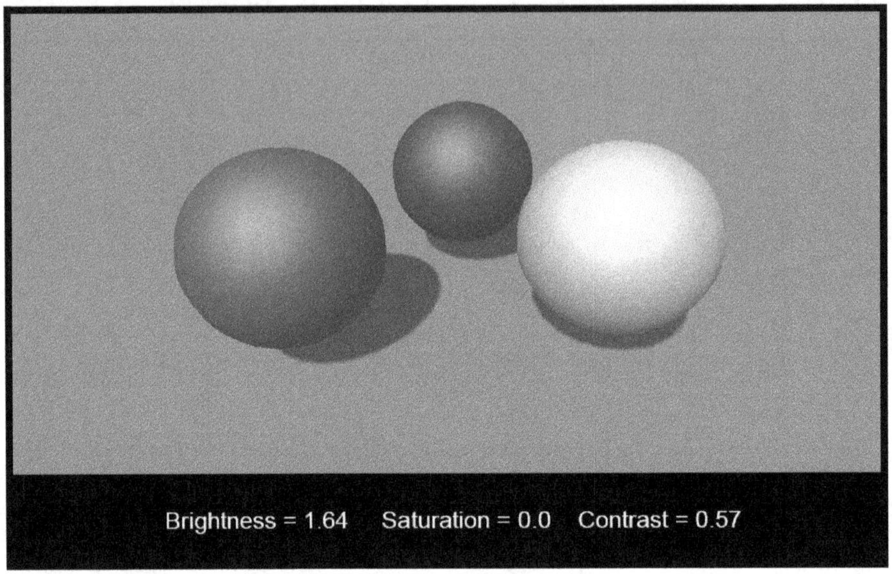

How it works...

Since we now know how the basic screen effects system works, let's just cover the per-pixel operations we created in the `ContrastSaturationBrightness()` function.

The function starts by taking a few arguments. The first and most important is the current `RenderTexture`. The other arguments simply adjust the overall effect of the screen effect and are represented by sliders in the screen effect's **Inspector** tab. Once the function receives the `RenderTexture` and the adjustment values, it declares a few constant values that we use to modify and compare against the original `RenderTexture`.

The `luminanceCoeff` variable stores the values that will give us the overall brightness of the current image. These coefficients are based on the CIE color matching functions and are pretty standard throughout the industry. We can find the overall brightness of the image by getting the dot product of the current image dotted with these luminance coefficients. Once we have the brightness, we simply use a couple of `lerp` functions to blend the grayscale version of the brightness operation and the original image, multiplied by the brightness value being passed into the function.

Screen effects such as this are crucial to achieving high-quality graphics for your games as they let you tweak the final look of your game without you having to edit each material in your current game scene.

Using basic Photoshop-like Blend modes with screen effects

The screen effects aren't just limited to adjusting the colors of a rendered image from our game. We can also use them to combine other images with our `RenderTexture`. This technique is no different than creating a new layer in Photoshop and choosing a **Blend** mode to blend two images together or, in our case, a texture with a `RenderTexture`. This becomes a very powerful technique as it gives the artists in a production environment a way to simulate their blending modes in the game rather than just in Photoshop.

For this particular recipe, we are going to take a look at some of the more common blend modes, such as **Multiply**, **Add**, and **Overlay**. You will see how simple it is to have the power of Photoshop **Blend** modes in your game.

Getting ready

To begin, we have to get our assets ready. So let's follow the next few steps to get our screen effects system up and running for our new **Blend** mode screen effect:

1. We will need another texture to perform our **Blend** mode effect. In this recipe, we will use a grunge-type texture. This will make the effect very obvious when we are testing it out.

2. The following screenshot is the grunge map used in the making of this effect. Finding a texture with enough detail and a nice range of grayscale values will make for a nice texture to test our new effect:

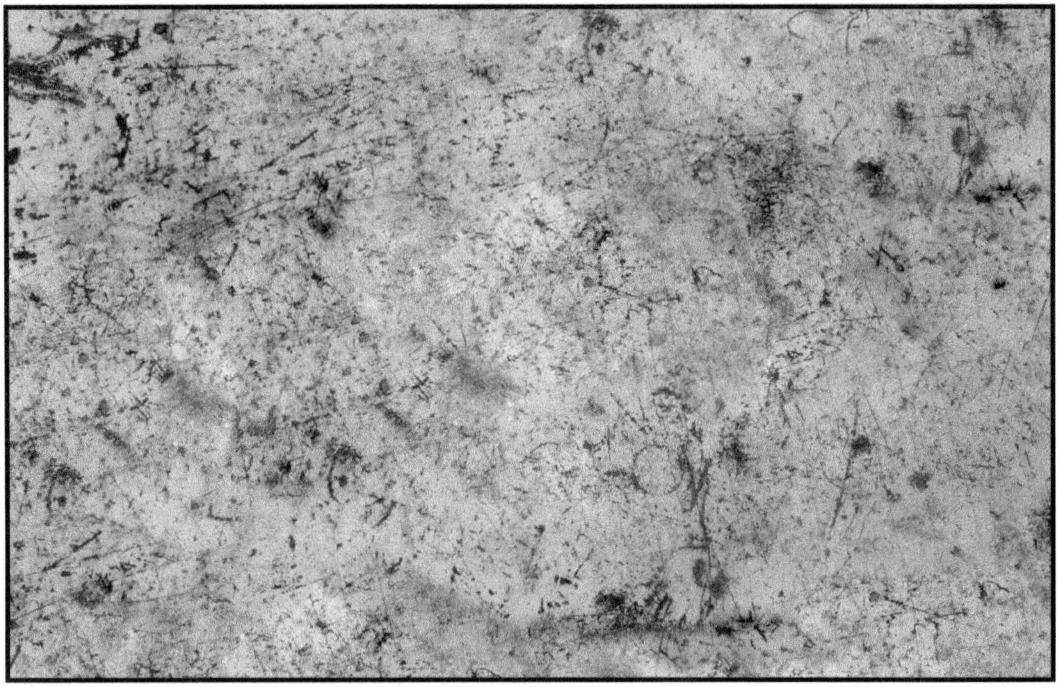

TIP

The preceding texture is available in the example code for this book in `Chapter 9 | Textures` folder.

How to do it...

The first **Blend** mode that we will implement is the **Multiply** blend mode as seen in Photoshop. Let's begin by modifying the code in our shader first:

1. Create a new shader by duplicating the `ScreenGreyscale` code by selecting it from the **Project** tab under the `Chapter 9 | Shaders` folder and pressing *Ctrl* + *D*. Once duplicated, rename the script to `ScreenBlendMode`. Then, double-click on this shader to open it in your script editor.

2. We need to add some new properties so that we have a texture to blend with and a slider for an opacity value. Enter the following code in your new shader:

```
Properties
{
  _MainTex ("Base (RGB)", 2D) = "white" {}
  _BlendTex ("Blend Texture", 2D) = "white"{}
  _Opacity ("Blend Opacity", Range(0,1)) = 1
}
```

3. Enter the corresponding variables in our `CGPROGRAM` so that we can access the data from our `Properties` block, replacing the previously created variables:

```
Pass
{
  CGPROGRAM
  #pragma vertex vert_img
  #pragma fragment frag
  #pragma fragmentoption ARB_precision_hint_fastest
  #include "UnityCG.cginc"

  uniform sampler2D _MainTex;
  uniform sampler2D _BlendTex;
  fixed _Opacity;
```

4. We modify our `frag()` function so that it performs the multiply operation on our two textures:

```
fixed4 frag(v2f_img i) : COLOR
{
  //Get the colors from the RenderTexture and the uv's
  //from the v2f_img struct
  fixed4 renderTex = tex2D(_MainTex, i.uv);
  fixed4 blendTex = tex2D(_BlendTex, i.uv);
  //Perform a multiply Blend mode
  fixed4 blendedMultiply = renderTex * blendTex;
  //Adjust amount of Blend Mode with a lerp
  renderTex = lerp(renderTex, blendedMultiply, _Opacity);
  return renderTex;
}
```

5. Save the shader and return to the Unity editor to let the new shader code compile and check for errors. If no errors occurred, then we can move on to creating our script file.

6. Now that the shader is finished, let's work on the script needed to make the effect show up. From the **Project** tab, go to the `Chapter 09 | Scripts` folder. Once there, select the `TestRenderImage` script and duplicate it by pressing *Ctrl* + *D*. Rename the newly created script to `RenderBlendMode`. Once renamed, double-click on it to enter your IDE of choice.
7. Our first step in modifying our script is to rename the class to match our filename, `RenderBlendMode`:

```
[ExecuteInEditMode]
public class RenderBlendMode : MonoBehaviour {
```

8. In our script file, we need to create the corresponding variables. We will need a texture so that we can assign one to the shader and a slider to adjust the final amount of the Blend mode we want to use:

```
#region Variables
public Shader curShader;
public Texture2D blendTexture;
public float blendOpacity = 1.0f;
private Material screenMat;
#endregion
```

9. We then need to send our variable data to the shader through the `OnRenderImage()` function:

```
void OnRenderImage(RenderTexture sourceTexture,
RenderTexture destTexture)
{
    if (curShader != null)
    {
        ScreenMat.SetTexture("_BlendTex", blendTexture);
        ScreenMat.SetFloat("_Opacity", blendOpacity);

        Graphics.Blit(sourceTexture, destTexture,
ScreenMat);
    }
    else
    {
        Graphics.Blit(sourceTexture, destTexture);
    }
}
```

10. To complete the script, we simply fill in our `Update()` function so that we can clamp the value of the `blendOpacity` variable between a value of `0.0` and `1.0`:

```
void Update()
{
    blendOpacity = Mathf.Clamp(blendOpacity, 0.0f, 1.0f);
}
```

11. With this complete, we assign the screen effect script to our **Main Camera** (remove the previous `Render BSC` script if it is attached) and add our screen effect shader to our script so that it has a shader to use for the per-pixel operations. In order for the effect to be fully functional, the script and shader look for a texture. You can assign any texture to the **Texture** field in the **Inspector** for the screen effect script. Once this texture is in place, you will see the effect of multiplying this texture over the game's rendered screenshot:

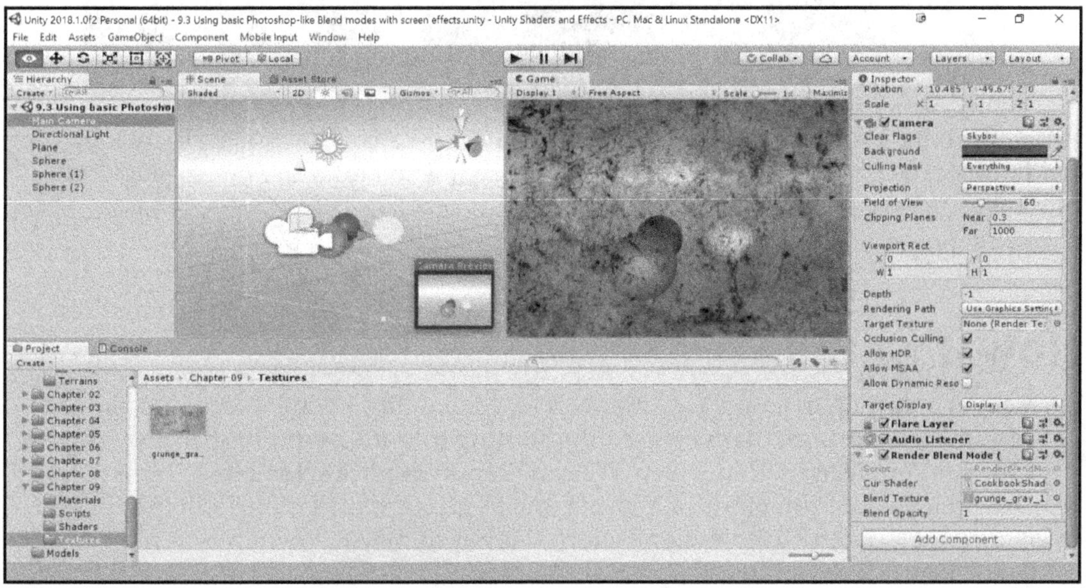

12. The following screenshot demonstrates the screen effect with a smaller `Blend Opacity` option:

With our first blend mode set up, we can begin to add a couple of simpler blend modes to get a better understanding of how easy it is to add more effects and really fine-tune the final result in your game. However, first let's break down what is happening here.

How it works...

Now we are starting to gain a ton of power and flexibility in our screen effects programming. I am sure that you are now starting to understand how much you can do with this simple system in Unity. We can literally replicate the effects of Photoshop layer blending modes in our game to give artists the flexibility they need to achieve high-quality graphics in a short amount of time.

With this particular recipe, we look at how to multiply two images together, add two images together, and perform a screen blending mode, using just a little bit of mathematics. When working with Blend modes, you have to think on a per-pixel level. For instance, when we are using the multiply blend mode, we literally take each pixel from the original `RenderTexture` and multiply it by each pixel of the Blend texture. The same goes for the add Blend mode. It is just a simple mathematical operation of adding each pixel from the source texture, or `RenderTexture`, to the Blend texture.

The screen Blend mode is definitely a bit more involved, but it is actually doing the same thing. It takes each image, `RenderTexture`, and Blend texture, inverts them, then multiplies them together, and inverts them again to achieve the final look. Just as Photoshop blends its textures together using blend modes, we can do the same with screen effects.

There's more...

Let's continue this recipe by adding a couple more blend modes to our screen effect:

1. In the screen effect shader, let's add the following code to our `frag()` function and change the value we are returning to our script. We will also need to comment out the multiply blend so that we don't return that as well:

```
fixed4 frag(v2f_img i) : COLOR
{
  //Get the colors from the RenderTexture and the uv's
  //from the v2f_img struct
  fixed4 renderTex = tex2D(_MainTex, i.uv);
  fixed4 blendTex = tex2D(_BlendTex, i.uv);
  //Perform a multiply Blend mode
  //fixed4 blendedMultiply = renderTex * blendTex;

  //Perform an additive Blend mode
  fixed4 blendedAdd = renderTex + blendTex;
  //Adjust amount of Blend Mode with a lerp
  renderTex = lerp(renderTex, blendedAdd, _Opacity);
  return renderTex;
}
```

2. Save the shader file in your IDE of choice and `MonoDevelop` and return to the Unity editor to let the shader compile. If no errors occurred, you should see a result similar to the following screenshot:

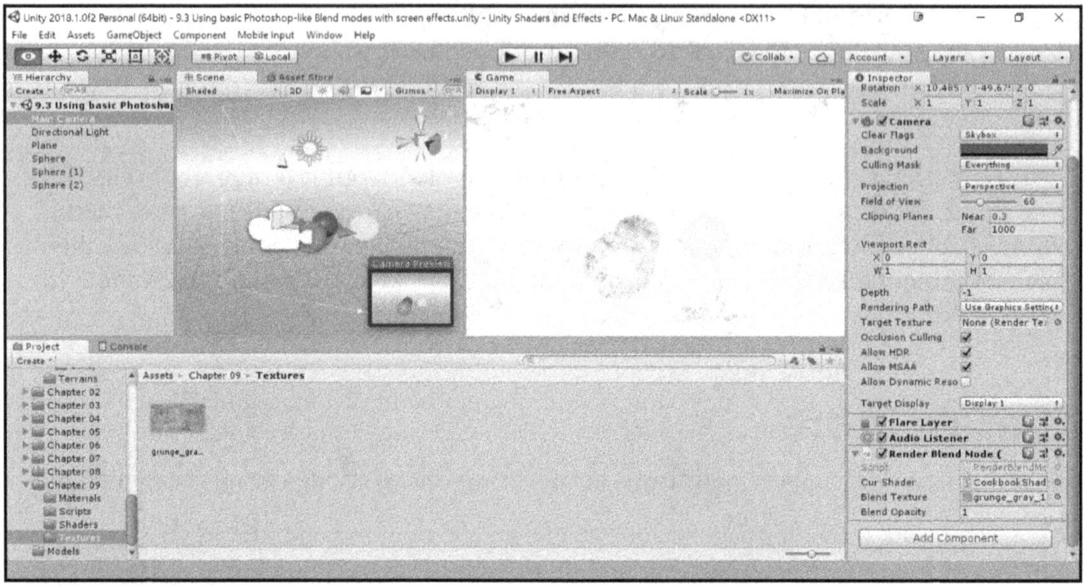

3. This is a simple add blending mode with a figure of `0.5` set for the `Blend Opacity`:

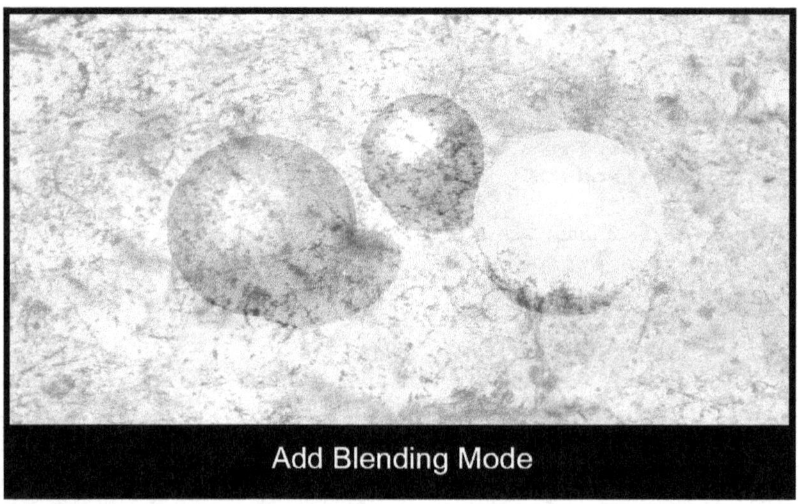

Add Blending Mode

As you can see, this has the opposite effect of multiply because we are adding the two images together.

4. Finally, let's add one more blend mode called a screen blend. This one is a little bit more involved, from a mathematical standpoint, but still simple to implement. Enter the following code in the `frag()` function of our shader:

```
fixed4 frag(v2f_img i) : COLOR
{
  //Get the colors from the RenderTexture and the uv's
  //from the v2f_img struct
  fixed4 renderTex = tex2D(_MainTex, i.uv);
  fixed4 blendTex = tex2D(_BlendTex, i.uv);
  //Perform a multiply Blend mode
  //fixed4 blendedMultiply = renderTex * blendTex;

  //Perform an additive Blend mode
  //fixed4 blendedAdd = renderTex + blendTex;

  //Perform screen blending mode
  fixed4 blendedScreen = (1.0 - ((1.0 - renderTex) * (1.0
- blendTex)));
  //Adjust amount of Blend Mode with a lerp
  renderTex = lerp(renderTex, blendedScreen, _Opacity);
  return renderTex;
}
```

The following screenshot demonstrates the results of using a screen type Blend mode to blend two images together in a screen effect:

Here's a screenshot displaying the effect:

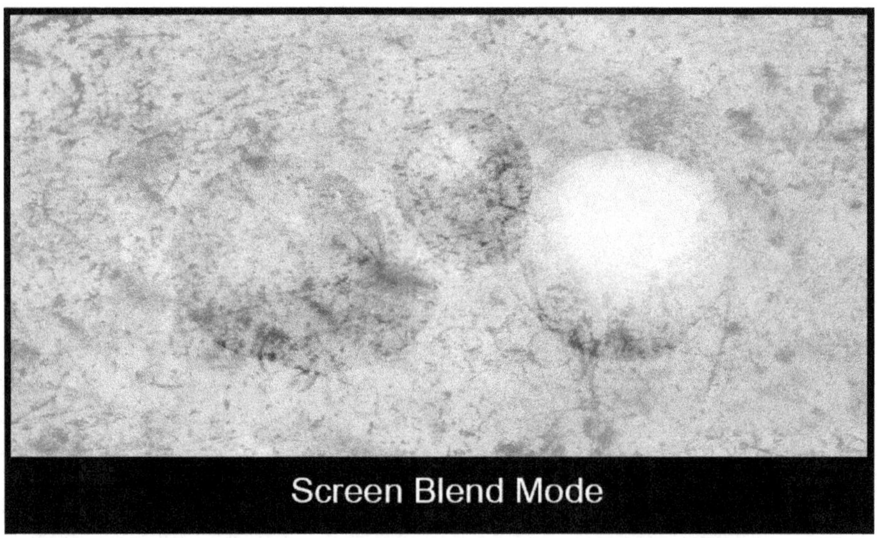

Using the Overlay Blend mode with screen effects

For our final recipe, we are going to take a look at another type of blend mode, the Overlay Blend mode. This blend mode actually makes use of some conditional statements that determine the final color of each pixel in each channel. So, the process of using this type of blend mode requires a bit more coding to work. Let's take a look at how this is done in the next few recipes.

How to do it...

To begin our Overlay Screen effect, we will need to get the code of our shader up and running without errors. We can then modify our script file to feed the correct data to the shader:

1. Create a new shader by duplicating the `ScreenGreyscale` code and selecting it from the **Project** tab under the `Chapter 9 | Shaders` folder and pressing *Ctrl* + *D*. Once duplicated, rename the script to `ScreenOverlay`. Then, double-click on this shader to open it in your script editor.
2. We first need to set up the properties in our `Properties` block. We will use the same properties from the previous few recipes in this chapter:

```
Properties
{
  _MainTex ("Base (RGB)", 2D) = "white" {}
  _BlendTex ("Blend Texture", 2D) = "white"{}
  _Opacity ("Blend Opacity", Range(0,1)) = 1
}
```

3. We then need to create the corresponding variables in our `CGPROGRAM`, removing the previously created ones:

```
Pass
{
  CGPROGRAM
  #pragma vertex vert_img
  #pragma fragment frag
  #pragma fragmentoption ARB_precision_hint_fastest
  #include "UnityCG.cginc"
  uniform sampler2D _MainTex;
  uniform sampler2D _BlendTex;
  fixed _Opacity;
```

4. In order for the Overlay Blend effect to work, we will have to process each pixel from each channel individually. To do this in a shader, we have to write a custom function that will take in a single channel, for instance, the red channel, and perform the overlay operation. Enter the following code in the shader just below the variable declarations:

```
fixed OverlayBlendMode(fixed basePixel, fixed blendPixel)
{
  if(basePixel < 0.5)
  {
    return (2.0 * basePixel * blendPixel);
  }
  else
  {
    return (1.0 - 2.0 * (1.0 - basePixel) * (1.0 -
blendPixel));
  }
}
```

5. We need to update our `frag()` function to process each channel of our textures in order to perform the blending:

```
fixed4 frag(v2f_img i) : COLOR
{
  //Get the colors from the RenderTexture and the uv's
  //from the v2f_img struct
  fixed4 renderTex = tex2D(_MainTex, i.uv);
  fixed4 blendTex = tex2D(_BlendTex, i.uv);
  fixed4 blendedImage = renderTex;
  blendedImage.r = OverlayBlendMode(renderTex.r,
blendTex.r);
  blendedImage.g = OverlayBlendMode(renderTex.g,
blendTex.g);
```

```
  blendedImage.b = OverlayBlendMode(renderTex.b,
blendTex.b);
  //Adjust amount of Blend Mode with a lerp
  renderTex = lerp(renderTex, blendedImage, _Opacity);
  return renderTex;
}
```

6. With the code completed in the shader, our effect should be working. Save the shader and return to the Unity editor to let the shader compile. Our script is already set up; select the **Main Camera** object. From the **Project** tab, drag and drop the **ScreenOverlay** shader onto the `Cur Shader` property from the **Render Blend Mode** component in the **Inspector** tab. Once the shader compiles, you should see a result similar to the following screenshot:

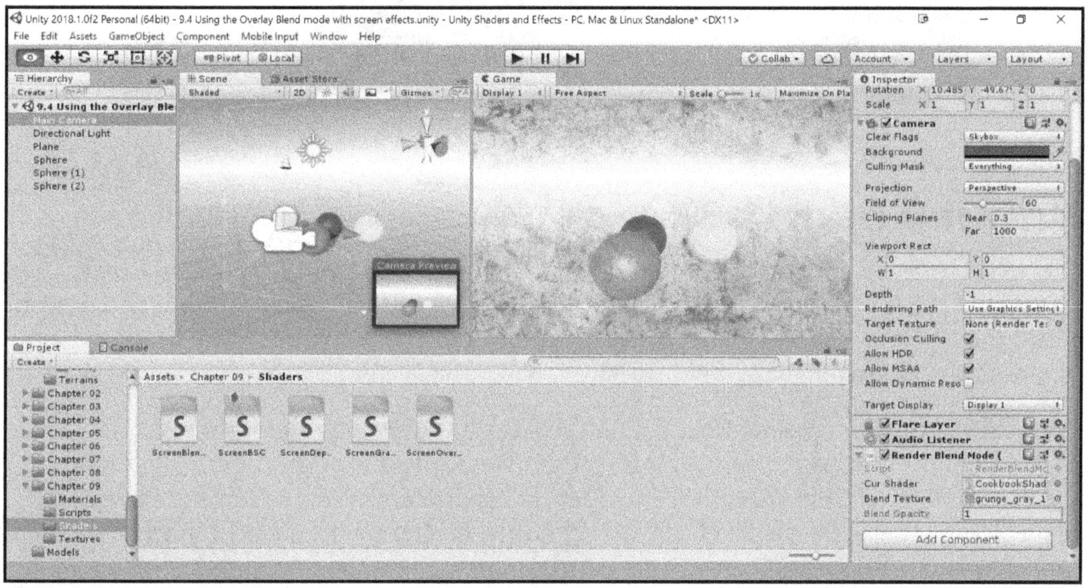

Here's a screenshot using a **Blend Opacity** of `0.5`:

How it works...

Our overlay blend mode is definitely a lot more involved, but if you really break down the function, you will notice that it is simply a multiply blend mode and screen blend mode. In this case, we are doing a conditional check to apply one or the other blend mode to a pixel.

With this particular screen effect, when the overlay function receives a pixel, it checks to see whether it is less than `0.5`. If it is, then we apply a modified multiply blend mode to that pixel; if it's not, then we apply a modified screen blend mode to the pixel. We do this for each pixel for each channel, giving us the final RGB pixel values for our screen effect.

As you can see, there are many things that can be done with screen effects. It really just depends on the platform and amount of memory you have allocated for screen effects. Usually, this is determined throughout the course of a game project, so have fun and get creative with your screen effects.

12
Behaviors – Intelligent Movement

In this chapter, you will develop AI algorithms for movement by covering the following recipes:

- Creating the behaviors template
- Pursuing and evading
- Adjusting the agent for physics
- Arriving and leaving
- Facing objects
- Wandering around
- Following a path
- Avoiding agents
- Avoiding walls
- Blending behaviors by weight
- Blending behaviors by priority
- Shooting a projectile
- Predicting a projectile's landing spot
- Targeting a projectile
- Creating a jump system

Introduction

Unity has been one of the most popular game engines for quite a while now, and it's probably the *de facto* game development tool for indie developers, not only because of its business model, which has a low entry barrier, but also because of its robust project editor, year-by-year technological improvements, and, most importantly, its ease of use and an ever-growing community of developers around the globe.

Thanks to Unity's heavy lifting behind the scenes (rendering, physics, integration, and cross-platform deployment, to name but a few) it's possible for us to focus on creating the AI systems that will bring our games to life, creating great real-time experiences in the blink of an eye.

The goal of this book is to give you the tools to build great AI, create better enemies, polish that final boss, or even build your own customized AI engine.

In this chapter, we will start by exploring some of the most interesting movement algorithms based on the steering behavior principles developed by Craig Reynolds, along with work from Ian Millington. These recipes are the stepping stones for most of the AI used in advanced games and other algorithms that rely on movement, such as the family of path-finding algorithms.

Creating the behaviors template

Before creating our behaviors, we need to code the stepping stones that help us to create not only intelligent movement, but also help us to build a modular system to change and add these behaviors. We will create custom data types and base classes for most of the algorithms covered in this chapter.

Getting ready

Our first step is to remember the update functions' order of execution:

- `Update`
- `LateUpdate`

How to do it...

We need to create three classes, `Steering`, `AgentBehaviour`, and `Agent`:

1. `Steering` serves as a custom data type for storing the movement and rotation of the agent:

```
using UnityEngine;
public class Steering
{
  public float angular;
  public Vector3 linear;
  public Steering ()
  {
    angular = 0.0f;
    linear = new Vector3();
  }
}
```

2. `AgentBehaviour` is the template class for most of the behaviors covered in this chapter:

```
using UnityEngine;
public class AgentBehaviour : MonoBehaviour
{
  public GameObject target;
  protected Agent agent;
  public virtual void Awake ()
  {
    agent = gameObject.GetComponent<Agent>();
  }
  public virtual void Update ()
  {
      agent.SetSteering(GetSteering());
  }
  public virtual Steering GetSteering ()
  {
    return new Steering();
  }
}
```

3. Finally, `Agent` is the main component, and it makes use of behaviors in order to create intelligent movement. Create the file and its bare bones:

```
using UnityEngine;
using System.Collections;
public class Agent : MonoBehaviour
```

```
{
    public float maxSpeed;
    public float maxAccel;
    public float orientation;
    public float rotation;
    public Vector3 velocity;
    protected Steering steering;
    void Start ()
    {
        velocity = Vector3.zero;
        steering = new Steering();
    }
    public void SetSteering (Steering steering)
    {
        this.steering = steering;
    }
}
```

4. Next, we code the `Update` function, which handles the movement according to the current value:

```
public virtual void Update ()
{
    Vector3 displacement = velocity * Time.deltaTime;
    orientation += rotation * Time.deltaTime;
    // we need to limit the orientation values
    // to be in the range (0 - 360)
    if (orientation < 0.0f)
        orientation += 360.0f;
    else if (orientation > 360.0f)
        orientation -= 360.0f;
    transform.Translate(displacement, Space.World);
    transform.rotation = new Quaternion();
    transform.Rotate(Vector3.up, orientation);
}
```

5. Finally, we implement the `LateUpdate` function, which takes care of updating the steering for the next frame according to the current frame's calculations:

```
public virtual void LateUpdate ()
{
    velocity += steering.linear * Time.deltaTime;
    rotation += steering.angular * Time.deltaTime;
    if (velocity.magnitude > maxSpeed)
    {
        velocity.Normalize();
        velocity = velocity * maxSpeed;
```

```
        }
        if (steering.angular == 0.0f)
        {
            rotation = 0.0f;
        }
        if (steering.linear.sqrMagnitude == 0.0f)
        {
            velocity = Vector3.zero;
        }
        steering = new Steering();
    }
```

How it works...

The idea is to be able to delegate the movement's logic inside the `GetSteering()` function on the behaviors that we will later build, simplifying our agent's class to a main calculation based on those.

Besides, we are guaranteed to be able to set the agent's steering value before it is used thanks to Unity script and function execution orders.

There's more...

This is a component-based approach, which means that we must remember to always have an `Agent` script attached to `GameObject` for the behaviors to work as expected.

See also

For further information on Unity's game loop and the execution order of functions and scripts, please refer to the official documentation available online at these links:

- `http://docs.unity3d.com/Manual/ExecutionOrder.html`
- `https://docs.unity3d.com/Manual/class-MonoManager.html`

Pursuing and evading

Pursuing and evading are great behaviors to start with because they rely on the most basic behaviors and extend their functionality by predicting the target's next step.

Getting ready

We need a couple of basic behaviors called `Seek` and `Flee`; place them right after the `Agent` class in the scripts' execution order.

The following is the code for the `Seek` behavior:

```
using UnityEngine;
using System.Collections;
public class Seek : AgentBehaviour
{
    public override Steering GetSteering()
    {
        Steering steering = new Steering();
        steering.linear = target.transform.position -
transform.position;
        steering.linear.Normalize();
        steering.linear = steering.linear * agent.maxAccel;
        return steering;
    }
}
```

Also, we need to implement the `Flee` behavior:

```
using UnityEngine;
using System.Collections;
public class Flee : AgentBehaviour
{
    public override Steering GetSteering()
    {
        Steering steering = new Steering();
        steering.linear = transform.position -
target.transform.position;
        steering.linear.Normalize();
        steering.linear = steering.linear * agent.maxAccel;
        return steering;
    }
}
```

How to do it...

`Pursue` and `Evade` are essentially the same algorithm, but differ in terms of the base class they derive from:

1. Create the `Pursue` class, derived from `Seek`, and add the attributes for the prediction:

```
using UnityEngine;
using System.Collections;

public class Pursue : Seek
{
    public float maxPrediction;
    private GameObject targetAux;
    private Agent targetAgent;
}
```

2. Implement the `Awake` function in order to set up everything according to the real target:

```
public override void Awake() { base.Awake(); targetAgent =
target.GetComponent<Agent>(); targetAux = target; target = new
GameObject(); }
```

3. Implement the `OnDestroy` function for properly handling the internal object:

```
void OnDestroy ()
{
    Destroy(targetAux);
}
```

4. Implement the `GetSteering` function:

```
public override Steering GetSteering()
{
    Vector3 direction = targetAux.transform.position -
transform.position;
    float distance = direction.magnitude;
    float speed = agent.velocity.magnitude;
    float prediction;
    if (speed <= distance / maxPrediction)
        prediction = maxPrediction;
    else
        prediction = distance / speed;
    target.transform.position = targetAux.transform.position;
```

```
        target.transform.position += targetAgent.velocity *
    prediction;
        return base.GetSteering();
    }
```

5. To create the `Evade` behavior, the procedure is just the same, but it takes into account the fact that `Flee` is the parent class:

```
public class Evade : Flee
{
    // everything stays the same
}
```

How it works...

These behaviors rely on `Seek` and `Flee` and take into consideration the target's velocity in order to predict where it will go next, and they aim at that position using an internal extra object.

Adjusting the agent for physics

We learned how to implement simple behaviors for our agents. However, we also need to take into consideration that our games will probably need the help of the physics engine in Unity. In that case, we need to take into consideration whether our agents have the `RigidBody` component attached to them, and adjust our implementation accordingly.

Getting ready

Our first step is to remember the execution order of event functions, but now we also consider `FixedUpdate`, because we're handling behaviors on top of the physics engine:

- `FixedUpdate`
- `Update`
- `LateUpdate`

How to do it...

This recipe entails adding changes to our `Agent` class.

1. Go to the `Agent` class.
2. Add a member variable for storing the rigid body component's reference:

```
private Rigidbody aRigidBody;
```

3. Get the reference to the rigid body component in the `Start` function:

```
aRigidBody = GetComponent<Rigidbody>();
```

4. Implement a function for transforming an orientation value to a vector:

```
public Vector3 OriToVec(float orientation)
{
  Vector3 vector = Vector3.zero;
  vector.x = Mathf.Sin(orientation * Mathf.Deg2Rad) * 1.0f;
  vector.z = Mathf.Cos(orientation * Mathf.Deg2Rad) * 1.0f;
  return vector.normalized;
}
```

5. Add the following two lines at the beginning of the `Update` function:

```
public virtual void Update ()
{
  if (aRigidBody == null)
    return;
  // ... previous code
```

6. Define the `FixedUpdate` function:

```
public virtual void FixedUpdate()
{
  if (aRigidBody == null)
    return;
  // next step
}
```

7. Continue implementing the `FixedUpdate` function:

```
Vector3 displacement = velocity * Time.deltaTime;
orientation += rotation * Time.deltaTime;
if (orientation < 0.0f)
  orientation += 360.0f;
else if (orientation > 360.0f)
  orientation -= 360.0f;
```

```
// The ForceMode will depend on what you want to achieve
// We are using VelocityChange for illustration purposes
aRigidBody.AddForce(displacement, ForceMode.VelocityChange);
Vector3 orientationVector = OriToVec(orientation);
aRigidBody.rotation =
Quaternion.LookRotation(orientationVector, Vector3.up);
```

How it works...

We added a member variable for storing the reference to a possible rigid body component, and also implemented `FixedUpdate`, similar to `Update`, but taking into consideration that we need to apply force to the rigid body instead of translating the object ourselves, because we're working on top of Unity's physics engine.

Finally, we created a simple validation at the beginning of each function so they're called only when it applies.

See also

For further information on the execution order of event functions, please refer to official Unity documentation:

- `https://docs.unity3d.com/Manual/ExecutionOrder.html`

Arriving and leaving

Similar to `Seek` and `Flee`, the idea behind these algorithms is to apply the same principles and extend the functionality to a point where the agent stops automatically after a condition is met, either being close to its destination (arrive), or far enough from a dangerous point (leave).

Getting ready

We need to create one file for the `Arrive` and `Leave` algorithms respectively, and remember to set their custom execution order.

How to do it...

They use the same approach, but in terms of implementation, the name of the member variables change, as well as some computations in the first half of the `GetSteering` function:

1. First, implement the `Arrive` behavior with its member variables to define the radius for stopping (target) and slowing down:

```
using UnityEngine;
using System.Collections;

public class Arrive : AgentBehaviour
{
    public float targetRadius;
    public float slowRadius;
    public float timeToTarget = 0.1f;
}
```

2. Create the `GetSteering` function:

```
public override Steering GetSteering()
{
    // code in next steps
}
```

3. Define the first half of the `GetSteering` function, in which we compute the desired speed depending on the distance from the target according to the radii variables:

```
Steering steering = new Steering();
Vector3 direction = target.transform.position -
transform.position;
float distance = direction.magnitude;
float targetSpeed;
if (distance < targetRadius)
    return steering;
if (distance > slowRadius)
    targetSpeed = agent.maxSpeed;
else
    targetSpeed = agent.maxSpeed * distance / slowRadius;
```

4. Define the second half of the `GetSteering` function, in which we set the steering value and clamp it according to the maximum speed:

```
Vector3 desiredVelocity = direction;
desiredVelocity.Normalize();
```

```
desiredVelocity *= targetSpeed;
steering.linear = desiredVelocity - agent.velocity;
steering.linear /= timeToTarget;
if (steering.linear.magnitude > agent.maxAccel)
{
    steering.linear.Normalize();
    steering.linear *= agent.maxAccel;
}
return steering;
```

5. To implement `Leave`, change the name of the member variables:

```
using UnityEngine;
using System.Collections;

public class Leave : AgentBehaviour
{
    public float escapeRadius;
    public float dangerRadius;
    public float timeToTarget = 0.1f;
}
```

6. Define the first half of the `GetSteering` function:

```
Steering steering = new Steering();
Vector3 direction = transform.position -
target.transform.position;
float distance = direction.magnitude;
if (distance > dangerRadius)
    return steering;
float reduce;
if (distance < escapeRadius)
    reduce = 0f;
else
    reduce = distance / dangerRadius * agent.maxSpeed;
float targetSpeed = agent.maxSpeed - reduce;
```

7. And finally, the second half of `GetSteering` stays just the same.

How it works...

After calculating the direction to go in, the next calculations are based on two radii distances in order to know when to go full throttle, slow down, and stop; that's why we have several `if` statements. In the `Arrive` behavior, when the agent is too far, we aim for full throttle, progressively slow down when inside the proper radius, and finally stop when close enough to the target. The inverse method applies to `Leave`:

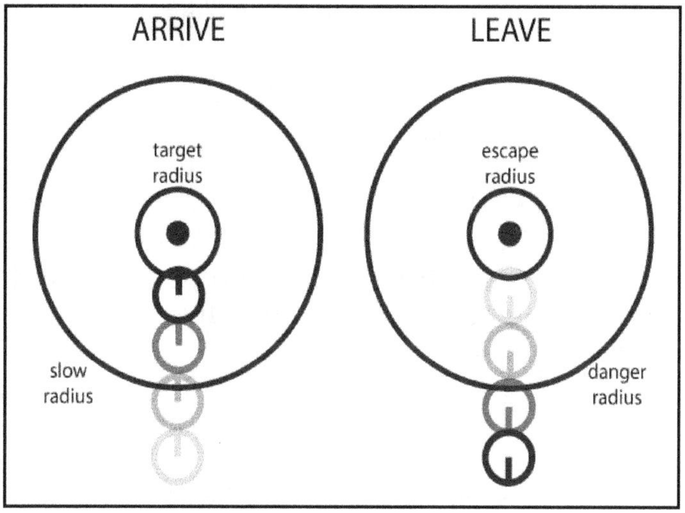

A visual reference for the Arrive and Leave behaviors

Facing objects

Real-world aiming, just like in combat simulators, works a little differently to the widely-used *automatic* aiming process in almost every game. Imagine that you need to implement an agent controlling a tank turret or a humanized sniper; that's when this recipe comes in handy.

Getting ready

We need to make some modifications to our `AgentBehaviour` class:

1. Add new member values to limit some of the existing ones:

```
public float maxSpeed;
public float maxAccel;
public float maxRotation;
public float maxAngularAccel;
```

2. Add a function called `MapToRange`. This function helps in finding the actual direction of rotation after two orientation values are subtracted:

```
public float MapToRange (float rotation) {
    rotation %= 360.0f;
```

```
        if (Mathf.Abs(rotation) > 180.0f) {
            if (rotation < 0.0f)
                rotation += 360.0f;
            else
                rotation -= 360.0f;
        }
        return rotation;
    }
```

3. Also, we need to create a basic behavior called `Align` that is the stepping stone for the facing algorithm. It uses the same principle as `Arrive`, but only in terms of rotation:

```
using UnityEngine;
using System.Collections;

public class Align : AgentBehaviour
{
    public float targetRadius;
    public float slowRadius;
    public float timeToTarget = 0.1f;

    public override Steering GetSteering()
    {
        Steering steering = new Steering();
        float targetOrientation =
target.GetComponent<Agent>().orientation;
        float rotation = targetOrientation -
agent.orientation;
        rotation = MapToRange(rotation);
        float rotationSize = Mathf.Abs(rotation);
        if (rotationSize < targetRadius)
            return steering;
        float targetRotation;
        if (rotationSize > slowRadius)
            targetRotation = agent.maxRotation;
        else
            targetRotation = agent.maxRotation * rotationSize
/ slowRadius;
        targetRotation *= rotation / rotationSize;
        steering.angular = targetRotation - agent.rotation;
        steering.angular /= timeToTarget;
        float angularAccel = Mathf.Abs(steering.angular);
        if (angularAccel > agent.maxAngularAccel)
        {
            steering.angular /= angularAccel;
            steering.angular *= agent.maxAngularAccel;
        }
```

```
            return steering;
        }
    }
```

How to do it...

We can now proceed to implement our facing algorithm that derives from `Align`:

1. Create the `Face` class along with a private auxiliary target member variable:

```
using UnityEngine;
using System.Collections;

public class Face : Align
{
    protected GameObject targetAux;
}
```

2. Override the `Awake` function to set up everything and swap references:

```
public override void Awake()
{
    base.Awake();
    targetAux = target;
    target = new GameObject();
    target.AddComponent<Agent>();
}
```

3. Also, implement the `OnDestroy` function to handle references and avoid memory issues:

```
void OnDestroy ()
{
    Destroy(target);
}
```

4. Finally, define the `GetSteering` function:

```
public override Steering GetSteering()
{
    Vector3 direction = targetAux.transform.position -
transform.position;
    if (direction.magnitude > 0.0f)
    {
        float targetOrientation = Mathf.Atan2(direction.x,
```

```
direction.z);
            targetOrientation *= Mathf.Rad2Deg;
            target.GetComponent<Agent>().orientation =
targetOrientation;
        }
        return base.GetSteering();
    }
```

How it works...

The algorithm computes the internal target orientation according to the vector between the agent and the real target. Then, it just delegates the work to its parent class.

Wandering around

This technique works like a charm for random crowd simulations, animals, and almost any kind of NPC that requires random movement when idle.

Getting ready

We need to add another function to our `AgentBehaviour` class called `OriToVec`, which converts an orientation value to a vector:

```
public Vector3 GetOriAsVec (float orientation) {
    Vector3 vector  = Vector3.zero;
    vector.x = Mathf.Sin(orientation * Mathf.Deg2Rad) * 1.0f;
    vector.z = Mathf.Cos(orientation * Mathf.Deg2Rad) * 1.0f;
    return vector.normalized;
}
```

How to do it...

We can regard it as a big three-step process in which we first manipulate the internal target position in a parameterized random way, face that position, and move accordingly:

1. Create the `Wander` class deriving from `Face`:

```
using UnityEngine;
```

```
using System.Collections;

public class Wander : Face
{
    public float offset;
    public float radius;
    public float rate;
}
```

2. Define the `Awake` function in order to set up the internal target:

```
public override void Awake()
{
    target = new GameObject();
    target.transform.position = transform.position;
    base.Awake();
}
```

3. Define the `GetSteering` function:

```
public override Steering GetSteering()
{
    Steering steering = new Steering();
    float wanderOrientation = Random.Range(-1.0f, 1.0f) *
rate;
    float targetOrientation = wanderOrientation +
agent.orientation;
    Vector3 orientationVec = OriToVec(agent.orientation);
    Vector3 targetPosition = (offset * orientationVec) +
transform.position;
    targetPosition = targetPosition +
(OriToVec(targetOrientation) * radius);
    targetAux.transform.position = targetPosition;
    steering = base.GetSteering();
    steering.linear = targetAux.transform.position -
transform.position;
    steering.linear.Normalize();
    steering.linear *= agent.maxAccel;
    return steering;
}
```

How it works...

The behavior takes two radii in order into consideration to get a random position to go next, looks toward that random point, and converts the computed orientation into a direction vector in order to advance:

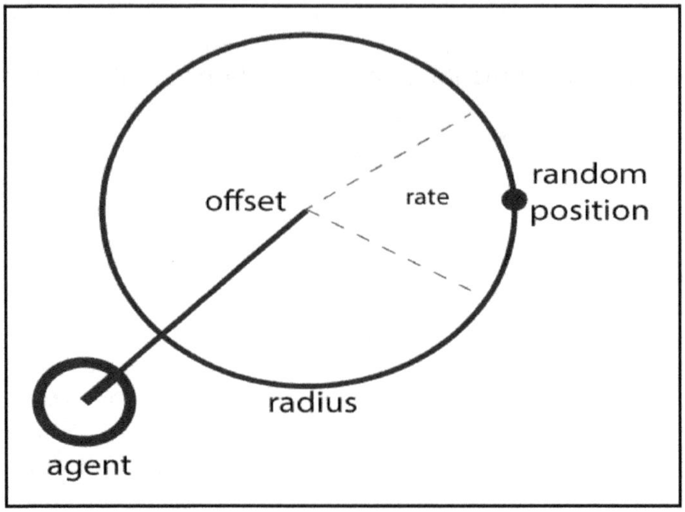

A visual description of the parameters for creating the Wander behavior

Following a path

There are times when we need scripted routes, and it's simply inconceivable to do it entirely by code. Imagine you're working on a stealth game. Would you code a route for every single guard? This technique will help you build a flexible path system for those situations.

Getting ready

We need to define a custom data type called `PathSegment`:

```
using UnityEngine;
using System.Collections;

public class PathSegment
{
```

```
    public Vector3 a;
    public Vector3 b;

    public PathSegment () : this (Vector3.zero, Vector3.zero){}
    public PathSegment (Vector3 a, Vector3 b)
    {
        this.a = a;
        this.b = b;
    }
}
```

How to do it...

This is a long recipe that could be regarded as a big two-step process. First, we build the `Path` class, which abstracts points in the path from their specific spatial representations, and then we build the `PathFollower` behavior that makes use of that abstraction in order to get actual spatial points to follow:

1. Create the `Path` class, which consists of nodes and segments; only the nodes are public and are assigned manually:

```
using UnityEngine;
using System.Collections;
using System.Collections.Generic;

public class Path : MonoBehaviour
{
    public List<GameObject> nodes;
    List<PathSegment> segments;
}
```

2. Define the `Start` function to set the segments when the scene starts:

```
void Start()
{
    segments = GetSegments();
}
```

3. Define the `GetSegments` function to build the segments from the nodes:

```
public List<PathSegment> GetSegments ()
{
    List<PathSegment> segments = new List<PathSegment>();
    int i;
    for (i = 0; i < nodes.Count - 1; i++)
    {
```

```
            Vector3 src = nodes[i].transform.position;
            Vector3 dst = nodes[i+1].transform.position;
            PathSegment segment = new PathSegment(src, dst);
            segments.Add(segment);
        }
        return segments;
    }
```

4. Define the first function for abstraction, which is called `GetParam`:

```
public float GetParam(Vector3 position, float lastParam)
{
    // body
}
```

5. We need to find out the segment the agent is closest to:

```
float param = 0f;
PathSegment currentSegment = null;
float tempParam = 0f;
foreach (PathSegment ps in segments)
{
    tempParam += Vector3.Distance(ps.a, ps.b);
    if (lastParam <= tempParam)
    {
        currentSegment = ps;
        break;
    }
}
if (currentSegment == null)
    return 0f;
```

6. Given the current position, we need to work out the direction to go to:

```
Vector3 currPos = position - currentSegment.a;
Vector3 segmentDirection = currentSegment.b -
currentSegment.a;
segmentDirection.Normalize();
```

7. Find the point in the segment using vector projection:

```
Vector3 pointInSegment = Vector3.Project(currPos,
segmentDirection);
```

8. Finally, `GetParam` returns the next position to reach along the path:

```
param = tempParam - Vector3.Distance(currentSegment.a,
currentSegment.b);
```

```
param += pointInSegment.magnitude;
return param;
```

9. Define the `GetPosition` function:

```
public Vector3 GetPosition(float param)
{
    // body
}
```

10. Given the current location along the path, we find the corresponding segment:

```
Vector3 position = Vector3.zero;
PathSegment currentSegment = null;
float tempParam = 0f;
foreach (PathSegment ps in segments)
{
    tempParam += Vector3.Distance(ps.a, ps.b);
    if (param <= tempParam)
    {
        currentSegment = ps;
        break;
    }
}
if (currentSegment == null)
    return Vector3.zero;
```

11. `GetPosition` converts the parameter as a spatial point and returns it:

```
Vector3 segmentDirection = currentSegment.b -
currentSegment.a;
segmentDirection.Normalize();
tempParam -= Vector3.Distance(currentSegment.a,
currentSegment.b);
tempParam = param - tempParam;
position = currentSegment.a + segmentDirection * tempParam;
return position;
```

12. Create the `PathFollower` behavior, which derives from `Seek` (remember to set the order of execution):

```
using UnityEngine;
using System.Collections;

public class PathFollower : Seek
{
    public Path path;
```

```
        public float pathOffset = 0.0f;
        float currentParam;
    }
```

13. Implement the `Awake` function to set the target:

```
public override void Awake()
{
    base.Awake();
    target = new GameObject();
    currentParam = 0f;
}
```

14. The final step is to define the `GetSteering` function that relies on the abstraction created by the `Path` class to set the target position and apply `Seek`:

```
public override Steering GetSteering()
{
    currentParam = path.GetParam(transform.position,
currentParam);
    float targetParam = currentParam + pathOffset;
    target.transform.position = path.GetPosition(targetParam);
    return base.GetSteering();
}
```

How it works...

We use the `Path` class in order to have a movement guideline. It is the cornerstone, because it relies on `GetParam` to map an offset point to follow in its internal guideline, and it also uses `GetPosition` to convert that referential point to a position in the three-dimensional space along the segments.

The path-following algorithm just makes use of the path's functions in order to get a new position, update the target, and apply the `Seek` behavior.

There's more...

It's important to take into account the order in which the nodes are linked in the inspector for the path to work as expected. A practical way to achieve this is to manually name the nodes with a reference number:

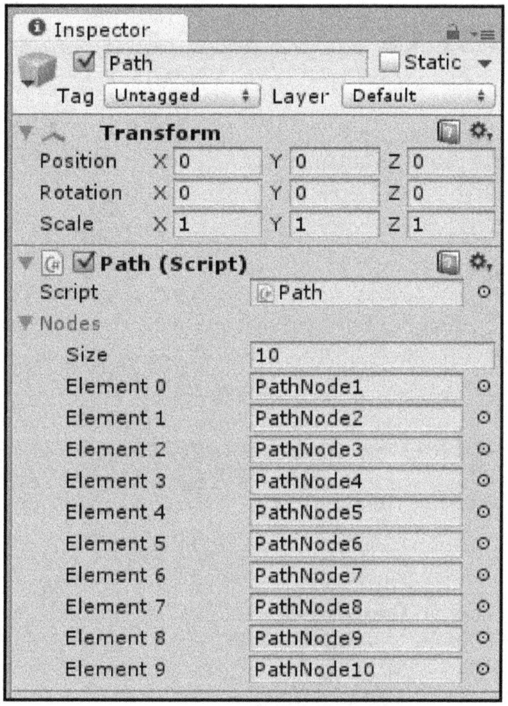

An example of a path set up in the Inspector window

Also, we could define the `OnDrawGizmos` function in order to have a better visual reference of the path:

```
void OnDrawGizmos ()
{
    Vector3 direction;
    Color tmp = Gizmos.color;
    Gizmos.color = Color.magenta;//example color
    int i;
    for (i = 0; i < nodes.Count - 1; i++)
    {
        Vector3 src = nodes[i].transform.position;
        Vector3 dst = nodes[i+1].transform.position;
        direction = dst - src;
        Gizmos.DrawRay(src, direction);
    }
    Gizmos.color = tmp;
}
```

Avoiding agents

In crowd-simulation games, it would be unnatural to see agents behaving entirely like particles in a physics-based system. The goal of this recipe is to create an agent capable of mimicking our peer-evasion movement.

Getting ready

We need to create a tag called **Agent** and assign it to those game objects that we would like to avoid, and we also need to have the **Agent** script component attached to them:

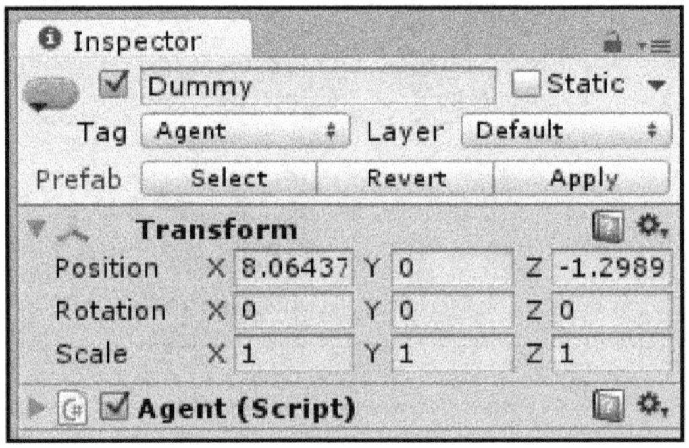

Example of how the Inspector window of a dummy agent should appear

Take a look on the following:

- Tag: Agent (created by us)
- Agent component is attached (the one created by us)

How to do it...

This recipe will entail creating a new agent behavior:

1. Create the `AvoidAgent` behavior, which is composed of a collision avoidance radius and the list of agents to avoid:

```
using UnityEngine;
using System.Collections;
using System.Collections.Generic;
```

```
public class AvoidAgent : AgentBehaviour
{
    public float collisionRadius = 0.4f;
    GameObject[] targets;
}
```

2. Implement the `Start` function in order to set the list of agents according to the tag we created earlier:

```
void Start ()
{
    targets = GameObject.FindGameObjectsWithTag("Agent");
}
```

3. Define the `GetSteering` function:

```
public override Steering GetSteering()
{
    // body
}
```

4. Add the following variables to the compute distances and velocities from agents that are nearby:

```
Steering steering = new Steering();
float shortestTime = Mathf.Infinity;
GameObject firstTarget = null;
float firstMinSeparation = 0.0f;
float firstDistance = 0.0f;
Vector3 firstRelativePos = Vector3.zero;
Vector3 firstRelativeVel = Vector3.zero;
```

5. Find the closest agent that is prone to collision with the current one:

```
foreach (GameObject t in targets)
{
    Vector3 relativePos;
    Agent targetAgent = t.GetComponent<Agent>();
    relativePos = t.transform.position - transform.position;
    Vector3 relativeVel = targetAgent.velocity -
agent.velocity;
    float relativeSpeed = relativeVel.magnitude;
    float timeToCollision = Vector3.Dot(relativePos,
relativeVel);
    timeToCollision /= relativeSpeed * relativeSpeed * -1;
    float distance = relativePos.magnitude;
    float minSeparation = distance - relativeSpeed *
timeToCollision;
```

```
        if (minSeparation > 2 * collisionRadius)
            continue;
        if (timeToCollision > 0.0f && timeToCollision <
    shortestTime)
        {
            shortestTime = timeToCollision;
            firstTarget = t;
            firstMinSeparation = minSeparation;
            firstRelativePos = relativePos;
            firstRelativeVel = relativeVel;
        }
    }
```

6. If there is one that is prone to collision, then move away:

```
if (firstTarget == null)
    return steering;
if (firstMinSeparation <= 0.0f || firstDistance < 2 *
collisionRadius)
    firstRelativePos = firstTarget.transform.position;
else
    firstRelativePos += firstRelativeVel * shortestTime;
firstRelativePos.Normalize();
steering.linear = -firstRelativePos * agent.maxAccel;
return steering;
```

How it works...

Given a list of agents, we take into consideration which one is closest, and, if it is close enough, we make it so that the agent tries to escape from the expected route of that first one according to its current velocity, so that they don't collide.

There's more...

This behavior works well when combined with other behaviors using blending techniques (some are included in this chapter); otherwise, it's a starting point for your own collision avoidance algorithms.

Avoiding walls

In this recipe, we will implement a behavior that imitates our own ability to evade walls. That is, seeing what we have in front of us that could be considered as a wall or obstacle, and walk around it using a safety margin, trying to maintain our principal direction at the same time.

Getting ready

This technique uses the `RaycastHit` structure and the `Raycast` function from the physics engine, so it's recommended that you look at the documents for a refresher in case you're a little rusty on the subject.

How to do it...

Thanks to our previous hard work, this recipe is a short one:

1. Create the `AvoidWall` behavior derived from `Seek`:

```
using UnityEngine;
using System.Collections;

public class AvoidWall : Seek
{
    // body
}
```

2. Include the member variables for defining the safety margin and the length of the ray to cast:

```
public float avoidDistance;
public float lookAhead;
```

3. Define the `Awake` function to set up the target:

```
public override void Awake()
{
    base.Awake();
    target = new GameObject();
}
```

4. Define the `GetSteering` function required for future steps:

```
public override Steering GetSteering()
{
    // body
}
```

5. Declare and set the variable needed for ray casting:

```
Steering steering = new Steering();
Vector3 position = transform.position;
Vector3 rayVector = agent.velocity.normalized * lookAhead;
Vector3 direction = rayVector;
RaycastHit hit;
```

6. Cast the ray and make the proper calculations if a wall is hit:

```
if (Physics.Raycast(position, direction, out hit, lookAhead))
{
    position = hit.point + hit.normal * avoidDistance;
    target.transform.position = position;
    steering = base.GetSteering();
}
return steering;
```

How it works...

We cast a ray in front of the agent, and when the ray collides with a wall, the target object is placed in a new position, with consideration given to its distance from the wall and the safety distance declared, delegating the steering calculations to the `Seek` behavior; this creates the illusion of the agent avoiding the wall.

There's more...

We could extend this behavior by adding more rays, such as whiskers, in order to achieve better accuracy. Also, it is usually paired with other movement behaviors, such as `Pursue`, using blending:

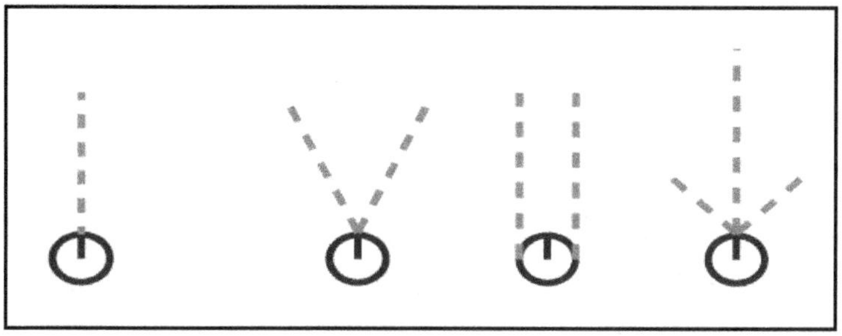

The original ray cast and possible extensions for more precise wall avoidance

See also

For further information on the `RaycastHit` structure and the `Raycast` function, please refer to the official documentation available online at these links:

- `http://docs.unity3d.com/ScriptReference/RaycastHit.html`
- `http://docs.unity3d.com/ScriptReference/Physics.Raycast.html`

Blending behaviors by weight

The blending techniques allow you to add behaviors and mix them without creating new scripts every time you need a new type of hybrid agent.

This is one of the most powerful techniques in this chapter, and it's probably the most widely-used behavior-blending approach because of its power and the low cost of implementation.

Getting ready

We must add a new member variable to our `AgentBehaviour` class called `weight` and preferably assign a default value. In this case, this is `1.0f`. We should refactor the `Update` function to incorporate `weight` as a parameter for the `Agent` class's `SetSteering` function. All in all, the new `AgentBehaviour` class should look something like this:

```
public class AgentBehaviour : MonoBehaviour
{
    public float weight = 1.0f;

    // ... the rest of the class

    public virtual void Update ()
    {
        agent.SetSteering(GetSteering(), weight);
    }
}
```

How to do it...

We just need to change the `SetSteering` function's signature and definition:

```
public void SetSteering (Steering steering, float weight)
{
    this.steering.linear += (weight * steering.linear);
    this.steering.angular += (weight * steering.angular);
}
```

How it works...

The weights are used to amplify the `steering` behavior result, and they're added to the main steering structure.

There's more...

The weights don't necessarily need to add up to `1.0f`. The `weight` parameter is a reference for defining the relevance that the `steering` behavior will have among other parameters.

See also

In this project, there is an example of avoiding walls, which is worked out using weighted blending.

Blending behaviors by priority

Sometimes, weighted blending is not enough because heavyweight behaviors dilute the contribution of the lightweights, but those behaviors need to do their part too. That's when priority-based blending comes into play, applying a cascading effect from high-priority to low-priority behaviors.

Getting ready

This approach is very similar to the one used in the previous recipe. We must add a new member variable to our `AgentBehaviour` class. We should also refactor the `Update` function to incorporate `priority` as a parameter to the `Agent` class's `SetSteering` function. The new `AgentBehaviour` class should look something like this:

```
public class AgentBehaviour : MonoBehaviour
{
    public int priority = 1;
    // ... everything else stays the same
    public virtual void Update ()
    {
        agent.SetSteering(GetSteering(), priority);
    }
}
```

How to do it...

Now, we need to make some changes to the `Agent` class:

1. Add a new namespace from the library:

```
using System.Collections.Generic;
```

2. Add the member variable for the minimum steering value to consider a group of behaviors:

```
public float priorityThreshold = 0.2f;
```

3. Add the member variable for holding the group of behavior results:

```
private Dictionary<int, List<Steering>> groups;
```

4. Initialize the variable in the `Start` function:

```
groups = new Dictionary<int, List<Steering>>();
```

5. Modify the `LateUpdate` function so that the steering variable is set by calling `GetPrioritySteering`:

```
public virtual void LateUpdate ()
{
    //  funnelled steering through priorities
    steering = GetPrioritySteering();
    groups.Clear();
    // ... the rest of the computations stay the same
    steering = new Steering();
}
```

6. Modify the `SetSteering` function's signature and definition to store the steering values in their corresponding priority groups:

```
public void SetSteering (Steering steering, int priority)
{
    if (!groups.ContainsKey(priority))
    {
        groups.Add(priority, new List<Steering>());
    }
    groups[priority].Add(steering);
}
```

7. Finally, implement the `GetPrioritySteering` function to funnel the steering group:

```
private Steering GetPrioritySteering ()
{
    Steering steering = new Steering();
    float sqrThreshold = priorityThreshold *
priorityThreshold;
    foreach (List<Steering> group in groups.Values)
    {
        steering = new Steering();
```

```
            foreach (Steering singleSteering in group)
            {
                steering.linear += singleSteering.linear;
                steering.angular += singleSteering.angular;
            }
            if (steering.linear.sqrMagnitude > sqrThreshold ||
                    Mathf.Abs(steering.angular) >
    priorityThreshold)
            {
                return steering;
            }
        }
        return steering;
    }
```

How it works...

By creating priority groups, we blend behaviors that are common to one another, and the first group, in which the steering value exceeds the threshold, is selected. Otherwise, steering from the lowest-priority group is chosen.

There's more...

We could extend this approach by mixing it with weighted blending, so we would have a more robust architecture, achieving extra precision in the way the behaviors impact on the agent at every priority level:

```
foreach (Steering singleSteering in group)
{
    steering.linear += singleSteering.linear * weight;
    steering.angular += singleSteering.angular * weight;
}
```

See also

There is an example of avoiding walls using priority-based blending in this project.

Shooting a projectile

This is the stepping stone for scenarios where we want to have control over gravity-reliant objects, such as balls and grenades, so we can then predict the projectile's landing spot or be able to effectively shoot a projectile at a given target.

Getting ready

This recipe differs a little bit as it doesn't rely on the base `AgentBehaviour` class.

How to do it...

1. Create the `Projectile` class, along with its member variables, to handle the physics:

```
using UnityEngine;
using System.Collections;

public class Projectile : MonoBehaviour
{
    private bool set = false;
    private Vector3 firePos;
    private Vector3 direction;
    private float speed;
    private float timeElapsed;
}
```

2. Define the `Update` function:

```
void Update ()
{
    if (!set)
        return;
    timeElapsed += Time.deltaTime;
    transform.position = firePos + direction * speed *
timeElapsed;
    transform.position += Physics.gravity * (timeElapsed *
```

```
timeElapsed) / 2.0f;
    // extra validation for cleaning the scene
    if (transform.position.y < -1.0f)
        Destroy(this.gameObject);// or set = false; and hide
it
}
```

3. Finally, implement the `Set` function in order to fire the game object (for example, calling it after it is instantiated in the scene):

```
public void Set (Vector3 firePos, Vector3 direction, float
speed)
{
    this.firePos = firePos;
    this.direction = direction.normalized;
    this.speed = speed;
    transform.position = firePos;
    set = true;
}
```

How it works...

This behavior uses high school physics in order to generate the parabolic movement.

There's more...

We could also take another approach: implementing public properties in the script or declaring member variables as public, and instead of calling the `Set` function, having the script disabled by default in the prefab and enabling it after all the properties have been set. That way, we could easily apply the object pool pattern.

See also

For further information on the object pool pattern, please refer to the following Wikipedia article and the official Unity technologies video tutorial available online:

- `http://en.wikipedia.org/wiki/Object_pool_pattern`
- `http://unity3d.com/learn/tutorials/modules/beginner/live-training-archive/object-pooling`

Predicting a projectile's landing spot

After a projectile is shot by the player, agents (our AI) need to either avoid it or look for it. For example, the agents need to run from a grenade to be kept alive, or run towards a soccer ball to take control. In either case, it's important for the agents to predict the projectile's landing spot to make decisions.

In this recipe, we will learn how to calculate such landing spots.

Getting ready

Before we get into predicting the landing position, it's important to know the time left before it hits the ground (or reaches a certain position). Thus, instead of creating new behaviors, we need to update the `Projectile` class.

How to do it...

1. First, we need to add the `GetLandingTime` function to compute the landing time:

```
public float GetLandingTime (float height = 0.0f)
{
    Vector3 position = transform.position;
    float time = 0.0f;
    float valueInt = (direction.y * direction.y) * (speed *
speed);
    valueInt = valueInt - (Physics.gravity.y * 2 * (position.y
- height));
    valueInt = Mathf.Sqrt(valueInt);
    float valueAdd = (-direction.y) * speed;
    float valueSub = (-direction.y) * speed;
    valueAdd = (valueAdd + valueInt) / Physics.gravity.y;
    valueSub = (valueSub - valueInt) / Physics.gravity.y;
    if (float.IsNaN(valueAdd) && !float.IsNaN(valueSub))
        return valueSub;
    else if (!float.IsNaN(valueAdd) && float.IsNaN(valueSub))
        return valueAdd;
    else if (float.IsNaN(valueAdd) && float.IsNaN(valueSub))
        return -1.0f;
    time = Mathf.Max(valueAdd, valueSub);
    return time;
}
```

2. Now, we add the `GetLandingPos` function to predict the landing spot:

```
public Vector3 GetLandingPos (float height = 0.0f)
{
    Vector3 landingPos = Vector3.zero;
    float time = GetLandingTime();
    if (time < 0.0f)
        return landingPos;
    landingPos.y = height;
    landingPos.x = firePos.x + direction.x * speed * time;
    landingPos.z = firePos.z + direction.z * speed * time;
    return landingPos;
}
```

How it works...

First, we are solving the equation from the previous recipe for a fixed height, and, given the projectile's current position and speed, we are able to get the time at which the projectile will reach the given height.

There's more...

Remember to take into account the `NaN` validation. It's placed that way because there may be one, two, or no solutions to the equation. Furthermore, when the landing time is less than zero, it means the projectile won't be able to reach the target height.

Targeting a projectile

Just as it's important to predict a projectile's landing point, it's also important to develop intelligent agents capable of aiming projectiles. It wouldn't be fun if our rugby-player agents weren't capable of passing the ball.

Getting ready

Just as in the previous recipe, we only need to expand the `Projectile` class.

How to do it...

Thanks to our previous hard work, this recipe is a real piece of cake:

1. Create the `GetFireDirection` function:

```
public static Vector3 GetFireDirection (Vector3 startPos,
Vector3 endPos, float speed)
{
    // body
}
```

2. Solve the corresponding quadratic equation:

```
Vector3 direction = Vector3.zero;
Vector3 delta = endPos - startPos;
float a = Vector3.Dot(Physics.gravity, Physics.gravity);
float b = -4 * (Vector3.Dot(Physics.gravity, delta) + speed *
speed);
float c = 4 * Vector3.Dot(delta, delta);
if (4 * a * c > b * b)
    return direction;
float time0 = Mathf.Sqrt((-b + Mathf.Sqrt(b * b - 4 * a * c))
/ (2*a));
float time1 = Mathf.Sqrt((-b - Mathf.Sqrt(b * b - 4 * a * c))
/ (2*a));
```

3. If shooting the projectile is feasible given the parameters, return a non-zero `direction` vector:

```
float time;
if (time0 < 0.0f)
{
    if (time1 < 0)
        return direction;
    time = time1;
}
else
{
    if (time1 < 0)
        time = time0;
    else
        time = Mathf.Min(time0, time1);
}
direction = 2 * delta - Physics.gravity * (time * time);
direction = direction / (2 * speed * time);
return direction;
```

How it works...

Given a fixed speed, we solve the corresponding quadratic equation in order to obtain the desired direction (when at least a single one-time value is available), which doesn't need to be normalized because we already normalized the vector while setting up the projectile.

There's more...

Take account of the fact that we are returning a *blank* direction when the time is negative; it means that the speed is not sufficient. One way to overcome this is to define a function that tests different speeds and then shoot the projectile.

Another relevant improvement is to add an extra parameter of the type `bool` for those cases when we have two valid times (which means two possible arcs), and we need to shoot over an obstacle such as a wall:

```
if (isWall)
    time = Mathf.Max(time0, time1);
else
    time = Mathf.Min(time0, time1);
```

Creating a jump system

Imagine that we're developing a cool action game where the player is capable of escaping using cliffs and rooftops. In that case, the enemies need to be able to chase the player and be smart enough to discern whether to take the jump and gauge how to do it.

Getting ready

We need to create a basic matching-velocity algorithm and the notion of jump pads and landing pads in order to emulate velocity math so that we can reach them.

The following is the code for the `VelocityMatch` behavior:

```
using UnityEngine;
using System.Collections;

public class VelocityMatch : AgentBehaviour {
```

```
    public float timeToTarget = 0.1f;

    public override Steering GetSteering()
    {
        Steering steering = new Steering();
        steering.linear = target.GetComponent<Agent>().velocity -
agent.velocity;
        steering.linear /= timeToTarget;
        if (steering.linear.magnitude > agent.maxAccel)
            steering.linear = steering.linear.normalized *
agent.maxAccel;

        steering.angular = 0.0f;
        return steering;
    }
}
```

Also, it's important to create a data type called `JumpPoint`:

```
using UnityEngine;
using System.Collections;

public class JumpPoint
{
    public Vector3 jumpLocation;
    public Vector3 landingLocation;

    //The change in position from jump to landing
    public Vector3 deltaPosition;

    public JumpPoint () : this (Vector3.zero, Vector3.zero)
    {
    }

    public JumpPoint(Vector3 a, Vector3 b)
    {
        this.jumpLocation = a;
        this.landingLocation = b;
        this.deltaPosition = this.landingLocation - this.jumpLocation;
    }
}
```

How to do it...

1. Create the `Jump` script along with its member variables:

```
using UnityEngine;
using System.Collections;

public class Jump : VelocityMatch
{
    public JumpPoint jumpPoint;
    public float maxYVelocity;
    public Vector3 gravity = new Vector3(0, -9.8f, 0);
    bool canAchieve = false;
}
```

2. Implement the `SetJumpPoint` function:

```
public void SetJumpPoint(Transform jumpPad, Transform
landingPad)
{
    jumpPoint = new JumpPoint(jumpPad.position,
landingPad.position);
}
```

3. Add a function to calculate the target:

```
protected void CalculateTarget()
{
    target = new GameObject();
    target.AddComponent<Agent>();
    target.transform.position = jumpPoint.jumpLocation;
    //Calculate the first jump time
    float sqrtTerm = Mathf.Sqrt(2f * gravity.y *
jumpPoint.deltaPosition.y + maxYVelocity * agent.maxSpeed);
    float time = (maxYVelocity - sqrtTerm) / gravity.y;
    //Check if we can use it, otherwise try the other time
    if (!CheckJumpTime(time))
    {
        time = (maxYVelocity + sqrtTerm) / gravity.y;
    }
}
```

4. Implement the `CheckJumpTime` function, to decide whether it's worth taking the jump:

```
private bool CheckJumpTime(float time)
{
    //Calculate the planar speed
    float vx = jumpPoint.deltaPosition.x / time;
    float vz = jumpPoint.deltaPosition.z / time;
    float speedSq = vx * vx + vz * vz;
    //Check it to see if we have a valid solution
    if (speedSq < agent.maxSpeed * agent.maxSpeed)
    {
        target.GetComponent<Agent>().velocity = new
Vector3(vx, 0f, vz);
        canAchieve = true;
        return true;
    }
    return false;
}
```

5. Finally, define the `GetSteering` function:

```
public override Steering GetSteering()
{
    Steering steering = new Steering();
    if (target == null)
    {
        CalculateTarget();
    }
    if (!canAchieve)
    {
        return steering;
    }
    //Check if we've hit the jump point
    if (Mathf.Approximately((transform.position -
target.transform.position).magnitude, 0f) &&
        Mathf.Approximately((agent.velocity -
target.GetComponent<Agent>().velocity).magnitude, 0f))
    {
        // call a jump method based on the Projectile
behaviour
        return steering;
    }
    return base.GetSteering();
}
```

How it works...

The algorithm takes into account the agent's velocity and calculates whether it can reach the landing pad or not. If it judges that the agent can, it tries to match the vertical velocity while seeking the landing pad's position.

13
Navigation

In this chapter, you will learn the following recipes:

- Representing the world with grids
- Representing the world with points of visibility
- Representing the world with a self-made navigation mesh
- Finding your way out of a maze with DFS
- Finding the shortest path in a grid with BFS
- Finding the shortest path with Dijkstra
- Finding the best-promising path with A*
- Improving A* for memory: IDA*
- Planning navigation in several frames: time-sliced search
- Smoothing a path

Introduction

In this chapter, we will learn path-finding algorithms for navigating complex scenarios. Game worlds are usually complex structures, be it a maze, an open world, and everything in between. That's why we need different techniques for approaching these kinds of problems.

We'll learn some ways of representing the world using different kinds of graph structures, and several algorithms for finding a path, each aimed at different situations.

It is worth mentioning that path-finding algorithms rely on techniques such as `Seek` and `Arrive`, learned in the previous chapter, in order to navigate the map.

Representing the world with grids

A grid is the most widely-used structure for representing worlds in games because it is easy to implement and visualize. However, we will lay the foundations for advanced graph representations while learning the basis of graph theory and its properties.

Getting ready

First, we need to create an abstract class, `Graph`, declaring the virtual methods that every graph representation implements. It is done this way because no matter how the vertices and edges are represented internally, the path-finding algorithms remain high level, thereby avoiding implementation of the algorithms for each type of graph representation.

This class works as a parent class for the different representations to be learned in the chapter and is a good starting point if you want to implement graph representations not covered in the book.

Then, we will implement a graph sub-class that handles itself internally as a grid.

How to do it...

The following code is for the `Graph` class:

1. Create the backbone with the member values:

```
using UnityEngine;
using System.Collections;
using System.Collections.Generic;

public abstract class Graph : MonoBehaviour
{
    public GameObject vertexPrefab;
    protected List<Vertex> vertices;
    protected List<List<Vertex>> neighbours;
    protected List<List<float>> costs;
    // next steps
}
```

2. Define the `Start` function:

```
public virtual void Start()
{
    Load();
}
```

3. Define the `Load` function, mentioned previously:

```
public virtual void Load() { }
```

4. Implement the function for getting the graph's size:

```
public virtual int GetSize()
{
    if (ReferenceEquals(vertices, null))
        return 0;
    return vertices.Count;
}
```

5. Define the function for finding the nearest vertex given a position:

```
public virtual Vertex GetNearestVertex(Vector3 position)
{
    return null;
}
```

6. Implement the function for getting the vertex given its ID:

```
public virtual Vertex GetVertexObj(int id)
{
    if (ReferenceEquals(vertices, null) || vertices.Count ==
0)
        return null;
    if (id < 0 || id >= vertices.Count)
        return null;
    return vertices[id];
}
```

7. Implement the function for retrieving a vertex's neighbors:

```
public virtual Vertex[] GetNeighbours(Vertex v)
{
    if (ReferenceEquals(neighbours, null) || neighbours.Count
== 0)
        return new Vertex[0];
    if (v.id < 0 || v.id >= neighbours.Count)
        return new Vertex[0];
```

```
        return neighbours[v.id].ToArray();
    }
```

We also need a `Vertex` class; use the following code:

```
using UnityEngine;
using System.Collections.Generic;
[System.Serializable]
public class Vertex : MonoBehaviour
{
    public int id;
    public List<Edge> neighbours;
    [HideInInspector]
    public Vertex prev;
}
```

We need to create a class for storing a vertex's neighbors with the costs. This class will be called `Edge`. Let's implement it:

1. Create the `Edge` class, deriving from `IComparable`:

```
using System;

[System.Serializable]
public class Edge : IComparable<Edge>
{
    public float cost;
    public Vertex vertex;
    // next steps
}
```

2. Implement its constructor:

```
public Edge(Vertex vertex = null, float cost = 1f)
{
    this.vertex = vertex;
    this.cost = cost;
}
```

3. Implement the comparison member function:

```
public int CompareTo(Edge other)
{
    float result = cost - other.cost;
    int idA = vertex.GetInstanceID();
    int idB = other.vertex.GetInstanceID();
    if (idA == idB)
        return 0;
```

```
        return (int)result;
    }
```

4. Implement the function for comparing two edges:

```
public bool Equals(Edge other)
{
    return (other.vertex.id == this.vertex.id);
}
```

5. Override the function for comparing two objects:

```
public override bool Equals(object obj)
{
    Edge other = (Edge)obj;
    return (other.vertex.id == this.vertex.id);
}
```

6. Override the function for retrieving the hash code. This is necessary when overriding the previous member function:

```
public override int GetHashCode()
{
    return this.vertex.GetHashCode();
}
```

Besides creating the previous classes, it's important to define a couple of prefabs based on the cube primitive in order to visualize the ground (maybe a low-height cube) and walls or obstacles. The prefab for the ground is assigned to the `vertexPrefab` variable and the wall prefab is assigned to the `obstaclePrefab` variable that is declared in the next section.

Finally, create a directory called `Maps` to store the text files for defining the maps.

Now, it's time to go in-depth and be specific about implementing our grid graph. First, we implement all the functions for handling the graph, leaving space for your own text files, and, in the following section, we'll learn how to read `.map` files, which is an open format used by a lot of games:

1. Create the `GraphGrid` class, deriving from `Graph`:

```
using UnityEngine;
using System;
using System.Collections.Generic;
using System.IO;

public class GraphGrid : Graph
```

```
{
    public GameObject obstaclePrefab;
    public string mapName = "arena.map";
    public bool get8Vicinity = false;
    public float cellSize = 1f;
    [Range(0, Mathf.Infinity)]
    public float defaultCost = 1f;
    [Range(0, Mathf.Infinity)]
    public float maximumCost = Mathf.Infinity;
    string mapsDir = "Maps";
    int numCols;
    int numRows;
    GameObject[] vertexObjs;
    // this is necessary for
    // the advanced section of reading
    // from an example test file
    bool[,] mapVertices;
    // next steps
}
```

2. Define the `GridToId` and `IdToGrid` functions for transforming a position in the grid into a vertex index, and vice versa:

```
private int GridToId(int x, int y)
{
    return Math.Max(numRows, numCols) * y + x;
}

private Vector2 IdToGrid(int id)
{
    Vector2 location = Vector2.zero;
    location.y = Mathf.Floor(id / numCols);
    location.x = Mathf.Floor(id % numCols);
    return location;
}
```

3. Define the `LoadMap` function for reading the text file:

```
private void LoadMap(string filename)
{
    // TODO
    // implement your grid-based
    // file-reading procedure here
    // using
    // vertices[i, j] for logical representation and
    // vertexObjs[i, j] for assigning new prefab instances
}
```

4. Override the `LoadGraph` function:

```
public override void LoadGraph()
{
    LoadMap(mapName);
}
```

5. Override the `GetNearestVertex` function. This is the traditional way, without considering that the resulting vertex is an obstacle. In the following steps, we will learn how to do it better:

```
public override Vertex GetNearestVertex(Vector3 position)
{
    position.x = Mathf.Floor(position.x / cellSize);
    position.y = Mathf.Floor(position.z / cellSize);
    int col = (int)position.x;
    int row = (int)position.z;
    int id = GridToId(col, row);
    return vertices[id];
   }
```

6. Override the `GetNearestVertex` function. It is based on the Breadth-First Search algorithm that we will learn about in-depth later in the chapter:

```
public override Vertex GetNearestVertex(Vector3 position)
{
    int col = (int)(position.x / cellSize);
    int row = (int)(position.z / cellSize);
    Vector2 p = new Vector2(col, row);
    // next steps
}
```

7. Define the list of explored positions (vertices) and the queue of the position to be explored:

```
List<Vector2> explored = new List<Vector2>();
Queue<Vector2> queue = new Queue<Vector2>();
queue.Enqueue(p);
```

8. Keep exploring while the queue still has elements to explore. Otherwise, return `null`:

```
do
{
    p = queue.Dequeue();
    col = (int)p.x;
    row = (int)p.y;
```

```
        int id = GridToId(col, row);
        // next steps
    } while (queue.Count != 0);
    return null;
```

9. Retrieve it immediately if it's a valid vertex:

```
if (mapVertices[row, col])
    return vertices[id];
```

10. Add the position to the list of explored, if it's not already there:

```
if (!explored.Contains(p))
{
    explored.Add(p);
    int i, j;
    // next step
}
```

11. Add all its valid neighbors to the queue, provided they are valid:

```
for (i = row - 1; i <= row + 1; i++)
{
    for (j = col - 1; j <= col + 1; j++)
    {
        if (i < 0 || j < 0)
            continue;
        if (j >= numCols || i >= numRows)
            continue;
        if (i == row && j == col)
            continue;
        queue.Enqueue(new Vector2(j, i));
    }
}
```

How it works...

The algorithm makes use of its private functions in order to adapt itself to the general functions derived from the parent's class, and it relies on simple mathematical functions to convert a two-dimensional vector position to a one-dimensional vector, or vertex index.

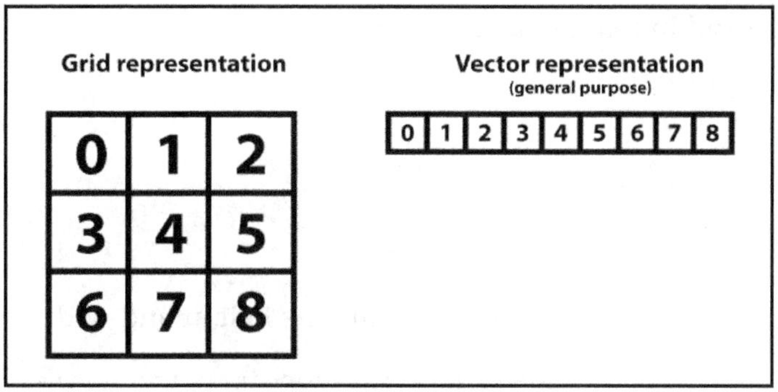

The LoadMap function needs to be implemented by you using your own map files, but, in the next section, we'll learn a way of implementing and reading certain kinds of text files containing maps based on grids. This will give you an idea of how to handle your files, and even use the same format for the commodity.

There's more...

We'll learn ways to implement the LoadMap function by using the .map file format as an example:

1. Define the function and create a StreamReader object for reading the file:

```
private void LoadMap(string filename)
{
    string path = Application.dataPath + "/" + mapsDir + "/" +
filename;
    try
    {
        StreamReader strmRdr = new StreamReader(path);
        using (strmRdr)
        {
            // next steps in here
        }
    }
    catch (Exception e)
    {
        Debug.LogException(e);
    }
}
```

2. Declare and initialize the necessary variables:

```
int j = 0;
int i = 0;
int id = 0;
string line;
Vector3 position = Vector3.zero;
Vector3 scale = Vector3.zero;
```

3. Read the header of the file containing its height and width:

```
line = strmRdr.ReadLine();// non-important line
line = strmRdr.ReadLine();// height
numRows = int.Parse(line.Split(' ')[1]);
line = strmRdr.ReadLine();// width
numCols = int.Parse(line.Split(' ')[1]);
line = strmRdr.ReadLine();// "map" line in file
```

4. Initialize the member variables, allocating memory at the same time:

```
vertices = new List<Vertex>(numRows * numCols);
neighbours = new List<List<Vertex>>(numRows * numCols);
costs = new List<List<float>>(numRows * numCols);
vertexObjs = new GameObject[numRows * numCols];
   mapVertices = new bool[numRows, numCols];
```

5. Declare the `for` loop for iterating over the characters in the following lines:

```
for (i = 0; i < numRows; i++)
{
    line = strmRdr.ReadLine();
    for (j = 0; j < numCols; j++)
    {
        // next steps in here
    }
}
```

6. Assign `true` or `false` to the logical representation depending on the character read:

```
bool isGround = true;
if (line[j] != '.')
    isGround = false;
mapVertices[i, j] = isGround;
```

7. Instantiate the proper prefab:

```
position.x = j * cellSize;
position.z = i * cellSize;
id = GridToId(j, i);
if (isGround)
    vertexObjs[id] = Instantiate(vertexPrefab, position,
Quaternion.identity) as GameObject;
else
    vertexObjs[id] = Instantiate(obstaclePrefab, position,
Quaternion.identity) as GameObject;
```

8. Assign the new game object as a child of the graph and clean up its name:

```
vertexObjs[id].name = vertexObjs[id].name.Replace("(Clone)",
id.ToString());
Vertex v = vertexObjs[id].AddComponent<Vertex>();
v.id = id;
vertices.Add(v);
neighbours.Add(new List<Vertex>());
costs.Add(new List<float>());
float y = vertexObjs[id].transform.localScale.y;
scale = new Vector3(cellSize, y, cellSize);
vertexObjs[id].transform.localScale = scale;
vertexObjs[id].transform.parent = gameObject.transform;
```

9. Create a pair of nested loops right after the previous loop, for setting up the neighbors for each vertex:

```
for (i = 0; i < numRows; i++)
{
    for (j = 0; j < numCols; j++)
    {
        SetNeighbours(j, i);
    }
}
```

10. Define the `SetNeighbours` function, called in the previous step:

```
protected void SetNeighbours(int x, int y, bool get8 = false)
{
    int col = x;
    int row = y;
    int i, j;
    int vertexId = GridToId(x, y);
    neighbours[vertexId] = new List<Vertex>();
```

```
        costs[vertexId] = new List<float>();
        Vector2[] pos = new Vector2[0];
        // next steps
    }
```

11. Compute the proper values when we need a vicinity of eight (top, bottom, right, left, and corners):

```
    if (get8)
    {
        pos = new Vector2[8];
        int c = 0;
        for (i = row - 1; i <= row + 1; i++)
        {
            for (j = col -1; j <= col; j++)
            {
                pos[c] = new Vector2(j, i);
                c++;
            }
        }
    }
```

12. Set up everything for a vicinity of four (no corners):

```
    else
    {
        pos = new Vector2[4];
        pos[0] = new Vector2(col, row - 1);
        pos[1] = new Vector2(col - 1, row);
        pos[2] = new Vector2(col + 1, row);
        pos[3] = new Vector2(col, row + 1);
    }
```

13. Add the neighbors to the lists. It's the same procedure as for the type of vicinity:

```
    foreach (Vector2 p in pos)
    {
        i = (int)p.y;
        j = (int)p.x;
        if (i < 0 || j < 0)
            continue;
        if (i >= numRows || j >= numCols)
            continue;
        if (i == row && j == col)
            continue;
        if (!mapVertices[i, j])
            continue;
```

```
        int id = GridToId(j, i);
        neighbours[vertexId].Add(vertices[id]);
        costs[vertexId].Add(defaultCost);
    }
```

See also

For further information about the map format used, and to get free maps from several acclaimed titles, please refer to the *Moving AI Lab's* website, led by Professor Sturtevant, available online at `http://movingai.com/benchmarks/`.

Representing the world with points of visibility

This is another widely-used technique for world representation based on points located throughout the valid area of navigation, be they manually placed or automated via scripting. We'll be using manually placed points connected automatically via scripting.

Getting ready

Just like the previous representation, it's important to have several things in order before continuing:

- Having the `Edge` class prepended to the `Graph` class in the same file
- Defining the `GetEdges` function in the `Graph` class
- Having the `Vertex` class

The vertex objects in the scene must have a collider component attached to them, as well as the `Vertex` tag assigned. It's recommended that they are unitary `Sphere` primitives.

How to do it...

We'll be creating the graph representation class as well as a custom `Vertex` class:

1. Create the `VertexVisibility` class deriving from `Vertex`:

```
using UnityEngine;
using System.Collections.Generic;

public class VertexVisibility : Vertex
{
    void Awake()
    {
        neighbours = new List<Edge>();
    }
}
```

2. Define the `FindNeighbours` function for automating the process of connecting vertices among them:

```
public void FindNeighbours(List<Vertex> vertices)
{
    Collider c = gameObject.GetComponent<Collider>();
    c.enabled = false;
    Vector3 direction = Vector3.zero;
    Vector3 origin = transform.position;
    Vector3 target = Vector3.zero;
    RaycastHit[] hits;
    Ray ray;
    float distance = 0f;
    // next step
}
```

3. Go over each object and cast a ray to validate whether it's completely visible and add it to the list of neighbors:

```
for (int i = 0; i < vertices.Count; i++)
{
    if (vertices[i] == this)
        continue;
    target = vertices[i].transform.position;
    direction = target - origin;
    distance = direction.magnitude;
    ray = new Ray(origin, direction);
    hits = Physics.RaycastAll(ray, distance);
    if (hits.Length == 1)
    {
```

```
            if (hits[0].collider.gameObject.tag.Equals("Vertex"))
            {
                Edge e = new Edge();
                e.cost = distance;
                GameObject go = hits[0].collider.gameObject;
                Vertex v = go.GetComponent<Vertex>();
                if (v != vertices[i])
                    continue;
                e.vertex = v;
                neighbours.Add(e);
            }
        }
    }
    c.enabled = true;
```

4. Create the `GraphVisibility` class:

```
using UnityEngine;
using System.Collections.Generic;

public class GraphVisibility : Graph
{
    // next steps
}
```

5. Build the `Load` function for making the connections between vertices:

```
public override void Load()
{
    Vertex[] verts = GameObject.FindObjectsOfType<Vertex>();
    vertices = new List<Vertex>(verts);
    for (int i = 0; i < vertices.Count; i++)
    {
        VertexVisibility vv = vertices[i] as VertexVisibility;
        vv.id = i;
        vv.FindNeighbours(vertices);
    }
}
```

6. Define the `GetNearesteVertex` function:

```
public override Vertex GetNearestVertex(Vector3 position)
{
    Vertex vertex = null;
    float dist = Mathf.Infinity;
    float distNear = dist;
    Vector3 posVertex = Vector3.zero;
    for (int i = 0; i < vertices.Count; i++)
```

```
        {
            posVertex = vertices[i].transform.position;
            dist = Vector3.Distance(position, posVertex);
            if (dist < distNear)
            {
                distNear = dist;
                vertex = vertices[i];
            }
        }
        return vertex;
    }
```

7. Define the `GetNeighbours` function:

```
public override Vertex[] GetNeighbours(Vertex v)
{
    List<Edge> edges = v.neighbours;
    Vertex[] ns = new Vertex[edges.Count];
    int i;
    for (i = 0; i < edges.Count; i++)
    {
        ns[i] = edges[i].vertex;
    }
    return ns;
}
```

8. Finally, override the `GetEdges` function:

```
public override Edge[] GetEdges(Vertex v)
{
    return vertices[v.id].neighbours.ToArray();
}
```

How it works...

The `GraphVisibility` parent class indexes every vertex on the scene and makes use of the `FindNeighbours` function on each one. This is in order to build the graph and make the connections without total user supervision, beyond placing the visibility points where the user sees fit. Also, the distance between two points is used to assign the cost to that corresponding edge.

There's more...

It's important to make points visible to one another in order for the graph to be connected. This approach is also suitable for building intelligent graphs considering stairs and cliffs; it just requires the moving of the `Load` function to an editor-friendly class in order to call it in edit mode, and then modifying or deleting the corresponding edges to make it work as intended.

Take a look at the previous recipe's *Getting ready* section so that you can better understand the starting point in case you feel you're missing something.

For further information about custom editors, editor scripting, and how to execute code in edit mode, please refer to the Unity documentation, available online at the following URLs:

- `http://docs.unity3d.com/ScriptReference/Editor.html`
- `http://docs.unity3d.com/ScriptReference/ExecuteInEditMode.html`
- `http://docs.unity3d.com/Manual/PlatformDependentCompilation.html`

Representing the world with a self-made navigation mesh

Sometimes, a custom navigation mesh is necessary for dealing with difficult situations such as different types of graphs, but placing the graph's vertices manually is troublesome because it requires a lot of time to cover large areas.

We will learn how to use a model's mesh in order to generate a navigation mesh based on its triangles' centroids as vertices, and then leverage the heavy lifting we learned from the previous recipe.

Getting ready

This recipe requires some knowledge of custom editor scripting and an understanding of implementing the points of visibility graph representation. Also, it is worth mentioning that the script instantiates a `CustomNavMesh` game object automatically in the scene and it requires a prefab to be assigned, just like any other graph representation.

Finally, it's important to create the following class, deriving from `GraphVisibility`:

```
using UnityEngine;
using System.Collections;
using System.Collections.Generic;

public class CustomNavMesh : GraphVisibility
{
    public override void Start()
    {
        instIdToId = new Dictionary<int, int>();
    }
}
```

How to do it...

We will create an editor window for easily handling the automation process without weighing down the graph's `Start` function, thereby delaying the scene loading:

1. Create the `CustomNavMeshWindow` class and place it in a directory called Editor:

```
using UnityEngine;
using UnityEditor;
using System.Collections;
using System.Collections.Generic;

public class CustomNavMeshWindow : EditorWindow
{
    // next steps here
}
```

2. Add the attributes to the editor window:

```
static bool isEnabled = false;
static GameObject graphObj;
static CustomNavMesh graph;
static CustomNavMeshWindow window;
static GameObject graphVertex;
```

3. Implement the function for initializing and showing the window:

```
[MenuItem("UAIPC/Ch02/CustomNavMeshWindow")]
static void Init()
{
    window = EditorWindow.GetWindow<CustomNavMeshWindow>();
```

```
        window.title = "CustomNavMeshWindow";
        SceneView.onSceneGUIDelegate += OnScene;
        graphObj = GameObject.Find("CustomNavMesh");
        if (graphObj == null)
        {
            graphObj = new GameObject("CustomNavMesh");
            graphObj.AddComponent<CustomNavMesh>();
            graph = graphObj.GetComponent<CustomNavMesh>();
        }
        else
        {
            graph = graphObj.GetComponent<CustomNavMesh>();
            if (graph == null)
                graphObj.AddComponent<CustomNavMesh>();
            graph = graphObj.GetComponent<CustomNavMesh>();
        }
    }
```

4. Define the `OnDestroy` function:

```
    void OnDestroy()
    {
        SceneView.onSceneGUIDelegate -= OnScene;
    }
```

5. Implement the `OnGUI` function for drawing the window's interior:

```
    void OnGUI()
    {
        isEnabled = EditorGUILayout.Toggle("Enable Mesh Picking",
    isEnabled);
        if (GUILayout.Button("Build Edges"))
        {
            if (graph != null)
                graph.LoadGraph();
        }
    }
```

6. Implement the first half of the `OnScene` function for handling the left-click on the scene window:

```
    private static void OnScene(SceneView sceneView)
    {
        if (!isEnabled)
            return;
        if (Event.current.type == EventType.MouseDown)
        {
            graphVertex = graph.vertexPrefab;
```

```
            if (graphVertex == null)
            {
                Debug.LogError("No Vertex Prefab assigned");
                return;
            }
            Event e = Event.current;
            Ray ray =
HandleUtility.GUIPointToWorldRay(e.mousePosition);
            RaycastHit hit;
            GameObject newV;
            // next step
        }
    }
```

7. Implement the second half for implementing the behavior when clicking on the mesh:

```
    if (Physics.Raycast(ray, out hit))
    {
        GameObject obj = hit.collider.gameObject;
        Mesh mesh = obj.GetComponent<MeshFilter>().sharedMesh;
        Vector3 pos;
        int i;
        for (i = 0; i < mesh.triangles.Length; i += 3)
        {
            int i0 = mesh.triangles[i];
            int i1 = mesh.triangles[i + 1];
            int i2 = mesh.triangles[i + 2];
            pos = mesh.vertices[i0];
            pos += mesh.vertices[i1];
            pos += mesh.vertices[i2];
            pos /= 3;
            newV = (GameObject)Instantiate(graphVertex, pos,
Quaternion.identity);
            newV.transform.Translate(obj.transform.position);
            newV.transform.parent = graphObj.transform;
            graphObj.transform.parent = obj.transform;
        }
    }
```

How it works...

We create a custom editor window and set up the `OnScene` delegate function for handling events on the scene window. Also, we are capable of creating the graph nodes by traversing the mesh vertex arrays, computing each triangle's centroid. Finally, we make use of the graph's `LoadGraph` function in order to compute neighbors.

Finding your way out of a maze with DFS

The **Depth-First Search** (**DFS**) algorithm is a path-finding technique suitable for low-memory devices. Another common use is to build mazes with some minor modifications to the list of nodes visited and discovered, but the main algorithm stays just the same.

Getting ready

This is a high-level algorithm that relies on each graph's implementation of the main functions (`build`, `init`, and so on), so that the algorithm is implemented in the `Graph` class.

It is important to take a moment and verify when the recipe is manipulating actual objects, or vertex IDs.

How to do it...

Even though this recipe is only defining a function, please take into consideration the comments in the code for better understanding of the implementation and code flow:

1. Declare the `GetPathDFS` function:

```
public List<Vertex> GetPathDFS(GameObject srcObj, GameObject
dstObj)
{
    // next steps
}
```

2. Establish whether input objects are `null`:

```
if (srcObj == null || dstObj == null)
    return new List<Vertex>();
```

3. Declare and initialize the variables we need for the algorithm:

```
Vertex src = GetNearestVertex(srcObj.transform.position);
Vertex dst = GetNearestVertex(dstObj.transform.position);
Vertex[] neighbours;
Vertex v;
int[] previous = new int[vertices.Count];
for (int i = 0; i < previous.Length; i++)
    previous[i] = -1;
previous[src.id] = src.id;
Stack<Vertex> s = new Stack<Vertex>();
s.Push(src);
```

4. Implement the DFS algorithm for finding a path:

```
while (s.Count != 0)
{
    v = s.Pop();
    if (ReferenceEquals(v, dst))
    {
        return BuildPath(src.id, v.id, ref previous);
    }

    neighbours = GetNeighbours(v);
    foreach (Vertex n in neighbours)
    {
        if (previous[n.id] != -1)
            continue;
        previous[n.id] = v.id;
        s.Push(n);
    }
}
```

How it works...

The algorithm is based on the iterative version of DFS. It is also based on the in-order traversing of a graph and the LIFO philosophy of using a stack for visiting nodes and adding discovered ones.

There's more...

We called the `BuildPath` function, but we haven't implemented it yet. It is important to note that this function is called by almost every other path-finding algorithm in this chapter; that's why it's not part of the main recipe.

This is the code for the `BuildPath` method:

```
private List<Vertex> BuildPath(int srcId, int dstId, ref int[]
prevList)
{
    List<Vertex> path = new List<Vertex>();
    int prev = dstId;
    do
    {
        path.Add(vertices[prev]);
        prev = prevList[prev];
    } while (prev != srcId);
    return path;
}
```

Finding the shortest path in a grid with BFS

The **Breadth-First Search** (**BFS**) algorithm is just another basic technique for graph traversal and is aimed at getting the shortest path in the fewest steps possible, with the trade-off of being expensive in memory; thus, it is aimed especially at games for high-end consoles and computers.

Getting ready

This is a high-level algorithm that relies on each graph's implementation of the general functions, so the algorithm is implemented in the `Graph` class.

How to do it...

Even though this recipe is only defining a function, please take into consideration the comments in the code for better understanding of the implementation and code flow:

1. Declare the `GetPathBFS` function:

```
public List<Vertex> GetPathBFS(GameObject srcObj, GameObject
dstObj)
{
    if (srcObj == null || dstObj == null)
        return new List<Vertex>();
    // next steps
}
```

2. Declare and initialize the variables we need for the algorithm:

```
Vertex[] neighbours;
Queue<Vertex> q = new Queue<Vertex>();
Vertex src = GetNearestVertex(srcObj.transform.position);
Vertex dst = GetNearestVertex(dstObj.transform.position);
Vertex v;
int[] previous = new int[vertices.Count];
for (int i = 0; i < previous.Length; i++)
    previous[i] = -1;
previous[src.id] = src.id;
q.Enqueue(src);
```

3. Implement the BFS algorithm for finding a path:

```
while (q.Count != 0)
{
    v = q.Dequeue();
    if (ReferenceEquals(v, dst))
    {
        return BuildPath(src.id, v.id, ref previous);
    }

    neighbours = GetNeighbours(v);
    foreach (Vertex n in neighbours)
    {
        if (previous[n.id] != -1)
            continue;
        previous[n.id] = v.id;
        q.Enqueue(n);
    }
}
return new List<Vertex>();
```

How it works...

The BFS algorithm is similar to the DFS algorithm because it's based on the same in-order traversing of a graph but, instead of a stack such as DFS, BFS uses a queue for visiting the discovered nodes.

There's more...

In case you haven't noticed, we didn't implement the `BuildPath` method. This is because we talked about it at the end of the recipe in this chapter, in the recipe *Finding your way out of a maze with DFS*.

Finding the shortest path with Dijkstra

Dijkstra's algorithm was initially designed to solve the single-source shortest path problem for a graph. Thus, the algorithm finds the lowest-cost route to everywhere from a single point. We will learn how to make use of it given two different approaches.

Getting ready

The first thing to do is to import the binary heap class from the **Game Programming Wiki** (**GPWiki**) into our project, given that neither the .Net framework nor Mono have a defined structure for handling binary heaps or priority queues.

The source file is already in the book's online repository service provider as it is no longer available online.

How to do it...

We will learn how to implement the Dijkstra algorithm using the same number of parameters as the other algorithms, and then explain how to modify it to make maximum use of it according to its original purpose:

1. Define the `GetPathDijkstra` function with its internal variables:

```
public List<Vertex> GetPathDijkstra(GameObject srcObj,
GameObject dstObj)
{
    if (srcObj == null || dstObj == null)
        return new List<Vertex>();
    Vertex src = GetNearestVertex(srcObj.transform.position);
    Vertex dst = GetNearestVertex(dstObj.transform.position);
    GPWiki.BinaryHeap<Edge> frontier = new
GPWiki.BinaryHeap<Edge>();
    Edge[] edges;
    Edge node, child;
    int size = vertices.Count;
    float[] distValue = new float[size];
    int[] previous = new int[size];

    // next steps
}
```

2. Add the source node to the heap (working as a priority queue) and assign a distance value of infinity to all of them but the source node:

```
node = new Edge(src, 0);
frontier.Add(node);
distValue[src.id] = 0;
previous[src.id] = src.id;
for (int i = 0; i < size; i++)
{
    if (i == src.id)
        continue;
    distValue[i] = Mathf.Infinity;
    previous[i] = -1;
}
```

3. Define a loop to iterate while the queue is not empty:

```
while (frontier.Count != 0)
{
    node = frontier.Remove();
    int nodeId = node.vertex.id;
    // next steps
}
return new List<Vertex>();
```

4. Code the procedure when arriving at the destination:

```
if (ReferenceEquals(node.vertex, dst))
{
    return BuildPath(src.id, node.vertex.id, ref previous);
}
```

5. Otherwise, process the visited nodes and add its neighbors to the queue, and return the path (not empty if there is a path from the source to the destination vertex):

```
edges = GetEdges(node.vertex);
foreach (Edge e in edges)
{
    int eId = e.vertex.id;
    if (previous[eId] != -1)
        continue;
    float cost = distValue[nodeId] + e.cost;
    if (cost < distValue[e.vertex.id])
    {
        distValue[eId] = cost;
        previous[eId] = nodeId;
        frontier.Remove(e);
        child = new Edge(e.vertex, cost);
        frontier.Add(child);
    }
}
```

How it works...

Dijkstra's algorithm works in a similar way to BFS, but considers non-negative edge costs in order to build the best route from the source vertex to every other vertex. That's why we have an array for storing what the previous vertex is.

There's more...

We will learn how to modify the current Dijkstra algorithm in order to approach the problem using pre-processing techniques and optimizing the path-finding time. It can be seen as three big steps—modifying the main algorithm, creating the pre-processing function (handy in editor mode, for example), and, finally, defining the path retrieval function:

1. Modify the main function's signature:

```
public int[] Dijkstra(GameObject srcObj)
```

2. Change the returning value:

```
return previous;
```

3. Remove the lines from step 4 of the *How to do it* section:

```
if (ReferenceEquals(node.vertex, dst))
{
    return BuildPath(src.id, node.vertex.id, ref previous);
}
```

   Also, delete the following line at the beginning:

```
Vertex dst = GetNearestVertex(dstObj.transform.position);
```

4. Create a new member value for the `Graph` class:

```
List<int[]> routes = new List<int[]>();
```

5. Define the pre-processing function, called `DijkstraProcessing`:

```
public void DijkstraProcessing()
{
    int size = GetSize();
    for (int i = 0; i < size; i++)
    {
        GameObject go = vertices[i].gameObject;
        routes.add(Dijkstra(go));
    }
}
```

6. Implement a new `GetPathDijkstra` function for path retrieval:

```
public List<Vertex> GetPathDijkstra(GameObject srcObj,
GameObject dstObj)
{
    List<Vertex> path = new List<Vertex>();
    Vertex src = GetNearestVertex(srcObj);
    Vertex dst = GetNearestVertex(dstObj);
    return BuildPath(src.id, dst.id, ref routes[dst.id]);
}
```

In case you haven't noticed, we didn't implement the `BuildPath` method. This is because we talked about it at the end of this chapter, in the recipe *Finding your way out of a maze with DFS*.

Finding the best-promising path with A*

The A* algorithm is probably the most widely-used technique for path finding given its implementation simplicity, efficiency, and because it has room for optimization. It's no coincidence that there are several algorithms based on it. At the same time, A* shares several roots with Dijkstra's algorithm, so you'll find similarities in their implementations.

Getting ready

Just like Dijkstra's algorithm, this recipe uses the binary heap extracted from the GPWiki. Also, it is important to understand what delegates are and how they work. Finally, we are entering into the world of informed search; that means that we need to understand what a heuristic is and what it is for.

In a nutshell, for the purpose of this recipe, a heuristic is a function for calculating the approximate cost between two vertices in order to compare them to other alternatives and take the minimum-cost choice.

We need to make small changes to the `Graph` class:

1. Define a member variable as a `delegate`:

```
public delegate float Heuristic(Vertex a, Vertex b);
```

2. Implement a Euclidean distance member function to use it as a default heuristic:

```
public float EuclidDist(Vertex a, Vertex b)
{
    Vector3 posA = a.transform.position;
    Vector3 posB = b.transform.position;
    return  Vector3.Distance(posA, posB);
}
```

3. Implement a Manhattan distance function to use as a different heuristic. It will help us in comparing results using different heuristics:

```
public float ManhattanDist(Vertex a, Vertex b)
{
    Vector3 posA = a.transform.position;
    Vector3 posB = b.transform.position;
    return Mathf.Abs(posA.x - posB.x) + Mathf.Abs(posA.y -
posB.y);
}
```

How to do it...

Even though this recipe covers defining a function, please take into consideration the comments in the code for better understanding of the implementation and code flow:

1. Define the `GetPathAstar` function, along with its member variables:

```
public List<Vertex> GetPathAstar(GameObject srcObj, GameObject
dstObj, Heuristic h = null)
{
    if (srcObj == null || dstObj == null)
        return new List<Vertex>();
    if (ReferenceEquals(h, null))
        h = EuclidDist;
```

```
    Vertex src = GetNearestVertex(srcObj.transform.position);
    Vertex dst = GetNearestVertex(dstObj.transform.position);
    GPWiki.BinaryHeap<Edge> frontier = new
GPWiki.BinaryHeap<Edge>();
    Edge[] edges;
    Edge node, child;
    int size = vertices.Count;
    float[] distValue = new float[size];
    int[] previous = new int[size];
    // next steps
}
```

2. Add the source node to the heap (working as a priority queue) and assign a distance value of infinity to all of them bar the source node:

```
node = new Edge(src, 0);
frontier.Add(node);
distValue[src.id] = 0;
previous[src.id] = src.id;
for (int i = 0; i < size; i++)
{
    if (i == src.id)
        continue;
    distValue[i] = Mathf.Infinity;
    previous[i] = -1;
}
```

3. Declare the loop for traversing the graph:

```
while (frontier.Count != 0)
{
    // next steps
}
return new List<Vertex>();
```

4. Implement the conditions for returning a path when necessary:

```
node = frontier.Remove();
int nodeId = node.vertex.id;
if (ReferenceEquals(node.vertex, dst))

{
    return BuildPath(src.id, node.vertex.id, ref previous);
}
```

5. Get the vertex's neighbors (also called successors in some textbooks):

```
edges = GetEdges(node.vertex);
```

6. Traverse the neighbors for computing the `cost` function:

```
foreach (Edge e in edges)
{
    int eId = e.vertex.id;
    if (previous[eId] != -1)
        continue;
    float cost = distValue[nodeId] + e.cost;
    // key point
    cost += h(node.vertex, e.vertex);
    // next step
}
```

7. Expand the list of explored nodes (`frontier`) and update the costs, if necessary:

```
if (cost < distValue[e.vertex.id])
{
    distValue[eId] = cost;
    previous[eId] = nodeId;
    frontier.Remove(e);
    child = new Edge(e.vertex, cost);
    frontier.Add(child);
}
```

How it works...

A* works in a similar fashion to Dijkstra's algorithm. However, instead of choosing the real lowest-cost node from all the possible options, it chooses the most promising one based on a given heuristic, and goes that way. In our case, the default heuristic is based solely on the Euclidean distance between two vertices with the option of using Manhattan distance.

There's more...

You are welcome to play with different heuristic functions depending on the game and context, and the following is an example of how to do so.

Define a heuristic function in the `Graph` class:

```
public float Heuristic(Vertex a, Vertex b)
{
  float estimation = 0f;
  // your logic here
  return estimation;
}
```

The important thing here is that the heuristic we develop is both *admissible* and *consistent*. For more theoretical insights about these topics, please refer to *Artificial Intelligence: A Modern Approach*, by Russel and Norvig.

In case you haven't noticed, we didn't implement the `BuildPath` method. This is because we talked about it at the end of this chapter, in the recipe *Finding your way out of a maze with DFS*.

See also

In this chapter, please refer to the following recipes:

- *Finding your way out of a maze with DFS*
- *Finding the shortest path with Dijsktra*

For further information about Delegates, please refer to the official documentation available online at `https://unity3d.com/learn/tutorials/modules/intermediate/scripting/delegates`.

Improving A* for memory – IDA*

IDA* is a variant of an algorithm called Iterative Deepening Depth-First Search. Its memory usage is lower than A* because it doesn't make use of data structures to store the looked-up and explored nodes.

Getting ready

For this recipe, it is important to have some understanding of how recursion works.

How to do it...

This is a long recipe that can be regarded as a big two-step process: creating the main function and an internal recursive one. Please take into consideration the comments in the code for better understanding of the implementation and code flow:

1. Let's start by defining the main function, `GetPathIDAstar`:

```
public List<Vertex> GetPathIDAstar(GameObject srcObj,
GameObject dstObj, Heuristic h = null)
{
    if (srcObj == null || dstObj == null)
        return new List<Vertex>();
    if (ReferenceEquals(h, null))
        h = EuclidDist;
    // next steps;
}
```

2. Declare and compute the variables to use alongside the algorithm:

```
List<Vertex> path = new List<Vertex>();
Vertex src = GetNearestVertex(srcObj.transform.position);
Vertex dst = GetNearestVertex(dstObj.transform.position);
Vertex goal = null;
bool[] visited = new bool[vertices.Count];
for (int i = 0; i < visited.Length; i++)
visited[i] = false;
visited[src.id] = true;
```

3. Implement the algorithm's loop:

```
float bound = h(src, dst);
while (bound < Mathf.Infinity)
{
    bound = RecursiveIDAstar(src, dst, bound, h, ref goal, ref
visited);
}
if (ReferenceEquals(goal, null))
    return path;
return BuildPath(goal);
```

4. Now it's time to build the recursive internal function:

```
private float RecursiveIDAstar(
        Vertex v,
        Vertex dst,
        float bound,
        Heuristic h,
```

```
            ref Vertex goal,
            ref bool[] visited)
{
    // next steps
}
```

5. Prepare everything to start the recursion:

```
// base case
if (ReferenceEquals(v, dst))
    return Mathf.Infinity;
Edge[] edges = GetEdges(v);
if (edges.Length == 0)
    return Mathf.Infinity;
```

6. Apply the recursion for each neighbor:

```
// recursive case
float fn = Mathf.Infinity;
foreach (Edge e in edges)
{
    int eId = e.vertex.id;
    if (visited[eId])
        continue;
    visited[eId] = true;
    e.vertex.prev = v;
    float f = h(v, dst);
    float b;
    if (f <= bound)
    {
        b = RecursiveIDAstar(e.vertex, dst, bound, h, ref
goal, ref visited);
        fn = Mathf.Min(f, b);
    }
    else
        fn = Mathf.Min(fn, f);
}
```

7. Return a value based on the recursion result:

```
return fn;
```

How it works...

As you can see, the algorithm is very similar to that of the recursive version of DFS, but uses the principle of making decisions on top of a heuristic from A*. The main function is responsible for starting the recursion and building the resulting path. The recursive function is the one responsible for traversing the graph, looking for the destination node.

There's more...

This time, we will need to implement a different `BuildPath` function, in case you have followed along with the previous path-finding recipes. Otherwise, we will need to implement this method, which we haven't defined yet:

```
private List<Vertex> BuildPath(Vertex v)
{
    List<Vertex> path = new List<Vertex>();
    while (!ReferenceEquals(v, null))
    {
        path.Add(v);
        v = v.prev;
    }
    return path;
}
```

Planning navigation in several frames – time-sliced search

When dealing with large graphs, computing paths can take a lot of time, even driving the game to a halt for a couple of seconds. This could lead to ruining the overall experience, to say the least. Luckily enough, there are methods for avoiding that.

> This recipe is built on top of the principles of using coroutines as a method for keeping the game running smoothly while finding a path in the background; some knowledge of coroutines is required.

Getting ready

We'll learn how to implement path-finding techniques using coroutines by refactoring the A* algorithm learned previously, but we will handle its signature as a different function.

How to do it...

Even though this recipe is only for defining a function, please take into consideration the comments in the code for a better understanding of the implementation and code flow:

1. Modify the `Graph` class and add a couple of member variables, one for storing the path and the other for knowing whether the coroutine has finished:

```
public List<Vertex> path;
public bool isFinished;
```

2. Declare the member function:

```
public IEnumerator GetPathInFrames(GameObject srcObj,
GameObject dstObj, Heuristic h = null)
{
    //next steps
}
```

3. Include the following member variables at the beginning:

```
isFinished = false;
path = new List<Vertex>();
if (srcObj == null || dstObj == null)
{
    path = new List<Vertex>();
    isFinished = true;
    yield break;
}
```

4. Modify the loop for traversing the graph:

```
while (frontier.Count != 0)
{
    // changes over A*
    yield return null;
    //////////////////////////////
    node = frontier.Remove();
```

5. Also, include the other path-retrieval validations:

```
if (ReferenceEquals(node.vertex, dst))
{
    // changes over A*
    path = BuildPath(src.id, node.vertex.id, ref previous);
    break;
    //////////////////////////////
}
```

6. Finally, reset the proper values and return control at the end of the function, after closing the main loop:

```
isFinished = true;
yield break;
```

How it works...

The `yield return null` statement inside the main loop works as a flag for delivering control to the higher-level functions, thus computing each new loop in each new frame using Unity's internal multitasking system.

See also

- The *Finding the best-promising path with A** recipe

For further information about coroutines and more examples, please refer to the official documentation available online at the following URLs:

- `http://docs.unity3d.com/Manual/Coroutines.html`
- `https://unity3d.com/learn/tutorials/modules/intermediate/scripting/coroutines`

Smoothing a path

When dealing with regular-size vertices on a graph, such as grids, it's pretty common to see some kind of *robotic* movement from the agents in the game. Depending on the type of game we're developing, this could be avoided using path-smoothing techniques, such as the one we're about to learn:

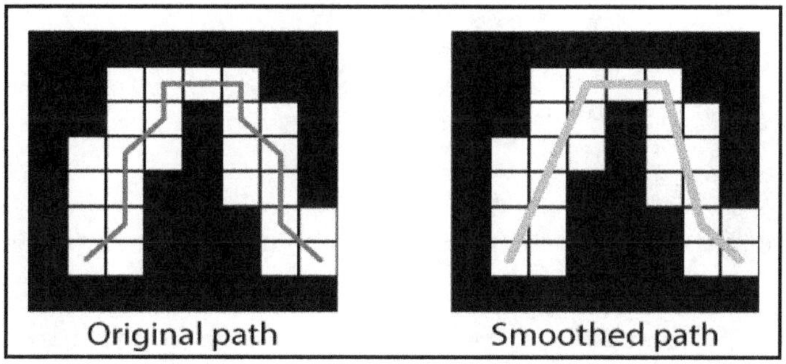

Getting ready

Let's define a new tag in the Unity editor called `Wall` and assign it to every object in the scene that is intended to work as a wall or obstacle in the navigation.

How to do it...

This is an easy, yet powerful, function:

1. Define the `Smooth` function:

```
public List<Vertex> Smooth(List<Vertex> path)
{
    // next steps here
}
```

2. Check whether it is worth computing a new path:

```
List<Vertex> newPath = new List<Vertex>();
if (path.Count == 0)
    return newPath;
if (path.Count < 3)
    return path;
```

3. Implement the loops for traversing the list and building the new path:

```
newPath.Add(path[0]);
int i, j;
for (i = 0; i < path.Count - 1;)
{
    for (j = i + 1; j < path.Count; j++)
    {
        // next steps here
    }
    i = j - 1;
    newPath.Add(path[i]);
}
return newPath;
```

4. Declare and compute the variables to be used by the ray casting function:

```
Vector3 origin = path[i].transform.position;
Vector3 destination = path[j].transform.position;
Vector3 direction = destination - origin;
float distance = direction.magnitude;
bool isWall = false;
direction.Normalize();
```

5. Cast a ray from the current starting node to the next one:

```
Ray ray = new Ray(origin, direction);
RaycastHit[] hits;
hits = Physics.RaycastAll(ray, distance);
```

6. Check whether there is a wall and break the loop accordingly:

```
foreach (RaycastHit hit in hits)
{
    string tag = hit.collider.gameObject.tag;
    if (tag.Equals("Wall"))
    {
        isWall = true;
        break;
    }
}
if (isWall)
    break;
```

How it works...

We create a new path, taking the initial node as a starting point, and apply ray casting to the next node in the path until we get a collision with a wall between our current node and the target node. When that happens, we take the last clear node, put it in the new path, and set it as the current node to start casting rays again. The process continues until there are no nodes left to check and the current node is the target node. That way, we build a more intuitive path.

14
Decision Making

In this chapter, you will learn the following recipes:

- Choosing through a decision tree
- Implementing a finite-state machine
- Improving FSMs: hierarchical finite-state machines
- Implementing behavior trees
- Working with fuzzy logic
- Making decisions with goal-oriented behaviors
- Implementing a blackboard architecture
- Experimenting with Unity's animation state machine

Introduction

Making decisions or changing the game flow according to the game's state could get really messy if we rely only on simple control structures. That's why we will learn different decision-making techniques that are flexible enough to adapt to different types of games, and robust enough to let us build modular decision-making systems.

The techniques covered in the chapter are mostly related to trees, automata, and matrices. Also, certain topics require a good understanding of how recursion, inheritance, and polymorphism work, so it is important that we review those topics if required.

Choosing through a decision tree

One of the simplest mechanisms for tackling decision-making problems is decision trees, because they are fast and easy to grasp and implement. As a consequence, it's one of the most widely-used techniques today; it is extensively used in other character-controlled scopes such as animations.

Getting ready

This recipe requires a good understanding of recursion and inheritance, as we will constantly be implementing and calling virtual functions throughout the sections.

How to do it...

This recipe requires a lot of attention due to the number of files that we will need to handle. Overall, we will create a parent class `DecisionTreeNode`, from which we will derive the other ones. Finally, we will learn how to implement a couple of standard decision nodes:

1. First, create the `DecisionTreeNode` parent class, as shown in the following code:

```
using UnityEngine;
using System.Collections;
public class DecisionTreeNode : MonoBehaviour
{
    public virtual DecisionTreeNode MakeDecision()
    {
        return null;
    }
}
```

2. Next, create the `Decision` pseudo-abstract class, deriving from the parent class, `DecisionTreeNode`, as demonstrated in the following code:

```
using UnityEngine;
using System.Collections;
public class Decision : DecisionTreeNode
{
    public Action nodeTrue;
    public Action nodeFalse;
```

```
        public virtual Action GetBranch()
        {
            return null;
        }
    }
```

3. Then, we need to define the `Action` pseudo-abstract class, as shown in the following code:

```
using UnityEngine;
using System.Collections;
public class Action : DecisionTreeNode
{
    public bool activated = false;

    public override DecisionTreeNode MakeDecision()
    {
        return this;
    }
}
```

4. We then implement the `LateUpdate` virtual function, as shown in the following code:

```
public virtual void LateUpdate()
{
    if (!activated)
        return;
    // Implement your behaviors here
}
```

5. Next, we create the final class, `DecisionTree`, as shown in the following code:

```
using UnityEngine;
using System.Collections;
public class DecisionTree : DecisionTreeNode
{
    public DecisionTreeNode root;
    private Action actionNew;
    private Action actionOld;
}
```

6. We then override the `MakeDecision` function with the following code:

```
public override DecisionTreeNode MakeDecision()
{
    return root.MakeDecision();
}
```

7. Finally, we then implement the `Update` function, as demonstrated in the following code:

```
void Update()
{
    actionNew.activated = false;
    actionOld = actionNew;
    actionNew = root.MakeDecision() as Action;
    if (actionNew == null)
        actionNew = actionOld;
    actionNew.activated = true;
}
```

How it works...

Decision nodes choose which path to take, calling the `MakeDecision` function recursively. It is worth mentioning that branches must be decisions, and leaves must be actions. Also, we should be careful not to create cycles within the tree:

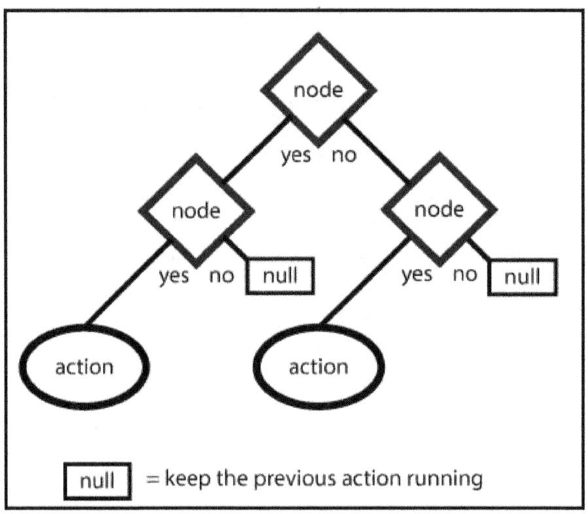

There's more...

We can create custom decisions and actions starting from the pseudo-abstract classes we've already created; for example, a decision on whether to attack or run away from the player.

The following code snippet demonstrates the custom Boolean decision:

```
using UnityEngine;
using System.Collections;

public class DecisionBool : Decision
{
    public bool valueDecision;
    public bool valueTest;

    public override Action GetBranch()
    {
        if (valueTest == valueDecision)
            return nodeTrue;
        return nodeFalse;
    }
}
```

Implementing a finite-state machine

Another interesting, yet easy-to-implement, technique is the **finite-state machine** (**FSM**). Finite-state machines move us to change the train of thought from what it was in the previous recipe. FSMs are great when our train of thought is more event-oriented, and we think in terms of holding a behavior until a condition is met, changing to another.

Getting ready

This is a technique mostly based on the behavior of automata, and will lay the foundations for the next recipe, which is an improved version of the current one.

How to do it...

This recipe is broken down into implementing three classes from the ground up. Don't worry, everything will make sense by the final step:

1. First, we'll implement the `Condition` class, as shown in the following code:

```
public class Condition
{
    public virtual bool Test()
    {
        return false;
    }
}
```

2. Next, we're going to define the `Transition` class, as demonstrated in the following code:

```
public class Transition
{
    public Condition condition;
    public State target;
}
```

3. We then need to define the `State` class, which is shown in the following code:

```
using UnityEngine;
using System.Collections.Generic;

public class State : MonoBehaviour
{
    public List<Transition> transitions;
}
```

4. Then, we implement the `Awake` function, as you'll see in the following code:

```
public virtual void Awake()
{
    transitions = new List<Transition>();
    // TO-DO
    // setup your transitions here
}
```

5. The next stage is to define the initialization function, as shown in the following code:

```
public virtual void OnEnable()
{
    // TO-DO
    // develop state's initialization here
}
```

6. We then define the finalization function, as you'll see in the following code:

```
public virtual void OnDisable()
{
    // TO-DO
    // develop state's finalization here
}
```

7. Next, we define the function for developing the proper behavior for the state, as shown in the following code:

```
public virtual void Update()
{
    // TO-DO
    // develop behaviour here
}
```

8. Finally, we implement the function for deciding if and which state is next enabled, as shown in the following code:

```
public void LateUpdate()
{
    foreach (Transition t in transitions)
    {
        if (t.condition.Test())
        {
            t.target.enabled = true;
            this.enabled = false;
            return;
        }
    }
}
```

How it works...

Each state is a `MonoBehaviour` script that is enabled or disabled according to the transitions it comes from. We take advantage of the `LateUpdate` function in order not to change the usual train of thought when developing behaviors, and we use it to check if it is time to transition to a different state. It is important to disable every state in the game object, apart from the initial one.

The following diagram shows the graphical representation for a finite-state machine.

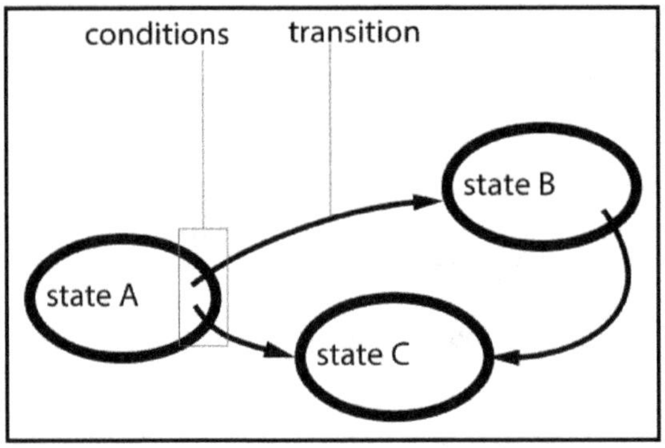

A finite-state machine representation

There's more...

In order to illustrate how to develop child classes deriving from the `Condition` function, let's take a look at a couple of examples; one that is aimed at validating a value in a range, the other at being a logic comparer between two conditions:

The code for `ConditionFloat` is as follows:

```
using UnityEngine;
using System.Collections;

public class ConditionFloat : Condition
{
    public float valueMin;
    public float valueMax;
    public float valueTest;

    public override bool Test()
```

```
        {
            if (valueMax >= valueTest && valueTest >= valueMin)
                return true;
            return false;
        }
    }
```

The following code is an example of code for `ConditionAnd`:

```
    using UnityEngine;
    using System.Collections;

    public class ConditionAnd : Condition
    {
        public Condition conditionA;
        public Condition conditionB;

        public override bool Test()
        {
            if (conditionA.Test() && conditionB.Test())
                return true;
            return false;
        }
    }
```

Improving FSMs: hierarchical finite-state machines

Finite-state machines can be improved in terms of having different layers or hierarchies. The principles are the same, but states are able to have their own internal finite-state machine, making them more flexible and scalable.

Getting ready

This recipe is based on top of the previous recipe, so it is important that we first grasp and understand how the finite-state machine recipe works.

How to do it...

We will create a state that is capable of holding internal states, in order to develop multilevel hierarchical state machines:

1. First, let's create the `StateHighLevel` class deriving from `State`, as shown in the following code:

```
using UnityEngine;
using System.Collections;
using System.Collections.Generic;

public class StateHighLevel : State
{
}
```

2. Next, add the new member variables to control the internal states, as demonstrated in the following code:

```
public List<State> states;
public State stateInitial;
protected State stateCurrent;
```

3. Then, we override the initialization function, as shown in the following code:

```
public override void OnEnable()
{
    if (stateCurrent == null)
        stateCurrent = stateInitial;
    stateCurrent.enabled = true;
}
```

4. Finally, we override the finalization function, as shown in the following code:

```
public override void OnDisable()
{
    base.OnDisable();
    stateCurrent.enabled = false;
    foreach (State s in states)
    {
        s.enabled = false;
    }
}
```

How it works...

The high-level state class allows us to activate the internal FSMs when it is enabled, and recursively disables its internal states when disabled. The working principle stays the same, thanks to the list of states and the way the parent class resolves the transitioning process.

See also

For further details, please refer to the following recipe in this chapter:

- *Implementing a finite-state machine* recipe.

Implementing behavior trees

Behavior trees can be seen as a synthesis of a number of other artificial intelligence techniques, such as finite-state machines, planning, and decision trees. In fact, they share some resemblance to FSMs, but instead of states, we think in terms of actions spanned across a tree structure.

Getting ready

This recipe requires us to understand coroutines.

How to do it...

Just like decisions trees, we will create three pseudo-abstract classes for handling the process:

1. First, let's create the `Task` base class, as shown in the following code:

```
using UnityEngine;
using System.Collections;
using System.Collections.Generic;

public class Task : MonoBehaviour
{
```

```
        public List<Task> children;
        protected bool result = false;
        protected bool isFinished = false;
    }
```

2. Next, we're going to implement the finalization function, as shown in the following code:

```
    public virtual void SetResult(bool r)
    {
        result = r;
        isFinished = true;
    }
```

3. We then implement the function for creating behaviors, as follows:

```
    public virtual IEnumerator Run()
    {
        SetResult(true);
        yield break;
    }
```

4. We then implement the general function for starting behaviors, as demonstrated in the following code:

```
    public virtual IEnumerator RunTask()
    {
        yield return StartCoroutine(Run());
    }
```

5. Next, we create the `ConditionBT` class, as shown in the following code:

```
    using UnityEngine;
    using System.Collections;

    public class ConditionBT : Task
    {
        public override IEnumerator Run()
        {
            isFinished = false;
            bool r = false;
            // implement your behaviour here
            // define result (r) whether true or false
            //---------
            SetResult(r);
            yield break;
        }
    }
```

6. Then, create the `base` class for actions, as can be seen in the following code:

```
using UnityEngine;
using System.Collections;

public class ActionBT : Task
{
    public override IEnumerator Run()
    {
        isFinished = false;
        // implement your behaviour here
        //---------
        return base.Run();
    }
}
```

7. Next, we're going to implement the `Selector` class, as shown in the following code:

```
using UnityEngine;
using System.Collections;

public class Selector : Task
{
    public override void SetResult(bool r)
    {
        if (r == true)
            isFinished = true;
    }

    public override IEnumerator RunTask()
    {
        foreach (Task t in children)
            yield return StartCoroutine(t.RunTask());
    }
}
```

8. Finally, we're also going to implement the `Sequence` class, which you can see in the following code:

```
using UnityEngine;
using System.Collections;

public class Sequence : Task
{
    public override void SetResult(bool r)
    {
        if (r == true)
```

```
                isFinished = true;
        }

        public override IEnumerator RunTask()
        {
            foreach (Task t in children)
                yield return StartCoroutine(t.RunTask());
        }
    }
```

How it works...

Behavior trees work in a similar fashion to decision trees; however, the leaf nodes are called *tasks*, and there are some branch nodes that are not conditions, but run a set of tasks in one of two ways: `Selector` and `Sequence`. Selectors run a set of tasks and return true when one of their sub-tasks returns true. They can be seen as `OR` nodes. Sequences run a set of tasks and return true when all of their sub-tasks return true. They can be seen as `AND` nodes.

See also

- For more theoretical insights, refer to Ian Millington's book, *Artificial Intelligence for Games.*

Working with fuzzy logic

There are times when we have to deal with gray areas, instead of binary-based values, to make decisions, and **fuzzy logic** is a set of mathematical techniques that help us with this task.

Imagine that we're developing an automated driver. A couple of available actions are steering and speed control, both of which have a range of degrees. Deciding how to take a turn, and at what speed, is what will make our driver different and possibly smarter. That's the type of gray area that fuzzy logic helps represent and handle.

Getting ready

This recipe requires a set of states indexed by continuous integer numbers. As this representation varies from game to game, we handle the raw input from such states along with their *fuzzification* in order to have a good general-purpose, fuzzy decision maker. Finally, the decision maker returns a set of fuzzy values representing the degree of membership of each state.

How to do it...

In this section, we will be creating two base classes and our fuzzy decision maker:

1. First, we'll create the `MembershipFunction` parent class, as shown in the following screenshot:

```
using UnityEngine;
using System.Collections;

public class MembershipFunction : MonoBehaviour
{
    public int stateId;
    public virtual float GetDOM(object input)
    {
        return 0f;
    }
}
```

2. Next, we'll implement the `FuzzyRule` class, as follows:

```
using System.Collections;
using System.Collections.Generic;

public class FuzzyRule
{
    public List<int> stateIds;
    public int conclusionStateId;
}
```

3. Then we're going to create the `FuzzyDecisionMaker` class, as shown in the following code:

```
using UnityEngine;
using System.Collections;
using System.Collections.Generic;

public class FuzzyDecisionMaker : MonoBehaviour
{
}
```

4. We then define the decision-making function signature and its member variables, as demonstrated in the following code:

```
public Dictionary<int,float> MakeDecision(object[] inputs,
MembershipFunction[][] mfList, FuzzyRule[] rules)
{
    Dictionary<int, float> inputDOM = new Dictionary<int,
float>();
    Dictionary<int, float> outputDOM = new Dictionary<int,
float>();
    MembershipFunction memberFunc;
    // next steps
}
```

5. Next, we're going to implement the loops for traversing the inputs, and populate the initial **degree of membership** (**DOM**) for each state. Take a look at the following code:

```
foreach (object input in inputs)
{
    int r, c;
    for (r = 0; r < mfList.Length; r++)
    {
        for (c = 0; c < mfList[r].Length; c++)
        {
            // next step
        }
    }
}
// steps after next
```

6. Then, we define the body of the innermost loop, which makes use of the proper membership functions to set (or update) the degrees of membership, as shown in the following code:

```
memberFunc = mfList[r][c];
```

```
int mfId = memberFunc.stateId;
float dom = memberFunc.GetDOM(input);
if (!inputDOM.ContainsKey(mfId))
{
    inputDOM.Add(mfId, dom);
    outputDOM.Add(mfId, 0f);
}
else
    inputDOM[mfId] = dom;
```

7. Then, we traverse the rules for setting the output degrees of membership, as shown in the following code:

```
foreach (FuzzyRule rule in rules)
{
    int outputId = rule.conclusionStateId;
    float best = outputDOM[outputId];
    float min = 1f;
    foreach (int state in rule.stateIds)
    {
        float dom = inputDOM[state];
        if (dom < best)
            continue;
        if (dom < min)
            min = dom;
    }
    outputDOM[outputId] = min;
}
```

8. Finally, we return the set of degrees of membership, as follows:

```
return outputDOM;
```

How it works...

We make use of the boxing/unboxing technique for handling any input via the object datatype. The *fuzzification* process is done with the help of our own membership functions, derived from the base class that we created in the beginning. Then, we take the minimum degree of membership for the input state for each rule, and calculate the final degree of membership for each output state given the maximum output from any of the applicable rules.

There's more...

We can create an example membership function to define whether an enemy is in enraged mode, knowing that its life points (ranging from zero to 100) are equal to or less than 30.

The following is the code for the example `MFEnraged` class:

```
using UnityEngine;
using System;
using System.Collections;

public class MFEnraged : MembershipFunction
{
    public override float GetDOM(object input)
    {
        if ((int)input <= 30)
            return 1f;
        return 0f;
    }
}
```

It's worth noting that it is a common requirement to have a complete set of rules; one for each combination of states from each input. This gives the recipe a lack of scalability, but it works well for a smaller number of input variables and a small number of states per variable.

See also

- For more theoretical insights regarding (de)*fuzzification* and scalability weaknesses, please refer to Ian Millington's book, *Artificial Intelligence for Games*.

Making decisions with goal-oriented behaviors

Goal-oriented behaviors are a set of techniques aimed to give agents not only a sense of intelligence, but also a sense of free will once a goal is defined and given a set of rules to choose from.

Imagine we're developing a trooper agent that need not only reach a goal of capturing the flag (main goal), but also while taking care of their own life and ammo (inner goals for reaching the first). One way of implementing it is to use a general-purpose algorithm for handling goals, so the agent develops something similar as free will.

Getting ready

We will learn how to create a goal-based action selector. Such a selector chooses an action, considering the main goal, avoiding unintentional actions with disrupting effects, and taking an action's duration into account. Just like the recipe in the preceding section, this requires the modeling of goals in terms of numerical values.

How to do it...

Along with the action chooser, we will create base classes for actions and goals:

1. First, we'll create the base class for modeling actions, as shown in the following code:

```
using UnityEngine;
using System.Collections;

public class ActionGOB : MonoBehaviour
{
  public virtual float GetGoalChange(GoalGOB goal)
  {
    return 0f;
  }

  public virtual float GetDuration()
  {
    return 0f;
  }
}
```

2. Next, we'll create the `GoalGOB` parent class with member variables, as shown in the following code:

```
using UnityEngine;
using System.Collections;

public class GoalGOB
{
```

```
    public string name;
    public float value;
    public float change;
  }
```

3. Next, we'll define the proper functions for handling discontentment and change over time, as demonstrated in the following code:

```
public virtual float GetDiscontentment(float newValue)
{
  return newValue * newValue;
}

public virtual float GetChange()
{
  return 0f;
}
```

4. Then, we'll define the `ActionChooser` class, as shown in the following code:

```
using UnityEngine;
using System.Collections;

public class ActionChooser : MonoBehaviour
{
}
```

5. Next, we're implementing the function for handling unintentional actions, as shown in the following code:

```
public float CalculateDiscontentment(ActionGOB action,
GoalGOB[] goals)
{
  float discontentment = 0;
  foreach (GoalGOB goal in goals)
  {
    float newValue = goal.value + action.GetGoalChange(goal);
    newValue += action.GetDuration() * goal.GetChange();
    discontentment += goal.GetDiscontentment(newValue);
  }
  return discontentment;
}
```

6. Then, we implement the function for choosing an action, as follows:

```
public ActionGOB Choose(ActionGOB[] actions, GoalGOB[] goals)
{
```

```
    ActionGOB bestAction;
    bestAction = actions[0];
    float bestValue = CalculateDiscontentment(actions[0],
  goals);
    float value;
    // next steps
  }
```

7. Next, we pick the best action based on the least compromising, as you can see in the following code:

```
foreach (ActionGOB action in actions)
{
  value = CalculateDiscontentment(action, goals);
  if (value < bestValue)
  {
    bestValue = value;
    bestAction = action;
  }
}
```

8. Finally, we return the best action, as shown in the following code:

```
return bestAction;
```

How it works...

The discontentment functions help avoid unintended actions, depending on how much a goal's value changes in terms of an action and the time it takes to be executed. Then, the function for choosing an action is handled by computing the best-promising in terms of the minimum impact (discontentment).

Implementing a blackboard architecture

In this recipe, we will model how we usually brainstorm and make decisions in an organized manner. First of all, this is called a **blackboard architecture**, or a **blackboard system**, based on the metaphor of a group of experts gathering in a room with a big blackboard. They're presented with a problem (facts, unknowns, and so on), and each is able to add/remove stuff from the board and give their opinion to solve the problem. The main issue is how to decide who takes the lead.

Let's say we have an RTS game to build a city, protect it, and conquer territories. For such a big task, it would be easier if we could implement modules for different problems as mentioned before: build and sustain, protect, and attack. In that regard, we need submodules (experts) that allow us to compartmentalize knowledge and decisions. Depending on the current state of the game, one expert is given control to take actions that will allow us to reach the current goal.

In the following sections, we will elaborate on a solution to such an issue.

Getting ready

We need to define certain data structures for setting up everything before implementing the main steps:

1. First, we'll create the data structure for handling data bits in a flexible manner, as shown in the following code:

```
public struct BlackboardDatum
{
  public int id;
  public string type;
  public object value;
}
```

2. Next, we'll create the class defining the expert, as follows:

```
public abstract class BlackboardExpert
{
  public virtual float GetInsistence(Blackboard board)
  {
    return 0f;
  }
  public virtual void Run(Blackboard board){}
}
```

3. Then, we create the data structure for saving actions taken by the experts, as shown in the following code:

```
public struct BlackboardAction
{
  public object expert;
  public string name;
  public System.Action action;
}
```

How to do it...

Now, let's create the class that handles the blackboard and the main logic behind our metaphor:

1. First, let's define the `Blackboard` class, as shown in the following code:

```
using System.Collections.Generic;

public class Blackboard
{
  public List<BlackboardDatum> entries;
  public List<BlackboardAction> pastActions;
  public List<BlackboardExpert> experts;
}
```

2. Next, let's implement its constructor, as follows:

```
public Blackboard()
{
  entries = new List<BlackboardDatum>();
  pastActions = new List<BlackboardAction>();
  experts = new List<BlackboardExpert>();
}
```

3. Then, we can define the main class for each iteration, as shown in the following code:

```
public void RunIteration()
{
  // next steps
}
```

4. Next, we're going to add the required variables, as you'll see in the following code:

```
BlackboardExpert bestExpert = null;
float maxInsistence = 0f;
```

5. Then, we'll implement the loop for deciding which expert will run next, as demonstrated in the following code:

```
foreach (BlackboardExpert e in experts)
{
  float insistence = e.GetInsistence(this);
  if (insistence > maxInsistence)
  {
```

```
            maxInsistence = insistence;
            bestExpert = e;
        }
    }
```

6. Now, if there's an expert chosen, make it run, as shown in the following code:

```
if (bestExpert != null)
    bestExpert.Run(this);
```

How it works...

First, we put in place all the data structures for creating the blackboard system to be unopinionated, and flexible enough for reuse. Then, we put in place the blackboard, and the main loop for deciding which expert will run next. It's pretty similar to the behavior-blending algorithm by priority, developed in `Chapter 12`, *Behaviors – Intelligent Movement*, but it's applied to solving a problem. Each expert computes how much it *thinks* that their opinion is important, and the most relevant one takes its turn to solve the problem. It's important to define the range of values returning from the `GetInsistence` function.

There's more...

We need to implement our own member functions by overriding the member functions from the `Expert` class. It's important to note that it's up to each expert to read and write the blackboard entries in the `GetInsistence` function. Then, it's time to execute actions during the `Run` member function. If the experts' `Run` member functions are computationally expensive, it's better to handle them via coroutines.

Finally, this could be revisited on each project by defining the blackboard as the game state, on which each expert is able to read and write data. Just keep in mind the priority part of the algorithm for it to run as expected.

Experimenting with Unity's animation state machine

We usually see a lot of things going on in Unity's animation state machine graph when we work alongside artists focused on animations, or when we use our own if we have a thing for this discipline; however, it's uncommon seeing things happening in code on top of it. We usually change states via the MonoBehaviour script, and deal with the behaviors in a separate manner.

In this recipe, we will use some of the basic movement behaviors created in `Chapter 12`, *Behaviors – Intelligent Movement*, as they are, and we will make our animator control their status.

Getting ready

This recipe doesn't cover the setting up of the animations in the **Animator** window. It's up to the reader to set them up. We will focus on the required steps for leveraging the power of the built-in finite-state machine to control our agent.

How to do it...

Let's set everything up first:

1. First, create a new **Animator Controller** using the **Create** button in the **Project** window, as shown in the following screenshot:

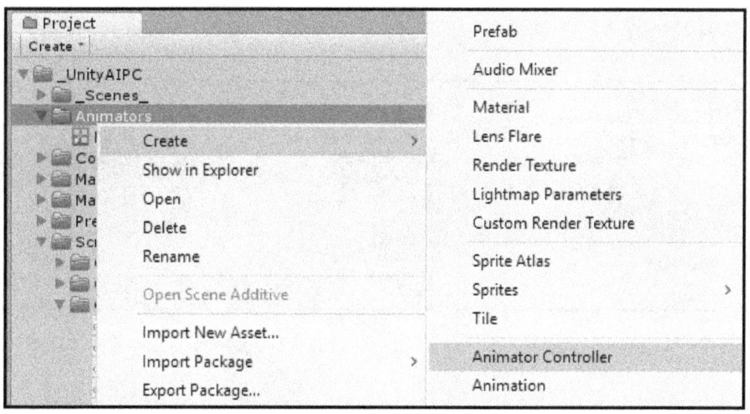

2. Next, create a new default state called **Wandering**.
3. Then, create a new state called **Pursuing**.
4. Next, connect both states to each other, and back, with two transitions, as you'll see in the following screenshot:

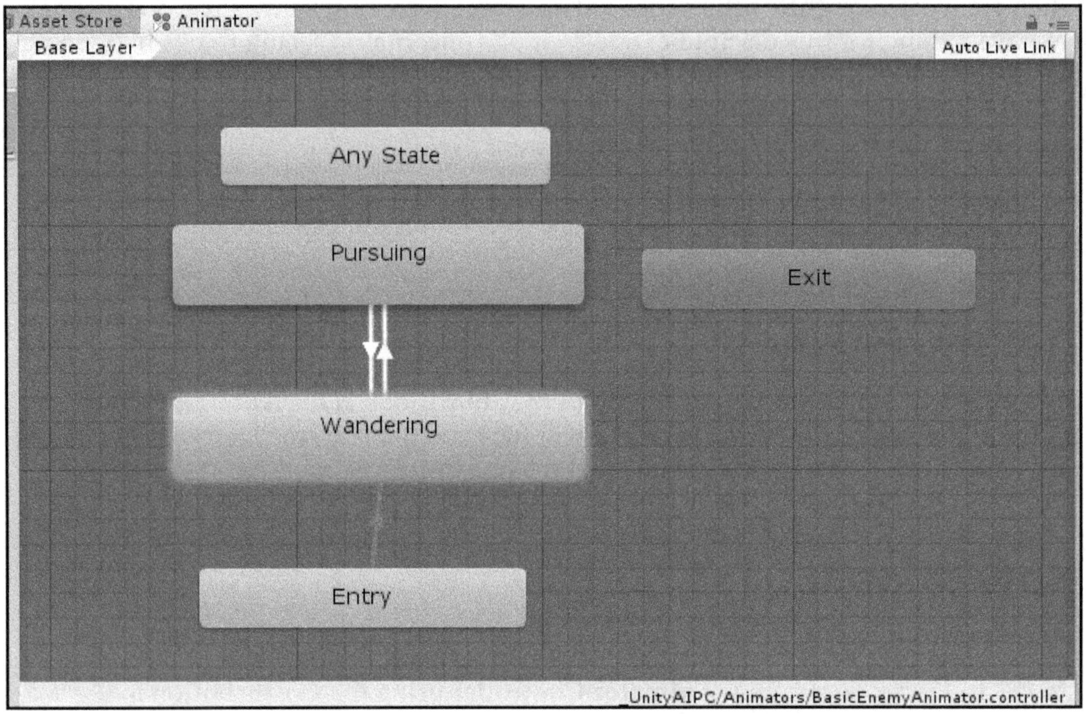

5. Now, we create two trigger parameters: `Pursue` and `Wander`, as shown in the following screenshot:

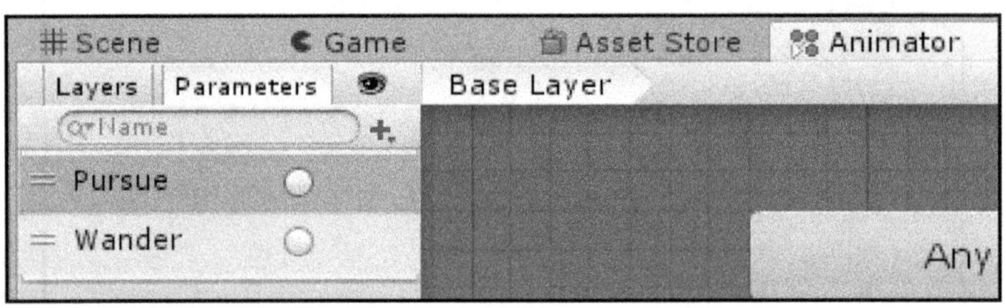

6. Next, assign the `Wander` parameter to the set of conditions in the **Pursuing -> Wandering** transition, as demonstrated in the following screenshot:

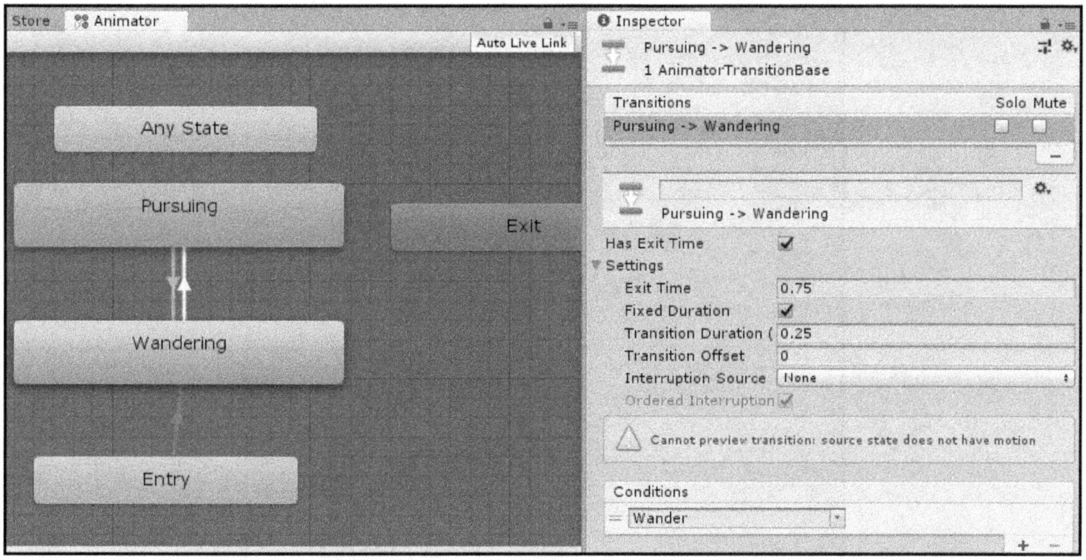

7. Next, make the inverse assignment in the **Wandering -> Pursuing** transition.

8. Then, we need to create a script behavior on the `Wander` state called `AFSMWandering`, as you can see in the following screenshot:

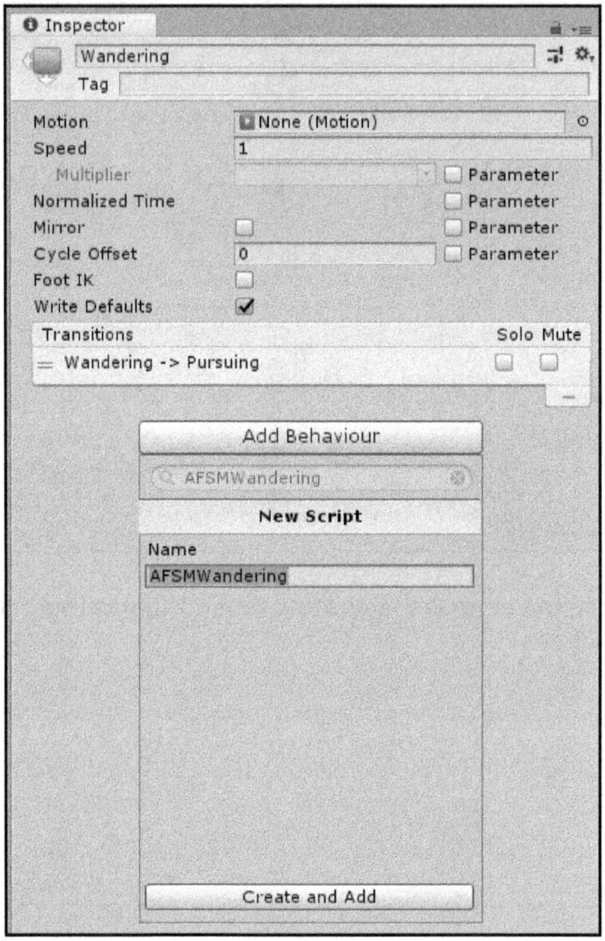

9. We then create a script behavior on the `Pursue` state called `AFSMPursue`, using the preceding method.
10. Next, create a new **GameObject** called `Wanderer`, and attach the following components:
    - **Animator**
    - **Agent**
    - **Wander** (disabled)
    - **Seek** (disabled)

The following image shows what the game object should look like. See how it shows the components mentioned in the preceeding step:

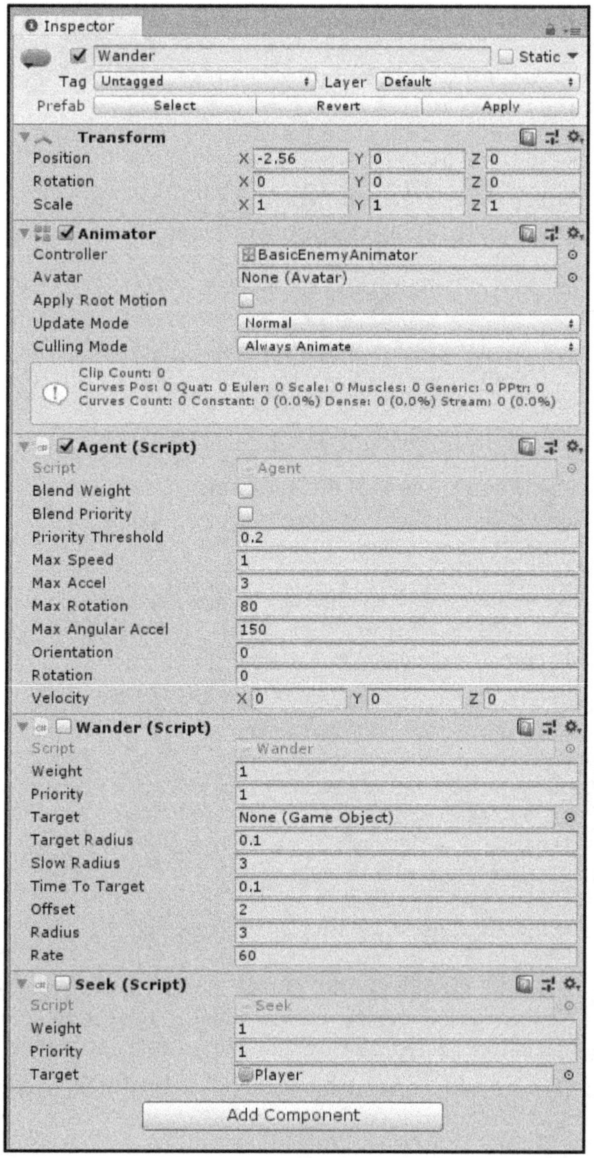

Animator, Agent, Wander, and Seek components attached to a game object

Now, we will implement the `Wander` state:

1. First, let's open the `AFSMWanderer.cs` file created previously.
2. Then, add the following member variables shown in the following code:

```
public float pursueDistance = 3f;
private Wander _wander;
private Seek _pursue;
```

3. Next, uncomment the `OnStateEnter` member function.
4. Then, we add code to it, as demonstrated in the following code:

```
AgentBehavior[] behaviors;
GameObject gameObject = animator.gameObject;
behaviors = gameObject.GetComponents<AgentBehavior>();
foreach (AgentBehavior b in behaviors)
  b.enabled = false;

_wander = gameObject.GetComponent<Wander>();
_pursue = gameObject.GetComponent<Seek>();
if (_wander == null || _pursue == null)
  return;
_wander.enabled = true;
animator.gameObject.name = "Wandering";
```

5. Uncomment the `OnStateUpdate` member function.
6. Then add code to it, as follows:

```
Vector3 targetPos, agentPos;
targetPos = _pursue.target.transform.position;
agentPos = animator.transform.position;
float distance = Vector3.Distance(targetPos, agentPos);
if (distance > pursueDistance)
  return;
animator.SetTrigger("Pursue");
```

Finally, we will implement a similar code in our `Pursue` state:

1. First, let's open the `AFSMPursue.cs` file created previously.
2. Next, add the member variables as shown in the following code:

```
public float stopDistance = 8f;
private Wander _wander;
private Seek _pursue;
```

3. Uncomment the `OnStateEnter` member function.

4. Next, add code as follows:

```
AgentBehavior[] behaviors;
GameObject gameObject = animator.gameObject;
behaviors = gameObject.GetComponents<AgentBehavior>();
foreach (AgentBehavior b in behaviors)
  b.enabled = false;

_wander = gameObject.GetComponent<Wander>();
_pursue = gameObject.GetComponent<Seek>();
if (_wander == null || _pursue == null)
  return;
_pursue.enabled = true;
animator.gameObject.name = "Seeking";
```

5. Uncomment the `OnStateUpdate` member function.
6. Finally, add the following code to it:

```
Vector3 targetPos, agentPos;
targetPos = _pursue.target.transform.position;
agentPos = animator.transform.position;
if (Vector3.Distance(targetPos, agentPos) < stopDistance)
  return;
animator.SetTrigger("Wander");
```

How it works...

We have the finite-state machine system that is the animator engine. First, we create the states and transitions that the agent will have. Second, we create our own behaviors deriving from the `StateMachineBehaviour` class, and attach them to the corresponding state. Also, we retrieve information needed from our game objects and script components to make decisions inside of each state. If required, we call the proper trigger to change states, thus changing the agent's behavior.

There's more...

By working on top of Unity's animation state machine, we gain a lot of flexibility. This way, we can reuse behaviors and decision making among several agents with minimum code and setup; however, what we gain in flexibility and modularity, we lose in script centralization. It is important to take that into account when working in teams, and even to remember that for debugging purposes (it happened while writing this book, LOL).

15
The New NavMesh API

In this chapter, you will learn how to make use of the new NavMesh API, through the following recipes:

- Setting up the NavMesh building components
- Creating and managing NavMesh for multiple types of agents
- Creating and updating NavMesh data at runtime
- Controlling the lifetime of the NavMesh instance
- Connecting multiple instances of NavMesh
- Creating dynamic NavMeshes with obstacles
- Implementing some behaviors using the NavMesh API

Introduction

The introduction of the NavMesh API, and its expansion, has opened a whole new world for AI and gameplay developers. It allows us to better tune our levels, even in real time, without the use of external tools (at least for a wide range of options).

In this chapter, we will learn how to manipulate this new set of tools that run on top of an already known and powerful navigation engine.

Setting up the NavMesh building components

Before manipulating our level and getting the hang of all the recipes, we need to download some assets from Unity's GitHub repository.

Getting ready

Some of us probably have some experience with the navigation engine that Unity has included for quite some time. It is important to have grasped the basics of creating a NavMesh by baking them via the **Navigation** window, and to understand the basics of the NavMeshAgent component.

How to do it...

To download the assets from the GitHub repository:

1. Go to the following web address using your preferred browser: `https://github.com/Unity-Technologies/NavMeshComponents`.
2. Go to the **releases** section, located under the **Code** tab as shown:

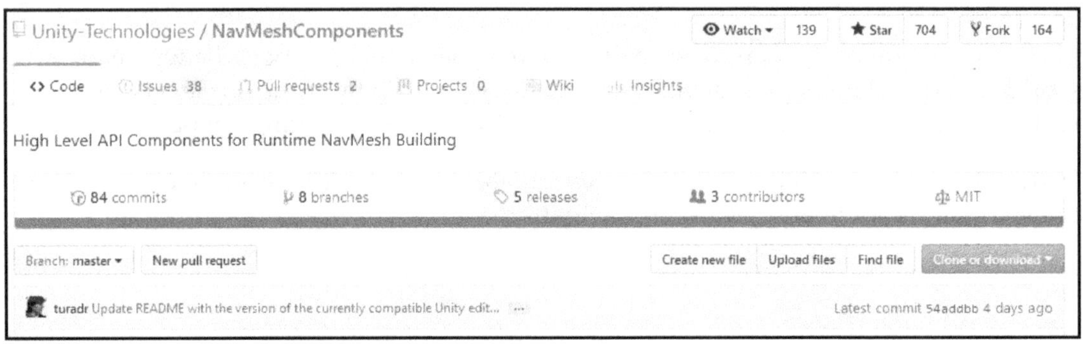

3. Download the compressed file to your computer, according to your version of Unity. In our case, it's `2018.1.0f2` at the time of writing.

4. Decompress the file outside the main project. We can see that it is a Unity project on its own:

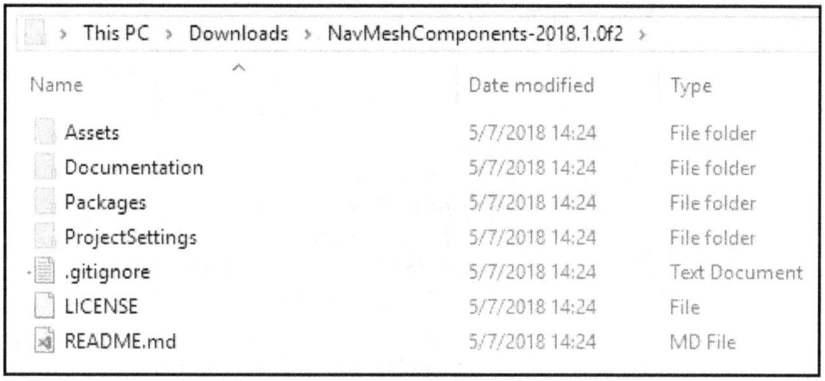

5. Navigate to the `Assets` folder, where we will see the following:

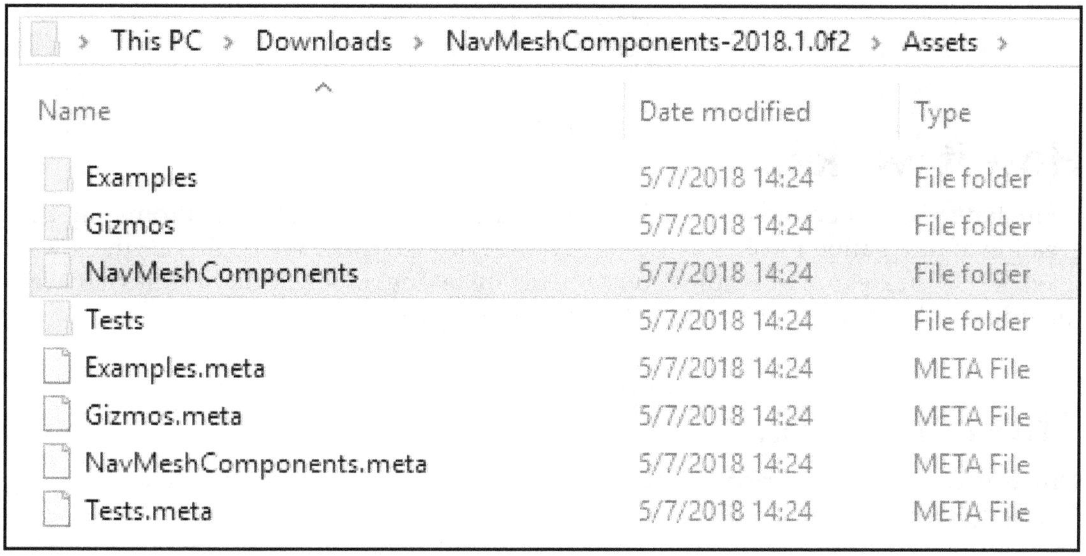

6. Copy or move the `NavMeshComponents` folder, with all its content, into your target project's `Asset` folder:

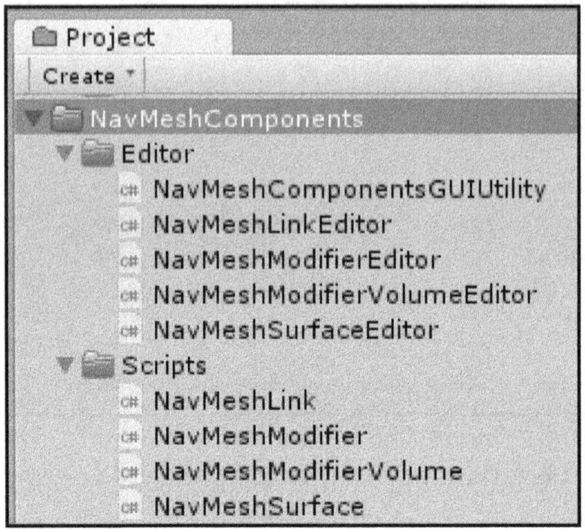

7. Let Unity reload the assets.

How it works...

By including this set of scripts, we have moved one step forward into automating the creation of navigation meshes as we please, even in real time. We could use the low-level API to create more complex components by taking a look at the scripts that are included in the zipped folder we just added to our project.

There's more...

One way to test that we carried out the previous steps successfully is to take the following steps:

1. Check there are no errors after asset reloading.
2. Create an empty game object, or select a random one for testing.
3. Go to the **Inspector** window and click on **Add Component**.
4. Write `NavMesh` in the search bar.

5. Make sure that all of the following components are listed:
    - **Nav Mesh Agent** (included in Unity)
    - **Nav Mesh Obstacle** (included in Unity)
    - **NavMeshLink**
    - **NavMeshModifier**
    - **NavMeshModifierVolume**
    - **NavMeshSurface**

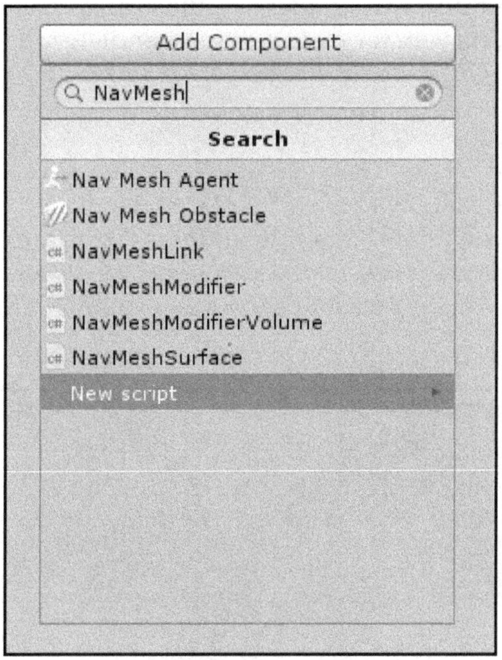

See also

For further information and references on the whole Navigation system, and the NavMesh building components, please refer to the official documentation available at these links:

- `https://docs.unity3d.com/Manual/Navigation.html`
- `https://docs.unity3d.com/Manual/NavMesh-BuildingComponents.html`

Creating and managing NavMesh for multiple types of agents

Our levels can have different areas that may change the behavior of our agents; say lava, a swamp, doors, and so on. In that case, we will need some kind of representation so that the agents are unable to pass those areas, change their speed, or simply devise a better route to avoid hazardous zones.

In this recipe, we will learn how to implement those areas in our level, so we have a more complex navigation mesh for our agents to handle better behavior.

Getting ready

Swamps, shallow water, and lava are easily placed in a level, and tagged on as a navigation area. However, doors are a little different. In this case, we will need to place an object below our door arc. It's even better if the door/arc mesh has a base mesh already. The following screenshot shows an example of what we're talking about:

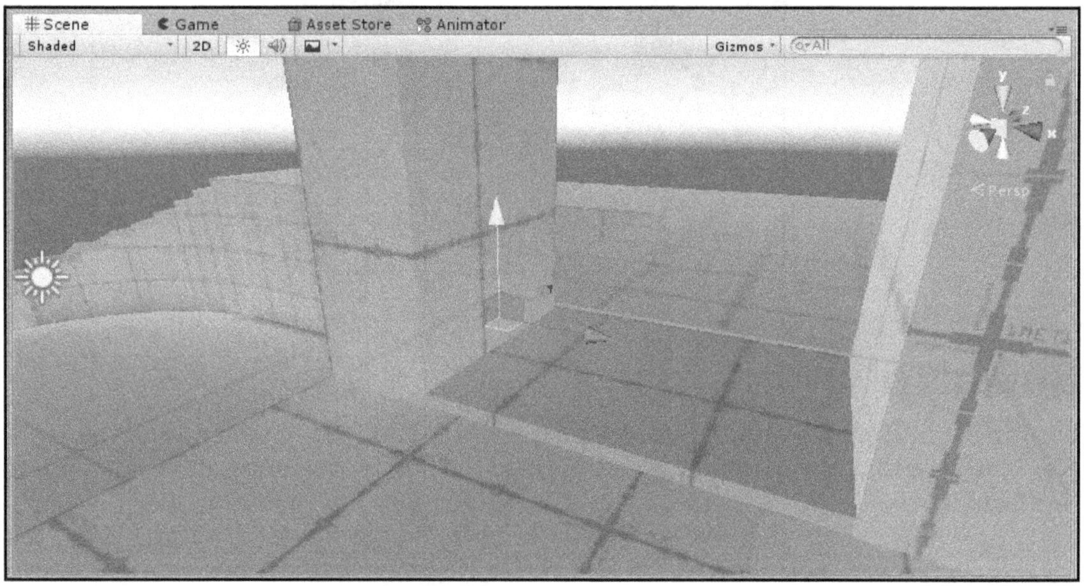

Door object below visual door for players

How to do it...

Now, we will learn how to make the proper changes to the NavMesh settings before baking:

1. Create the game world with different areas. In our case, we will have regular areas (walkable), doors, and swamps.
2. Open the **Navigation** window: **Menu** | **Window** | **Navigation**.
3. Go to the **Areas** tab.
4. Create a `Swamp` area with cost `6`.
5. Create a `Door` area with cost `2`.

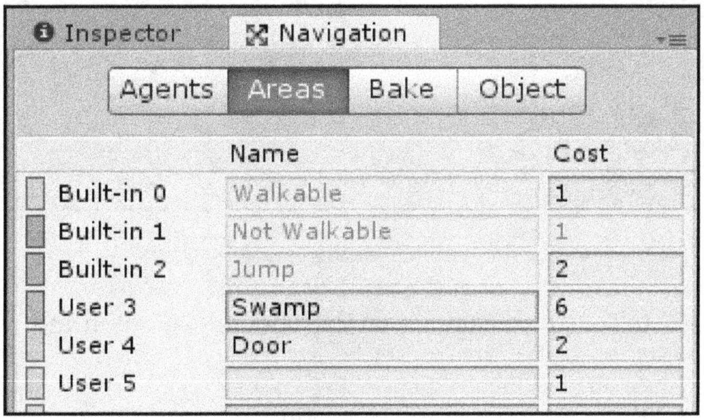

6. Select the objects that will behave like swamps.
7. Go to the **Navigation** window, and select the **Objects** tab.
8. Change the **Navigation Area** value to **Swamp**.
9. Select the objects that will behave like doors.
10. Go to the **Navigation** window, and select the **Objects** tab.
11. Change the **Navigation Area** value to **Door**.

12. Bake the NavMesh:

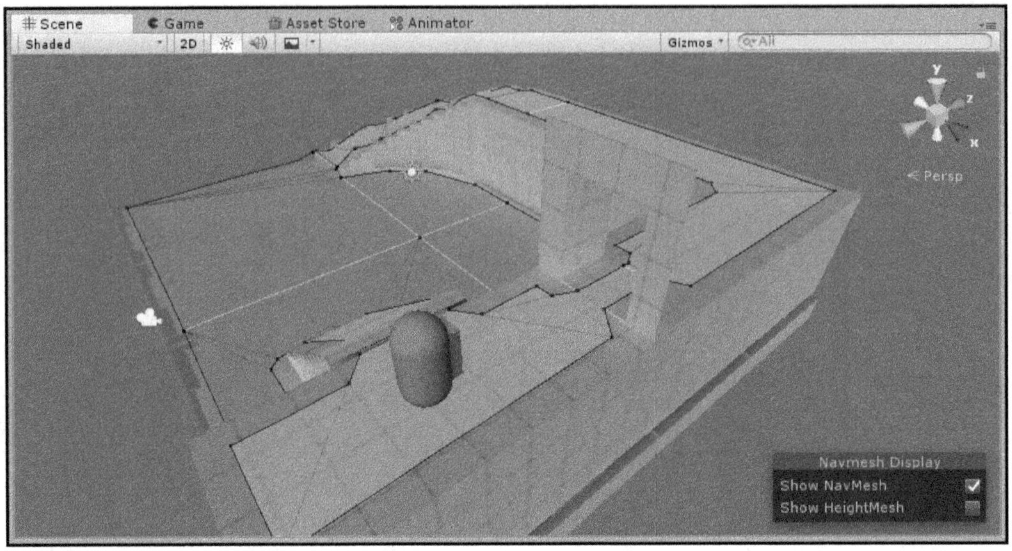

Resulting baked NavMesh

Then, we need to set up the agents so they behave as intended with the designated areas:

1. Add the agent object to the scene.
2. Add the **NavMesh** component to the object.
3. Go to the **Inspector** window.
4. Select the available areas that the agent can traverse. In our case, deselect the **Door** area mask:

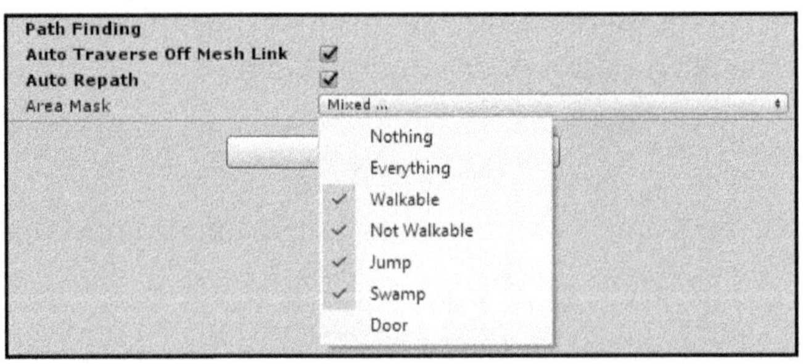

NavMeshAgent configuration for enemies that cannot walk through doors

How it works...

As seen in the preceding section, the navigation mesh is divided into different areas thanks to our settings. When implementing the search algorithm for devising a path to the target location, the agent takes into account the weights we defined for each area. As stated in the documentation, Unity implements A*, so the agent takes the cheapest path. It also takes into account only the areas we selected. That's why we deselected the doors, so players can hide behind them and find refuge.

There's more...

We could also make use of the current area, so the agent behaves differently (changes speed, for example). In that case, we need to get to know the `SamplePathPostion` from the **NavMeshAgent** component.

Creating and updating NavMesh data at runtime

With the advent of procedural-generated content, more specifically levels, it becomes necessary to come up with techniques that enable us to adjust the navigation areas. This is also important when we have very dynamic levels that can be destroyed in real time in a non-scripted way.

Getting ready

It is important to have the `NavMeshComponents` directory in our project as shown in the previous recipe, *Setting up our project.*

Also, it is important to attach the **NavMeshSurface** component to all the parent objects we want to build the new navigation mesh with.

How to do it...

We will create a new component called **NavMeshBuilder**:

1. Create a new file called `NavMeshBuilder.cs`:

```
using UnityEngine;
using UnityEngine.AI;
using System.Collections;
using System.Collections.Generic;

public class NavMeshBuilder : MonoBehaviour
{
  // Next steps
}
```

2. Add a member variable for storing the navigation surfaces:

```
public NavMeshSurface[] surfaces;
```

3. Implement the method for building all the `NavMesh` at once:

```
public void Build()
{
  for (int i = 0; i < surfaces.Length; i++)
  {
    surfaces[i].BuildNavMesh();
  }
}
```

4. Implement the method for building all the `NavMesh` in between frames:

```
public IEnumerator BuildInFrames(System.Action eventHandler)
{
  for (int i = 0; i < surfaces.Length; i++)
  {
    surfaces[i].BuildNavMesh();
    yield return null;
  }
  if (eventHandler != null)
      eventHandler.Invoke();
}
```

How it works...

By importing the `NavMeshComponents` directory, we are able to manipulate meshes and their surfaces via the **NavMeshSurface** component, using their *up* vector to detect the movement areas.

In the second member function, we take advantage of the coroutines' system to avoid freezing our game in case a surface is too complex to handle fast. Also, we make use of the delegate system to trigger an event when all the navigation meshes have been built on all the surfaces.

Controlling the lifetime of the NavMesh instance

Occasionally, we need to create navigation on the go because the topology is unknown. This is crucial when dealing with procedural-generated levels. One of the options is to bake the NavMesh at runtime, as we learned before. However, it could be a problem if level topology is really big or complex. Luckily, the **NavMesh** components developed by Unity can help us with this task, taking a different approach.

In this recipe, we will learn how to create a NavMesh around an agent without a NavMesh volume, making use of the NavMesh components.

Getting started

It is important to have the `NavMeshComponents` directory in our project, as shown in the previous recipe, *Setting up our project*.

How to do it...

1. Create the game level with proper colliders on the floor and/or the terrain where the agent will navigate.
2. Create the agent object with the following components set up: **Capsule** or **Box Collider**, **Rigidbody**, and **NavMesh Agent**.

3. Create the `NMRealTimeBuilder` class:

```
using UnityEngine;
using UnityEngine.AI;
using System.Collections;
using System.Collections.Generic;
using NavMeshBuilder = UnityEngine.AI.NavMeshBuilder;

public class NMRealTimeBuilder : MonoBehaviour
{
  // next steps
}
```

4. Declare the required member variables:

```
public Transform agent;
public Vector3 boxSize = new Vector3(50f, 20f, 50f);
[Range(0.01f, 1f)]
public float sizeChange = 0.1f;
private NavMeshData navMesh;
private AsyncOperation operation;
private NavMeshDataInstance navMeshInstance;
private List<NavMeshBuildSource> sources = new
List<NavMeshBuildSource>();
```

5. Implement the `static` member function for comparing the difference between two cubes:

```
static private Vector3 Quantize(Vector3 a, Vector3 q)
{
  float x = q.x * Mathf.Floor(a.x/q.x);
  float y = q.y * Mathf.Floor(a.y/q.y);
  float z = q.z * Mathf.Floor(a.z/q.z);
  return new Vector3(x, y, z);
}
```

6. Implement the member function that makes use of the previous function:

```
private Bounds QuantizeBounds()
{
  Vector3 position = agent.transform.position;
  return new Bounds(Quantize(position, boxSize * sizeChange),
boxSize);
}
```

7. Define the member function for updating the `NavMesh` around the agent:

```
private void UpdateNavMesh(bool isAsync = false)
{
  // next step
}
```

8. Implement the member function declared before:

```
NavMeshSourceTag.Collect(ref sources);
NavMeshBuildSettings settings;
settings = NavMesh.GetSettingsByID(0);
Bounds bounds = QuantizeBounds();
if (isAsync)
  operation = NavMeshBuilder.UpdateNavMeshDataAsync(navMesh,
settings, sources, bounds);
else
 NavMeshBuilder.UpdateNavMeshData(navMesh, settings, sources,
bounds);
```

9. Implement the `Awake` member function:

```
private void Awake()
{
  if (agent == null)
    agent = transform;
}
```

10. Implement the `OnEnable` member function:

```
private void OnEnable()
{
  navMesh = new NavMeshData();
  navMeshInstance = NavMesh.AddNavMeshData(navMesh);
  UpdateNavMesh(false);
}
```

11. Implement the `OnDisable` member function:

```
private void OnDisable()
{
  navMeshInstance.Remove();
}
```

How it works...

We leverage the power of the **NavMesh** components to create a smaller component that helps us in building a custom NavMesh around the object.

We take the size of the box around our agent, and the required difference between the box around the previous frame and the current one. If that difference is greater than the percentage we declared in `sizeChange`, the `NavMeshBuilder` takes the new position, disposes of the previous navigation mesh, and creates a new one.

That way, we can have an unknown topology, but can navigate it with the same type of agent. Furthermore, it takes considerably less time because we're using the size variable (a `Vector3`) to create the bounds.

There's more...

The `NMRealTimeBuilder` component could be attached to the very agent game object or to a different one. That's why we implemented the `Awake` function.

Finally, we could use a mix between the recipe and some of the behaviors developed in `Chapter 12`, *Behaviors – Intelligent Movement*, by getting the direction of the target and then telling the agent to walk to the farthest point of the NavMesh in that direction.

Connecting multiple instances of NavMesh

We have learned how to build a NavMesh, but there are cases where levels are really complex to the point of needing to divide them in several sections; sometimes, this is because there are pitfalls or because we are loading our level programmatically.

Getting ready

It is important to work on top of objects that have at least one **NavMeshSurface** component attached.

How to do it...

We need to connect one **NavMeshSurface** component to another one:

1. Locate, via the editor or code, two **NavMeshSurface** components to connect
2. Add the **NavMeshLink** component to the object that will work as the origin
3. Select the agent type that will be able to use the connection
4. Set the **Start Point** and **End Point** values
5. Repeat the previous steps for every agent type for which you need to connect the nodes

How it works...

Imagine one **NavMeshSurface** component working as a big node in a graph. By using the **NavMeshLink** component, we add an edge between two nodes. It's worth noting that the coordinates in **Start Point** and **End Point** are relative to the object; thus, they move/rotate with the parent object.

There's more...

We might need some special actions between transitions, such as animations. Imagine a one-directional link between a ledge and the ground. We have the power to know exactly when the agent hits the link, and then we can play an animation.

One way to do this is by deactivating the **Auto Traverse Off-Mesh Links** option on the **NavMeshAgent** component, playing the animation, executing the physics, and continuing with the logic as planned.

Creating dynamic NavMeshes with obstacles

There are times when our levels have dynamic obstacles and we need the agent to avoid those obstacles as well. Let's imagine an MMORPG or a MOBA, where the minions from our hero also need to avoid obstacles in order to reach the target. We could implement a difficult algorithm to blend the navigation with the obstacle avoidance, or we could leverage the power of a dynamic NavMesh to get the same result, with little to no code disruption.

In this recipe, we will learn how to adapt a NavMesh to be dynamic and react to moving obstacles, so our agents can avoid them and reach the target successfully.

Getting ready

It is important to know how the NavMesh basics work, and how to build/bake a NavMesh.

How to do it...

1. Put the level in place.
2. Create an empty game object and call it `NavMesh`.
3. Add the **NavMeshSurface** component to the **NavMesh** object.
4. Hit **Bake**.
5. Select all the obstacles.
6. Add the **Nav Mesh Obstacle** component to them.
7. Check the **Carve** option in the component.
8. Select the dynamic obstacles.
9. Uncheck the **Carve Only Stationary** option.
10. Configure each obstacle as needed, using the other options in the component.

How it works...

After baking the initial navigation mesh, the whole system takes into account all the obstacles in the scene and carves the areas around the obstacles in order to fine-tune the available navigation area. Besides, the navigation system keeps track of the dynamic obstacles' transformations (the ones with the **Carve Only Stationary** option unchecked) in order to recalculate the navigation area as needed.

There's more...

The aforementioned process is definitely not performance friendly, and works best in cases where we don't know for sure the topology, such as in procedural-generated levels. Although we put in place the example with a known level, we can rely on prefabs and programming to recreate most of the previous steps and apply them in a procedural-generated level.

On the other hand, if we know for sure the level's layout and want to improve performance, we could leave the **Carve** option unchecked in the **Nav Mesh Obstacle** component, and play with the obstacle avoidance parameters (found in the **Nav Mesh Agent** component) until we get a result that satisfies our needs.

Finally, we could just play around with a mixed method to find a balance between performance and experience, selecting key obstacles to be avoided with our "good enough" parameters and other obstacles that affect the navigation mesh in real time.

See also

For more details on dynamic navigation meshes, please refer to the official Unity video found at `https://unity3d.com/learn/tutorials/topics/navigation/making-it-dynamic`.

Implementing some behaviors using the NavMesh API

In `Chapter 12`, *Behaviors – Intelligent Movement*, we learned about different types of movement for our agents. We can implement some of them in a different way using the NavMesh API and the **NavMeshAgent** component. Thus, we'll be able to prototype similar behaviors in a faster, cleaner, and more Unity-ish way.

We will learn how to implement the patrolling behavior so that we can have a different angle and get ideas on how to fast-prototype different behaviors beyond the basic flow.

Getting ready

It is important to have grasped the basics of NavMesh and baking and handling the **NavMeshAgent** component before working on this recipe.

How to do it...

We will create a patrol behavior component to be used along with a **NavMeshAgent** component:

1. Create a script named `NMPatrol.cs`, and include the `NavMeshAgent` as a required component:

```
using UnityEngine;
using UnityEngine.AI;

[RequireComponent(typeof(NavMeshAgent))]
public class NMPatrol : MonoBehaviour
{
  // next steps
}
```

2. Add the member variables required:

```
public float pointDistance = 0.5f;
public Transform[] patrolPoints;
private int currentPoint = 0;
private NavMeshAgent agent;
```

3. Create a function for finding the closest patrol point in the array:

```
private int FindClosestPoint()
{
  // next step
}
```

4. Add the internal variables required:

```
int index = -1;
float distance = Mathf.Infinity;
int i;
Vector3 agentPosition = transform.position;
Vector3 pointPosition;
```

5. Implement the loop for finding the closest point:

```
for (i = 0; i < patrolPoints.Length; i++)
{
  pointPosition = patrolPoints[i].position;
  float d = Vector3.Distance(agentPosition, pointPosition);
  if (d < distance)
  {
    index = i;
    distance = d;
  }
}
return index;
```

6. Implement the function for updating the agent's destination point:

```
private void GoToPoint(int next)
{
  if (next < 0 || next >= patrolPoints.Length)
    return;
  agent.destination = patrolPoints[next].position;
}
```

7. Implement the `Start` function for initialization:

```
private void Start()
{
  agent = GetComponent<NavMeshAgent>();
  agent.autoBraking = false;
  currentPoint = FindClosestPoint();
  GoToPoint(currentPoint);
}
```

8. Implement the `Update` function:

```
private void Update()
{
  if (!agent.pathPending && agent.remainingDistance <
pointDistance)
    GoToPoint((currentPoint + 1) % patrolPoints.Length);
}
```

How it works...

We have a patrolling component that requires the navigation agent controller to work as intended. First, we calculate the closest point to the agent and move it to that position. After that, we use the `pointDistance` value to make the agent aware that it needs to move to the next point in the loop. Finally, we use the modulo operation to get the next patrol point without too much validation and just keep increasing the number of the current point.

There's more...

We need to take into account the order in which we put the patrol points in the array, so that they work as intended. Also, we could work on this a little bit by creating a function for deciding what the next patrol point will be. This will come in handy if we decide to keep improving the patrolling behavior according to our game's requirements:

```
private int CalculateNextPoint()
{
  return (currentPoint + 1) % patrolPoints.Length;
}

private void Update()
{
  if (!agent.pathPending && agent.remainingDistance < pointDistance)
    GoToPoint(CalculateNextPoint());
}
```

16
Coordination and Tactics

In this chapter, you will learn the following recipes:

- Handling formations
- Extending A* for coordination: A*mbush
- Introducing waypoints by making a manual selector
- Analyzing waypoints by height
- Analyzing waypoints by cover and visibility
- Creating waypoints automatically
- Exemplifying waypoints for decision making
- Implementing influence maps
- Improving influence with map flooding
- Improving influence with convolution filters
- Building a fighting circle

Introduction

As we will see, this is not a chapter focused on a sole subject, but rather a chapter that has its own original recipes and also draws on previous recipes in order to create new or improved techniques.

In this chapter, we will learn different recipes for coordinating different agents as a whole organism, such as formations and techniques that allow us to make tactical decisions based on graphs (such as waypoints) and influence maps. These techniques use different elements from the previous chapters and recipes, especially from graph construction and path-finding algorithms found in `Chapter 13`, *Navigation*.

Handling formations

This is a key algorithm for creating flocks or a group of military agents. It is designed to be flexible enough to give you the chance to create your own formations.

The end result of this recipe is having a set of target positions and rotations for each agent in the formation. Then, it is up to you to create the necessary algorithms to move the agent to the previous targets.

> We can use the movement algorithms learned in `Chapter 12`, *Behaviors – Intelligent Movement*, in order to target these positions.

Getting ready

We will need to create three base classes that are the data types to be used by the high-level classes and algorithms. The `Location` class is very similar to the `Steering` class and is used to define a target position and rotation given the formation's anchor point and rotation. The `SlogAssignment` class is a data type to match a list's indices and agents. Finally, the `Character` class is a component to hold the target `Location` class.

The following is the code for the `Location` class:

```
using UnityEngine;
using System.Collections;

public class Location
{
    public Vector3 position;
    public Quaternion rotation;

    public Location ()
    {
```

```
        position = Vector3.zero;
        rotation = Quaternion.identity;
    }

    public Location(Vector3 position, Quaternion rotation)
    {
        this.position = position;
        this.rotation = rotation;
    }
}
```

The following is the code for the `SlotAssignment` class:

```
using UnityEngine;
using System.Collections;

public class SlotAssignment
{
    public int slotIndex;
    public GameObject character;

    public SlotAssignment()
    {
        slotIndex = -1;
        character = null;
    }
}
```

The following is the code for the `Character` class:

```
using UnityEngine;
using System.Collections;

public class Character : MonoBehaviour
{
    public Location location;

    public void SetTarget (Location location)
    {
        this.location = location;
    }
}
```

How to do it...

We will implement two classes—`FormationPattern` and `FormationManager`:

1. Create the `FormationPattern` pseudo-abstract class:

```
using UnityEngine;
using System.Collections;
using System.Collections.Generic;

public class FormationPattern: MonoBehaviour
{
    public int numOfSlots;
    public GameObject leader;
}
```

2. Implement the `Start` function:

```
void Start()
{
    if (leader == null)
        leader = transform.gameObject;
}
```

3. Define the function for getting the position for a given slot:

```
public virtual Vector3 GetSlotLocation(int slotIndex)
{
    return Vector3.zero;
}
```

4. Define the function for retrieving, if a given number of slots is supported by the formation:

```
public bool SupportsSlots(int slotCount)
{
    return slotCount <= numOfSlots;
}
```

5. Implement the function for setting an offset in the locations, if necessary:

```
public virtual Location GetDriftOffset(List<SlotAssignment>
slotAssignments)
{
    Location location = new Location();
    location.position = leader.transform.position;
    location.rotation = leader.transform.rotation;
```

```
        return location;
    }
```

6. Create the class for managing the formation:

```
using UnityEngine;
using System.Collections;
using System.Collections.Generic;

public class FormationManager : MonoBehaviour
{
    public FormationPattern pattern;
    private List<SlotAssignment> slotAssignments;
    private Location driftOffset;
}
```

7. Implement the `Awake` function:

```
void Awake()
{
    slotAssignments = new List<SlotAssignment>();
}
```

8. Define the function for updating the slot assignments given the list's order:

```
public void UpdateSlotAssignments()
{
    for (int i = 0; i < slotAssignments.Count; i++)
    {
        slotAssignments[i].slotIndex = i;
    }
    driftOffset = pattern.GetDriftOffset(slotAssignments);
}
```

9. Implement the function for adding a character to the formation:

```
public bool AddCharacter(GameObject character)
{
    int occupiedSlots = slotAssignments.Count;
    if (!pattern.SupportsSlots(occupiedSlots + 1))
        return false;
    SlotAssignment sa = new SlotAssignment();
    sa.character = character;
    slotAssignments.Add(sa);
    UpdateSlotAssignments();
    return true;
}
```

10. Implement the function for removing a character in the formation:

```
public void RemoveCharacter(GameObject agent)
{
    int index = slotAssignments.FindIndex(x =>
x.character.Equals(agent));
    slotAssignments.RemoveAt(index);
    UpdateSlotAssignments();
}
```

11. Implement the function for updating the slots:

```
public void UpdateSlots()
{
    GameObject leader = pattern.leader;
    Vector3 anchor = leader.transform.position;
    Vector3 slotPos;
    Quaternion rotation;
    rotation = leader.transform.rotation;
    foreach (SlotAssignment sa in slotAssignments)
    {
        // next step
    }
}
```

12. Finally, implement the `foreach` loop:

```
Vector3 relPos;
slotPos = pattern.GetSlotLocation(sa.slotIndex);
relPos = anchor;
relPos += leader.transform.TransformDirection(slotPos);
Location charDrift = new Location(relPos, rotation);
Character character = sa.character.GetComponent<Character>();
character.SetTarget(charDrift);
```

How it works...

The `FormationPattern` class contains the relative positions for a given slot. For example, a `CircleFormation` child class will implement the `GetSlotLocation` class, given the number of slots and its locations over 360 degrees. It is intended to be a basic class, so it is up to the manager to add a layer for permissions and rearrangement. That way, the designer can focus on simple formation scripting, deriving from the base class.

The `FormationManager` class, as stated earlier, handles the high-level layer and arranges the locations as it better fits the formation's needs and permissions. The calculations are based on top of the leader's position and rotation, and they apply the necessary transformations given the pattern's principles.

There's more...

It is worth mentioning that the `FormationManager` and `FormationPattern` classes are intended to be components of the same object. When the leader field in the manager is set to `null`, the leader is the object itself. This way, we could have a different leader object in order to have a clean inspector window and class modularity.

See also

For further information on the theory behind this recipe, you can refer to the following materials:

- `Chapter 12`, *Behaviors – Intelligent Movement*, in the recipe, *Arriving and Leaving*.
- Ian Millington's book, *Artificial Intelligence for Games*.

Extending A* for coordination – A*mbush

After learning how to implement A* for path finding, we will now use its power and flexibility to develop some kind of coordinated behavior in order to ambush the player. This algorithm is especially useful when we want an inexpensive solution for the aforementioned problem, and which also has ease of implementation.

This recipe sets the path for every agent, to be taken into account for ambushing a given vertex or point in the graph.

Getting ready

We need a special component for the agents called `Lurker`. This class will hold the paths that are to be used later in the navigation process.

The following is the code for the `Lurker` class:

```
using UnityEngine;
using System.Collections;
using System.Collections.Generic;

public class Lurker : MonoBehaviour
{
    [HideInInspector]
    public List<int> pathIds;
    [HideInInspector]
    public List<GameObject> pathObjs;

    void Awake()
    {
        if (pathIds == null)
            pathIds = new List<int>();
        if (pathObjs == null)
            pathObjs = new List<GameObject>();
    }
}
```

How to do it...

We will create the main function for setting the ambush path for all the agents and then the function for setting each agent's path:

1. Define the main function for the ambush:

```
public void SetPathAmbush(GameObject dstObj, List<Lurker>
lurkers)
{
    Vertex dst = GetNearestVertex(dstObj.transform.position);
    foreach (Lurker l in lurkers)
    {
        Vertex src = GetNearestVertex(l.transform.position);
        l.path = AStarMbush(src, dst, l, lurkers);
    }
}
```

2. Declare the function for finding each path:

```
public List<Vertex> AStarMbush(
        Vertex src,
        Vertex dst,
        Lurker agent,
        List<Lurker> lurkers,
        Heuristic h = null)
{   // next steps
}
```

3. Declare the necessary members for handling the extra cost of computations:

```
int graphSize = vertices.Count;
float[] extra = new float[graphSize];
float[] costs = new float[graphSize];
int i;
```

4. Initialize the regular cost and the extra cost variables:

```
for (i = 0; i < graphSize; i++)
{
    extra[i] = 1f;
    costs[i] = Mathf.Infinity;
}
```

5. Add the extra cost to each vertex that is contained in another agent's path:

```
foreach (Lurker l in lurkers)
{
    foreach (Vertex v in l.path)
    {
        extra[v.id] += 1f;
    }
}
```

6. Declare and initialize the variables for computing A*:

```
Edge[] successors;
int[] previous = new int[graphSize];
for (i = 0; i < graphSize; i++)
    previous[i] = -1;
previous[src.id] = src.id;
float cost = 0;
Edge node = new Edge(src, 0);
GPWiki.BinaryHeap<Edge> frontier = new
GPWiki.BinaryHeap<Edge>();
```

7. Start implementing the A* main loop:

```
frontier.Add(node);
while (frontier.Count != 0)
{
    if (frontier.Count == 0)
        return new List<GameObject>();
    // next steps
}
return new List<Vertex>();
```

8. Validate that the goal has already been reached, otherwise it's not worth computing the costs, and you'd be better off continuing with the usual A* algorithm:

```
node = frontier.Remove();
if (ReferenceEquals(node.vertex, dst))
    return BuildPath(src.id, node.vertex.id, ref previous);
int nodeId = node.vertex.id;
if (node.cost > costs[nodeId])
    continue;
```

9. Traverse the neighbors and check whether they have been visited:

```
successors = GetEdges(node.vertex);
foreach (Edge e in successors)
{
    int eId = e.vertex.id;
    if (previous[eId] != -1)
        continue;
    // next step
}
```

10. If they haven't been visited, add them to the `frontier`:

```
cost = e.cost;
cost += costs[dst.id];
cost += h(e.vertex, dst);
if (cost < costs[e.vertex.id])
{
    Edge child;
    child = new Edge(e.vertex, cost);
    costs[eId] = cost;
    previous[eId] = nodeId;
    frontier.Remove(e);
    frontier.Add(child);
}
```

How it works...

The A*mbush algorithm analyzes the path of every agent and increases the cost of that node. When an agent computes its path using A*, it is better to choose a different route than the one chosen by other agents, thus creating the sense of an ambush among the target positions.

There's more...

There is an easy-to-implement improvement over the algorithm, which leads to the P-A*mbush variation. Simply order the lurkers' list, from the closest to the farthest, and we should have a better result at almost no extra cost in computation. This is due to the fact that the ordering operation is handled just once, and could be easily implemented via a priority queue, retrieving it as a list to the main A*mbush algorithm with no additional changes.

Analyzing waypoints by height

This recipe lets us evaluate a waypoint according to its position. Strategically speaking, lower positions are at a disadvantage. In this case, we will use a flexible algorithm to get the quality of a waypoint, given the heights of its surroundings.

Getting ready

This recipe is simple enough, so there is no extra content to be aware of. The algorithm is flexible enough to receive a list of positions, which is given by the waypoints' neighbors or just the complete graph of waypoints. The surrounding's heuristic is kept outside for our perusal and it provides the game's specific design.

How to do it...

We will implement a function to evaluate a location given its height and surrounding points:

1. Declare the function for evaluating the quality:

```
public static float GetHeightQuality (Vector3 location,
Vector3[] surroundings)
```

```
{
    // next steps
}
```

2. Initialize the variables for handling the computation:

```
float maxQuality = 1f;
float minQuality = -1f;
float minHeight = Mathf.Infinity;
float maxHeight = Mathf.NegativeInfinity;
float height = location.y;
```

3. Traverse the surroundings in order to find the maximum and minimum heights:

```
foreach (Vector3 s in surroundings)
{
    if (s.y > maxHeight)
        maxHeight = s.y;
    if (s.y < minHeight)
        minHeight = s.y;
}
```

4. Compute the quality in the given range:

```
float quality = (height-minHeight) / (maxHeight - minHeight);
quality *= (maxQuality - minQuality);
quality += minQuality;
return quality;
```

How it works...

We traverse the list of surroundings to find the maximum and minimum width and then compute the location value in the range of `-1` to `1`. We could change this range to meet our game's design, or invert the importance of the height in the formula.

Analyzing waypoints by cover and visibility

When dealing with military games, especially FPSes, we need to define a waypoint value, by its capacity, to be a good cover point with maximum visibility for shooting or reaching other enemies visually. This recipe helps us to compute the waypoint's value given these parameters.

Getting ready

We need to create a function for checking whether a position is in the same room as the others:

```
public bool IsInSameRoom(Vector3 from, Vector3 location, string
tagWall = "Wall")
{
    RaycastHit[] hits;
    Vector3 direction = location - from;
    float rayLength = direction.magnitude;
    direction.Normalize();
    Ray ray = new Ray(from, direction);
    hits = Physics.RaycastAll(ray, rayLength);
    foreach (RaycastHit h in hits)
    {
        string tagObj = h.collider.gameObject.tag;
        if (tagObj.Equals(tagWall))
            return false;
    }
    return true;
}
```

How to do it...

We will create the function that computes the quality of the waypoint:

1. Define the function with its parameters:

```
public static float GetCoverQuality(
        Vector3 location,
        int iterations,
        Vector3 characterSize,
        float radius,
```

```
            float randomRadius,
            float deltaAngle)
{
    // next steps
}
```

2. Initialize the variable for handling the degrees of rotation, possible hits received, and valid visibility:

```
float theta = 0f;
int hits = 0;
int valid = 0;
```

3. Start the main loop for the iterations to be computed on this waypoint and return the computed value:

```
for (int i = 0; i < iterations; i++)
{
    // next steps
}
return (float)(hits / valid);
```

4. Create a random position near the waypoint's origin to see whether the waypoint is easily reachable:

```
Vector3 from = location;
float randomBinomial = Random.Range(-1f, 1f);
from.x += radius * Mathf.Cos(theta) + randomBinomial *
randomRadius;
from.y += Random.value * 2f * randomRadius;
from.z += radius * Mathf.Sin(theta) + randomBinomial *
randomRadius;
```

5. Check whether the random position is in the same room:

```
if (!IsInSameRoom(from, location))
    continue;
valid++;
```

6. Compute a position, about the size of our template character, around the waypoint:

```
Vector3 to = location;
to.x += Random.Range(-1f, 1f) * characterSize.x;
to.y += Random.value * characterSize.y;
to.z += Random.Range(-1f, 1f) * characterSize.z;
```

7. Cast a ray to the visibility value to check whether such a character will be visible:

```
Vector3 direction = to - location;
float distance = direction.magnitude;
direction.Normalize();
Ray ray = new Ray(location, direction);
if (Physics.Raycast(ray, distance))
    hits++;
theta = Mathf.Deg2Rad * deltaAngle;
```

How it works...

We create a number of iterations and then start putting random numbers around the waypoint to verify that it is reachable and hittable. After that, we compute a coefficient to determine its quality.

Creating waypoints automatically

Most of the time, waypoints are assigned manually by the game designer, but what happens if the level has been generated procedurally? We need to come up with an automated solution for our agents.

In this recipe, we will learn a technique called condensation that helps us deal with this problem, allowing the waypoints to compete with each other given their assigned values, meaning the relevant ones will prevail.

Getting ready

We will deal with static member functions. It is important that we know the use and value of static functions.

How to do it...

We will create the `Waypoint` class and add the methods for condensing the set of waypoints:

1. Create the `Waypoint` class, deriving from both `MonoBehaviour` and from the `IComparer` interface:

```
using UnityEngine;
using System.Collections;
using System.Collections.Generic;

public class Waypoint : MonoBehaviour, IComparer
{
  public float value;
  public List<Waypoint> neighbours;
}
```

2. Implement the `Compare` function from the interface:

```
public int Compare(object a, object b)
{
  Waypoint wa = (Waypoint)a;
  Waypoint wb = (Waypoint)b;
  if (wa.value == wb.value)
    return 0;
  if (wa.value < wb.value)
    return -1;
  return 1;
}
```

3. Implement the `static` function that checks whether an agent is able to reach one waypoint from the other:

```
public static bool CanMove(Waypoint a, Waypoint b)
{
  // implement your own behaviour for
  // deciding whether an agent can move
  // easily between two waypoints
  return true;
}
```

4. Define the member function for condensing the waypoints:

```
public static void CondenseWaypoints(List<Waypoint> waypoints,
float distanceWeight)
{
  // next steps
}
```

5. Initialize the required variables and sort the waypoints in descending order:

```
distanceWeight *= distanceWeight;
waypoints.Sort();
waypoints.Reverse();
List<Waypoint> neighbours;
```

6. Start the loop for processing each waypoint:

```
foreach (Waypoint current in waypoints)
{
  // next steps
}
```

7. Retrieve the waypoint neighbors, sort them, and start the loop for making them compete:

```
neighbours = new List<Waypoint>(current.neighbours);
neighbours.Sort();
foreach (Waypoint target in neighbours)
{
  if (target.value > current.value)
    break;
  if (!CanMove(current, target))
    continue;
  // next steps
}
```

8. Compute the target's position:

```
Vector3 deltaPos = current.transform.position;
deltaPos -= target.transform.position;
deltaPos = Vector3.Cross(deltaPos, deltaPos);
deltaPos *= distanceWeight;
```

9. Compute the target's overall value and decide whether it's worth keeping:

```
float deltaVal = current.value - target.value;
deltaVal *= deltaVal;
if (deltaVal < distanceWeight)
{
  neighbours.Remove(target);
  waypoints.Remove(target);
}
```

How it works...

We assign the `Waypoint` component to every node of the graph, or every node that is worth taking as a waypoint (because the condensation algorithm emphasizes performance).

The waypoints are ordered according to their relevance (such as the height to be used as a sniping or advantage location), and then their neighbors are checked to see which ones are going to be dismissed from the condensation. Naturally, the less valuable waypoints are kept to the end of the computation cycle.

There's more...

In the current implementation, the value member variable is an oversimplification. We know we could have several member variables with fuzzy values to determine diverse relevance points for every waypoint.

In that case, it's a good idea to synthesize all those calculations in an overall value, as presented here, or work in a better heuristic for determining the relevance of a waypoint over the others in the `Compare` implementation, so the sorting algorithm can work as expected.

See also

For further information on how to evaluate waypoints, please refer to the following recipes in this chapter:

- *Analyzing waypoints by height*
- *Analyzing waypoints by cover and visibility*

Exemplifying waypoints for decision making

Just as we learned in `Chapter 14`, *Decision Making*, evaluating a waypoint's value it is not flexible enough, but rather a more complex process. In this case, the solution is to apply techniques learned previously and incorporate them into the waypoint for tackling the problem.

The key idea behind this recipe is to add a condition to the node so that it can be evaluated, for example, using a decision tree and develop more complex heuristics for computing a waypoint's value.

Getting ready

It is important to read the recipe *Implementing a finite-state machine*, in `Chapter 14`, *Decision Making*, before diving in.

How to do it...

We will make a little adjustment to the `Waypoint` class:

1. Add a member variable to the `Waypoint` class:

    ```
    public Condition condition;
    ```

2. Assign the condition class to be used, for example `ConditionFloat`:

    ```
    condition = new ConditionFloat();
    ```

How it works...

The pseudo-abstract class `Condition`, which we learned about previously, has a member function called `Test`. This function evaluates whether a condition is met.

See also

For further information on decision making and conditions, please refer to the following recipe:

- `Chapter 14`, *Decision Making, Implementing a finite-state machine.*

Implementing influence maps

Another way to use graphs is to represent how much reach or influence an agent, or, in this case, a unit, has over an area of the world. In this context, influence is represented as the total area of a map covered by an agent, or a group of agents from the same party.

This is a key element for creating good AI decision mechanisms based on top of military presence in real-time simulation games, or games where it is important to know how much of the world is taken up by a group of agents, each representing a given faction.

Getting ready

This is a recipe that requires experience of graph building, so it is based on the general `Graph` class. That means that we will need to use a specific graph definition (no matter which one you prefer), or define our own methods to handle vertices and the neighbors' retrieval logic, as learned in `Chapter 13`, *Navigation*.

We will learn how to implement the specific algorithms for this recipe, which are based on top of the `Graph` class general functions and the `Vertex` class.

Finally, we will need a base Unity component for our agent and `Faction enum`.

The following is the code for the `Faction enum` and `Unit` classes. They can be written in the same file, which is called `Unit.cs`:

```
using UnityEngine;
using System.Collections;

public enum Faction
{
    // example values
    BLUE, RED
```

```
}

public class Unit : MonoBehaviour
{
    public Faction faction;
    public int radius = 1;
    public float influence = 1f;

    public virtual float GetDropOff(int locationDistance)
    {
        return influence;
    }
}
```

How to do it...

We will build the `VertexInfluence` and `InfluenceMap` classes, which are used for handling vertices and the graph, respectively:

1. Create the `VertexInfluence` class, deriving from `Vertex`:

```
using UnityEngine;
using System.Collections;
using System.Collections.Generic;

public class VertexInfluence : Vertex
{
    public Faction faction;
    public float value = 0f;
}
```

2. Implement the function for setting up values (it returns true if it was a success, and false otherwise):

```
public bool SetValue(Faction f, float v)
{
    bool isUpdated = false;
    if (v > value)
    {
        value = v;
        faction = f;
        isUpdated = true;
    }
    return isUpdated;
}
```

3. Create the `InfluenceMap` class deriving from `Graph` (or a more specific graph implementation):

```
using UnityEngine;
using System.Collections.Generic;

public class InfluenceMap : Graph
{
    public List<Unit> unitList;
    // works as vertices in regular graph
    GameObject[] locations;
}
```

4. Define the `Awake` function for initialization:

```
void Awake()
{
    if (unitList == null)
        unitList = new List<Unit>();
}
```

5. Implement the function for adding a unit on the map:

```
public void AddUnit(Unit u)
{
    if (unitList.Contains(u))
        return;
    unitList.Add(u);
}
```

6. Implement the function for removing a unit from the map:

```
public void RemoveUnit(Unit u)
{
    unitList.Remove(u);
}
```

7. Start building the function for computing the influence:

```
public void ComputeInfluenceSimple()
{
    VertexInfluence v;
    float dropOff;
    List<Vertex> pending = new List<Vertex>();
    List<Vertex> visited = new List<Vertex>();
    List<Vertex> frontier;
    Vertex[] neighbours;
```

```
        // next steps
    }
```

8. Continue by creating a loop for iterating over the list of units:

```
foreach(Unit u in unitList)
{
    Vector3 uPos = u.transform.position;
    Vertex vert = GetNearestVertex(uPos);
    pending.Add(vert);
    // next step
}
```

9. Finally, apply BFS-based code for spreading influence given the radius reach:

```
// BFS for assigning influence
for (int i = 1; i <= u.radius; i++)
{
    frontier = new List<Vertex>();
    foreach (Vertex p in pending)
    {
        if (visited.Contains(p))
            continue;
        visited.Add(p);
        v = p as VertexInfluence;
        dropOff = u.GetDropOff(i);
        v.SetValue(u.faction, dropOff);
        neighbours = GetNeighbours(vert);
        frontier.AddRange(neighbours);
    }
    pending = new List<Vertex>(frontier);
}
```

How it works...

The influence map graph works exactly as a general graph, as well as the influence-based vertex, because there are just a couple of extra parameters for mapping the influence across the graph. The most relevant part relies on the computation of the influence, and it is based on the BFS algorithm.

For each unit on the map, we spread its influence given the radius. When the computed influence (drop-off) is greater than the vertex original faction, the vertex faction is changed.

There's more...

The drop-off function should be tuned according to your specific game needs. We can define a smarter function with the following example code, using the `locationDistance` parameter:

```
public virtual float GetDropOff(int locationDistance)
{
    float d = influence / radius * locationDistance;
    return influence - d;
}
```

It is important to note that the `locationDistance` parameter is an integer indicating the distance measured in vertices.

Finally, we could avoid using factions and instead use a reference to the unit itself. That way, we could map the influence based on individual units, but we think it makes the most sense when thinking in terms of factions or teams.

See also

- `Chapter 13`, *Navigation*, and the *Representing the world with grids* and *Finding the shortest path in a grid with BFS* recipes

Improving influence with map flooding

The previous influence computation is good when dealing with simple influence that is based on individual units helping a faction. However, this could lead to holes in the map instead of covering a whole section. One technique to approach that problem is flooding; it's a technique based on Dijkstra's algorithm.

Getting ready

In this recipe, we will combine two concepts into a class. First, tagging a vertex to represent that fact that it's owned by a faction; second, the drop-off function from units. Such a class is called `Guild`. This is a component to be attached to the game object; one component for each desired guild:

```
using UnityEngine;
using System;
using System.Collections;

public class Guild : MonoBehaviour
{
    public string guildName;
    public int maxStrength;
    public GameObject baseObject;
    [HideInInspector]
    public int strenghth

    public virtual void Awake()
    {
        strength = maxStrength;
    }
}
```

It also needs a drop-off function. This time, however, we wanted to create an example using Euclidean distance:

```
public virtual float GetDropOff(float distance)
{
    float d = Mathf.Pow(1 + distance, 2f);
    return strenght / d;
}
```

Finally, we will need a `GuildRecord` data type for the Dijkstra algorithm's representation of a node:

1. Create the `GuildRecord` struct, deriving from the `IComparable` interface:

```
using UnityEngine;
using System.Collections;
using System;

public struct GuildRecord : IComparable<GuildRecord>
{
    public Vertex location;
    public float strength;
```

```
        public Guild guild;
    }
```

2. Implement the Equal functions:

```
public override bool Equals(object obj)
{
    GuildRecord other = (GuildRecord)obj;
    return location == other.location;
}

public bool Equals(GuildRecord o)
{
    return location == o.location;
}
```

3. Implement the required IComparable functions:

```
public override int GetHashCode()
{
    return base.GetHashCode();
}

public int CompareTo(GuildRecord other)
{
    if (location == other.location)
        return 0;
    // the substraction is inverse for
    // having a descending binary heap
    return (int)(other.strength - strength);
}
```

How to do it...

Now, we just need to modify some files and add functionalities:

1. Include the guild member in the VertexInfluence class:

```
public Guild guild;
```

2. Include new members in the InfluenceMap class:

```
public float dropOffThreshold;
private  Guild[] guildList;
```

3. Also, in `InfluenceMap`, add the following line to the `Awake` function:

```
guildList = gameObject.GetComponents<Guild>();
```

4. Create the map flooding function:

```
public List<GuildRecord> ComputeMapFlooding()
{
}
```

5. Declare the principal necessary variables:

```
GPWiki.BinaryHeap<GuildRecord> open;
open = new GPWiki.BinaryHeap<GuildRecord>();
List<GuildRecord> closed;
closed = new List<GuildRecord>();
```

6. Add the initial nodes for each guild in the priority queue:

```
foreach (Guild g in guildList)
{
    GuildRecord gr = new GuildRecord();
    gr.location = GetNearestVertex(g.baseObject);
    gr.guild = g;
    gr.strength = g.GetDropOff(0f);
    open.Add(gr);
}
```

7. Create the main Dijkstra iteration and return the assignments:

```
while (open.Count != 0)
{
    // next steps here
}
return closed;
```

8. Take the first node in the queue and get its neighbors:

```
GuildRecord current;
current = open.Remove();
GameObject currObj;
currObj = GetVertexObj(current.location);
Vector3 currPos;
currPos = currObj.transform.position;
List<int> neighbours;
neighbours = GetNeighbors(current.location);
```

9. Create the loop for computing each neighbor, and put the current node in the closed list:

```
foreach (int n in neighbours)
{
    // next steps here
}
closed.Add(current);
```

10. Compute the drop-off from the current vertex, and check whether it is worth trying to change the guild assigned:

```
GameObject nObj = GetVertexObj(n);
Vector3 nPos = nObj.transform.position;
float dist = Vector3.Distance(currPos, nPos);
float strength = current.guild.GetDropOff(dist);
if (strength < dropOffThreshold)
    continue;
```

11. Create an auxiliary `GuildRecord` node with the current vertex's data:

```
GuildRecord neighGR = new GuildRecord();
neighGR.location = n;
neighGR.strength = strength;
VertexInfluence vi;
vi = nObj.GetComponent<VertexInfluence>();
neighGR.guild = vi.guild;
```

12. Check the closed list and validate the time when a new assignment must be avoided:

```
if (closed.Contains(neighGR))
{
    int location = neighGR.location;
    int index = closed.FindIndex(x => x.location == location);
    GuildRecord gr = closed[index];
    if (gr.guild.name != current.guild.name
            && gr.strength < strength)
        continue;
}
```

13. Check the priority queue for the same reasons:

```
else if (open.Contains(neighGR))
{
    bool mustContinue = false;
    foreach (GuildRecord gr in open)
    {
        if (gr.Equals(neighGR))
        {
            mustContinue = true;
            break;
        }
    }
    if (mustContinue)
        continue;
}
```

14. Create a new `GuildRecord` assignment and add it to the priority queue when everything else fails:

```
else
{
    neighGR = new GuildRecord();
    neighGR.location = n;
}
neighGR.guild = current.guild;
neighGR.strength = strength;
```

15. Add it to the priority queue if necessary:

```
open.Add(neighGR);
```

How it works...

The algorithm traverses the whole graph, starting from the guilds' positions. Given our previous inverse subtraction, the priority queue always starts from the strongest node and computes the assignment until it reaches a value below the `dropOffThreshold`. It also checks for ways to avoid a new assignment if the conditions are not met, if the vertex value is greater than the current strength, or if the guild assignment is the same.

See also

- The *Introducing influence maps* recipe
- `Chapter 13`, *Navigation*, and the *Finding the shortest path with Dijkstra* recipe

Improving influence with convolution filters

Convolution filters are usually applied in image processing software, but we can use the same principles to change a grid's influence given a unit's value and its surroundings. In this recipe, we will look at a couple of algorithms to modify a grid using matrix filters.

Getting ready

It is important to have grasped the concept of an influence map before implementing this recipe so that you can understand the context in which it is applied.

How to do it...

We will implement the `Convolve` function:

1. Declare the `Convolve` function:

```
public static void Convolve(
        float[,] matrix,
        ref float[,] source,
        ref float[,] destination)
{
    // next steps
}
```

2. Initialize the variables for handling the computations and the traversal of arrays:

```
int matrixLength = matrix.GetLength(0);
int size = (int)(matrixLength - 1) / 2;
int height = source.GetLength(0);
int width = source.GetLength(1);
int I, j, k, m;
```

3. Create the first loop for iterating over the destination and source grids:

```
for (i = 0; i < width-- size; i++)
{
    for (j = 0; j < height-- size; j++)
    {
        // next steps
    }
}
```

4. Implement the second loop for iterating over the filter matrix:

```
destination[i, j] = 0f;
for (k = 0; k < matrixLength; k++)
{
    for (m = 0; m < matrixLength; m++)
    {
        int row = i + k-- size;
        int col = j + m-- size;
        float aux = source[row, col] * matrix[k,m];
        destination[i, j] += aux;
    }
}
```

How it works...

We create a new grid to be swapped with the original source grid following the application of the matrix filter on each position. Then, we iterate over each position that is to be created as a destination grid and compute its result, taking the original grid's value and applying the matrix filter to it.

It is important to note that the matrix filter must be an odd-square array for the algorithm to work as expected.

There's more...

The following `ConvolveDriver` function helps us iterate using the `Convolve` function implemented previously:

1. Declare the `ConvolveDriver` function:

```
public static void ConvolveDriver(
        float[,] matrix,
        ref float[,] source,
        ref float[,] destination,
        int iterations)
{
    // next steps
}
```

2. Create the auxiliary variables for holding the grids:

```
float[,] map1;
float[,] map2;
int i;
```

3. Swap the maps, regardless of whether iterations are odd or even:

```
if (iterations % 2 == 0)
{
    map1 = source;
    map2 = destination;
}
else
{
    destination = source;
    map1 = destination;
    map2 = source;
}
```

4. Apply the previous function during the iterations and swap the maps:

```
for (i = 0; i < iterations; i++)
{
    Convolve(matrix, ref source, ref destination);
    float[,] aux = map1;
    map1 = map2;
    map2 = aux;
}
```

See also

- The *Introducing influence maps* recipe

Building a fighting circle

This recipe is based on the Kung-Fu Circle algorithm devised for the game *Kingdoms of Amalur: Reckoning*. Its purpose is to offer an intelligent way for enemies to approach a given player and set attacks on it. It is very similar to the formation recipe, but it uses a stage manager that handles approach and attack permissions based on enemy weights and attack weights. It is also implemented so that the manager is capable of handling a list of fighting circles; this is especially aimed at multiplayer games.

Getting ready

Before implementing the fighting circle algorithm, it is important to create some components that accompany the technique. First, the `Attack` class is a pseudo-abstract class for creating general-purpose attacks for each enemy, and it works as a template for the custom attacks in our game. Second, we need the `Enemy` class, which is the holder of the enemy's logic and requests. As we will see, the `Enemy` class holds a list of the different attack components found in the game object.

The code for the `Attack` class is as follows:

```
using UnityEngine;
using System.Collections;

public class Attack : MonoBehaviour
{
    public int weight;

    public virtual IEnumerator Execute()
    {
        // your attack behaviour here
        yield break;
    }
}
```

The steps to build the `Enemy` component are as follows:

1. Create the `Enemy` class:

```
using UnityEngine;
using System.Collections;

public class Enemy : MonoBehaviour
{
    public StageManager stageManager;
    public int slotWeight;
    [HideInInspector]
    public int circleId = -1;
    [HideInInspector]
    public bool isAssigned;
    [HideInInspector]
    public bool isAttacking;
    [HideInInspector]
    public Attack[] attackList;
}
```

2. Implement the `Start` function:

```
void Start()
{
    attackList = gameObject.GetComponents<Attack>();
}
```

3. Implement the function for assigning a target fighting circle:

```
public void SetCircle(GameObject circleObj = null)
{
    int id = -1;
    if (circleObj == null)
    {
        Vector3 position = transform.position;
        id = stageManager.GetClosestCircle(position);
    }
    else
    {
        FightingCircle fc;
        fc = circleObj.GetComponent<FightingCircle>();
        if (fc != null)
            id = fc.gameObject.GetInstanceID();
    }
    circleId = id;
}
```

4. Define the function for requesting a slot from the manager:

```
public bool RequestSlot()
{
    isAssigned = stageManager.GrantSlot(circleId, this);
    return isAssigned;
}
```

5. Define the function for releasing a slot from the manager:

```
public void ReleaseSlot()
{
    stageManager.ReleaseSlot(circleId, this);
    isAssigned = false;
    circleId = -1;
}
```

6. Implement the function for requesting an attack from the list (the order is the same as in the inspector):

```
public bool RequestAttack(int id)
{
    return stageManager.GrantAttack(circleId, attackList[id]);
}
```

7. Define the virtual function for the attack behavior:

```
public virtual IEnumerator Attack()
{
    // TODO
    // your attack behaviour here
    yield break;
}
```

How to do it...

Now, we implement the `FightingCircle` and `StageManager` classes:

1. Create the `FightingCircle` class along with its member variables:

```
using UnityEngine;
using System.Collections;
using System.Collections.Generic;

public class FightingCircle : MonoBehaviour
{
```

```
    public int slotCapacity;
    public int attackCapacity;
    public float attackRadius;
    public GameObject player;
    [HideInInspector]
    public int slotsAvailable;
    [HideInInspector]
    public int attackAvailable;
    [HideInInspector]
    public List<GameObject> enemyList;
    [HideInInspector]
    public Dictionary<int, Vector3> posDict;
}
```

2. Implement the `Awake` function for initialization:

```
void Awake()
{
    slotsAvailable = slotCapacity;
    attackAvailable = attackCapacity;
    enemyList = new List<GameObject>();
    posDict = new Dictionary<int, Vector3>();
    if (player == null)
        player = gameObject;
}
```

3. Define the `Update` function so that the slots' positions get updated:

```
void Update()
{
    if (enemyList.Count == 0)
        return;
    Vector3 anchor = player.transform.position;
    int i;
    for (i = 0; i < enemyList.Count; i++)
    {
        Vector3 position = anchor;
        Vector3 slotPos = GetSlotLocation(i);
        int enemyId = enemyList[i].GetInstanceID();
        position +=
player.transform.TransformDirection(slotPos);
        posDict[enemyId] = position;
    }
}
```

4. Implement the function for adding enemies to the circle:

```
public bool AddEnemy(GameObject enemyObj)
{
    Enemy enemy = enemyObj.GetComponent<Enemy>();
    int enemyId = enemyObj.GetInstanceID();
    if (slotsAvailable < enemy.slotWeight)
        return false;
    enemyList.Add(enemyObj);
    posDict.Add(enemyId, Vector3.zero);
    slotsAvailable -= enemy.slotWeight;
    return true;
}
```

5. Implement the function for removing enemies from the circle:

```
public bool RemoveEnemy(GameObject enemyObj)
{
    bool isRemoved = enemyList.Remove(enemyObj);
    if (isRemoved)
    {
        int enemyId = enemyObj.GetInstanceID();
        posDict.Remove(enemyId);
        Enemy enemy = enemyObj.GetComponent<Enemy>();
        slotsAvailable += enemy.slotWeight;
    }
    return isRemoved;
}
```

6. Implement the function for swapping enemies' positions in the circle:

```
public void SwapEnemies(GameObject enemyObjA, GameObject
enemyObjB)
{
    int indexA = enemyList.IndexOf(enemyObjA);
    int indexB = enemyList.IndexOf(enemyObjB);
    if (indexA != -1 && indexB != -1)
    {
        enemyList[indexB] = enemyObjA;
        enemyList[indexA] = enemyObjB;
    }
}
```

7. Define the function for getting an enemy's spatial position according to the circle:

```
public Vector3? GetPositions(GameObject enemyObj)
{
```

```
        int enemyId = enemyObj.GetInstanceID();
        if (!posDict.ContainsKey(enemyId))
            return null;
        return posDict[enemyId];
    }
```

8. Implement the function for computing the spatial location of a slot:

```
private Vector3 GetSlotLocation(int slot)
{
    Vector3 location = new Vector3();
    float degrees = 360f / enemyList.Count;
    degrees *= (float)slot;
    location.x = Mathf.Cos(Mathf.Deg2Rad * degrees);
    location.x *= attackRadius;
    location.z = Mathf.Cos(Mathf.Deg2Rad * degrees);
    location.z *= attackRadius;
    return location;
}
```

9. Implement the function for virtually adding attacks to the circle:

```
public bool AddAttack(int weight)
{
    if (attackAvailable - weight < 0)
        return false;
    attackAvailable -= weight;
    return true;
}
```

10. Define the function for virtually releasing the attacks from the circle:

```
public void ResetAttack()
{
    attackAvailable = attackCapacity;
}
```

11. Now create the `StageManager` class:

```
using UnityEngine;
using System.Collections;
using System.Collections.Generic;

public class StageManager : MonoBehaviour
{
    public List<FightingCircle> circleList;
    private Dictionary<int, FightingCircle> circleDic;
```

```
        private Dictionary<int, List<Attack>> attackRqsts;
    }
```

12. Implement the `Awake` function for initialization:

```
void Awake()
{
    circleList = new List<FightingCircle>();
    circleDic = new Dictionary<int, FightingCircle>();
    attackRqsts = new Dictionary<int, List<Attack>>();
    foreach(FightingCircle fc in circleList)
    {
        AddCircle(fc);
    }
}
```

13. Create the function for adding circles to the manager:

```
public void AddCircle(FightingCircle circle)
{
    if (!circleList.Contains(circle))
        return;
    circleList.Add(circle);
    int objId = circle.gameObject.GetInstanceID();
    circleDic.Add(objId, circle);
    attackRqsts.Add(objId, new List<Attack>());
}
```

14. Also, create the function for removing circles from the manager:

```
public void RemoveCircle(FightingCircle circle)
{
    bool isRemoved = circleList.Remove(circle);
    if (!isRemoved)
        return;
    int objId = circle.gameObject.GetInstanceID();
    circleDic.Remove(objId);
    attackRqsts[objId].Clear();
    attackRqsts.Remove(objId);
}
```

15. Define the function for getting the closest circle if given a position:

```
public int GetClosestCircle(Vector3 position)
{
    FightingCircle circle = null;
    float minDist = Mathf.Infinity;
    foreach(FightingCircle c in circleList)
```

```
        {
            Vector3 circlePos = c.transform.position;
            float dist = Vector3.Distance(position, circlePos);
            if (dist < minDist)
            {
                minDist = dist;
                circle = c;
            }
        }
        return circle.gameObject.GetInstanceID();
    }
```

16. Define the function for granting an enemy a slot in a given circle:

```
public bool GrantSlot(int circleId, Enemy enemy)
{
    return circleDic[circleId].AddEnemy(enemy.gameObject);
}
```

17. Implement the function for releasing an enemy from a given circle ID:

```
public void ReleaseSlot(int circleId, Enemy enemy)
{
    circleDic[circleId].RemoveEnemy(enemy.gameObject);
}
```

18. Define the function for granting attack permissions and adding them to the manager:

```
public bool GrantAttack(int circleId, Attack attack)
{
    bool answer =
circleDic[circleId].AddAttack(attack.weight);
    attackRqsts[circleId].Add(attack);
    return answer;
}
```

19. Implement the function for executing all the queued attacks:

```
public IEnumerator ExecuteAtacks()
{
    foreach (int circle in attackRqsts.Keys)
    {
        List<Attack> attacks = attackRqsts[circle];
        foreach (Attack a in attacks)
            yield return a.Execute();
    }
```

```
            foreach (FightingCircle fc in circleList)
                fc.ResetAttack();
        }
```

How it works...

The `Attack` and `Enemy` classes control the behaviors when needed, so the `Enemy` class can be called from another component in the game object. The `FightingCircle` class is very similar to `FormationPattern`, in that it computes the target positions for a given enemy. It just does it in a slightly different way. Finally, the `StageManager` grants all the necessary permissions for assigning and releasing enemy and attack slots for each circle.

There's more...

It is worth noting that the fighting circle can be added as a component of a game object that works as the target player itself, or a different empty object that holds a reference to the player's game object.

Also, you could move the functions for granting and executing attacks to the fighting circle. We wanted to keep them in the manager so that the attacks' executions are centralized, and the circles just work for handling target positions; just like formations.

See also

For further information, please refer to the following material:

- Refer to the *Handling formations* recipe
- For further information on the Kung-Fu Circle algorithm, please refer to the book *Game AI Pro*, by Steve Rabin

17
Agent Awareness

In this chapter, you will learn the following algorithm recipes for simulating senses and agent awareness:

- The seeing function using a collider-based system
- The hearing function using a collider-based system
- The smelling function using a collider-based system
- The seeing function using a graph-based system
- The hearing function using a graph-based system
- The smelling function using a graph-based system
- Creating awareness in a stealth game

Introduction

In this chapter, we will learn different approaches to simulating sense stimuli on an agent. We will learn how to use tools that we are already familiar with to create these simulations, colliders, and graphs.

In the first approach, we will take advantage of ray casting, colliders, and the `MonoBehaviour` functions bound to this component, such as `OnCollisionEnter`, in order to leverage the need to acquire objects nearby in the three-dimensional world. Then, we will learn how to simulate the same stimuli using the graph theory and functions so that we can take advantage of this way of representing the world.

Finally, we'll learn how to implement agent awareness using a mixed approach that considers the previously learned sensory-level algorithms.

The seeing function using a collider-based system

This is probably the easiest way to simulate vision. We take a collider, be it a mesh or a Unity primitive, and use it as the tool for determining whether or not an object is inside the agent's vision range.

Getting ready

It's important to have a collider component attached to the same game object using the script in this recipe, as well as the other collider-based algorithms in this chapter. In this case, it's recommended that the collider is a pyramid-based one in order to simulate a vision cone. The fewer the polygons, the faster it will be in the game.

How to do it...

We will create a component that is able to see enemies nearby:

1. Create the `Visor` component, declaring its member variables. It is important to add the following corresponding tags to Unity's configuration:

```
using UnityEngine;
using System.Collections;

public class Visor : MonoBehaviour
{
    public string tagWall = "Wall";
    public string tagTarget = "Enemy";
    public GameObject agent;
}
```

2. Implement the function for initializing the game object in case the component is already assigned to it:

```
void Start()
{
    if (agent == null)
        agent = gameObject;
}
```

3. Declare the function for checking collisions in every frame:

```
public void OnTriggerStay(Collider coll)
{
    // next steps here
}
```

4. Discard the collision if it is not a target:

```
string tag = coll.gameObject.tag;
if (!tag.Equals(tagTarget))
    return;
```

5. Get the game object's position and compute its direction from the visor:

```
GameObject target = coll.gameObject;
Vector3 agentPos = agent.transform.position;
Vector3 targetPos = target.transform.position;
Vector3 direction = targetPos - agentPos;
```

6. Compute its length and create a new ray to be shot soon:

```
float length = direction.magnitude;
direction.Normalize();
Ray ray = new Ray(agentPos, direction);
```

7. Cast the ray created and retrieve all the hits:

```
RaycastHit[] hits;
hits = Physics.RaycastAll(ray, length);
```

8. Check for any walls between the visor and target. If there are none, we can proceed to call our functions or develop the behaviors that are to be triggered:

```
int i;
for (i = 0; i < hits.Length; i++)
{
    GameObject hitObj;
    hitObj = hits[i].collider.gameObject;
    tag = hitObj.tag;
    if (tag.Equals(tagWall))
        return;
}
// TODO
// target is visible
// code your behaviour below
```

How it works...

The following diagram shows how the two-step vision system works:

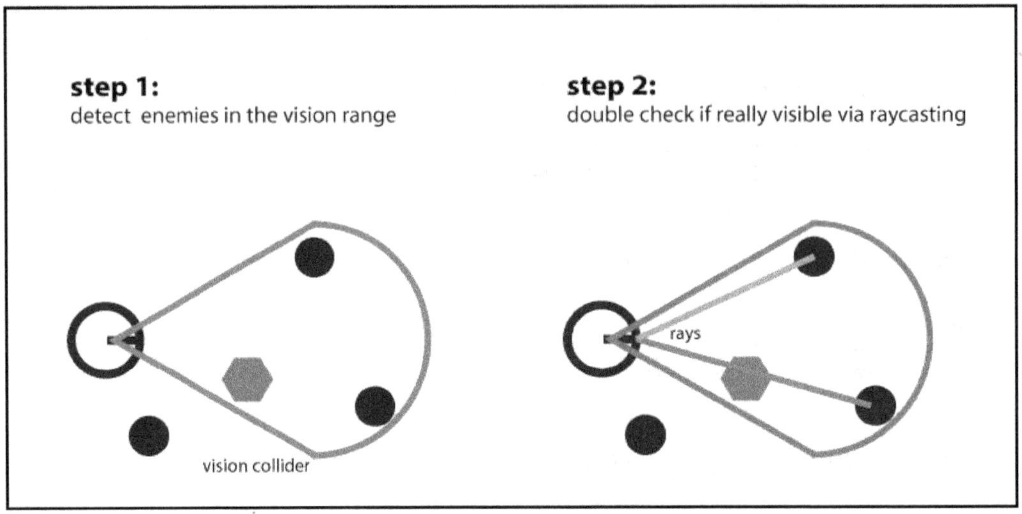

The collider component checks every frame to see whether it is colliding with any game object in the scene. We leverage the optimizations in Unity's scene graph and engine, and focus only on how to handle the valid collisions.

After checking this, if a target object is inside the vision range represented by the collider, we cast a ray in order to check whether it is really visible or whether there is a wall between the target and the agent.

The hearing function using a collider-based system

In this recipe, we will emulate a sense of hearing by developing two entities: a sound emitter and a sound receiver. It is based on the principles proposed by Millington for simulating a hearing system, and it uses the power of Unity colliders to detect receivers near an emitter.

Getting ready

As with the other recipes based on colliders, we will need collider components attached to every object that is to be checked, and rigid body components attached to either emitters or receivers.

How to do it...

We will create the `SoundReceiver` class for our agents, and `SoundEmitter` for things such as alarms:

1. Create the class for the sound-receiver object:

```
using UnityEngine;
using System.Collections;

public class SoundReceiver : MonoBehaviour
{
    public float soundThreshold;
}
```

2. Define the function for the behavior that is handling the reception of sound:

```
public virtual void Receive(float intensity, Vector3 position)
{
    // TODO
    // code your own behaviour here
}
```

3. Now, let's create the class for the sound-emitter object:

```
using UnityEngine;
using System.Collections;
using System.Collections.Generic;

public class SoundEmitter : MonoBehaviour
{
    public float soundIntensity;
    public float soundAttenuation;
    public GameObject emitterObject;
    private Dictionary<int, SoundReceiver> receiverDic;
}
```

4. Initialize the list of receivers nearby and the emitter object, in case the component is attached directly:

```
void Start()
{
    receiverDic = new Dictionary<int, SoundReceiver>();
    if (emitterObject == null)
        emitterObject = gameObject;
}
```

5. Implement the function for adding new receivers to the list when they enter the emitter bounds:

```
public void OnTriggerEnter(Collider coll)
{
    SoundReceiver receiver;
    receiver = coll.gameObject.GetComponent<SoundReceiver>();
    if (receiver == null)
        return;
    int objId = coll.gameObject.GetInstanceID();
    receiverDic.Add(objId, receiver);
}
```

6. Also, implement the function for removing receivers from the list when they are out of reach:

```
public void OnTriggerExit(Collider coll)
{
    SoundReceiver receiver;
    receiver = coll.gameObject.GetComponent<SoundReceiver>();
    if (receiver == null)
        return;
    int objId = coll.gameObject.GetInstanceID();
    receiverDic.Remove(objId);
}
```

7. Define the function for emitting sound waves to nearby agents:

```
public void Emit()
{
    GameObject srObj;
    Vector3 srPos;
    float intensity;
    float distance;
    Vector3 emitterPos = emitterObject.transform.position;
    // next step here
}
```

8. Compute sound attenuation for every receiver:

```
foreach (SoundReceiver sr in receiverDic.Values)
{
    srObj = sr.gameObject;
    srPos = srObj.transform.position;
    distance = Vector3.Distance(srPos, emitterPos);
    intensity = soundIntensity;
    intensity -= soundAttenuation * distance;
    if (intensity < sr.soundThreshold)
        continue;
    sr.Receive(intensity, emitterPos);
}
```

How it works...

The following diagram shows how the sound emulation system works with colliders:

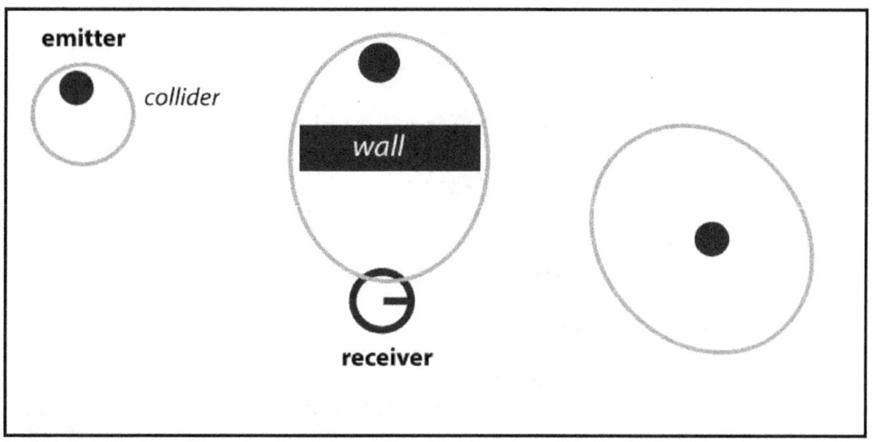

The collider triggers help to register agents in the list of agents assigned to an emitter. The sound emission function then takes into account the agent's distance from the emitter in order to decrease its intensity using the concept of sound attenuation.

There's more...

We can develop a more flexible algorithm by defining different types of walls that affect sound intensity. It works by casting rays and adding up their values to the sound attenuation:

1. Create a dictionary for storing wall types as strings (using tags) and their corresponding attenuation:

```
public Dictionary<string, float> wallTypes;
```

2. Reduce sound intensity this way:

```
intensity -= GetWallAttenuation(emitterPos, srPos);
```

3. Define the function that was called in the previous step:

```
public float GetWallAttenuation(Vector3 emitterPos, Vector3
receiverPos)
{
    // next steps here
}
```

4. Compute the necessary values for ray casting:

```
float attenuation = 0f;
Vector3 direction = receiverPos - emitterPos;
float distance = direction.magnitude;
direction.Normalize();
```

5. Cast the ray and retrieve the hits:

```
Ray ray = new Ray(emitterPos, direction);
RaycastHit[] hits = Physics.RaycastAll(ray, distance);
```

6. For every wall type found via tags, add up its value (stored in the dictionary):

```
int i;
for (i = 0; i < hits.Length; i++)
{
    GameObject obj;
    string tag;
    obj = hits[i].collider.gameObject;
    tag = obj.tag;
    if (wallTypes.ContainsKey(tag))
```

```
            attenuation += wallTypes[tag];
        }
        return attenuation;
```

The smelling function using a collider-based system

Smelling is one of the trickiest senses to translate from the real to the virtual world. There are several techniques, but most of them are inclined to use colliders or graph logic.

Smelling can be simulated by computing a collision between an agent and odor particles, scattered throughout the game level.

Getting ready

As with the other recipes based on colliders, we will need collider components attached to every object that is to be checked, and rigid body components attached to either emitters or receivers.

How to do it...

We will develop the scripts for representing odor particles and agents that are able to smell:

1. Create the particle's script and define its member variables for computing its lifespan:

```
using UnityEngine;
using System.Collections;

public class OdourParticle : MonoBehaviour
{
    public float timespan;
    private float timer;
}
```

2. Implement the `Start` function for proper validations:

```
void Start()
{
    if (timespan < 0f)
        timespan = 0f;
    timer = timespan;
}
```

3. Implement the `timer` and destroy the object after its life cycle ends:

```
void Update()
{
    timer -= Time.deltaTime;
    if (timer < 0f)
        Destroy(gameObject);
}
```

4. Create the class for representing the sniffer agent:

```
using UnityEngine;
using System.Collections;
using System.Collections.Generic;

public class Smeller : MonoBehaviour
{
    private Vector3 target;
    private Dictionary<int, GameObject> particles;
}
```

5. Initialize the dictionary for storing odor `particles`:

```
void Start()
{
    particles = new Dictionary<int, GameObject>();
}
```

6. Add to the dictionary the colliding objects that have the `OdourParticle` component attached:

```
public void OnTriggerEnter(Collider coll)
{
    GameObject obj = coll.gameObject;
    OdourParticle op;
    op = obj.GetComponent<OdourParticle>();
    if (op == null)
        return;
    int objId = obj.GetInstanceID();
```

```
        particles.Add(objId, obj);
        UpdateTarget();
    }
```

7. Release the odor particles from the local dictionary when they are out of the agent's range or after they've been destroyed:

```
    public void OnTriggerExit(Collider coll)
    {
        GameObject obj = coll.gameObject;
        int objId = obj.GetInstanceID();
        bool isRemoved;
        isRemoved = particles.Remove(objId);
        if (!isRemoved)
            return;
        UpdateTarget();
    }
```

8. Create the function for computing the odor `centroid` according to the current elements in the dictionary:

```
    private void UpdateTarget()
    {
        Vector3 centroid = Vector3.zero;
        foreach (GameObject p in particles.Values)
        {
            Vector3 pos = p.transform.position;
            centroid += pos;
        }
        target = centroid;
    }
```

9. Implement the function for retrieving the odor centroids, if any:

```
    public Vector3? GetTargetPosition()
    {
        if (particles.Keys.Count == 0)
            return null;
        return target;
    }
```

How it works...

The following diagram shows how the smell system works:

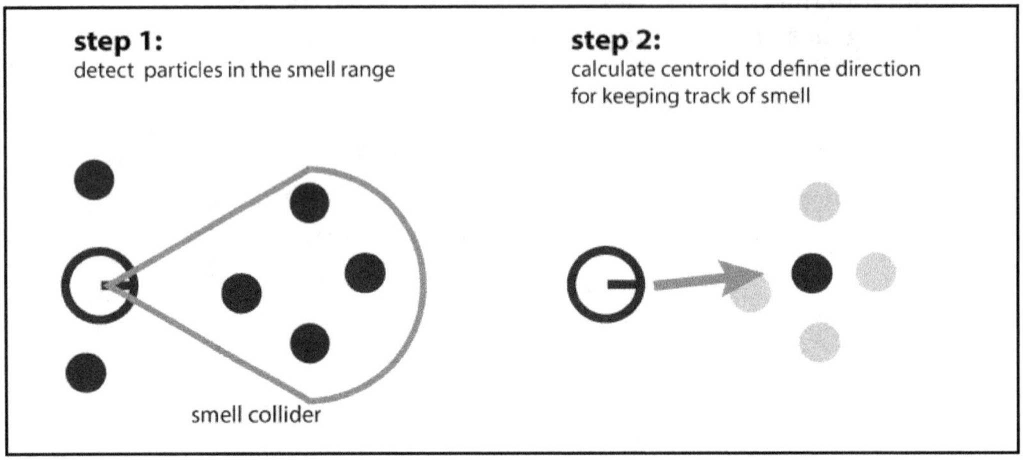

Just like the hearing recipe based on colliders, we use the trigger colliders in order to register odor particles in an agent's perception (implemented using a dictionary). When a particle is included or removed, the odor centroid is computed. However, we implement a function for retrieving that centroid because, when no odor particle is registered, the internal centroid position is not updated.

There's more...

Particle emission logic is left behind to be implemented according to our game's needs, and it's basically instantiating odor-particle prefabs. Also, it is recommended that you attach the rigid body components to the agents. Odor particles are prone to be massively instantiated, reducing the game's performance.

The seeing function using a graph-based system

We will start looking at those recipes using graph-based logic in order to simulate sense. Again, we start by developing a sense of vision.

Getting ready

It is important to have grasped `Chapter 13`, *Navigation,* in order to understand the inner workings of the graph-based recipes.

How to do it...

We will just implement a new file:

1. Create the class for handling vision:

```
using UnityEngine;
using System.Collections;
using System.Collections.Generic;

public class VisorGraph : MonoBehaviour
{
    public int visionReach;
    public GameObject visorObj;
    public Graph visionGraph;
}
```

2. Validate the visor object in case the component is not attached:

```
void Start()
{
    if (visorObj == null)
        visorObj = gameObject;
}
```

3. Define and start building the function for detecting the visibility of a given set of nodes:

```
public bool IsVisible(int[] visibilityNodes)
{
    int vision = visionReach;
    int src = visionGraph.GetNearestVertex(visorObj);
    HashSet<int> visibleNodes = new HashSet<int>();
    Queue<int> queue = new Queue<int>();
    queue.Enqueue(src);
}
```

4. Implement a **Breadth-First Search** (**BFS**) algorithm:

```
while (queue.Count != 0)
{
    if (vision == 0)
        break;
    int v = queue.Dequeue();
    List<int> neighbours = visionGraph.GetNeighbors(v);
    foreach (int n in neighbours)
    {
        if (visibleNodes.Contains(n))
            continue;
        queue.Enqueue(v);
        visibleNodes.Add(v);
    }
}
```

5. Compare the set of visible nodes with the set of nodes reached by the vision system:

```
foreach (int vn in visibleNodes)
{
    if (visibleNodes.Contains(vn))
        return true;
}
```

6. Return `false` if there is no match between the two sets of nodes:

```
return false;
```

How it works...

The recipe uses the BFS algorithm in order to discover nodes within its vision reach and then compares this set of nodes to the set where agents reside.

The input array is computed before being used by the algorithm and is beyond the scope of this recipe because it relies on pinpointing; for example, the position of each agent or object that needs to be checked visibly.

The hearing function using a graph-based system

Hearing works in a similar way to vision, but doesn't take into account the nodes' direct visibility because of the properties of the sound. However, we still need a sound receiver in order to make it work. Instead of making an agent a direct sound receiver, in this recipe, the sound travels along the sound graph and is perceived by the graph nodes.

Getting ready

It is important to have grasped the chapter regarding path finding in order to understand the inner workings of the graph-based recipes.

How to do it...

1. Create the emitter class:

```
using UnityEngine;
using System.Collections;
using System.Collections.Generic;

public class EmitterGraph : MonoBehaviour
{
    // next steps
}
```

2. Declare the member variables:

```
public int soundIntensity;
public Graph soundGraph;
public GameObject emitterObj;
```

3. Implement the validation of the emitter object's reference:

```
public void Start()
{
    if (emitterObj == null)
        emitterObj = gameObject;
}
```

4. Declare the function for emitting sounds:

```
public int[] Emit()
{
    // next steps
}
```

5. Declare and assign the variables needed:

```
List<int> nodeIds = new List<int>();
Queue<int> queue = new Queue<int>();
List<int> neighbours;
int intensity = soundIntensity;
int src = soundGraph.GetNearestVertex(emitterObj);
```

6. Add the source node to the list of reached nodes and the queue:

```
nodeIds.Add(src);
queue.Enqueue(src);
```

7. Code the BFS loop for reaching out to nodes:

```
while (queue.Count != 0)
{
    // next steps
}
return nodeIds.ToArray();
```

8. Finish the loop if the sound runs out of intensity:

```
if (intensity == 0)
    break;
```

9. Take a node from the queue and get its neighbors:

```
int v = queue.Dequeue();
neighbours = soundGraph.GetNeighbors(v);
```

10. Check the neighbors and add them to the queue if necessary:

```
foreach (int n in neighbours)
{
    if (nodeIds.Contains(n))
        continue;
    queue.Enqueue(n);
    nodeIds.Add(n);
}
```

11. Reduce the sound intensity:

```
intensity--;
```

How it works...

This recipe returns the list of nodes affected by sound intensity using the BFS algorithm. The algorithm stops when there are no more nodes to visit, or when the intensity of the sound is dimmed by the graph traversal.

There's more...

After learning how to implement smelling using both colliders and graph logic, you could develop a new hybrid algorithm that relies on a heuristic that takes distance as input. If a node goes beyond the sound's maximum distance, there's no need to add its neighbors to the queue.

See also

Refer to the following recipes in `Chapter 13`, *Navigation*:

- *Breadth-First Search algorithm*
- *A* algorithm (for taking a heuristic function as an argument)*

The smelling function using a graph-based system

In this recipe, we take a mixed approach to tag vertices with a given odor particle that collides with it.

Getting ready

The vertices should have a broad collider attached so that they catch the odor particles nearby.

How to do it...

1. Add the following member variable to the odor-particle script to store its parent ID:

```
public int parent;
```

2. Create the new odor-enabled class, deriving from the original vertex:

```
using UnityEngine;
using System.Collections;
using System.Collections.Generic;

public class VertexOdour : Vertex
{
    private Dictionary<int, OdourParticle> odourDic;
}
```

3. Initialize the odor dictionary in the proper function:

```
public void Start()
{
    odourDic = new Dictionary<int, OdourParticle>();
}
```

4. Add the odor to the vertex's dictionary:

```
public void OnCollisionEnter(Collision coll)
{
    OdourOdourParticle op;
    op = coll.gameObject.GetComponent<OdourParticle>();
    if (op == null)
        return;
    int id = op.parent;
    odourDic.Add(id, op);
}
```

5. Remove the odor from the vertex's dictionary:

```
public void OnCollisionExit(Collision coll)
{
    OdourParticle op;
    op = coll.gameObject.GetComponent<OdourParticle>();
    if (op == null)
        return;
    int id = op.parent;
    odourDic.Remove(id);
}
```

6. Implement the function for checking whether any odor is tagged:

```
public bool HasOdour()
{
    if (odourDic.Values.Count == 0)
        return false;
    return true;
}
```

7. Implement the function for checking whether a given type of odor is indexed in the vertex:

```
public bool OdourExists(int id)
{
    return odourDic.ContainsKey(id);
}
```

How it works...

The odor particles collide with the vertices, being indexed in their odor dictionary. From that point on, our agents can check whether a given odor is registered in a vertex nearby.

See also

- `Chapter 13`, *Navigation,* and the *BFS and graph construction* recipe

Creating awareness in a stealth game

Now that we know how to implement sensory-level algorithms, it's time to see how they can be taken into account in order to develop higher-level techniques for creating agent awareness.

This recipe is based on the work of Brook Miles and the team at Klei Entertainment for the game *Mark of the Ninja*. The mechanism revolves around the notion of having interest sources that can be seen or heard by the agents and a sensory manager to handle those.

Getting ready

As a lot of things revolve around the idea of interests, we'll need two data structures for defining the interests' sense and priority, and a data type for the interest itself.

This is the data structure for sense:

```
public enum InterestSense
{
    SOUND,
    SIGHT
};
```

This is the data structure for priority:

```
public enum InterestPriority
{
    LOWEST = 0,
    BROKEN = 1,
    MISSING = 2,
    SUSPECT = 4,
    SMOKE = 4,
    BOX = 5,
    DISTRACTIONFLARE = 10,
    TERROR = 20
};
```

The following is the interest data type:

```
using UnityEngine;
using System.Collections;

public struct Interest
{
    public InterestSense sense;
    public InterestPriority priority;
    public Vector3 position;
}
```

Before developing the necessary classes for implementing this idea, it's important to note that sensory-level functions are left blank in order to keep the recipe flexible and open to our custom implementations. These implementations could be developed using some of the recipes learned previously.

How to do it...

This is a long recipe where we'll implement two extensive classes. It is advised to read the following steps carefully:

1. Let's start by creating the class that defines our agents and its member variables:

```
using UnityEngine;
using System.Collections;
using System.Collections.Generic;

public class AgentAwared : MonoBehaviour
{
    protected Interest interest;
    protected bool isUpdated = false;
}
```

2. Define the function for checking whether a given interest is relevant or not:

```
public bool IsRelevant(Interest i)
{
    int oldValue = (int)interest.priority;
    int newValue = (int)i.priority;
    if (newValue <= oldValue)
        return false;
    return true;
}
```

3. Implement the function for setting a new interest in the agent:

```
public void Notice(Interest i)
{
    StopCoroutine(Investigate());
    interest = i;
    StartCoroutine(Investigate());
}
```

4. Define the custom function for investigating. This will have our own implementation, and it will take account of the agent's interest:

```
public virtual IEnumerator Investigate()
{
    // TODO
    // develop your implementation
    yield break;
}
```

5. Define the custom function for leading. This will define what an agent does when it's in charge of giving orders and will depend on our own implementation:

```
public virtual IEnumerator Lead()
{
    // TODO
    // develop your implementation
    yield break;
}
```

6. Create the class for defining interest sources:

```
using UnityEngine;
using System.Collections;
using System.Collections.Generic;

public class InterestSource : MonoBehaviour
{
    public InterestSense sense;
    public float radius;
    public InterestPriority priority;
    public bool isActive;
}
```

7. Implement a property for retrieving the interest value:

```
public Interest interest
{
    get
    {
        Interest i;
        i.position = transform.position;
        i.priority = priority;
        i.sense = sense;
        return i;
    }
}
```

8. Define the function for checking whether or not the agent is affected by the interest source. This could be defined in the agent's class, but it requires some changes in several of the following steps. This is one of the sensory-level functions:

```
protected bool IsAffectedSight(AgentAwared agent)
{
    // TODO
```

```
    // your sight check implementation
    return false;
}
```

9. Implement the next sensory-level function for checking whether an agent is affected by sound. It has the same architectural considerations as the previous step:

```
protected bool IsAffectedSound(AgentAwared agent)
{
    // TODO
    // your sound check implementation
    return false;
}
```

10. Define the function for getting the list of agents affected by the interest source. It is declared virtual, in case we need to specify it further or simply change the way it works:

```
public virtual List<AgentAwared> GetAffected(AgentAwared[]
agentList)
{
    List<AgentAwared> affected;
    affected = new List<AgentAwared>();
    Vector3 interPos = transform.position;
    Vector3 agentPos;
    float distance;
    // next steps
}
```

11. Start creating the main loop for traversing the list of agents and return the list of those affected:

```
foreach (AgentAwared agent in agentList)
{
    // next steps
}
return affected;
```

12. Discriminate an agent if it is beyond the source's action radius:

```
agentPos = agent.transform.position;
distance = Vector3.Distance(interPos, agentPos);
if (distance > radius)
    continue;
```

13. Check whether the agent is affected, given the source's type of sense:

```
bool isAffected = false;
switch (sense)
{
    case InterestSense.SIGHT:
        isAffected = IsAffectedSight(agent);
        break;
    case InterestSense.SOUND:
        isAffected = IsAffectedSound(agent);
        break;
}
```

14. If the agent is affected, add it to the list:

```
if (!isAffected)
    continue;
affected.Add(agent);
```

15. Next, create the class for the sensory manager:

```
using UnityEngine;
using System.Collections;
using System.Collections.Generic;

public class SensoryManager : MonoBehaviour
{
    public List<AgentAwared> agents;
    public List<InterestSource> sources;
}
```

16. Implement its `Awake` function:

```
public void Awake()
{
    agents = new List<AgentAwared>();
    sources = new List<InterestSource>();
}
```

17. Declare the function for getting a set of scouts, given a group of agents:

```
public List<AgentAwared> GetScouts(AgentAwared[] agents, int
leader = -1)
{
    // next steps
}
```

18. Validate the number of agents and return the list:

```
if (agents.Length == 0)
    return new List<AgentAwared>(0);
if (agents.Length == 1)
    return new List<AgentAwared>(agents);
```

19. Remove the leader, if given its index:

```
List<AgentAwared> agentList;
agentList = new List<AgentAwared>(agents);
if (leader > -1)
    agentList.RemoveAt(leader);
```

20. Calculate the number of scouts to retrieve:

```
List<AgentAwared> scouts;
scouts = new List<AgentAwared>();
float numAgents = (float)agents.Length;
int numScouts = (int)Mathf.Log(numAgents, 2f);
```

21. Get the random scouts from the list of agents:

```
while (numScouts != 0)
{
    int numA = agentList.Count;
    int r = Random.Range(0, numA);
    AgentAwared a = agentList[r];
    scouts.Add(a);
    agentList.RemoveAt(r);
    numScouts--;
}
```

22. Retrieve the scouts:

```
return scouts;
```

23. Define the function for checking the list of interest sources:

```
public void UpdateLoop()
{
    List<AgentAwared> affected;
    AgentAwared leader;
    List<AgentAwared> scouts;
    foreach (InterestSource source in sources)
    {
        // next steps
    }
}
```

24. Avoid inactive sources:

```
if (!source.isActive)
    continue;
source.isActive = false;
```

25. Avoid sources that don't affect any agent:

```
affected = source.GetAffected(agents.ToArray());
if (affected.Count == 0)
    continue;
```

26. Get a random `leader` and the set of `scouts`:

```
int l = Random.Range(0, affected.Count);
leader = affected[l];
scouts = GetScouts(affected.ToArray(), l);
```

27. Call the leader to its role if necessary:

```
if (leader.Equals(scouts[0]))
    StartCoroutine(leader.Lead());
```

28. Finally, inform the scouts about noticing the interest, in case it's relevant to them:

```
foreach (AgentAwared a in scouts)
{
    Interest i = source.interest;
    if (a.IsRelevant(i))
        a.Notice(i);
}
```

How it works...

There is a list of interest sources that could get the attention of a number of agents in the world. That list is kept in a manager that handles the global update for every source, taking into account just the active ones.

An interest source receives the list of agents in the world and retrieves only the affected agents after a two-step process. First, it sets aside all the agents that are outside its action radius and then only takes into account those agents that can be reached with a finer (and more expensive) sensory-level mechanism.

The manager handles the affected agents, sets up scouts and their leader, and finally informs all of them about their relevant interests.

There's more...

It is worth mentioning that the `SensoryManager` class works as a hub to store and organize the list of agents and the list of interest sources, so it ought to be a singleton. Its duplication could bring about undesired complexity or behavior.

An agent's interest is automatically changed by the sensory manager using the priority values. Still, it can be reset when needed, using the `Notice` public function.

There is room for improvement still, depending on our game. The scout lists can overlap each other, and it's up to us and our game to handle this scenario the best way we can. However, the system we built takes advantage of the priority values to make decisions.

See also

For further information on the train of thought behind this recipe, please refer to Steve Rabin's book, *Game AI Pro*.

18 Board Games and Applied Search AI

In this chapter, you will learn the following recipes for developing board game AI:

- Working with the game-tree class
- Implementing Minimax
- Implementing Negamax
- Implementing AB Negamax
- Implementing NegaScout
- Implementing a Tic-Tac-Toe rival
- Implementing a Checkers rival
- Implementing Rock-Paper-Scissors AI with UCB1
- Implementing Regret Matching

Introduction

In this chapter, you will learn about a family of algorithms for developing board game techniques and creating artificial intelligence. They are based on the principle of a game-tree graph that spans as we evaluate a state and decide to visit its neighbors. They also take into account board games for two rivals. But, with a little bit of work, some of them can be extended to accommodate more players.

Working with the game-tree class

The game state can be represented in a lot of different ways, but you will learn how to create extendible classes to use the high-level board AI algorithms for different circumstances.

Getting ready...

It is important to be clear on object-oriented programming, specifically on inheritance and polymorphism. This is because we'll be creating generic functions that can be applied to a number of board game decisions, and then we'll be writing specific sub-classes that inherit and further specify these functions.

How to do it...

We will build two classes to represent game-tree with the help of the following steps:

1. Create the abstract class `Move`:

```
using UnityEngine;
using System.Collections;

public abstract class Move
{
}
```

2. Create the pseudo-abstract class `Board`:

```
using UnityEngine;
using System.Collections;

public class Board
{
    protected int player;
    //next steps here
}
```

3. Define the default constructor:

```
public Board()
{
    player = 1;
}
```

4. Implement the virtual function for retrieving the next possible moves:

```
public virtual Move[] GetMoves()
{
    return new Move[0];
}
```

5. Implement the virtual function for playing a move on the board:

```
public virtual Board MakeMove(Move m)
{
    return new Board();
}
```

6. Define the virtual function for testing whether the game is over:

```
public virtual bool IsGameOver()
{
    return true;
}
```

7. Implement the virtual function for retrieving the current player:

```
public virtual int GetCurrentPlayer()
{
    return player;
}
```

8. Implement the virtual function for testing the board's value for a given player:

```
public virtual float Evaluate(int player)
{
    return Mathf.NegativeInfinity;
}
```

9. Also, implement the virtual function for testing the board's value for the current player:

```
public virtual float Evaluate()
{
    return Mathf.NegativeInfinity;
}
```

How it works...

We have created the stepping stones for the next algorithms. The `Board` class works as a node to represent the current game state, and the `Move` class to represent an edge. When the `GetMoves` function is called, we model the function for getting the edges to reach the neighbors of the current game state.

See also

For more theoretical insights about the techniques in this chapter, please refer to Russel and Norvig's *Artificial Intelligence: A Modern Approach* (adversarial search) and Ian Millington's *Artificial Intelligence for Games* (board games).

Implementing Minimax

Minimax is an algorithm based on minimizing the possible loss for the worst case (maximum loss). Besides game development and game theory, Minimax is a decision rule that is also used in statistics, decision theory, and philosophy.

This technique was originally formulated for the two-player zero-sum game theory, meaning that one player's win is the opponent's loss. However, in this case, it is flexible enough to handle more than two players.

Getting ready...

It is important to know the difference between a dynamic member function and a static member function, as well as recursion. A dynamic member function is bound to the instance of the class, while the static member function is bound to the class itself. The static method allows us to call it without instantiating an object. This is great for general-purpose algorithms, such as the ones we'll be developing in this recipe.

In the case of recursion, it's not always clear (differing with iteration) that this is an iterative process that requires a base case (also called the stop condition) and a recursive case (the one to keep iterating).

How to do it...

We will create the base class for handling all of our main algorithms and implement the `Minimax` function as follows:

1. Create the `BoardAI` class:

```
using UnityEngine;
using System.Collections;

public class BoardAI
{

}
```

2. Declare the `Minimax` function:

```
public static float Minimax(
        Board board,
        int player,
        int maxDepth,
        int currentDepth,
        ref Move bestMove)
{
    // next steps here
}
```

3. Consider the base case:

```
if (board.IsGameOver() || currentDepth == maxDepth)
    return board.Evaluate(player);
```

4. Set the initial values depending on the player:

```
bestMove = null;
float bestScore = Mathf.Infinity;
if (board.GetCurrentPlayer() == player)
    bestScore = Mathf.NegativeInfinity;
```

5. Loop through all the possible moves and return the best score:

```
foreach (Move m in board.GetMoves())
{
    // next steps here
}
return bestScore;
```

6. Create a new game state from the current move:

```
Board b = board.MakeMove(m);
float currentScore;
Move currentMove = null;
```

7. Start the recursion:

```
currentScore = Minimax(b, player, maxDepth, currentDepth + 1,
ref currentMove);
```

8. Validate the score for the current player:

```
if (board.GetCurrentPlayer() == player)
{
    if (currentScore > bestScore)
    {
        bestScore = currentScore;
        bestMove = currentMove;
    }
}
```

9. Validate the score for the adversary:

```
else
{
    if (currentScore < bestScore)
    {
        bestScore = currentScore;
        bestMove = currentMove;
    }
}
```

How it works...

The algorithm works as a bounded **Depth-First Search** (**DFS**). In each step, the move is chosen by selecting the option that maximizes the player's score and assuming the opponent will choose the option of minimizing it until a terminal (leaf) node is reached.

The move tracking is done using recursion, and the heuristic for selecting or assuming an option depends on the `Evaluate` function.

See also

For further information, please refer to the following material:

- *Working the game-tree class* recipe in this chapter

Implementing Negamax

When we have a zero-sum game with only two players involved, we are able to improve Minimax, taking advantage of the principle that one player's loss is the other's gain. In this way, it is able to provide the same results as the Minimax algorithm. However, it does not track whose move it is. Negamax is an improvement from Minimax.

Getting ready...

It is important to know the difference between a dynamic member function and a static member function, as well as recursion. A dynamic member function is bound to the instance of the class, while a static member function is bound to the class itself. The static method allows us to call it without instantiating an object. This is great for general-purpose algorithms, such as the one we are developing in this recipe.

In the case of recursion, it's not always clear (differing with iteration) that this is an iterative process that requires a base case (also called the stop condition) and a recursive case (the one to keep iterating).

How to do it...

We will add a new function to the `BoardAI` class as follows:

1. Create the `Negamax` function:

```
public static float Negamax(
        Board board,
        int maxDepth,
        int currentDepth,
        ref Move bestMove)
{
    // next steps here
}
```

2. Validate the base case:

```
if (board.IsGameOver() || currentDepth == maxDepth)
    return board.Evaluate();
```

3. Set the initial values:

```
bestMove = null;
float bestScore = Mathf.NegativeInfinity;
```

4. Loop through all the available moves and return the best score:

```
foreach (Move m in board.GetMoves())
{
    // next steps here
}
return bestScore;
```

5. Create a new game state from the current move:

```
Board b = board.MakeMove(m);
float recursedScore;
Move currentMove = null;
```

6. Start the recursion:

```
recursedScore = Negamax(b, maxDepth, currentDepth + 1, ref
currentMove);
```

7. Set the current score and update the best score and move, if necessary:

```
float currentScore = -recursedScore;
if (currentScore > bestScore)
{
    bestScore = currentScore;
    bestMove = m;
}
```

How it works...

The base algorithm works the same, but we're making some improvements. At each step of going back in the recursion, the scores from the previous steps have their sign inverted. Instead of choosing the best option, the algorithm changes the sign of the score, eliminating the need for tracking whose move it is.

There's more...

As Negamax alternates the viewpoints between players at each step, the evaluate function used is the one with no parameters.

See also

For further exploration and understanding, please refer to the following material:

- *Working the game-tree class* recipe in this chapter
- *Implementing Minimax* recipe in this chapter

Implementing AB Negamax

There is still room for improving the Negamax algorithm. Despite its efficiency, the downside of the Negamax algorithm is that it examines more nodes than is necessary (for example, board positions). To overcome this problem, we use Negamax with a search strategy called alpha-beta pruning.

Getting ready...

It is important to know the difference between a dynamic member function and a static member function, as well as recursion. A dynamic member function is bound to the instance of the class, while the static member function is bound to the class itself. The static method allows us to call it without instantiating an object. This is great for general-purpose algorithms, such as the ones we'll be developing in this recipe.

In the case of recursion, it's not always clear (differing with iteration) that this is an iterative process that requires a base case (also called the stop condition) and a recursive case (the one to keep iterating).

How to do it...

We will add a new function to the `BoardAI` class as follows:

1. Create the `ABNegamax` function:

```
public static float ABNegamax(
```

```
            Board board,
            int player,
            int maxDepth,
            int currentDepth,
            ref Move bestMove,
            float alpha,
            float beta)
{
    // next steps here
}
```

2. Validate the base case:

```
if (board.IsGameOver() || currentDepth == maxDepth)
    return board.Evaluate(player);
```

3. Set the initial values:

```
bestMove = null;
float bestScore = Mathf.NegativeInfinity;
```

4. Loop through every available move and return the best score:

```
foreach (Move m in board.GetMoves())
{
    // next steps here
}
return bestScore;
```

5. Create a new game state from the current move:

```
Board b = board.MakeMove(m);
```

6. Set the values for calling the recursion:

```
float recursedScore;
Move currentMove = null;
int cd = currentDepth + 1;
float max = Mathf.Max(alpha, bestScore);
```

7. Start the recursion:

```
recursedScore = ABNegamax(b, player, maxDepth, cd, ref
currentMove, -beta, max);
```

8. Set the current score and update the best score and move if necessary. Also, stop the iteration if necessary:

```
float currentScore = -recursedScore;
if (currentScore > bestScore)
{
    bestScore = currentScore;
    bestMove = m;

    if (bestScore >= beta)
        return bestScore;
}
```

How it works...

Since we know the basic principle of the algorithm, let's concentrate on the search strategy. There are two values: alpha and beta, respectively. The alpha value is the lowest score a player can achieve, thus avoiding considering any move where the opponent has the opportunity to lessen it. Similarly, the beta value is the upper limit, and no matter how tempting the new option is, the algorithm assumes that the opponent won't provide the opportunity to take it.

Given the alternation between each player (minimizing and maximizing), only one value needs to be checked at each step.

See also

- The *Working the game-tree class* recipe
- The *Minimax* recipe
- The *Negamaxing* recipe

Implementing NegaScout

Including a search strategy also makes room for new challenges. NegaScouting is the result of narrowing the search by improving the pruning heuristic. It is based on a concept called **search window**, which is the interval between the alpha and beta values. So, reducing the search window increases the chance of a branch being pruned.

Getting ready...

It is important to know the difference between a dynamic member function and a static member function, as well as recursion. A dynamic member function is bound to the instance of the class, while the static member function is bound to the class itself. The static method allows us to call it without instantiating an object. This is great for general-purpose algorithms, such as the ones we'll be developing in this recipe.

In the case of recursion, it's not always clear (differing with iteration) that this is an iterative process that requires a base case (also called the stop condition) and a recursive case (the one to keep iterating).

How to do it...

We will add a new function to the `BoardAI` class as follows:

1. Create the `ABNegascout` function:

```
public static float ABNegascout (
        Board board,
        int player,
        int maxDepth,
        int currentDepth,
        ref Move bestMove,
        float alpha,
        float beta)
{
    // next steps here
}
```

2. Validate the base case:

```
if (board.IsGameOver() || currentDepth == maxDepth)
    return board.Evaluate(player);
```

3. Set the initial values:

```
bestMove = null;
float bestScore = Mathf.NegativeInfinity;
float adaptiveBeta = beta;
```

4. Loop through every available move and return the best score:

```
foreach (Move m in board.GetMoves())
{
    // next steps here
}
return bestScore;
```

5. Create a new game state from the current move:

```
Board b = board.MakeMove(m);
```

6. Set the values for the recursion:

```
Move currentMove = null;
float recursedScore;
int depth = currentDepth + 1;
float max = Mathf.Max(alpha, bestScore);
```

7. Call the recursion:

```
recursedScore = ABNegamax(b, player, maxDepth, depth, ref
currentMove, -adaptiveBeta, max);
```

8. Set the current score and validate it:

```
float currentScore = -recursedScore;
if (currentScore > bestScore)
{
    // next steps here
}
```

9. Validate for pruning:

```
if (adaptiveBeta == beta || currentDepth >= maxDepth - 2)
{
    bestScore = currentScore;
    bestMove = currentMove;
}
```

10. Otherwise, take a look around:

```
else
{
    float negativeBest;
    negativeBest = ABNegascout(b, player, maxDepth, depth, ref
bestMove, -beta, -currentScore);
    bestScore = -negativeBest;
}
```

11. Stop the loop if necessary. Otherwise, update the adaptive value:

```
if (bestScore >= beta)
    return bestScore;
adaptiveBeta = Mathf.Max(alpha, bestScore) + 1f;
```

How it works...

This algorithm works by examining the first move of each node. The following moves are examined using a scout pass with a narrower window based on the first move. If the pass fails, it is repeated using a full-width window. As a result, a large number of branches are pruned and failures are avoided.

See also

- The *AB Negamaxing* recipe

Implementing a Tic-Tac-Toe rival

To make use of the previous recipes, we will devise a way to implement a rival for the popular game Tic-Tac-Toe. Not only does it help us extend the base classes, but it also gives us a way to create rivals for our own board games.

Getting ready...

We will need to create a specific move class for the Tic-Tac-Toe board derived from the parent class we created at the beginning of the chapter:

```
using UnityEngine;
using System.Collections;

public class MoveTicTac : Move
{
    public int x;
    public int y;
    public int player;

    public MoveTicTac(int x, int y, int player)
    {
```

```
        this.x = x;
        this.y = y;
        this.player = player;
    }
}
```

How to do it...

We will create a new class, deriving it from `Board`, override its parent's methods, and create new ones:

1. Create the `BoardTicTac` class, deriving it from `Board`, and add the corresponding member variables for storing the board's values:

```
using UnityEngine;
using System;
using System.Collections;
using System.Collections.Generic;

public class BoardTicTac : Board
{
    protected int[,] board;
    protected const int ROWS = 3;
    protected const int COLS = 3;
}
```

2. Implement the default constructor:

```
public BoardTicTac(int player = 1)
{
    this.player = player;
    board = new int[ROWS, COLS];
    board[1,1] = 1;
}
```

3. Define the function for retrieving the next player in turn:

```
private int GetNextPlayer(int p)
{
    if (p == 1)
        return 2;
    return 1;
}
```

4. Create a function for evaluating a given position regarding a given player:

```
private float EvaluatePosition(int x, int y, int p)
{
    if (board[y, x] == 0)
        return 1f;
    else if (board[y, x] == p)
        return 2f;
    return -1f;
}
```

5. Define a function for evaluating the neighbors of a given position regarding a given player:

```
private float EvaluateNeighbours(int x, int y, int p)
{
    float eval = 0f;
    int i, j;
    for (i = y - 1; i < y + 2; y++)
    {
        if (i < 0 || i >= ROWS)
            continue;
        for (j = x - 1; j < x + 2; j++)
        {
            if (j < 0 || j >= COLS)
                continue;
            if (i == j)
                continue;
            eval += EvaluatePosition(j, i, p);
        }
    }
    return eval;
}
```

6. Implement a constructor for building new states with values:

```
public BoardTicTac(int[,] board, int player)
{
    this.board = board;
    this.player = player;
}
```

7. Override the member function for getting the available moves from the current state:

```
public override Move[] GetMoves()
{
    List<Move> moves = new List<Move>();
    int i;
    int j;
    for (i = 0; i < ROWS; i++)
    {
        for (j = 0; j < COLS; j++)
        {
            if (board[i, j] != 0)
                continue;
            MoveTicTac m = new MoveTicTac(j, i, player);
            moves.Add(m);
        }
    }
    return moves.ToArray();
}
```

8. Override the function for retrieving a new state from a given move:

```
public override Board MakeMove(Move m)
{
    MoveTicTac move = (MoveTicTac)m;
    int nextPlayer = GetNextPlayer(move.player);
    int[,] copy = new int[ROWS, COLS];
    Array.Copy(board, 0, copy, 0, board.Length);
    copy[move.y, move.x] = move.player;
    BoardTicTac b = new BoardTicTac(copy, nextPlayer);
    return b;
}
```

9. Define the function for evaluating the current state given a player:

```
public override float Evaluate(int player)
{
    float eval = 0f;
    int i, j;
    for (i = 0; i < ROWS; i++)
    {
        for (j = 0; j < COLS; j++)
        {
            eval += EvaluatePosition(j, i, player);
            eval += EvaluateNeighbours(j, i, player);
```

```
            }
        }
        return eval;
    }
```

10. Implement the function for evaluating the current state of the current player:

```
    public override float Evaluate()
    {
        float eval = 0f;
        int i, j;
        for (i = 0; i < ROWS; i++)
        {
            for (j = 0; j < COLS; j++)
            {
                eval += EvaluatePosition(j, i, player);
                eval += EvaluateNeighbours(j, i, player);
            }
        }
        return eval;
    }
```

How it works...

We define a new type of move for the board that works well with the base algorithms because they make use of it only at a high level as a data structure. The recipe's bread and butter comes from overriding the virtual functions from the `Board` class to model the problem. We use a two-dimensional integer array for storing the players' moves on the board (`0` representing an empty place), and we work out a heuristic for defining the value of a given state regarding its neighbors.

There's more...

The functions for evaluating a board's (state) score have an admissible heuristic, but it's probably not optimal. It is up to us to revisit this problem and refactor the body of the aforementioned functions to have a better-tuned rival.

See also

- The *Working the game-tree class* recipe

Implementing a Checkers rival

You will learn how to extend the previous recipes with an advanced example. In this case, you will learn how to model a Checkers (draughts) board and its pieces to comply with the necessary functions to be used with our board-AI framework.

This approach uses a chess board (of the size 8 x 8) and its respective number of pieces (12). However, it can be easily parameterized to change these values if we want to have a different-sized board.

Getting ready...

First, we need to create a new type of movement for this particular case called `MoveDraughts`:

```
using UnityEngine;
using System.Collections;

public class MoveDraughts : Move
{
    public PieceDraughts piece;
    public int x;
    public int y;
    public bool success;
    public int removeX;
    public int removeY;
}
```

This data structure stores the piece to be moved, the new `x` and `y` coordinates if the movement is a successful capture, and the position of the piece to be removed.

How to do it...

We will implement two core classes for modeling the pieces and the board, respectively. This is a long process, so it is advised to read each step carefully:

1. Create a new file called `PieceDraughts.cs` and add the following statements:

```
using UnityEngine;
using System.Collections;
using System.Collections.Generic;
```

2. Add the `PieceColor` data type:

```
public enum PieceColor
{
    WHITE,
    BLACK
};
```

3. Add the `PieceType` data `enum`:

```
public enum PieceType
{
    MAN,
    KING
};
```

4. Start building the `PieceDraughts` class:

```
public class PieceDraughts : MonoBehaviour
{
    public int x;
    public int y;
    public PieceColor color;
    public PieceType type;
    // next steps here
}
```

5. Define the function for setting up the piece logically:

```
public void Setup(int x, int y,
        PieceColor color,
        PieceType type = PieceType.MAN)
{
    this.x = x;
```

```
        this.y = y;
        this.color = color;
        this.type = type;
    }
```

6. Define the function for moving the piece on the board:

```
public void Move (MoveDraughts move, ref PieceDraughts [,]
board)
{
    board[move.y, move.x] = this;
    board[y, x] = null;
    x = move.x;
    y = move.y;
    // next steps here
}
```

7. If the move is a capture, remove the corresponding piece:

```
if (move.success)
{
    Destroy(board[move.removeY, move.removeX]);
    board[move.removeY, move.removeX] = null;
}
```

8. Stop the process if the piece is `KING`:

```
if (type == PieceType.KING)
    return;
```

9. Change the type of piece if it is `MAN` and it reaches the opposite border:

```
int rows = board.GetLength(0);
if (color == PieceColor.WHITE && y == rows)
    type = PieceType.KING;
if (color == PieceColor.BLACK && y == 0)
    type = PieceType.KING;
```

10. Define the function for checking whether a move is inside the bounds of the board:

```
private bool IsMoveInBounds(int x, int y, ref PieceDraughts[,]
board)
{
    int rows = board.GetLength(0);
    int cols = board.GetLength(1);
```

```
        if (x < 0 || x >= cols || y < 0 || y >= rows)
            return false;
        return true;
    }
```

11. Define the general function for retrieving the possible moves:

```
    public Move[] GetMoves(ref PieceDraughts[,] board)
    {
        List<Move> moves = new List<Move>();
        if (type == PieceType.KING)
            moves = GetMovesKing(ref board);
        else
            moves = GetMovesMan(ref board);
        return moves.ToArray();
    }
```

12. Start implementing the function for retrieving the moves when the piece's type is `Man`:

```
    private List<Move> GetMovesMan(ref PieceDraughts[,] board)
    {
        // next steps here
    }
```

13. Add the variable for storing the two possible moves:

```
    List<Move> moves = new List<Move>(2);
```

14. Define the variable for holding the two possible horizontal options:

```
    int[] moveX = new int[] { -1, 1 };
```

15. Define the variable for holding the vertical direction depending on the piece's color:

```
    int moveY = 1;
    if (color == PieceColor.BLACK)
        moveY = -1;
```

16. Implement the loop for iterating through the two possible options and return the available moves. We will implement the body of the loop in the next step:

```
    foreach (int mX in moveX)
    {
        // next teps
    }
```

```
return moves;
```

17. Declare two new variables for computing the next position to be considered:

```
int nextX = x + mX;
int nextY = y + moveY;
```

18. Test the possible option if the move is out of bounds:

```
if (!IsMoveInBounds(nextX, y, ref board))
    continue;
```

19. Continue with the next option if the move is being blocked by a piece of the same color:

```
PieceDraughts p = board[moveY, nextX];
if (p != null && p.color == color)
    continue;
```

20. Create a new move to be added to the list:

```
MoveDraughts m = new MoveDraughts();
m.piece = this;
```

21. Create a simple move if the position is available:

```
if (p == null)
{
    m.x = nextX;
    m.y = nextY;
}
```

22. Test whether the piece can be captured, and modify the move accordingly:

```
else
{
    int hopX = nextX + mX;
    int hopY = nextY + moveY;
    if (!IsMoveInBounds(hopX, hopY, ref board))
        continue;
    if (board[hopY, hopX] != null)
        continue;
    m.y = hopX;
    m.x = hopY;
    m.success = true;
    m.removeX = nextX;
```

```
        m.removeY = nextY;
    }
```

23. Add the move to the list:

```
    moves.Add(m);
```

24. Start to implement the function for retrieving the available moves when the piece's type is `King`:

```
    private List<Move> GetMovesKing(ref PieceDraughts[,] board)
    {
        // next steps here
    }
```

25. Declare the variable for holding the possible moves:

```
    List<Move> moves = new List<Move>();
```

26. Create the variables for searching in four directions:

```
    int[] moveX = new int[] { -1, 1 };
    int[] moveY = new int[] { -1, 1 };
```

27. Start implementing the loop for checking all the possible moves, and retrieve those moves. The next step will implement the body of the inner loop:

```
    foreach (int mY in moveY)
    {
        foreach (int mX in moveX)
        {
            // next steps here
        }
    }
    return moves;
```

28. Create the variables for testing the moves and advances:

```
    int nowX = x + mX;
    int nowY = y + mY;
```

29. Create a loop for going in that direction until the board's bounds are reached:

```
    while (IsMoveInBounds(nowX, nowY, ref board))
    {
        // next steps here
```

```
}
```

30. Get the position's piece reference:

```
PieceDraughts p = board[nowY, nowX];
```

31. If it is a piece of the same color, stop going further:

```
if (p != null && p.color == color)
    break;
```

32. Define a variable for creating the new available move:

```
MoveDraughts m = new MoveDraughts();
m.piece = this;
```

33. Create a simple move if the position is available:

```
if (p == null)
{
    m.x = nowX;
    m.y = nowY;
}
```

34. Test whether the piece can be captured and modify the move accordingly:

```
else
{
    int hopX = nowX + mX;
    int hopY = nowY + mY;
    if (!IsMoveInBounds(hopX, hopY, ref board))
        break;
    m.success = true;
    m.x = hopX;
    m.y = hopY;
    m.removeX = nowX;
    m.removeY = nowY;
}
```

35. Add the move and advance a step towards the current direction:

```
moves.Add(m);
nowX += mX;
nowY += mY;
```

36. Create a new class called `BoardDraughts` in a new file:

```
using UnityEngine;
using System.Collections;
```

```
using System.Collections.Generic;

public class BoardDraughts : Board
{
    public int size = 8;
    public int numPieces = 12;
    public GameObject prefab;
    protected PieceDraughts[,] board;
}
```

37. Implement the `Awake` function:

```
void Awake()
{
    board = new PieceDraughts[size, size];
}
```

38. Start implementing the `Start` function. It is important to note that this may vary depending on your game's spatial representation:

```
void Start()
{
    // TODO
    // initialization and board set up
    // your implementation may vary

    // next steps here
}
```

39. Throw an error message if the template object doesn't have an attached `PieceDraught` script:

```
PieceDraughts pd = prefab.GetComponent<PieceDraughts>();
if (pd == null)
{
    Debug.LogError("No PieceDraught component detected");
    return;
}
```

40. Add iterator variables:

```
int i;
int j;
```

41. Implement the loop for placing the white pieces:

```
int piecesLeft = numPieces;
for (i = 0; i < size; i++)
```

```
{
    if (piecesLeft == 0)
        break;
    int init = 0;
    if (i % 2 != 0)
        init = 1;
    for (j = init; j < size; j+=2)
    {
        if (piecesLeft == 0)
            break;
        PlacePiece(j, i);
        piecesLeft--;
    }
}
```

42. Implement the loop for placing the black pieces:

```
piecesLeft = numPieces;
for (i = size - 1; i >= 0; i--)
{
    if (piecesLeft == 0)
        break;
    int init = 0;
    if (i % 2 != 0)
        init = 1;
    for (j = init; j < size; j+=2)
    {
        if (piecesLeft == 0)
            break;
        PlacePiece(j, i);
        piecesLeft--;
    }
}
```

43. Implement the function for placing a specific piece. This could change in your game depending on its visualization:

```
private void PlacePiece(int x, int y)
{
    // TODO
    // your own transformations
    // according to space placements
    Vector3 pos = new Vector3();
    pos.x = (float)x;
    pos.y = -(float)y;
    GameObject go = GameObject.Instantiate(prefab);
    go.transform.position = pos;
    PieceDraughts p = go.GetComponent<PieceDraughts>();
```

```
        p.Setup(x, y, color);
        board[y, x] = p;
    }
```

44. Implement the `Evaluate` function with no parameters:

```
    public override float Evaluate()
    {
        PieceColor color = PieceColor.WHITE;
        if (player == 1)
            color = PieceColor.BLACK;
        return Evaluate(color);
    }
```

45. Implement the `Evaluate` function with a parameter:

```
    public override float Evaluate(int player)
    {
        PieceColor color = PieceColor.WHITE;
        if (player == 1)
            color = PieceColor.BLACK;
        return Evaluate(color);
    }
```

46. Start implementing the general function for evaluation:

```
    private float Evaluate(PieceColor color)
    {
        // next steps here
    }
```

47. Define the variables for holding the evaluation and assigning points:

```
    float eval = 1f;
    float pointSimple = 1f;
    float pointSuccess = 5f;
```

48. Create variables for holding the board's bounds:

```
    int rows = board.GetLength(0);
    int cols = board.GetLength(1);
```

49. Define variables for iteration:

```
    int i;
    int j;
```

50. Iterate throughout the board to look for moves and possible captures:

```
for (i = 0; i < rows; i++)
{
    for (j = 0; j < cols; j++)
    {
        PieceDraughts p = board[i, j];
        if (p == null)
            continue;
        if (p.color != color)
            continue;
        Move[] moves = p.GetMoves(ref board);
        foreach (Move mv in moves)
        {
            MoveDraughts m = (MoveDraughts)mv;
            if (m.success)
                eval += pointSuccess;
            else
                eval += pointSimple;
        }
    }
}
```

51. Retrieve the evaluation value:

```
return eval;
```

52. Start developing the function for retrieving the board's available moves:

```
public override Move[] GetMoves()
{
    // next steps here
}
```

53. Define the variables for holding the moves and the board's boundaries, and handling iteration:

```
List<Move> moves = new List<Move>();
int rows = board.GetLength(0);
int cols = board.GetLength(1);
int i;
int j;
```

54. Get the moves from all the available pieces on the board:

```
for (i = 0; i < rows; i++)
{
    for (j = 0; i < cols; j++)
    {
        PieceDraughts p = board[i, j];
        if (p == null)
            continue;
        moves.AddRange(p.GetMoves(ref board));
    }
}
```

55. Return the moves found:

```
return moves.ToArray();
```

How it works...

The board works in a similar fashion to the previous board, but it has a more complex process due to the rules of the game. The movements are tied to the piece's moves, thus creating a cascading effect that must be handled carefully. Each piece has two types of movement depending on its color and type.

As we can see, the high-level rules are the same. It just requires a little bit of patience and thinking to develop good evaluation functions and procedures for retrieving the board's available moves.

There's more...

The `Evaluate` function is far from perfect. We implemented a heuristic based solely on the number of available moves and captured the opponent's pieces, providing room for improvements to avoid movements where a player's piece could be captured on the rival's next move.

Also, we should make our own changes to the `PlacePiece` function in the `BoardDraughts` class. We implemented a direct method that probably doesn't fit your game's spatial setup.

Implementing Rock-Paper-Scissors AI with UCB1

Rock-Paper-Scissors is a classic game for testing AI techniques; that's why we'll use this case scenario for the current and following recipes. We will implement what are called **bandit algorithms** based on the notion of exploring *n*-armed bandits. It's usually modeled towards a slot machine, but we will study it as an RPS player. The main idea is to get hold of the option that results in a better payoff.

In this recipe, we will learn about the UCB1 algorithm and how it works.

Getting ready...

First, we need to implement a data structure for defining our actions:

```
public enum RPSAction
{
  Rock, Paper, Scissors
}
```

How to do it...

We will implement a `Bandit` class for building the logic behind the algorithm:

1. Create a new class named `Bandit`:

```
using UnityEngine;

public class Bandit : MonoBehaviour
{
  // next steps
}
```

2. Define the required member variables:

```
bool init;
int totalActions;
int[] count;
float[] score;
int numActions;
RPSAction lastAction;
int lastStrategy;
```

3. Define the function for initializing the UCB1 algorithm:

```
public void InitUCB1()
{
  if (init)
    return;
 // next step
}
```

4. Define the local variables and initialize them:

```
  totalActions = 0;
  numActions = System.Enum.GetNames(typeof(RPSAction)).Length;
  count = new int[numActions];
  score = new float[numActions];
  int i;
  for (i = 0; i < numActions; i++)
  {
    count[i] = 0;
    score[i] = 0f;
  }
  init = true;
```

5. Define a member function for computing the next action to be taken by the agent:

```
public RPSAction GetNextActionUCB1()
{
  // next steps
}
```

6. Include the required local variables:

```
int i, best;
float bestScore;
float tempScore;
InitUCB1();
```

7. Check the number of actions available. If an action hasn't been explored, return it:

```
for (i = 0; i < numActions; i++)
{
  if (count[i] == 0)
  {
    lastStrategy = i;
```

```
        lastAction = GetActionForStrategy((RPSAction)i);
        return lastAction;
    }
}
```

8. Initialize the variables for computing the best score:

```
best = 0;
bestScore = score[best]/(float)count[best];
float input = Mathf.Log(totalActions/(float)count[best]);
input *= 2f;
bestScore += Mathf.Sqrt(input);
```

9. Check all the actions available:

```
for (i = 0; i < numActions; i++)
{
  // next step
}
```

10. Compute the best score:

```
tempScore = score[i]/(float)count[i];
input = Mathf.Log(totalActions/(float)count[best]);
input *= 2f;
tempScore = Mathf.Sqrt(input);
if (tempScore > bestScore)
{
  best =i;
  bestScore = tempScore;
}
```

11. Return the best action:

```
lastStrategy = best;
lastAction = GetActionForStrategy((RPSAction)best);
return lastAction;
```

12. Define the function for retrieving the best response for a given initial action:

```
public RPSAction GetActionForStrategy(RPSAction strategy)
{
  RPSAction action;
  // next steps
}
```

13. Implement the basic rules of the game:

```
switch (strategy)
{
  default:
  case RPSAction.Paper:
    action = RPSAction.Scissors;
    break;
  case RPSAction.Rock:
    action = RPSAction.Paper;
    break;
  case RPSAction.Scissors:
    action = RPSAction.Rock;
    break;
}
```

14. Return the best action:

```
return action;
```

15. Define the member function for computing the utility of an action, based on the opponent's one. Initially, it's a draw:

```
public float GetUtility(RPSAction myAction, RPSAction
opponents)
{
  float utility = 0f;
  // next steps
}
```

16. Check whether the opponent played paper:

```
if (opponents == RPSAction.Paper)
{
  if (myAction == RPSAction.Rock)
    utility = -1f;
  else if (myAction == RPSAction.Scissors)
    utility = 1f;
}
```

17. Check whether the opponent played rock:

```
else if (opponents == RPSAction.Rock)
{
  if (myAction == RPSAction.Paper)
    utility = 1f;
  else if (myAction == RPSAction.Scissors)
```

```
        utility = -1f;
    }
```

18. Check whether the opponent played scissors:

```
else
{
  if (myAction == RPSAction.Rock)
    utility = -1f;
  else if (myAction == RPSAction.Paper)
    utility = 1f;
}
```

19. Return the utility value:

```
return utility;
```

How it works...

We developed our recipe using a pseudo-exploratory algorithm and stored the payoff from taking a certain action. The recipe first tests every action there is, and then keeps making moves using the formula from the UCB1 algorithm. It is good enough to be challenging, and at the same time it is defeatable because the algorithm explores different options—Thus, creating better changes for the player to improve their skills, or just to be lucky.

There's more...

We need a function for handling the overall actions of the game and informing the algorithm of the actions from the opponent. In this case, the player's actions:

```
public void TellOpponentAction(RPSAction action)
{
  totalActions++;
  float utility;
  utility = GetUtility(lastAction, action);
  score[(int)lastAction] += utility;
  count[(int)lastAction] += 1;
}
```

See also

For more theoretical reading regarding the UCB1 algorithm, please refer to the work of Prof Nathan Sturtevant, at the following URL: `https://www.movingai.com/gdc14/`.

Implementing regret matching

Continuing with the bandit algorithms, we will explore an improvement to the UCB1 algorithm, called regret matching. We will use the same case of playing rock-paper-scissors, but it can be repurposed for other types of games, such as fighting games.

Getting ready...

It's important to have read the previous recipe and to have taken into account the member variables and data structures. The member functions are not relevant for the purpose of this algorithm as we will implement a different set to have a different recipe, but it's based on the knowledge gained previously.

How to do it...

We will implement the following steps in the same `Bandit` class we created before.

1. Define the required member variables:

```
float initialRegret = 10f;
float[] regret;
float[] chance;
RPSAction lastOpponentAction;
RPSAction[] lastActionRM;
```

2. Define the member function for initialization:

```
public void InitRegretMatching()
{
  if (init)
    return;
  // next steps
}
```

3. Declare the local variables and initialize them:

```
numActions = System.Enum.GetNames(typeof(RPSAction)).Length;
regret = new float[numActions];
chance = new float[numActions];
int i;
for (i = 0; i < numActions; i++)
{
  regret[i] = initialRegret;
  chance[i] = 0f;
}
init = true;
```

4. Define the member function for computing the next action to be taken:

```
public RPSAction GetNextActionRM()
{
  // next steps
}
```

5. Declare the local variables and call the initialization function:

```
float sum = 0f;
float prob = 0f;
int i;
InitRegretMatching();
```

6. Explore all the available options and hold the response to be taken:

```
for (i = 0; i < numActions; i++)
{
  lastActionRM[i] = GetActionForStrategy((RPSAction)i);
}
```

7. Sum the overall regret:

```
for (i = 0; i < numActions; i++)
{
  if (regret[i] > 0f)
    sum += regret[i];
}
```

8. Return a random action if the sum is less than or equal to zero:

```
if (sum <= 0f)
{
  lastAction = (RPSAction)Random.Range(0, numActions);
  return lastAction;
}
```

9. Explore the set of actions and sum the chance of regretting them:

```
for (i = 0; i < numActions; i++)
{
 chance[i] = 0f;
  if (regret[i] > 0f)
    chance[i] = regret[i];
  if (i > 0)
    chance[i] += chance[i-1];
}
```

10. Compute a random probability and compare that to the chance of taking the actions. Return the first one to be greater than the probability computed:

```
prob = Random.value;
for (i = 0; i < numActions; i++)
{
  if (prob < chance[i])
  {
    lastStrategy = i;
    lastAction = lastActionRM[i];
    return lastAction;
  }
}
```

11. Return the last action if everything else fails:

```
return (RPSAction)(numActions-1)
```

How it works...

We explore the available options and compute the payoff of taking them. Once we have taken a certain amount of action, the algorithm adjusts and retrieves actions based on stochastic events. However, we play with chance against such actions, given the opponent's moves.

There's more...

Not only it is important to define and balance strategies, but also the results of keeping track of the opponent's actions. That's why we need to implement a member function for adding them into the mix we talked about in the previous section:

```
public void TellOpponentActionRM(RPSAction action)
{
  lastOpponentAction = action;
  int i;
  for (i = 0; i < numActions; i++)
  {
    regret[i] += GetUtility((RPSAction)lastActionRM[i],
(RPSAction)action);
    regret[i] -= GetUtility((RPSAction)lastAction, (RPSAction)
action);
  }
}
```

Finally, it's important to balance the strategies and the utility function. It's pretty straightforward for RPS, but it could get as complex as our game.

See also

For more theoretical reading regarding the UCB1 algorithm, please refer to the work of Prof Nathan Sturtevant at the following URL: `https://www.movingai.com/gdc14/`.

19
Learning Techniques

In this chapter, you will explore the world of machine learning through the following recipes:

- Predicting actions with an N-Gram predictor
- Improving the predictor – Hierarchical N-Gram
- Learning to use a Naïve Bayes classifier
- Implementing reinforcement learning
- Implementing artificial neural networks

Introduction

In this chapter, we will explore the field of machine learning. This is a very extensive and intrinsic field in which even AAA titles have a hard time, because of the amount of time that the techniques require to be tuned and experimented with.

However, the recipes that are contained in this chapter will give us a great head start in our endeavor to learn and apply machine learning techniques to our games. They are used in several different ways, but the one feature that they are most useful for is difficulty adjustment.

Finally, it is advised that you complement these recipes by reading more theoretical books on the subject, to gain in-depth insights that lie beyond the scope of this chapter.

Predicting actions with an N-Gram predictor

Predicting actions is a great way to give players a challenge by going from random selection to selection based on past actions. One way to implement machine learning is by using probabilities to predict what the player will do next, and that's what an N-Gram predictor does.

To predict the player's next choice, N-Gram predictors hold a record of the probabilities of making particular decisions (which are usually moves), given all the combinations of the choices for the previous *n* moves.

Getting ready...

This is a recipe that makes use of general types. It is recommended that you have at least a basic understanding of how they work, because it's important that we use them well.

The first thing to do is implement a data type for holding the actions and their probabilities, which is called `KeyDataRecord`.

The `KeyDataRecord.cs` file should look like this:

```
using System.Collections;
using System.Collections.Generic;

public class KeyDataRecord<T>
{
    public Dictionary<T, int> counts;
    public int total;
    public KeyDataRecord()
    {
        counts = new Dictionary<T, int>();
    }
}
```

How to do it...

The process of building an N-Gram predictor is divided into five big steps, as follows:

1. Create the general class within a file that has the same name:

```
using System.Collections;
using System.Collections.Generic;
using System.Text;

public class NGramPredictor<T>
{
    private int nValue;
    private Dictionary<string, KeyDataRecord<T>> data;
}
```

2. Implement the constructor for initializing the member variables:

```
public NGramPredictor(int windowSize)
{
    nValue = windowSize + 1;
    data = new Dictionary<string, KeyDataRecord<T>>();
}
```

3. Implement a static function for converting a set of actions into a string key:

```
public static string ArrToStrKey(ref T[] actions)
{
    StringBuilder builder = new StringBuilder();
    foreach (T a in actions)
    {
        builder.Append(a.ToString());
    }
    return builder.ToString();
}
```

4. Define the function for registering a set of sequences:

```
public void RegisterSequence(T[] actions)
{
    string key = ArrToStrKey(ref actions);
    T val = actions[nValue - 1];
    if (!data.ContainsKey(key))
        data[key] = new KeyDataRecord<T>();
    KeyDataRecord<T> kdr = data[key];
    if (kdr.counts.ContainsKey(val))
        kdr.counts[val] = 0;
    kdr.counts[val]++;
    kdr.total++;
}
```

5. Finally, implement the function for computing the prediction of the best action to take:

```
public T GetMostLikely(T[] actions)
{
    string key = ArrToStrKey(ref actions);
    KeyDataRecord<T> kdr = data[key];
    int highestVal = 0;
    T bestAction = default(T);
    foreach (KeyValuePair<T,int> kvp in kdr.counts)
    {
        if (kvp.Value > highestVal)
        {
            bestAction = kvp.Key;
            highestVal = kvp.Value;
        }
    }
    return bestAction;
}
```

How it works...

The predictor registers a set of actions according to the size of the window (the number of actions to register to make predictions) and assigns them the resulting value. For example, for a window with a size of `3`, the first three are saved as a key to predict that it's possible that a fourth one may follow.

The prediction function computes how likely it is for an action to be the one that follows, given a set of previous actions. The more registered actions, the more accurate the predictor will be (with some limitations).

There's more...

It is important to consider that the object of type `T` must override both the `ToString` function and the `Equals` function in an admissible way for it to work correctly as an index in the internal dictionaries.

Improving the predictor – Hierarchical N-Gram

The N-Gram predictor can be improved by having a handler with several other predictors ranging from 1 to *n*, and obtaining the best possible action after comparing the best guess from each one of them.

Getting ready...

We need to make some adjustments prior to implementing the hierarchical N-Gram predictor.

Add the following member function to the `NGramPredictor` class:

```
public int GetActionsNum(ref T[] actions)
{
    string key = ArrToStrKey(ref actions);
    if (!data.ContainsKey(key))
        return 0;
    return data[key].total;
}
```

How to do it...

Just like the N-Gram predictor, the building of the hierarchical version is a few steps long:

1. Create the new class:

```
using System;
using System.Collections;
using System.Text;

public class HierarchicalNGramP<T>
{
    public int threshold;
    public NGramPredictor<T>[] predictors;
    private int nValue;
}
```

2. Implement the constructor for initializing member values:

```
public HierarchicalNGramP(int windowSize)
{
    nValue = windowSize + 1;
    predictors = new NGramPredictor<T>[nValue];
    int i;
    for (i = 0; i < nValue; i++)
        predictors[i] = new NGramPredictor<T>(i + 1);
}
```

3. Define a function for registering a sequence, just like its predecessor:

```
public void RegisterSequence(T[] actions)
{
    int i;
    for (i = 0; i < nValue; i++)
    {
        T[] subactions = new T[i+1];
        Array.Copy(actions, nValue - i - 1, subactions, 0,
i+1);
        predictors[i].RegisterSequence(subactions);
    }
}
```

4. Finally, implement the function for computing the prediction:

```
public T GetMostLikely(T[] actions)
{
    int i;
    T bestAction = default(T);
    for (i = 0; i < nValue; i++)
    {
        NGramPredictor<T> p;
        p = predictors[nValue - i - 1];
        T[] subactions = new T[i + 1];
        Array.Copy(actions, nValue - i - 1, subactions, 0, i +
1);
        int numActions = p.GetActionsNum(ref actions);
        if (numActions > threshold)
            bestAction = p.GetMostLikely(actions);
    }
    return bestAction;
}
```

How it works...

The hierarchical N-Gram predictor works almost exactly like its predecessor, the difference being that it holds a set of predictors and computes each main function using its children. Each method works by decomposing the set of available actions, and, whether by registering sequences or finding out the most likely future action, each method works by decomposing the set of actions and feeding the children with them.

Learning to use Naïve Bayes classifier

Learning to use examples could be hard even for humans. For example, given a list of examples for two sets of values, it's not always easy to see the connection between them. One way of solving this problem would be to classify one set of values and then give it a try, and that's where classifier algorithms come in handy.

Naïve Bayes classifiers are prediction algorithms for assigning labels to problem instances; they apply probability and Bayes' theorem with a strong-independence assumption between the variables that are to be analyzed. One of the key advantages of Bayes' classifiers is their scalability.

Getting ready...

Since it is hard to build a general classifier, we will build ours assuming that the inputs are positive- and negative-labeled examples. So, the first thing we need to do is define the labels that our classifier will handle using an enum data structure called `NBCLabel`:

```
public enum NBCLabel
{
    POSITIVE,
    NEGATIVE
}
```

How to do it...

The classifier we'll build won't take long, just five steps:

1. Create the class and its member variables:

```
using UnityEngine;
using System.Collections;
using System.Collections.Generic;

public class NaiveBayesClassifier : MonoBehaviour
{
    public int numAttributes;
    public int numExamplesPositive;
    public int numExamplesNegative;

    public List<bool> attrCountPositive;
    public List<bool> attrCountNegative;
}
```

2. Define the `Awake` method for initialization:

```
void Awake()
{
    attrCountPositive = new List<bool>();
    attrCountNegative = new List<bool>();
}
```

3. Implement the function for updating the classifier:

```
public void UpdateClassifier(bool[] attributes, NBCLabel
label)
{
```

```
        if (label == NBCLabel.POSITIVE)
        {
            numExamplesPositive++;
            attrCountPositive.AddRange(attributes);
        }
        else
        {
            numExamplesNegative++;
            attrCountNegative.AddRange(attributes);
        }
    }
```

4. Define the function for computing the Naïve probability:

```
    public float NaiveProbabilities(
            ref bool[] attributes,
            bool[] counts,
            float m,
            float n)
    {
        float prior = m / (m + n);
        float p = 1f;
        int i = 0;
        for (i = 0; i < numAttributes; i++)
        {
            p /= m;
            if (attributes[i] == true)
                p *= counts[i].GetHashCode();
            else
                p *= m - counts[i].GetHashCode();
        }
        return prior * p;
    }
```

5. Finally, implement the function for prediction:

```
    public bool Predict(bool[] attributes)
    {
        float nep = numExamplesPositive;
        float nen = numExamplesNegative;
        float x = NaiveProbabilities(ref attributes,
    attrCountPositive.ToArray(), nep, nen);
        float y = NaiveProbabilities(ref attributes,
    attrCountNegative.ToArray(), nen, nep);
        if (x >= y)
            return true;
        return false;
    }
```

How it works...

The `UpdateClassifier` function takes the example input values and stores them. This is the first function to be called. The `NaiveProbabilities` function is the one responsible for computing the probabilities for the prediction function to work. Finally, the `Predict` function is the second one to be called by us to get the results of the classification.

Implementing reinforcement learning

Imagine that we need to come up with an enemy that needs to select different actions over time as the player progresses through the game and their patterns change, or a game for training different types of pets that have free will, to some extent.

For these types of tasks, there exists a series of techniques aimed at modeling learning based on experience. One of these algorithms is *Q*-learning, which will be implemented in the following recipe.

Getting ready...

Before delving into the main algorithm, you should have certain data structures implemented. We need to define a structure for the game state, another for the game actions, and a class for defining an instance of the problem. They can coexist in the same file.

The following is an example of the data structure for defining a game state:

```
public struct GameState
{
    // TODO
    // your state definition here
}
```

The following is an example of the data structure for defining a game action:

```
public struct GameAction
{
    // TODO
    // your action definition here
}
```

Finally, we will build the data type for defining a problem instance:

1. Create the file and class:

```
public class ReinforcementProblem
{
}
```

2. Define a virtual function for retrieving a random state. Depending on the type of game we're developing, we would be interested in random states concerning the current state of the game:

```
public virtual GameState GetRandomState()
{
    // TODO
    // Define your own behaviour
    return new GameState();
}
```

3. Define a virtual function for retrieving all the available actions from a given game state:

```
public virtual GameAction[] GetAvailableActions(GameState s)
{
    // TODO
    // Define your own behaviour
    return new GameAction[0];
}
```

4. Define a virtual function for carrying out an action, and then retrieving the resulting state and reward:

```
public virtual GameState TakeAction(
        GameState s,
        GameAction a,
        ref float reward)
{
    // TODO
    // Define your own behaviour
    reward = 0f;
    return new GameState();
}
```

How to do it...

We will now implement two classes. The first one stores values in a dictionary for learning purposes and the second one actually holds the *Q*-learning algorithm. Go through the following steps to create the two classes:

1. Create the `QValueStore` class:

```
using UnityEngine;
using System.Collections.Generic;

public class QValueStore : MonoBehaviour
{
    private Dictionary<GameState, Dictionary<GameAction,
float>> store;
}
```

2. Implement the constructor:

```
public QValueStore()
{
    store = new Dictionary<GameState, Dictionary<GameAction,
float>>();
}
```

3. Define the function for getting the resulting value of taking an action in a game state. Carefully craft this so that an action cannot be taken in that particular state:

```
public virtual float GetQValue(GameState s, GameAction a)
{
    // TODO: your behaviour here
    return 0f;
}
```

4. Implement the function for retrieving the best action to take in a certain state:

```
public virtual GameAction GetBestAction(GameState s)
{
    // TODO: your behaviour here
    return new GameAction();
}
```

5. Implement the function for the following:

```
public void StoreQValue(
```

```
            GameState s,
            GameAction a,
            float val)
    {
        if (!store.ContainsKey(s))
        {
            Dictionary<GameAction, float> d;
            d = new Dictionary<GameAction, float>();
            store.Add(s, d);
        }
        if (!store[s].ContainsKey(a))
        {
            store[s].Add(a, 0f);
        }
        store[s][a] = val;
    }
```

6. Let's move on to create the `QLearning` class that will run the algorithm:

```
using UnityEngine;
using System.Collections;

public class QLearning : MonoBehaviour
{
    public QValueStore store;
}
```

7. Define the function for retrieving random actions from a given set:

```
private GameAction GetRandomAction(GameAction[] actions)
{
    int n = actions.Length;
    return actions[Random.Range(0, n)];
}
```

8. Implement the learning function. Be advised that this is split into several steps. Start by defining it. Take into consideration that this is a coroutine:

```
public IEnumerator Learn(
        ReinforcementProblem problem,
        int numIterations,
        float alpha,
        float gamma,
        float rho,
        float nu)
{
    // next steps
}
```

9. Validate that the store list is initialized:

```
if (store == null)
    yield break;
```

10. Get a random state:

```
GameState state = problem.GetRandomState();
for (int i = 0; i < numIterations; i++)
{
    // next steps
}
```

11. Return `null` for the current frame to keep running:

```
yield return null;
```

12. Validate against the length of the walk:

```
if (Random.value < nu)
    state = problem.GetRandomState();
```

13. Get the available actions from the current game state:

```
GameAction[] actions;
actions = problem.GetAvailableActions(state);
GameAction action;
```

14. Get an action depending on the value of the randomness of exploration:

```
if (Random.value < rho)
    action = GetRandomAction(actions);
else
    action = store.GetBestAction(state);
```

15. Calculate the new state for taking the selected action on the current state and the resulting reward value:

```
float reward = 0f;
GameState newState;
newState = problem.TakeAction(state, action, ref reward);
```

16. Get the `q` value, given the current game, and take action, and the best action for the new state that was computed before:

```
float q = store.GetQValue(state, action);
GameAction bestAction = store.GetBestAction(newState);
float maxQ = store.GetQValue(newState, bestAction);
```

17. Apply the *Q*-learning formula:

```
q = (1f - alpha) * q + alpha * (reward + gamma * maxQ);
```

18. Store the computed `q` value, giving its parents as indices:

```
store.StoreQValue(state, action, q);
state = newState;
```

How it works...

In the *Q*-learning algorithm, the game world is treated as a state machine. It is important to bear in mind the meaning of the parameters:

- `alpha`: This is the learning rate
- `gamma`: This is the discount rate
- `rho`: This is the randomness of exploration
- `nu`: This is the length of the walk

Implementing artificial neural networks

Imagine that we made an enemy or game system that emulates the way the brain works. That's how neural networks operate. They are based on the neuron—we call it the `Perceptron`—and are formed of the sum of several neurons; its inputs and outputs are what makes a neural network.

In this recipe, we will learn how to build a neural system, starting from the `Perceptron` through to the way that they can be joined to create a network.

Getting ready...

We will need a data type for handling raw input; this is called `InputPerceptron`:

```
public class InputPerceptron
{
    public float input;
    public float weight;
}
```

How to do it...

We will implement two big classes. The first one is the implementation for the `Perceptron` data type, and the second one is the data type handling the neural network. Go through the following steps to implement these two classes:

1. Implement a `Perceptron` class derived from the `InputPerceptron` class that was previously defined:

```
public class Perceptron : InputPerceptron
{
    public InputPerceptron[] inputList;
    public delegate float Threshold(float x);
    public Threshold threshold;
    public float state;
    public float error;
}
```

2. Implement the constructor for setting the number of inputs:

```
public Perceptron(int inputSize)
{
    inputList = new InputPerceptron[inputSize];
}
```

3. Define the function for processing the inputs:

```
public void FeedForward()
{
    float sum = 0f;
    foreach (InputPerceptron i in inputList)
    {
        sum += i.input * i.weight;
    }
    state = threshold(sum);
}
```

4. Implement the functions for adjusting weights:

```
public void AdjustWeights(float currentError)
{
    int i;
    for (i = 0; i < inputList.Length; i++)
    {
        float deltaWeight;
        deltaWeight = currentError * inputList[i].weight *
state;
```

```
            inputList[i].weight = deltaWeight;
            error = currentError;
        }
    }
```

5. Define a function for funneling the weights with regard to the type of input:

```
    public float GetIncomingWeight()
    {
        foreach (InputPerceptron i in inputList)
        {
            if (i.GetType() == typeof(Perceptron))
                return i.weight;
        }
        return 0f;
    }
```

6. Create the class for handling the set of `Perceptron` elements as a network:

```
    using UnityEngine;
    using System.Collections;

    public class MLPNetwork : MonoBehaviour
    {
        public Perceptron[] inputPer;
        public Perceptron[] hiddenPer;
        public Perceptron[] outputPer;
    }
```

7. Implement the function for transmitting inputs from one end of the neural network to the other:

```
    public void GenerateOutput(Perceptron[] inputs)
    {
        int i;
        for (i = 0; i < inputs.Length; i++)
            inputPer[i].state = inputs[i].input;
        for (i = 0; i < hiddenPer.Length; i++)
            hiddenPer[i].FeedForward();
        for (i = 0; i < outputPer.Length; i++)
            outputPer[i].FeedForward();
    }
```

8. Define the function for propelling the computation that actually emulates learning:

```
public void BackProp(Perceptron[] outputs)
{
    // next steps
}
```

9. Traverse the output layer for computing values:

```
int i;
for (i = 0; i < outputPer.Length; i++)
{
    Perceptron p = outputPer[i];
    float state = p.state;
    float error = state * (1f - state);
    error *= outputs[i].state - state;
    p.AdjustWeights(error);
}
```

10. Traverse the internal `Perceptron` layers:

```
for (i = 0; i < hiddenPer.Length; i++)
{
    Perceptron p = outputPer[i];
    float state = p.state;
    float sum = 0f;
    for (i = 0; i < outputs.Length; i++)
    {
        float incomingW = outputs[i].GetIncomingWeight();
        sum += incomingW * outputs[i].error;
        float error = state * (1f - state) * sum;
        p.AdjustWeights(error);
    }
}
```

11. Implement a high-level function for ease of use:

```
public void Learn(
        Perceptron[] inputs,
        Perceptron[] outputs)
{
    GenerateOutput(inputs);
    BackProp(outputs);
}
```

How it works...

We implemented two types of `Perceptron` to define the ones that handle external input and the ones internally connected to one another. That's why the basic `Perceptron` class derives from the latter one. The `FeedForward` function handles the inputs and irrigates them along the network. Finally, the function for back propagation is the one responsible for adjusting the weights. This *weight adjustment* is the emulation of learning.

20
Procedural Content Generation

In this chapter, you will learn different techniques for procedural content generation with the following recipes:

- Creating mazes with Depth-First Search
- Implementing the constructive algorithm for dungeons and islands
- Generating landscapes
- Using N-Grams for content generation
- Generating enemies with the evolutionary algorithm

Introduction

We can define **Procedural Content Generation** (**PCG**) in games as the creation of content via algorithms, with or without human input. It's a topic of interest for both academia and the industry, the latter ranging from big development studios to small independent developers. It can be used for generating vegetation, delivering high-level details, creating complete mazes and worlds to explore, and increasing the title's replay value, and hours of gameplay.

The different techniques covered in this chapter will give us a glimpse of the possibilities, and guide us in the right direction for more in-depth work.

Creating mazes with Depth-First Search

We will start our journey with PCG by using a search algorithm as a starting point for creating mazes. We will use the foundations acquired in `Chapter 13`, *Navigation*, and twist them a little, to create mazes.

Getting ready

For the graph, we will use the grid representation, and Boolean values to define whether a cell is a wall or not, respectively.

How to do it...

We will comprise everything in just a class that will handle the abstract representation, called `DSFDungeon`:

1. Define the `DFSDungeon` component and its member values:

```
using UnityEngine;
using System.Collections.Generic;

public class DFSDungeon : MonoBehaviour
{
  public int width;
  public int height;
  public bool[,] dungeon;
  public bool[,] visited;
  private Stack<Vector2> stack;
  private Vector2 current;
  private int size;

  // next steps
}
```

2. Define the initialization function:

```
private void Init()
{
  // next steps
}
```

3. Initialize the required variables and random initial position:

```
stack = new Stack<Vector2>();
size = width * height;
dungeon = new bool[height, width];
visited = new bool[height, width];
current.x = Random.Range(0, width - 1);
current.y = Random.Range(0, height - 1);
```

4. Assign a wall to all the cells in the dungeon:

```
int i, j;
for (j = 0; j < height; j++)
  for (i = 0; i < width; i++)
    dungeon[j, i] = true;
```

5. Insert the initial position into the stack:

```
stack.Push(current);
i = (int)current.x;
j = (int)current.y;
```

6. Mark that cell as visited, reducing the number of available cells:

```
visited[j, i] = true;
size--;
```

7. Define the member function for getting the eight connected neighbors for a given cell:

```
private Vector2[] GetNeighbors(Vector2 node)
{
  // next steps
}
```

8. Initialize the necessary variables for defining the top-left and bottom-right corners to be traversed:

```
List<Vector2> neighbors = new List<Vector2>();
int originX, targetX, originY, targetY;
originX = (int)node.x - 1;
originY = (int)node.y - 1;
targetX = (int)node.x + 1;
targetY = (int)node.y + 1;
int i, j;
```

9. Iterate through the cells and add only the valid and available cells:

```
for (j = originY; j < targetY; j++)
{
  if (j < 0 || j >= height)
    continue;
  for (i = originX; i < targetX; i++)
  {
    if (i < 0 || i >= width)
    if (i == node.x && j == node.y)
      continue;
```

```
            if (visited[j,i])
              continue;
            neighbors.Add(new Vector2(i, j));
          }
        }
```

10. Retrieve the neighbors as an array:

```
        return neighbors.ToArray();
```

11. Define the function for building the maze:

```
        public void Build()
        {
          Init();
          // next steps
        }
```

12. Iterate while there still are available positions:

```
        while (size > 0)
        {
          // next steps
        }
```

13. Get the neighbors for the current cell:

```
        Vector2[] neighbors = GetNeighbors(current);
```

14. Validate whether the number of neighbors is greater than zero:

```
        if (neighbors.Length > 0)
        {
          // next step
        }
```

15. If so, add the current cell to the stack:

```
        stack.Push(current);
```

16. Select a random neighbor and remove the wall between that neighbor and the current cell:

```
        int rand = Random.Range(0, neighbors.Length - 1);
        Vector2 n = neighbors[rand];
        int i, j;
        i = (int)current.y;
        j = (int)current.x;
        dungeon[j, i] = false;
```

```
i = (int)n.y;
j = (int)n.x;
dungeon[j, i] = false;
```

17. Mark the neighbor as visited:

```
visited[j, i] = true;
current = n;
size--;
```

18. Get a new position from the stack, if the stack still has elements:

```
else if (stack.Count > 0)
  current = stack.Pop();
```

How it works...

We use the principles from DFS to traverse the graph. That is, we use a stack to store cells and add or remove them accordingly. We start by defining all the cells as walls, and then, from a random position, start taking them down. We repeat the process until we have traversed the whole graph.

Implementing the constructive algorithm for dungeons and islands

One of the most-used world structures in games, besides open worlds, are dungeons. In this recipe, we will use a technique that will allow us to create both.

Getting ready

This technique works easily with a grid graph, like the one we used with the DFS maze builder. However, we will experiment with a different approach to show you how to handle space partitioning and size storage.

How to do it...

We will need to create two different classes: one for handling the nodes, and one for handling the whole tree and high-level operations.

Let's start with the node file:

1. Create a new class named `DungeonNode2D`:

```
using UnityEngine;
using System.Collections.Generic;

[System.Serializable]
public class DungeonNode2D
{
  // next steps
}
```

2. Define its member variables:

```
public Rect area;
public Rect block;
public Dungeon2D root;
public DungeonNode2D left;
public DungeonNode2D right;
protected int depth;
```

3. Implement its constructor for initialization:

```
public DungeonNode2D (Rect area, Dungeon2D root, int depth =
0)
{
this.area = area;
this.root = root;
this.depth = depth;
this.root.leaves.Add(this);
if (!this.root.tree.ContainsKey(depth))
  this.root.tree.Add(depth, new List<DungeonNode2D>());
this.root.tree[depth].Add(this);
}
```

4. Implement the member function for splitting the node:

```
public void Split(Dungeon2D.Split splitCall)
{
  this.root.leaves.Remove(this);
  Rect[] areas = splitCall(area);
  if (areas == null)
    return;
  left = new DungeonNode2D(areas[0], root, depth + 1);
  right = new DungeonNode2D(areas[1], root, depth + 1);
}
```

5. Implement the member function for creating a block (walkable space or cell):

```
public void CreateBlock()
{
  block = new Rect();
  block.xMin = Random.Range(area.xMin, area.center.x);
  block.yMin = Random.Range(area.yMin, area.center.y);
  block.xMax = Random.Range(area.center.x, area.xMax);
  block.yMax = Random.Range(area.center.y, area.yMax);
}
```

Now, we will need to develop the class for building the dungeon:

1. Create a new class named `Dungeon2D`, deriving from `MonoBehaviour`:

```
using UnityEngine;
using System.Collections.Generic;

public class Dungeon2D : MonoBehaviour
{
  // next steps
}
```

2. Define the member variables required:

```
public float minAcceptSize;
public Rect area;
public Dictionary<int, List<DungeonNode2D>> tree;
public HashSet<DungeonNode2D> leaves;
public delegate Rect[] Split(Rect area);
public Split splitCall;
public DungeonNode2D root;
```

3. Implement the member function for initialization:

```
public void Init()
{
  leaves.Clear();
  tree.Clear();
  if (splitCall == null)
    splitCall = SplitNode;
  root = new DungeonNode2D(area, this);
}
```

4. Implement the member function for building the dungeon:

```
public void Build()
{
  root.Split(splitCall);
  foreach (DungeonNode2D node in leaves)
    node.CreateBlock();
}
```

5. Implement the `Awake` function for instantiating the objects for storing the leaf nodes and the branch nodes:

```
private void Awake()
{
  tree = new Dictionary<int, List<DungeonNode2D>>();
  leaves = new HashSet<DungeonNode2D>();
}
```

6. Define the default member function for splitting nodes:

```
public Rect[] SplitNode(Rect area)
{
  // next steps
}
```

7. Initialize the necessary variables:

```
Rect[] areas = null;
DungeonNode2D[] children = null;
```

8. Check whether the area's width or height are below the minimum. If so, return that area:

```
float value = Mathf.Min(area.width, area.height);
if (value < minAcceptSize)
  return areas;
```

9. Check the greater value between the width and height:

```
areas = new Rect[2];
bool isHeightMax = area.height > area.width;
float half;
```

10. Split by the height, if the height is the maximum value:

```
if (isHeightMax)
{
  half = area.height/2f;
  areas[0] = new Rect(area);
  areas[0].height = half;
  areas[1] = new Rect(area);
  areas[1].y = areas[0].y + areas[0].height;
}
```

11. Split by the width, if the width is the maximum value:

```
else
{
  half = area.width/2f;
  areas[0] = new Rect(area);
  areas[0].width = half;
  areas[1] = new Rect(area);
  areas[1].x = areas[0].x + areas[0].width;
}
```

12. Return the area for the new nodes:

```
return areas;
```

How it works...

We use a technique called **Binary-Space Partitioning** (**BSP**), and the node is the bread and butter of it all, along with the split function defined.

Also, we use the main component to drive all the high-level work. However, given that the splitting happens recursively, we just need to take care of the split function for the base and recursive case, and then create the connections between the blocks.

There's more...

Given that we implemented the split function as a delegate, we can improve and fine-tune the BSP by implementing new functions and assigning them to the builder as we see fit.

For example, you could try your own split function that doesn't split by half, but with a random value using the half as the pivot.

See also

For more in-depth theories about constructive algorithms, you can check out the following material:

- *Procedural Content Generation in Games: A textbook and an overview of current research*, Noor Shaker, Julian Togelius, and Mark J Nelson (2016). Springer. ISBN 978-3-319-42714-0. (`http://pcgbook.com`)

Generating landscapes

Besides dungeons and mazes, landscapes are the next big thing regarding procedural content. They're the *de facto* solution for open worlds. There are several algorithms for generating landscapes, and we will learn how to implement the Square-Diamond algorithm for generating landscapes. As a matter of fact, it is a popular algorithm for creating heightmap textures.

Getting ready

In this recipe, we will keep using a grid-based graph. However, this time we won't be using it for defining walls, but for terrain height. The interesting thing about this technique is that it can be applied seamlessly for both 2D and 3D worlds.

How to do it...

We will develop our terrain generator in just a single component:

1. Create a new class named `TerrainGenerator`:

```
using UnityEngine;

public class TerrainGenerator : MonoBehaviour
{
  // next steps
}
```

2. Define the member variables required for controlling size, height, and processing:

```
[Range(3, 101)]
public int size;
[Range(0.1f, 20f)]
public float maxHeight;
protected float[,] terrain;
```

3. Implement the initialization function:

```
public void Init()
{
  if (size % 2 == 0)
    size++;
  terrain = new float[size, size];
  terrain[0, 0] = Random.value;
  terrain[0, size-1] = Random.value;
  terrain[size-1, 0] = Random.value;
  terrain[size-1, size-1] = Random.value;
}
```

4. Define the function for building the terrain. This is a huge function that implements the algorithm in the next steps of the recipe:

```
public void Build()
{
  // next steps
}
```

5. Initialize the necessary variables:

```
int step = size - 1;
float height = maxHeight;
float r = Random.Range(0, height);
```

6. Create the loop that traverses the whole grid. All the following steps for the recipe exist inside this loop:

```
for (int sideLength = size-1; sideLength >= 2; sideLength /=
2)
{
  // next steps
}
```

7. Implement the square-step loop:

```
// SQUARE
int half = size / 2;
int x, y;
for (y = 0; y < size - 1; y += sideLength)
{
  for (x = 0; x < size -1; x += sideLength)
  {
    // next step
  }
}
```

8. Compute the values for the corners:

```
float average = terrain[y,x];
average += terrain[x + sideLength, y];
average += terrain[x, y + sideLength];
average += terrain[x + sideLength, y + sideLength];
average /= 4f;
average += Random.value * 2f * height;
terrain[y + half, x + half] = average
```

9. Implement the diamond-step loop:

```
// DIAMOND
for (int j = 0; j < size - 1; j = half)
{
  for (int i = (j + half)%sideLength; i < size - 1; i +=
sideLength)
  {
    // next step
  }
}
```

10. Compute the values for the corners:

```
float average = terrain[(j-half+size)%size, i];
average += terrain[(j+half)%size,i];
average += terrain[j, (i+half)%size];
average += terrain[j,(j-half+size)%size];
average = average + (Random.value * 2f * height) - height;
terrain[j, i] = average;
```

11. Wrap values on the edge for increased smoothness. This is an optional step, but worth it if the terrain needs to be used for an infinite landscape:

```
if (i == 0)
```

```
 terrain[j, size - 1] = average;
if (j == 0)
 terrain[size-1, i] = average;
```

12. Decrease the height value:

```
height /= 2f;
```

How it works...

After initializing the corners with some values, we go from the outer corners, working inwards and propagating those values with some randomness.

The key thing is that by working in steps, subdividing the grid into squares and diamonds, we get a randomness similar (to some extent) to the randomness we find in landscapes in nature.

It's important to fine-tune the initial values to get better results according to our specific needs for our game.

Using N-Grams for content generation

In `Chapter 19`, *Learning Techniques*, we learned how N-Grams is a probabilistic language model for predicting the next item in a sequence of n-1 elements, and how it can be applied in learning techniques for predicting player behavior. However, it can also be used for procedural content generation—creating new elements by imitating the style of a given set.

In this recipe, we will use the power of N-Grams for creating new levels from a given set, thus imitating the style of the designer.

Getting ready

It's important to remind ourselves about the N-Gram predictor that we developed in `Chapter 19`, *Learning Techniques*, as we will use it as a tool for building levels based on the previous design—in this case, a level to be used as the main pattern.

How to do it...

We will develop three different classes: a component for our prefabs, the level predictor, and the level generator that puts everything together.

`LevelSlice` is the component to attach to the prefabs:

```
using UnityEngine;

public class LevelSlice : MonoBehaviour
{
  public string id;

  override public string ToString()
  {
    return id;
  }
}
```

Now we need to develop the predictor:

```
public class LevelPredictor : NGramPredictor<LevelSlice>
{
  public LevelPredictor(int windowSize) : base(windowSize)
  {
  }
}
```

And, finally, we develop the level generator:

```
using UnityEngine;
using System.Collections.Generic;

public class LevelGenerator : MonoBehaviour
{
  public LevelPredictor predictor;
  public List<LevelSlice> pattern;
  public List<LevelSlice> result;
  private bool isInit;

  private void Start()
  {
    isInit = false;
  }

  public void Init()
  {
    result = new List<LevelSlice>();
```

```
        predictor = new LevelPredictor(3);
        predictor.RegisterSequence(pattern.ToArray());
    }

    public void Build()
    {
        if (isInit)
            return;
        int i;
        for (i = 0; i < pattern.Count - 1; i++)
        {
            LevelSlice slice;
            LevelSlice[] input = pattern.GetRange(0, i + 1).ToArray();
            slice = predictor.GetMostLikely(input);
            result.Add(slice);
        }
    }
}
```

How it works...

We used the N-Gram predictor developed in `Chapter 19`, *Learning Techniques*, as a base for the level predictor in this recipe. This allowed us to focus on the high-level logic and let the predictor do its work.

We have an initial pattern from a level comprised of prefabs that have attached the `LevelSlice` component. Then, we use that pattern to create a new level with a similar style, and of the same size as the previous one.

It's important to put a unique identifier on each prefab for the recipe to work.

There's more...

We can use this technique to build an infinite runner with the following train of thought:

1. Store the key levels (change of world or difficulty)
2. Assign them a higher-level director to the current level builder
3. Swap initial generated levels with the new ones, or keep using pattern levels to generate more until the game finishes

As demonstrated in the research cited in the following section, this technique works well with 3-grams (as used in the recipe).

See also

For further information on how to use N-Grams for procedural content generation, and the use case applied in this recipe, please visit the following resources:

- *Implementing N-Grams for Player Prediction, Procedural Generation, and Stylized AI*, Joseph Vasquez II. (`http://www.gameaipro.com/GameAIPro/GameAIPro_Chapter48_Implementing_N-Grams_for_Player_Prediction_Proceedural_Generation_and_Stylized_AI.pdf`).
- *Linear Levels Through N-Grams*, Dahlskog, Togelius, Nelson. (`http://julian.togelius.com/Dahlskog2014Linear.pdf`).

Generating enemies with the evolutionary algorithm

So far, we have created topological algorithms, so it's time to explore a different kind of content, such as enemies.

In this recipe, we will make use of the evolutionary algorithm to create waves of enemies based on the ones that are difficult to tackle for the player.

Getting ready

We need to define the template for the enemies to focus the next section on how to implement the main evolutionary algorithm. In this case, we will use a serializable class named `EvolEnemy`:

```
using UnityEngine;
using UnityEngine.UI;

[System.Serializable]
public class EvolEnemy
{
  public Sprite sprite;
  public int healthInit;
  public int healthMax;
  public int healthVariance;
}
```

How to do it...

We will work on two classes: the enemy generator containing the evolutionary algorithm and the enemy controller for handling the real-time instances from the enemy templates created in the previous section. We'll also use some game logic.

We need to define the controller for such a template with `EvolEnemyController`:

1. Create the class named `EvolEnemyController`:

```
using UnityEngine;
using System;
using System.Collections;

public class EvolEnemyController :
    MonoBehaviour, IComparable<EvolEnemyController>
{
  // next steps
}
```

2. Define its member variables:

```
public static int counter = 0;
[HideInInspector]
public EvolEnemy template;
public float time;
protected Vector2 bounds;
protected SpriteRenderer _renderer;
protected BoxCollider2D _collider;
```

3. Implement the member function from the `IComparable` interface:

```
public int CompareTo(EvolEnemyController other)
{
  return other.time > time ? 0 : 1;
}
```

4. Implement the initialization function:

```
public void Init(EvolEnemy template, Vector2 bounds)
{
  this.template = template;
  this.bounds = bounds;
  Revive();
}
```

5. Implement the function for reactivating the object:

```
public void Revive()
{
  gameObject.SetActive(true);
  counter++;
  gameObject.name = "EvolEnemy" + counter;

  Vector3 newPosition = UnityEngine.Random.insideUnitCircle;
  newPosition *= bounds;
  _renderer.sprite = template.sprite;
  _collider = gameObject.AddComponent<BoxCollider2D>();
}
```

6. Implement the `Update` function:

```
private void Update()
{
  if (template == null)
    return;
  time += Time.deltaTime;
}
```

7. Implement the function for defeating the enemy with a click:

```
private void OnMouseDown()
{
 Destroy(_collider);
 gameObject.SendMessageUpwards("KillEnemy", this);
}
```

Finally, we work on the enemy generator:

1. Create a new class named `EvolEnemyGenerator`:

```
using UnityEngine;
using System.Collections.Generic;

public class EvolEnemyGenerator : MonoBehaviour
{
  // next
}
```

2. Declare all the necessary member variables:

```
public int mu;
public int lambda;
public int generations;
```

```
public GameObject prefab;
public Vector2 prefabBounds;
protected int gen;
private int total;
private int numAlive;
public EvolEnemy[] enemyList;
private List<EvolEnemyController> population;
```

3. Implement the `Start` member function:

```
private void Start()
{
  Init();
}
```

4. Declare the initialization function:

```
public void Init()
{
  // next steps
}
```

5. Declare its internal variables:

```
gen = 0;
total = mu + lambda;
population = new List<EvolEnemyController>();
int i, x;
bool isRandom = total != enemyList.Length;
```

6. Create the initial generation or wave of enemies:

```
for (i = 0; i < enemyList.Length; i++)
{
  EvolEnemyController enemy;
  enemy =
Instantiate(prefab).GetComponent<EvolEnemyController>();
  enemy.transform.parent = transform;
  EvolEnemy template;
  x = i;
  if (isRandom)
    x = Random.Range(0, enemyList.Length - 1);
  template = enemyList[x];
  enemy.Init(template, prefabBounds);
  population.Add(enemy);
}
```

7. Initialize the number of enemies alive relative to the size of population:

```
numAlive = population.Count;
```

8. Define the function for creating a new generation:

```
public void CreateGeneration()
{
  // next steps
}
```

9. Check whether the number of generations created is greater than allowed:

```
if (gen > generations)
  return;
```

10. Sort the individuals in ascending order, and create a list of surviving individuals:

```
population.Sort();
List<EvolEnemy> templateList = new List<EvolEnemy>();
int i, x;
for (i = mu; i < population.Count; i++)
{
  EvolEnemy template = population[i].template;
  templateList.Add(template);
  population[i].Revive();
}
```

11. Create new individuals from the surviving types:

```
bool isRandom = templateList.Count != mu;
for (i = 0; i < mu; i++)
{
  x = i;
  if (isRandom)
    x = Random.Range(0, templateList.Count - 1);
  population[i].template = templateList[x];
  population[i].Revive();
}
```

12. Increase the number of generations, and reset the number of individuals alive:

```
gen++;
numAlive = population.Count;
```

13. Implement the function for defeating enemies:

```
public void KillEnemy(EvolEnemyController enemy)
{
  enemy.gameObject.SetActive(false);
  numAlive--;
  if (numAlive > 0)
    return;
  Invoke("CreateGeneration", 3f);
}
```

How it works...

The `EvolEnemy` class works as a template for defining the individual phenotype. We start by using `mu` and `lambda` for defining the size of the population, and a first wave is created at random.

Then, after each wave is defeated, the evaluation function takes place, sorting the enemies from least to best fit. The first `mu` number of individuals are eradicated, and offspring are created by copying the surviving population. This is called a generation.

The algorithm stops after the defined number of generations are created.

There's more...

We used `EvolEnemy` as a base class for defining the individuals in the population and a simple rule for sorting them. This algorithm can be improved further by defining more complex templates and phenotype definitions to take mutations into account, such as speed, color, size, and strength.

Also, the enemy controller is separated from the template, given the example created to illustrate the algorithm, and to give you more room for experimentation. However, the idea is to give you the tools to grasp the algorithm, so you can apply it in your own game, once it's well understood.

See also

For further information on the genetic algorithm and its applications in procedural content generation, you can check out the following material:

- *Artificial Intelligence: A Modern Approach* (third edition), Stuart Russel, Peter Norvig (2010), Prentice Hall.
- *Procedural Content Generation in Games: A textbook and an overview of current research*, Noor Shaker, Julian Togelius, and Mark J Nelson (2016). Springer. ISBN 978-3-319-42714-0. (`http://pcgbook.com`)

Summary

In this book, we started our journey with Unity by creating a first person collection game. Then, we looked at how to create shaders from scratch, starting by creating the most basic shaders and learning how the shader code is structured. You gained new skills that increased the quality of your shaders and even made your shader writing process more efficient. Then, the book introduced you to the tools you need to build great AI, either for creating better enemies, polishing that final boss, or even building your own customized AI engine. With this, you take your Unity and AI skills to new levels, and also deliver that feature that will engage players with your game.

Other Books You May Enjoy

If you enjoyed this book, you may be interested in these other books by Packt:

Hands-On Game Development without Coding
Nagendra Kumar Nainar, Yogesh Ramdoss, Yoram Orzach

ISBN: 978-1-78646-167-4

- Configure Wireshark 2 for effective network analysis and troubleshooting
- Set up various display and capture filters
- Understand networking layers, including IPv4 and IPv6 analysis
- Explore performance issues in TCP/IP
- Get to know about Wi-Fi testing and how to resolve problems related to wireless LANs
- Get information about network phenomena, events, and errors
- Locate faults in detecting security failures and breaches in networks

Unity 2018 Cookbook - Third Edition

Matt Smith

ISBN: 978-1-78847-190-9

- Get creative with Unity's shaders and learn to build your own shaders with the new Shader Graph tool
- Create a text and image character dialog with the free Fungus Unity plugin
- Explore new features integrated into Unity 2018, including TextMesh Pro and ProBuilder
- Master Unity audio, including ducking, reverbing, and matching pitch to animation speeds
- Work with the new Cinemachine and timeline to intelligently control camera movements
- Improve ambiance through the use of lights and effects, including reflection and light probes
- Create stylish user interfaces with the UI system, including power bars and clock displays

Leave a review - let other readers know what you think

Please share your thoughts on this book with others by leaving a review on the site that you bought it from. If you purchased the book from Amazon, please leave us an honest review on this book's Amazon page. This is vital so that other potential readers can see and use your unbiased opinion to make purchasing decisions, we can understand what our customers think about our products, and our authors can see your feedback on the title that they have worked with Packt to create. It will only take a few minutes of your time, but is valuable to other potential customers, our authors, and Packt. Thank you!

Index

G

H

I

J

L

M

R

S

T

U

V

W

Z

CPSIA information can be obtained
at www.ICGtesting.com
Printed in the USA
LVHW021814150720
660782LV00010B/374